AMERICA'S ARMED FORCES
A History

JAMES M. MORRIS

Christopher Newport College

D1511412

PRENTICE HALL, *Englewood Cliffs, New Jersey 07632*

Library of Congress Cataloging-in-Publication Data

Morris, James M., (date)
   America's armed forces : a history / by James M. Morris.
     p.   cm.

   Includes bibliographical references and index.
   ISBN 0-13-029265-6
   1. United States--Armed Forces--History.   2. United States-
-History, Military.   I. Title.
UA23.M644   1991
355'.00973--dc20
                                    90-41714
                                      CIP

Editorial/production supervision and
   interior design and pagemakeup: ELIZABETH BEST
Cover design: RAY LUNDGREN GRAPHICS, LTD.
Prepress buyer: DEBRA KESAR
Manufacturing buyer: MARY ANNE GLORIANDE
Acquisitions: STEPHEN DALPHIN

> *To Nancy,*
> *Outstanding wife, mother, and friend.*

© 1991 by Prentice Hall, Inc.
A Division of Simon & Schuster
Englewood Cliffs, New Jersey 07632

Printed in the United States of America

10 9 8 7 6 5 4 3 2 1

ISBN 0-13-029265-6

Prentice-Hall International (UK) Limited, *London*
Prentice-Hall of Australia Pty. Limited, *Sydney*
Prentice-Hall Canada, Inc., *Toronto*
Prentice-Hall Hispanoamericana, S.A., *Mexico*
Prentice-Hall of India Private Limited, *New Delhi*
Prentice-Hall of Japan, Inc., *Tokyo*
Simon & Schuster Asia Pte. Ltd., *Singapore*
Editora Prentice-Hall do Brasil, Ltda., *Rio de Janeiro*

Contents

List of Illustrations

Figures

Maps

Preface

In this book I have endeavored to produce an American military history textbook that is reasonably complete and always understandable to the reader. I have followed the major theme of the interrelationship between America's armed forces and the political, economic, and diplomatic affairs of the nation from colonial times to the present. Since no text of this length can possibly include the entire corpus of U.S. military history, I had to exercise a great deal of judgment as to what the reader should know about this fascinating and important topic. I am confident that no truly important event or development has been overlooked.

A singular feature of this book, which is basically operational rather than administrative in its coverage of events, is the inclusion throughout the text of mini-biographies of many of America's military leaders. Books of this kind too often introduce important persons in American military history, detail their contributions to some major event, and then drop them from further discussion. The student is left with little appreciation of their backgrounds, personalities, and subsequent careers. The mini-biographies should alleviate this persistent problem and should find wide appeal with students.

The text is divided into 13 chapters, usable on either a semester or term basis. I have deliberately attempted to keep the length of each chapter within reasonable limits to allow the instructor to assign outside readings on each subject. Suggestions for further reading follow each chapter. I have endeavored to include the best and latest scholarship on each area or subject, but, here again, judgment comes into play, and I have inevitably excluded someone's "best" book on one topic or another. Such are the hazards of judicious selection. The maps and illustrations should also enhance the students' appreciation of the subject. At the suggestion of my military history students, I have omitted arrows on the maps in order to force the readers themselves to trace the course of battles and campaigns for greater comprehension of the flow of events.

My special thanks go to Dr. Clark Reynolds of the College of Charleston and Dr. David Skaggs of Bowling Green State University for helping to get this book "off the ground" conceptually. Thanks are also due to the insightful readers for Prentice Hall, who pointed out many oversights and some errors and offered a number of excellent suggestions for improving the text: Edward L. Dreyer, Professor, University of Miami, Robin Fabel, Professor, Auburn University, Mark T. Gilderhus, Professor, Colorado State University, Charles Johnson, Professor, University of Tennessee, and Robert F. Smith, Professor, University of Toledo.

I am also grateful to Steve Dalphin and his team at Prentice Hall, whose writing abilities supersede mine; to my colleague Keith McLoughland of Christopher Newport College, and to Dr. Joseph G. "Chip" Dawson of Texas A&M University for reading and commenting on the manuscript; to Mary Daniel, Trish Kearns, and Cathy Doyle of Captain John Smith Library for their valuable help in obtaining materials and information for me beyond all reasonable expectations; and to Thomas P. Madigan of the Christopher Newport College Computer Center for helping me master my personal computer. Thanks, too, to my daughter, Anne C. Christensen, for using her considerable talents in preparing the maps for publication. Finally, and as always, my gratitude goes to my wife, Nancy, for simply putting up with me during the writing process, when I am not the most attentive husband and father.

The standard disclaimer holds for this book: All errors of fact or interpretation are my ultimate responsibility alone.

JAMES M. MORRIS
Christopher Newport College

British-French Wars in Colonial America

Warfare has always played a key role in history. Men, tribes, factions, city-states, nations, coalitions of nations—all have felt the need to take up arms to aggrandize themselves, to defend themselves against aggressors, to defeat their enemies in combat. Sometimes the cause for which they have fought has been honorable; sometimes it has been fraudulent. Sometimes they have fought in a spirit of enthusiasm; sometimes, out of grim and bloody necessity. Sometimes the stakes have been high and critical; sometimes they have been petty and transient.

Whatever the cause, whatever the times, whatever the weapons used, the child of warfare has always been suffering and death. This is because the very purpose of war is to inflict sufficient injury upon the enemy to compel him to bend his will to yours, to do what you want him to do, other methods of persuasion having been tried or rejected. Weapons, strategies, tactics, locales, specific goals and purposes—all have changed with time, circumstance, and technological growth. But the goal of bending the will of the enemy to your own never changes. Because some persons have always felt a compulsion to impose their will on others, the history of people and nations has been marked by war. War, as a consequence, has been a prime determinant of the fate of peoples and nations.

To study war and warmaking, then, is to study one crucial aspect of humankind's existence over time. Warfare studied with discernment reveals that the outcome of any conflict is determined by many factors. It has been said that victory belongs to the strong, but "the strong" goes far beyond physical and material strength, far beyond superior weapons, resources, and economic production, although these are important factors. It also embraces nonmaterial elements such as leadership, cohesiveness around a body of shared ideals, determination to win over all obstacles, and willingness to accept injury or even death for a greater good. The story of nations at war, whether on a major or minor scale, is a mirror image of those nations at peace. To see a nation through the prism of armed conflict is to know that nation and the qualities it possesses.

As this has been true of all countries since the beginning of recorded history, so it is true of the United States. Born in the crucible of conflict in the late eighteenth century, tested in its early years by Old World enemies, faced with conflict with the Indian nations time and again as it expanded westward into their territories, torn by the fratricidal Civil War that decided whether it would be one nation or two, called to play a major role in the defense of its values in two great world conflicts in the twentieth century, and propelled into military and political leadership in the defense of Western ideals since World War II, the United States for two centuries has relied on its military forces to defend its values and freedoms and to extend them to others.

BASES OF THE ANGLO–FRENCH CONFLICT

The discovery of the Western Hemisphere by Europeans at the end of the fifteenth century opened up a whole new epoch for Europe: the age of exploration and colonization. It came at a time when certain of the European nations were united under centralized monarchies and, thanks to technological advances, could traverse the oceans with comparative ease. Economically they were ready and able to seek new sources of raw materials and new markets, and religiously they were determined to evangelize and spread their own particular Christian creeds. Throughout the sixteenth and seventeenth centuries they fervidly competed with one another for the lands and riches of the New World.

Spain, united under Ferdinand and Isabella and having driven out the hated Moors by 1492 after 500 years of the *Reconquista,* was in the best position to take advantage of its discoveries. It had a powerful navy, a growing merchant fleet, and the blessing and support of ambitious monarchs. In the sixteenth century it laid claim to vast stretches of South and Central America, the rich Caribbean islands, and the southern and southwestern parts of North America. Responsible for Spain's successes were its explorers, *conquistadores,* and clerics, collectively seeking to conquer the continents for God, gold, and glory. Spain was, however, forced to leave the rich prize of Brazil to Portugal, according to the Treaty of Tordesillas in 1494.

Unhampered at home by religious controversy, since it went untouched by the Protestant Reformation, which convulsed the rest of Europe in the sixteenth century, Spain set out to create a New Spain on the far side of the Atlantic and around to the Pacific shores. It succeeded very well. The great bulk of the Western Hemisphere was thereafter dominated by Catholic and Iberian culture as the native Indian cultures were gradually subsumed by the swelling tide of Spanish and Portuguese interlopers.

The center of French attention in the New World in the sixteenth and seventeenth centuries was the St. Lawrence River Valley. The seas off the Gulf of St. Lawrence were prized as one of the best fishing grounds in the New World. Its navigable waters led hundreds of miles into a forested interior teeming with wildlife valued for their pelts. Farther on were the five Great Lakes, with the tremendous expanse of territory they drained. Not far beyond the western shores of the Great Lakes lay the headwaters of the Mississippi, that great river whose tributaries gathered water all the way from the crest of the Appalachians in the east to the Rockies in the west.

Into these territories in the seventeenth century—the French being delayed in their exploration and colonization activities by the religious conflict between the Catholic crown and the Protestant Huguenot dissenters at home—came explorers, government officials, fur traders, and proselytizing priests to claim this land for France. Through their work a great arc of rich lands stretching from Newfoundland up the St. Lawrence, across the Great Lakes, and down the Mississippi River to the Gulf of Mexico was claimed for the French monarchy. New France, a vast land of tremendous potential but few people, began to come to life under the banner of the Bourbon kings.

Left to claim the Atlantic coast from Maine to Georgia were the English. Beginning with the first successful English colony, established in 1607 at Jamestown in Virginia on the shores of the James River, English colonists, seeking economic opportunity above all, and sometimes religious freedom too, established themselves along the entire Atlantic coast over the course of the seventeenth century and into the eighteenth. They eventually absorbed the Dutch colony of New Netherland, anchored at New Amsterdam and extending up the Hudson River to and beyond Fort Orange (Albany), as well as the Swedish colony to the south, all the while steadily moving west into the interior.

The French had the English hemmed in between the Appalachians and the Atlantic coast. And they had won the allegiance of the various Indian tribes in their territories by their more humane treatment of these native peoples, so that the "savages" were willing to ally themselves with the French against English encroachments. But to the English colonists eager to thrive and to extend their territories, the presence of the French and their Indian allies was more of a challenge to be overcome than a barrier to be respected.

As the English and French colonies in North America grew and eventually prospered in the seventeenth century—albeit unevenly and in different ways—it was inevitable that their divergent national, cultural, economic, and religious beliefs and goals would lead to conflict. New France may have been sparsely populated, especially west of its trade centers, the cities of Quebec and Montreal, but its network of fortified trading posts on all the key river passages gave it a stranglehold on the American interior that the English and their American colonists did not appreciate. Furthermore, the French colonists' fur trade was a source of great wealth flowing away from English purses, their Catholic religious beliefs were heretical in the judgment of the Anglican and Protestant Englishmen, and their Indian allies seemed always to be a mortal danger.

Likewise, the French colonists had much to lose at the hands of English fishermen encroaching on their fishing grounds off Acadia (renamed Nova Scotia by the English after 1713) and Newfoundland. And British traders were attempting to capture the lucrative French fur trade with the Indians (along with the Indians' loyalties). British settlers and land speculators moving across the Appalachians into the Ohio Country also bode ill for future French development in America.

Overriding all of these colonial antagonisms was the fact that England and France were national, economic, and religious rivals for the domination of Europe. Spain and Holland were gradually losing out to these two major powers (primarily because of their loss of sea power and economic vitality), although they were willing to join in any fight to recoup their European and colonial losses when the opportunity arose. When, as a result of these national antagonisms, the so-called Wars for Empire between England and France broke out in 1689 and continued on and off until 1763, colonists under both flags in the New World were more than ready to join in the fray on behalf of their mother countries and of their own provincial interests.

KING WILLIAM'S WAR, 1689–1697

The first of the Wars for Empire began in 1689 and lasted until 1697. In Europe it was known as the War of the League of Augsburg; in the colonies it was simply called King William's War. It was essentially a conflict in which King Louis XIV of France was attempting to expand his realm by breaking the "Hapsburg ring" surrounding France to the east, south, and northwest by invading the Belgian Netherlands. The French king was also determined to help the exiled James II regain the English throne. Because Louis's move into the Netherlands would endanger King William's throne as well as his home territory of Holland (the Dutchman William III and his wife, Mary, having come to the throne of England at the behest of Parliament the year before in the Glorious Revolution), England joined Sweden, Austria, Spain, and a number of German states in the League of Augsburg to help stop him, and fighting began both in Europe and in America.

STRATEGY, TACTICS, AND LOGISTICS DEFINED

Strategy (derived from the Greek *strategos,* meaning the art or skill of the general): the art or science of planning and directing large-scale military operations using the means and resources available, specifically of maneuvering forces into the most advantageous position relative to the enemy prior to actual engagement in battle for the purpose of attaining military and political goals.

> **Strategy of annihilation:** the adoption of military means designed to lead to the destruction of the enemy's armed forces.

> **Strategy of attrition:** the adoption of military means designed to destroy gradually the will and resistance of the enemy's armed forces.

Tactics (derived from the Greek *taktos,* meaning ordered or arranged): the art or science of arranging and maneuvering military forces when action is imminent or underway, especially with reference to short-range objectives.

Logistics (derived from the Greek *logistikos,* meaning skilled in calculation): the acquisition, movement, distribution, and maintenance of all services and resources necessary to sustain military forces.

The conflict began in the colonies with the French making the first strategic move, a three-pronged ferocious attack in 1690 on Schenectady and two other frontier settlements. On the English side, Sir William Phips, a colorful 39-year-old prominent citizen of Massachusetts, led a 700-man force of volunteers by sea to Acadia, where they easily seized the Port Royal fort and its environs before returning to Boston in triumph— although the French soon reoccupied Port Royal.

Meanwhile, delegates from New York and the New England colonies had met and decided to embark on a major two-part attack on the French in Canada. One militia force was to move overland to seize Montreal; a second would move by sea up the St. Lawrence to take Quebec. The two most important cities in New France would then be in the colonists' hands. The seizure of these two key points would bring the enemy to defeat without major bloodshed. But the plan fizzled. Fewer militiamen and Iroquois Indian allies than expected showed up at the New York assembly point to launch the attack on Montreal. Furthermore, the militia volunteers were swept by smallpox, and it was then discovered that they had too few boats to cross Lake Champlain. The expedition to capture Montreal could not be carried out.

Faring no better, the 2,000-man Quebec force under Phips was delayed in starting and arrived late in the season. Chilly October winds greeted the volunteers as they made their way up the St. Lawrence. Bitter cold soon followed. The group was too small to assault Quebec successfully, and supplies were too few. Finally, when hit by smallpox, the American colonist-volunteers went home. The last organized campaign of King William's War came to an inglorious end.

For the next seven years neither side launched any major campaigns in the colonies. Indian raids by both sides occurred, the English militiamen demonstrating time and again that, despite their best efforts, they were unable to defend life and property on the frontier adequately against the French and their Indian friends. Colonists on both sides of the Canadian frontier welcomed peace in 1697.

QUEEN ANNE'S WAR, 1702–1713

The War of the Spanish Succession, in the colonies called Queen Anne's War, represented an attempt by Louis XIV to put his grandson on the throne of Spain. Britain, following a grand strategy of maintaining a balance of power in Europe by refusing to allow France—or any other nation—to dominate the continent, joined a coalition of nations to prevent this expansion of French power and influence over the Iberian Peninsula, the Spanish colonies in the New World, the southern (Belgian) Netherlands, and much of Italy.

The colonial phase of the fighting began in the south in 1702 with an 800-man South Carolina expedition of militia and Indians against St. Augustine, Spain having allied itself with France. Temporarily successful, the expedition was one of many launched by the English against Spanish outposts in the next ten years, the English also beating off a French-Spanish attack on Charleston in 1706.

As in King William's War a decade earlier, the New England frontier was again the scene of Indian attacks, most notably the Deerfield massacre in western Massachusetts in February 1704. But in 1709 the Crown finally agreed to help the colonists neutralize French power in Canada. The plan for a two-pronged attack on Montreal and Quebec was resurrected, this time with help promised from the British army and navy. Again the plan failed, not once but twice. The first time, the colonies mustered 1,500 militiamen below Lake Champlain in May 1709 to assault Montreal, while 1,200 New England militiamen assembled in Boston for a seaborne assault on Quebec, only to find that the British had reversed their decision about sending aid. The fleet had been sent to Portugal instead. The militiamen went home.

But in 1711, two years later (British marines and 1,500 New England militiamen meanwhile having seized Port Royal in Acadia), the plan was revived, and a British fleet commanded by Vice-Admiral Sir Hovenden Walker sailed into Boston with 5,500 British regulars and marines aboard 70 ships to aid the colonial irregulars. New England recruited 1,500 militiamen to help in the attack on Quebec. A western force of 2,000 militia under Colonel Francis Nicholson (former governor of Virginia and leader of the assault on Port Royal the year before) again assembled to slash through the woods to Montreal while Admiral Walker and the eastern force sailed to Quebec. But Walker's fleet got lost in the St. Lawrence fog, and eight of his ships ran aground, killing 900 soldiers and sailors. Walker delayed, then gave up and sailed for home (where his flagship mysteriously exploded at Spithead, killing all aboard, and where he was promptly cashiered), leaving the New England militiamen no choice but to sail back to Boston in failure. Nicholson's western force was subsequently recalled. The offensives of 1709 and 1711 had come to naught, and the British imperial forces were as unimpressed with the performance of the colonials as the colonists were with them.

When the war was ended by treaty in 1713, England received French recognition of its claims to Hudson's Bay and title to Acadia, Newfoundland, and two islands in the Caribbean. But France was far from defeated in the overarching Wars for Empire. It still held the St. Lawrence and Canada while maintaining a toehold on the Gulf of Mexico and claiming a number of strategic outposts along the Mississippi, which gave it access to the American interior. The English colonists were not pleased with the situation, nor would they be as long as the French and their Indian allies were on their northern, southern, and western borders.

During the seventeenth century, both the British and the French had formed working friendships and trade partnerships with the Indians in their northeastern areas of national and colonial contention. These alliances reinforced the longstanding animosity between the Five Nations of the Iroquois Confederacy of New York, on the one hand, and the Algonquin and Huron tribes in the French territories along and north of the St. Lawrence and in the Great Lakes region (plus Iroquoin tribes defeated by the Five Nations) on the other. Each side curried the favor of its Indian allies by aiding them economically and militarily. As a result, British-French colonial conflicts in the New World neatly dovetailed with traditional Indian hatreds to create a high level of violence and bloodshed on the frontiers separating the contending groups, red and white.

KING GEORGE'S WAR, 1744–1748

England and France (along with France's ally Spain) were technically at peace for the 31 years after 1713. Both countries were recuperating from their recent conflicts, yet each was determined that it alone would be the dominant world power. Accordingly, they continued to reinforce their American possessions. The English built Fort Oswego in New York to influence the Indians in the northern part of the colony and to lay claim to the southern shore of Lake Ontario. The French countered with a fort at Crown Point below

Lake Champlain and built an imposing fortress at Louisbourg on Cape Breton Island to control the mouth of the strategically important St. Lawrence.

The French also demonstrated their influence in the south by befriending the Creek Indians, who attacked Carolina in 1715 in what came to be called the Yamassee War. This, combined with the French establishment of New Orleans at the mouth of the Mississippi River, was a clear sign that any British hold on the south was in jeopardy. Accordingly, the English built a series of forts and established the colony of Georgia under James Oglethorpe in 1732 as a buffer against Spain and its French ally in that region.

Conflict broke out in 1739 between England and Spain in a limited war known as the War of Jenkins' Ear. It was so named because a Spanish navy captain ripped off the ear of the English captain Robert Jenkins when he refused to allow the Spaniard to search his ship, the brig *Rebecca*, in the West Indies. Jenkins carried the ear back to London and displayed it to Parliament, setting off a call for retribution.

From 1739 until 1744 the southern colonies helped the mother country war against Spain. In 1741, some 3,400 colonial volunteers from nine colonies, organized as the "American Regiment" and commanded by Governor William Gooch of Virginia, joined British army and navy regulars in a grand attempt to take the port of Cartagena in Columbia from the Spanish. It turned into a disastrous defeat. Some 2,900 of the American colonists died on the expedition, and 55 percent of the British-American forces were recorded as casualties.

The War of Jenkins' Ear merged into the War of the Austrian Succession (1744–1748), the third round of the Wars for Empire. It was known in the colonies as King George's War. Fighting now shifted to the north, highlighted by a 1745 attack on Louisbourg led by the merchant and militia colonel William Pepperrell of Kittery, Maine. There was no real prospect of victory as the ill-trained militia army of almost 4,000 men, aided by four British warships, sailed out to assault Cape Breton Island and the fortification-in-depth that was Louisbourg. But after a seven-week siege, the fortress fell, having been pummeled by almost 10,000 artillery rounds. The attackers were aided by inept French defensive measures and a lack of supplies, thanks to the Royal Navy's regularly capturing French supply vessels. Louisbourg, the grand prize, the key to control of the St. Lawrence and New France, was now in colonial hands. Reflecting the religious dimension of the longstanding French-English struggle, Chaplain Parson Moody of Boston chopped up the altar and sacred images in Louisbourg's Catholic church at the end of the siege.

In these and the other colonial wars, the weapons used were of some variety. The standard British military piece was the 15-pound, single-shot, muzzle-loading "Brown Bess" flintlock musket with a 14-inch ring (or socket) bayonet. Its 3-foot, 8-inch smoothbore barrel could hurl a 3/4-inch lead ball to an effective range of up to 50 yards. And, of greatest importance, a well-trained infantryman could fire three rounds per minute. The American colonists also used the Kentucky (or Pennsylvania) long rifle, of greater accuracy because of its rifled (grooved) barrel. It fired a 1/2-inch bullet, as opposed to the musket's 3/4-inch projectile. Artillery consisted of 4-, 8-, or 12-pound muzzle-loading pieces without rifling and firing solid shot, grapeshot (small balls attached to one another but designed to scatter on concussion, spreading their lethality over a considerable field), or canister shot (loose pellets in a can, which would also spread on concussion).

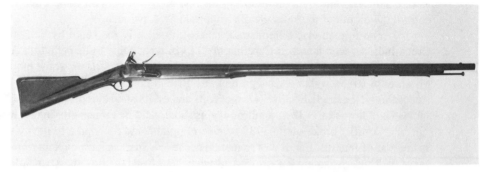

FIGURE 1–1 Brown Bess flintlock musket. (*Smithsonian Institution, Washington, D.C.*)

King George's War dragged on for the next three years with little to claim by either side. A third two-pronged attack on Canada was planned by the colonists, but the British first delayed, then abandoned, the scheme. The war in the colonies stalemated into a series of frontier Indian attacks and finally ended in 1748 when the exhausted British and French mother countries called a halt to the fighting. The English colonists, however, were furious when Britain, in the resulting peace pact, the Treaty of Aix-la-Chapelle, returned strategic Louisbourg and Cape Breton Island to France in exchange for Madras in India.

After all of this fighting, the main question of who would dominate Europe had still not been settled, nor had the French "menace" been removed from the English colonists' northern and western borders. To no one's surprise, conflict between the two countries broke out again six years later, this time on the colonial frontier. It soon escalated into the Seven Years' War, a war in which the question of European and colonial dominance was finally settled.

THE FRENCH AND INDIAN WAR, 1754–1763

The French and Indian War, as the colonists called it, began in 1754 in the disputed Ohio Country when the French destroyed a half-built colonial fort at the crucial point of land where the Monongahela and Allegheny Rivers meet to form the Ohio River (the site of present-day Pittsburgh). There they built their own fort, Fort Duquesne, to reinforce their claim to all land from the St. Lawrence through the Great Lakes region to New Orleans. A summer relief expedition sent to regain the site was headed by young but respected Colonel George Washington of Virginia, but it was too weak to oust the French. Washington was forced to surrender his small defensive stockade, Fort Necessity, and return home with his men.

By the next year, 1755, despite the fact that England and France were officially at peace, the British had formulated plans to assault Canada's frontier at three key points: Fort Duquesne, Fort Niagara, and Fort St. Frederic at Crown Point. Major General Edward Braddock, an officer of outstanding reputation with over 40 years of military experience on the Continent, arrived in Williamsburg, Virginia, to fill out two regiments of his regulars with two regiments of colonial volunteers and help seize the objectives. New

York Indian agent William Johnson would lead a force against Crown Point. Governor William Shirley of Massachusetts would command the Niagara expedition. Braddock himself would conduct the march on Fort Duquesne; Washington accompanied him but held no command.

The three offensives resulted in little success for British and colonial arms. Johnson's force bested a French force in the Battle of Lake George, but the New Yorker failed to hurl his forces at Crown Point, and the French built Fort Ticonderoga a few miles south after he left. Governor Shirley's troops got only as far as Oswego on Lake Ontario before abandoning the Niagara operation. Braddock's tightly packed regular and colonial forces were ambushed and cut down by the French and their Indian allies 6 miles from Fort Duquesne, Lieutenant Colonel Thomas Gage's advance guard retreating through Braddock's main body and causing confusion and panic. Braddock died of battle wounds. British and colonial deaths totaled almost 1,000; French losses were only 39 killed and wounded. Thus the years 1754 and 1755 saw the French gain an even stronger grip on the frontier. In addition, the British abandoned a major assault on Louisbourg without even getting started.

But in 1757, William Pitt (the Elder) took over the British government and began to pour money, men, supplies, and clear strategic thinking into the colonial war. Pitt was determined to use the superior Royal Navy to cut off Canada from aid by blockading the French coast and by pouncing on every French merchant vessel or transport found on the high seas. Pitt also sent 20,000 army regulars to America. Counting on help from the navy to maintain command of the sea and the colonists, the British army was determined to drive the French out of North America.

An attack in July 1758 by about 6,000 well-trained British regulars and 10,000 colonial volunteers against only 3,500 French troops at Ticonderoga turned into a four-hour bloodbath as General James Abercromby, failing to spot his artillery effectively, merely threw wave after wave of men through fallen trees against the well-emplaced French in six valiant but foolish frontal attacks.

But British arms were successful elsewhere. A 9,000 regular, 500 militiamen expedition against Louisbourg, led by the reliable Major General Jeffrey Amherst and supported by the Royal Navy, resulted in a six-week siege and the city's surrender in July 1758. That same year, an English force of 5,000 militiamen and 1,700 regulars found Fort Duquesne abandoned. The British promptly built Fort Pitt on that key location. In 1759 Niagara was finally seized, as were Fort Ticonderoga and Crown Point. Along with these land victories by the English and their colonials, British sea power was having a telling effect. The French in Canada were finding themselves losing strength for lack of supplies. The Marquis de Montcalm, learning Quebec would be the target for the next British move—to be followed by Montreal—concentrated his forces at Quebec to await the British invasion armada headed by the resolute 40-year-old Major General James Wolfe, hero of the seizure of Louisbourg the year before.

Quebec, situated high above the St. Lawrence, was a natural bastion that had never been taken, but on the night of September 12–13, 1759, the brilliant Wolfe led over 4,000 of his regulars up the steep cliffs below the city via a goat trail under cover of darkness to assemble on the grassy Plains of Abraham before the city. Later that day they fended off Montcalm's 4,500 regulars and volunteers as they attacked in the standard eighteenth-century manner of musket volleys followed by a bayonet charge. Both Wolfe and Montcalm died of wounds received in the crucial battle.

The remainder of the French forces managed to slip away to Montreal before Quebec surrendered six days later, but the remnants of France's once powerful forces could only remain there and await their fate as British armies from Lake Ontario, Lake Champlain, and Quebec inexorably converged upon them. The 2,400 French at Montreal surrendered in September to 10,000 British regulars, and the American colonial phase of the Seven Years' War was over. All key French strongholds had been seized and neutralized. France had lost all control of its colonies to the British.

When the war was finally concluded by the Treaty of Paris of 1763, France surrendered the great bulk of its American colonial empire to Britain. All French lands in North America became British except for the two small fishing islands of St. Mihiel and St. Pierre off the coast of Newfoundland and the sugar islands of Martinique, Guadeloupe, and Sta. Lucia in the West Indies. Spain ceded Florida to Britain, and, as compensation, New Orleans and all French lands west of the Mississippi were ceded to Spain. The British flag now flew from Florida to Hudson's Bay and beyond, from the Atlantic Ocean to the Mississippi River. The French had been expelled by the British army and the Royal Navy, aided by colonial militia volunteers. To many colonists, however, the victories had been gained primarily by colonial volunteer arms, a contention no British regular would grant.

THE COLONIAL MILITIA: SUMMARY AND CRITIQUE

Because of their bad experience with standing armies in seventeenth-century England at the time of the Stuarts, during the Commonwealth and Protectorate, and during the period of the Restoration, a widespread distrust of standing mercenary armies was brought to America by the English colonists. They were seen as an unchanging threat to the liberties of the people. Necessary protection, the colonists urged, could be ensured by citizen-soldiers, part-timers, who would drill regularly to learn the rudiments of the military art and be on call to defend home and hearth when necessary.

Accordingly, each of the colonies formed militia units from its able-bodied men to be free of the real or potential tyranny associated with standing armies and to ward off any danger to the public safety, usually in the form of Indian raids. Indeed, by the eighteenth century, service in the local "trained band," or "trainband," was considered a matter not only of duty but also of civic pride, each man bringing his own weapon to militia muster. Each unit elected its own officers, or the officers were chosen by the colonial governors.

Such was the popular concept of the militia, but the myth obscured some significant facts overlooked in the popular mind. For example, while all men supposedly trained in local units on a regular basis and were available to respond to local danger, in an actual emergency beyond the local environs individuals were drafted out of the local units to serve in "volunteer" units. Entire local units did not go. Entire units could not go. To remove a whole trainband from an area would leave it defenseless. And those who did not wish to go if drafted into the volunteer expeditionary forces were usually excused if they paid a fine or hired a substitute. Consequently, the "better sort" tended not to serve in wartime, and battlefield units were generally made up of the "lesser sort," who could not buy their way out or were being paid as someone else's substitute.

Furthermore, the reliability of militia units varied widely. During the time of Bacon's Rebellion in Virginia in the 1670s, Governor Berkeley had difficulty recruiting only 500 soldiers to guard the frontier against the Indians. Virginians preferred to rely on friendly Indians, a few forts, and a handful of mounted volunteer "rangers" to do the job because militia service for most men took them far from home and left their families and settlements defenseless. At the same time, however, New England militiamen proved to be very reliable during King Philip's War, perhaps because the danger was proximate and because New England towns could serve as bases of operations.

By the eighteenth century, the local militia units were no longer the principal military forces in the colonies because important changes were taking place there—this despite the persistence of the militia myth, now becoming sanctified by time. With France and Spain, not local Indians, now the principal enemies, fighting usually took place farther away and took more time, a distinct burden on most colonial householders, who had farms to till or businesses to run, to say nothing of families to protect. If the fighting was close at hand and the enemy a proximate danger, the mustered local regular units approached the cherished ideal. But if the fighting was more distant and the danger more remote, the colonies showed less interest in sending militiamen or supporting them monetarily. Furthermore, volunteer units now increasingly tended to be made up of recruits from the lower classes, consisting to a large degree of men who could not buy their way out, had little or nothing to protect at home, and could use the money. Thus the volunteers mustered into service in the eighteenth century were increasingly Indians, blacks, mixed breeds, landless whites, and drifters.

Yet despite their actual makeup—militia duty at home was still considered a civic duty that no man should shirk, although it was a social obligation rather than an obligation to serve in combat—the predominantly-lower-class volunteers drafted from militia units sometimes performed creditably during the colonial wars. During King William's War, volunteer militiamen from Massachusetts served with Phips in his seizure of Port Royal in Acadia in 1690 and reported for duty to attack Montreal and Quebec shortly afterward, although that two-pronged offensive failed. As noted, the militiamen were less successful in defending the frontier against Indian raids.

In Queen Anne's War, the South Carolina militia volunteers had some success in attacking St. Augustine and carried out a number of raids against the Spanish in the years that followed. Later in the war, 1,500 northern volunteers from local militia units participated in the Montreal expedition under Francis Nicolson and were with Admiral Walker on his ill-fated attack on Quebec. American volunteers, the "American Regiment," took part in the attack on Cartagena in 1740 during the War of Jenkins' Ear, and Georgia and Carolina militiamen had accompanied Oglethorpe against St. Augustine the year before. In King George's War, the 4,000-man militia's successful seizure of Louisbourg in 1745 was beyond the belief of the British military regulars and was the high point of the colonial militia record.

Finally, as we have seen, the militia during the French and Indian War served with Johnson at Crown Point, with Braddock in western Pennsylvania, and with Abercromby at the bloodbath at Ticonderoga. They took part in the subsequent seizures of

Niagara, Fort Ticonderoga, and Crown Point. Some militiamen were with Wolfe at Quebec in 1759 and with the forces advancing on Montreal thereafter.

The British regulars had little good to say about the colonial militia troops. They complained that they were lazy, undisciplined, unreliable, and distinctly unmilitary. Considering the actual makeup of militia volunteer units in the eighteenth century, their complaints may well have been justified to some extent, although certain units such as (Captain Robert) Rogers's Rangers from New Hampshire in the French and Indian War were notable exceptions. It is also true that, all things considered, it was the British army regulars and the Royal Navy that finally brought victory over the French in the wars for the North American colonies.

Yet the colonial militia had served beside the royal forces throughout the Wars for Empire. At times they had served very well. They had played a key supporting role in securing an expanded British North America that stretched from Hudson's Bay to Florida, from the Atlantic to the Mississippi. Whatever their exact contribution in attaining the final victory over the French and their Indian and European allies, the colonial soldier-volunteers had stood by the Crown and the colonies in time of need, with some colonists even enlisting in British regular units. The colonists justifiably took great pride in their militias' accomplishments, and the myth of the militiamen defending hearth and home was enshrined as holy writ by the eighteenth century as the American colonies found themselves in disputes with the mother country—disputes that soon led to warfare and independence.

Suggestions for Further Reading

BRODIE, BERNARD, and FAWN BRODIE, *From Crossbow to H-Bomb*. Bloomington: Indiana University Press, 1973.

CRESS, LAWRENCE D., *Citizens in Arms: The Army and Militia in American Society to the War of 1812*. Chapel Hill: University of North Carolina Press, 1982.

FREGAULT, GUY, *Canada: The War of the Conquest,* Margaret M. Cameron, trans. Toronto: Oxford University Press, 1969.

GIPSON, LAWRENCE H., *The British Empire Before the American Revolution,* 15 vols. New York: Knopf, 1936–1970.

GRAHAM, GERALD S., *Empire of the North Atlantic: The Maritime Struggle for North America,* 2nd ed. Toronto: University of Toronto Press, 1958.

LEACH, DOUGLAS E., *Arms for Empire: A Military History of the British Colonies in North America, 1607–1763*. New York: Macmillan, 1973.

——, *The Northern Colonial Frontier, 1607–1763*. New York: Holt, Rinehart & Winston, 1966.

PECKHAM, HOWARD H., *The Colonial Wars, 1689–1762*. Chicago: University of Chicago Press, 1964.

PRESTON, RICHARD A., and SYDNEY F. WISE, *Men in Arms: A History of Warfare and Its Interrelationships with Western Society*. New York: Praeger, 1970.

ROBINSON, W. STITT, *The Southern Colonial Frontier, 1607–1763*. Albuquerque: University of New Mexico Press, 1979.

ROPP, THEODORE,   *War in the Modern World*. Durham: Duke University Press, 1959.

SCHWOERER, LOIS G.,   *"No Standing Armies!" The Anti-Army Ideology in Seventeenth Century England*. Baltimore: Johns Hopkins University Press, 1974.

SHEA, WILLIAM L.,   *The Virginia Militia in the Seventeenth Century*. Baton Rouge: Louisiana State University Press, 1983.

America's Wars for Independence, 1763–1815

The American Revolution has been one of the most intensely studied conflicts in American history, yet it remains enshrouded in myth. Typically viewed as a war of freedom versus tyranny, of enlightened political theory versus archaic monarchical pretensions, or of human progress overwhelming political regression, the armed conflict between the American colonies and England is often unwittingly perceived as having a providential outcome from the start. While there are elements of truth in these popular concepts, further investigation reveals that the reasons for the war were far from simple and that the outcome was hardly preordained.

The three conflicts that followed—the Quasi-War, the Barbary Wars, and the War of 1812—were all of significance as guarantors of American independence, yet they have generally received much less attention. They have sometimes been judged as tangential to American development or as somewhat insignificant—this because the outcome of the first was inconclusive, the second produced no great change in national status, and the third ended militarily as a draw at best.

Yet all of these conflicts with foreign powers—plus two domestic rebellions and a number of Indian wars—were important to the subsequent development of the United States and to its military arm. Each deserves careful scrutiny because each represented a crucial step in the evolution of modern America and its armed forces.

BACKGROUND TO CONFLICT WITH GREAT BRITAIN

In a very real sense, the American Revolution began not in 1775 but in 1763. In essence, the war started out as a quarrel over colonial rights, developed into a limited armed conflict, and finally escalated into a full-fledged war. The dispute began after the French and Indian War in 1763. France had been defeated in Europe and in North America. Great Britain now had legal title to a New World empire twelve times the size of the home islands. It was of inestimable value economically and politically, although careful development and control would be needed to bring it to its full potential. To take advantage of the new-found opportunities that now lay before it, Britain was forced to make a number of critical policy changes at home and in its American continental colonies. That is where the trouble started.

Since wars are always costly and Britain had been fighting France on and off since 1689, the nation was deep in debt by 1763, and revenues were insufficient to pay its obligations. The government could not even keep up with the interest payments on the debt due each year, much less retire the principal. And now that a new worldwide empire was in its hands (the treaty of 1763 granted it almost all French territories in North America plus Spanish Florida and also guaranteed it trading rights and territories in India), Britain would have to bring this empire under Crown control for maximum utilization of its potential. This, too, would cost money and demand policy changes.

Furthermore, in North America, with its now-expanded boundaries, there was a particular problem. For decades the English colonists along the Atlantic coast had been casting covetous eyes on the expansive land mass beyond the Appalachians, land the British had promised to their Indian allies for their help during the recent colonial wars. And colonial fur traders and other frontiersmen had actually been cutting through the mountains and encroaching on the Ohio Country. Moreover, certain enterprising colonial speculators were already making treaties with the Indians to buy their land and sell it to colonists moving in from the east. If the settlers and speculators were not kept out, trouble with the Indians would surely ensue. They had to be barred from the new lands west of the Appalachians somehow, even if it meant garrisoning the frontier with British regulars, unpopular as this might be with the colonists.

Finally, while it was not immediately discernible in 1763, the American colonists had been assuming more and more privileges of self-government over the years, such as electing their own officials, taxing themselves, and appealing under law to their own charters and ordinances. They now viewed these legal privileges as constitutional rights. The colonists tended to view their sustained privileges as rights, especially since they appeared to be sanctioned by the British common-law tradition. In essence, the mother country had been of necessity carrying out a policy of "salutary neglect" while fighting off the French challenge from 1689 to 1763. For eight decades the colonists had been practicing a considerable degree of self-government on a day-to-day basis. By the 1760s they were hardly in a mood to give up their rights. Britain, then, faced a real challenge if it was going to bring the American colonists into line with its imperial objectives of debt reduction plus economic and legal direction from London. It did not take long to reveal the rift between the mother country and its American colonies.

In 1763 the Crown, fearing trouble with the Indians in the west and faced with Pontiac's Indian rebellion, announced the establishment of the Proclamation Line. Under this decree, all the land west of the crest of the Appalachians was declared to be Indian territory and closed to colonial settlement. Needless to say, this ran contrary to the aspirations of thousands of ordinary colonial expansionists, who saw the territory as a land of immense economic opportunity for themselves and their families. Also very unhappy were wealthy land speculators from Virginia, North Carolina, and Pennsylvania, who saw their treaties with the Indians nullified and their investments wiped out (although the Crown subsequently confirmed some of these treaties). Besides, garrisoning the Appalachian frontier to keep the colonists and Indians apart would mean sending to America some 7,500 troops at an annual cost of 300,000 to 400,000 pounds sterling, an expenditure the Crown felt the colonists should rightly pay, since the soldiers would be there for their "protection." The colonists resented the Crown's contention that they should pay for soldiers they did not need or want, whose duty it would be to keep them out of lands that rightly "belonged" to them, not to the Indians.

The following year, in 1764, Parliament passed the Sugar (or Revenue) Act to raise and collect revenues on sugar and molasses coming into the colonies. This would serve as a means of having the colonies pay their way, cover the cost of the soldiers on the frontier, and reduce the Empire's debt burden. There was immediate protest in the colonies, with some dissenters objecting that the tax was unfair and "unconstitutional."

The next year, 1765, saw Parliament pass the Stamp Act, an "internal tax" on various items such as newspapers and legal and trade documents. Parliament was hardly moved by the legal arguments leveled against the Stamp Act by the colonists, but when the Stamp Act Congress met in New York City in October 1765 and recommended boycotting British goods, when groups such as the Sons of Liberty began to enforce the extralegal boycott with violence and mayhem, and when the British merchants began to complain that trade was being affected adversely, the government backed down in 1766 and repealed the hated act. Although Parliament passed the Declaratory Act at the same time to reassert its right to impose any kind of tax it felt proper, this statement of legal and constitutional principle had little impact in the colonies. The Crown had backed down. The mother country had shown a lack of will and could, it appeared, be forced to rescind any measure obnoxious to the colonies. These were the lessons learned by the colonists in the Stamp Act crisis, lessons that were not forgotten.

Still in need of revenues, since tax collections from America covered only about 10 percent of the cost of maintaining the army in the colonies, Parliament again passed a revenue measure in 1767, popularly called the Townshend Duties, imposing taxes on a number of imported items. Again the colonists protested and adopted nonimportation agreements. By 1770 the boycotts were obviously working again as losses by British businesses continued to climb. And the colonies were in an uproar over a minor soldier–civilian incident in Boston (there were by now over 4,000 British soldiers stationed in Boston, a city of 15,000 people) that was trumpeted as the "Boston Massacre." As a result, Parliament repealed the Townshend Duties, retaining a tax on tea as a matter of principle to show that there was nothing unconstitutional in imposing such measures.

This calmed things down considerably until the government in 1773 passed the Tea Act, which allowed the East India Company, overburdened with excess tea, to sell its product directly in America. Protest arose from all the major colonial cities, Boston extremists outdoing all others by not allowing the tea cargoes of several ships to be unloaded and then dumping the tea into the harbor on December 16, 1773.

British reaction to this act of defiance was swift. In 1774 Parliament passed the "Intolerable Acts," or the "Coercive Acts," as the angry colonists called them, which closed the port of Boston until the tea was paid for. This caused great hardship to thousands of citizens who had had nothing to do with the Boston Tea Party and, therefore, aroused much resentment against the mother country. The Intolerable Acts also made many Massachusetts officials answerable to the Crown, not to the colony's legislature, and allowed British officials accused of capital crimes to be put on trial in England or elsewhere outside the colony. Equally important, a new quartering act was also passed, forcing Massachusetts to support the soldiers of the realm sent to that rebellious colony.

In reacting to the trouble in Boston in this way, the British governmental officials believed that they were dealing with a local situation that called for a law-and-order reaction. If Boston could be isolated and punished for its unlawful acts while any outstanding grievances were redressed at the same time, the other areas of the colonies would be pacified by reasonable Crown compromises and intimidated by the example of Boston. The British army, then, was to be used in Massachusetts as an overwhelming force at a single point to crush colonial rebellion in its embryo stage.

For this purpose, Major General Thomas Gage, commander of the British army in America and now the appointed governor of Massachusetts, prepared his troops in Boston for military action. Meanwhile, the colonials' First Continental Congress, meeting in Philadelphia since September 1774, was urging the colonies to gather military supplies and prepare for possible conflict to preserve colonial rights. By this time King George III had proclaimed that a state of rebellion existed in the colony of Massachusetts, and that colony's provisional legislature had appointed a Committee of Public Safety to gather arms and reorganize the militia. The stage was set for armed conflict.

General Gage soon found out from his spies that military supplies were being stored by the Massachusetts rebels at the town of Concord, some 20 miles northwest of Boston, and on April 18, 1775, he dispatched Lieutenant Colonel Francis Smith and 700 men to seize them. Early the next morning Smith sent some of his force ahead to capture the supplies before the aroused colonials had a chance to remove them. These regulars arrived at Lexington, halfway to Concord, only to find themselves face to face with about 70 determined militiamen, "minute men," on the village green. A fracas lasting only minutes—with light casualties—ensued, and the British moved on to Concord. Here they had a second skirmish, this time with several hundred militiamen. The Redcoats decided to withdraw, only to find themselves under constant fire from thousands of concealed militiamen as they retreated to Lexington, where they were saved temporarily by reinforcements sent out by Gage. This enlarged British column of 1,500 men fought its way back into Boston (suffering 20 percent casualties in the whole affair), and Gage soon found himself besieged in the city by 20,000 angry and determined militiamen.

What had begun, then, as a limited movement in force to seize an insurgent arms cache had turned into a bloody conflict with heavy casualties and the would-be enforcing army surrounded in hostile territory. Whether or not these limited engagements would turn into something bigger depended in large measure on the Second Continental Congress, now seated in Philadelphia. Congress's decision was to resist until colonial rights were recognized, and the army surrounding Boston was recognized as having official status on June 14, 1775, the birthday of the United States Army. George Washington, considered the most able military leader in the colonies and widely recognized as a prominent southerner (whose support would ensure southern loyalty to the cause), was named commander-in-chief and set about his duties in and around Boston. Albeit unofficially, the colonies and the mother country were now at war, a fact attested to by Britain's sending reinforcements to Gage, along with three of the country's most reputable generals: William Howe, Henry Clinton, and John Burgoyne.

The colonial achievement in seizing Fort Ticonderoga and Crown Point under Ethan Allen and Benedict Arnold in May 1775 and British success in finally driving the American colonial army off Breed's Hill a month later (at the horrible price of 1,000 British casualties out of 2,500 men committed) did little to change the overall situation, although the misnamed Battle of Bunker Hill, along with Lexington and Concord, added to the American myth of the superiority of the American citizen-volunteer over the British regular in combat. But both events were clear signs that colonial resistance was real, and, like it or not, the British had a war on their hands.

BRITISH AND AMERICAN STRENGTHS AND WEAKNESSES

The British were certain of swift victory and, indeed, remained confident of success until their defeat at Yorktown six years later. After all, they had a population of 11 million people (compared to the colonies' paltry 2.5 million, of whom about 20 percent were slaves), an army numbering 50,000 men, the Royal Navy of 131 ships of the line and 139 other vessels, and vast financial resources from which to draw. In the colonies, they assumed, they could count on many colonists' loyalty to the Crown and support from friendly Indian tribes.

Yet they failed to realize that their armed strength would most likely be dissipated in trying to conquer and occupy an area thousands of square miles in extent. Furthermore, much of the population, rather than being almost uniformly supportive as in previous wars in America, proved to be uncooperative and hostile in this situation, leading to severe logistical problems in carrying out military operations. Reflecting the typical eighteenth-century military outlook of limited warfare, wherein emphasis was placed on putting the enemy in an untenable position by maneuver, they assumed that if they could seize the major cities, control the seacoast, and defeat the colonists' army in standup, regular combat, the rebellion would soon collapse.

But as the British were to find out, seizing major cities and seaports had a limited impact on the colonists' determination to fight on. After a few unsuccessful engagements in "regular-style" fighting, the colonial regulars and militia changed their strategy and tactics, avoided standup engagements, and moved into the interior, hoping to hit the British forces only at key points of vulnerability rather than risk major defeats. As the colonial armies moved inland, they were falling back upon their own lines of supply. As the British marched out after them from their coastal cities, they were moving away from their sources of supply, resulting in a logistical nightmare.

And the Royal Navy, while never seriously challenged in combat by the American navy and the navies of the individual colonies, could not shut down the depredations of the American privateering vessels operating under letters of marque. The privateers regularly seized and harassed British supply vessels. Fighting a war across 3,000 miles of ocean with limited support from the indigenous population, the British soon learned, was far different from conducting a war across secure seas and operating with the cooperation of the native population, as they had done during the colonial wars.

Furthermore, despite its great strength, the Royal Navy had become seriously weakened thanks to peacetime parsimony, administrative neglect and incompetence, and bitter feuds between the senior officers over many issues. It was still strong enough to fend off the rebellious colonies' puny efforts, blockade the American coast, and ensure at least adequate resupply across the Atlantic. But when France joined the Americans in 1778, its rebuilt and revitalized naval force was able to match its British counterpart.

Britain was also weakened by a lack of consensus at home regarding the war. At the outbreak of hostilities, such influential figures as Edmund Burke, the Earl of Chatham (Pitt the Elder), and Charles James Fox stood in opposition to the government's policy of the use of the force of arms against the American colonists. Better to give the colonies home rule—or even independence, they believed—than to fight a very difficult and expensive war in which the enemy, even if conquered, wanted only limited self-government. This antiwar opinion at home, even though held by only a few at first, not only prevented a clear and consistent British strategy during the war (the ministers vacillating between coercion and conciliation) but also played directly into the colonists' hands. The only way the colonists could win, Washington and other colonial leaders came to realize, was to avoid major defeats, keep their forces intact, and continue their resistance until the cost and duration of the war would swing British opinion around to the side of the dissenters, thus ending the conflict.

This American grand strategy explains why Washington, after 1776 and his jarring experiences in and around New York City, refused to engage in crucial battles in which he might lose his army and, therefore, the war. The colonials could bend Britain's will to their own only by avoiding major defeats; perhaps receiving help from other nations, especially France; and dragging the war out until the British political and military leaders, faced with hostile public opinion, gave up. This is exactly what happened. Cornwallis's surrender at Yorktown in 1781 did not mean that Britain's main army had been captured and that Britain *could* not fight any longer. Rather, Yorktown had such a negative impact politically in London that Britain *would* no longer fight the war and thus moved to negotiate a peace settlement.

The greatest strength on the colonists' side was the cause for which they fought (even though, initially at least, only a minority of the colonists allied themselves to the Patriot cause). Their network of committees played an important role in organizing recruits and pressuring the would-be loyalists to the Crown to remain neutral. Even their enemies were amazed at their belief in freedom and in the righteousness of the cause of home rule and, after 1776, of independence. Personal privations and sacrifice were commonplace, and, while morale sometimes slumped in the face of defeat, basic belief in the colonial cause never seemed to waiver.

As a fighting force, the Continental Army acquitted itself well despite its lack of professional training, a problem which Washington was perennially trying to overcome. Never large in numbers (probably 38,000 at its largest) and always bedeviled by a shortage of qualified officers, the Continental Army nevertheless carried the burden of the fighting during the war, relying on the militia forces to aid it at crucial times.

For shoulder arms the American infantry forces used a wide variety of weapons, including captured British "Brown Bess" flintlock muskets and a mixed assortment of

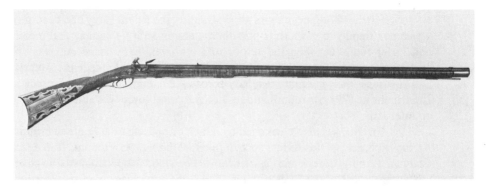

FIGURE 2–1   Pennsylvania (or Kentucky) long rifle. (*Smithsonian Institution, Washington, D.C.*)

other muskets, including fusils (a light flintlock musket) and carbines (a short musket) of odd caliber. Marksmen favored the Pennsylvania (or Kentucky) long rifle. A number of French .69-caliber Charleville muskets were also used, some colonial manufacturers producing copies of the Charleville and Brown Bess weapons for use by the Americans.

For artillery the Americans organized an artillery branch in 1776 under Henry Knox, but their weapons were usually of foreign make and of various sizes and shapes. Generally speaking, American artillery followed French manufacture and consisted of 4-, 8-, and 12-pound field guns; 16-, 24-, and 36-pound siege guns; and 8-, 12-, and 16-inch mortars.

FIGURE 2–2   Revolutionary War French Cannon. (*Smithsonian Institution, Washington, D.C*)

Fortunately for the colonists' cause, the individual colonies had begun to reorganize and revitalize their volunteer forces when trouble first began to brew in 1775. Militiamen still tended to be unavailable and unreliable when the scene of action was far from home. They still tended to be the "poorer sort" who could not obtain exemptions or buy a substitute, although there were exceptions. Many were paid substitutes. Their commanders reported that the militiamen were typically both unprofessional and insubordinate. Nevertheless, the militia played a significant role in America's victory over the mother country by supporting the Continentals, by preventing requisitioning by the British forces, and by seriously complicating the reestablishment of royal authority. Sometimes militiamen were courageous and sacrificing; sometimes they were cowardly and unreliable. All in all, however, these nonregulars, fighting for a cause they believed in, were always a threat to the British attempts to put down the rebellion and served to buttress the American cause sufficiently to allow for eventual victory.

The greatest weakness of the American war effort was the inability of the Second Continental Congress to sustain the army throughout the war. The army persistently suffered from a lack of supplies because Congress could not adequately finance the war. Because it had no power to tax, Congress was forced to print paper money to pay its bills. This script devalued quickly. Congress managed to secure some foreign loans, but the army suffered at all times from a shortage of necessary supplies.

Congress also did poorly in administering the war, relying on a five-member board to direct the conflict and on individual staff departments to care for the military's needs. The result was confusion, venality, corruption, and inefficiency. In desperation, Congress in late 1779 turned over to the states the job of paying for the provisioning of their own Continental contingents, but no state ever met its obligations. The lack of political and administrative support for the Continental Army is one of the saddest pages in American military history. Fortunately, a combination of significant victories at crucial times by the Continentals aided by the militia, a high quality of military leadership, perseverance for a noble cause against disheartening odds, and inherent weaknesses in the British military-political effort to suppress the revolt allowed the American rebels to gain victory and independence.

WARFARE OF MANEUVER LEADS TO STALEMATE, 1775–1777

All in all, the first year of the war went tolerably well for the colonial rebels, although General Washington was forced to recruit a whole new army around Boston when the enlistments of the first Continentals expired and almost all refused to reenlist. In late 1775 he sent Colonel Henry Knox to Fort Ticonderoga to fetch the artillery pieces captured there earlier. This Knox and his men managed to do, dragging the 50 cannon 300 miles across snow and ice back to Boston, where they were placed atop Dorchester Heights to bombard the city and harbor. This move forced Major General William Howe, now in command, to abandon the city for a better logistical base at Halifax, Nova Scotia, on March 17, 1776, taking many of the city's Loyalists with him but leaving behind stores of cannon and ammunition.

☆ An American Portrait

Henry Knox—Knox, who won fame during the war as Washington's artillerist, was born in Boston in 1750. Shouldering the responsibilities for his mother when his father deserted her when he was only 12, Knox became a bookseller and while a young man witnessed the Boston Massacre. Thereafter joining the Boston Grenadier Corps, Knox offered his services to the Patriot cause in 1775 and soon became a close friend and advisor to Washington. In November of that year he was appointed a colonel and, at the suggestion of John Adams, was placed in charge of the army's artillery. He led the expedition to return the captured artillery from Fort Ticonderoga to Boston, and was later placed in charge of the artillery around New York City, although neither his guns nor Washington's men could thwart the massive invasion by the British army and navy. Rendering valuable aid to Washington at Trenton and Princeton, the portly officer was soon raised in rank to brigadier general and in January 1777 was sent to Massachusetts to start a government arsenal at Springfield.

Knox was back at Washington's side at Brandywine and Monmouth, served on the court martial of Major John Andre after the treason of Benedict Arnold had been discovered, and participated as the Continental army's artillerist in the siege of Yorktown in 1781, where his guns proved to be decisive. Appointed a major general after Cornwallis's surrender, Knox was one of the founders of the Society of the Cincinnati, an association of former army officers, and served as its first secretary. He was appointed by Congress to the position of secretary at war and under the new Constitution became the nation's first secretary of war, in that position preparing a comprehensive plan for a national militia, a scheme that was rejected by Congress. In December 1794 Knox retired. He died 12 years later, on October 25, 1806, at Thomaston, Maine, when a chicken bone became lodged in his intestines.

Fueled by the current American hope that Canada would join the fighting as the fourteenth colony, Washington dispatched Colonel Benedict Arnold and a force of 1,100 men to move up the Kennebec River through the Maine woods to assault the city of Quebec. Congress at the same time sent Brigadier General Philip Schuyler with 2,000 militiamen to take Montreal, thus recreating the two-pronged strategy of the colonial wars. The left-hand prong under Brigadier General Richard Montgomery (who replaced Schuyler) seized Montreal with little difficulty on November 13, 1775, but Arnold's force suffered greatly as his men trekked through the Maine wilderness. They arrived at Quebec in pitiable condition, having suffered sickness, starvation, and desertion, and failed in their first attempt to take the city.

Joined by Montgomery, the combined forces stormed Quebec on December 30, 1775, during an unmerciful blizzard, but the attack failed when Montgomery was killed and Arnold was wounded. The Americans managed to keep Quebec under siege as reinforcements dribbled in, but when additional British troops arrived in May 1776, Arnold and his exhausted forces pulled out for Ticonderoga. All dreams of adding Canada to the rebellion as the fourteenth colony now faded away.

☆   An American Portrait

George Washington—Born in 1732 in Westmoreland County, Virginia, Washington was raised in the *noblesse oblige* tradition of the southern colonial aristocracy to which he belonged. Despite a lack of formal schooling, Washington carved out a useful life as a surveyor, land developer, and planter. At the age of 22 he was awarded the rank of lieutenant colonel in the Virginia militia, leading his men across the mountains to confront the French at the Forks of the Ohio—unsuccessfully, as it turned out. The next year, 1755, he accompanied the British general Edward Braddock on his ill-fated offensive against the French into the interior, followed by his appointment as colonel and commander-in-chief of the Virginia militia.

From 1759 to 1775 he served in the Virginia House of Burgesses and was a delegate to both the First and Second Continental Congresses. Chosen to command the colonies' makeshift army around Boston on June 15, 1775, because of his military experience and southern prominence, he served in this preeminent position of military authority throughout the war.

Faced with the task of leading the colonies in an improvised and sometimes ambiguous military struggle for independence, Washington displayed extraordinary qualities of leadership, adapting his strategy and tactics to the changing conditions of the war. Although he continually stressed the need for a trained and disciplined national force capable of meeting the British in open combat, he nevertheless realized that his greatest military and national obligation was to keep intact his Continental army—the nucleus of American resistance—by avoiding any action that would risk defeat. Yet he was willing to make spirited assaults when the situation was favorable, as at Trenton (1776) and Yorktown (1781).

In addition to displaying a sure sense of the possible strategically, Washington also exhibited a rare talent in handling his sometimes difficult subordinates and in dealing with America's battlefield allies, the French. Honored even at the time as the living symbol of the Revolution, Washington resigned as commander of the American forces in April 1783 at the end of the war and returned to his plantation, Mount Vernon, on the banks of the Potomac River, only to be called upon to serve as the nation's first president six years later. He filled this political office with the same skill, patience, and distinction he had displayed as a military leader. He died in 1799 and was buried on the grounds of his beloved Virginia estate.

In the south, however, the rebels fared better that first year. John Murray, the Earl of Dunmore and governor of Virginia, recruited a contingent of Loyalists from Tidewater Virginia to aid the Tory cause, but in December 1775 this force was defeated by the Virginia militia plus 200 Continentals south of Norfolk at the Battle of Great Bridge. Then, early in 1776, another patriot militia force defeated a North Carolina militia force under Loyalist governor Josiah Martin at Moore's Creek Bridge. Both colonies thereafter saw royal authority disappear in the face of militia strength. The British, after the first year of the war, could take comfort only in the St. Lawrence defense. Their destruction of Falmouth, Maine, in October 1775 and of Norfolk, Virginia, three months later did not improve their strategic position but only added to the patriots' determination to fight on.

In 1776, of course, the colonists declared their independence from the authority of the Crown and Parliament. It was also a year in which the British government made a major effort to stamp out what had now become a very stubborn rebellion in its American colonies.

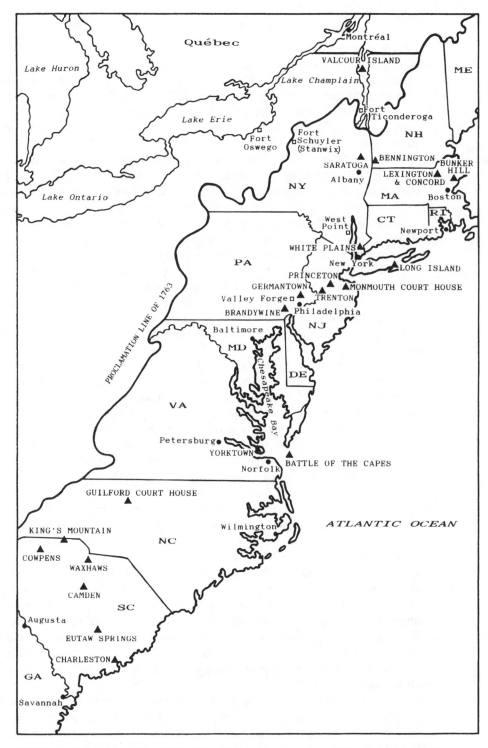

MAP 2–1 Revolutionary War, 1775–1781. (*Used with permission of Anne C. Christensen.*)

In August 1776, the British sent 32,000 troops (formerly Gage's army, which had been evacuated from Boston to Halifax earlier that year) and a powerful fleet of ships (about half the Royal Navy) against New York City by direct assault, while Sir Guy Carleton led 13,000 men down the Lake Champlain route to recapture Fort Ticonderoga and move to Albany, thereafter to swing east into New England. If the assault on New York, led on land by General Sir William Howe and at sea by his brother, the dark-complexioned Vice-Admiral Sir Richard "Black Dick" Howe, was to succeed, the best harbor in America would be in British hands and the army would move up the Hudson and into New England. If Carleton gained his objective, he would join up with William Howe, and New England would be subdued and cut off from the remainder of the rebellious states. The first move succeeded; the second failed.

Washington pulled his Continental Army down from Boston to protect New York, placing 10,000 Continentals and militia on Brooklyn Heights under General Israel Putnam, the other 9,000 men being placed on Manhattan Island. Howe landed 20,000 men on August 27, 1776, and routed the American forward units on Long Island by a flanking maneuver. But then, in typical eighteenth-century style, he put Brooklyn Heights under siege instead of assaulting it directly. This allowed the Americans to escape across the East River to Manhattan.

For the next three months the indolent Howe moved slowly against the colonials in a number of probing actions instead of using the maneuverability of the Royal Navy via the Hudson and East Rivers to trap and annihilate Washington's army. This command dalliance—at least partially explained by the fact that the Howe brothers were also peace commissioners and were trying to persuade the colonists to abandon the fight—permitted the Americans to move north up the Hudson to Harlem Heights, then to White Plains to escape capture or annihilation. General Howe then turned south to move against New Jersey and Philadelphia, sending his brother, Richard, and the navy to capture Newport, Rhode Island. Howe's move south saved Washington and his battered and now-miniscule army of only 2,000 men. They moved across New Jersey and then crossed the Delaware River into Pennsylvania to safety. Washington could not save New Jersey from the British, but, of crucial importance, his tiny army was intact. Howe broke off his drive toward Philadelphia with winter coming on and secured his New York–New Jersey base to await the coming of spring.

☆   An American Portrait

Marie Joseph Paul Roch Gilbert Du Motier, the Marquis de Lafayette—Lafayette, Washington's friend and deputy, was born in 1757 in Auvergne, France, of inherited wealth and nobility. He served in the French army during the time of the Ancien Régime but became interested in the American war for independence both for its ideals and because it offered France a chance to avenge its losses in the Seven Years' War. Sailing for the new United States in April 1777, Lafayette three months later had received a commission as a major general as promised by Silas Deane, the American agent in Paris, but had been given no command. But the French nobleman was soon virtually adopted as a son by Washington and served beside him at Brandywine, Valley Forge, and Monmouth Court House, rendering very valuable aid to the commander as his liaison officer between the French and American armies and also commanding troops in the field.

Sailing for France on furlough in January 1779, Lafayette returned to Boston the next year to prepare for the coming of Rochambeau and his French army. In the last year and a half of the war, Lafayette served as a member of the court-martial board for John Andre, was given command of the army operating in Virginia, and in the spring of 1781, with his 2,500 Continentals and militia, slowly retreated before the advancing Cornwallis, only to turn and harass him until the British general moved out of central Virginia to effect an evacuation at Yorktown. Lafayette played a prominent role in the siege of Yorktown, the battle that led to final victory for the Americans in the war.

After his duty in America, Lafayette returned to France as an enthusiast for the republican ideas he had seen in America and played a part in the ensuing French Revolution, being imprisoned for five years by the radicals because of his moderation. He returned to America in 1824 as the nation's guest of honor and was feted in a one-year grand tour of the country. He died in May 1834 (after declining the presidency of France following the Revolution of 1830) and was buried in Paris, his grave covered with earth from Bunker Hill, as he had requested.

Meanwhile, the other British army under General Carleton was moving down from the St. Lawrence to seize Fort Ticonderoga and move on to Albany. Congress decided that a stand should be made on Lake Champlain. Accordingly, it directed that ship's carpenters be sent from Philadelphia and that ordnance and supplies be sent from New York and Connecticut to build and outfit a fleet there. In six weeks a flotilla of 15 small craft (10 new and 5 existing) was ready, thanks to the diligence of the carpenters and the fleet's commander, General Benedict Arnold.

☆   An American Portrait

Benedict Arnold—One of the most skillful and resourceful leaders in America's war for independence, Arnold is remembered chiefly as the most infamous of all traitors to that cause. Born in 1741 in Connecticut, he ran away at the age of 14 to fight in the French and Indian War, then returned to become a successful druggist, bookseller, and merchant in New Haven. As a captain in the Connecticut militia, Arnold was sent to capture Fort Ticonderoga in the early weeks of the conflict with Great Britain. The fort was taken, but Arnold's leadership was marred by his quarreling with Ethan Allen of Vermont and Benjamin Hinman of Connecticut over rank and precedent.

Appointed a colonel in the Continental Army in 1775, Arnold carried out the first of his three great military accomplishments of the war by leading a contingent of men through the Maine woods to attack Quebec. The siege eventually failed and Arnold was wounded, but his expedition through the rugged northeastern wilderness still stands as one of the great military achievements of the Revolutionary War.

The next year Arnold built a fleet on Lake Champlain to be used against a British force descending from Canada. In the subsequent engagement at Valcour Island, he lost the battle but stopped the British invasion, his second great feat. Passed over by Congress for advancement to major general by five men junior to him in 1777, Arnold was predictably miffed and threatened to resign. Nevertheless, he played a significant role—his third great military accomplishment—in helping to relieve Fort Stanwix in upper New York in 1777 and then played a dashing role in the subsequent Battle of Saratoga, one of the most crucial battles of the war.

Assigned as commander at Philadelphia in 1778 and soon angered by criticism that he was too friendly with the local Tories and by charges of dishonesty placed against him (in addition to being displeased over continued "slights" to him by Congress and by the new alliance with France, of which he disapproved), Arnold, with the help of his wife, began to pass military information to the British. Finally, in 1780, while commander of the garrison at West Point controlling the Hudson River, he agreed to turn over the citadel to the enemy. The plot was discovered, but Arnold managed to escape to the safety of the British lines. His British contact, Major John André, adjutant general to General Clinton, was not so lucky; he was captured and hanged. Arnold was amply rewarded with 6,000 pounds sterling and was given the rank of brigadier general in the British army. Late in the war, he led the British troops in Virginia and in the burning of New London, Connecticut.

At the conclusion of hostilities, Arnold sailed to London, then returned to Canada at a later time to conduct a shipping business there before embarking for London for a final time. He died there in 1801, having never been accepted in England and suffering continuing opprobrium in America as the greatest traitor to the nation's cause of independence.

As the 30-ship British inland fleet came down the lake on October 11, 1776, Arnold and his flotilla had taken a position between Valcour Island and the New York shore. They allowed the British fleet to pass so that its ships would have to beat back against the wind as the Americans sailed out to attack. The eight-hour fight saw the smaller American squadron beaten—Arnold and his remaining vessels slipped away during the night—but the rebels had delayed the British by forcing them to build a fleet and then meet them in combat. As a result, the British attack on Ticonderoga and move on Albany had to be delayed until it was too late in the season to continue the operation. Their withdrawal north after Valcour Island, then, meant the abandonment of the British pincer movement, which could have spelled disaster for the American cause and the end of the rebellion. Arnold's little navy, manned by volunteers and army personnel, had won one of the most important victories of the war.

And Washington, keeping the British off balance, assaulted Britain's Hessian mercenaries at Trenton, New Jersey, on Christmas night in 1776. He then avoided British reinforcements sent against him and attacked Princeton, these moves forcing Howe back into New York.

Nor did the British fare well in the south in their third major offensive of 1776. Believing that region to be a hotbed of Loyalists only waiting for the British army and navy to arrive so that they could overthrow the rebel governments and return the south to loyalty to the Crown, Major General Henry Clinton, Howe's second-in-command, and Admiral Sir Peter Parker were sent to aid the southern cause by a land and sea expedition. They chose to attack Charleston, South Carolina, the great southern seaport and the largest city in the region. The South Carolina militia, aided by Continentals under Major General Charles Lee, built a palmetto log fort, Fort Moultrie, on Sullivan's island at the approach to the harbor and awaited the British amphibious assault. The British attack of June 28, 1776, was badly mishandled. Their regulars were landed on nearby Long Island but were unable to ford the deep water to assault Fort Moultrie. This left the Americans there free to devastate the British fleet with their cannon fire. Parker and Clinton gave up and sailed off for New York, leaving the Loyalists in the south without aid for the next three years.

As the new year of 1777 dawned, the British occupied New York and its environs and Newport, but the Americans held the south and the interior. Thanks to British fumbling and American courage and adaptability, the rebels had not been brought to bay. But 1777 was another major campaign year, and again the British decided to attempt to use the Lake Champlain–Hudson River route down from Canada to divide the Americans' territory and destroy them piecemeal by cutting off New England from the other rebellious areas. According to their plans, one force of 700 regulars and 1,000 Tories and Indians under Lieutenant Colonel Barry St. Leger was to move east from Oswego on Lake Ontario along the Mohawk River to Albany. Here they would be joined by a second force of 7,200 British and Hessian regulars and 650 Loyalist militia and Indians under Major General John Burgoyne moving down from the north. Howe, meanwhile, was to move up from the south after taking Philadelphia, and New England would be cut off from the rest of the rebellious colonies.

But St. Leger turned back after an unsuccessful siege of Fort Stanwix. (The defenders received help from Benedict Arnold and 950 Continentals sent to their aid, and the attackers saw their Indian allies desert.) And Burgoyne, moving slowly because of his tremendous supply train, ran into stern and effective resistance from Horatio Gates and New England militiamen, most pointedly at Bennington, Vermont, where a force of 2,000 militiamen from New England, under Brigadier General John Stark of New Hampshire, wiped out a British foraging party of 650 men and their reinforcements, Burgoyne losing one-tenth of his forces in these engagements.

☆ An American Portrait

Horatio Gates—Gates, one of the few trained soldiers in Washington's command entourage, was born in 1728 in Maldon, Essex, England. He entered the British army as an officer at an early age and served with Braddock in 1755 in the assault on Fort Duquesne (in which he was severely wounded) and then on various frontier posts in the American colonies before returning to England. In August 1772, at the urging of his friend George Washington, he returned to the colonies, bought a plantation, and settled down with his family in Virginia.

When fighting broke out between the colonies and the mother country, Gates was commissioned a brigadier general and appointed adjutant-general of the Continental army on Washington's staff, advancing in rank to major general in 1776. Despite his rare abilities as an organizer of armies, the ever-contentious Gates ran into repeated conflicts with Congress. Appointed to command in the northern department, he rightly won high regard as commander of the nation's forces at the great Patriot victory at Saratoga.

During 1777 and 1778 there were attempts made by persons disgruntled with Washington's leadership to have Gates appointed commander in his place. Gates apparently took no direct part in these efforts to displace his friend and commander, but he allowed his friends to do so. Notwithstanding these attempts to replace him, Washington gave Gates command of the northern department, and then of the forces at Boston in 1778 and 1779. But when Gates took command of the southern armies in 1780, over Washington's objections, and was badly defeated at Camden, South Carolina—the defeat turning into a rout—there was no way his career could be saved. He was replaced by Nathaniel Greene and returned to Virginia.

Thereafter Gates tried twice to clear his name in the Camden matter by demanding a trial on his handling of his troops there. He failed to get his trial in both instances, but Congress finally vindicated him officially. After the war, in 1790, Gates emancipated his slaves, left Virginia, and moved to New York City. He died in April 1806, the stain of Camden having never been removed from his name.

Dogging Burgoyne at every step as he moved southward, the patriot regulars and militia, shocked and angered by the murder and scalping of a white woman, Jane McCrea, by Burgoyne's Indians, established a strong defensive position at Bemis Heights, south of Saratoga, New York. These had been skillfully prepared by Thaddeus Kosciusko, a Polish engineer who had attached himself to the American cause. Burgoyne could not break the patriot's lines in the Battle of Freeman's Farm on September 19 and took heavy casualties. He broke off the attack but was still surrounded by 10,000 militia and reinforcing Continentals. Unable to extricate himself on October 7 in the Battle of Bemis Heights (where Benedict Arnold again distinguished himself and was wounded for a second time), Burgoyne retreated to Saratoga and was forced to surrender himself and almost 6,000 men on October 17, 1777.

In the meantime, Howe, a victim of missed communications between himself and the other commanders, turned south by sea and moved up the Delaware River toward Philadelphia instead of moving north to make his critical juncture with Burgoyne. He was able to push aside the Americans at Brandywine Creek southwest of Philadelphia and take the capital, beating off a surprise Trenton-like attack by Washington at Germantown north of the city, but at the price of a failed grand British offensive of 1777.

BRITAIN MOVES SOUTH AND LOSES THE WAR, 1778–1781

The year 1778 began with what seemed to be bleak prospects for Washington and his Continentals wintering at Valley Forge, 20 miles northwest of Philadelphia, while their adversaries remained safe and warm in the nearby capital (and in New York and Newport). But events were taking place at Valley Forge, in the French capital of Paris, and in the councils of the British high command that would eventually lead to American victory.

At Valley Forge, despite the cold and unnecessary privations caused by Congress's fumbling of the logistical demands of Washington's army, Friedrich Wilhelm von Steuben, an ex-Prussian military officer, now having joined the Americans, introduced simplified drill, musketry, and bayonet tactics to the Continentals, steps that would make them a more formidable fighting force thereafter.

☆ An American Portrait

Frederich Wilhelm (von) Steuben—"Baron" von Steuben, who was in fact not a member of the nobility (his grandfather had inserted the noble prefix *von* of his own accord to impress people), was born in Prussia in 1730. After a successful military career there, including service as a general staff officer under Frederick the Great in the Seven Years' War, followed by years of involuntary retirement from the Prussian army, he set sail for America—promoting himself from captain to lieutenant general—where his military talents were in demand with the outbreak of the revolution against England. He joined Washington at Valley Forge in February 1778 and became his inspector general, in charge of teaching the raw American troops the rudiments of military drill and battlefield tactics. He accomplished this difficult task through a model company of 100 selected men.

By the spring, Washington's Continentals knew how to maneuver and fire on command and how to use the bayonet, skills they put to good use in the Battle of Monmouth in June of that year. By the next year Congress had created the Inspector General's Department, and Steuben became the nation's first inspector general, in charge of training all of the troops. In this capacity he wrote his *Regulations for the Order and Discipline of the Troops of the United States,* or his "Blue Book," which was adopted as the manual of drill field service regulations for the army. The "Blue Book" was reprinted over 70 times before being replaced in 1812 by another manual based upon French, rather than Prussian, military principles.

In addition to serving as inspector general, Steuben also sat on the court martial board for Major John André, gave aid to Nathaniel Greene in Virginia in 1780, and commanded one of Washington's three divisions at Yorktown during the successful siege there. After the war he retired to a 16,000-acre estate given him by the State of New York, helped found the Society of the Cincinnati, made up of Revolutionary War officers, and wrote widely on military affairs until his death on his Mohawk Valley estate in 1794.

Steuben is remembered primarily for his work in instilling military qualities in the Continental Army by adapting Prussian principles based on severe discipline to the liberty-loving American volunteer soldier. Yet his greater contribution to his adopted country and to its military may well have been his *Regulations,* long on the reading list of American officers and the "Bible" of the fledgling American Army.

In Paris, the French, now convinced by Saratoga that the Americans might win the war, and desiring to be on the winning side to recover some of their losses in the Wars for Empire, signed a treaty of alliance with the United States. The Americans had been receiving aid from France prior to this, but now, with France as an ally, American chances brightened considerably, especially when Spain and Holland also soon declared war on Britain. As a result, the British were involved in a world war by 1778 and soon found themselves fighting not just in America but also in the Caribbean, the Mediterranean, India, and Florida against four determined foes. Their strategy had to be reappraised for 1778.

Again assuming, as they had two years before, that the south was Loyalist territory that needed only the presence of British force of arms to separate it from the rebel cause, the new British strategy called for a move into that region to defeat the rebels there. They would form local Loyalist militia units to maintain control over areas taken by the British regulars and then gradually extend their conquests northward, reestablishing British authority and loyalty to the Crown as they went. This policy of pacification would bring the war to an end without calling for major exactions or numbers of troops, a vital consideration in a world war where army and navy strength had to be maintained to fend off possible French attacks at home as well as in far-flung areas of the world.

Preparing for this new strategy, General Henry Clinton (who had replaced General Howe) was ordered to consolidate his forces in New York City. Accordingly, on June 18, 1778, he abandoned Philadelphia to the rebels and marched his 10,000 men north, successfully beating off an American attack on his columns by regulars and New Jersey militiamen under General Charles Lee on June 27 at Monmouth Court House, New Jersey, the last major battle of the war in the north. For the next three years the American and British forces eyed one another from New York and its environs but made no major moves and fought no major battles while the British strategy of pacification of the south was put into operation.

☆   An American Portrait

Charles Lee—Lee, surely one of the most controversial of Washington's lieutenants, was born in Dernhall, Cheshire, England, in 1731. Commissioned a lieutenant in his father's infantry regiment in 1751, Lee was with Braddock on his expedition into western Pennsylvania four years later. He was then transferred to the Mohawk Valley of New York, where he was adopted by the Mohawks and carried on a long-term dalliance with the daughter of a Seneca chief. He was with General Abercromby at his fruitless and foolish assault on Fort Ticonderoga in 1758, and two years later he ably assisted General Amherst in his capture of Montreal before returning to England in 1761.

In Europe, Lee served well under General John Burgoyne in Portugal and then, reduced to half pay at the end of the Seven Years' War, he went to Poland and served as aide-de-camp to Stanislaus Poniatowski, the pro-Russian Pole claiming the throne. Although Lee returned to England the next year, this budding soldier of fortune went back to Poland in 1769 and, as a major general, aided Poniatowski and the Russian army in an offensive against Turkey. All of this experience—and wide reading in military theory and tactics—led Lee to conclude that the conventional stand-up combat of that day was ill-conceived, a belief that led him into grave difficulties later on in America.

Migrating to western Virginia in 1773, Lee brought his strong antimonarchist ideas with him, leading him to become an enthusiastic patriot and zealot for liberty and democracy by 1775, when he obtained a commission as a major general in the Continental Army. He initially served the American cause with distinction, showing great organizational and military engineering skills during the siege of Boston, aiding Colonel William Moultrie and his Charleston defenders in 1776 in preparing for the impending British attack (although Lee was not present when the British offensive failed), and assisting Washington in his battles around New York City later in the year.

At this point, however, Lee's reputation began to fade as he lost faith in Washington for his defense of the New York–Hudson River area and became a carping critic of his commander for his strategy and conventional tactics. (Lee espoused guerrilla-type combat based on the colonial militia.) In addition, he was extremely dilatory—if not derelict in his duty—in not supporting Washington in his retreat across New Jersey. Taken prisoner by the British in December 1776, Lee may well have been guilty of treason by drawing up a plan for them whereby the Howe brothers could defeat the American forces, although some argue that it was all a ruse to deceive General Howe.

Exchanged in April 1778 just in time to join Washington at Valley Forge as he was about to take the offensive against the British forces withdrawing from Philadelphia for New

York, Lee first rejected, then accepted, field command of the American troops assembled to attack the British columns. At the ensuing Battle of Monmouth, Lee, behind Anthony Wayne (who was on the point of the attack), suddenly began to retreat. (He had argued earlier against attacking the British in open combat.) The retreat was rapidly turning into a rout when Washington arrived, quarreled with Lee, took over command of the troops, and stopped the withdrawal.

Lee demanded a court martial to clear his name, but, his wish having been granted, he was convicted of disobedience of orders for not attacking, misbehavior before the enemy because of retreating, and disrespect for his commander-in-chief. However, he was only suspended from the army for 12 months as punishment. He never returned to command. Retiring to his Virginia estate the next year, in 1779, Lee spent his time writing insulting letters to Congress, the press, and his erstwhile friends. For his ill-considered efforts he was dismissed from the army in January 1780. He died two years later in Philadelphia, a political and tactical radical to the end.

In December 1778, Clinton and 3,500 of his men easily secured Savannah and overran the rest of Georgia. Then, in May 1780, Charleston fell to the British after a one-month siege, along with the entire American Continental force of 5,400 men there under General Benjamin Lincoln. It was the greatest loss of the war for the Americans. Meanwhile 350 Virginians were wiped out at the Waxhaws near the North Carolina border by the Loyalist British Legion commanded by Lieutenant Colonel Banastre Tarleton. The legionnaires killed off those patriots who surrendered, despite their having displayed a white flag of surrender. Turning over the task of pacification to Major General Charles Cornwallis, Clinton sailed north. The situation in the south was apparently well in hand. British authority was being reestablished, and Loyalist militia units were being formed behind the British regulars.

The British situation improved still further when Congress, over the objections of Washington, appointed General Horatio Gates, the hero of Saratoga, to command a new southern army. This army met Cornwallis's force on August 16, 1780, near Camden, South Carolina, and suffered complete defeat, the militia abandoning the field in panic before the attacks of the British regulars.

During these years of conflict east of the Appalachians from New England to Georgia, a secondary theater of war was also blazing on the frontier all the way from New York to the Florida border. Here the British allied themselves with various Indian tribes, long indignant over colonial incursions into their territories, to war against the colonial rebels. In the New York–Pennsylvania area the war split the Iroquois Confederacy. The Oneidas and Tuscaroras sided with the Americans; the other four tribes, with the British. The Mohawks, under Chief Joseph Brant, with their Tory allies, made numerous attacks in 1778 out of their base at Fort Niagara on Pennsylvania and New York frontier settlements, burning and slaughtering as they went. This led to a punitive expedition against them the next year. It was headed by General John Sullivan and made up of 4,200 trained regulars. Sullivan and his men were successful in securing the Iroquois country for the Americans by besting the Loyalist rangers and the Iroquois in a series of engagements before rejoining Washington's main force, but sporadic fighting on the northern frontier between Loyalists and Patriots and their Indian allies continued until the end of the war.

In the west, the British lieutenant governor at Detroit, Henry Hamilton (the "Hairbuyer"), sent raiding parties from there into Kentucky with telling effect in 1777 and 1778. To curb this menace, Virginia governor Patrick Henry and the General Assembly sent 25-year-old Lieutenant Colonel George Rogers Clark to capture Kaskaskia and Vincennes (in present-day Illinois and Indiana) in 1778. Clark was then to capture Detroit. But Hamilton recaptured Vincennes and held it briefly before Clark took it back. Clark also managed to take Hamilton prisoner. But Clark's forces were never large enough to seize Detroit, the heart of British operations in the Indian country, so fighting continued on this frontier until the war ended.

In the south, the Cherokees rose up against the Americans in 1776 but were put down by militiamen from Georgia and the Carolinas. The continued weak British position in the interior of the south kept the Indians in check during the war, although the Cherokees rose up again in 1780, only to be severely chastised for a second time. As in the north and the west, Indian warfare backed by the British brought temporary terror to the southern frontier at various times, but these Indian wars—a continuation of a frontier theme of a century's duration of whites using the natives to advance their own fortunes—played only a minor role in the strategies and outcome of the conflict.

The year 1780 saw the whole war turn around. In the north, a 5,000-man French force under the Comte de Rochembeau arrived in Newport to secure that port and nail down New England. And in the south, the depredations of the Loyalist militia units (who used their new-found power against their patriot neighbors) pushed the American guerrillas to fight on and persuaded many formerly neutral southerners to join the rebel cause. Under such men as Francis Marion ("the Swamp Fox"), the dour Andrew Pickens, and Thomas Sumter ("the Gamecock"), ferocious guerrilla warfare against British regulars and the Tory militia units blazed up in South Carolina, North Carolina, and Georgia. This resistance was highlighted in October 1780 at King's Mountain, South Carolina, where 1,700 American irregulars from North Carolina and Virginia wiped out a force of 1,000 Loyalist militiamen sent into the interior to recruit more Tory supporters. Congress sent Nathaniel Greene south to lead the American resistance, replacing the incompetent Horatio Gates, and Brigadier General Daniel Morgan soon joined him. Although the combatants did not realize it at the time, the drama of the American Revolution was moving into its final act.

☆ An American Portrait

Nathaniel Greene—Greene, Washington's quartermaster-general and southern commander after 1780, was born in Rhode Island in 1742. Becoming prominent in the iron business and as a deputy in that colony's General Assembly, in May 1775 he led a brigade of militia to nearby Boston and was soon commissioned a brigadier general in the Continental Army besieging Boston. Serving as commander of the garrison at Boston after the British evacuated the city in 1776, Greene was soon assigned the defenses of New York City and by August had been advanced to the rank of major general. He served alongside Washington in the Christmas attack on Trenton that year and remained with him through 1777 and 1778 before accepting the post of quartermaster-general in February 1778. While Greene enjoyed considerable success in improving Washington's logistical situation, he also assisted him on the field of battle at Monmouth and fought alongside General John Sullivan in his attack with D'Estaing on Newport, Rhode Island. He resigned the post of quartermaster-general in anger in August 1780 when Congress charged him with maladministration.

Taking over the command at West Point after the treason of Benedict Arnold, Greene soon emerged as a skillful field commander when, in October 1780, Washington chose him to replace Horatio Gates in the south after the near fatal disaster at Camden. With the cooperation of Francis Marion, Thomas Sumter, and Andrew Pickens, leaders of the colonial irregulars, his southern forces gained important victories for the American cause. In January 1781 his subordinate Daniel Morgan of Virginia defeated the detested Banastre Tarleton at Cowpens, South Carolina. This was followed by Greene's strategic retreat designed to pull the forces of Cornwallis into the interior before turning on him at Guilford Court House. Later, in September 1781, Greene inflicted a severe defeat on the British at Eutaw Springs, South Carolina. Following Yorktown, Greene's forces cleared all of South Carolina of British forces except Charleston, but that important port city was held under siege until the British finally evacuated it on December 14, 1782. Greene, his military service over at the end of hostilities, lived in Rhode Island and Georgia after the war. He died at Mulberry Grove near Savannah in June 1786.

Greene daringly divided his army between himself and Morgan, forcing Cornwallis to do the same. The British general sent the hated Tarleton and 1,100 infantrymen after Morgan while he inched forward to cut off his escape. But Morgan stopped at Cowpens, South Carolina, in January 1781 and, in a move reminiscent of the great Roman victory at Cannae in 216 B.C., drew Tarleton into a trap and annihilated his forces in an amazing display of regulars and militiamen operating as an effective combined force. Over 900 casualties were inflicted on the British, a serious blow to Cornwallis.

Rejoined by Morgan, Greene let Cornwallis chase him north (leaving the guerrillas in South Carolina to operate safely), finally crossing into Virginia and then back into North Carolina. Greene and his 4,500 Continentals and militia met Cornwallis and his 1,900 regulars at Guilford Court House, North Carolina, on March 15, 1781. The British won this hard-fought battle, but Cornwallis lost one-fourth of his men and was forced to retreat to Wilmington to be resupplied by sea. He had about 9,500 men in his command, but 8,000 of them were scattered throughout South Carolina and Georgia. If he called them in, he would surely lose control of those territories; if he left them at their posts, he had limited effectives at hand to bring the rebel forces to bay. And logistical problems were bedeviling the British war of pacification in the south every time they ventured into the interior.

Cornwallis soon moved out again to invade Virginia, which he saw as the heart of southern resistance. As Cornwallis moved north, Greene moved south into the Carolinas and Georgia, where his regulars and militiamen battered the British at Eutaw Springs, South Carolina, in September and gained effective control of the entire area of the south except for Wilmington, Savannah, and Charleston. The British strategy of incremental pacification was proving to be singularly ineffective, its weakness traceable to its lack of sufficient regular troops to hold conquered areas effectively while also moving against the rebels and in its reliance on overbearing and sometimes vengeful Loyalist militia to hold and pacify these conquered areas. The British were also hampered by logistical problems as they were drawn away from their critical supply bases on the sea.

By early 1781 the British had sent Benedict Arnold (now a British brigadier general) to Virginia with 1,600 men, and Washington had countered with 1,200 men under Lafayette. Cornwallis arrived in Virginia from the south but failed to bring the Americans to decisive battle in the interior. Now in overall command of all British forces in Virginia (some 7,000 men), the British commander sent Arnold, whom he did not like, off to New York. Then, under orders from Clinton in New York (who realized Cornwallis's precarious position with two French fleets in America able to combine and cut him off from aid), Cornwallis moved to Yorktown on the York River off the Chesapeake Bay on August 1, 1781. Here he would await resupply or, if necessary, evacuation to New York or Charleston via his seaborne lifeline.

Moving quickly when informed that a French fleet under Rear Admiral Francois the Count de Grasse was headed toward Chesapeake Bay (on the advice of Rochembeau), Washington scuttled his plans for a French-American land and sea attack on New York. He ordered his New York army of 8,000 men, having been joined by Rochembeau's army from Newport, to move south via Chesapeake Bay (leaving 2,000 men above New York to distract Clinton) and join with Lafayette to put Cornwallis under siege. Washington also ordered the French naval squadron of Commodore Louis the Count de Barras at Newport to sail to Yorktown with artillery and provisions.

When De Grasse arrived at the Chesapeake with 24 ships, he debarked 3,000 troops to join Lafayette, stationed himself at the mouth of the bay, and, in the Battle of the Capes on September 5, 1781, beat off an attempt by the British fleet from New York under Rear Admiral Thomas Graves to enter the bay and relieve the trapped land forces there. De Grasse was joined by Barras's fleet on September 10, and Graves, now outclassed, sailed back to New York. Cornwallis, under siege from parallel trenches erected under the direction of Washington, Henry Knox, and French engineers, and surrounded by 7,000 French troops, 5,700 Continentals, and 3,000 militiamen, had no choice but to surrender.

On October 19, 1781, British troops marched out of their defenses in the village of Yorktown and stacked their arms. For all practical purposes the war was over. The American rebels had won, although troops remained in the field for two more years. Faced with a world war that was going badly, with French successes in the Caribbean, Spain seizing West Florida, Gibraltar under siege, and control of India slipping away, British political opinion definitely shifted after the disastrous defeat at Yorktown. A fear gripped the British that all the imperial gains of 1689 to 1763 were about to be lost in a prolonged no-win conflict in the American colonies. The existing government fell from power, and a new cabinet pledged to seeking peace took its place. British will had finally been broken.

Peace between Great Britain and the United States was formalized in the Treaty of Paris of September 1783. The American grand strategy of avoiding defeat and thus prolonging the war while seeking the aid of other nations had been successful. The indecisive British grand strategy of attempting to bring law and order to New England, and then trying to defeat the rebels in conventional combat, and finally attempting to pacify the south had failed. The first war of American independence—a war that spelled the beginning of the end of eighteenth-century limited and professional warfare because of its high ideological content and its reliance on citizen-soldiers, a war that took 25,000 American lives, and a war in which American military commanders displayed a remarkable talent for adaptive strategy and tactics—had been won.

THE WAR AT SEA

When the Revolutionary War began, the rebellious colonies had no navy. Although a Continental Navy and 11 state navies were subsequently created, they had little effect on the outcome of the war, spending most of their time bobbing alongside wharves because they were too few and too weak to take on the Royal Navy and break its hold on the American coast and North Atlantic waters. The Continental Navy dispatched only 60 ships to sea during the entire war, and they seized or destroyed only about 200 vessels. However, the record of America's privateers was outstanding, and the contributions of the French navy after 1778 were vital to the colonies' eventual triumph.

Not until October 13, 1775, was a Continental Navy created, this out of consternation over the British destruction of Falmouth, Maine, that month. From the beginning and throughout the war this navy was run by a Congressional committee and was completely outside General Washington's control. The committee showed a marked disposition to put its members' relatives in charge of vessels, as was the case when the inexperienced Esek Hopkins was given command of the 24-gun frigate *Alfred*. Hopkins left the Delaware in February 1776 for Virginia with seven other vessels under orders to clear Chesapeake Bay of British ships. But he completely bypassed the bay and seized Nassau in the Bahamas instead. He then lost a nighttime duel with the smaller British frigate *Glasgow* off New London, Connecticut, on the way home. Hopkins was court-martialed, and his fleet never sailed again. Nor did David Bushnell's one-man submarine, *The Turtle*, manage to sink its target, Admiral Howe's flagship, HMS *Eagle*, on the night of September 6, 1776, despite the bravery and tenacity of army sergeant Ezra Lee, its lone crew member.

Two years later, on March 17, 1778, the 32-gun frigate *Randolph*, under Nicholas Biddle, was destroyed by the 64-gun HMS *Yarmouth* off Barbados. And a summer 1779 expedition by a sizable American squadron under Captain Dudley Saltonstall against a British base being built at the mouth of the Penobscot River in Maine turned into a complete rout with the arrival of a small British fleet.

On the positive side, that same year, 1779, saw the victory of John Paul Jones and the *Bonhomme Richard* (ex-merchant vessel *Duc de Duras*) over the 44-gun HMS *Serapis* off Flamborough Head on the Yorkshire coast of England. Herein the Americans finally found a genuine naval hero, whose defiant words of rejection of a surrender offer halfway through the battle, "I have not yet begun to fight," thrilled the Americans and seemed to embody their spirit of defiance in the protracted conflict.

Yet if America's saltwater navy did not compile an enviable record in the war, her privateers did. Privateers were vessels whose captains or owners had secured letters of marque (legal permission) to seize British merchant and supply vessels. All types of vessels (sloops, schooners, and converted fishing vessels) remained active as privateers during the conflict, their favored haunts being the American coast, the waters off the Gulf of St. Lawrence, and the Caribbean. Some vessels even operated in European waters.

As weapons of war, the privateers proved very effective. Some 2,000 American privateers captured over 2,200 British vessels, forcing the Royal Navy to extend itself by assuming convoy duty to protect British merchant vessels. The American privateers, authorized by Congress or by the states, hardly won the war, but they contributed significantly to victory by harassing the British merchant vessels and forcing the Royal Navy to deal with them as a constant threat to the Crown's logistical lifeline to the rebellious colonies.

It was the French navy that played the most vital role in the Americans' victory. Indeed, without the French navy's help after the Treaty of Alliance in 1778 it is unlikely the Americans would have achieved a decisive victory as they did at Yorktown. France entered into the American war with a rebuilt and revitalized navy of 80 ships of the line and 67,000 men, but its first sortie into the conflict was disappointing in the extreme. In April 1778, two months after the Treaty of Alliance, Admiral Charles Hector, Comte d'Estaing, arrived with a fleet off New York harbor to aid Washington in attacking the city but refused to enter to take on Admiral Richard Howe's fleet because of the deep draft of his ships. Instead, he sailed off to Newport to bombard the city and bottle up the British fleet in that Rhode Island harbor while General Sullivan launched a simultaneous land attack. When Howe moved up to challenge him, neither admiral would commit to a fight. They were then scattered by a storm. Subsequently, Howe took his fleet back to New York, and d'Estaing sailed off to Boston, then to the Caribbean, the patriots' war effort being aided not at all by his presence in the northern American waters and Sullivan being left in an untenable position at Newport.

The next year, in October 1779, d'Estaing, in cooperation with General Benjamin Lincoln and 1,350 men of his southern army, attacked the main British base at Savannah with 20 ships and over 5,000 troops. But they mounted a direct assault instead of laying siege to the base because the hurricane season precluded any extended operations in the area, and they suffered a humiliating defeat. D'Estaing thereupon sailed to the West Indies, and this second Franco-American joint venture was also a failure.

In time, however, the French fleet began to tip the balance in the rebels' favor. By 1780 the French and Spanish fleets had gained control of the Caribbean waters, and in July of that year d'Estaing seized Newport after it had been abandoned by the British. The British by this time were so committed worldwide that they could not even challenge French control of that vital New England port.

Finally, when General Cornwallis moved to Yorktown in 1781 to await resupply or evacuation, the presence of the French fleet brought victory for Franco-American arms. As we have seen, as Washington moved down to Virginia from New York with his troops and those of Rochembeau from Newport, Admiral de Grasse moved up from the Caribbean and stationed his fleet between Cape Henry and Cape Charles at the mouth of Chesapeake Bay. When the British fleet under Admiral Thomas Graves arrived on the scene to aid Cornwallis, it could not force its way into the bay, and it suffered a major defeat in the Battle of the Capes. The French admiral also managed to draw off Graves' fleet for five critical days, allowing Barras from Newport, with artillery and provisions for the siege, and Washington's Continentals and Rochembeau's French forces sailing down the Chesapeake Bay from Head of Elk to slip by. Graves had no choice but to return to New York, and Cornwallis had no choice but to surrender. For all practical purposes this ended the war on American soil in the rebels' favor, even though the French and British fleets tangled again in the great Caribbean sea struggle called the Battle of the Saints the following year. Britain retained New York and Charleston and continued to harass the Americans on the frontier until the peace treaty was signed two years later.

French naval power had proved to be one of the most decisive elements in the struggle that created the United States of America. Unfortunately, the new nation would be forced to fight two more wars before its independence and national rights would finally be recognized by the European powers.

DOMESTIC CONFLICT AND FRONTIER ACTION

At the end of the Revolutionary War, Congress moved quickly to scale back the military. Congress's actions were hastened by vivid memories of the "Newburg Conspiracy" of 1782–1783, in which a group of disgruntled army officers at Newburg, New York, above West Point, egged on by certain nationalist politicians (who wanted to use the officers' discontent to give Congress permanent taxing power), appear to have threatened to disobey orders and not disband until their back pay was forthcoming. In the face of this seeming *coup d'etat*, General Washington had defused the situation by movingly appealing directly to the men and to Congress, which granted the officers back pay and full pay for five years instead of half pay for life, as they had demanded. The "conspiracy" ended, but the incident—plus a march in 1783 on the Pennsylvania State House and on the Congress and Pennsylvania legislature meeting there by troops from that state demanding immediate discharge and full pay—aroused fear of a standing army as a danger to the nation and added to the haste to disband the Army the next year.

These events brought to the fore the national concern over the type of military best suited to the new United States. Should there be a standing army, and, if so, how large and under whose control? Those who wanted a strong central authority tended to favor an adequate standing army and navy able to defend the nation's interests and an adequate taxing power to support them. Those who wanted a weak central government, with most powers remaining in the hands of the states, and who saw a standing army and high taxes as threats to personal liberty favored relying on militias under state control. Thus the issue of centralization versus decentralization was joined immediately after the war and remained an area of contention throughout the remaining years of the Confederation and the first decades under the new Constitution.

In 1783 Congress appointed a committee, chaired by Alexander Hamilton, to investigate the military question. The committee's star witness, the venerable George Washington, recommended a small standing army of 2,630 men and a national militia. The committee accepted his ideas and, with some changes, presented them to Congress, but that strongly antinationalist body rejected these suggestions and cut the Army back to a mere handful of men in June 1784.

But since there had to be some force other than state-controlled militia to police the Indians and keep an eye on the British on the frontier, Congress had no choice but to raise an adequate force for duties there. Accordingly, in 1784 it called for a 700-man unit raised by four states and the next year made it a regular force under Josiah Harmar of Pennsylvania. This small standing force was never effective in guarding the frontier against either the Indians or the British, a serious weakness in the eyes of the nationalists, leading them to doubt even more seriously the whole decentralized confederation type of government.

In 1786 an "army" of debt-ridden farmers in Massachusetts took up arms in their demand for relief and attacked the Springfield arsenal in January of the next year. Congress called for a 1,300-man force of volunteers—the first time the Army was called upon to carry out constabulary duties against American citizens—to put down the rebellion, but it arrived too late to forestall the move by Daniel Shays and his men on the arsenal. The rebellion had to be quelled by the Massachusetts militia. The central government's power to enforce its laws through its military if necessary had proved to be totally inadequate and moved many national leaders to consider some fundamental constitutional changes for the United States.

The new government created in Philadelphia in 1787 balanced the powers of the central government against those of the states as one of its central principles. This included the military. Congress was given the power to establish an army and a navy and the right to collect taxes to support them. But to guard against the power of an unchecked military, military appropriations were limited to two years. Congress alone could declare war, and it was to provide the means for calling out the militia to execute the laws and ensure the peace if necessary. In such cases the militia would be under federal authority; otherwise militia units would be controlled by the states. But Congress's power over the military was also checked by the provisions that the president would be the commander in chief and would appoint military officers (with the advice and consent of the Senate). Thus the Constitution guarded against military tyranny by placing it under two authorities—one legislative, one executive.

The states, on the other hand, were allowed to keep their militias and could appoint officers for them. The result was that the existing two-track structure of federal forces plus state militia was built into the new system of government, a proviso that, with various refinements, continues to the present day.

When the new government was constituted in 1789, it took over the Army—there was no navy—by placing it under Secretary of War Henry Knox; placed the militia under the president when federalized; and, under the Uniform Militia Act of 1792, called for all white men between the ages of 18 and 45 to serve in the militia. But this militia law contained no enforcement or federal supervisory provisions, so in effect the states were in complete control of their militias. As soon became evident, neither the small regular army nor the state militia units were equal to the task when called upon to "provide for the common defense" and "insure domestic tranquility" as events on the frontier called both the regulars and militiamen to constabulary duty in the last decade of the eighteenth century and the first decades of the nineteenth.

The state militia units proved to be poorly organized, poorly trained, and poorly led, as was revealed in the Whiskey Rebellion of 1794 in western Pennsylvania. This revolt by the frontiersmen was against internal excise taxes, inadequate protection from the Indians, foreign control of the Mississippi, the indifference of eastern centers of government to their problems, and—as they saw it—the crushing of their liberties in general. It was against the federal excise tax on whiskey in particular. It ended with little bloodshed as militia units from eastern Pennsylvania, New Jersey, Maryland, and Virginia—the "watermelon armies," as they were dubbed in derision—slowly made their way to the scene. But the suppression of the rebellion must be credited more to ambiguity of purpose and confusion on the part of the frontier rebels than to the prowess and fighting effectiveness of the federal government's almost 13,000 "volunteer" forces from the states, most of whom were reluctantly drafted into the service or were paid substitutes, in both cases coming from the lower classes of society.

Nor did the puny federal forces distinguish themselves in constabulary duty in fighting the Indians on the frontier. Victory was finally achieved, but only limited credit could be given to Brigadier General Josiah Harmar, Major General Arthur St. Clair, and their regular Army contingents.

The Amerindians beyond the Appalachians in the Old Northwest proved restive under American rule after the nation achieved its independence. Much of the trouble was caused by the white men moving into the Indians' territories in the Ohio Country. These incursions were fiercely resented by the Indians. Their ill feelings were fueled by the British, who refused to give up their forts in the Northwest as agreed to in the Treaty of Paris of 1783 because the wartime Loyalists' confiscated properties had not been paid for after the war as promised, and who gave the Indians arms and supplies. When the new settlers in the trans-Appalachian territories began issuing veiled threats of alliance with England or Spain if help was not forthcoming, the federal government decided that something had to be done about the Indians, and it turned to the military for help. Even though the regular Army of 2,283 officers and men was on the frontier (the number having been raised at Washington's pleading), this was clearly not enough power to police the frontier or solve the Indian problem.

Accordingly, General Harmar was ordered to cooperate with Governor Arthur St. Clair of the Northwest Territory and raise an army to move against the Miami Indian tribes in the Ohio Country. In 1790, some 1,400 men marched out of Fort Washington (now Cincinnati) to carry out a two-pronged attack on the Indians. It failed completely. So the next year, in 1791, a second offensive, led by St. Clair and made up of 600 regulars and 1,400 militiamen, was launched. This second movement proved to be as dilatory as the first. By November St. Clair's "Legion" finally reached the banks of the Wabash River in Ohio, its numbers down to only 1,400 by this time because of illness and desertions. Early on the morning of November 4, 1791, the soldiers were suddenly attacked by 1,000 Indians commanded by Chief Little Turtle. Some 600 men died and another 300 were wounded before the surprise attack ended. It was one of the most decisive defeats suffered by the American Army in its long history. St. Clair's military career was ended.

Despite the pleas of many seaboard Americans to abandon the frontier, President Washington persisted. Congress was now finally willing to authorize an army of 5,000 men, and Washington chose the Revolutionary War hero Major General "Mad Anthony" Wayne of Pennsylvania to lead a third expedition. In 1794, Wayne, having trained his frontier soldiers thoroughly for two years, moved out from Fort Washington with 3,000 of his best men. Moving on a British fort called Fort Miamis (on the site of present-day Toledo), he was attacked by the Indians almost within sight of the fortification. Wayne and his men beat off their first assault and then launched a bayonet charge, driving the Indians out of their defensive positions among fallen trees and onto the prairie, where his mounted militiamen destroyed their ranks. After this crucial Battle of Fallen Timbers, Wayne burned the Indians' village and their crops. Impressed by this battle, the Indians in the western Ohio Country agreed to the Treaty of Greenville of August 1795 (dictated

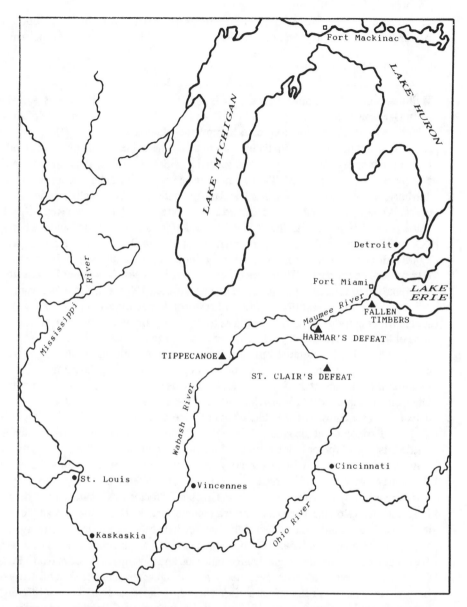

MAP 2–2   Western Frontier, 1778–1817. (*Used with permission of Anne C. Christensen*)

to them by Wayne), wherein they espoused peace and ceded their lands to the United States, setting off another flood of pioneers into the Northwest Territory.

In the meantime, Wayne's successor as commander, Brigadier General James Wilkinson (an intriguer and sometime charleton in the pay of the Spanish since 1791 and later involved in a conspiracy with Vice President Aaron Burr to establish a separate nation in the West) returned to the East to denounce Wayne and further his campaign to become general of the Army. Wayne died in December 1796 without having the opportunity to answer Wilkinson's charges, and Wilkinson succeeded him as general of the Army.

☆   An American Portrait

William Henry Harrison—Although he is usually associated with the trans-Appalachian west, Harrison was born in Virginia in 1773 and spent his early years in the Old Dominion. Initially educated at home, he entered Hampden-Sydney College in 1787 and then went to Richmond and on to Philadelphia in 1791 to study medicine. Abandoning his studies, he joined the infantry that same year and served as aide-de-camp to Anthony Wayne in the Northwest Territory in 1798. Two years later he was appointed governor of the Indiana Territory, where he oversaw land grants and treaties with the Indians, including the 1809 Treaty of Fort Wayne, wherein the Indians granted 2.5 million acres on the Wabash River to the United States (a treaty provision the Shawnee Indian leader Tecumseh said he would not honor).

As a result of this and other Indian difficulties, in October 1811 Harrison led about 1,000 militia, volunteers from Kentucky and Indiana, and regulars against Tecumseh and his brother The Prophet at Tippecanoe Creek. The Shawnees' November 7 predawn attack was repulsed in furious fighting, and Harrison suffered 190 casualties in the engagement.

After unsuccessfully urging on President James Madison a general war on the Indian tribes early in 1812, Harrison was ready for action when war with Britain came in June of that year. Brevetted (given a higher honorary rank without higher pay or authority) a major general of the Kentucky militia, Harrison marched his men to the successful relief of the Americans at Fort Wayne. As a brigadier general in the regular Army he was placed in supreme command of the Army of the Northwest but made some rash movements across Ohio and in January 1813 saw his subordinate Brigadier General James Winchester defeated at Frenchtown on the Raisin River by the British under Colonel Henry Proctor.

Harrison spent the next six months rebuilding his shattered army and standing on the defensive as Proctor twice besieged him and his men at Fort Meigs at Miami Rapids. But when Oliver Hazard Perry's victory on September 10, 1813, at Put-in-Bay crushed British naval power on Lake Erie. Harrison went on the offensive. By September 29, Detroit was reoccupied by the Americans, and on October 5 Proctor was overtaken and defeated by Harrison's forces on the Thames River in a mounted attack. This victory broke the power of the British in the Northwest and led to the pacification of the Indians in the territory.

Harrison was promoted to major general in 1813 on the strength of his victories in the West, but the next year he resigned his commission and took up residence at North Bend near Cincinnati. The war hero's years thereafter were taken up with politics. Between 1816 and 1819 he served in Congress; in 1819 he sat as a senator in the Ohio legislature; between 1825 and 1828 he served in the U.S. Senate; during 1828–1829 he was minister to Columbia; and finally, in 1840, he was elected the ninth president of the United States on the Whig ticket, his campaign slogan "Tippecanoe and Tyler too" playing on his role as a frontier war hero 2 1/2 decades before. He died of pneumonia on April 4, 1841, after only a month in office.

Within a decade and a half, further incursions of whites into Indian lands led to another confrontation. The Indian resistance leaders were Tecumseh, chief of the Shawnee tribe, and his brother The Prophet, who formed a sizable Indian defensive alliance among the various tribes. At the urging of the western settlers, William Henry Harrison, governor of the Indiana Territory, decided to strike first. With a band of 300 regulars and 650 militiamen he set out from Vincennes in September 1811 toward Tecumseh's main village at Tippecanoe Creek in western Indiana. As his party neared the site on the morning of November 7, 1811, it was attacked by the Indians, who were driven off in furious hand-to-hand combat. Harrison saw 70 of his men killed in this engagement, less important for subduing the Indian menace on the frontier than for its effects on the declaration of war on Britain the next year (the Indians at Tippecanoe were found to have new British rifles in their possession) and for helping William Henry Harrison's political career, which eventually brought him to the presidency in 1840.

The Army also helped extend the frontier in these years through two major expeditions and, indeed, began the Army's exploration tradition, a vital nineteenth-century component of its service to the nation. In 1803 the United States obtained the Louisiana Territory from France (who had bought it from Spain three years before) for only $15 million, despite President Thomas Jefferson's constitutional scruples over the transaction. The demands for a more secure American hold on the vital port of New Orleans at the mouth of the Mississippi and western farmers' long-standing demands for free and unhindered passage on that waterway seemed more important to Jefferson and most Americans than the means of acquisition of the territory. The Army took formal possession of the territory in December 1803.

But Jefferson really did not know what the country had purchased, so he sent Captain Meriwether Lewis and Lieutenant William Clark to explore and map the region. Their expedition of 51 men left St. Louis in May 1804 and returned in September 1806, having ascended the Missouri River, traversed the Rockies, and reached the Pacific Ocean via the Columbia River before returning through present-day Montana. In the meantime, Captain Zebulon Pike had explored the area of present-day Colorado. Both missions were of lasting importance to the nation, which now had a much better legal claim and much better knowledge of the tremendous area it had purchased. The Army's role in pacifying the Indians and in opening up the West was not over, however. It was only beginning. For the remainder of the century the Army would play a major role in opening up the nation's western lands, eventually extending all the way to the Pacific.

Yet whatever the plusses or minuses of the military's actions during these years, the political-philosophic issue of centralization through federal power versus decentralization by the maintenance of state and local powers did not fade. Federal policies in all areas of governance—the military, taxes, tariffs, assumption of state debts, the creation of a central bank, and so on—led first to political factions and then to contending political parties. The Federalists emerged as the champions of greater central authority, government policies to create a varied and dynamic commercial-industrial economy, and rule by a natural elite. The Democratic-Republicans spoke as the champions of localism, republicanism through state power, an agrarian economy, and a greater range of governmental participation by a broader range of citizens. This basic difference in outlook and aspirations for the nation also resulted in partisan differences over foreign policy as America became entangled in Europe's conflicts. These, in turn, determined the makeup and function of America's armed forces and led to participation in three more foreign conflicts before 1815.

CONFLICT WITH FRANCE: THE QUASI-WAR

While the American army was pacifying the frontier and exploring the new western lands during these years, momentous events were taking place in Europe that soon dragged the young nation into conflict with two Old World powers. The year 1789, in which the United States inaugurated a new government under its Constitution, saw the beginning of the French Revolution. This political upheaval against the Bourbon monarchy would end ten years later with the coming to power of a Corsican artillery officer, Napoleon Bonaparte, to lead the convulsive French nation. In the meantime, France had declared war on the other European powers, including Great Britain, who were determined to restore Bourbon authority and stamp out the contagious fires of revolution sparked by the revolutionary ideas of the French radicals.

Since both Britain and France relied heavily on supplies being shipped in from their colonies and from neutral countries, and since the United States was fast becoming the leading neutral supplier and shipper as the war dragged on, it was inevitable that both sides would refuse to recognize the neutral rights of the young and militarily weak nation across the Atlantic. Both Britain and France used every conceivable legality to seize American ships and cargoes going to their enemy, thus dragging the proud new nation into their war of exhaustion.

The British were the first primary violators of American rights on the high seas, but President Washington was determined to keep the country out of war. Accordingly, he sent John Jay to London to work out a treaty guaranteeing American rights and settling all other outstanding bones of contention. Jay, his bargaining power undercut by the pro-British secretary of the treasury, Alexander Hamilton, returned with a treaty in 1795 that was, at best, half a loaf, but probably all that could have been obtained under the circumstances. Britain agreed to give up its forts in the Northwest at long last and to allow some American trade with its Caribbean possessions, but it would not give up its "right" to seize neutral (i.e., American) vessels carrying goods to France. The Jay Treaty (only lukewarmly accepted by Washington and barely passed by the Senate) prevented war with Britain, but France, angered by its provisions, then began to seize American vessels too.

As the situation had pointed toward war since 1793, Congress belatedly agreed to rebuild the moribund Navy, as the merchant-backed Federalists under Alexander Hamilton had long urged and as the country-backed and anti-standing-military Democratic-Republicans had long resisted. Six new 204-foot frigates were authorized in 1794, but by 1797 only the *United States, Constellation,* and *Constitution* had been launched. It was not much of a navy, but it was called to duty when President John Adams's fumbling diplomacy failed and the United States found itself in an undeclared war with France, the "Quasi-War," in 1798.

Congress was initially willing to authorize the president to activate 80,000 militiamen for only three months to supplement the regular force of 3,300 men. But when fighting actually began, Congress created the Provisional Army, with infantry, harbor defense, and ordnance units under aging ex-president George Washington as lieutenant general. This army grew to 4,000 men by 1800, but it had nothing to do, since the Quasi-War was fought entirely at sea. It was disbanded in June 1800 even before the war officially ended, and, with the antimilitary Jeffersonians coming to power in 1801, was soon scaled back to only 3,000 officers and men.

Meanwhile, the Quasi-War at sea went on. During the two-year conflict some 80 French ships were seized, and Captain Thomas Truxtun won accolades for his victories in *Constellation* over *L' Insurgente* in 1799 and *La Vengeance* in 1800 in Caribbean waters. But the war proved little for American arms and was hardly more than an irritant for Napoleonic France. The real military significance of the Quasi-War was that it led to the creation of the United States Navy as a separate and permanent branch of the military with its own secretary. The first secretary of the navy was Benjamin Stoddert, a Maryland merchant, who got the service off to such an expansive start during the Quasi-War that its independent status was never questioned thereafter, although the antinaval Jeffersonians did their best to keep it small when they came to power in 1801. With the Jeffersonians in control, the Navy soon consisted of only six ships and a few hundred men.

The same fate befell the United States Marine Corps, created on July 11, 1798, to serve with either the Army or the Navy, on land or at sea. Its first commandant was William Ward Burrows of Philadelphia, who was authorized to recruit 33 officers and 848 men. During this Undeclared War with France another 204 officers and men were added, and the seagoing marines served with distinction in the sea skirmishes that marked that conflict. Yet when Jefferson came to power he cut back the strength of the marines to just 26 officers and 453 men, hardly a sufficient number of "sea soldiers" to serve the nation well as the United States embarked on a punitive expedition against the pirates who made their homes on the Barbary Coast of North Africa.

CONFLICT WITH THE BARBARY PIRATES: THE TRIPOLITAN WAR

Jefferson, the leader-philosopher of the Democratic-Republicans, envisioned a miniscule military force as proper to a peaceful nation, but attacks by Barbary pirates from Tripoli, Tunis, Morocco, and Algiers on American vessels in the Mediterranean and annual payments of $2 million to the Barbary leaders as tribute (one-fifth of the nation's revenue) finally convinced the peace-loving Jefferson that the Barbary pirates had to be humbled. When the pasha of Tripoli declared war on the United States in 1801, a four-ship Mediterranean Squadron was created to put down the piracy and end the payments.

This frustrating naval police action was marked by two major events. The first was the daring escapade of naval lieutenant Stephen Decatur at Tripoli in February 1804. Decatur and a small band of sailors and marines under cover of night worked themselves out to the captured and grounded American frigate *Philadelphia* (stranded on a barrier reef while pursuing a Tripolitan vessel too close to shore) and burned it to the waterline, thus rendering it useless to the enemy.

The second event of note was the expedition led by Marine Lieutenant Presley O'Bannon and William Eaton, U.S. diplomatic agent, against the ruler of Tripoli. Recruiting a force of 600 mercenaries in Alexandria, Egypt, Eaton and O'Bannon led them on a seven-week, 600-mile trek across the Libyan desert to Derna, the capital of Tripoli, in which was located the castle of Yusuf Caramanli, ruler of Tripoli. Aided by Hamet Bey, exiled brother of the pasha, the American force successfully attacked the city and castle with the aid of a bombardment from the naval warships of Captain Issac Hull in the harbor. The seizure of Derna played a major role in persuading the pasha to sign a peace treaty on June 4, 1805. A ceremonial sword, the Mameluk, was presented to O'Bannon by Hamet Bey. The sword serves to this day as the pattern for the swords carried by officers of the Marine Corps.

The war ended in 1805 when the crew of the *Philadelphia* was returned, the United States consented to pay a $60,000 bribe, and the Barbary leaders agreed to cease preying on American ships. However, the trouble with the Barbary pirates did not really end until 1815–1816, when a naval expedition compelled Algeria, Tunis, and Tripoli to halt their depredations.

Still Jefferson could not be convinced in 1805 that a strong naval presence was vital to protecting American interests. He put his faith in guarding America's coastlines with 188 50-foot, two-cannon oared boats that could be stored under protective sheds when not deployed in order to save maintenance costs. He preferred to rely on economic and diplomatic persuasion rather than force to ensure America's rights on the high seas. As events were quickly to show, these were weak levers to use against the Royal Navy fighting for Britain's life against Napoleonic France and therefore quite willing to seize American ships on the high seas.

CONFLICT WITH GREAT BRITAIN: THE WAR OF 1812

Despite Jefferson's attitudes toward the military, the United States Military Academy was born during his first term, as George Washington had long urged. Congress in 1802 created the Corps of Engineers to provide for trained military engineers and assigned its first ten cadets and seven officers to West Point. After some decades of struggle, the academy would emerge as the premier training institution for army officers, and it has remained so to the present time.

Jefferson's attention, however, was focused on America's troubles with Great Britain on the seas. The British were not only seizing American ships (some 500 between 1803 and 1807), but they were also impressing American sailors into the Royal Navy. In an action that infuriated the Americans, in 1807 the British frigate *Leopard* pursued and fired on the American frigate *Chesapeake* off the Virginia coast, causing 21 casualties, and then seized 4 alleged deserters from the Royal Navy. Jefferson first tried the stratagem of denying American shipping to both France and Britain by an embargo, but this brought more hardship to American shippers than to the offenders and had to be abandoned. The maritime merchants of the northeast seemed willing to live with occasional seizures of their ships and cargoes, but the agrarian western and southern populace (Jefferson's political allies) were convinced that British actions were preventing their crops from reaching their markets and thus were causing an agricultural recession. In addition, the people on the frontier were convinced that the British were arming the Indians. The discovery of British weapons at Tippecanoe seemed proof positive that such was the case. And many Americans were looking for an excuse to conquer Canada anyway. "War Hawks," such as Felix Grundy, Henry Clay, and John C. Calhoun, were also particularly sensitive to the lack of respect accorded to America's rights as an independent nation.

As a result of these pressures, during the presidency of James Madison, on June 18, 1812, Congress passed a declaration of war against Great Britain. A decade and a half of encroachments on American neutral rights by the principal combatants in Europe's war for dominance had first led to a war with France in 1798. They now resulted in a war with Great Britain, the War of 1812.

Britain had 300,000 men in its army at the beginning of the war. Its navy had 150,000 men and 125 ships of the line. The United States had only 11,000 men in its army, and the 450,000 militiamen called up were only for short terms. The Navy had only 20 ships and 4,000 men. The disparity of numbers, however, was offset by Britain's exertions in Europe and in its colonies. And Canada, a prime target for the Americans, could muster only 10,000 militia to aid Britain's 6,000 regulars there. Furthermore, because of the war with France, the Royal Navy could assign only 80 ships to cover the long coastline from Halifax to Florida. This was an impossibly small number to beat off all the privateers operating off the Atlantic coast, but it was more than sufficient to best America's small navy and seal off its coast.

Faced with the awesome disparity between its size and power and that of the Royal Navy, the American navy turned to harassing British vessels on the North Atlantic sea lanes. One early success in this war of unequals was gained when Captain John Rodgers drew the British Halifax naval squadron hundreds of miles out to sea, thereby allowing American merchantmen to reach their ports safely. Another early success was registered with the August 19, 1812, victory of Captain Isaac Hull's 44-gun frigate *Constitution* over the British 38-gun *Guerriere* off Nova Scotia. By the end of the first year of the war, some 600 privateers (including Captain Joshua Barney's famous *Rossie* out of Baltimore) were also enjoying some success in preying on British commerce. Before the fighting ended two years later, saltwater privateers had captured over 1,300 British vessels, although over half of the American privateering voyages ended in failure or in surrender during the course of the conflict.

But despite these efforts and occasional victories in ship-to-ship combat, such as that of USS *United States* over HMS *Macedonian* in October 1812 and USS *Constitution* over HMS *Java* later that year, British naval power was soon predominant, and American ports from New England to New Orleans were under stringent British blockade with American naval and merchant vessels tied up to their wharves.

British naval units, supplied in part by Americans opposed to the war and in dire economic straits, were strangling American commerce. This explains why great numbers of American shippers obtained British licenses in order to sail in and out of the country unhampered by the British blockade and why disgruntled New England merchants and shippers were willing to back the secession-threatening Hartford Convention in 1814. Victory in this second war of independence could never come from America's miniscule navy; it would have to come from its land forces aided by inland naval units able to predominate in certain key situations.

In its land warfare, the Army at least had an adequate supply of weapons, including .69-caliber flintlock muskets and .59-caliber flintlock pistols from the Springfield, Massachusetts, and Harpers Ferry, Virginia, federal arsenals. And sufficient ordnance was available with the creation during the war of an Ordnance Department and a Corps of Artillery.

As the land war began, the Americans launched three attacks on Canada. All three failed. Brigadier General William Hull, governor of the Michigan Territory, was directed to lead a force of 1,500 Ohio militiamen from Detroit across and down the Detroit River to seize woefully weak Fort Malden in July 1812. General Isaac Brock, the Canadian commander, seized Hull's supplies being floated down the river and crossed over to cut off Hull from reinforcements from Ohio. Hull then found out that the small American garrison at Fort Michilimackinac, between Lake Michigan and Lake Huron, had meekly surrendered. Believing that Brock had ten times the number of men he actually commanded at Fort Malden, Hull retreated to Detroit and subsequently surrendered his entire force at that location on August 16, 1812. Furthermore, a small American force moving to aid Hull from Fort Dearborn (now Chicago) was massacred on the trail by Indians. The entire Northwest Territory was now in British hands.

A second movement across the Niagara Frontier to attack British forts in Ontario also failed miserably. The Americans assembled 6,500 men for the operation, but the two commanders, Major General Stephen van Rensselaer of the New York militia and Brigadier General Alexander Smyth of the regular Army, argued as to how and where the attacks should be made. Ignoring Smyth, Rensselaer attacked with 600 of his men across the Niagara River to take Queenstown on October 13, 1812. When the attack sputtered, most of the New York militiamen refused to leave United States territory to aid their comrades, and Smyth refused to send help from Buffalo. As a result, 900 men were forced to surrender; 350 had been killed or wounded. In the weeks that followed, the New Yorkers wandered off home, and the regulars went into winter quarters. Smyth never again held command.

The year 1813 was marked by two crushing defeats on the Canadian-American frontier. In October 1812, a force had been assembled under General William Henry Harrison, the hero of Tippecanoe, to retake Detroit. Its advance contingent of 1,000 men reached the Raisin River southeast of Detroit, where it was wiped out by a British-Indian force. Over 100 Americans were killed and 500 captured, the wounded being slaughtered by the Indians. "Remember the Raisin!" was the rallying cry of the soldiers in the Northwest thereafter. Harrison decided to build two forts at the western end of Lake Erie and await further developments.

A second attack from Sacketts Harbor on the eastern end of Lake Ontario was designed to seize Kingston to the north but was detoured by Dearborn and his naval commander, Commodore Isaac Chauncey, to York (present-day Toronto) instead. With 1,700 men, Brigadier General Zebulon Pike attacked York on April 27, 1813. The troops proceeded to burn and loot the town after a powder magazine explosion killed Pike and a number of other Americans. Meanwhile, the remaining garrison at Sacketts Harbor had to beat off a determined attack from Kingston led by the governor-general of Canada, Sir George Prevost. And while Prevost was attacking Sacketts Harbor, Dearborn and Chauncey had left York and were attacking Fort George and Queenstown on the far western end of the lake. In this operation, despite an auspicious opening amphibious assault led by Master Commandant Oliver Perry of the Navy and Colonel Winfield Scott of the Army, Dearborn dallied, and the initiative was lost. The British forts were soon back in British hands.

Fortunately for the Americans, on September 10, 1813, Master Commandant Oliver Hazard Perry, with his home-built fleet of ships, was able to seize control of Lake Erie to the west in a smashing victory over a six-ship British squadron at Put-in-Bay,

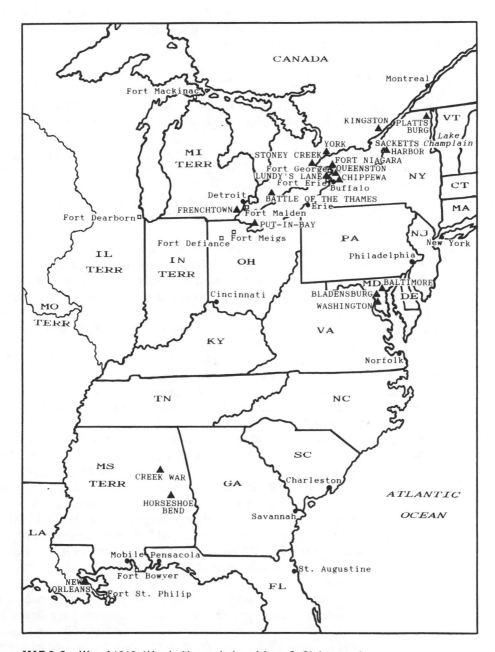

MAP 2–3   War of 1812. (*Used with permission of Anne C. Christensen.*)

despite an unwillingness to engage displayed by Jesse D. Elliot, the commander of the frigate *Lawrence*. With Lake Erie now in American hands, Harrison, aided by Perry, moved his forces against the British in lower Canada. Catching up with them on October

5, the Americans destroyed the 2,000-man British regular and Indian force in the Battle of the Thames in southwestern Ontario. Among the dead was Tecumseh, the great leader of Indian resistance on the northwest frontier.

☆ An American Portrait

Oliver Hazard Perry—Born in South Kingstown, Rhode Island, in 1785, Perry went to sea on his father's ship as a midshipman at the age of 13. There he served in the West Indies during the Quasi-War and twice between 1802 and 1806 was stationed in the Mediterranean during the wars with the Barbary pirates. In 1807 he was commissioned a permanent lieutenant and for the next four years spent his time building and commanding gunboats in Rhode Island and Connecticut in addition to carrying out other naval duties.

With the coming of war in June 1812, Perry was appointed master commandant at Rhode Island, but early in 1813 he was ordered to report to Commodore Isaac Chauncey at Sacketts Harbor, New York, on the eastern shore of Lake Ontario. This was the beginning of Perry's swift climb to fame as the great naval warrior of the Lakes.

During the spring and summer of 1813, Perry was at Erie, Pennsylvania, supervising the building of a 10-vessel fleet including the 480-ton brigs *Lawrence* and *Niagara*. On August 12, 1813, he sailed out onto Lake Erie bound for Put-in-Bay, north of Sandusky, Ohio, which would serve as his headquarters as he prepared to meet Commander Robert H. Barclay and his British fleet ported at Amherstburg on the Detroit River in a contest for control of Lake Erie.

On September 10 Barclay approached Put-in-Bay, and from 11:45 A.M. until 3:00 P.M., the two fleets pounded it out. Perry's flagship, the *Lawrence*, was wrecked in the fighting, but he transferred his flag to the *Niagara* and continued the battle until the British surrendered. Perry informed Harrison of his victory with the message, "We have met the enemy and they are ours."

By this victory the Americans gained control of Lake Erie and the upper Lakes, and the negotiators at Ghent had a further claim to retention of the Northwest. In the aftermath of Put-in-Bay, Harrison and his men were ferried across the lake to attack the British in Ontario, leading to the climactic Battle of the Thames of October 5. In this battle Perry acted as aide-de-camp to General Harrison and rode in the front rank of the mounted warriors.

These victories brought Perry national renown and a captaincy in the Navy. He went on to further naval duty in the Mediterranean and Latin America and died of yellow fever in Venezuela on August 23, 1819. Interred at Port of Spain, seven years later his body was reinterred at Newport in his native state of Rhode Island.

But a two-pronged attack against Montreal that autumn—one force moving from Sacketts Harbor down the St. Lawrence, the other from Plattsburgh on Lake Champlain—completely misfired. Each force retreated to Plattsburgh in the face of British resistance. And on the Atlantic coast the British continued their blockade and roamed up and down Chesapeake Bay burning and looting along its shores. Their June 1813 attack on Norfolk ended in failure, so they burned the town of Hampton across the waters of Hampton Roads instead. But these actions had little long-range effect. On the sea as well as on land, the year 1813 saw no crucial and decisive victories by either side.

The following year, 1814, saw the fighting escalate in size and ferocity, but again both sides gained victories and suffered defeats without the military struggle becoming decisive either way. The major American offensive for 1814 saw a sizable force of 3,500 men under Brigadier General Jacob Brown and Brigadier General Winfield Scott cross the Niagara Frontier on July 3 and seize Fort Erie before moving north to join Commodore Chauncey and his naval force on Lake Ontario, thereby to seize control of the entire Niagara peninsula. Brown, ably assisted by Scott, who had uniformed his recruits in what would later become West Point gray and had drilled them so thoroughly that the British commander in the heat of battle exclaimed, "Those are regulars, by God!," defeated a large force of British at the Chippewa River. Chauncey refused to reinforce Brown for his move on Queenstown, however, so Brown had to pull back to the Chippewa. Here his forces again tangled with the British on July 25 in a deadly brawl at Lundy's Lane that saw each side lose over 800 men. Brown retreated to Fort Erie, but even with the arrival of reinforcements he could not hold his position. The whole force finally retreated to the Niagara Frontier, the bloody campaign having been fought for naught.

☆   An American Portrait

Jacob Brown—One of the least remembered of the military leaders of the War of 1812, Brown was born in 1775 in Bucks County, Pennsylvania. In 1799 he purchased several thousand acres of land near Watertown, New York, near the shore of Lake Ontario, and established the village of Brownville there.

Brown's military career began in 1809, when he was appointed commander of a local militia regiment. Two years later he was made brigadier general of militia, and on May 29, 1813, having assumed the responsibility for the defense of nearby Sacketts Harbor against British attack, he and his 500 militiamen and 400 regulars beat off a British invasion and forced them to withdraw. As a brigadier general in the regular army he was present at the fiasco of Wilkinson's expedition to Montreal but was not blamed for the outcome.

Accordingly, in January 1814, Brown was raised in rank to major general and given command over all forces in western New York. Under his leadership, Fort Erie, Ontario, was seized on July 2–3, and Brown's forces were victorious at the Chippewa River to the north. But Brown now discovered that Commodore Chauncey's supporting fleet had not even left Sacketts Harbor at the other end of Lake Ontario, so his offensive had to be curtailed.

On July 25 in the Battle of Lundy's Lane, Brown, although wounded, gained a tactical victory. But the next day he had to fall back to Fort Erie. From August 15 through September 17, Brown and his men were under siege there, but they were not overrun. Despite all the American problems along the Niagara frontier, Brown had provided sterling leadership in a very difficult situation.

In 1821, Brown, as the senior officer in service, was named commander of the U.S. Army, a position he held until his death in February 1828.

When the reinforcements had been sent to Brown at Fort Erie from Plattsburgh, it left the Lake Champlain route wide open to the enemy. On September 1, three days after the reinforcements for Brown left, an army of 12,000 British veterans of the

European wars under General Prevost, assisted by a naval squadron of four frigates, brigs, and sloops and twelve gunboats, began moving down Lake Champlain. With Napoleon now defeated, Britain intended to retrieve some of the lands lost at the Treaty of Paris three decades before and cripple the upstart infant American nation.

Upon arriving at Plattsburgh on September 6, General Prevost decided to wait for his naval squadron to destroy the American defensive flotilla of 14 ships under Thomas Macdonough anchored there before proceeding. But by skillful gunnery and maneuvering, Macdonough and his crews got the better of the British naval forces in a two-hour battle on September 11, sinking two ships and damaging a number of others. Faced with a tenuous supply line even if he took Plattsburgh, Prevost decided to return to Canada. The northern frontier was saved and thereafter remained in American hands.

The following month, a second British force made a major move, this time on Chesapeake Bay. A force of 4,000 men under Major General Robert Ross sailed up the bay and landed on the Patuxent River. Their destination was the nation's capital. Sweeping aside 5,000 hastily assembled regulars, sailors, marines, and militiamen, the British moved on Washington, burning the Capitol, the presidential mansion, and other government buildings. They then returned to their ships and sailed on to Baltimore. Here they were finally stopped by 10,000 militiamen manning earthworks constructed outside the city and by the resolute defensive efforts of 1,000 regulars and sailors inside Fort McHenry guarding the city's harbor. It was in testimony to this defensive stand that Francis Scott Key wrote the national anthem. Finally abandoning their attack on Baltimore, the British sailed away to the West Indies to plan another offensive, this time on New Orleans to close the Mississippi River. This would give the British leverage for gaining territorial concessions at the peace negotiations then underway.

For the New Orleans operation, the British assembled 8,000 regulars and 50 ships. Major General Andrew Jackson, the American commander at New Orleans (who had made his reputation by his furious attacks on the Creeks the year before at Horseshoe Bend in the Mississippi Territory), had only 5,000 men with which to stop the British. Fortunately for Jackson and the American cause, the British naval commander and his subordinates positioned their forces with the Mississippi River on one side and a cypress swamp on the other. In front of them were the American defenders behind high earthworks with 20 artillery pieces.

☆   An American Portrait

Andrew Jackson—Jackson was born in Waxhaw, South Carolina, in 1767. When he was a ten-year old, Jackson took part in the Battle of Hanging Rock during the Revolutionary War and was later taken prisoner. In 1781 his mother died, and he was left alone at the age of 14. After teaching school and reading law in North Carolina, he migrated to Nashville, Tennessee, in 1788 and found success as a backwoods lawyer and land speculator. In the years that followed, he served briefly in the U.S. House of Representatives and Senate and as a judge on the supreme court of his adopted state. His chief interests, however, were land ownership and his plantation, "The Hermitage."

Jackson's military service began in 1802, when he was appointed a major general in the Tennessee militia. During the War of 1812 he led the Tennessee forces to Fort Mims

FIGURE 2–3 Andrew Jackson. (*National Archives, Washington, D.C.*)

in the Mississippi Territory, and on March 27, 1814, as a major general in the regular army, he led his men to a major victory over the Creek Indians. His subsequent defense of New Orleans on January 8, 1815, catapulted him to national fame.

In 1818, "Old Hickory" again assumed military leadership when he led an expedition across the Spanish Florida border to Pensacola to chastise the Seminoles and ended up hanging two British subjects. This set off a diplomatic crisis, with both Britain and Spain threatening war.

In the 1820s Jackson turned his attention to politics, acting as the first governor of the territory of Florida, serving again in the U.S. Senate, and in 1828 being elected the seventh president of the United States. He died on June 8, 1845, at The Hermitage.

When Lieutenant General Edward Pakenham arrived on the scene, he foolishly opted for a frontal attack with a minor flanking movement on the American lines. It came on January 8, 1815. The result was a disaster for British arms. In only three hours, Pakenham and 2,000 regulars fell victim to American firepower directed at them from behind the parapets. The Americans suffered only 45 casualties. The British pulled out, attacked Fort Bowyer harbor inside Mobile Bay, and then returned to the West Indies upon receiving news that a peace treaty had been agreed upon.

Indeed, the Treaty of Ghent, signed on Christmas Eve, 1814, had already ended the war. Despite the seesaw nature of the conflict for the first two years and major victories for both sides in 1814—the Americans at Lake Champlain and the British destruction of Washington—neither side had gained a clear position of authority. With the fundamental cause of the war, British seizure of American ships and men and American neutral rights on the high seas, now of no consequence with the defeat of Napoleon and his armies, there was no reason to continue the war, so both sides simply called it off.

The War of 1812 did not represent a pageant of military glory for the Americans, despite the exertions of its regulars and volunteers, especially in 1814 against three determined British offenses. But the outcome of the conflict prevented Britain from attaining any diplomatic leverage that could be used to regain any of the territories it had lost in the Revolutionary War or contesting American ownership of the Louisiana Territory (which it had not recognized). Of equal importance, the United States again had an army and a navy, and by its actions in the Quasi-War, the Barbary wars, and the War of 1812, it would now have to be recognized as a viable independent nation able to defend its rights and prerogatives in the affairs of the nations of the world.

Suggestions for Further Reading

ALDEN, JOHN R., *A History of the American Revolution*. New York: Knopf, 1969.

BALDWIN, LELAND, *Whiskey Rebels: The Story of a Frontier Uprising*. Pittsburgh: University of Pittsburgh Press, 1962.

BOWLER, R. ARTHUR, *Logistics and the Failure of the British Army in America*. Princeton, NJ: Princeton University Press, 1975.

COLES, HARRY L., *The War of 1812*. Chicago: University of Chicago Press, 1965.

CUNLIFFE, MARCUS, *George Washington*. Boston: Little, Brown, 1958.

DECONDE, ALEXANDER, *The Quasi-War*. Chicago: Scribner's, 1966.

DILLON, RICHARD, *We Have Met the Enemy: Oliver Hazard Perry. Wilderness Commodore*. New York: McGraw-Hill, 1978.

DULL, JONATHAN, *The French Navy and American Independence*. Princeton, NJ: Princeton University Press, 1975.

FLEXNER, JAMES T., *George Washington in the American Revolution (1775–1783)*. Boston: Little, Brown, 1968.

FOWLER, WILLIAM M., Jr., *Rebels Under Sail: The American Navy during the Revolution*. New York: Scribner's, 1976.

FREEMAN, DOUGLAS S., *George Washington: A Biography,* vols. 4, 5. New York: Scribner's, 1948–1957.

GUTTRIDGE, LEONARD F., and JAY D. SMITH, *The Commodores: The U.S. Navy in the Age of Sail*. New York: Harper & Row, Pub., 1969.

HORSMAN, REGINALD, *The War of 1812*. New York: Knopf, 1969.

KOHN, RICHARD H., *Eagle and Sword: The Federalists and the Creation of the Military Establishment in America, 1783–1812*. New York: Free Press, 1975.

LORD, WALTER, *The Dawn's Early Light*. New York: W. W. Norton & Co., Inc., 1972.

MACKESY, PIERS, *The War for America, 1775–1783*. Cambridge: Harvard University Press, 1964.

MAHAN, ALFRED T., *Sea Power in its Relation to the War of 1812,* 2 vols. Boston: Little, Brown, 1919.

MAHON, JOHN K., *The War of 1812*. Gainesville: University of Florida Press, 1972.

MARTIN, JAMES K., and MARK E. LENDER, *A Respectable Army: The Military Origins of the Republic, 1763–1789*. Arlington Heights, IL: Harlan Davidson, 1982.

ROYSTER, CHARLES, *A Revolutionary People at War*. Chapel Hill: University of North Carolina Press, 1979.

SHY, JOHN,   *A People Numerous and Armed*. New York: Oxford University Press, 1976.

SLAUGHTER, THOMAS P.,   *The Whiskey Rebellion: Frontier Epilogue to the American Revolution*. New York: Oxford University Press, 1986.

SMELSER, MARSHALL,   *The Congress Founds a Navy*. South Bend, IN: University of Notre Dame Press, 1959.

STAGG, J. C. A.,   *Mr. Madison's War*. Princeton, NJ: Princeton University Press, 1983.

TILLEY, JOHN A.,   *The British Navy and the American Revolution*. Columbia: University of South Carolina Press, 1987.

TUCHMAN, BARBARA W.,   *The First Salute*. New York: Knopf, 1988.

TUCKER, GLENN,   *Dawn Like Thunder: The Barbary Wars and the Birth of the U.S. Navy*. Indianapolis: Bobbs-Merrill, 1963.

WALLACE, WILLARD R.,   *Appeal to Arms: A Military History of the American Revolution*. New York: Harper & Bros., 1951.

WARD, CHRISTOPHER.,   *The War of the Revolution*, 2 vols. New York: Macmillan, 1952.

★3

Evolution
of the American Military,
1815–1860

The War of 1812 had seen notable victories for America's regulars and militiamen. But there had also been humiliating defeats. At the least, the final war of American independence had taught the American people the necessity of adequate military defenses on land and sea. Still, the proper balance between regulars and volunteers in a nation that took great pride in its peaceful intentions, its military prowess when called upon to fight, and its citizen-soldier tradition was far from clear, and it would remain so for decades.

The question of the status of the regulars after the fighting had ended was clarified in March 1815 in a law passed by Congress that allowed for an army of up to 10,000 men, a considerable improvement over its prewar status. It also divided the Army into two co-equal commands, a Northern Division under Major General Jacob Brown and a Southern Division under Major General Andrew Jackson. But there was no general-in-chief for coordination. This led to many difficulties, and the newly formed general staff made up of the Army's department chiefs, although supplemented by additional departments added by Secretary of War John C. Calhoun in 1818, led not to greater coordination and cooperation, but often to further confusion.

The Army still had numerous problems to solve before enjoying full acceptance as a national necessity and attaining the professionalism demanded by its permanent status. In the next 4 1/2 decades it made giant strides toward attaining both goals.

JOMINI AND CLAUSEWITZ: COFOUNDERS OF MODERN MILITARY THOUGHT

Napoleon Bonaparte, the Corsican artillery captain turned dictator, then emperor, of France, had astonished the Western world by his military victories. By 1812 he had subjugated continental Europe with his armies, and even his subsequent defeats by the coalition of nations arrayed against him hardly dulled the luster of his battlefield successes.

Napoleon had gained his great victories in two ways. These changed the nature of war forever. First, he had harnessed the energies of the entire French nation behind his war banners. His adoption of Lazare Carnot's *levee en masse* (dating from the Revolution) had drawn every Frenchman—man, woman, and child—into active support of his wars. As the American Revolution had foreshadowed, no longer would wars be the business only of the soldiers and politicians. Napoleon's acceptance of the concept of "the nation at war" had brought tremendous strength to the French military campaigns and would be emulated by all nations thereafter. The older eighteenth-century concept of limited and humane warfare carried out by professional soldiers, then, was a casualty of Napoleon's battlefield successes.

Second, Napoleon's tactical abilities—some would say military genius—in directing his armies on the battlefields of Europe led to an emphasis on maneuver and flexibility never before practiced on such a grand scale. Whether Napoleon's moves were the result of excellent preplanning or of brilliant improvisation, they resulted not only in the seizure of key positions but also in the capture or annihilation of great masses of his enemies' forces. This sounded the death knell for the old concept of singular attention to capturing places and interdicting lines of supply as the keys to military victory.

In addition, because of their brilliance, Napoleon's battles and victories led to a new, systematic study of warfare that became the basis of modern military thought. The two founders of the modern examination of warfare according to rational analysis were Antoine Henri Jomini and Karl von Clausewitz. The conclusions on warmaking drawn by these two intellectual giants, often in conflict with one another depending on how each analyzed Napoleon's successes, formed the basis of the emerging nineteenth-century science—or refined art—of warmaking. Jomini's thoughts dominated in the pre–Civil War period, Clausewitz's in the latter decades of the century through the work of Emory Upton.

Major General Antoine Henri Jomini was a French Swiss born in 1779. He served in the French army during the time of Napoleon. While never attaining independent command, he held high staff positions that gave him first-hand experience in moving armies in the field and in the confused maelstrom of combat, in the "fog of war," the cloud of uncertainty of information experienced in the heat of battle. In 1813 he joined the Russian army of Alexander I, where he held the rank of general, and in the remaining 54 years of his life after the Napoleonic Wars served as a military consultant and scholar of high renown. Before his death in 1869, Jomini had written 27 volumes on the wars of Frederick the Great, the French Revolution, and Napoleon, plus an 1804–1805 theoretical work entitled *Traite des grande operations militaires* (Treatise on Large-Scale Military Operations). The greatest and most influential work by this soldier-scholar-theorist, however, was his two-volume *Precis de l'art de la guerre* (Summary of the Art of War), published in 1838.

In his *Precis,* Jomini argued that fundamental principles of successful warmaking can be discovered. These principles, he said, are unaffected by time, place, and weaponry. However, he warned, these precepts are not mathematical variables or ingredients, as in a recipe, that used in proper proportion would necessarily lead to a given consequence.

Rather, they are general principles always and everywhere understandable and applicable in any wartime situation.

With regard to strategy, for example, he listed four rules:

1. Maneuver to bring the major part of your forces to bear upon the enemy's decisive areas and communications without endangering your own.
2. Maneuver to bring your major forces against only part of the enemy's forces.
3. Maneuver to bring your major forces to bear upon the decisive area of the battlefield or of the enemy's lines.
4. Maneuver to bring your mass to bear swiftly and simultaneously.

These moves, he argued, can be accomplished with a good plan for the campaign drawn up beforehand and with correct lines of operation (usually and preferably a single interior line, although a double line might be used if it can be rejoined quickly). This combination of solid campaign planning and correct lines of operation (the interior always being preferred over the exterior) in order to bring the army's weight to bear at the right time in the right place, said Jomini, is the key to swift and climactic military victory.

A successful general, then, is one who has a good campaign plan with secure lines to dominate a zone of operation. The correct campaign plan, added Jomini, should include maneuvering whereby your army can successfully dominate three sides of a rectangular zone held by your enemy. If the successful general can command the three sides of a rectangle, his enemy will either be crushed or forced to abandon the territory. In either case, the territory is won, and that is the purpose of conflict.

To Jomini, then, war is primarily a matter of maneuvering to gain territory and places, not a matter of annihilating the enemy forces. And by staying on the strategic initiative at all times, if possible, to have control of the situation—the "offensive defensive" being used only when there is no other choice—the war will be won.

Critics have alleged that Jomini drew more lessons from the warmaking of Frederick the Great than from Napoleon. They have also pointed out that war has a dynamic of its own that can fracture and fragment operational plans and maneuvers no matter how carefully designed or supervised, thus nullifying Jomini-type generalship. Be that as it may, there is no question that Jomini's *Precis*, in which he spelled out the principles of successful warmaking, had a tremendous impact on the growing number of professional military officers emerging in the leading nations of the West in the first half of the nineteenth century. American military officers were no exception. They, too, sought to convert the eighteenth-century gentlemanly leadership of armies into an art or science requiring rigorous training and perceptive insight. Jomini's principles were indirectly taught to and absorbed by America's emerging officer cadre at West Point through lectures and by textbooks such as those written by Dennis Hart Mahan, Henry Halleck, and others. Jomini's formal approach to war was finding a receptive audience at the United States Military Academy, with its emphasis on engineering.

The second giant in military theory in the nineteenth century—but one whose influence was felt only much later in the century—was Major General Karl von Clausewitz. Born in 1780, Clausewitz was admitted to the Berlin War Academy for young officers and soon came under the influence of Gerhard Johann Scharnhorst, the noted reorganizer of the Prussian army. Clausewitz then fought in the Napoleonic wars, serving both Russia and his native Prussia. From 1818 until 1830 he held the position of managing director of the *Kriegsakademie,* a position that allowed him more than adequate time for writing his monumental tome *Vom Kriege* (On War), published in 1831, although not available in English translation until 1873. Convinced that the "controlling ideas" on warfare can be discovered by human reason, and impressed by Napoleon's successes, Clausewitz in his great work attempted to produce a treatise on the nature of war that blended the rational with the experiental in order to attain principles of universal validity.

Clausewitz's first principle is that war is essentially an act of violence, its outcome determined not by scientific calculation but by immaterial and moral factors. Generalship, for example, is a matter of insightful genius, not of following rules of effective strategy and tactics. The object of war, he argued, is to compel your opponent by violent means to bend his will to yours. This can usually be accomplished by destroying his armed forces, not by seizing his territory or key locations. Destruction of the enemy's forces, then, is "the first-born son of war."

Second, since war is subject to modification by human choice (good or bad) or action (effective or defective), it is necessarily guided by probability, not by scientific calculation. In other words, every conflict is altered by what Clausewitz calls "the frictions of war" (human fallacies, errors, oversights, and the like that always occur in battle), which lead to probabilities rather than certainties in its outcome.

Third, war as it is fought is also determined by the political aims of the state that the warrior serves. War is always a means, not an end. As Clausewitz expressed it in an oft-quoted statement, "War is nothing else than the continuation of state policy by different means." This suggests, among other things, that the more powerful the motives behind a war and the stronger the hatreds within the states fighting the war, the greater will be the amount of violence that will be accepted or encouraged (that is, the closer the conflict will come to total or absolute war).

Real war, then, can be understood by the following formula: $WR = WA \times F \times P$ (War Real = War Absolute as modified by Friction (chance) as modified by Politics (the political aims and attitudes of the state). This formula leads not only to a better understanding of any real war but also to the vital place of leadership, accident, and policymaking within it. For the military leader, it reveals the parameters within which he must operate during wartime.

Other concomitant principles follow from this formula. First, says Clausewitz, basic strategy must be directed against the enemy's "center of gravity." This point of greatest vulnerability may vary widely. While in most cases the center of gravity will be the enemy's armed forces (whose will to fight must be broken), in certain wars public opinion in the enemy nation is the real center of gravity toward which the fight must be directed. (America's strategy in the Revolutionary War is a perfect example of the use of this strategy; America's loss of the Vietnam War is another.)

Second, while the defensive strategic posture may be the stronger because "to preserve is easier than to acquire," it has only a negative objective—avoiding defeat. Therefore, a "swift and vigorous assumption of the offensive," when it can succeed, regains the initiative and can lead to the breaking of the enemy's will to fight.

Third, since war is partially determined by chance and by nonmaterial or moral factors, great generalship lies in being able to inspire one's troops to fight to their maximum abilities and reject defeat. It also lies in being able to gauge the total situation, material and nonmaterial, with calm judgment. In Clausewitz's words, the "strong mind [of the great general]...keeps its equilibrium amidst the most powerful emotions, so that in spite of the storm in the breast, perception and judgment can act with perfect freedom, like the needle of the compass in a storm-tossed ship."

Read and taught in America's service academies and enthusiastically digested by military officers, first Jomini's *Precis* prior to the 1870s and Clausewitz's *Vom Kriege* thereafter served as leaven for the development of the principles of war and as intellectual grist for the military professionalism emerging in the nation in the nineteenth century.

WEST POINT, ANNAPOLIS, AND MILITARY PROFESSIONALISM

The United States Military Academy, situated above the Hudson River at West Point, New York, was established in 1802 when a handful of engineering officers and cadets were assigned to the post. Its first years were marked by miserable living conditions and slack standards for the cadets, but 65 of its 89 graduates served during the War of 1812, distinguishing themselves as military engineers by the fact that no fortifications or earthworks built under their direction ever fell to the enemy during that conflict.

The cadets formally became members of the Army Corps of Engineers during the war, and some steps were taken by the Academy's commandant (and its first graduate in 1802) Colonel Joseph G. Swift to put the school on stronger academic and military footing. But under Captain Alden Partridge's *de facto* leadership from 1810 to 1815 (Swift was often absent on duties elsewhere) and during his time as superintendent from 1815 to 1817, the Academy degenerated into academic and disciplinary chaos. All rules, academic and otherwise, were regularly and systematically flouted, according to his detractors. (It was during Partridge's tenure, though, that the cadets received gray uniforms, by tradition honoring the regulars at the Chippewa River and Lundy's Lane, who wore gray kersey because no regulation blue uniforms were available.) Only when President James Monroe visited West Point in 1817 and was informed as to the conditions existing there was corrective action taken.

The man ordered to rectify the situation was Brevet Major Sylvanus Thayer, who was appointed superintendent in July 1817, having just returned from two years of study of military schools and fortifications in France. Thayer had a Herculean task before him, but he carried it out with firmness and authority. He replaced incompetent faculty members and enlisted personnel assigned to the post, organized a set and rigorous curriculum built around four years of study, instituted strict military rules of conduct, and imbued both faculty and cadets with his own conviction that West Point graduates should be officers, gentlemen, and professionals in every way.

Unfortunately, Thayer's work at West Point ended after only 16 years. President Andrew Jackson, listening to his aide (and nephew) who had been dismissed from the Academy for insubordination and resenting the "aristocratic" nature of the institution, began openly to override the academy's rules, even reinstating dismissed or court-martialed cadets. As a result of Jackson's high-handed actions, Thayer resigned in 1833. Although Thayer continued his distinguished career as an army officer and as an engineer, the foundation he built at West Point was too strong to be destroyed. Not without further difficulties, the academy went on to become the premier military and engineering school in the nation. By 1846 it had graduated almost a thousand cadets, and by 1860 more than 76 percent of U.S. Army officers were West Point graduates. Thayer's years at the academy placed it on the road to the professionalism that was becoming the mark of the nineteenth-century military officer.

The Navy's move toward professional military training was long delayed by that service's time-honored practice of training at sea and Congress's opposition to building up a professional naval force, steeped, as it was, in the militia tradition. Reformers were calling for more regular and extensive training of officers for decades, even if it meant establishing an elite and "undemocratic" school to do so, but nothing happened. Then, the Navy began to move to steam-driven warships requiring more technical training. In addition, Philip Spencer, the son of the secretary of war, and two others on board the naval warship *Somers* were summarily hanged in 1842 for alleged mutiny. In the public controversy that followed over the judgment of the captain, Alexander S. Mackenzie, in hanging the three, even the most obstinate footdraggers realized that something had to be done to elevate the caliber of the navy's officers. The initiative in this direction was taken by historian and educator George Bancroft in 1845 shortly after he was appointed secretary of war.

After studying how West Point was run and despairing of ever getting congressional approval, Bancroft arranged through the War Department for the transfer of Fort Severn at Annapolis, Maryland, from the Army to the Navy. He created the United States Naval Academy there. Its first superintendent was Commander Franklin Buchanan, and its curriculum was set up on a 2-3-1 basis (two years at Annapolis, three years at sea, and one year on a practice ship). Within five years, 90 graduates had received naval commissions, and in 1851 a regular four-year academic program with summer cruises was instituted. Like its army counterpart, the Naval Academy represented a significant step forward in the development of professional military officers.

The 1840s also saw the antiquated Board of Naval Commissioners, dating back to 1815 and made up of three high-ranking officers to advise the naval secretary, replaced in 1842 by five naval bureaus (Ordnance and Hydrography; Medicine and Surgery; Yards and Docks; Construction, Equipment, and Repair; and Provisions and Clothing) plus a Corps of Engineers (for its steam vessels) for specialized and more professional management of the navy's affairs.

Equally important to the development of a professional officer corps after 1815 was the abandonment of many political practices that had plagued the military since the founding of the nation. After 1783 there was no clear consensus as to how large the military should be or even what role it should play in time of war. This was evident in the Indian wars and again in the War of 1812. Furthermore, appointments to rank were solely a matter of political patronage. Each of the developing political parties, the Federalists and the Democratic-Republicans, blatantly made military appointment and advancement a matter of political connections, and "lateral appointments" (the appointment of favored civilians directly to high ranks) were commonplace. Officers, acting out of sheer necessity, were highly political, their professional qualifications being of little importance.

After 1815, however, the situation began to change. For one thing, there was now no real threat of serious contractions in the officer ranks, and fewer lateral appointments were made. Officers could look forward to stable careers as military professionals (albeit with low pay and slow advancement in rank) and began to develop the attitudes necessary for such a role. They set out to acquire skills useful to them and to their branch of service, and they began to distinguish between their political and military lives. Accordingly, these officers became more responsible to their branch of the service and to the nation and less to their political friends and their local areas. They manifested a pride in themselves as experts in the art of war carrying out a sacred duty to the nation. The words emblazoned on the West Point crest—*Duty, Honor, Country*—became their watchwords.

As a result of this emerging dedication to military service to the nation, American military officers became more and more apolitical regarding matters not strictly military in nature. In other words, military leaders came to accept the idea that they must stay out of partisan politics because of their role as instruments of national policy. They realized that professionalism demanded a constitutionally mandated military subservient to political authority as well as technical competence.

This did not mean, however, that officers would not still use political influence to advance their own careers or the interests of their particular branches of service. It did mean that the military officers would remain subservient to their civilian commanders and that they would not allow the military to be used as an instrument of intrigue by politicians seeking to advance the policy issues they favored.

Military professionalism, then, evolving from West Point and Annapolis, as well as from the military stability of the times, resulted in greater competence in the art of war. It also represented a posture of military subservience to the wishes of the people of the nation and their elected leaders. The principle of civilian control of the military became part of the very mentality of the career officer in the years 1815 to 1860, a professional mentality that has persisted to this day.

INDIAN WARS AND FRONTIER EXPANSION

The persistent Indian problems on the nation's frontiers, caused by continued white incursions into the Indians' lands and a determination to remove them from their paths of settlement by means fair or foul in the name of "progress" and "civilization," flared up again in 1814 on the southern frontier and occasioned Andrew Jackson's attack on the Creeks at Horseshoe Bend. Trouble broke out again three years later with an uprising by the surviving Lower Creeks, who had settled in along the south Georgia–Spanish Florida border and had brought some Seminole Indians (a branch of the Creeks) and fugitive black slaves into their band. In November 1817, an army keelboat moving up the Apalachicola River as part of an operation to resupply Fort Scott at the southwestern tip of Georgia was attacked by the Indians, and 34 soldiers and their wives were slain or captured. As a result, General Jackson was authorized to march to Fort Scott to subdue them. The First Seminole War was on.

Jackson added 1,000 Tennessee volunteers to his 800-man force of regulars, as well as 1,000 Georgia militiamen, and prepared a major attack on the Indian-black force of thousands camped on the Suwannee River under the Seminole chief Billy Bowlegs. Not bothered in the least by the prospect of violating Spanish territory—nor had he been during the War of 1812—Jackson seized St. Marks in Florida in April 1818 as a prelude to his march on the Indian encampment. When he found the Indians gone from the Suwanee, "Old Hickory" had two captured British "agitators" tried and executed for stirring up the Indians. He then moved into Pensacola with his troops in pursuit of the Seminoles and their allies. He left troops there and at St. Marks and returned to Nashville, satisfied with his work. Jackson's summary execution of the two British citizens was strongly protested by the British government and led to a diplomatic crisis. But the Spanish government raised little fuss over Jackson's moves into Florida, since the United States and Spain were currently negotiating for its acquisition by the United States anyway, the deal being struck in the Adams-Onis Treaty of 1819.

Jackson's supply difficulties during the First Seminole War were not lost on the secretary of war from 1817 to 1825, John C. Calhoun. Calhoun made major moves to improve the Army's logistics. The South Carolinian, knowing that Congress was about to cut back on the Army's authorized strength, was also responsible for the "expansible army" concept. According to this plan, cuts in the numbers of enlisted personnel would be by one-half of each company, so that if a crisis came, the 6,000-man Army could be expanded to 19,000 using the cadre of senior, trained enlisted men as the core of the new units formed. Congress reduced the Army beyond Calhoun's wishes and the "expansible army" concept was not implemented, but the idea of using trained cadres as the basis for rapid and effective expansion was later resurrected in the form of the ready reserves.

Calhoun, one of the premier secretaries of war in the antebellum period, was also responsible for the expansion of the nation's seacoast fortifications. By 1826, some 31 seacoast artillery works were in place, and an artillery school had been established at Fortress Monroe, Virginia, on Hampton Roads in 1824. In 1821, Brigadier General Winfield Scott, head of the Eastern Department (Eastern and Western having replaced Northern and Southern), issued the first official set of Army regulations covering every aspect of the soldier's life. Calhoun was also a major supporter of Thayer's curricular and disciplinary reforms at West Point.

The second Indian war to occur during this period took place in the West. Thousands of white settlers were moving into western Illinois, displacing the Sac and Fox Indians there. In 1831 a band of Sac Indian warriors under Chief Black Hawk (actually Black Sparrow Hawk) crossed back into Illinois from Iowa across the Mississippi River, where they had been herded, and caused minor damage before being forced back across the river again. But the next year Black Hawk, with 500 warriors and 1,500 women and children, again moved back across the Mississippi, seeking to resettle on their ancestral lands. Secretary of War Lewis Cass called out regulars from Jefferson Barracks, Missouri, and another 1,000 regulars under General Winfield Scott, who arrived too late, their ranks depleted by cholera. In addition, Illinois called out 1,000 volunteers to drive the Indians back across the Mississippi. The resulting "Black Hawk War" of 1832 consisted of a battering of the hapless Indians in brief fights at Wisconsin Bluffs and on the Bad Axe River as Black Hawk fled north into the Wisconsin Territory to escape his pursuers. The remnants of the Indians, including women and children, were brutally slaughtered as they tried to wade the river to safety. In a surprising sequel to these events, Black Hawk was treated kindly by his captor, Lieutenant Jefferson Davis. He also met President Jackson on cordial terms and lived out his life peacefully in Iowa.

The third Indian war, a drawn-out bloody affair called the Second Seminole War, began in 1835 when Seminole Indians, exasperated by continued white movement into their homelands and led by the half-breed chief Osceola, attacked an army detachment under Captain Francis L. Dade and killed 108 men in the "Dade Massacre." As a result, the Army was sent to Florida under General Winfield Scott, where it soon found itself involved in a deadly guerrilla-type war being carried out by the Indians. The Seminoles wisely refused open combat with the detachments sent against them and attacked small units and outposts before disappearing into the impenetrable swamps. Before the war came to an end in 1842, some 60,000 regulars, militiamen, and volunteers had served in Florida. Four different commanders tried and failed to bring the Indians to bay, and the Army turned the conflict into a merciless war of extermination against the Indians, combatants and noncombatants alike.

The Army invited Osceola and the other chiefs to a conference in 1837 under a flag of truce and took them prisoner, but the war went on. Osceola died in captivity in 1838, and the attending physician hung the dead chief's skull on a bedpost to frighten his children. But still the Indians persisted in their defiance of the Army's efforts to end their rebellion. It was, in the last analysis, only the Army's continuing strategy of eradication against the 3,800 Seminoles (who essentially were only resisting resettlement in distant Arkansas) that ended the Second Seminole War. Because of the obvious futility of any further efforts to remove them by force, the Seminole nation was subsequently allowed to remain in Florida, became very peaceful, and still reside there.

During these same years the Army also helped to open the trans-Mississippi West by surveying, building roads and forts, and aiding settlers in Iowa, Kansas, and Nebraska. Fort Leavenworth in the Kansas Territory, established in 1827, served as the jumping-off point for exploring expeditions that led to the opening of the Sante Fe Trail to the southwest and the Oregon Trail to the northwest. As they moved across the plains and into the mountains, the Army commanders also made treaties with the Indians and otherwise aided the thousands of pioneers moving west—sometimes even into territories claimed by Britain and Mexico. It was in the context of the continued movement by Americans into the territory of the latter nation that a serious dispute arose that eventually saw the American military fight a major war against Mexico in the 1840s.

THE MEXICAN WAR, 1846–1848

With the encouragement, or at least acquiescence, of the Mexican government, American settlers had been moving into Texas in great numbers beginning in the 1820s, Moses Austin having been awarded a large tract of land after promising to settle no more than 300 families on it. By 1835 there were over 30,000 Americans living in Texas and becoming increasingly restive under Mexican rule, including that government's restrictions on slavery and further immigration from the United States. The Texans' resentment of Mexican "interference" with their lives boiled over into revolution in 1836.

Within a year the Texans, under Sam Houston, had resisted to their deaths the Mexican forces led by president and general Santa Anna at the Alamo on the outskirts of San Antonio de Bexar. The Texans had also seen 390 of their volunteer soldiers shot down in cold blood on the prairie near Goliad. But final victory had been won over Santa Anna in an 18-minute ferocious contest at San Jacinto to the war cries of "Remember the Alamo!" and "Remember Goliad!" Declaring their independence, the Texas Republic then turned to the United States and asked for admission into the Union, setting off a decade-long debate over the issue.

Many Americans, especially Southerners and kinsmen of the Texans, wanted the republic annexed regardless of Mexico's objections, but an equal number saw the annexation of Texas as hardly worth the price of war. Opinion was sharply divided over the issue, with many Northerners and Whigs seeing annexation as part of a slaveholders' plot to expand slavery to the southwest.

When the young expansionist and annexationist presidential candidate James K. Polk of Tennessee won the Democratic party's nomination and then the general election in 1844—even though it was far from clear that Polk's expansionist views were the reason for his victory—lame-duck president John Tyler chose to accept the election results as a clear mandate for Texas annexation and began to push Congress in that direction. On March 1, 1845, Congress voted in favor of annexation. Mexico immediately broke all diplomatic ties with the United States. A crisis of major proportions was at hand.

Tyler had already ordered Brevet Brigadier General Zachary Taylor to move his forces from Louisiana into Texas. Taylor and his 4,000 regulars, volunteers, and Texas Rangers established themselves at the town of Corpus Christi at the mouth of the Nueces River. Then, in February 1846, the government ordered him to move 100 miles south to the mouth of the Rio Grande. Taylor was now occupying land never before claimed by the United States or by the Texas Republic. Whatever the legality of Texas being an independent republic now annexed by the United States—its independence had never been recognized by Mexico—an American armed force was definitely in territory over which the United States had little or no legal claim.

☆   An American Portrait

Zachary Taylor—Born in Virginia in 1784, Taylor was moved with his family to Jefferson County, Kentucky, the next year. Commissioned a lieutenant in the 17th Infantry in 1808, within two years he had attained the rank of captain, and two years later he was brevetted a major for his service in the West during the War of 1812.

After serving for twenty years at many duty stations in the South, the Southwest, and the West, including commanding 400 regulars in the Black Hawk War, Taylor, now a colonel, was sent to Florida in 1837 to fight the Seminoles. It was here he earned the sobriquet "Old Rough and Ready" from his men. In 1838 he was raised in rank to brevet brigadier general and given command of the forces fighting the Seminoles, a position he held until 1840.

After serving on the Southwest frontier for four years at Fort Smith, Arkansas, "Old Zack" (as he was also called by his men) in June 1845 was ordered to move to Corpus Christi as the dispute with Mexico over the annexation of Texas began to heat up. In January 1846 he was directed to advance farther south along the coast to the Rio Grande. In the ensuing Battle of Palo Alto in May 1846, Taylor defeated General Arista, was promoted to brevet major general, and was designated commander of the Army of the Rio Grande. When he subsequently seized Saltillo, he became a national hero and his popularity at home soared,

FIGURE 3–1 Zachary Taylor. (*National Archives, Washington, D.C.*)

making him, as a prominent and outspoken Whig, appear politically dangerous to the Democratic president, James K. Polk. Taylor furthered his political popularity by publicly attacking the Polk administration in a New York newspaper for its lack of support for the armies in Mexico.

After the Battle of Buena Vista, Taylor's political stock rose even higher, the Whig party openly urging him to run for president. Taylor himself became very vocal on the political issues of the day. In June 1848 he received his party's nomination for president, and the following November he was elected the twelfth president of the United States. Taylor, always faithful to the Army regulars and very vocal in his opinions on military matters, often expressed little faith in volunteers and was highly critical of the officership of the West Point graduates. But as president he had little opportunity to affect the American military because his term was very short and was marked by the overriding controversy over the expansion of slavery that resulted in the Compromise of 1850. Taylor died of cholera on July 9, 1850, while still in office.

Accordingly, in April 1846 a Mexican force crossed the Rio Grande and attacked an American detachment from Fort Texas, which had been built at the mouth of that river. Taylor pulled back temporarily for supplies, then struck out again for Fort Texas, meeting the Mexican forces at Palo Alto on May 7. In a day-long artillery duel featuring Brevet Major Samuel Ringgold's "flying artillery" (formed eight years before by Ringgold to give greater mobility to artillery, the cannon crews riding on horseback), he bested them with his 6-, 12-, and 18-pounders loaded with canister and solid shot. Losing 700 of their 4,000 men in a single day's engagement, the Mexicans retreated back across the Rio Grande. Taylor was delayed in following them because, always careless in preparing for battle, he had no pontoon bridges or boats with which to cross the river. Meanwhile, on May 13, 1846, Congress declared war on Mexico for "invading United States territory."

At the same time, Congress authorized an army of 15,000 regulars and 50,000 one-year volunteers to fight the war. The regular Army was small in numbers at the outbreak of the conflict—only 730 officers and fewer than 8,000 men in uniform—but it was much more professionally officered than it had been in earlier conflicts and more experienced because of its conflicts with the Indians. It was also better armed. The Army's old flintlock firearms were always subject to misfiring from worn flints or from dampness in the priming powder in the flashpan (resulting in only a "flash in the pan" instead of the priming powder's igniting the gunpowder behind the shot in the firing chamber via the vent hole). These old flintlocks were giving way to the newer muskets whose hammer struck a copper cap of fulminate of mercury, which caused a sure and instant explosion in the firing chamber. This ensured a quicker and more dependable shot.

Many, if not most, of the Army's infantrymen were still equipped with the old Springfield 1835 .67-inch caliber flintlock muskets rather than with the newer percussion types, thanks to General Winfield Scott's prejudice against the newer weapons, but at least the cavalry units were equipped with Hall carbines (most of .54-inch caliber), which were percussion-fired and breechloading for more accurate and rapid fire. Most of the artillery batteries relied heavily on mobile 6-pounders drawn by horses. Artillery performed so well during this war that the number of artillery regiments was doubled from four to eight by an enthusiastic Congress in 1847.

As the war began, a giant three-pronged offensive to seize northern Mexico was planned. Brigadier General Zachary Taylor (soon to be promoted to brevet major general and given overall command in Mexico by Polk, a Democrat, to thwart the presidential ambitions of General Scott, commanding general of the Army and a Whig) was to march west from Matamoros at the mouth of the Rio Grande to Monterrey. Brigadier General John E. Wool was to move southwest from San Antonio to join up with Taylor. Colonel Stephen Kearney was ordered to proceed south and west from Fort Leavenworth to Sante Fe and then on west to San Diego on the southern California coast. Later a fourth major movement, from the port of Veracruz on the Gulf of Mexico directly west to the capital at Mexico City, would be added and launched under Major General Scott.

General Taylor—"Old Zack" or "Old Rough and Ready" to his men—moved west from Matamoros to Monterrey 125 miles away. He arrived there on September 19, 1846, with a total of 6,200 regulars and volunteers and put the city under siege. Five days later the Mexican army commander asked for an eight-week armistice, during which he would withdraw from the city. Taylor agreed, having already lost 800 men to battle and sickness. President Polk repudiated the armistice, however, and ordered him forward. Taylor seized Monterrey and moved on to the important crossroads town of Saltillo, where he was joined by General Wool and his 2,500 men. Taylor was now in a splendid position to proceed south toward Mexico City, but at this point 4,000 regulars and 4,000 volunteers were taken away from him to be moved back east to Tampico on the coast to join General Scott for an invasion of Veracruz. Taylor was ordered back to Monterrey to stand on the defensive with his 7,000 remaining men.

Furious at these moves (and believing that Scott was trying to best him for political advantage), Taylor decided to accept his orders to return to Monterrey as "advice" and moved south toward Mexico City instead. He assumed that General Santa Anna in Mexico City with

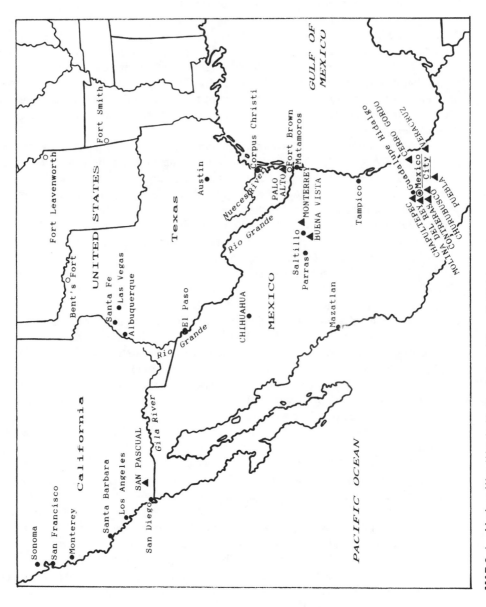

MAP 3–1 Mexican War. *(Used with permission of Anne C. Christensen.)*

a force of 20,000 at his command would not move north across 200 miles of barren desert to confront him but, rather, would turn east against Scott at Veracruz.

Taylor, often guilty of misunderstanding and underrating his enemy, had guessed wrong. Santa Anna and 15,000 men began marching north against him instead. When he became aware of this on February 21, 1847, Taylor established himself and his force of less than 5,000 men at Hacienda Buena Vista, south of Saltillo. Here he had a broad plain in front of him, a series of mountain spurs (La Angostura) on his left (eastern) flank, upon which he placed his artillery, and a right (western) flank consisting of a series of deep gullies.

After both commanders spent most of the first day jockeying for position, the climax of the two-day Battle of Buena Vista was reached on the second, February 23, 1847. Santa Anna first tried to hit Taylor's La Angostura left flank but was rebuffed by artillery and infantry. The Mexican general then threw his army against Taylor across the broad central plateau. The Americans positioned there broke and ran in the face of a two-division Mexican charge, but the day was saved when Taylor's mounted dragoons, the 1st Mississippi Rifles under Colonel Jefferson Davis, broke up the Mexican attack. Santa Anna then threw another entire division at the American lines in the midst of a mighty thunderstorm. Again the situation was saved by the timely arrival of the now-wounded Jefferson Davis and the Mississippi Rifles, plus punishing artillery bombardment from the Americans on La Angostura. Santa Anna, having lost at least 1,500 men to the Americans' 800, withdrew from the field. American artillery and the bravery of the regulars and volunteers—combined with the inspiring personal bravery of "Old Zack," who stationed himself on his horse in the center of the American lines, seemingly unconcerned about Mexican bullets whizzing around him—had won the first great victory of the war.

☆   An American Portrait

Stephen W. Kearney—Undoubtedly the nation's foremost soldier of the West, Kearney was born in New Jersey in 1794. Not finding academics to his liking at Columbia College, he joined the Army as a lieutenant in 1812 and was decorated for his gallantry at Queenston Heights and advanced in rank to captain. Between the War of 1812 and 1846 he served most of his time on the frontier, leading exploring expeditions, building forts, and carrying out other duties while steadily advancing in rank to colonel.

In 1846 he was promoted to brigadier general and given command of the Army of the West in the conflict with Mexico. Arriving in Sante Fe with 1,660 men from Fort Leavenworth, Kansas Territory, he set out in September with 300 dragoons for the California coast (sending most of them back when California appeared to be safely in American hands) and arrived in San Diego after pitched battles with resisting Mexican forces and being saved by a relief force sent out by Commodore Robert Stockton of the Navy.

With Stockton and 600 men, Kearney set out for Los Angeles, occupying the city on January 10, 1847. Three days later, California surrendered to a separate force under the command of explorer-turned-conqueror John C. Frémont. But when Frémont (appointed governor of California by Stockton) refused to obey Kearney's orders and Washington upheld Kearney's authority, Kearney ordered Frémont east under virtual arrest to face a court martial for insubordination. Frémont was found guilty and resigned from the Army.

Kearney subsequently moved on into lower Mexico and was brevetted major general, but, his health broken by a tropical disease, he returned to the United States and died in St. Louis in October 1848.

☆   An American Portrait

John C. Frémont—John Charles Frémont, the "Pathmarker of the West," was born in Georgia in 1813. Between 1829 and 1831 he studied science and mathematics at the College of Charleston in South Carolina and began surveying work through the influence of his friend Joel R. Poinsett. By 1838 he had been summoned to Washington by Poinsett, now secretary of war, and commissioned a lieutenant in the U.S. Corps of Topographical Engineers. He then accompanied Joseph Nicolet, the French scientist, on an expedition to study the region between the Upper Mississippi and Missouri Rivers, the trip adding to Frémont's knowledge and whetting his appetite for exploration.

During these years Frémont picked up a powerful patron in the person of Senator Thomas Hart Benton of Missouri, in 1841 eloping with Benton's strong-willed daughter Jessie. Through Benton's influence, Frémont was given command of an expedition to the Wind River section of the Rocky Mountains the next year. This trip was so successful that Congress authorized a second Frémont expedition. This second expedition, lasting 14 months, took Frémont and his party across the present-day states of Utah, Oregon, and Nevada and down through California and was concluded in 1844.

Frémont's third Western expedition, the most notable in bringing him fame, began in 1845 in St. Louis, heading for Bent's Fort on the Arkansas River and the eastern slopes of the Rockies. Frémont and his men, fully armed in case of an outbreak of war with Mexico, ended up in the region of the Great Salt Lake and California. In 1846 he participated in the Bear Flag Rebellion around Sutter's Fort, working with Commodore Robert F. Stockton and General Stephen W. Kearney in bringing California under American control. In a subsequent power struggle between Stockton and Kearney, Frémont backed Stockton, the loser, and, as a result, was returned to the East under court martial for disobedience. He was found guilty, but President James K. Polk remitted his sentence of dismissal from the Army; nevertheless, Frémont resigned his commission.

Frémont's fourth and fifth explorations (1848–1849 and 1853–1854) were under private auspices. Between these expeditions, Frémont developed gold-mining interests in California and served briefly as U.S. senator from that newly admitted state. In 1856 he was the first presidential nominee of the new Republican party, losing to James Buchanan in the November election. With the outbreak of the Civil War he was appointed a major general and given command of the Western Department, headquartered at St. Louis. His 100-day command there was marked by controversy and military setbacks. His brief command in the Shenandoah Valley thereafter was equally undistinguished.

After the war he became involved in railroad speculation, was wracked by bankruptcy, and served briefly as governor of the Arizona Territory. Impoverished, he died in New York City in 1890. Although a financial, political, and military failure, John C. Frémont still stands as the "Pathmarker of the West," a military man who helped open that region to the expanding nation.

Colonel Kearney arrived in San Diego after a rugged march across deserts and mountains to find California in American hands, thanks to the "Bear Flag Revolt," the presence of the Navy's Pacific squadron, and the victories of John C. Frémont's "explorers" in the north. This development, combined with Taylor's triumph at Buena Vista and Colonel Alexander W. Doniphan's detached 850-man First Missouri Mounted Volunteers' ("Doniphan's Thousand") seizure of Chichuahua and the upper Rio Grande area, meant that all of northern Mexico was now under American control. Doniphan's men had moved over 1,800 miles and had won pitched battles at El Brazito north of El Paso and at Rio Sacramento before joining Taylor at Parras. They were then sent on to Monterrey and eventually home to St. Louis, having covered over 6,000 miles. Attention then shifted to Scott's invasion of Veracruz and his planned march on Mexico City.

General Scott—"Old Fuss and Feathers"—had 13,000 soldiers at his rendezvous point at Lobos Island south of Tampico for his amphibious attack on Veracruz, the first major joint-service amphibious operation in American history. (Oliver Hazard Perry and Scott, then Perry and William Henry Harrison, had conducted such operations on a much smaller scale in 1813.) Joined by the Navy under Matthew C. Perry, a near-perfect landing was made on March 9, 1847, south of the city. Some 10,000 men, with their artillery and supplies, were landed in specially designed surf boats in only four hours in the largest American amphibious landing until World War II. When it became clear that more firepower would be needed to compel the surrender of Veracruz and its protecting fortress of San Juan de Ulua, six 32-pound naval guns were brought ashore and emplaced around the besieged city. Under the overwhelming combined force of this Army and Navy artillery barrage, the city fell to the Americans on March 27.

☆ An American Portrait

Winfield Scott—Scott, a native of Virginia and perhaps the most prominent American military figure between the Revolutionary War and the Civil War, was born near Petersburg on June 13, 1786. After a brief stint at the College of William and Mary, he studied law, joined a Petersburg cavalry unit, and in 1809, as a captain of light artillery in the regulars, was sent to New Orleans. Scott came into his own during the War of 1812. Commissioned a lieutenant colonel, he participated in the Battle of Queenstown (where he was captured and later paroled), fought at Fort George and other frontier battles with the British, and, as a brigadier general, emerged as a national hero in the battles at the Chippewa and Lundy's Lane, after which he was brevetted a major general.

In the interwar years he wrote extensively on military topics (including the first standard set of American drill regulations and the three-volume *Infantry-Tactics*) and on temperance. He also led a contingent to the West in the Black Hawk War, fought in Florida against the Seminoles, skillfully managed the diplomatic crisis with the British known as the *Caroline* Affair, negotiated the end of the Aroostock War on the Canadian frontier, and led 16,000 Cherokees from South Carolina and Tennessee to the Southwest.

In June 1841 he was appointed general-in-chief of the Army, in this position eradicating the worst of the harsh disciplinary punishments in the service and showing strong support for the United States Military Academy even though he had not received professional military training. With the outbreak of the Mexican War, "Old Fuss and Feathers"

FIGURE 3–2 Winfield Scott. (*National Archives, Washington D.C.*)

(a nickname he had picked up because of his pompous bearing) set out for the war zone. There he led the March 1847 landing at Veracruz and the drive toward Mexico City. Because he was a leading Whig and because of his support for Nicholas Trist over peace negotiations, he became a target of criticism by President Polk and the Democrats. After the fighting ended, he properly disciplined three officers for insubordination, giving Polk an opportunity to attack him again by bringing him before a board of inquiry (where the charges were eventually withdrawn).

In 1852 Scott was nominated for president on the Whig ticket but lost to Franklin Pierce in a bitter contest. Thereafter continuing his military service, he was promoted to brevet lieutenant general (the first lieutenant general in the Army since Washington) in 1855, settled a dispute with Britain over the Oregon boundary in 1859, and in 1861 remained loyal to the Union in the secession crisis, authoring an overall Union strategy for the war and supervising the defense of the capital before retiring as general-in-chief in November 1861 at 75 years of age. Assuming the post of superintendent of West Point, he died there in May 1866 and was buried on the Academy grounds.

☆   An American Portrait

Matthew Calbraith Perry—Perry, brother of the War of 1812 hero Oliver Hazard Perry, was born in 1794 in Newport, Rhode Island. In 1809 he entered the Navy as a midshipman and saw service in many battles during the war with Great Britain (including a tour of duty under his older brother). After the war he attained independent command and fought pirates in the West Indies and held many other posts, including second officer of the New York navy yard beginning in 1833. Often called "the father of the steam navy," he was responsible for many technological innovations in the naval service and in 1837 took command of the USS *Fulton,* one of the Navy's first steampowered ships of war.

In 1841 he became commandant of the New York Navy Yard. Two years later he took command of the African Squadron, assigned the task of suppressing the slave trade off the coasts of that continent, and in 1845 he helped establish the United States Naval Academy at Annapolis. During the Mexican War—in which the Navy had relatively little to do—he was commander of the steam-sail USS *Mississippi* and commander-in-chief of the squadron that controlled the eastern coast of Mexico, placing it under close blockade. In his capacity as commander-in-chief he also directed the naval forces during the successful amphibious landings at Veracruz on March 9, 1847.

Perry won his greatest fame when, between 1852 and 1854, he headed a squadron sent to Japan to open that isolationist kingdom to American trade, his diplomatic success affirmed in the Treaty of Kanawaga of 1854. Perry—"Old Bruin," naval officer, and diplomat—died in March 1858 in New York City.

Scott then moved inland and met Santa Anna's 12,000-man force at Cerro Gordo on the National Highway on April 18. Here the Americans won complete victory by flanking Santa Anna's superior frontal position and bringing their artillery to bear against his soldiers from higher ground. The Mexicans fled back west toward the capital, but Scott was delayed in following them when the enlistments ran out on 4,000 of his volunteers. This deficit, combined with his additional losses as a result of combat and disease, left Scott with only 16,000 men, so he took the city of Puebla and settled down for ten weeks to await reinforcements and the outcome of the peace negotiations then underway.

When reinforcements arrived and the peace negotiations broke down, Scott renewed his push toward Mexico City. Abandoning his line of communication back to Veracruz because of his shortage of manpower, he moved off on August 7, 1847, with 10,000 regulars, volunteers, and marines and was soon only 14 miles from the capital. Displaying his usual thoroughness in preparing for battle by reconnaissance of the terrain and the enemy's position, Scott then sent part of his forces off to the left in a flanking movement to assault the city from the west. The Mexican army made gallant stands at Contreras and Churubusco (suffering almost 5,000 casualties in the two engagements) but could not withstand the American infantry-artillery assaults. Santa Anna—now the elected president of Mexico for a second time—accepted Scott's offer of an armistice. But the Mexican leader seemed to have no intention of coming to terms, so Scott resumed his drive on the capital even though he now had only 8,000 men against Santa Anna's 15,000.

Scott first seized the outer defensive position of Mexico City at El Molino del Rey and then launched a successful three-pronged attack on September 13 on the Castle of Chapultepec, the infantry pushing on to take two key gates to the city. Facing impending military defeat, Santa Anna surrendered on September 14. The war was over. Generals Taylor and Scott, ably assisted by a large cadre of West Point–trained young officers, had carried out a series of brilliant operations that had resulted in overwhelming victory and validated the military professionalism taught at the Academy. Among those who saw combat were Ulysses S. Grant, Robert E. Lee, Braxton Bragg, George B. McClellan, Jefferson Davis, Pierre G. T. Beauregard, George G. Meade, and Joseph E. Johnston.

The war was formally ended in February 1848 with the signing of the Treaty of Guadalupe-Hidalgo. Nicholas Trist, the American peace commissioner, and General Scott ignored instructions from Washington to break off the peace talks and resume fighting because they realized that a negotiated peace was at hand. By the provisions of the treaty the United States gained over a million square miles of new territory, including all of present-day California, Arizona, New Mexico, Utah, and Nevada, and parts of Colorado and Wyoming. The cost was 13,000 dead (over 86 percent from accident or disease). By August 1, 1848, all American troops were out of Mexico, and the Army was soon cut back to about 13,000 men.

The Mexican conflict had revealed that a seminal change had taken place since 1815 in the time-honored tradition of the citizen-soldier protecting American lives and values through his local common militia. In the years following the War of 1812, the common militia units, still existing in the states under laws that demanded enrollment and drill, gradually fell into decline and disuse. Payment of a fee for exemption from serving, lax enforcement of enrollment and drill obligations, and parsimonious support for the militia—except on the frontier, where Indian difficulties remained a very real threat—became the norm. Local militia service as a civic virtue became less and less a matter of concern, and, with the decline in the quality and effectiveness of the local units, militia musterings, with their attempts at parade-ground soldiering, frequently became the subject of local levity.

This did not mean, however, that citizen-soldier volunteerism in democratic and local-minded America had ceased to exist as part of the nation's civic virtue system. Rather, it had been gradually transferred to local-based volunteer units. These, like the militia, would answer the state or nation's call in time of need. Independent volunteer companies—riflemen, grenadiers (originally grenade-throwers), light artillery, cavalry, lancers, dragoons (mounted infantrymen), and so on—had first originated in small numbers in the early nineteenth century. They were usually independent of state militia systems (although some states eventually designated them as the state militia), and were, in reality, select little societies of men drawn together for military or quasi-military purposes.

The 50 to 100 members of each company received no pay and financed their own often-colorful and unique uniforms and equipment. The French-emulating Zouave units, with their red caps, sashes, and baggy trousers and their unique drill, were the most conspicuous in this regard. They also screened their own applicants and elected their own officers. Often the members of a volunteer company were all from the same trade (firemen, clerks, and so on) or nationality (such as the German Volunteers and the Irish Jasper Greens of Savannah and the *Bataillon d'Artillerie d'Orleans* from Louisiana), and competition was fierce among them. These independent companies were uniquely elitist, democratic, socially binding, and military all at the same time, a reflection of the nation they served.

These volunteer companies were sometimes used for constabulary duties in urban riots, on the Canadian frontier, or on slave patrol in the South, besides carrying out ceremonial duties on state, national, or ethnic days of celebration and parade. Yet they clearly proved very valuable to a nation in need of military manpower during the Seminole wars and especially in the Mexican War. Despite the self-conscious posturing that marked their hometown displays of martial prowess, volunteers such as Doniphan's Thousand and Davis' Mississippi Rifles displayed notable battlefield abilities that compared favorably with those of the regulars in the Mexican conflict.

The calls for limited service by both belligerents at the outbreak of the Civil War tended to fracture the volunteer companies because companywide enlistments were initially rejected by the governments. The volunteer companies in the antebellum period nevertheless served well for four decades and proved to be a military training ground for many officers who would make valuable contributions to Civil War leadership. Out of this antebellum volunteer company tradition and volunteers' service during the Civil War would come the postbellum National Guard movement as the third stage of local-based, democratic soldiering for the republic.

Meanwhile, the soldiers of the now-reduced regular Army returned to their old duties in the West of surveying, building roads and forts, and defending settlers against the Indians. They were also involved in constabulary duties of another type, this time in a near-war in the Utah Territory in 1857–1858. The Mormons, having fled their city of Nauvoo, Illinois, and having established their "State of Deseret" at Salt Lake City under the inspired leadership of Brigham Young, refused to follow American law, particularly regarding polygamy. The Army was sent in to persuade them to do so. A march was conducted from Fort Leavenworth to Salt Lake City under miserable conditions by some 3,000 troops under Brevet Brigadier General Albert Sidney Johnston. After negotiations were carried out, a settlement was agreed upon whereby Young would remain as head of the Church of the Latter Day Saints, and he and his followers would recognize the authority of the United States and abide by its laws. Thus the "Mormon War" was a war that never was, and federal authority was ensured in all the territory taken from Mexico.

The Army was also absorbing the lessons of its recent successful war and the potential of its new weapons in its service schools. Few realized that just around the corner was the bloodiest war in American history. During this fratricidal Civil War, its experience and its new weapons and technology would be put to the ultimate test as veteran officers and enlisted men, plus newly enrolled officers and men by the hundreds of thousands, would be pitted against one another in a cataclysmic struggle over the fate of the nation.

THE NAVY AND MARINE CORPS FROM 1815 TO 1860

The Navy was not called upon to play a major role in defending America's interests against other countries in the 4 1/2 decades following the War of 1812, yet it managed moderate growth and development while protecting and extending America's interests throughout the world. Great 74-gun sailing ships continued to be built and manned—although at a very dilatory pace—and steam power came to the Navy, first in the form of the 700-ton sidewheeler USS *Fulton* in 1837 and then in the wooden paddlewheel sister ships *Missouri* and *Mississippi* in the 1840s. The screw propeller of John Ericsson was first used by the Navy on the sloop *Princeton* (1843), and the first iron-hulled steam warship, the sidewheeler *Michigan*, was launched that same year for service on the Great Lakes.

The Navy protected American commerce, struggled to eradicate the illegal African slave trade, and fought pirates in the Caribbean. It carried out the successful exploration voyage of Charles Wilkes to Antarctica, the South Pacific, and the Northwest Coast from 1838 to 1842 and developed the sciences of navigation and oceanography under the leadership of Matthew Fontaine Maury, the "Pathfinder of the Seas." It also laid claim to the Sandwich Islands (Hawaii) in the 1840s, opened China to trade with America in the Treaty of Wanghia in 1844, opened Japan to the West through the power diplomacy of Commodore Matthew Calbraith Perry in 1852–1854, and "showed the flag" in foreign ports throughout the world.

☆ An American Portrait

Matthew Fontaine Maury—Maury, the "Pathfinder of the Seas," first superintendent of the U.S. Naval Observatory, the nation's first hydrographer, and the "father of oceanography," was born in Virginia in 1806 but raised in Tennessee. Entering naval service at a young age, he noticed deficiencies in the Navy's education of its midshipmen, particularly its lack of system-ized instruction in navigation. Accordingly, in 1836 he published a text on the subject entitled *A New Theoretical and Practical Treatise on Navigation.* This brought him international fame.

Declining to join the naval exploring expedition to the South Seas and Antarctica led by Charles Wilkes because of a personal dislike of the man, Maury continued to work for educational and administrative reform while carrying out his other naval duties. Then, in 1842, as superintendent of the Depot of Charts and Instruments (later the U.S. Naval Observatory) he began studying the atmosphere. From the logs of naval ships he collected valuable navigational data that appeared in his books *The Wind and Current Chart of the North Atlantic* and *Explanations and Sailing Directions to Accompany the Wind and Current Charts,* published in 1847 and 1851. In 1858 he produced his classic *The Physical Geography of the Sea.*

When the Civil War broke out in April 1861, Maury resigned his naval commission to join his native Virginia in secession. He was soon appointed to head the Confederate Naval Bureau of Coast, Harbor, and River Defense and worked on developing an electric mine during the course of the conflict. After the war he served the government of Emperor Maximilian in Mexico and attempted to colonize families who wanted to emigrate from the defeated South. This scheme failed, and in 1868 Maury moved to Lexington, Virginia, to become a professor of meteorology at the Virginia Military Institute. He served in this position until his death in 1873.

Thanks to the trailblazing work of naval officer Matthew Fontaine Maury in oceanography and hydrography and to his charting of the earth's winds, seas, and weather, the science of navigation was advanced enormously in the mid-nineteenth century and travel was made safer and speedier for millions of people on maritime and naval vessels traversing the oceans of the world.

The Navy faced no serious challenge during the Mexican War, since no Mexican war vessels were ever put to sea on the waters of the Gulf of Mexico. The Navy did, however, seal off the Mexican coast in a tight and effective blockade to prevent outside aid from reaching Santa Anna. It also performed with dispatch its joint amphibious assault on Veracruz in March 1847. In the subsequent siege of Veracruz, naval guns and their crews accounted for 45 percent of the ordnance directed against the city's walls, while naval ships in the harbor subjected the besieged city and fortress to withering fire. Then, as Scott moved inland against Santa Anna, the Navy seized the ports of Alvarado, Tuxpan, and Tobasco on the Gulf Coast, thus completely securing Mexican waters against outside aid.

In the meantime, the Navy also played a key role in seizing California for the Americans, Commodore Thomas ap Catesby Jones even mistakenly taking the port of Monterey in California before the war was declared. (It was returned, with proper apologies rendered.) Thereafter, Commodore Robert F. Stockton cooperated with Captain John C. Frémont and the leaders of the "Bear Flag Republic" in taking Santa Barbara, Los Angeles, and San Diego for the Americans. Subsequently, in 1847, Commodore W. Branford Shubrick also seized important ports in Baja California and on the western coast of Mexico. The Navy had indeed played a vital role in the war with Mexico and had ensured for the United States a firm hold on the California coast as a jumping-off point for extending the nation's western frontier far out across the waters of the Pacific.

The Marine Corps was also occupied with myriad duties in the decades after 1815. Led for most of this period by Major (later Brigadier General) Archibald Henderson, the Corps's fifth commandant, the Navy's sea soldiers took part in assaults against pirates in Cuba in 1821 and in another attack on buccaneers in Sumatra in 1832. They fought off dissolution by Andrew Jackson and his political allies in the period from 1829 to 1834, battled alongside the Army in the Seminole wars, and took part in the attacks on Mexico City in 1847 (commemorated in the opening words of the Marine Corps Hymn, "From the halls of Montezuma..."). They landed in Buenos Aires in 1852 to protect American lives and property there during national rioting, accompanied Commodore Perry on his mission to Japan from 1852 until 1854, and attacked the "Barrier Forts" on the Pearl River near Canton, China, in 1856 when the guns from the forts fired on three American warships.

As was true of its sister services, the U.S. Army and the U.S. Navy, the Marine Corps had begun to come of age professionally and had served the nation well in its years of evolution from 1815 to 1860. However, the strength of all three services, like the strength of the nation, would be sorely tried in the tumultuous and sanguinary Civil War fought from 1861 until 1865.

Suggestions for Further Reading

AMBROSE, STEPHEN E., *Duty, Honor, Country: A History of West Point.* Baltimore: Johns Hopkins University Press, 1966.

BAUER, K. JACK, *Surfboats and Horse Marines: U.S. Naval Operations in the Mexican War, 1846–1848.* Annapolis: U.S. Naval Institute Press, 1969.

———, *The Mexican War, 1846–1848.* New York: Macmillan, 1974.

CONNELLY, OWEN, *Blundering to Glory: Napoleon's Military Campaigns.* Wilmington, DE: Scholarly Resources, 1987.

CUNLIFFE, MARCUS, *Soldiers and Civilians: The Martial Spirit in America, 1775–1865.* Boston: Little, Brown, 1968.

ELLIOTT, CHARLES W., *Winfield Scott: The Soldier and the Man.* New York: Macmillan, 1937.

ELLIS, JOSEPH, and ROBERT MOORE, *School for Soldiers: West Point and the Profession of Arms.* New York: Oxford, 1974.

FLEMING, THOMAS, *West Point: The Men and Times of the United States Military Academy.* New York: Morrow, 1969.

GOETZMANN, WILLIAM H., *Army Exploration of the American West, 1803–1863*. New Haven: Yale University Press, 1959.

HALLECK, HENRY W., *Elements of Military Art and Science*. New York: Appleton, 1862.

HAMILTON, HOLMAN, *Zachary Taylor: Soldier of the Republic*. Indianapolis: Bobbs-Merrill, 1941.

HEINL, ROBERT D., *Soldiers of the Sea: The United States Marine Corps, 1775–1962*. Annapolis: U.S. Naval Institute Press, 1962.

LEWIS, EMANUEL R., *Seacoast Fortifications of the United States*. Washington, DC: Smithsonian Institution Press, 1970.

MAHAN, DENNIS HART, *Advanced-Guard, Outpost, with the Essential Principles of Strategy and Grand Tactics*. New York: John Wiley, 1863.

NEVINS, ALLAN, *Frémont: Pathfinder of the West*. New York: Longmans, Green, 1955.

PRUCHA, FRANCIS P., *The Sword of the Republic: The United States Army on the Frontier, 1783–1846*. New York: Macmillan, 1968.

SCOTT, WINFIELD, *Memoirs of Lieut.-General Winfield Scott*, 2 vols. New York: Sheldon, 1864.

SINGLETARY, OTIS A., *The Mexican War*. Chicago: University of Chicago Press, 1960.

STEVENS, FRANK C., *The Black Hawk War*. Chicago: F. E. Stevens, 1903.

STRODE, HUDSON, *Jefferson Davis, American Patriot*. New York: Harcourt, 1955.

WILTSE, CHARLES M., *John C. Calhoun, Nationalist, 1782–1828*. Indianapolis: Bobbs-Merrill, 1944.

☆4

The Civil War, 1861–1862

The War Between the States began in April 1861 and ended four years later, only after the Union had suffered 610,000 dead or wounded and the Confederacy had sustained 452,000 casualties. The Civil War was the bloodiest in American history, with the highest percentage of the American population killed (almost one of every five white men of military age in the South; one of sixteen in the North) and more men slain in battle than in all the wars to follow in the next century, including World War I and World War II.

Since that time, historians have combed through the records seeking the causes of this tragic conflict. They have advanced various theories as to why the war was fought and why the seemingly irreversible march toward fratricidal blood-letting could not have been stopped before it was too late.

Some historians have argued that the causes lay in the separate economic paths the North and South had followed, especially since 1815. Northerners had moved steadily to develop industry and trade as the co-mainstays of their economy, along with multicrop, large-scale commercial agriculture, while Southerners had largely rejected industry and commerce and opted to hold fast to their agricultural economic order based on a few cash crops, especially cotton. This, in turn, led to differences between the two sections over national economic policy in matters such as tariffs and internal transportation networks such as roads, canals, and railroads.

These economic differences were also reflected in each section's social and political structure. The North had a basically open, three-tiered social and political structure consisting of an upper class, a middle class, and a lower, or working, class. Political power was widely distributed among the classes. In the South, on the other hand, political and economic power were firmly in the hands of the planter aristocracy. There was virtually no middle class, and the bulk of the people who made up the white Southern population, the yeoman farmers, were willing to defer to the planter aristocracy in all matters political and economic—and eventually in secession from the Union and war.

Finally, the South used black slaves as a major source of its labor supply. The North had done away with bondage within its borders at the turn of the century. As the sections grew and expanded into the western territories across the Mississippi, each was determined to take its slave or nonslave labor source with it. For four decades prior to the outbreak of hostilities, the nation had wrestled with the problem of the expansion of slavery into the trans-Mississippi West. The Missouri Compromise of 1819–1820 had temporarily satisfied both sides, but the issue of the extension of slavery was joined all over again when the American victories in the Mexican War led to acquisition of vast territories in the West from Mexico, and a second compromise, the Compromise of 1850, was worked out.

But the 1850s saw the issue exacerbated by numerous events, and the situation worsened as the years went by. The Fugitive Slave Law (part of the Compromise of 1850) was regularly thwarted by defiant Northerners who prevented federal and state officials from cooperating in the return of alleged runaway slaves from the South. Abolitionists in the North and fervent proslavery enthusiasts in the South added emotional fuel to the sectional fires. The politically expedient Kansas-Nebraska Act of 1854, embracing "popular sovereignty," satisfied few and resulted instead in bloody warfare in Kansas. It also led to the breakup of the existing Democratic and Whig parties and brought about the formation of the all-Northern, anti-expansion-of-slavery Republican party.

Added to these political events were the Supreme Court's Dred Scott decision of 1857 and John Brown's abortive attempt to set up an independent slave nation in the mountains of Virginia. By this time the nation had become so polarized over the issue of the expansion of slavery that when Abraham Lincoln was elected president on the Republican ticket in November 1860, the Southern states, led by South Carolina, began to secede from the Union.

The seceding states seized federal properties within their borders and formed a new government, the Confederate States of America. Various compromise efforts failed, and when President Lincoln refused to abandon Fort Sumter in the harbor of Charleston, South Carolina (thereby rejecting the Confederates' claim that it was a foreign installation within the boundaries of their independent and sovereign nation, a claim Lincoln would not and could not accept and still preserve the Constitutional integrity of the Union). Confederate forces began to bombard the fort on April 12, 1861. Lincoln called for troops to put down this defiance of federal authority, and the war was on.

COMPARATIVE STRENGTHS OF THE NORTH AND SOUTH

As was obvious at the outbreak of hostilities, the North enjoyed a decided power advantage over the South by almost any measure. Twenty-three states stayed loyal to the Union, while the Confederacy could claim only eleven. In population the North had 20.7 million persons; the South had only 9.1 million, but this included some 3.6 million slaves, who, at least initially, would not be allowed to bear arms for the Confederacy. This brought the population ratio down to about 4 to 1 in the Union's favor.

In industrial strength—and this would be a modern war demanding prodigious amounts of weapons, ordnance, equipment, food, and other supplies—the North again had all the advantages. The Union could rely on the output of 110,000 manufacturing establishments and 1.3 million trained industrial workers; the Confederacy had but 18,000 establishments and 110,000 workers.

In transportation, and especially railroads (this new and dependable means of carriage would be vital to moving armies and their uncounted tons of supplies to and between the battlefields), the North again had the upper hand by a wide margin. Some 70 percent of the 31,000 miles of track in the nation were located in the North, linking all major areas together with high efficiency. The South, always relying more on its riverways than on rails, had only 31 percent and was further handicapped by giant gaps in its linkage between many of its major cities and a variety of different gauges between lines. Furthermore, 96 percent of the nation's locomotives were built in the North, leaving the South with only 4 percent and with no repair or replacement facilities. The figures for rolling stock were similar.

On the seas, the South owned virtually no merchant marine cargo vessels and very few shipyards capable of building naval or merchant vessels. Whatever the justice of its cause, without trade in and out of the Confederacy, it would in time necessarily die economically.

Yet this disparity of resources was not as overwhelming as it appears at first glance because the South, of necessity, would essentially be fighting a defensive war. This meant that the Confederacy would need fewer men in arms to preserve its territories, while the North would have to invade the South to put down the rebellion and then maintain control over all the territories seized by them. Furthermore, the Southerners would be fighting on their own ground and for preservation of their own homes, very important tactical and psychological considerations. They would also hold the interior lines of communication, while the North would be left with the more difficult exterior lines of a great arc stretching from Virginia all the way across the northern boundary of the Confederacy to the Southwest. Finally, the Confederates had been able to seize federal forts, naval bases, and arsenals in their territories in great numbers in the weeks following secession, so the disparity in military supplies was somewhat less than it appeared.

Whatever the exact inequality in economic and military strengths between the contending sections, morale would also be an important factor—indeed, a factor every bit as vital as numbers of men or quantities of supplies. Southern leaders knew this well and banked on the popularity and righteousness of the cause of secession and confederation—as well as on aid from other nations—to more than offset Federal population and material advantages and lead them to victory in their war for independence.

BASIC STRATEGIES FOR VICTORY

Neither side was strategically prepared for the war when it came. The South had to create a government and a military structure from scratch, leaving no time or opportunity to devise strategic plans. The North was no better off, having no military agency or individual assigned the task of planning strategy in case of a civil war. Thus strategy on both sides was a matter of improvisation once hostilities began.

The essential goal of the federal government in the war was to restore the Union by forcing the seceded states to return to loyalty. This could be done only by breaking the Confederates' dream of independent existence by convincing them that their cause was hopeless.

The resulting Northern strategy was essentially offensive. The Federals would have to carry the war into the South to break the rebels' will to resist. This would be done by four strategic offensive moves carried out simultaneously or serially, depending upon circumstances.

First, Richmond, the Confederate capital after May 1861 and located 100 miles south of Washington, DC, was to be captured, and any forces defending it were to be smashed. This was a reflection of the Jominian principle of seizing key locations.

Second, the Mississippi River cutting through the South was to be seized, thereby slicing the rebellious territory in two and denying the eastern section vital food supplies and reinforcement from the western section.

Third, the important rail center of Chattanooga on the upper Tennessee River just north of the Georgia border was to be captured as a base of operations from which a drive toward Atlanta and then the sea could be launched to cut the South in two once again.

Fourth, all Southern harbors were to be seized and a tight blockade imposed on the entire southern Atlantic and Gulf coasts from Norfolk, Virginia, to Galveston, Texas, a distance of 3,500 miles, to prevent Southern cotton from being exported and war materials from being imported. The seizure of the Mississippi, along with the blockade, was the essence of Scott's ill-fated "Boa-constrictor," later dubbed the "Anaconda," Plan.

The Confederate aim in the war was simply to avoid defeat, to stand on the defensive long enough and make the price of victory high enough that the citizens of the North would despair of winning and demand of their government that the war be ended, thus ensuring Southern independence and recognition as a separate country. In the process of carrying out this basic grand strategy, they would hold off the Federal forces, try to penetrate the Union naval blockade, and bank on foreign aid and recognition, perhaps drawing cotton-importing England into the war and tipping the military balance in the South's favor.

In practice, the Confederate strategy contained a number of crucial weaknesses. First, if the Union government employed astute diplomacy and carried out effective military operations whereby the Southern ports were seized and a strict blockade established, perhaps Britain would refuse to come to the aid of the South, rendering the Confederates' economic and logistical problems insurmountable. Second, by attempting to hold the entire arc of the Confederate border impervious to penetration by the numerically superior Federal forces, the Southern armies would be widely scattered and perhaps unable to hold the line at key points. Conversely, abandoning any of the border areas in favor of a stronger but shorter arc would be an admission of weakness and an invitation to defection from the cause, especially along the vital Kentucky-Tennessee border areas vital as a source of food supplies. Third, if the South stayed on the defensive, it might well have an adverse effect on its armies, whose leaders believed in the offensive mode of war both strategically and tactically.

Equally important, it might be deemed necessary to go on the offensive into Northern territory to showcase Southern determination, to impress foreign countries, and to undermine Northern morale and support for the war. When this offensive strategy was in fact adopted on two notable occasions during the war, the result was a fortunate draw in the first instance (Antietam in 1862) and a terrible defeat in the second (Gettysburg in 1863). These two invasions, rather than grievously wounding the North, resulted in higher Northern morale, greater Yankee determination to win, and no chance of foreign recognition. It must be added, too, that perhaps both of these offensive operations might have succeeded in their purpose had it not been for the Southern need to hold back additional troops and supplies to protect other areas along the great border arc and for the fact that various Southern governors regularly refused to commit their states' men and supplies to the greater strategic effort in order to "protect their state from invasion," even though they were free of any real threat at the time.

Thus each side developed its basic strategy early in the war and began to carry it into execution. Either strategy could have worked, but only one did. This can be explained, in part, because strategies, however solid in theory, face their ultimate test in actual combat. Here is where wars are won and lost. Here is where leadership and judgment, like strategy, are found adequate or wanting.

PRESIDENTIAL LEADERSHIP

In both the United States and the Confederate constitutions, the designated commander-in-chief was the president. In the last analysis, then, it was Abraham Lincoln and Jefferson Davis into whose hands direction of the opposing forces fell. Ironically, it was the nonmilitary Lincoln who emerged as an effective war president, while the militarily experienced Davis was found lacking.

Abraham Lincoln had virtually no military experience on assuming his duties as president and commander-in-chief. He had served very briefly in the Black Hawk War as a militia captain but had no formal military training. Yet he was endowed with remarkable vision and will and undoubtedly became the single most important factor in Union victory. It was he who kept the North together in its determination to suppress the rebellion whatever the cost, and it was he who finally determined Northern strategy and imposed it on his military chiefs.

Unlike almost all of his leading generals (who believed in limited war, avoiding battles, and seizing crucial territories), Lincoln was not concerned with capturing territory and key areas as such. He believed that victory, breaking the will of the South, lay in engaging and defeating the enemy's armies. And it was Lincoln who proposed placing a cordon around the South (borrowing the idea from Winfield Scott's Anaconda Plan but refusing to believe, like Scott, that placing the South in an economic squeeze would bring Unionist sentiment there to the fore and end the war in one year). With the cordon in place and with the North's superiority in numbers and resources, Lincoln believed, the South could be penetrated at different points simultaneously and its armies engaged and defeated, thus ending the war.

If it took four years for this strategy to work out against a determined Southern enemy, the fault lay not with the plan but with Lincoln's inability to find a Union general who could understand and accept the concept that destruction of the enemy's forces was the key to victory.

And it was Lincoln who inaugurated and developed the modern command and staff concept, although in a rather tenuous, trial-and-error fashion. In November 1861, Lincoln removed the aged, 350-pound, physically infirm Winfield Scott as general-in-chief and replaced him with the popular 35-year-old Major General George B. McClellan. McClellan was also commander of the Army of the Potomac, having been named to the post in July 1861 after the Union's disastrous defeat at First Manassas. A splendid organizer and trainer of men, 5-foot, 8-inch "Little Mac" was beloved by his troops, but Lincoln was looking for a strategist, a driver toward victory, a leader of men in battle, and McClellan was none of these.

☆   An American Portrait

George B. McClellan—McClellan was born in December 1826 to a well-to-do Philadelphia family. Upon graduation from the United States Military Academy in 1846 as second in his class, he rendered distinguished service during the Mexican War and was brevetted twice. He returned to West Point for three years to serve as an instructor in military engineering before being assigned various engineering tasks and railroad surveys. He was then sent to Europe to observe the Crimean War.

Resigning his captaincy in 1857, McClellan rose rapidly in the railroad business, in 1860 becoming president of the Ohio and Mississippi Railroad. Living in Cincinnati when the war broke out, McClellan was appointed a major general of the Ohio volunteers and gained victories in western Virginia. On the strength of his reputation and his early wartime experience, he was called to Washington by Lincoln in July 1861 to lead the Army of the Potomac after the Union's defeat at First Manassas. Later that year he was also appointed general-in-chief, replacing Winfield Scott.

McClellan was a superb organizer and trainer of troops, and his men idolized him. The Peninsula campaign, however, revealed that in battle McClellan was very reluctant to assume the initiative, always believing that the worse that could happen would happen. This reluctance was largely responsible for his losses in his 1862 drive toward Richmond. An exasperated Lincoln removed him from command, but after Pope's defeat at Second Manassas, McClellan was again placed in charge of the Army of the Potomac. But the Battle of Antietam later that year revealed that McClellan had not changed when he refused to pursue the Confederates energetically after the battle. Lincoln relieved him again, and McClellan never again held field command in the Union army.

McClellan emerged as the candidate for president of the Democratic party in 1864, but Lincoln, his political fortunes buoyed by Sherman's seizure of Atlanta, won handily. After the war McClellan rose to prominence in business and engineering, served as governor of New Jersey between 1878 and 1881, and died on October 29, 1885, in Orange, New Jersey, still acknowledged as having been a great trainer of men but a bitter disappointment on the battlefield.

McClellan's sole strategic plan, finally coaxed out of him by Lincoln, was a reflection of the general's Jominian indoctrination at West Point. According to his plan, McClellan would take 275,000 men by sea, sail up the James River and take Richmond, then reembark his men, and go down the coast doing the same sort of thing all the way to New

Orleans. While the idea of seaborne amphibious operations had some strategic merit, the fact that McClellan had neither the men nor the supplies, and was lacking sea transportation to carry out the operations, combined with the fact that seizing places would still leave the Confederate armies intact, impelled Lincoln to reject the plan. McClellan never came up with another.

Unhappy with McClellan's lack of initiative and vision as general-in-chief, Lincoln removed him from the office at the time the popular general began his Virginia Peninsula campaign in March 1862 and left the position vacant for five months. He acted as his own commander of land armies with the aid of Secretary of War Edwin M. Stanton and the "Army Board," the bureau chiefs of the Army. In effect, Lincoln had created the Army's first general staff.

☆   An American Portrait

Henry W. Halleck—"Old Brains," as he came to be called, was born in Westernville, New York, in January 1815. After receiving a degree from Union College, where he made Phi Beta Kappa, he was graduated third in his class of 32 at West Point in 1839 and served in the Mexican War. Between the wars he flourished as a teacher at West Point, became an expert on fortifications, and published books on military subjects, including *Elements of Military Art and Science* (1846) and a translation of Jomini's *Vie Politique et Militaire de Napoleon*. Resigning his commission of engineers in 1853, Halleck served as secretary of state in California and was a leading lawyer in San Francisco.

With the outbreak of the war, Halleck was appointed a major general in August 1861, and three months later he was named commander of the Department of the Missouri. Here he received much credit and publicity for the battlefield victories of Grant and other generals under him, but when he entered the field for the first time at Corinth, Mississippi, he proved to be plodding and very cautious.

Appointed general-in-chief in July 1862 to replace McClellan, he soon demonstrated considerable administrative abilities but mediocre leadership qualities, so Lincoln took over as the *de facto* military leader of the Union armies. When Grant was brought east in May 1864, Halleck was appointed to the new post of chief of staff and continued to function well as Lincoln's organizational lieutenant. After the war, Halleck commanded the Military Division of the James, the Division of the Pacific, and the Division of the South. He died in Louisville, Kentucky, on January 9, 1872.

The president went back to the use of a general-in-chief in July 1862 when he brought Major General Henry W. Halleck from the western theater to occupy the post. But Halleck, for all his justified reputation for brilliance as an expert in military affairs, was no grand strategist and proved to be chronically indecisive, although a very competent administrator. So Lincoln kept Halleck on as general-in-chief in title only for the Army administratively, while he as commander-in-chief acted as general-in-chief for the next year and a half of the war. Thus it was Abraham Lincoln, acting as chief strategist and commander of all land armies, aided by the Army Board, who saw the Union armies through their time of greatest crisis.

In March 1864, at Lincoln's request, Congress created the rank of lieutenant general (at that time the highest in the Army) and specified that the person appointed to this position could also be general-in-chief—that is, commander of land armies. Lincoln quickly appointed Ulysses S. Grant, the victor at Vicksburg and Chattanooga, to both positions.

Grant lost no time in moving east to direct the war near to his commander-in-chief and in adopting a strategy of attrition, attacking the Confederate armies on all fronts, especially Robert E. Lee's Army of Northern Virginia. Grant's strategy was to attack and attack and attack again, taking casualties as he moved south toward Richmond but in the process bleeding the Confederates to death. Lincoln had at last found a general who understood and would carry out his strategy of attacking armies, not places. As Lincoln said of Grant, "He fights."

In the meantime, Halleck was "kicked upstairs" to be chief of staff in March 1864 and admirably performed the job of maintaining liaison among Lincoln, Grant, and the Union Army's departmental commanders. Thus, by the end of the war, Lincoln had imposed a winning strategy on the military commanders under him and had created a modern command and staff structure in the Army while serving as the unwavering political and spiritual leader of the North. Well did this military amateur deserve the accolades bestowed upon him as the nation's war president.

Jefferson Davis, on the other hand, was a military professional who performed weakly in his role as war president, although the fault was not entirely his own. Davis, born in Kentucky, was graduated from West Point in 1828 and served in the regular Army for seven years thereafter. Resigning his commission, he then entered into careers in planting and politics in Mississippi, served in Congress, made a reputation for gallantry as a colonel in the 1st Mississippi Rifles at Buena Vista during the Mexican War, served in the United States Senate both before and after a successful stint as secretary of war under Franklin Pierce, and finally was inaugurated as provisional president of the Confederate States of America in February 1861 at Montgomery, Alabama, and as president one year later in Richmond.

As war president, Davis was constantly hampered by the unwillingness of the leaders of the Southern states to accept direction from their central government and by their insistence on keeping men and supplies back from the Confederate armies in the field to protect their own home areas. But most of Davis's problems came from his own personality. Prideful, doctrinaire, and resentful of unsolicited or critical advice, Davis wanted to be both commander-in-chief and general-in-chief for the Confederacy. He was bent on making all the strategic military decisions and carrying out the war as he alone saw fit. His old friend, Adjutant General Samuel Cooper, the highest-ranking general in the Confederate Army, was of limited assistance to Davis because of his old age. Cooper's Northern background also made him the object of persistent suspicion.

When, by 1862, the war effort was not going as well as expected and he became the object of criticism on this account, Davis finally asked the Confederate Congress to create the position of general-in-chief. But when the lawmakers did so, he vetoed the bill as an infringement on his presidential powers! Davis then created on his own the position of military advisor and named Robert E. Lee to the post, although he insisted that all military operations ordered by Lee have his personal approval. Then, when Lee shortly afterward departed to assume theater command of the Army of Northern Virginia, Davis left the post of military advisor vacant for 20 months and ran the war himself, soliciting no professional advice from those under him. Indeed, Davis went through five secretaries of war in four years because of his interference with their duties and decisions and ended up squabbling with almost all of his generals.

In 1864, with the war going very badly, Davis finally created the position of chief of staff, but he appointed to it General Braxton Bragg (blamed by many for numerous disasters in 1862 and 1863 in Tennessee), a reflection of Davis' penchant for cronyism. Bragg never challenged Davis, so the president continued to direct strategy and the movement of the Confederate field armies.

Finally, in February 1865, with the Confederacy facing military disaster, Congress formally created the office of general-in-chief to direct the armies, and Davis named Lee to the post. But Lee would not challenge Davis's stated position that the general-in-chief must be subordinate to the commander-in-chief, so Davis ended the war as he began it, in personal charge of military affairs.

Thus the war leadership of Jefferson Davis, unlike that of Abraham Lincoln, revealed not only little strategic vision or political charisma but also no development of a command and staff organization. Surely Jefferson Davis was not entirely responsible for Southern military defeat, but his insistence on directing military affairs for the Confederacy while brooking no honest criticism and not sharing any power of command decision making was a contributory factor to the South's defeat by 1865.

WEAPONS AND TACTICS

The Union and Confederate armies used similar weapons during the war. Thanks to technological improvements since the Mexican conflict, the rifle had largely superseded the musket, and the faster and more reliable percussion lock had replaced the flintlock. Breech-loading and repeating weapons and rifled artillery were also coming into use.

The percussion-fired rifle, such as the US Model 1861 of .58-caliber (the size of a bullet as measured by its diameter), with an effective range of 300 yards, represented a major improvement in shoulder arms. Here credit must be given to two French army captains, C. E. Minié and Henri Delvigne, who in the 1840s invented a nonfouling (non-barrel-clogging) rifle bullet usually called the minie ball. Made of lead, it was hollow-based and of cylindroconoidal shape with an iron cup at the base. Rammed down the barrel while wrapped in a patch, when the rifle was fired, the gas of the

FIGURE 4–1 U.S. Model 1861 rifle. (*Smithsonian Institution, Washington, D.C.*)

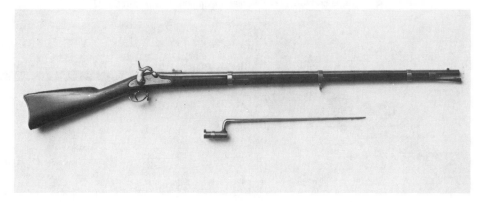

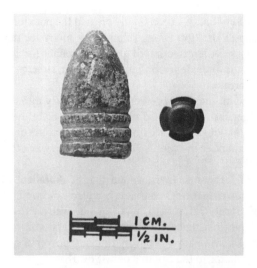

FIGURE 4–2 Minie ball. (*Smithsonian Institution, Washington, D.C.*)

explosion expanded the cup at the base, the cup wedging into the base and the lead taking the rifling grooves as the bullet was projected out of the barrel. This revolutionary projectile had been adopted by the Army in 1855. The use of the more accurate rifle with minie bullets as standard on both sides partially explains the carnage of the Civil War.

Rapid-fire weapons used by both sides also contributed to the bloodshed. Single-shot weapons could be fired faster by breech loading than by muzzle loading, although during the war, breech-loaders were used mainly as cavalry carbines, usually the .54-caliber Burnside or the .52-caliber Sharps. There were also repeating carbines used, such as the seven-shot, buttstock loading, .52-caliber Spencer and the 15-round, .44-caliber Henry. Six-shot revolver pistols, such as the Model 1861 and Model 1863 .44-caliber Remington, the .44-caliber Starr, and the .44-caliber Colt, became the standard sidearms. The hand-cranked, six-barrel, .58-caliber Gatling gun, the first successful machine gun, was capable of firing 600 rounds per minute, but because of design problems, it saw little use. It was adopted by the Army only after the war in 1866, by which time it had been significantly improved.

FIGURE 4–3 Sharps carbine. (*Smithsonian Institution, Washington, D.C.*)

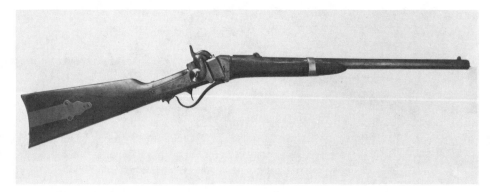

FIGURE 4–4 Model 1863 .44-cal. Remington revolver. (*Smithsonian Institution, Washington, D.C.*)

The most prominent artillery piece used by both sides was the highly mobile US Model 1857 smoothbore "Napoleon" 12-pounder. A Napoleon charged with canister or grape could cause great slaughter among massed troops. The use of shrapnel shot, or "spherical case shot" (a thin-shelled iron ball, usually a 12-pounder, filled with smaller lead or iron balls and set off by a time fuse), would cause a spread of concentrated destruction at up to 1,200 yards. Other smoothbore cannon included squat Howitzers of limited range, field guns accommodating loads of 6 to 24 pounds, and various heavier pieces simply styled "guns."

Rifled cannon were more accurate than smoothbores and by 1863 constituted about half of the Union artillery pieces. The 3-inch ordnance gun was the most popular among them, having an effective range of 2,500 yards. Like the smoothbores, the rifled cannon were muzzle loaders, the experimental breech loaders proving to be unsatisfactory. The most prominent rifled cannon was the Parrott gun, with a single reinforcing band on the breech and ranging in caliber from 10-pounder to 300-pounder. It was matched in size, if not in accuracy, by the smoothbore 15-inch Rodman gun. Both the Northern and Southern navies relied heavily on bulbous Dahlgren bronze howitzers and rifled guns in 12- and 24-pound sizes, plus Dahlgren smoothbore 11-inch shellguns.

The principal tactical combat art in the Civil War was infantry. Infantry would attack the enemy's lines or fortifications in long lines of battle two ranks deep for maximum effective firepower in massed volleys. The lines would be arrayed in a column of brigades, with three brigades in each division moving forward and attacking in successive waves.

Attacks were usually preceded by an artillery bombardment, but the shelling was seldom effective, leaving the defending infantry and artillery unscathed and ready to pour devastating fire on the attackers almost from the moment their assault began. It is estimated that only one out of eight attacks against prepared positions was ever successful during the war, and in some assaults the attacker's casualties ran as high as 80 percent. With this advantage to the defense, it is little wonder that the number of defenders on the line could be as few as 12,000 to the mile and still hold off a major assault.

Given the difficulty of successful frontal attacks and the fact that West Point–trained officers preferred to avoid them anyway, some generals attempted to flank the enemy's lines and roll them up lengthwise. Defending generals, therefore, attempted to secure their flanks by natural obstacles or by troops. All commanders, offensive and defensive, kept troops in reserve to take advantage of any breakthrough or to reinforce any breaks in their lines. Fighting "piecemeal" was the worst of all possible tactical calamities. And skirmishers were used to feel out the enemy positions and to screen their own troops.

Cavalry and artillery were fated to play lesser offensive tactical roles than in earlier conflicts because of the difficulty of moving through the wooded terrain of the American landscape. Cavalry also lost their battlefield advantage with the development of rifled firearms, to which they were highly vulnerable. Cavalry units, therefore, were used for scouting and screening. They were also used in quickly seizing key locations and in these relatively large independent operations proved to be very effective. Artillery was used primarily in a defensive mode, where the guns could be dug in and prepared to deliver withering fire upon attacking lines of infantry.

Technology, then, had delivered new and more devastating firepower into the hands of the Civil War combatants, accounting in large measure for the defensive advantage and for the high casualty totals. (Approximately 600,000 died as battle casualties on both sides in the four-year war.) In the final analysis, however, wars are usually not won or lost on the basis of weapons, technology, numbers, logistics, and leadership alone. With rare exceptions, they are won or lost on the battlefield. The Civil War, the War of Southern Independence, was no exception.

THE BATTLES IN THE EAST

On March 6, 1861, President Jefferson Davis put out a successful call for 100,000 volunteers to serve for 12 months. Later that year another 300,000 men had signed on for one year, but by 1862 it was obvious that more troops would be needed by the Confederacy. Accordingly, a conscription law was passed requiring the conscripts to serve for three years. Excluded by the myriad provisions of the conscription law were members of the state militia and those who owned 20 or more slaves; it also allowed those drafted to purchase a substitute. Thus the war for the South—as was true for the North and has been true in most modern wars—was fought mainly by the poorer and less privileged members of society. Eventually some 900,000 men served in the Confederate armies for three years or more, the highest number at any given time coming in 1863 with about 465,000 on the muster rolls. By 1864 the number was down to only 200,000, half of whom had deserted.

The Union Army stood at only 16,000 as the secession crisis came to a head, but by late 1861 an army of almost 500,000 three-year volunteers had been authorized. Fewer than 50,000 men in the Federal land armies were conscripts, largely because volunteers came into the service through a very effective enrollment system. Eventually about 1.5 million regulars, volunteers, militiamen, and draftees donned the Union blue, the highest number standing at 500,000 on active duty in 1864.

Initially neither side was in a hurry to initiate combat after Fort Sumter. Armies and navies had to be raised, trained, and supplied. Yet few on either side doubted that the initial clash of armies, when it came, would be somewhere between Richmond, the Confederate capital, and Washington, the Federal capital, 100 miles to the north, capital cities being primary targets under Jominian thinking.

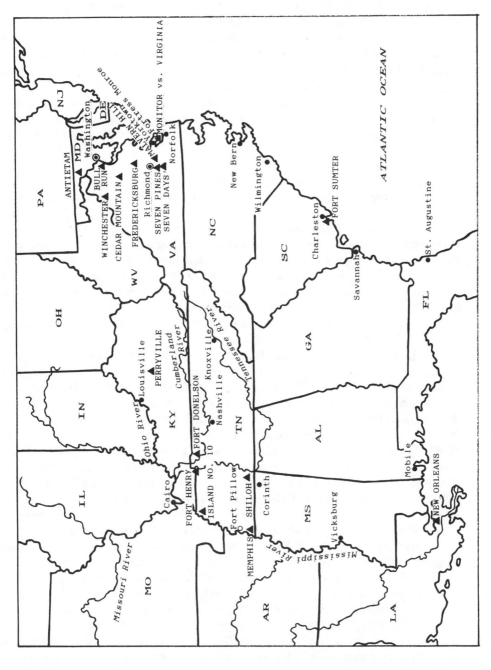

MAP 4–1 Civil War, 1861–1862. (*Used with permission of Anne C. Christensen.*)

In the meantime, the Federals assembled an army of 30,000 men at Alexandria, just south of Washington, under Brigadier General Irwin McDowell to guard the capital. Another army of 15,000 men was posted at the northern end of the Shenandoah Valley to the west under the aged major general of Pennsylvania volunteers Robert Patterson, the Irish-born veteran of both the War of 1812 and the Mexican War. The Confederates assembled an army of 22,000 at Manassas Junction, a vital rail center 29 miles southwest of Washington, under Brigadier General Pierre G. T. Beauregard of Louisiana (and McDowell's West Point classmate). Another army was located to the west in the Shenandoah Valley under Brigadier General Joseph E. Johnston. Johnston had 11,000 men in his command in the valley. Neither side wanted to make a move, but popular pressures for action eventually dictated otherwise.

☆   An American Portrait

Pierre G. T. Beauregard—One of the most colorful of the Confederate generals, "Gustav" Beauregard was born in 1818 in Louisiana. He was graduated from the United States Military Academy in 1838, like Lee, second in his class, and was commissioned a lieutenant of engineers. During the Mexican War he served on the engineering staff of Winfield Scott and fought in the battles of Veracruz and Cerro Gordo. It was Beauregard who advised the taking of Mexico City via Chapultepec. After the war, Beauregard carried out engineering duties in his native Louisiana until 1861, in that year serving as superintendent of West Point for five days before resigning to join the Confederacy in February 1861.

Appointed a brigadier general in the Confederate Army and assigned to Charleston, South Carolina, it was Beauregard who was in command during the firing on Fort Sumter. He was also in command of the left flank during the First Battle of Manassas, being promoted to full general on the strength of his performance there. The following year he was second in command to Albert Sidney Johnston in that general's surprise attack on Shiloh Church, assuming command upon the mortal wounding of Johnston and leading the subsequent Confederate defense at Corinth, Mississippi.

In 1863 he was assigned the defense of South Carolina and Georgia coasts, and in 1864 he was sent to Virginia to aid Lee in his defense against the forces of Ulysses S. Grant. He then held administrative positions until the end of the war. After the fighting was over, Beauregard served for five years as president of a railroad and after 1870 held various civil positions in Louisiana and New Orleans. He died on February 20, 1893.

With the Northern politicians and journalists calling for an offensive—for the one big and easy victory that would break the back of the rebellion—Lincoln in June 1861 instructed Winfield Scott to order McDowell to march on the Southern army southwest of the capital. Scott assured McDowell that Patterson would keep Johnston from leaving the valley: his only problem would be Beauregard. McDowell and his force set out on July 16, 1861, spies and the Washington newspapers having informed Beauregard of the departure.

By July 21, Beauregard had his troops in line behind Bull Run, a meandering stream east of Manassas, awaiting McDowell. He had been reinforced by Johnston, who had neatly slipped away from Patterson in the Shenandoah Valley and brought his 11,000 men from Winchester by rail, the first time strategic mobility had been gained by the use of a railroad. McDowell's battle plan was to move down the Warrenton Turnpike, feint against the 8-mile Confederate line, and move on Beauregard's left flank, rolling it up. The attack by his right flanking columns initially went well, and McDowell's troops began fighting their way south down the Manassas-Sudley Road, forcing back Beauregard's left flank. By midday, Beauregard was pulling in reinforcements from his right flank, and McDowell was also pouring in more troops to crack the enemy's line, by this time running almost north to south with the Federals to the west and the Confederates to the east.

The Union forces made their major attack against the now-reinforced Confederate line at 2:00 in the afternoon. The battle was decided in the next two hours of furious fighting. At 4:00 the Confederates attacked McDowell's right flank and began to roll it up. The exhausted Federals first began to withdraw from the field in an orderly fashion and then panicked when the Cub Run Bridge was hit by artillery fire, jamming their escape route. The retreat soon turned into a rout, with troops and civilian spectators making their way back to Washington in panic.

Although the Confederates had won a decisive victory in this First Battle of Manassas (or Bull Run), they were too exhausted and disorganized to pursue the fleeing "Yankees," even though President Jefferson Davis had arrived on the scene and was urging them to do so. The battle simply petered out. Southern confidence in its military prowess swelled in the aftermath of First Manassas, aided by stories of the gallant stand of Brigadier General Thomas J. Jackson, an eccentric professor of artillery and natural philosophy at Virginia Military Institute, at the head of his brigade during the height of the Southern defensive effort. A fellow general, commenting on Jackson, said he was standing "like a stone wall," and "Stonewall" Jackson it was thereafter. Union casualties totaled 2,896 men, and Confederate losses stood at 1,982 in this first important, but not decisive, battle of the Civil War in the East.

☆   An American Portrait

Thomas J. "Stonewall" Jackson—Jackson was born in 1824 in Clarksburg, Virginia (now West Virginia), and entered the United States Military Academy in 1842. He was graduated four years later, standing seventeenth in his class of 59 cadets, and entered into the conflict with Mexico. He fought well at Veracruz, Cerro Gordo, and Chapultepec, and for four years after the war served the Army at various stations. He resigned his commission in 1852, however, to accept the position of professor of artillery tactics and natural philosophy at Virginia Military Institute at Lexington.

After almost a decade as an austere and somewhat absentminded professor, Jackson led his cadet corps to Richmond at the outbreak of the Civil War. There he was soon commissioned a brigadier general and performed outstandingly at First Manassas, moving Brigadier General Barnard E. Bee to make his famous remark, "There is Jackson standing like a stone wall." Soon thereafter Jackson was advanced in rank to major general and was given command in the Shenandoah Valley.

There, in March 1862, he began his famous Shenandoah Valley campaign, causing the suspension of McDowell's move to aid McClellan on the Virginia Peninsula and inflicting brilliant counterstrokes upon his Union pursuers. At the Seven Days' battles Jackson was slow in reacting to orders, probably because he was physically worn out, but he displayed his usual battlefield superiority at Second Manassas and in capturing Harpers

FIGURE 4–5 Thomas J. Jackson. *(National Archives, Washington, D.C.)*

Ferry before moving on to aid Lee at Antietam. Advanced to lieutenant general and corps commander, Jackson continued to serve Lee well, especially at the defense of Fredericksburg.

But at the moment of perhaps the greatest Confederate victory of the war at Chancellorsville, Jackson, while reconnoitering his lines on the night of May 2, 1863, was accidentally wounded by one of his own men in the fading light of day. Eight days later, on May 10, he died of pneumonia at Guiney's Station, south of Fredericksburg (his left arm having been amputated in an attempt to save his life), thereby denying Lee of his most able subordinate and the Confederacy of one of its most able field commanders. His body was interred at Lexington.

For the remainder of the year 1861 the two armies eyed one another south of Washington but made no major moves. Lincoln replaced McDowell with the highly touted Major General George B. McClellan, who set about whipping the Army of the Potomac into shape for the next campaigning season. As 1862 dawned, McClellan's army totaled 150,000 men, but still the general was reluctant to move. Just to the south were 50,000 Confederates under General Joe Johnston, although McClellan (with poor intelligence from Alan Pinkerton) insisted that their numbers were twice that figure. Finally McClellan came up with a plan to move his entire army by water to Urbanna, east of Richmond on the lower Rappahannock River, to pull Johnston south, where he could be defeated and the Confederate capital taken. But Lincoln demanded that 40,000 troops be left to cover Washington. And when Johnston pulled back behind the Rappahannock to a location near McClellan's planned landing site, the offensive was aborted.

☆   An American Portrait

Joseph E. Johnston—Born in 1807 in Prince Edward County, Virginia, "Joe" Johnston, the first United States Military Academy graduate appointed to general officer rank, entered

West Point in 1825 and was graduated thirteenth in his class of 46 in 1829. He served as an artillery officer until 1837, when he resigned to begin a career in civil engineering. But he was recommissioned the next year as a lieutenant in the Topographical Engineers and was advanced in rank to captain in 1846. During the Mexican War he served at the Battle of Cerro Gordo, where he was wounded twice, and led the assaulting column at Chapultepec. Here he was wounded three more times. By 1855 he had been promoted to lieutenant colonel in the cavalry. In 1860 he was a brigadier general and quartermaster-general of the Army.

On April 22, 1861, after Virginia had seceded from the Union, Johnston resigned to join his native state and soon advanced in rank to brigadier general in the Confederate Army. He served the Southern cause well, slipping away from Harpers Ferry and General Patterson to join Jackson at First Manassas, where he displayed his skill at tactical maneuver. Thereafter he was promoted to general, Confederate States Army. Johnston conducted the rearguard withdrawal in the Peninsula campaign but was wounded at Seven Pines and replaced by Robert E. Lee.

In November 1862, Johnston took over command in the West and in May 1863 arrived with his army in Jackson, Mississippi, only to see that capital city fall to Grant after General Pemberton in Vicksburg twice disobeyed orders to join him. In December 1863, Johnston was assigned to the Army of Tennessee at Chattanooga, and the following spring he displayed tactical skill in delaying General Sherman in his march to Atlanta. For failing to stop Sherman, however, Johnston was relieved of his command by Jefferson Davis on July 17. By the next spring Johnston had been reassigned to the Army of Tennessee and used every effort to halt the Union juggernaut moving through the Carolinas toward Richmond. He finally was forced to surrender to Sherman on April 26, 1865, two weeks after Appomattox.

After the war Johnston entered the insurance business in Savannah, then moved to Richmond and on to Washington, D.C. During the 1880s he was appointed commissioner of railroads. He died in March 1891 in the nation's capital, but his battlefield decisions have remained a subject of controversy ever since.

McClellan then proposed to transport his army to Fortress Monroe on Hampton Roads at the tip of the Virginia Peninsula (the fort remained in Union hands throughout the war), from there to march up the Peninsula with the James River on his left and the York River on his right and seize Richmond 75 miles to the west. Lincoln agreed to the plan but pulled 30,000 men from McClellan's command under General McDowell and sent them to Fredericksburg on the upper Rappahannock to cover Johnston and shield the nation's capital.

Despite losing these 30,000 men, McClellan still had a massive army of 105,000 men at his disposal as he jumped off from Fortress Monroe on April 4, 1862. Facing him were only 17,000 Confederates under Major General John B. Magruder. Magruder had three thin defensive lines erected across the Peninsula east of Williamsburg from the York River on the north to the Warwick River on the south, but McClellan spent a full month laying siege to the lines, allowing time for Johnston's army to be brought in as reinforcements. Johnston assumed command on April 26.

Not until May 4 did McClellan launch his assault, only to find the Confederate lines deserted. Johnston had withdrawn to the west. He had saved his army, although he had consigned eastern Virginia to the Federals. Norfolk soon fell (leading to the destruction of the ironclad *Virginia*, ex-*Merrimack*, which now had no port), and the Union soon controlled the James River all the way to Drewry's Bluff, only 7 miles from Richmond, but Johnston's army was intact.

Johnston pulled his forces back all the way to the area east of Richmond, aided by heavy spring rains that made rapid pursuit by McClellan impossible. Then, when Johnston found that McClellan had split his forces, one contingent north of the Chickahominy River covering his base on the York and the other south of the Chickahominy threatening Richmond, he launched counterattacks on McClellan's right at Seven Pines and Fair Oaks Station. These proved indecisive, however, and Johnston, severely wounded, was replaced by General Robert E. Lee as commander of the Army of Northern Virginia.

☆   An American Portrait

Robert E. Lee—Lee, usually considered one of the nation's most eminent tacticians, was born January 19, 1807, at Stratford, Westmoreland County, Virginia, the fifth child of Henry "Light Horse Harry" Lee of Revolutionary War fame. He was graduated from West Point in 1829, second in his class and having never been given a demerit in his four-year career at the Point. Between 1829 and 1846 he was assigned various duties in military engineering, meanwhile marrying the great-granddaughter of George Washington in 1831 and being commissioned a captain in 1838.

During the Mexican War he first served with General John E. Wool at Buena Vista and then went on to participate in the battles at Veracruz and Cerro Gordo and the battles for Mexico City, being brevetted a colonel for gallantry. After the war he served as superintendent at West Point, was made lieutenant colonel of cavalry in 1855, and played a prominent role in putting down the John Brown insurrection at Harpers Ferry in 1859. In 1860–1861 he was commander of the Department of Texas.

When war broke out between the states, Lee was offered field command of the Union Army but declined in order to join his native Virginia in secession as a general and advisor to President Jefferson Davis. On May 1, 1862, he was given command of the Army

FIGURE 4-6 Robert E. Lee. (*National Archives, Washington, D.C.*)

of Northern Virginia after the serious wounding of General Joseph E. Johnston during the Peninsula campaign.

Learning many valuable lessons in maneuver and organization during the Seven Days' battles, Lee performed magnificently tactically at Second Manassas and Antietam, and then went on to add to his laurels at Fredericksburg and especially at Chancellorsville, his greatest victory. He was also in command of the Confederate forces at the critical loss at Gettysburg in July 1863. On February 6, 1865, he was appointed by Davis to the position of general in chief of all Confederate armies, a meaningless position because by this time the Southern cause was lost. Ever since the previous summer, Lee had been trying to thwart the unrelenting attacks by Grant and was then under close siege at Petersburg. When the Petersburg position was no longer tenable, Lee moved off to the west to try to continue the fight, but he accepted the inevitable when he obviously could not escape Grant's Army of the Potomac. On April 12, 1865, he surrendered his army to Grant at Appomattox Court House, Virginia.

After the war, Lee quickly applied for a presidential pardon and in 1865 was appointed president of Washington College at Lexington, Virginia. He died there on October 12, 1870, the years after his death seeing his reputation rise for his military exploits and as a symbol of the South, defeated but unbowed by shame.

In the meantime, Lincoln agreed to send McDowell's 30,000 men south to join McClellan on the Chickahominy, but the Confederates reacted by dispatching Stonewall Jackson and his 17,000 men out of the Shenandoah Valley toward Washington to threaten the capital and prevent McDowell's move south. Accordingly, three Union armies were sent after Jackson. They never caught him, leaving him free to return to the valley and leaving McClellan without the 30,000 reinforcements as he cautiously made his way toward Richmond.

☆   An American Portrait

James Ewell Brown Stuart—Born in Patrick County, Virginia, in 1833, "Jeb" Stuart attended Emory and Henry College for two years before entering West Point in 1850. He was graduated in 1854, received a commission in the regular Army, and was assigned to Texas. Subsequently he served as a cavalry officer in Kansas and was with Robert E. Lee during the John Brown insurrection.

In May 1861 he resigned his captaincy and accepted a like position in the Confederate Army. He gained attention for his well-timed cavalry charge at First Manassas that year and was advanced in rank to brigadier general in September, by the end of the year commanding 2,400 officers and men. It was Stuart and his men who covered the withdrawal of Lee to the Chickahominy and who made a complete circuit of the Union forces in June 1862 to ascertain their positions during the Seven Days' battles. The next month Stuart was raised in rank to major general.

Stuart continued to perform yeoman service for the Confederate war cause, covering Jackson's move to Bristoe Station and drawing praise from Lee for his service at Antietam. The no-drinking, no-swearing, no-loose-living-in-my-company general, armed with his 14-inch, 3-1/2-pound, double-barreled LeMat sidearm (the upper barrel being a shotgun barrel of .65-caliber, the lower barrel a 9-shot, .44-caliber revolver), performed admirably on the right at Fredericksburg and took over II Corps from A. P. Hill at Chancellorsville when Jackson was wounded. Unfortunately, it was also Stuart who decided to ride all the way around the Union forces as the Battle of Gettysburg was forming, thereby denying Lee valuable information on the exact disposition of Meade's army.

Wounded as his 4,500 men held off Philip Sheridan and his force of 12,000 at Yellow Tavern on May 11, 1864, Stuart, "the Cavalier of Dixie," died the next day in Richmond, ending the career of one of the Confederacy's most colorful and effective cavalry officers.

When Lee discovered (thanks to Major General J. E. B. Stuart's cavalry ride completely around the Union army) that McClellan's right flank was weak, he left only 25,000 men before Richmond as a covering force and hit McClellan's right with 47,000 men on June 26 and 27, opening the so-called Seven Days' campaign at Mechanicsville and Gaines Mill. Stonewall Jackson's Army of the Valley was uncharacteristically tardy and failed to hit the Union right flank as planned, and the Confederate attackers took heavy casualties as they assaulted the Union artillery defenses, but they caused McClellan to withdraw toward the south and the safety of the James River to "save his army."

Lee followed McClellan, badgering him all the way and always shielding Richmond. Then, on July 1, 1862, Lee foolishly launched his men against superior Union defenses at Malvern Hill in what he hoped would be the crushing blow to McClellan's demoralized army. The waves of charging Confederate infantrymen were blown apart time after time by murderous Union artillery fire, causing one Confederate general to comment after the battle, "It was not war—it was murder." Lee lost 5,355 men that day in the finale of the Seven Days' campaign. In that one week alone the Confederates took over 20,000 casualties (3,286 killed) while inflicting almost 16,000 casualties on the Union army. But Richmond had been saved, the Peninsula campaign was over, and the Confederates were ready to take the initiative in the East. McClellan continued his retreat to Harrison's Landing on the James and, on Lincoln's orders, began the process of evacuation. Lincoln and his advisors had decided to withdraw from the Peninsula; place Major General John Pope, brought in from the West, in charge of the Army of the Potomac; and take Richmond from the north instead.

☆   An American Portrait

John Pope—John Pope, the loser of the Second Battle of Manassas, was born in Kentucky in 1822 and was raised in Illinois. He attended West Point between 1838 and 1842 and was graduated seventeenth in a class of 62 cadets. During the Mexican War he was brevetted captain for gallantry, but even at this point in his career he revealed himself to be almost unfailingly impetuous and loud-mouthed.

When the Civil War came, Pope was made brigadier general of volunteers and in 1862 was given command of the Army of the Mississippi, where he received credit for the capture of New Madrid, Missouri, and Island No. 10 on the Mississippi. On the strength of these accomplishments, he was appointed major general and was called east in March 1862. Yet at Second Manassas on August 29–30 of that year, he committed his troops piecemeal against Stonewall Jackson on the first day and then, believing the Confederates were in retreat, ordered a pursuit that resulted in complete defeat as Longstreet's and Jackson's men tore apart the Union ranks. He suffered 16,000 casualties out of 60,000 men committed to the battle.

Relegated to the West thereafter, Pope fought against the Indians and on the frontier for the next quarter century, retiring in 1886. He died in 1892 and was buried in Sandusky, Ohio.

Characteristically, McClellan dawdled in returning his army to northern Virginia, and Lee took advantage of the situation by making a move on Pope. The result was the Second Battle of Manassas (or Bull Run) of August 29–30, 1862. In this battle, fought on the site of the First Battle of Manassas the year before, Pope engaged in piecemeal attacks on the Confederates, commanded by Stonewall Jackson and entrenched behind a railroad embankment, only to be met by withering musket and artillery fire.

The climax of the battle came on the second day, when the Federals launched three futile attacks on the Confederate lines and Major General James Longstreet ordered his Confederate right wing forward in a grand attack on the shattered and demoralized Union units. Pope's army was soon in full retreat back toward Washington, having suffered 16,000 casualties out of 60,000 men committed, while inflicting only 9,000 casualties on the Confederate 50,000-man force. Pope was relieved, and McClellan was returned to command, but Lee was now ready to make a major strategic move. He would invade Maryland, break the Union will to fight, gain European diplomatic recognition for the Confederacy, and perhaps entice Maryland into the Confederacy.

☆   An American Portrait

James Longstreet—Although born in South Carolina in 1821, Longstreet was raised in Georgia and Alabama. He was graduated from West Point in 1842, standing fifty-fourth in his class of 62, and served on various stations until the outbreak of the Mexican War. During that short conflict he served with both Taylor and Scott, and thereafter continued in the Army and was promoted to the rank of major in 1858. He resigned in June 1861 and was offered a commission in the Confederate Army.

Longstreet showed great skill in handling his troops at First Manassas with Jackson and soon thereafter was raised in rank to major general and placed in charge of a division under Joseph E. Johnston. He served Johnston well, conducting an effective rear guard action in the evacuation of Williamsburg and winning the confidence of Lee during the Seven Days' battles. At Second Manassas, however, he was slow in attacking, a reflection of his tendency to move in a dilatory manner when he thought his commander was wrong. Nevertheless, Longstreet fought well at Antietam, being raised to the rank of lieutenant general in its aftermath. He also bore the brunt of the fight at Fredericksburg and became the most important of Lee's lieutenants after Jackson's death at Chancellorsville. Although he was slow in responding to Lee's orders during the fateful three days at Gettysburg in July 1863, his objections to Lee's tactics appear to have been valid.

In September of that year, Longstreet was sent to Georgia, then to Knoxville. In April 1864 he was ordered back to Virginia from the West to help Lee and served beside him all the way to Appomattox. After the war he entered the insurance business and served as a cotton broker in New Orleans. He became the object of considerable bitterness during the period of Reconstruction when he became an active Republican, believing that the only hope for the South lay in accepting its defeat and working with the Republicans to rebuild the shattered Old Confederacy.

From 1869 to 1904 he held a series of political appointments and never escaped controversy in his native South, not only because of his politics, but also because it became necessary to blame someone other than the revered Lee for the critical defeat at Gettysburg. Longstreet died at Gainesville, Georgia, in January 1904.

Accordingly, on September 4, 1862, Lee's Army of Northern Virginia crossed the Potomac and concentrated at Frederick, Maryland, three days later. Lee then divided his army and sent Stonewall Jackson to seize Harpers Ferry to the west to secure the Shenandoah Valley. Jackson was then to join Lee and Longstreet as they moved north, his armies reunited before the Army of the Potomac could react and challenge them.

In the meantime, the Union forces began their pursuit of Lee, moving cautiously under the now-restored but ever-wary McClellan. Arriving in Frederick two days after the Confederates had left, McClellan was presented with a grand opportunity for military success when a copy of Lee's orders outlining his plans was discovered wrapped around three cigars. Knowing that Lee's army was divided, McClellan could now destroy Lee's troops piecemeal before they were reunited.

With his plans discovered, Lee had to abandon his proposed invasion, but when he was informed that Jackson had successfully taken Harpers Ferry on September 15 and had seized 10,000 men, 13,000 small arms, and 73 artillery pieces, he decided to concentrate his forces at Sharpsburg, Maryland, for a showdown fight with McClellan.

Lee dug in his troops along Antietam Creek, and on September 16 Jackson joined him on the field. Facing the 40,000 Confederate defenders were 75,000 Federals determined to annihilate them as they met in combat the next morning. The day that dawned was destined to be the bloodiest of the Civil War—indeed, in all of American military history—with 4,700 men dead, 18,440 wounded, and 3,000 missing before the sun set.

McClellan's attacks were piecemeal and uncoordinated, hitting the Confederates first on their left, then in the center along a sunken road (thereafter called "Bloody Lane" from the piles of dead Confederate defenders lying there after the three-hour fight subsided), and finally on the Confederate right, where Major General Ambrose Burnside was slow and unsure about crossing the stone-arched Rohrback Bridge. Lee was thus able to shift his troops and hold off his attackers. McClellan also refused to commit his reserves. As in other Civil War battles, artillery fire was murderous against attacking infantry. Only at 3:00 in the afternoon was Burnside able to smash through and flank the Confederate right wing. He could now roll up the Confederate line toward the town of Sharpsburg and gain the victory. But at this moment Major General Ambrose P. Hill's division of Jackson's army arrived from Harpers Ferry and drove Burnside back across the bridge and from the field.

Both sides were exhausted by the day's fighting and incapable of resuming the battle the next day. Lee slipped his army back across the Potomac into Virginia, but McClellan was a day late in sending a force in pursuit. The Battle of Antietam (Sharpsburg) ended as a tactical draw. Strategically, Lee's invasion of the North had been thwarted, but his army had not been destroyed by the Federals, and he had been allowed to withdraw to safety. Lincoln was furious. McClellan was relieved of command, never again to lead a Union army.

But while Antietam was a tactical draw and a strategic failure for both sides, it was nevertheless a turning point of the war. Five days later, on September 22, 1862, riding the crest of the North's elation over the Union repulse of Lee's invasion of Maryland, Lincoln issued a preliminary emancipation proclamation stating that as of January 1, 1863, all slaves in all areas under rebellion would be free. By this one bold stroke Lincoln struck at the major labor source of the rebellious South, ended all chances for diplomatic recognition of the Confederacy by European nations, and converted the war for the preservation of the Union simultaneously into a war against slavery.

McClellan's reluctant replacement as the head of the Army of the Potomac as of November 7 was the easygoing and likeable Major General Ambrose E. Burnside of Rhode Island. He quickly secured Lincoln's approval for a new advance on Richmond. He would move east and south along the Rappahannock, avoid Lieutenant General James Longstreet's corps at Culpeper (Lee's second wing under Jackson was farther west in the Valley near Winchester), cross the Rappahannock at Fredericksburg, and follow the rail line south to Richmond.

☆   An American Portrait

Ambrose E. Burnside—Surely one of the most unfortunate generals in the Civil War, Burnside was born in 1824 in Liberty, Indiana. He was graduated from West Point in 1847 but saw only garrison duty during the Mexican War and thereafter was assigned to the western frontier. In 1853 he resigned his commission to open a rifle factory in Rhode Island that would manufacture breech-loading rifles of his own design. The firm went bankrupt, but Burnside's successors in the business turned out 55,000 "Burnside" carbines, the first to use metallic cartridges, during the war. In the meantime Burnside had become a major general in the Rhode Island militia and in 1861 was appointed a colonel in the 1st Rhode Island Volunteers, a unit that saw action at First Manassas.

In August 1861, Burnside was made brigadier general and carried out a series of successful coastal campaigns in North Carolina, capturing Roanoke Island, New Bern, and Beaufort, and was raised in rank to major general. At Antietam under McClellan, Burnside revealed a hesitancy on the left flank, but, this performance notwithstanding, two months later Lincoln asked him to take command of the Army of the Potomac. Burnside did so only very reluctantly, believing that the job was beyond his capabilities. His defeat at Fredericksburg and his subsequent attempt to cross the Rappahannock River upstream—a botched operation that became known as "Burnside's Mud March"—led to his being replaced by Joseph "Fighting Joe" Hooker. Burnside was then given command of the Department of the Ohio, where he acquitted himself well in the defense of Knoxville against Longstreet. The year 1864 found Burnside back in the East serving under Grant on his drive south from The Wilderness through the siege of Petersburg. Burnside's slowness resulted in a bloody disaster on July 30, 1864, in what has come to be called the Battle of the Crater. He was relieved of command after this fiasco.

Three days after Appomattox, Burnside resigned his commission. He was subsequently elected governor of his adopted state of Rhode Island three times and served in the

U.S. Senate between 1874 and 1881. He died in September 1881 and was buried in Bristol, Rhode Island.

Moving with dispatch, Burnside's Federals reached Falmouth, across the river from Fredericksburg, only four days after beginning their march on November 15, 1862. Lee was caught flatfooted, his army divided and facing a major offensive move. But he was given breathing room by the fact that the pontoon bridges ordered by Burnside for the crossing of the Rappahannock arrived only on November 25. By this time Lee had shifted both Longstreet and Jackson to Fredericksburg, where their 70,000 men were dug in with artillery on the heights above the town.

On December 12, Burnside managed to get most of his 130,000 men across the river on five pontoon bridges. The next morning the Union forces began their assaults on Longstreet's men, who were well entrenched behind and to the north of the town at Marye's Heights, and on Jackson's troops, who were behind a railroad embankment on Prospect Hill. The result was an artillery and infantry slaughter of the Union attackers. The Federals took 12,653 casualties to only 5,309 for the Confederates. Two days later, under cover of a violent rainstorm, the despondent Union soldiers recrossed the river. Burnside's great offensive against Richmond had ended in bloody, frustrating failure.

As 1862 came to a close on the Eastern battlefields, the war there was essentially a stalemate. The Confederates had won resounding victories at Manassas twice and at Fredericksburg, had thwarted McClellan's drive toward Richmond up the Virginia Peninsula, and had gained a tactical draw under very difficult circumstances at Antietam. They had displayed considerable tactical skill and had demonstrated that they were in the war for keeps.

Still, the Union will had not been broken, a great Southern invasion of the North had been stopped, and all chances of foreign intervention on behalf of the Confederacy were dead. Furthermore, Union forces were intact and could be replenished and re-equipped to fight on, and the war in the West was beginning to tilt in the North's favor. The war was far from over for both sides, but the patterns of the conflict were beginning to emerge—patterns that would eventually spell defeat for the Confederacy.

THE BATTLES IN THE WEST

The officers and men of the Union army in the West spent 1861 preparing themselves to seize the vital Mississippi River and central Tennessee. Possession of that river, they knew, would slice the Confederacy in two, and moving from the vital rail juncture at Chattanooga through Atlanta to the sea would bisect the South again.

By late in the year, Brigadier General Don Carlos Buell, reputed to be one of the Army's top strategists, was headquartered in Louisville with 50,000 men under his command as head of the Department of the Ohio. In St. Louis, Major General Henry W. Halleck, later to be named Lincoln's general-in-chief, headed the newly formed Department of the Missouri. He replaced John C. Frémont, whose short tenure in command of the department well illustrated the incompetence of most of the political generals forced on Lincoln and the Army by political circumstances. Halleck had 90,000 men under him, including 20,000 under Brigadier General Ulysses S. Grant and 30,000 in Missouri under ex–Iowa congressman and West Pointer Major General Samuel S. Curtis. Facing these Union forces were 43,000 widely scattered Confederates under General Albert Sidney Johnston, appointed by his friend Jefferson Davis to head the huge Department Number 2, which stretched from the Appalachians to the Indian Territories.

☆   An American Portrait

Ulysses S. Grant—Born in April 1822 in Point Pleasant, Ohio, and christened Hiram Ulysses Grant, "Sam" Grant entered the United States Military Academy in 1839 and was graduated twenty-first in his class. Notwithstanding his superb horsemanship, Grant was assigned to the 4th U.S. Infantry and served with Taylor and Scott during the Mexican War, where he won brevets for gallantry at Molino del Ray and Chapultepec. Thereafter assigned to remote garrisons in the West, unhappy with such duty, and away from his family, he resigned his captaincy in 1854 and moved to Missouri. Here he was unsuccessful in a number of jobs and finally moved his family to Galena, Illinois.

With the outbreak of the Civil War, Grant was appointed a colonel in the 21st Illinois Infantry in June 1861 and two months later gained a commission as brigadier general. His first offensive, against Belmont, Missouri, in November 1861, was not an outstanding operation, but it did impress Lincoln, who marked Grant as a general who was willing to fight. Three months later, in February 1862, Grant's forces seized Forts Henry and Donelson, and he was catapulted to nationwide fame, although the luster of his victories was clearly dulled by his army's being almost destroyed by A. S. Johnston's surprise attack at Shiloh two months later, before Grant was able to regroup and launch a counterattack the next day.

The period from December 1862 to July 1863 was frustrating for Grant as he attempted time and again to seize the Confederate fortress of Vicksburg, but victory was

FIGURE 4–7   Ulysses S. Grant. (*National Archives, Washington, D.C.*)

finally attained by his bold move to below the city, from there to march east to seize Jackson, the Mississippi capital, before turning to attack and besiege Vicksburg from the east. Appointed a major general in the regular Army after this victory, Grant added to his laurels in the West by his lifting of the siege of Chattanooga. On the basis of these victories. Lincoln appointed him lieutenant general and brought him east to be general-in-chief of the Union armies.

Grant carried out a multitheater campaign in the East, with Sherman marching toward Atlanta and then beyond, Butler moving up the James River toward Richmond, and Sheridan operating in the Shenandoah, while he and the Army of the Potomac ground down Lee's defenders in a prolonged slithering movement from The Wilderness to Petersburg, Grant losing his strategic patience—and thereby suffering defeat—only at Cold Harbor. As he gradually extended his lines around the Confederates at Petersburg, he knew that the Southern cause was doomed. Confirmation came on April 12, 1865, when Robert E. Lee surrendered his army to Grant at Appomattox Court House.

In the aftermath of the war, Grant was drawn into politics and nominated for the presidency on the Republican ticket—having voted only once before, this in 1856 for James Buchanan on the Democratic side, as he said, "Because I knew Frémont." He accepted the nomination with four words: "Let us have peace." Grant's presidency was marred by a series of scandals, attributed in large part to his naivete and his inability to judge his subordinates. Leaving the presidency in 1877, Grant lived the remainder of his days in peace, racing against throat cancer to complete his war memoirs. He died in Mount McGregor, New York, on July 23, 1885, still hailed as one of the nation's greatest generals and strategists.

Grant marched out early in 1862 to capture Fort Henry on the Tennessee River and Fort Donelson 12 miles away on the Cumberland River at the northern border of Tennessee. If successful, the Union would use these two rivers for penetration of the center of the Confederate defensive arc. Grant's forces were aided by naval gunboats under the command of Flag Officer Andrew H. Foote. The Confederate commander at Fort Henry, with only 3,400 poorly equipped troops and many of his cannon underwater from flooding, moved most of his men to Fort Donelson as Grant approached and then put up a token if spirited artillery resistance before surrendering Fort Henry on February 6.

Grant and Foote moved on to the 100-acre Fort Donelson on the Cumberland. The Confederates there, reinforced by 12,000 men sent by Johnston, put up a defiant resistance to the combined land and naval attack upon them of February 14. But on the night of February 15, the fort's commander and his second-in-command, Brigadier General John B. Floyd and Major General Gideon J. Pillow, deciding the fort was indefensible—Grant now had 27,000 men—escaped with 2,500 of their men. They left the third-in-command, Brigadier General Simon Bolivar Buckner, with the distasteful task of surrendering the fort to Grant. Grant demanded unconditional surrender, received 15,000 Confederate prisoners, and found himself a national hero. With the fall of these forts and of Nashville up the Cumberland River a week later, Kentucky and western Tennessee and the vital lower Cumberland and Tennessee Rivers were in Union hands.

General Halleck next sent Major General John Pope and his 18,000-man Army of the Mississippi to seize New Madrid, Missouri, and Island Number 10, located on a strategic inverted S-curve below Cairo, Illinois. New Madrid fell after an 11-day siege on March 14. The next day the Union Army and Navy began their attacks on Island Number 10 on the Tennessee side of the river. By April 8 the Union gunboats had knocked out the Confederate artillery batteries and Pope's men had crossed the river, compelling the Southerners to surrender the island and its adjacent mainland defenses with 6,000 men. The Confederate strongholds on the vital Mississippi River were crumbling. It was now open to the Union forces as far south as Fort Pillow, Tennessee.

In the meantime, Halleck devised a plan to unite Grant's 39,000-man Army of the Tennessee moving south through western Tennessee and Buell's 36,000-man Army of the Ohio in Nashville at Corinth, Mississippi, an important rail juncture just south of the Tennessee border, and seize it for the Federals. But General Albert Sidney Johnston concentrated 44,000 men at Corinth to thwart Halleck's plan and decided to attack Grant's men in their camp at Pittsburg Landing near Shiloh Church on the Tennessee River 23 miles northeast of Corinth before Buell arrived.

☆   An American Portrait

Albert Sidney Johnston—Born in Mason County, Kentucky, in 1803, Johnston attended Transylvania University before transferring to West Point. Commissioned an infantry lieutenant upon his graduation in 1826, Johnston fought in the Black Hawk War before resigning in 1834 because of his wife's illness. At the time of the Texas revolution, he enlisted in the Texas army as a private but was soon commissioned adjutant general. In 1837, as senior brigadier general, he was placed in command of that new nation's army. He went on to serve for 15 months as secretary of war for the Republic of Texas.

With the outbreak of the Mexican War, Johnston was commissioned colonel in the 1st Texas Rifle Volunteers and served at Monterrey. In 1849 he was made paymaster of the U.S. Army and in 1856 was designated the commander of the Department of Texas. As a brevet brigadier general, he led the troops into Utah through grueling conditions to quell the "Mormon War" from 1858 until 1860, and in the latter year he was placed in command of the Department of the Pacific at San Francisco.

Johnston resigned his commission when Texas seceded in April 1861 despite the fact that he had been offered the Union Army post of second in command to Winfield Scott. Shortly thereafter he was appointed general and commander of the Western Department for the Confederacy. Johnston's greatest moment came on April 6, 1861, when he led his troops from Corinth to attack the unsuspecting Grant at Shiloh. In the attack, an artery in Johnston's leg was severed by gunfire, and he bled to death. Temporarily entombed in New Orleans, his body was reburied in Austin, Texas, in 1867.

The Confederates set out from Corinth on April 3, but it took three days of slogging through the wet, wooded countryside before they were ready to strike the unsuspecting Union encampment. Their attack began early in the morning on Sunday, April 6. After six hours of bitter fighting, three Union divisions had been overrun. But the Confederate attack slowed at the moment of victory as the units lost direction and coordination. When the Union forces under Brigadier General Benjamin M. Prentiss held off a major Confederate thrust for two hours in the "Hornet's Nest," Grant was given time to fashion a strong defensive position backed by artillery and two Union gunboats.

General Beauregard, directing the Southern forces after the fatal wounding of General Johnston early in the afternoon, necessarily called off the attack at twilight to await the dawn.

During the night, however, all except one division of Buell's army arrived, so Grant decided to go on the offensive. By the end of that day, April 7 (the same day on which Island Number 10 was surrendered on the Mississippi), the outnumbered Confederates, despite brave and dogged efforts, were being driven back, and Beauregard ordered a withdrawal to Corinth. The Battle of Shiloh (or Pittsburg Landing) was over. It was the first great bloodbath of the war. Over 13,000 Union soldiers were counted as casualties, including 1,754 killed, in the two-day battle. Confederate casualties were 10,694, including 1,723 killed. The public, both North and South, was shocked by the "butcher's bill" of Shiloh, but the battle, along with the seizure of New Madrid and Island Number 10 by General Pope, was decisive in the war in the West, with Corinth falling to the Federals, led personally by General Halleck, on May 30 as Beauregard evacuated the city and moved to safety at Tupelo 50 miles south.

The Confederates, though, were far from finished in the West for 1862. With Lee moving into Maryland in the East, they planned a massive counteroffensive into central Tennessee and Kentucky to break the Yankee grip on the area and perhaps bring Kentucky into the Confederacy. Commanding the Army of Tennessee, which would carry out the offensive, was General Braxton Bragg. Bragg moved most of his army from Mississippi to Chattanooga by rail and launched his drive northward in August. Initially Bragg and Major General E. Kirby Smith enjoyed great success in outflanking Union forces in Tennessee and then marching into Kentucky. But the Confederates were stopped in furious fighting at Perryville on October 8 and forced to return to Tennessee. Here on December 31 and January 2, 1863, Bragg attacked Major William S. Rosecran's forces and was badly defeated at Stone's River southeast of Nashville, taking over 10,000 casualties, most to massed Union artillery.

☆   An American Portrait

William S. Rosecrans—Rosecrans, possibly a strategic genius but a field command failure, was born in 1819 in Ohio and attended the United States Military Academy from 1838 to 1842, being graduated fifth in his class and securing the coveted rank of lieutenant of engineers. After a year spent working on fortifications in Hampton Roads, he spent four years teaching engineering at West Point. He then served in a number of posts in New England.

In 1854 Rosecrans resigned his commission and went into business as an architect and engineer in Cincinnati, but when the war came he was able to secure an appointment as a brigadier general in the regular Army. In July 1861 he won the Battle of Rich Mountain in western Virginia under George McClellan—who described him as a "silly fussy goose"—and participated in the siege of Corinth in May the next year. In October 1862 he was named commander of the Army of the Cumberland and fought the Battle of Stone's River against Braxton Bragg two months later. His greatest strategic maneuver was his working the Confederates out of vital Chattanooga. In September 1863, however, he allowed a critical gap to occur in the line at Chickamauga and was besieged in Chattanooga, having allowed the Confederates to occupy the high ground around the city, until relieved of command in October by Grant.

Through 1864 Rosecrans was commander of the Department of the Missouri. He resigned from the Army in 1867. For the next two years he served as minister to Mexico under President Andrew Johnson, and from 1881 to 1885 he represented California in the U.S. House of Representatives. He died in 1898 in Redondo, California.

The great Southern counteroffensives of 1862 had failed, as had an October 3–4 attempt to wrest Corinth, Mississippi, back from the Federals. As in the East, Confederate forces had fought well, and their morale was still high. But the Union forces had seized key positions on the Mississippi River, on the Tennessee and Cumberland Rivers, and in central Tennessee and upper Mississippi and could not be dislodged. The Union strategy of cutting the South into pieces, while far from coming to fruition, was beginning to be realized. Unless Union advances could be stopped and reversed, the South was in serious trouble in its Western theater.

THE WAR ON THE WATERS

The Union Navy was weak at the beginning of the war, with 42 warships in commission (only 23 were steam-powered) and only 12 on home station, but the North had the capacity to build or buy whatever navy it needed. Under the able leadership of Secretary of the Navy Gideon Welles of Connecticut, by the end of 1861 the service had 250 vessels of all types, 1,200 officers (including 350 Southerners who refused to "go south"), and over 21,000 men ready to sail and fight for the cause of union.

The South, on the other hand, had the 321 ex–U.S. Navy officers but less than a dozen small vessels and little industrial or shipyard capacity to produce more. Confederate Naval Secretary Stephen R. Mallory attempted unsuccessfully to buy ironclad steamers in Europe. He then contracted for ironclads and steamers in the South and for swift commerce raiders in England. Still, the Confederacy would find it impossible to match the Federals' naval power.

The South, accordingly, turned to commerce raiding on the high seas to obtain supplies and to weaken the morale of its Northern opponents while driving maritime insurance rates to unprecedented heights. Commerce raiding might also draw off vessels from the Union blockade that was sure to come and, combined with blockade running (cotton being shipped out and ordnance, raw materials, and manufactures in), might help attain victory for the Confederacy.

In their commerce raiding, the Southerners were very successful in seizing Northern vessels, even though never more than 30 raiders were operating at one time. The most famous were the British-built CSS *Florida* and CSS *Alabama,* the former captured in a Brazilian port in 1864 and "accidentally" sunk by Union officers in Hampton Roads thereafter, and the latter sunk by the Union's USS *Kearsarge* on June 19, 1864, in a fevered duel off the coast of France. While the damage done by these and other vessels to American commerce was considerable, they never drew any blockading vessels off station and did not affect the outcome of the war in any major way.

Similarly, blockade runners had a limited effect on the war, primarily because they were too few in number to carry an appreciable amount of Southern goods, especially cotton, out of the Confederacy. Of equal or greater importance, the blockade-running captains and owners were as interested in bringing fabulously high-profit consumer goods such as salt, coffee, and luxury textiles into the Confederacy as they were in bringing in iron, copper, steel, guns, ammunition, and the like needed to fight the war.

The most important naval aspect of strategy, as it turned out, was the Union's use of the blockade of the South's Atlantic and Gulf coasts combined with the seizure of Southern ports. Using as its base of operations Fortress Monroe on Hampton Roads, the Union in 1861 began the process of attacking and seizing the 89 Southern ports and harbors along the 3,500-mile Confederate coast. In August a joint Army–Navy expedition of seven days into North Carolina waters resulted in the successful capture of Fort Clark and Fort Hatteras and the closing of Albemarle and Pamlico Sounds to vessels seeking egress into the Atlantic. Two months later another joint expedition, led by Brigadier General Thomas W. Sherman of the Army and Flag Officer Samuel F. DuPont of the Navy, led to the capture of Port Royal, South Carolina, on November 7. This ensured a secure coaling and supply base for blockading both Savannah and Charleston. Other ports continued to fall to Federal arms. By March 1862 only Savannah, Charleston, and Wilmington, North Carolina, were open as major ports on the Atlantic.

Bleak as the picture looked for the Confederacy at sea, great hopes were placed in a new naval weapon that might break the blockade, the ironclad *Virginia* being built in the Gosport Naval Yard near Norfolk. Using the hull of the 40-gun steam frigate USS *Merrimack,* burned to the waterline when the Union abandoned Gosport in April 1861, Confederate naval contractors reconstructed her into a steam-driven, 257-foot ironclad with angled, steel-over-pine sloping sides on her low superstructure and 10 guns. With the *Virginia,* it was hoped, Chesapeake Bay could be controlled by the South, Richmond could be opened to the sea, and perhaps the capital city of Washington could be menaced.

On the morning of March 8, 1862, captained by Franklin Buchanan, founder of the Naval Academy and now a Confederate naval officer, the *Virginia* sailed slowly out into Hampton Roads (her top speed being only 6 knots) to take on the Union vessels there. Before the day was out she had done considerable damage to the wooden Union vessels on station in those waters. But as she made her way back to Norfolk with the lowering tide, another vessel was making her way into Hampton Roads to tie up under the protective guns of Fortress Monroe. This was the Union's answer to the *Virginia,* the ironclad *Monitor.*

The *Monitor,* built on Long Island by John Ericsson, looked like "a matchbox on a shingle." The diminutive ironclad vessel, 172 feet in length, rode very low in the water and had on its deck a single revolving 20-foot-diameter turret only 9 feet high. It mounted only two guns, retractable 11-inch Dahlgrens. Ordered to do battle with the *Virginia* when she reappeared the next morning, Sunday, April 9, 1862, Lieutenant John L. Worden and his crew of 58 men sailed out to meet their adversary.

To everyone's surprise and consternation (including spectators lining Newport News Point), neither ship could do serious damage to the other despite its best efforts. Shots glanced off their ironclad sides and attempts at ramming were unsuccessful. The famed "first battle of the ironclads" ended as a draw in the early afternoon, with each side claiming victory. The duel may well have been a tactical draw, but it was a strategic victory for the North. The remainder of the blockading fleet in Hampton Roads was intact and, with the *Monitor* present, the *Virginia* could not move up the Chesapeake. Her overwhelming destructive power had been neutralized.

The *Virginia,* however, kept station in Hampton Roads, preventing Yankee movement up the James River toward Richmond for the next month. But when Union forces moved on Norfolk as part of the Peninsula campaign, the by-now-famous vessel was scuttled in the lower James off Craney Island on May 11, 1862. Like her Southern counterpart, the *Monitor* met her demise in 1862. On December 30, while under tow south along the Atlantic coast, the tiny vessel foundered in a storm off Cape Hatteras and sank in 200 feet of water, never to be recovered.

Meanwhile, the Union fleet was in Gulf waters preparing to capture the vital Southern port of New Orleans upriver from the mouth of the Mississippi. The expedition was led by Flag Officer David G. Farragut in his steam sloop USS *Hartford.* Farragut and his West Gulf Coast Blockading Squadron first had to reduce Forts Saint Philip and Jackson, 90 miles below New Orleans and 12 miles above Head of Passes. When a six-day mortar bombardment failed to silence their guns, Farragut decided to run by them by night. He made his move on the night of April 24, 1862, after two Union gunboats first broke a boom of logs and chains stretched across the river. Farragut's 17 steam vessels ran by the forts while sustaining little damage. Subsequently, Army troops carried 5 miles north of the forts via the bayous easily besieged and captured the two protecting forts.

New Orleans, left weakly defended by Richmond out of a belief that Union forces could never pass the forts, fell into Federal hands on April 25. The most important Southern port had been captured, and the Union now had a base on the lower Mississippi from which it could move north. This matched its hold on the upper Mississippi, from which it was steadily moving south. Time and superior naval power were working in the Federals' favor by 1862 all along the South's Atlantic and Gulf Coast waters.

Union naval superiority was also obvious on the Western inland waters. By November 1861 a squadron of eight steam-driven ironclads, each 175 feet in length and mounting 13 guns, had been assembled at Cairo to assist the Army (under War Department, not naval, authority at that time) in seizing the Western rivers from their Confederate adversaries. As has been seen, gunboats played a vital part in the capture of Forts Henry and Donelson in February 1862 and in taking New Madrid and Island Number 10 on the Mississippi in March and April of that year. Gunboats also played an active role in the capture of Fort Pillow, halfway between Island Number 10 and Memphis, two months later. And on June 4, 1862, a sensational river battle between opposing ironclads and rams took place before the enthralled citizens of Memphis, with the Confederate gunboat fleet losing three vessels before fleeing downriver, leaving the city defenseless and with no choice but to surrender. Combined with the naval victories below New Orleans that led to that city's surrender and the Army's victories along their watercourses, the gunboats on the Western rivers were now moving the Federals into a position to seize in its entirety what Lincoln called "the backbone of the rebellion," the Mississippi River.

By the end of 1862, then, Union successes on the Atlantic and Gulf coasts, on the inland waters, on the battlefields of the West, and on the battlefields of the East all pointed to eventual victory. But much fighting and dying were yet to occur before the guns fell silent.

Suggestions for Further Reading

CATTON, BRUCE, *The Centennial History of the Civil War,* 3 vols. Garden City, NY: Doubleday, 1961–1965.

COCHRAN, HAMILTON, *Blockade Runners of the Confederacy.* Indianapolis: Bobbs-Merrill, 1958.

CONNELLY, THOMAS L., *Army of the Heartland: The Army of Tennessee, 1861–1862.* Baton Rouge: Louisiana State University Press, 1967.

CONNELLY, THOMAS L., and ARCHER JONES, *The Politics of Command: Factions and Ideas in Confederate Strategy.* Baton Rouge: Louisiana State University Press, 1973.

DAVIS, WILLIAM C., *Battle at Bull Run.* Garden City, NY: Doubleday, 1977.

——, *Duel Between the First Ironclads.* Garden City, NY: Doubleday, 1975.

DOWDEY, CLIFFORD, *Lee.* Boston: Little, Brown, 1965.

EATON, CLEMENT, *Jefferson Davis.* New York: Free Press, 1977.

FOOTE, SHELBY, *The Civil War: A Narrative,* 3 vols. New York: Random House, 1958–1974.

FREEMAN, DOUGLAS SOUTHALL, *Lee's Lieutenants: A Study in Command,* 3 vols. New York: Scribner's, 1942–1944.

GOFF, RICHARD D., *Confederate Supply.* Durham, NC: Duke University Press, 1969.

GRIFFITH, PADDY, *Battle Tactics of the Civil War.* New Haven, CT: Yale University Press, 1989.

HASSLER, WARREN W., JR., *Commanders of the Army of the Potomac.* Baton Rouge: Louisiana State University Press, 1962.

——, *General George B. McClellan: Shield of the Union.* Baton Rouge: Louisiana State University Press, 1957.

HATTAWAY, HERMAN, and ARCHER JONES, *How the North Won.* Urbana: University of Illinois Press, 1983.

MCDONOUGH, JAMES L., *Shiloh—in Hell before Night.* Knoxville: University of Tennessee Press, 1977.

MCMURRY, RICHARD M., *Two Great Rebel Armies: An Essay in Confederate Military History.* Chapel Hill: University of North Carolina Press, 1989.

MCWHINEY, GRADY, *Braxton Bragg,* 2 vols. New York: Columbia University Press, 1969.

MCWHINEY, GRADY, and PERRY D. JAMIESON, *Attack and Die: Civil War Military Tactics and the Southern Heritage.* University, AL: University of Alabama Press, 1982.

MILLIGAN, JOHN D., *Gunboats Down the Mississippi.* Annapolis: U.S. Naval Institute Press, 1965.

MURFIN, JAMES V., *The Gleam of Bayonets: The Battle of Antietam and the Maryland Campaign of 1862.* New York: Yoseloff, 1965.

RANDALL, JAMES G., *Lincoln the President,* 4 vols. New York: Dodd, Mead, 1945–1955.

REED, ROWENA, *Combined Operations in the Civil War.* Annapolis: U.S. Naval Institute Press, 1978.

ROLAND, CHARLES P., *Albert Sidney Johnston: Soldier of Three Republics.* Austin: University of Texas Press, 1964.

SEARS, STEPHEN W., *George B. McClellan: The Young Napoleon*. New York: Ticknor & Fields, 1988.

———, *Landscape Turned Red: The Battle of Antietam*. New York: Ticknor & Fields, 1983.

SWORD, WILEY, *Shiloh: Bloody April*. New York: Morrow, 1974.

TANNER, ROBERT G., *Stonewall in the Valley*. Garden City, NY: Doubleday, 1976.

VANDIVER, FRANK E., *Rebel Brass: The Confederate Command System*. Baton Rouge: Louisiana State University Press, 1956.

WEST, RICHARD S., JR., *Mr. Lincoln's Navy*. New York: Longman, Green, 1957.

WHAN, VORING E., *Fiasco at Fredericksburg*. University Park: Pennsylvania State University Press, 1961.

WILLIAMS, T. HARRY, *Lincoln and His Generals*. New York: Knopf, 1952.

WOODWORTH, STEVEN E., *Jefferson Davis and His Generals: The Failure of Confederate Command in the West*. Lawrence, KS: University Press of Kansas, 1990.

★5

The Civil War, 1863–1865

On January 1, 1863, Abraham Lincoln released his final Emancipation Proclamation freeing all slaves in all territories under Confederate control. Lincoln labeled his action "a fit and necessary war measure" based on his powers as commander-in-chief during wartime. (Freedom for the slaves was constitutionally guaranteed only with the ratification of the Thirteenth Amendment in December 1865.) He thereby immediately broadened the war aims of the North.

The Emancipation Proclamation also had direct military effects. For the last six months of 1862, a limited number of blacks had been recruited into the Army under the Second Confiscation and Militia Acts of 1862, but now the door was open to widescale use of blacks from both the North and the South, free and ex-slave. Before the war was over, almost 180,000 blacks had served in the Army—originally in all-black supply and labor units, but increasingly in combat as the war went on—and another 10,000 served in the Navy.

It was well that they did. Federal conscription schemes never worked well, as evidenced by the New York City draft riots of 1863, accounting for less than 50,000 Union soldiers, or about 6 percent of the total. Black soldiers accounted for 9 percent and generally acquitted themselves well in combat, taking part in more than three dozen major engagements. Their contribution to Northern victory was significant, and Lincoln's Emancipation Proclamation represented a landmark step in American history. It may not have constitutionally freed any slaves, but it did aid the Northern war effort and, above all, guaranteed the end of slavery once the war was over.

TWO ECONOMIES AT WAR

The Northern economy went into a severe slump at the outbreak of the war. This decline was caused by economic uncertainty over the effects of the war and by the abrupt loss of Southern markets for Northern goods. But by the crisis year of 1863, the Northern economy had recovered fully and was in the midst of a wartime boom. War, because of its essential destructiveness, always demands great quantities of manufactured and agricultural commodities and always produces full employment because of the need for military manpower and laborers in all the expanding sectors of the economy. The Civil War was no exception.

The greatest stimulus to the North's economic boom was the government's demand for war supplies of all types. Contracts for guns, ammunition, clothing, boots and shoes, and all the other manufactured necessities of war ran into millions of dollars and set off a supply bonanza. Shipments of iron ore from the Lake Superior region (via the new canal locks at Sault Ste. Marie) doubled in tonnage; new steel mills sprang up in the Midwest; the clothing and shoe industries, using sewing machines in record numbers, turned out quantities of goods as never before; the coal industry grew 21 percent; farm machinery, such as reapers, mowers, and rotary plows, were sold by the tens of thousands each year; machine-made interchangeable parts became standard in manufacturing, most notably in the production of weapons; and profits soared to new heights. The federal government relied on private enterprise to meet its needs, engaging in direct manufacturing to only a limited extent. All in all, the Northern economy was able to meet both civilian and military industrial needs throughout the war with little strain.

Sufficiency was also the story in regard to Northern agriculture, despite the loss of farm manpower to military demands. Women and children took over many of the farming tasks theretofore performed by men. The sharp increase in the number of immigrants beginning in 1863 also helped to take up the manpower shortage, farmers being the second largest immigrant occupation group among the newcomers, many of them moving directly to the Midwest.

Significant increases in the quantities of wheat, corn, hogs, and other farm commodities were noted, aided by better and more farm machinery and the passage of the Homestead Act in 1862 (long delayed by Southern interests prior to the war but quickly passed after secession), which granted 160 acres free to any settler who would live on the land for five years and improve it. Northern farmers were able to raise production to such heights that they were able not only to supply domestic wartime demands but also to export great amounts of grain and bread products to Europe to make up for poor harvests there. Farmers also benefited from rising land prices and from wartime inflation, which enabled them to pay off their debts more easily.

Finally, the United States government was able to finance the war with relatively little difficulty. The basic wealth of the North provided a strong tax base (approximately 25 percent of the cost of the war was paid for by taxes), and a strong credit position for government borrowing opened that avenue of war financing to Lincoln's government. Despite the issuance of greenbacks worth $450 million and the persistence of wartime inflation, the government had no problem sustaining its credit, and the dollar maintained a respectable value.

The Southern economy, on the other hand, was in a problematic, if not perilous, state throughout the conflict. The South had enough raw materials for industrial use but not the ability to convert them into usable goods. It had too little available capital, too few skilled mechanics, and too little industrial equipment to increase its productivity sufficiently to met its wartime military and domestic needs. Southern uniforms, shoes, guns, munitions, and supplies were never available in adequate quantities despite heroic efforts by private companies and Confederate- and state-operated manufacturers to supply them. Shortages of military goods were commonplace despite the Herculean efforts of Commissary General of Subsistence Lucius B. Northrup and Chief of the Bureau of Ordnance Josiah Gorgas. These realities had a deleterious effect on Southern morale in the armies and at home.

In agriculture, too, the South faced insurmountable problems as the war went on. The market for cotton, the South's chief commercial export, closed down in proportion to the increasing success of the Union blockade, and Britain was unwilling to intervene to ensure a supply of the staple. Cotton and tobacco planting were largely abandoned in favor of farming of food products, but shortages of food persisted. This was due largely to low crop yields because of less advanced farming methods, inadequate transportation to distribute the food effectively, the loss of some of the South's best grain-growing areas to the Federal armies early in the war, and the closing off of supplies from the trans-Mississippi western Confederacy after the fall of Vicksburg in 1863. Shortages in food and manufactured goods became increasingly serious as the war ground on to its conclusion.

With a weaker economic base, the Confederate government found that financing the war was also very difficult. Taxes were difficult to collect, so the government had to rely on borrowing and on printing paper money. All except $248 million of the $2.3 billion Confederate war cost was raised by floating loans or by printing money. The inevitable result was a rapid decline in the value of the Confederate dollar and runaway inflation. By the end of the war, Confederate currency was virtually worthless. The Southern people now found their savings and credit gone, on top of their manufacturing shortcomings and their devastated agricultural economic base.

In summary, Northern manufacturing and agriculture grew stronger during the war, and its war financing was adequate; Southern manufacturing and agriculture, on the other hand, was weak in the beginning and only became weaker, while its monetary and fiscal policies bred economic disaster. Not only on the battlefields, but also in the few factories and on the farms of the Confederacy, the coming of 1863 portended an ominous future for the cause of Southern independence.

It must also be added that, because of the work of the Union's Army (or War) Board and through the inspired efforts of such men as Quartermaster General Montgomery C. Meigs, Chiefs of Ordnance James W. Ripley and Alexander B. Dyer, and Commissary General Joseph P. Taylor, the men in the Union armies usually had enough food, sufficient shoes and clothing, adequate weapons and ammunition, and sufficient field and personal equipment. None of this was true for the Confederate soldier. As the war went on, the logistical situation became more and more critical to the South as the Union armies bisected the area twice and drove deep into its territory and as the Union Navy clamped its blockade ever tighter on the Southern coastline. The year 1863 was as critical to Southern fortunes in the vital economic realm as it was on the battlefields of this conflict, which was rapidly becoming a total war to the finish.

THE BATTLES IN THE WEST

By the beginning of the third calendar year of the war, almost all of the long course of the Mississippi River had been assaulted and seized by Federal land and naval forces converging from the north and the south. The whole cause of eventual Southern victory was tied to keeping this vital artery free of Yankee domination at Vicksburg, the key transportation hub located on a bluff high above the Mississippi's waters. If Vicksburg, the last Southern stronghold on the river, fell to the Union, the western Confederacy would be cut off from the east. Both sides knew the stakes; each side was determined that its flag, and its flag alone, would wave over Vicksburg, "the Gibraltar of the West."

Major General Ulysses S. Grant, appointed to head the Department of the Tennessee, had attempted to take Vicksburg by land during the last two months of 1862, but he had been forced to pull back when his extended supply lines were perilously threatened by Confederate cavalry. The first time, in November, while moving south from La Grange, Tennessee, along the Mississippi Central Railroad line toward Vicksburg, Grant had established a large supply depot at Holly Springs but had been harassed by the forces of Major General Earl VanDorn and the cavalry of Brigadier General Nathan Bedford Forrest. Nevertheless, Grant had continued to probe south toward Vicksburg and the Confederate forces there commanded by Lieutenant General John C. Pemberton.

☆   An American Portrait

Nathan Bedford Forrest—Undoubtedly the Confederacy's most famous and effective cavalry officer, Forrest was born in Tennessee in 1821 but moved with his family to Mississippi as a child. When his father died in 1837, Forrest became the head of his large family and, by dint of hard work, advanced himself from farm laborer to plantation owner.

When war came in 1861, he enlisted in the Confederate Army as a private but was soon placed in command of troops as a lieutenant colonel. He led the Confederates out of Fort Donelson when it was attacked by the Federals in February 1862 and fought at Shiloh Church, where he was severely wounded. When he returned to duty as a brigadier general in July 1862, he inaugurated a series of bold cavalry raids against Union communities and behind enemy lines, his troopers using their horses for mobility but fighting on foot.

After Chickamauga, Forrest got into a serious altercation with Braxton Bragg, calling him a "damned scoundrel" and a "coward." The dispute necessitated the intervention of Jefferson Davis, but, rather than ending his military career, the mercurial Forrest found himself transferred out of Bragg's command but raised in rank to major general. Carrying out more daring raids, Forrest was responsible for the April 1864 slaughter of Union black soldiers after their capture at Fort Pillow. Forrest did not order their deaths, but he did nothing to prevent the atrocity.

Forrest was made lieutenant general in the last weeks of the war and, after Appomattox, went into plantation agriculture and railroading. During these years he was also involved in the formation of the Ku Klux Klan. He died in October 1871 in Memphis, Tennessee, his fame as a cavalry warrior intact.

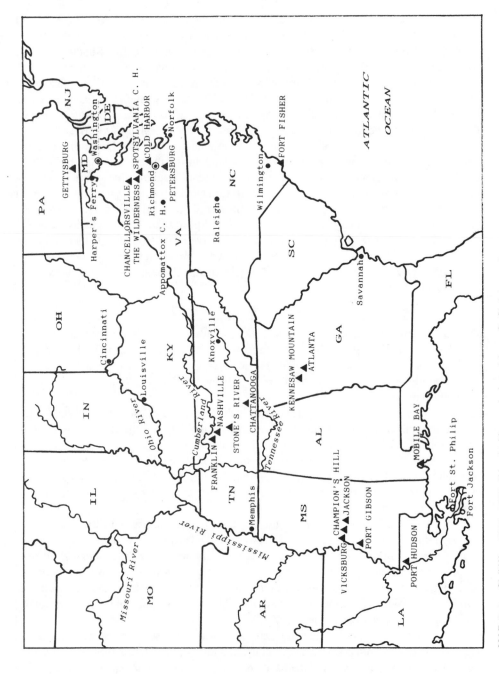

MAP 5-1 Civil War, 1863–1865. *(Used with permission of Anne C. Christensen.)*

116

Then, on December 11, Grant's supply lines were hit hard a second time by Forrest's cavalry, and on December 20, VanDorn and 3,400 cavalry had again assaulted Grant's base at Holly Springs, this raid resulting in a $1.5 million loss in Union supplies. Grant then abandoned his land campaign against Vicksburg because of his tenuous supply lines. He returned to La Grange still determined to take Vicksburg. But the next time, he decided, he would use a more secure water route to seize the city.

Three more times between December 1862 and March 1863 Grant tried to take Vicksburg, and three times he failed. The first attempt came in late December 1862, when he dispatched 31,000 men under Major General William T. Sherman, supported by the gunboats of Rear Admiral David Dixon Porter, to ascend the Yazoo River flowing down from the north-northeast and joining the Mississippi at Vicksburg. Sherman was to land his army at Johnson's plantation and seize the high ground northeast of the city. But the Confederates, divining the plan, had brought up reinforcements and had 14,000 men waiting on Chickasaw Bluffs. Sherman's infantry now had the difficult task of penetrating the swampland that lay before them (artillery could not be brought through the swamps) and then assailing the dug-in and artillery-laden Confederates on the bluffs. The Federal assault on December 27–29 turned into a bloody failure as Confederate guns tore into the Union ranks. Federal casualties numbered almost 1,800; Confederate losses were only slightly more than 200. Sherman withdrew from the Yazoo on January 2, 1863.

Grant's next attempt to take Vicksburg came in February and March 1863. It was called the Yazoo Pass Expedition, an attempt to reach Vicksburg by water from the north using the Coldwater, Tallahatchie, and Yazoo Rivers. But the Confederates blocked the waterways by felling giant trees to complement the stumps already in the water and built a small fort at the confluence of the Tallahatchie and Yazoo that stopped a Federal three-gunboat flotilla and 5,000 troops from proceeding with the operation.

In the meantime, Grant had his men attempting to dig three canals to bypass Vicksburg via the Louisiana rivers and bayous across the Mississippi to the west to transport his men south of the city for an assault, the northern and northeastern approaches appearing to be impossible. Final proof of the futility of these operations was furnished by the March 14–25 Steele's Bayou Expedition. In this operation, Admiral Porter tried to take four gunboats to Vicksburg via the narrow rivers and bayous northeast of the city and found himself stopped and in danger of being trapped by natural obstructions and by the trees that the Confederates had chopped down into the narrow waterways behind him. Porter had to be rescued by General Sherman and his men.

Grant finally decided to march his army through the swamps across from Vicksburg down to a point on the Mississippi below the city. Here he would cross over the river to its eastern bank near Port Gibson and attack Vicksburg from the south and east. To do so he would have to be ferried across the river. Since Confederate batteries at Port Hudson, Louisiana, prevented naval aid and supplies from Baton Rouge and New Orleans from reaching him from the south for the operation, he directed Admiral Porter to run a flotilla past the rebel guns at Vicksburg and meet him below the city to ferry his troops to the east bank.

☆   An American Portrait

David Dixon Porter—An adopted brother of David G. Farragut, Porter was born in 1813 and went to sea with his father at the age of 10. In 1829 he joined the Navy. Thereafter he received a variety of assignments, but he found advancement in rank painfully slow in the mainly peacetime Navy.

With the outbreak of the war in 1861, however, things changed rapidly. Porter was placed in command of the *Powhatan,* sent to relieve Fort Pickens at Pensacola, and then assigned to duty in the Gulf Squadron. It was he who received the surrender of the Mississippi forts below New Orleans in April 1862.

In late 1862 and 1863, Porter, now in command of the Mississippi Squadron, cooperated with Grant and the Army in finally running by Vicksburg to put it under siege until the citadel city fell on July 4, 1863. Transferred to command of the North Atlantic Blockading Squadron in 1864, Porter took part in the assaults on Fort Fisher, during the operation commanding the largest American fleet ever assembled to that time.

After the war, Porter served as superintendent of the Naval Academy from 1865 until 1870, and was appointed admiral in 1870. He died in February 1891.

On March 29 three corps of Union troops began moving south through the swamps and bayous across the Mississippi to the west of Vicksburg, hacking out a road as they went. Their destination was Hard Times, Louisiana. Across the river was Bruinsburg, Mississippi, on the river's eastern bank. On April 16 Porter successfully ran his flotilla past the guns of Vicksburg, losing only 1 of his 12 vessels. The next day, Brigadier General Benjamin H. Grierson, former music teacher and Illinois volunteer, left La Grange, Tennessee, on a 16-day, 600-mile cavalry raid through central Mississippi all the way to Baton Rouge. Grierson's raid was designed to draw off defenders from Vicksburg and confuse the enemy. Then, on April 22, Porter's navy ran a second, 5-transport flotilla loaded with supplies past Vicksburg. Grant now had all his men and supplies at Bruinsburg for his grand move on Vicksburg.

General Pemberton and the 40,000 Confederate troops in the Vicksburg area expected Grant to move north against them there. But after taking Port Gibson northeast of the little town, Grant, abandoning most of his supplies, struck out toward the east and the state capital of Jackson instead. On May 13 his forces defeated the Confederates at the town of Raymond, 15 miles southwest of Jackson. The next day they seized the capital, cutting off General Joseph E. Johnston's troops from aiding Pemberton by driving them off to the north. In two weeks' time, Grant's men had moved 130 miles from Bruinsburg and had isolated Pemberton from Johnston and reinforcement.

Grant then turned west, defeated Pemberton's forces in vicious battle at Champion's Hill and at Big Black River Bridge, and moved on the outer defenses of Vicksburg. On May 19 and 22, unsuccessful assaults were made on the Confederate lines. These failing, Grant decided to take the city by siege, an investment that lasted from May 22 to July 4, 1863. As the city, its citizens, and its 20,000-man defending force were pounded day after day by Union artillery from the land side (Grant's army now totaled 71,000 men) and by gunboats from the Mississippi, the situation in Vicksburg went from bad to worse to hopeless. Before Pemberton finally surrendered his surviving 20,000 men on July 4, Vicksburg's residents and the Confederate troops there were taking refuge in caves and were reduced to eating horses and mules. During the siege the Confederate defenders saw over 1,200 of their comrades killed, 3,500 wounded, and 4,000 captured or missing.

The fall of Vicksburg was one of the most calamitous defeats suffered by the Confederacy. Combined with the fall of Port Hudson, 25 miles north of Baton Rouge, on July 8 (after a 47-day siege by the inept politician-turned-soldier Major General Nathaniel Banks and his 15,000 men from New Orleans), it meant that the Mississippi River was now firmly in Union hands. As Lincoln said, "The Father of Waters again goes unvexed to the sea." The first great bisecting of the Confederacy had been attained. It was now time to begin planning the second deep penetration of the South by seizing the vital rail center of Chattanooga, Tennessee, from there to move down through Georgia to Atlanta.

In charge of the Federals' 60,000-man Army of the Cumberland, assigned the job of prying the Confederates out of Chattanooga, was Major General William S. Rosecrans, a West Point graduate and a prominent politician who had previously fought Braxton Bragg at the Battle of Stone's River on the final day of 1862. Rosecrans was successful in maneuvering Bragg and his 43,000 men out of Chattanooga without a fight on September 9, 1863, and followed them south to Lee and Gordon's Mills across the Georgia line. Given the strategic value of Chattanooga, both sides sought immediate reinforcements. Jefferson Davis ordered General James Longstreet, Lee's second-in-command, to take his corps west from Virginia to reinforce Bragg via the Virginia and Tennessee Railroad and help him retake Chattanooga. They arrived on September 18, bringing Bragg's strength to 66,000 effectives. For one of the few times in the war, Rebels outnumbered Yankees in battle.

☆   An American Portrait

Braxton Bragg—Bragg, the Confederates' best organizer in the West but a general whose irritability and quarrelsome personality made it difficult for his subordinates to remain loyal to him, was born in North Carolina in 1817. He attended West Point from 1833 through 1837 and, as a lieutenant of artillery, fought in the Seminole wars. As a captain he fought in the Mexican War in the battles of Fort Brown and Monterrey and the next year was brevetted a lieutenant colonel for distinguished service at Buena Vista. He resigned his commission in 1856 and bought a plantation in Louisiana.

Early in 1861 he was appointed a colonel, then major general, of the Louisiana militia, followed by an appointment to the position of brigadier general in the Confederate Army. Showing great vigor in the Western campaigns, Bragg was soon advanced to major general and to a corps command and on April 12, 1862, was made a full general.

Named to head the Army of Tennessee in June 1862, Bragg fought Buell to a draw at Perryville, but at the turn of the new year revealed a lack of aggressive spirit when he failed to exploit his advantages at Stone's River. Notwithstanding the outcry against him, Jefferson Davis kept him in command. But in September 1863 he was maneuvered out of Chattanooga by General Rosecrans and, despite his apparent victory at Chickamauga, failed to pursue the defeated Union forces vigorously, thus allowing them to escape to Chattanooga.

Chased away from Chattanooga by Grant's fearsome and effective attacks on November 23–25, Bragg, on December 2, 1863, turned over his command to Joseph E.

Johnston. In 1864 Bragg was called to Richmond to serve as advisor and nominal general-in-chief to Jefferson Davis, fleeing with the Confederate president to Georgia with the evacuation of Richmond and being captured on May 9. He was subsequently paroled and began a career in engineering, but died in September 1876 in Galveston, Texas.

Bragg moved out on September 18 to the east of Chickamauga Creek, hoping to crush the left flank of Rosecran's line, which ran north to south along the LaFayette Road. The bloody two-day battle began on September 19 as Bragg's forces attacked the four-mile Union line from the east and the Federals counterattacked. There was no apparent victor the first day. But on September 20, as Bragg continued to pound on the Union left, Rosecrans, informed that there was a break in his line, pulled Brigadier General Thomas J. Wood's men out of position on the right to fill the gap. Longstreet's Virginians poured through the gap left by Wood's departure and began to sweep the field.

The Union forces were saved only by the resolute stand of Major General George H. Thomas and his men, who redeployed and held off the surging Confederates until dusk along Snodgrass Hill, following the rest of the beaten Union army into Chattanooga the next day. Unfortunately for the South, Bragg refused to follow up on this, his greatest victory, giving the Union forces time to escape back to Tennessee and reinforcement in Chattanooga. Southern losses at Chickamauga were over 18,000; Union casualties numbered over 16,000, but the fight for Chattanooga was far from over even as Bragg placed his men on the hills around three sides of the crucial railroad town waiting for Rosecrans to begin evacuation.

☆ An American Portrait

George H. Thomas—A native of Southampton County, Virginia, Thomas was born in 1816 and was raised in the antebellum South, yet he chose to remain with the Union in 1861. After attending Southampton Academy and beginning the study of law, Thomas entered West Point in 1836 and was graduated twelfth in his class of 42 four years later. As a lieutenant in the field artillery he fought against the Seminoles in Florida, and during the Mexican War he served under Zachary Taylor. He was brevetted captain and major for gallantry at Monterrey and Buena Vista. After further service in Texas, he spent four years at West Point as an instructor of artillery and cavalry before joining a newly formed cavalry unit in Texas on garrison and exploration duty.

Choosing to stay with the Union during the secession crisis, he was in the Shenandoah Valley during the First Manassas campaign; upon promotion to brigadier general in August 1861, he was sent to the West. There he fought at Shiloh, Corinth, Perryville, and Stone's River, receiving a promotion to major general after Shiloh.

Thomas gained enduring fame on September 20, 1863, the second day of the Battle of Chickamauga, when he held off the Confederates breaking through and earned the nickname "The Rock of Chickamauga." He went on to play a prominent role in the lifting of the siege of Chattanooga at Lookout Mountain and Missionary Ridge. Serving as second in command to Sherman in the Atlanta campaign, he was hurried off to Nashville to defend it against John Bell Hood in the last Confederate attempt to break through in that sector of the entwining Union lines.

After the war, Thomas, now a major general in the regulars, headed the Division of Texas and in 1869 was transferred to California to command the Division of the Pacific. He died at his post on March 28, 1870, still well remembered as "The Rock of Chickamauga."

Rosecrans was in a trap. He had the Tennessee River at his back and was confronted with strong Confederate positions on Missionary Ridge northeast to southwest over the town, on Lookout Mountain to the southwest, and on Raccoon Mountain and Lookout Valley to the west. Lincoln sent Major General Joseph Hooker and two corps from the Army of the Potomac to aid him, while Bragg for his part was determined to starve out the Union forces by putting Chattanooga under siege and cutting off all river and rail traffic into the town.

Hopeless as the situation seemed, Lincoln was undeterred. On October 16 he created the Division of the Mississippi and put General Ulysses S. Grant in charge. Grant fired Rosecrans, appointed Thomas in his place as commander of the Army of the Cumberland, and traveled to Chattanooga to see the situation at first hand. He lost no time in reversing the plight of the Union forces. On October 27 Hooker's men established a bridgehead at Brown's Ferry on the Tennessee River and held on as an east–west supply line—soon dubbed the "Cracker Line"—was established across Moccasin Point, allowing food and ammunition to be brought into the besieged troops in Chattanooga.

In the meantime, dissension broke out within the Confederate high command. Feelings were running so high against the inactive and irresolute Bragg that Jefferson Davis himself had to visit the scene and talk to his generals. Davis refused to relieve Bragg, but three leading subordinates (Generals Leonidas Polk, Daniel H. Hill, and Thomas C. Hindman) were fired, and Longstreet was allowed to take two divisions to Knoxville to attack Burnside there—just as the 40,000-man Union forces in Chattanooga were being reinforced by General Sherman and 17,000 men from Memphis and Vicksburg.

On November 23 the Union army made its first move. Two divisions hit the foothills below Missionary Ridge and dug in. The next day saw furious fighting as Hooker seized Lookout Mountain on Bragg's left while Sherman's troops left Brown's Ferry west of Chattanooga, moved north around the town, and established a strong position on Bragg's right on the north end of Missionary Ridge. Thomas' troops held the center.

The climactic fight of November 25 for Missionary Ridge lasted most of the day. It was highlighted by the actions of the troops of Brigadier General Thomas J. Wood and Major General Philip H. Sheridan, who, finding themselves under severe fire at the base of Missionary Ridge, carried out an unauthorized charge up the hill that broke through and collapsed the entire Confederate line. The Union victories at Lookout Mountain and Missionary Ridge turned into a rout, with the Confederates retreating into northern Georgia. Chattanooga was saved for the Union, Grant was promoted to lieutenant general and called east in March 1864 to be general-in-chief, and Sherman took over his command and began preparations for the spring 1864 advance on Atlanta. Bragg asked to be relieved of command and was granted his request.

Operating as one part of Grant's two-part Western strategy for 1864 (the other was a movement by Banks against Mobile), Major General William T. Sherman of Ohio was preparing by early May to launch his 100,000-man march on Atlanta. The "Gate City" was the South's last major rail center. It was 105 miles southeast of Chattanooga. Sherman would be facing Joseph E. Johnston's 53,000-man Army of Tennessee. Sherman's forces consisted of four cavalry divisions and three armies: the Armies of the Cumberland (Major General Thomas), of the Tennessee (Major General James B. McPherson), and of the Ohio (Major General John M. Schofield). Seeking to avoid logistical problems along his route of march, Sherman took over the civilian railroads in the area and stockpiled necessary supplies. On Grant's orders, he intended to carry out total war against the enemy, both military and civilian, in order to destroy the South's military and economic structure by laying waste its sources of production and breaking its will to fight. The successful capture of Atlanta might also guarantee Lincoln's reelection in November and end efforts then underway in certain quarters to arrange for a negotiated peace.

☆ An American Portrait

William Tecumseh Sherman—"Cump" Sherman was born in February 1820 in Lancaster, Ohio. He was appointed to West Point in 1836 and was graduated four years later, standing sixth in his class of 42 cadets. After duty in Florida and South Carolina, he served in the Mexican War as an aide to Philip Kearney and participated in the drive on Mexico City.

After serving in the Pacific Division, he resigned his commission in 1853 and went into banking in San Francisco, thence into law and real estate in Leavenworth, Kansas. In 1859 he became superintendent of the Louisiana State Seminary of Learning (the forerunner of Louisiana State University at Baton Rouge) and, with the outbreak of the war, was offered a commission in the Confederate Army.

Sherman instead accepted the regular rank of colonel in the Union Army and served at First Manassas. Thereafter he was raised in rank to brigadier general of volunteers and sent to Kentucky. Serving as commander of the District of Cairo, Illinois, he was with

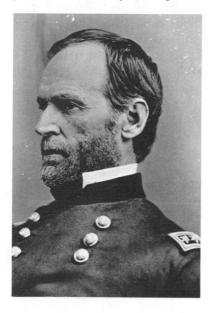

FIGURE 5–1 William T. Sherman. (*National Archives, Washington, D.C.*)

Grant at Shiloh and under Halleck at Corinth, advancing in rank to major general. By July 1862 Sherman had been appointed by Grant to defend Memphis, and he served well beside Grant during the prolonged effort to seize Vicksburg, which lasted from December 1862 through July 1863.

Sent to the relief of Chattanooga two months later. Sherman was given command of the Army of the Tennessee and by March 1864 was in command of all Union troops in the West. In this capacity he directed the May-to-September 1864 march on Atlanta, followed by the Union Army's move to the sea at Savannah and then into the Carolinas. Sherman illustrated by his generalship during this all-out offensive that he was one of the first modern war leaders.

After the war, in 1866, Sherman—a perennial enemy of the press—was raised in rank to lieutenant general, and in 1869 he was made general and appointed general-in-chief of the Army under President Grant, his old friend and war companion, serving until his retirement in 1883. He died in February 1891 in New York City.

Sherman began his march on May 9. He was disappointed when Johnston slipped out of a trap at Buzzard Roost and Rocky Face Gap, but he continued to press on. Johnston was gradually forced to retreat in the face of the massive Union strength throughout the month of May, although his troops put up spirited resistance at Resaca, Cassville, New Hope Church, Mount Zion Church, and Pickett's Mills. In early June, Johnston was forced to withdraw toward Atlanta again, finally setting up a defensive position at Kennesaw Mountain. Here Sherman foolishly tried to assail the Confederates by a frontal assault and met a bloody rebuff. But Sherman then returned to his basic flanking tactics, and soon Johnston was forced to pull back beyond Marietta to the banks of the Chattahoochee River, only seven miles from Atlanta. Again Sherman flanked his spirited opponent, forcing Johnston south of the river. This led Jefferson Davis on July 17 to remove Johnston in favor of the daring and more aggressive Lieutenant General John Bell Hood.

☆ An American Portrait

John Bell Hood—Known as the "fighting general" and amassing a military career record marred by rashness, Hood was born in 1831 in Bath County, Kentucky. Graduating from West Point forty-fourth in a class of 52 in 1853, Hood saw duty in New York, California, and Texas before resigning his commission in April 1861 to join the Confederate Army.

He was assigned to Yorktown, Virginia, under General John B. Magruder as head of his cavalry on the Peninsula, and the next year, as brigadier general and head of the "Texas Brigade," he fought at Gaines Mill, Second Manassas, and Antietam. Raised in rank to major general and to head of a corps under Longstreet in October 1862, he was badly wounded at Gettysburg. Returning to duty, at Chickamauga he directed Longstreet's corps and three divisions of the Army of Tennessee and, again being wounded, suffered the loss of his right leg. Again returning to active service and now a lieutenant general, in February 1864 he took command of a corps under Joseph E. Johnston.

When Johnston was removed from command for not stopping Sherman's determined march on Atlanta, Hood was appointed in his place and immediately went on the offensive and suffered a series of defeats. He then abandoned the campaign against Sherman and marched northwest to strike at Thomas and Schofield, hoping to reinforce Lee in Virginia. But he met defeat at both Franklin and Nashville and asked to be relieved of command.

Hood surrendered to Union officials a month after the war ended and then moved on to Texas, where he became a commission merchant. He died of yellow fever on August 30, 1879, six days after the death of his wife, the unfortunate couple leaving behind a family of ten children, including infant twins.

True to his character and reputation, Hood immediately launched an attack on Thomas's army along Peachtree Creek, only to meet bloody defeat and suffer 4,800 casualties. Undeterred, Hood launched another attack on the Union forces of General McPherson east of the city on July 22 in "The Battle of Atlanta." Again Hood failed to stem the Union tide.

Sherman then sent first his cavalry, then his infantry, west of Atlanta to circle around to the south and cut all of the city's rail lines. Hood slowed this movement near Ezra Church on July 28 and again at Jonesboro on August 31 and September 1, but in these engagements he sustained very heavy casualties, destroying his military power. With Sherman's seizure of the Macon and Western Railroad, Hood was forced to abandon Atlanta on September 1, 1864. The next day the Gate City was in Federal hands, Hood moved off toward the northwest and Alabama, Lincoln's reelection seemed reassured, and the South began to despair of victory.

Sherman then convinced Grant and Lincoln that he should strike out for Savannah and the sea, in the meantime sending Thomas and two corps plus cavalry back to cover central Tennessee against anything Hood might attempt. This way he could continue to carry total warfare to the South (to "make Georgia howl," as he said) by smashing Confederate sources of production and cutting all supply lines from the Deep South to Virginia while completing the second bisecting of the South.

Sherman's "March to the Sea" began on November 15 and ended 26 days later, when his armies came to a halt outside Savannah 250 miles away. Sherman's troops started out from Atlanta by moving to the east and southeast with two columns that converged at the state capital of Milledgeville, which was destroyed. They were opposed by only 18,000 men under Lieutenant General William Hardee and 3,000 scattered Georgia militiamen. Sherman's troops continued on, cutting a 60-mile-wide swath of destruction and desolation as they moved to Savannah and the sea.

Inside the Confederate fortifications at Savannah were 10,000 men under General Hardee. By December 10 they were surrounded by Sherman's 62,000-man army. One week later Hardee refused Sherman's demand to surrender, so Sherman reluctantly prepared an assault. But before he could launch his attack, Hardee's men constructed a pontoon bridge across the Savannah River and escaped into North Carolina. On December 21, Sherman's forces moved into defenseless Savannah. The March to the Sea was completed, the South had been bisected again, and the reality of total warfare had been brought home to the people in the Deep South. Sherman could now move north through Georgia and the Carolinas to catch the remaining Confederate forces in a giant pincer as the Army of the Potomac moved south in Virginia.

The Western armies still had two major tasks to carry out. Hood's army remained on the loose and dangerous, and Charleston had still not been taken. After the fall of Atlanta, Hood had withdrawn into northwest Alabama, and by November 1864 he and his

39,000 Confederates, with Davis's approval, were prepared to invade Tennessee to draw off Union forces from the Deep South and destroy Sherman's supplies for his operations in the Southeast. General Thomas, now in Nashville, was ordered to stop them. As Hood moved into Tennessee on this last great mission in the western Confederacy, he was joined by Major General Nathan B. Forrest's cavalry. But a Union force under General Schofield held off 18 Confederate brigades on November 30 at Franklin, 18 miles south of Nashville. Here Hood foolishly relied on a frontal attack. The result was his worst defeat and a butcher's bill for the day of 6,000 casualties (as opposed to the Union's 2,300). That night Schofield and his men withdrew, and by dawn the next day his leading elements were safely within Thomas' lines at Nashville. Hood's men, meanwhile, attacked the Union fortifications at Franklin, only to find them empty. They moved on to surround Nashville.

When Thomas, with 70,000 men in Nashville, dawdled for two weeks in going after Hood's inferior forces outside the city (because of the need for thorough preparation and because of bad weather, he said), Grant bluntly ordered him to "attack Hood at once." Still Thomas delayed, and Grant considered sacking the dilatory general. But on December 15 and 16, Thomas sent his army out of Nashville to "get Hood" and, highlighted by Major General James H. Wilson's cavalry maneuvers, in two days shattered Hood's forces. They retreated toward Mississippi with Thomas's army in hot pursuit for ten days. On December 29 the remains of Hood's army entered Tupelo and safety. But the Confederate Army of Tennessee was now in ruins. Some elements were sent to various locations to hold out in Mississippi and Alabama; the rest were moved east into the Carolinas. The Western campaign was over. The western Confederate armies, now defeated and fragmented, were for all practical purposes out of the war.

The final task for Sherman's forces was to seize Charleston as they moved north. In April 1863 the Navy, under Rear Admiral Samuel F. DuPont, had attempted to seize the city and harbor with a flotilla of seven monitors and two ironclads, but Confederate gunners had made a shambles of the Union fleet and brought an end to DuPont's Civil War military career. This had been followed by a naval and land attack the following July. This second attack also failed, although Charleston was effectively blockaded from that time on.

As Sherman moved north from Savannah in early 1865, he passed west of the city and cut off all reinforcements for the garrison within. On orders from General P. G. T. Beauregard, commanding in the Carolinas, General Hardee and his men slipped out of Charleston on the night of February 17, 1865, to join other Confederate forces to the north in trying to stop Sherman's inexorable drive through the Carolinas. The next day the Federals moved into the city, and a month later Brigadier General Robert Anderson, who as a major had been forced to haul down the American flag over Fort Sumter four years before, returned to the now-devastated fort to raise the Stars and Stripes over Charleston harbor once again.

☆ An American Portrait

David Glasgow Farragut—Born in Campbell's Station, Tennessee, in 1801, Farragut went to sea in 1810 and saw action in the War of 1812, serving as a prizemaster at the age of 12. In the years after 1815 Farragut advanced in seamanship and rank, attaining a coveted naval captaincy by 1855.

FIGURE 5–2 David G. Farragut. (*National Archives, Washington, D.C.*)

When war broke out in 1861, Farragut was living in Norfolk, Virginia, and was implored to stay with his native South. But he moved north and by the end of the year was in command of the West Gulf Blockading Squadron. In April 1862 he pushed his force past Forts Jackson and St. Philip and on April 25 captured the crucial Southern port of New Orleans for the Union. Three months later he was advanced in rank to rear admiral, the first in American naval history, Congress finally abandoning its reluctance to award admiral rank.

During the early months of 1863, various attempts to capture Vicksburg and open the Mississippi River were tried and failed, but in the meantime Farragut and his naval forces continued to tighten the blockade of the Gulf. On August 5, 1864, he and his Gulf naval forces gained their greatest victory when they forced their way into Mobile Bay and seized the Alabama port city, with Farragut in the rigging of his flagship USS *Hartford* giving the order, "Damn the torpedoes [floating mines]! Full speed ahead!"

Although Farragut was thereafter promoted to vice admiral, poor health allowed him only limited action for the remainder of the war. His postwar duties were mainly administrative. He died at Portsmouth, New Hampshire, in August 1870, a Southerner by birth but the Union's greatest naval commander.

Mobile Bay had been seized by the Union Navy under Rear Admiral David G. Farragut on August 5, 1864, and Fort Fisher, guarding Wilmington, North Carolina, had fallen to Federal forces on January 15, 1865, (followed by Wilmington itself on February 23) after the incompetent politician-general Benjamin F. "Beast" Butler was sacked by Lincoln. With the Federal seizure of Charleston and Wilmington, the Southern seacoasts were now completely sealed off except for the secondary port of Galveston, Texas. The end of the war was near. Sherman continued to push north in pursuit of the remnants of the Confederate forces in the Carolinas. In the meantime, Grant's Army of the Potomac held the last elements of Robert E. Lee's Army of Northern Virginia within the earthworks at Petersburg south of Richmond awaiting what was now an inevitable end.

THE BATTLES IN THE EAST

Early in 1863, General Ambrose Burnside, shaken by his defeat at Fredericksburg the previous month, was replaced as head of the Army of the Potomac by Major General Joseph "Fighting Joe" Hooker. A veteran of many earlier campaigns, a fearless fighter, and an accomplished braggart, Hooker had been chosen by Lincoln for his aggressiveness. He set about living up to his nickname. He reorganized the Army of the Potomac and whipped it into fighting shape at Falmouth, across the Rappahannock from Fredericksburg, while in preparation for a grand offensive to encircle Lee and destroy once and for all his Army of Northern Virginia.

☆   An American Portrait

Joseph Hooker—Hooker was born in November 1814 in Hadley, Massachusetts. He was graduated from the United States Military Academy in 1837, standing twenty-ninth in a class of 50. After serving in the Second Seminole War and on the Canadian border, during the war with Mexico he served under both Taylor and Scott, being brevetted for gallantry to captain, lieutenant colonel, and colonel. In 1853 he resigned from the Army to take up farming in California.

In May 1861 he was appointed brigadier general of volunteers and was assigned to help defend Washington. During the Peninsula campaign he fought at Williamsburg, Seven Pines, White Oak Swamp, and Malvern Hill, earning the nickname "Fighting Joe" for his exploits.

Participating in Second Manassas and Bristoe Station, he was a corps commander at Antietam and soon thereafter was appointed a brigadier general in the regulars. Known for his severe criticism of General Burnside at Fredericksburg, Hooker was thereafter given command of Burnside's Army of the Potomac. Although he swiftly reorganized the army upon taking command, his failure to attack Lee when the Confederate's army was divided at Chancellorsville in May 1863 led Lincoln to have grave doubts about his competence as a field commander. Accordingly, he was dismissed by the president on June 28, 1863, and replaced by Meade three days before the fateful battle at Gettysburg.

But "Fighting Joe" went on to serve well in the Western theater, especially at Chattanooga and Lookout Mountain, and served as a corps commander under Sherman in his march on Atlanta. Passed over for higher command, Hooker asked to be relieved, and his request was granted. He retired from the Army in 1868 and died in October 1879 in Garden City, New York.

Hooker's plan was to send Major General George Stoneman and 10,000 men across the river to raid Lee's supply lines south of Fredericksburg and divert him from the main Union attacks. Then Major General John Sedgwick, with one-third of the remaining 124,000-man Federal force, would cross the river at Fredericksburg and hold

Lee in place while Hooker took a second third of the force ten miles up the Rappahannock and cross at the Rapidan River to move in behind Lee. The final third of the army would act as Hooker's reserve to aid either Sedgwick or Hooker as needed.

Stoneman's cavalry was two weeks late jumping off because heavy rains made the Rappahannock impossible to ford. They thus played no important part in the ensuing Chancellorsville campaign. But on April 27, 1863, Hooker's men moved out to the west. Two days later they crossed the Rapidan. Then next day they were in the Wilderness, a forbidding area of woods and deep underbrush ten miles west of Fredericksburg at the crossroads settlement of Chancellorsville. With his reserves, Hooker now had 75,000 men at Lee's rear, while another 40,000 under Sedgwick were moving against his front at Fredericksburg. Lee had only 60,000 men, Longstreet, with two divisions, having been sent off on a foraging expedition.

Unwilling to abandon the field and retreat toward Richmond, Lee decided to split his army, a dangerous tactic but necessary under the circumstances. Leaving Major General Jubal A. Early with 10,000 men to hold off Sedgwick's 40,000 at Fredericksburg, Lee moved west on May 1 with the remainder of his army to confront Hooker. That same day the confident Federal advance forces were moving out of the Wilderness into open country. The Federals met up with Lee's Confederates in a vicious fight with Stonewall Jackson's veterans in the afternoon, and Hooker, losing his nerve, ordered a retreat into the Wilderness. He thereby surrendered the initiative—despite the protests of his corps commanders—and set up a defensive position around Chancellorsville.

That night Lee and Jackson, informed that Hooker's right flank was uncovered, decided to split the Confederate forces again. The next morning Jackson, with 26,000 men, began a 14-mile circuitous march to get on Hooker's flank, while Lee and his 20,000 men demonstrated before Chancellorsville to keep Hooker's Federals in place. Meanwhile, Major General Oliver O. Howard, on Hooker's right, disregarded intelligence reports that Confederates were to the west. He assumed that they were only a few Confederates retreating from the field. In a lightning assault on the unsuspecting Union forces in the fading light, Jackson's men suddenly attacked Howard's forces and chased them back two miles toward Chancellorsville before darkness ended the rout. That night, Stonewall Jackson was mistakenly shot by Confederate soldiers. Surgeons tried to save him, but he died on May 10, the greatest Southern casualty of the victory at Chancellorsville and perhaps of the war.

The next day, May 3, the Confederates again struck Hooker's lines around Chancellorsville, forcing him to abandon the town and withdraw to the north, this time with his flanks well covered by the Rapidan and Rappahannock Rivers. As Lee was preparing to assault this new line, he learned that Sedgwick's forces had broken through at Fredericksburg and were advancing from the east. Accordingly, he sent part of his forces six miles east to Salem Church to block Sedgwick's march. Here a sharp fight ensued, with the Federals taking 4,700 casualties, but Hooker sent no aid to Sedgwick. And when the Confederates resumed their attack on Sedgwick's forces the next morning, they found he had pulled back across the Rappahannock at Bank's Ford. Hooker, having never even committed one-third of his giant army, retreated back across the Rappahannock on the night of May 5–6 to return to Falmouth.

The Battle of Chancellorsville, Lee's greatest tactical victory, was over. Hooker's dream of a magnificent, war-ending offensive lay in ruins. Union casualties totalled over 17,000; Confederate figures stood at 12,700. But surely the South's greatest loss at Chancellorsville was Stonewall Jackson. The Army of Northern Virginia would never again be as effective without Jackson at Lee's side—as was soon demonstrated at the little town of Gettysburg, Pennsylvania. Here Lee, fresh from his greatest victory, would suffer his worst strategic and tactical defeat.

Lee, with Jefferson Davis' blessing, decided after Chancellorsville to mount a major invasion of the North. This would encourage war-weariness among the Northerners, disrupt any enemy plans for another offensive, delay any movement toward Richmond for the year, and allow his army to live off the rich fields and orchards of Pennsylvania rather than of Virginia. He intended to march north out of the Shenandoah Valley into Pennsylvania, then swing east to threaten Philadelphia and Baltimore, forcing Hooker and the Army of the Potomac to pursue him and attack him on ground of his own choosing, thereby administering a decisive thrashing of the Union forces on their own territory. However, while a great victory in the North would surely be a great strategic coup, a loss, any loss, would be a great strategic blow to the South and a major gain for the North considering the circumstances. Lee, then, was taking a sizable gamble by invading Pennsylvania. His gamble failed.

On June 3, 1863, Lee began moving his 75,000 men toward the Shenandoah and then north. He had divided his army into three corps commanded by Longstreet (I Corps), A. P. Hill (III Corps), and one-legged Lieutenant General Richard S. Ewell (II Corps). Lee left Hill and III Corps behind as a temporary rear guard as he moved northwest, and Hooker, discovering what Lee had done, wanted to drive on Hill and make a move toward Richmond. But Lincoln rejected this strategy. As always, the president believed that the destruction of Lee's army had to be the primary objective. Instead, he ordered Hooker to keep parallel with Lee as he moved northwest, always guarding Washington.

By June 30, Lee had all of his infantry and artillery across the Potomac. Ewell had moved north and east and was at Carlisle, Pennsylvania, north of Hagerstown, Maryland. Hill's corps was nearby. Everything was going well except that Lee had not known until two days before that Hooker was not still in Virginia but, rather, was near Frederick, Maryland, and moving toward him. Lee's late intelligence was the fault of Major General Jeb Stuart, who, on June 22, had been ordered by Lee to cover the Confederate right flank with his cavalry and keep him posted on the location of the Federals. Instead of returning to Lee in 36 hours as stipulated, Stuart decided to ride around the Federals, as he had done successfully during the Peninsula campaign the year before. Accordingly, he and his cavalrymen rode as far east as Fairfax Court House, Virginia, then moved on to Rockville, Maryland, and into southern Pennsylvania, taking prisoners and, as a result, being slowed down as they went. Stuart did not arrive back at Lee's headquarters until July 2. By this time the ensuing great battle of Gettysburg was well underway.

When Lee had finally learned on June 28 that the Federals were moving on him and were at Frederick, he knew he had to reassemble his scattered units immediately. He could not face the enemy piecemeal. Accordingly, he had sent out messengers to tell his commanders to meet at the town of Gettysburg, where the roads from Chambersburg,

Carlisle, and York met. Thus it was that the crossroads town of Gettysburg, Pennsylvania, became the site of one of the most decisive battles of the Civil War.

What Lee did not know, however, is that on that same day, June 28, Hooker had been replaced as head of the Army of the Potomac by Major General George Gordon Meade, a very different type of leader. The crusty general was chosen by Lincoln to replace the problematic Hooker because he was reliable and, above all, did not scare easily.

☆   An American Portrait

George Gordon Meade—Born in Cadiz, Spain (where his father was a U.S. naval agent) in 1815, Meade was graduated from the United States Military Academy in 1835, standing nineteenth in a class of 56 cadets. After serving in the Seminole War, he resigned his commission in 1836 to work in railroad engineering but rejoined the Army in 1842. During the Mexican War he was at Palo Alto and Monterrey and was with Scott at Veracruz. After the war he resumed his military engineering duties for the Army.

With the outbreak of the Civil War, Meade was assigned to help defend the nation's capital. As a major in the regular Army, he served under McClellan in the Peninsula campaign, at Second Manassas under Pope, and again under McClellan at Antietam in 1862.

Now a major general of volunteers, Meade commanded V Corps at Chancellorsville in May 1863 and the next month was picked by Lincoln to take over command of the Army of the Potomac from General Hooker as Lee was invading Pennsylvania. Although Meade handled his troops well during the crucial Battle of Gettysburg, his failure to pursue the defeated Southerners earned him the wrath of the president. Presidential displeasure notwithstanding, Meade continued to serve as commander of the Army of the Potomac under Grant through 1864 and 1865 as they pursued, and finally crushed, the Confederate forces in Virginia.

After the war Meade held many top Army command positions and in 1868 was sent to Atlanta to administer Reconstruction policies there. He died in Philadelphia in November 1872 of pneumonia and residual damage inflicted by old war wounds.

Meade knew that if he could force Lee to stop and concentrate his forces, the Confederate commander would either have to attack him (on ground of Meade's choosing, not his own, Meade hoped) or retreat back to Virginia, both eventualities being in the Union's favor. On June 30, as Lee was drawing his scattered units together, Meade sent Brigadier General John Buford's cavalry to find Lee. Meade also sent Major General John Reynolds and about one-third of his 88,000-man army after Buford. If Buford found Lee, Meade ordered, Reynolds was to engage him until he arrived with the main force. Late that day Buford found Lee west of Gettysburg, and Reynolds began to move up.

The Battle of Gettysburg began the next morning, July 1, 1863, when the advance units of both armies opened fire on each other north and west of Gettysburg. Hill's and Reynolds's forces fought one another along Seminary Ridge, running north to south on the west side of the town, and around to the northern outskirts of the village. The fighting was heavy, but the Union forces were holding their own while Lee was pushing men up the Chambersburg Road east toward Gettysburg. Then, in the afternoon, Ewell's and Jubal

Early's forces arrived from the north and hit the Union right flank. Lee ordered a general offensive, which pushed the Union forces back through Gettysburg and up onto Culp's Hill and Cemetery Hill east and south of the town and along Cemetery Ridge running south from there. Meade, 15 miles to the southeast, ordered Major General Winfield S. Hancock to assume command (Reynolds had been killed that day during the fighting) and left it to him to decide whether Gettysburg was a good place tactically for their showdown fight with Lee. His answer was yes.

In the meantime, the Confederates might have been able to sweep to victory that first day by driving the Federals off Cemetery Hill and Ridge, but in the confusion and exhaustion of the battle and the subsequent Union retreat through the town, the opportunity was lost. July 1 ended with the Union forces on the heights east and south of Gettysburg and the Confederates north of the town and along Seminary Ridge to the west but with a good opportunity to drive the Federals from their positions the next day.

But the second day, July 2, started in confusion and disagreement in the Southern high command and ended in frustrating failure as three Confederate attacks went awry. Longstreet asked permission to move his men all the way around the Union left flank to attack them from the rear, but Lee would not allow it. He still did not know where Meade's main forces were, and he feared that Longstreet might find himself in an ambush. Rather, Lee directed Longstreet to go down Seminary Ridge and hit the Union left at or around the Round Tops (two elevated knobs at the south end of Cemetery Ridge, which, if seized and fortified with artillery, could rake the whole Union line to the north). At the same time, Ewell was to seize Culp's Hill on the north, and A. P. Hill in the center would support either operation as needed.

Longstreet was almost successful in seizing Little Round Top and Big Round Top, thanks to Union Major General Daniel Sickles's foolish decision to leave the high ground there and move out and down the ridge to try to flank Longstreet. He was hit by 12,000 of Longstreet's men. Furious fighting in the Wheat Field and in the Peach Orchard and in and around the cluster of giant rocks known thereafter as "the Devil's Den" put the Confederates in a position to collapse the Union left flank on Cemetery Ridge. Fortunately for the Federals, Meade ordered up reinforcements with artillery, and the left flank held. In the meantime, Ewell's four attacks up the steep, wooded slopes of Culp's Hill carried the Confederates only half way up, where they had to dig in at dusk to try again the next day. And secondary attacks by Hill and Jubal Early on the Union center along Cemetery Ridge also failed. The value of holding the high ground was never so graphically displayed as at Gettysburg.

Lee was now in a strategic and tactical bind. With Meade's entire army having arrived on the field, he could not withdraw in defeat, and he could not hold his ground and wait for an offensive by the stronger Union forces. Furthermore, he could not maneuver because the armies were too close together. He therefore decided that the next day he would launch a massive assault up the center (rejecting Longstreet's strenuous objections to this move) and he would send Ewell to complete the seizure of Culp's Hill and the Union right flank, the Union left flank now being unassailable. This is exactly what Meade expected him to do. Lee would now have to either hit the Union strong points or retreat, Meade knew. Strategically and tactically Lee could work his way out of his box and win only if all worked perfectly on the third day of battle. It did not.

Lee's orders specified that Major General George Pickett's fresh division and brigades of Longstreet and Hill from Seminary Ridge (over 13,000 men in all) were to proceed east across the valley, cross the Emmitsburg Road, and strike the center of the Union line along Cemetery Ridge. At the same time, Ewell was to renew his attack up Culp's Hill, and Stuart, who had finally rejoined the army, was to circle around the Union lines with his cavalry to disrupt their defenses from the rear.

On the morning of July 3, the third day, Ewell's men on their own initiative began their attack up Culp's Hill before Pickett was ready to move. It was unsuccessful. Then, in the early afternoon, the Confederate artillery opened up on Cemetery Ridge in preparation for the attack on the center of the Union lines, but most of the shots were too high. The Union infantry and artillery were hardly disturbed, the Federal artillery answering in a terrible fusillade of fire. When the Confederate infantry finally set off in the afternoon led by Pickett's division (some historians blame Longstreet for the delay), they had to cross the mile-wide valley, redress their lines after crossing the Emmitsburg Road, and march up the steep slope of Cemetery Ridge into the very teeth of the Union defenses. Hit by Union infantry and artillery fire with canister and grapeshot on both flanks and from Cemetery Ridge, the brave Confederate soldiers drove on—to their deaths. At one point some of them reached the crest of Cemetery Ridge only to be driven back. The entire surviving Confederate assault force soon had no choice but to retreat to Seminary Ridge. There Lee could only tell them, "It is all my fault." In the meantime, Stuart's cavalry was caught by Federal cavalry forces and driven away after a three-hour fight, having contributed nothing to the day's operations.

Lee contracted his flanks and waited for Meade's counterattack. It never came. Meade was willing only to chase Lee out of Pennsylvania, striking him if the opportunity arose. He would not attack Lee's lines. Lee, sensing that Meade was not going to attack, began to pull back cautiously on July 4. Meade's men followed at a respectable distance in the ensuing days. On the night of July 13, Lee crossed the Potomac into safety near Williamsport, Pennsylvania.

Yet even though Lee had been allowed to escape after Gettysburg, the battle still stood as a great Northern victory. The second Confederate bid for independence by a stunning victory in the North had failed. Gettysburg, combined with the surrender of Vicksburg on July 4, was, in retrospect, the beginning of the end for the Confederacy. It never really recovered from these dual defeats of early July 1863. Finally, whereas the Confederates inflicted 23,000 casualties on their enemy in the three days of Gettysburg, while suffering 28,000 themselves—more than 7,000 men died on both sides in the three-day battle—Confederate losses represented one-third of Lee's entire combat strength. He could not make up the losses. These losses, combined with Grant's strategy of attrition in the battles that followed in 1864 and 1865, a strategy of attacking and bleeding the Confederates to death, meant that sooner or later the South would have to quit the war.

Both sides spent the rest of 1863 maneuvering against each other in northern Virginia and then went into winter quarters. But Grant was ready to move with the coming of spring. His 1864 grand strategy called for three simultaneous offensive movements. In the West, Sherman would strike southeast from Chattanooga toward Atlanta while Major General Nathaniel Banks (ex-governor of Massachusetts, a political appointee, and a military incompetent) was to move up the Red River to take Shreveport and northwest

Louisiana, then move east to take Mobile and march north to the Alabama capital at Montgomery. (This Red River campaign turned into a fiasco, and the dilatory Banks was justifiably removed by Lincoln.)

In the East, Meade and the Army of the Potomac were to push south from the Rapidan toward Richmond, the object being to destroy Lee's army. Meade had 120,000 men; Lee, facing him, had only 63,000. In addition, Major General Benjamin F. Butler and his 33,000-man Army of the James were prepared to drive up that river toward Richmond. A third army was in the Shenandoah Valley guarding Meade's right flank.

Grant, traveling along and in effect commanding Meade's Army of the Potomac, jumped off on May 4 to drive Lee out of the Wilderness and into open combat while slithering left to gain access to southbound rail lines and to resupply lines from the tributaries of the Chesapeake in eastern Virginia. The result was the Battle of the Wilderness on May 5 through 7, 1864. For two days the armies attacked and counterattacked one another in the Wilderness west of Chancellorsville before the battle ended as a tactical draw. So grim had been the fighting that the Union forces suffered an appalling 15 percent casualty rate (17,500 casualties of 115,000 effectives) and the Confederates' rate stood at 12 percent (7,500 casualties of 60,000).

But Grant refused to pull back despite the carnage and, instead, continued to slide south and east. Attention now shifted to Spotsylvania Court House, a crossroads village southeast of the Wilderness. Lee's men got to the vital spot first and erected defenses to stop Grant. Undeterred, Grant assailed the Confederate positions again and again from May 8 through 19. The fighting was often severe, and casualties were high, but Grant, repulsed at Spotsylvania, again moved off to Lee's right on May 21 to continue his movement toward Richmond while bleeding the Confederates to death in pitched battle.

Lee hastened right to prevent Grant's sliding left to reach Richmond, and the two armies met again briefly at North Anna and then dramatically at Cold Harbor on Richmond's outer defense perimeter, the final major conflict in Grant's move toward Richmond. Here, on June 1 through 3, 1864, along a seven-mile front, the two contestants and their armies slugged it out once again. Lee had taken the vital crossroads of Cold Harbor ahead of him and was well dug in, but Grant nevertheless ordered a frontal attack, believing that one good push would send the Confederates reeling back toward Richmond and end the war. Instead, the Confederate line held in the face of a Federal 40,000-man attack, 7,000 Union soldiers becoming casualties in less than half an hour. It was, one Southern defender said, "inexplicable and incredible butchery."

Grant had suffered 55,000 casualties in the month since his 1864 campaign had begun in the Wilderness, but still he pressed on, moving his army south to and across the James River to City Point, arriving by June 15 (and receiving no help from the incompetent General Butler and his Army of the James). Lee's defensive line now ran from north of Richmond around to the east and down to below Petersburg, 20 miles south of the capital. Grant intended to break this line by besieging Petersburg, a vital rail center. If Petersburg fell, Lee, his army, and Richmond would be denied resupply and would be doomed. Grant knew this, and so did Lee.

To break Grant's encirclement and to draw off some of Grant's army, Lee sent Major General Jubal Early and his cavalry north down the Shenandoah Valley to menace Washington, but, in contrast to 1862 and Jackson's raids on the capital, this time there was no panic and few troops were drawn off to confront Early. The Confederate cavalry raider and his men were driven off, but to make sure this did not happen again, Grant detailed Major General Philip H. Sheridan and his troops to destroy Early's forces in the Shenandoah. Sheridan did just that, defeating Early in three major engagements and finally putting the entire valley to the torch to prevent the Confederates from ever again exploiting its agricultural riches and using it as a broad roadway into the North.

☆ An American Portrait

Jubal A. Early—Early was born in 1816 in Franklin County in southeastern Virginia. He was graduated from the United States Military Academy eighteenth in his class in 1837 as an artillery officer, and fought briefly against the Seminoles in Florida before resigning his commission in 1838. He then read law and began to practice in Rocky Mount, Virginia, being elected to the commonwealth's legislature for one term as a Whig. In January 1847 he became a major in the 1st Virginia Regiment and served in northern Mexico and on garrison duty at Monterrey, being mustered out of service in April 1848.

When the secession crisis arose, Early voted against Virginia leaving the Union at that state's convention; nevertheless, he joined the Confederate Army and as a colonel served with the 24th Virginia Infantry at First Manassas. From 1861 to 1864 he fought with the Army of Northern Virginia on the Peninsula, at Malvern Hill, Second Manassas, Fredericksburg, Chancellorsville, Gettysburg, the Wilderness, and Cold Harbor, rising steadily in rank until appointed lieutenant general in May 1864. Sent into the Shenandoah Valley under independent command the following month, Early made a spirited advance on Washington (which was thwarted) and then carried out further raids on the Federals in the Valley.

Grant sent a 40,000-man army under General Sheridan to check and destroy Early there, resulting in the defeat of Early's men at Winchester, Fisher's Hill, and Cedar Creek and the gradual forcing of the Confederates up the Valley. Finally, in March 1865, in the waning weeks of the war, Early's outnumbered and exhausted forces were almost destroyed at Waynesborough and Lee was forced to relieve him of command, 1,600 men having been captured and his remaining troops having lost confidence in him.

At the end of the war, Early, refusing to accept the defeat of the Confederacy, fled to Mexico and then to Canada. He eventually returned to Lynchburg, Virginia, to resume his practice of the law, but his bitterness toward the Federal government never waned. He died in Lynchburg on March 2, 1894, almost three decades after the war, one of the most unreconstructed Southerners and a longtime leader in creating the myth of the Lost Cause.

☆ An American Portrait

Philip H. Sheridan—Born in Albany, New York, in 1831 and raised in Ohio, Sheridan was one of the few military leaders on either side who did not serve in the Mexican War. Entering West Point in 1848 and being graduated in 1853 thirty-fourth in his class of 49, Sheridan served thereafter on the Rio Grande and in the Northwest.

Unhappy with staff duty with the infantry in southwest Missouri after the outbreak of war in 1861, Sheridan the next year became a colonel in the 2nd Michigan Cavalry and performed in an outstanding manner at Perryville and Stone's River. Raised in rank to major general of volunteers in March 1863, he distinguished himself as a corps commander at Chickamauga and Missionary Ridge.

Because of Sheridan's élan and aggressive style of warmaking, Grant brought him east in 1864 as cavalry commander of the Army of the Potomac. Sheridan reorganized the cavalry service and performed stellar service for Grant as they fought their way south to Richmond and Petersburg by severing Confederate communications with daring and effective raids on Southern rail lines, telegraph lines, and supplies.

In August 1864 Sheridan was appointed head of the Army of the Shenandoah. Here he defeated Jubal Early the next month, carried out a scorched earth policy in the Valley that won him everlasting hatred in the South, and finally inflicted a critical defeat on Early at Waynesborough on March 2, 1865, opening the way into central Virginia for the Union forces.

After the war Sheridan headed the Military Division of the Gulf, served in Texas and Louisiana during the beginning of the Reconstruction process, was promoted to lieutenant general in 1869, and was made general-in-chief of the Army in 1884, succeeding William T. Sherman. Sheridan was promoted to general in 1888, dying that same year in Nosquitt, Massachusetts.

On through the winter of 1864–1865, Grant continued to close the siege lines around Petersburg, ever sidling west to cut off all connections between Petersburg and Richmond and the Confederate armies and their sources of supply farther south. Disease, privation, and desertion were daily companions to the Confederates manning the miles of defensive breastworks around Petersburg for ten long months. Still they held off the Yankees, including an ill-fated attempt on July 30, 1864, by some Pennsylvania coal miners serving in the Union army to blow a hole in the line with 8,000 pounds of blasting powder. But the Confederates' defensive capabilities were limited.

As winter turned to spring and the Union forces finally cut off all outside help to the embattled Confederates, Grant ordered a major assault all along the Petersburg defensive lines to take place on April 2, 1865. The Confederate lines were crushed by this assault, and the government abandoned Richmond, Jefferson Davis fleeing south but subsequently being captured by the cavalry of General James Wilson near Irwinville, Georgia, on May 10, 1865.

Lee and the remnants of his army attempted to escape to the southwest to join up with General Joe Johnston in the Carolinas, but Federal troops shadowed them and finally brought them to a halt at Appomattox Court House, 85 miles west of Petersburg. Here on Sunday, April 9, 1865—Palm Sunday—Lee and Grant sat down in Wilmer McLean's farmhouse parlor to discuss surrender terms. Grant was magnanimous toward his defeated enemies. The actual surrender of the Army of Northern Virginia took place three days later, on April 12.

Johnston subsequently capitulated, with his 18,000 men, to Sherman at Durham Station, North Carolina, near Raleigh, on April 26. Lieutenant General Richard Taylor surrendered his 12,000 troops north of Mobile on May 4; Lieutenant General Simon Bolivar Buckner surrendered General E. Kirby Smith's trans-Mississippi troops at New Orleans on May 26; Smith surrendered Galveston on June 2; and Cherokee chief and Brigadier General Stand Watie capitulated with his Confederate Indian troops near Fort Towson in the Indian Territory on June 23. No more Confederate soldiers stood under arms. The Civil War was over. The carnage had been ended. The Union had been preserved.

THE FIRST MODERN WAR

While precedent can be found in earlier conflicts for certain characteristics of the Civil War, the American war between the states can justifiably be labeled the first modern war. This claim is based on developments in four areas.

In the area of weaponry, it was during the Civil War that rifling was first used extensively in shoulder arms, sidearms, and artillery pieces. Widespread use of repeating rifles was also a Civil War first, as was the limited employment of automatic weapons in the form of the Gatling gun. It was in this war, too, that mobile siege artillery mounted on rail cars was first introduced.

In tactics and strategy we find many practices that were unchanged, but the war was marked by first-time use of extensive trenches and field fortifications (and even wire entanglements) by armies on the field of battle. These gave clear advantages to the defenders and, combined with semiautomatic weapons, were a foretaste of World War I. Tactically, the Civil War also witnessed the first dramatic clash of ironclad warships, the use of the railroad to transport troops to and from battlefields and between battlefields and theaters of war, the widespread use of the telegraph to direct armies, and the use of balloons for reconnaissance. Strategically, the war saw the use of war of attrition against opposing armies, most dramatically in Grant's Eastern strategy in 1864 and 1865, and the directing of the destruction of war against civilian populations to destroy their morale and warmaking capabilities, as in Sherman's March to the Sea. Also, strategy in the North was carried out for the first time through the workings of an embryonic general staff.

In logistics the Civil War witnessed the initiation of mass production in industry and agriculture by both sides in order to bend the entire resources of the sections to sustaining the war effort. It also saw the development of more efficient logistical systems by the governments and the military to support the armies in the field, even if the South's system never functioned as effectively as it could have. The war also saw the first widespread use of the railroads to carry supplies of all types to troops in camp or in the field.

In weaponry, tactics and strategy, logistics, and governmental power, then, the Civil War stands as the first modern war, presenting a foreshadowing of armed conflict in the modern world.

Suggestions for Further Reading

BIGELOW, JOHN, JR., *The Campaign of Chancellorsville: A Strategic and Tactical Study.* New Haven: Yale University Press, 1910.

CARTER, SAMUEL, III, *The Final Fortress: The Campaign for Vicksburg, 1862–1863.* New York: St. Martin's Press, 1980.

CATTON, BRUCE, *Grant Moves South.* Boston: Little, Brown, 1960.

CODDINGTON, EDWIN B., *The Gettysburg Campaign: A Study in Command.* New York: Scribner's, 1968.

CORNISH, DUDLEY T., *The Sable Arm: Black Troops in the Union Army, 1861–1865.* New York: W. W. Norton & Co., Inc., 1966.

DAVIS, BURKE, *Sherman's March*. New York: Random House, 1980.

DOWNEY, FAIRFAX D., *Storming of the Gateway: Chattanooga, 1863*. New York: David McKay, 1960.

FELLMAN, MICHAEL, *Inside War: The Guerrilla Conflict in Missouri During the American Civil War*. New York: Oxford University Press, 1989.

FOOTE, SHELBY, *The Civil War,* 3 vols. New York: Random House, 1958–1974.

GOVEN, GILBERT E., and JAMES W. LIVINGOOD, *A Different Valor: The Story of General Joseph E. Johnston*. Indianapolis: Bobbs-Merrill, 1956.

GRANT, ULYSSES S., *Personal Memoirs of U. S. Grant,* 2 vols. New York: Webster, 1885.

HAGERMAN, EDWARD, *The American Civil War and the Origins of Modern Warfare*. Bloomington and Indianapolis: Indiana University Press, 1988.

HORN, STANLEY F., *The Decisive Battle of Nashville*. Baton Rouge: Louisiana State University Press, 1956.

LAMERS, WILLIAM M., *The Edge of Glory: A Biography of General William S. Rosecrans, U.S.A.* New York: Harcourt, Brace, 1961.

MCDONOUGH, JAMES L., *Chattanooga—A Death Grip on the Confederacy.* Knoxville: University of Tennessee Press, 1984.

MCDONOUGH, JAMES L., and JAMES P. JONES, *War So Terrible: Sherman and Atlanta*. New York: W. W. Norton & Co., Inc., 1987.

MCPHERSON, JAMES M., *The Negro's Civil War*. New York: Pantheon, 1965.

PFANZ, HARRY W., *Gettysburg: The Second Day*. Chapel Hill: University of North Carolina Press, 1987.

ROBERTSON, JAMES I., JR., *General A. P. Hill: The Story of a Confederate Warrior*. New York: Random House, 1987.

SOMMERS, RICHARD, *Richmond Redeemed: The Siege at Petersburg*. Garden City, NY: Double-day, 1981.

STACKPOLE, EDWARD J., *Chancellorsville: Lee's Greatest Battle*. Harrisburg, PA: Stackpole, 1958.

STEERE, EDWARD, *The Wilderness Campaign*. Harrisburg, PA: Stackpole, 1960.

TUCKER, GLENN, *Chickamauga*. Indianapolis: Bobbs-Merrill, 1961.

☆6

Military Arm
of an Expanding Nation,
1865–1914

With the conclusion of the Southern bid for independence in 1865, the United States military forces had successfully met their greatest challenge to date, but other missions lay ahead as the nation grew and prospered during the decades that followed. At the end of the fighting there still remained the duty of military occupation of the South during Reconstruction. There was also the emerging responsibility of protecting America's pioneers as they flooded into the trans-Mississippi West by overland wagon and on the transcontinentals' rails of steel seeking to exploit and develop the riches of that vast area from the Mississippi River to the Rockies. Here they would be met by strenuous—if futile—resistance by the Native Americans living there.

Back east there was the constabulary task of containing the domestic violence attendant on the nation's rapid move toward industrialization, a transition that time and again brought in its wake confrontation between owners and workers. When federal forces were too few to contain the violence, state after state turned to creating its own military forces, and, as a result, both the Army and the Navy soon found that they had formidable martial competitors for money, influence, and public support.

Meanwhile, America's armed services were also in the throes of internal controversy over what a modern military force should be. The advocates of professionalism and reform locked horns with the counselors of retrenchment, privilege, and established military practices, their disputes testing the patience and wisdom of the nation's policy-makers.

These internal developments, which led to the emergence of the new, modern U.S. Army, U.S. Navy, and Marine Corps, were tested in action at the turn of the century when American politics and policies led to military intervention in Cuba, the Philippines,

China, and the Caribbean basin. Not without evidence of a lack of adequate preparation, training, and perspective, the three armed services successfully met these tests of arms. It is well that they did, for just around the corner lay participation in World War I, the greatest military confrontation to date in the history of the world.

DEMOBILIZATION AND RECONSTRUCTION

Throughout its history the United States has always had a love–hate relationship with its military. During wartime its men under arms have been lionized as defenders of its most sacred values. No sacrifice has been deemed too great to sustain them in their deeds of valor. With the coming of peace, however, the cry has gone up to "send the boys home" and curb the military. The military has then been seen as an unnecessary drain on the nation's economy if not as a self-serving, antidemocratic, and antiliberal bureaucracy dedicated only to its own purposes, even to the point of creating phantom enemies at home or abroad to ensure its continued parasitic existence. America, it would seem, can envision only all-out war or all-out peace and, therefore, sees its military only as self-sacrificing heroes or self-serving villains. As a result, during times of peace the nation's armed forces have always had to fight for their existence against the cries of peace and parsimony that have stirred the nation's heart.

And so it was after the Civil War. Frenzied enthusiasm was displayed by the admiring crowds in the nation's capital in May 1865 as 100,000 men of Sherman's and Meade's armies, symbolically representing the half-million men then dressed in Union blue, marched down Pennsylvania Avenue; yet retrenchment was the order of the day. General Philip Sheridan led 52,000 men to the Mexican border to send a clear signal from the United States government to the French emperor Napoleon III that his attempt to take over Mexico as a colony would not be tolerated, and occupation troops would obviously be needed in the conquered South for some time. Nevertheless, the Army was soon contracted precipitously.

By late 1866, only 11,043 volunteers (10,000 of whom were blacks) were still in uniform. That same year Congress authorized the regulars to a strength of only 54,302. For 1869 the authorization was down to 37,000, and by 1876 the maximum strength had been slashed to only 27,442. In 1877 Congress even failed to pass an appropriations bill for the service. The Army had to buy supplies on credit, and pay simply fell into arrears until Congress voted funds the next year, the officers in the meantime borrowing money so that they and their men could live.

The Navy fared no better. A resurgence of the South was unthinkable; 3,000 miles of water separated the country from any possible foreign enemy; and peace was now believed to be inevitable. From a force of 700-plus warships in its inventory (including 65 ironclads) and 60,000 officers and men in 1865, it had been reduced by 1880 to only 48 ships capable of combat and only about 8,000 personnel. In size it stood twelfth in the world—behind Denmark, China, and Chile. The great ironclads of Civil War fame lay rotting at their wharves, and other river craft had been sold off. A handful of monitors and sailing craft was all that was left of the mighty Civil War Navy. The Navy's weakness, like the Army's, reflected the values of the American public they served.

Occupation of the defeated South was onerous duty for the Army. During the conflict, civilian governors had been established as the Federals regained possession of the seceded states, but martial law meant that the local military commanders and their troops really maintained law and order. Everyone had seemed to assume that shortly after the war ended, civilian governments would be reestablished and the troops would go home. But President Andrew Johnson shortly got involved in a dispute with the Radical Republicans in Congress over what kind of reconstruction should be imposed on the South, and the Army found itself dragged into the jurisdictional fight.

Johnson essentially wanted to carry out his predecessor's conciliatory "forgive and forget" plans for the South, a generous scheme that was well enunciated in Lincoln's second inaugural address of March 4, 1865: "With malice toward none, with charity for all...let us strive on to finish the work we are in, to bind up the nation's wounds...." Constitutionally, Lincoln, then Johnson, believed they had the right to reconstruct the Old Confederacy because the South, by its acts of secession and war, had violated federal law, and the Constitution provides that the president "shall have power to grant reprieves and pardons for offenses against the United States." Reconstruction, according to Lincoln and Johnson, was a presidential prerogative. The South and the Southern Democrats agreed, since Johnson, they knew, would treat them with compassion.

But the so-called Radical Republicans in control of Congress did not agree. They argued that leniency would merely put the old Southern aristocracy—who had started and directed the war—back in power, to the detriment of the mass of the Southern whites and, clearly, of the now-emancipated blacks. A new South could not be created without removing the still-recalcitrant Southern leaders from power, without driving home to all Southerners the fact that they had lost the war and that things could not continue as before. A new, less aristocratic and more democratic leadership had to arise from among the Southern people. Besides, it was a moral affront to all those who had fought and died for the Union to allow the leaders of the bloody rebellion to resume their places unchastened and unrepentant. Constitutionally, the Radical Republicans argued, Congress alone had the right of reconstruction, since the Southern states, by their own admission, had left the Union. The setting of the conditions for bringing territories into the Union was, they asserted, clearly a congressional, not a presidential, prerogative. Thus the issue was joined, and the Army found itself caught up in its complexities.

One thing was clear. Many ex-Confederates were unrepentant and made life miserable for the occupying Army troops (many of whom were black) not only by openly insulting them but also by creating a wave of violence against the 3.5 million freedmen in the South, who had to be protected. This was led by resistance societies such as the Ku Klux Klan, one of whose founders was ex-Confederate general Nathan Bedford Forrest, and the Knights of the White Camellia. Faced with Southern intransigence and widespread turbulence too great for it to control, the Army turned to Congress and the Radical Republicans for help.

Secretary of War Edwin M. Stanton and General-in-Chief Ulysses S. Grant soon found themselves at cross-purposes with President Johnson, who took steps to remove them both. Congress, therefore, to protect them and its more stringent plans for the South (Johnson's "reconstructed" state governments' validity having already been rejected by Congress), passed the Tenure of Office Act and the Command of the Army Act in March

1867, over Johnson's veto. The first of these acts—of very questionable constitutionality—forbade the president to remove any cabinet member (in other words, Stanton) from office without the consent of the Senate. The second mandated that all presidential orders to the Army had to be issued through the general-in-chief, who could not be removed without the consent of the Senate. These acts were followed by the Reconstruction Acts of 1867, which divided the South into five military districts wherein military law was superior to all civilian law. These Reconstruction Acts also directed the military to register freedmen—and all other eligibles—to vote. When Grant followed up these laws by directing the five major generals in charge in the South to follow only the orders of Congress, Johnson was shorn of any effective power over the military in the region.

Johnson, enraged by these usurpations of his authority, fired Stanton without the Senate's approval and put the reluctant Grant in his place. Grant gave the office back to Stanton after Congress reconvened, and Stanton would not vacate the office to Johnson's next appointee, General Lorenzo Thomas. The House of Representatives then drew up articles of impeachment against the president. Johnson was impeached but not convicted, although the Senate came within one vote of removing him from office. Had they carried the vote, it would have placed the Radical Republican president *pro tempore* of the Senate, Benjamin Wade of Ohio, in the presidency.

But the impeachment and trial neutralized Johnson politically anyway, and the "Rule of the Major Generals" began in earnest in the South. Under Army and Radical Republican–appointee rule, the former Confederacy lived under military and Republican domain until 1877. Safe and loyal Republican militia units were created to help the Army maintain law and order in the area, albeit with questionable efficiency given the Army's virtually impossible task of policing the entire South and given the reduction of its numbers, especially in the mid-1870s, when Democrat-supported all-white militia units were formed in the South to counter the Army and the Republican militias.

The Army was pulled out of the Old Confederacy in early 1877, after the famous Compromise of 1877 was consummated. In 1869 the Radical Republicans had clear sailing to reconstruct the South according to their own lights and to advance their political fortunes because of their firm control of Congress and a pliant—if not naive—Ulysses S. Grant in the White House. But time would work against them. The Northern populace gradually grew tired of the crusade for a fundamental reconstruction of the South and for full citizenship rights and economic opportunities for the ex-slaves and poor whites. The Republican party split in 1872 over the scandals emanating from Grant's appointees to office and from the contracts for building the transcontinental railroads. The Panic of 1873 caused widespread unemployment and hardship, and the national Democrats began to rebound from being labeled "the party of secession." As the Democrats began to win elections (including gaining a majority in the House of Representatives in 1874), the Republicans were forced to consider abandoning Reconstruction as a politically profitless venture.

When the presidential election of 1876 between Republican Rutherford B. Hayes of Ohio and Democrat Samuel J. Tilden of New York ended in an electoral college deadlock over disputed election returns from four states, the Republicans cut a deal with the Southern Democrats to award the presidency to Hayes without a fight in return for an end to Reconstruction. Accordingly, the newly inaugurated Hayes pulled the troops out of the South in April 1877, consigning the rule in the region to the "Redeemers," the old aristocratic ruling class. This ensured that black civil rights would be a dead letter thereafter, and white supremacy was soon fully reestablished throughout the South.

Thus Reconstruction was ended by a crass political deal in an atmosphere of public apathy over the whole issue. The Army, attempting to execute an ambiguous national policy, always understrength in the occupied South with a maximum of only 17,000 troops, and perennially unable to carry out effectively its duty of pacification, was only too happy to leave. Minuscule in size with a total of only about 26,000 men, the Army needed its troops elsewhere, not only on coastal artillery defense duties in the East but also to face the continuing Indian menace in the West.

CONSTABULARY DUTY IN THE WEST

The 270,000 Native Americans who lived west of the Mississippi were no particular danger to the two million whites there, but they lived and hunted on lands coveted by the expanding white population for ranching, farming, or the extraction of their mineral wealth. American Indian policy since the early decades of the century had been simply to push them west onto marginal lands designated as reservations. The majority of the Indian tribes had reluctantly accepted this policy and had moved west, only to find that further encroachments by the expanding whites forced them to move again and again, often under terrible conditions because the agents appointed to look after the Indians' welfare were frequently both incompetent and dishonest.

In the years after the Civil War, perhaps 100,000 Indians (only a percentage of whom were warriors, the rest being women, children, and the elderly) decided that they would fight back rather than see their lands taken again and their way of life obliterated. These Plains Indian warriors, mounted on ponies, using rifles, and displaying great martial skill and bravery, constituted excellent light cavalry forces and were more than a minor challenge to the troops assigned to police them from their widely scattered posts in an area stretching from the Canadian border to Mexico. Fortunately for the Army, tribal alliances between the Indian nations were hard to create and sustain, and the soldiers had superior weapons and logistical support and greater numbers as the Indian wars continued to blaze in the West.

However individual officers and men looked upon their campaigning against the often-defenseless Indians, the policy of the government was clear, and orders were passed down and obeyed. The Indians were to be placed on and confined to reservations. Those defying these steps were to be treated as enemies and forced to comply by whatever means necessary. To carry out their orders, the 1,000-man army stationed on the frontier (including two regiments of infantry and two of cavalry made up of "buffalo soldiers," ex-slave and free black enlistees, most former Union soldiers, serving under white officers) soon discovered four successful strategies that, used complementarily, would ensure success against the Indians. First, well-planned campaigns should be carried out, winter campaigns being especially effective; second, converging columns should be used to trap the Indians and force them to fight or surrender; third, Indian camps, along with their food, shelter, and horses, should be attacked and destroyed; and fourth, friendly Indians should be used as scouts and regular forces.

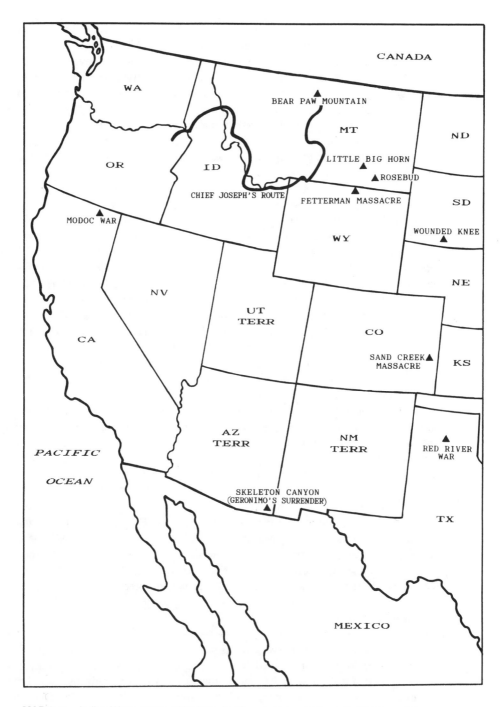

MAP 6–1   Indian Wars, 1866–1890.(*Used with permission of Anne C. Christensen.*)

The Indian wars lasted from 1866 to 1890 and included over 1,000 separate engagements. The Southern Plains Indians were the first to resist the swelling white tide and the first to suffer defeat at the hands of the frontier army of about 4,000 men in that area. The Indian tribes on the Southern Plains—the Arapahoes, Cheyennes, Comanches, and Kiowas—were fine soldiers but could not unite effectively to fight off the intruders, nor could they control the "peace" factions among them who were unwilling to resist. When their growing reign of terror against the white settlers became too great a problem, the government in 1874 turned the task of pacification over to the Army. The result was the Red River War, in which 3,000 troops moving in five converging columns defeated the Indians in a year-long struggle and forced them to agree to move onto reservations in the Indian Territory (now Oklahoma).

The Army's problems with the Indians of the Sioux confederation on the Northern Plains, however, were much more difficult to solve and were settled only after much blood had been shed. The Sioux, numbering 30,000 and roaming the plains in search of buffalo, were capable of united action and were led by their three great war chiefs Sitting Bull, Red Cloud, and Crazy Horse. The Sioux had been resisting white infiltration onto their hunting grounds ever since 1866, when the government tried to build a road, the Bozeman Trail from Wyoming to Montana, through their territory. The first round went to the skillful Oglala Sioux under Red Cloud, who held the men of Fort Phil Kearney in Wyoming just south of the Montana border under limited siege and harassment for three years; wiped out 80 men under Captain William J. Fetterman in the December 1866 "Fetterman Massacre" near there, in which the bodies of the soldiers were mutilated; and eventually forced the abandonment of the fort and the road-building project.

Thereafter things were comparatively quiet on the Northern Plains, but in 1875 gold was discovered in the Black Hills in the Sioux reserve and fortune-seeking miners by the thousands began to pour in, the Army being unable to stop them. Red Cloud, Sitting Bull, and Crazy Horse thereupon led a large number of Sioux into Montana to prepare for a showdown with the protectors of the white intruders. When these Indians refused to disperse, Lieutenant General Philip Sheridan, commander of the Division of the Missouri, ordered a giant converging-column expedition to force their return.

Brigadier General George Crook, with 1,000 men and 260 Crow and Shoshone warriors, would move north from Fort Fetterman in Wyoming. Colonel John Gibbon, with 475 soldiers and 25 Crows, would move southeast from Forts Shaw and Montana toward the Sioux encampment in the southeastern part of that territory. Brigadier General Alfred H. Terry would approach from the east from the Dakota Territory with 925 men and 40 Indian scouts. Sheridan's plan was solid, but what neither he nor anyone else realized was that thousands of Sioux warriors were prepared to fight them to the death.

☆   An American Portrait

George Crook—Crook, renowned for his campaigns against the Indians in the West but little known for his sympathies toward his Native American foes (he wanted them to have equal rights under the law and equal privileges as American citizens), was born near Dayton, Ohio, in 1829. Upon being graduated from West Point in 1852 as a lieutenant of infantry, he served in the Northwest until the outbreak of the Civil War.

In September 1861, Crook was made a colonel of volunteers in the 36th Ohio Infantry and was raised to brevet major in the regulars in May 1862 for his victory at Lewisburg in western Virginia. As a brevet brigadier general of volunteers, he served at South Mountain and Antietam. The next year, in command of a cavalry division of the Army of the Cumberland, he participated in the Battle of Chickamauga. Crook saw action in 1864 in West Virginia and in command of a corps of Sheridan's Army of the Shenandoah, there participating in all major battles and rising in rank to brevet major general in the regulars. He was with Sheridan at Petersburg in 1865.

After the war, Crook reverted to his regular rank of lieutenant colonel of infantry and spent three years as commander of the district around Boise, Idaho, putting down an Indian war there. In 1871 he was sent south by President Grant to pacify the Indians in northern Arizona. In 1875, now a brigadier general, he was named commander of the Department of the Platte, in this northern frontier post playing a prominent role in the Sioux war of 1876.

In 1882 Crook was sent back to Arizona to again pacify the Indians in that territory, and the next year he successfully pursued Geronimo and the Chiricahua Apaches into the Sierra Madre Mountains across the border in Mexico. When Geronimo again fled into the Sierra Madres in 1885, Crook's successor, General Nelson A. Miles, pursued him across the border for a second time.

The years from 1886 through 1888 saw Crook again transferred north to take up his duties as commander of the Department of the Platte. In April 1888 he reached the pinnacle of his career when he was promoted to major general and named commander of the Division of the Missouri, headquartered in Chicago. This modest, nondrinking, and unassuming leader of the Army's wars against the Indians died on March 20, 1890, far ahead of the nation's civilian and military leaders in his respectful attitudes toward the Amerindians.

☆   An American Portrait

Alfred H. Terry—Born in Hartford, Connecticut, in 1827, Terry attended Yale Law School for one year. He left after he passed the bar examination. His first military experience came in 1861, when he was named colonel in the 2nd Connecticut Militia. He subsequently served at First Manassas. Terry then became colonel of the 7th Connecticut Volunteers and took part in many actions along the Atlantic coast, being raised in rank to brigadier general of volunteers in April 1862.

After participating in Flag Officer Samuel F. du Pont's attack on Charleston in 1863, he spent a full year with the Army of the James under Benjamin F. Butler. In January 1865, Terry took over command of the Union assault on Fort Fisher, North Carolina (after Butler's failure of the month before), bringing the operation to a successful conclusion and being brevetted a brigadier general in the regular Army. He finished his Civil War service by occupying Wilmington, North Carolina; joining up with Sherman's advancing forces; and finally serving in the Army of the Ohio.

In the postwar years he was assigned to the Army's constabulary forces in the West, commanding the Department of Dakota for a total of 17 years (a 3-year stint as commander of the Department of the South interrupted this duty). In 1876 he was in personal command of the punitive expedition into the Yellowstone-Bighorn area against the Sioux, an expedition marred by "Custer's Last Stand" at the Little Bighorn on June 25.

FIGURE 6–1 Alfred H. Terry. (*National Archives, Washington, D.C.*)

In the aftermath of the massacre, Terry steadfastly refused to excoriate the dead Custer for his disobedience to orders that contributed to the tragedy. In 1877 he personally led the negotiations with Sitting Bull that sent the Indians to reservations and brought the Sioux expedition to an end.

Terry's last service came in 1886, when, as a major general, he took command of the Division of the Missouri. The general retired in 1888 as one of the few general officers on duty in the postwar years who was not a West Point graduate and as an officer who was uniquely able to elicit the cooperation of both his superiors and those under him in his long years of service. He moved back to New Haven after his retirement from the Army, where he died on December 16, 1890, one of the best-loved officers of his time.

Crook's column from the south was attacked on June 17, 1876, at Rosebud Creek, just north of the Montana border, by 1,500 Sioux and Cheyenne warriors. Defeated in a six-hour battle, it was forced to turn back. Meanwhile, the other two columns continued to advance, attempting to drive the Sioux into the valley of the Little Bighorn River, 50 miles to the north of the Rosebud. The 7th Cavalry Regiment under Lieutenant Colonel George Armstrong Custer, part of Terry's force, was ordered to cross the Rosebud and move north along the river while the combined forces of Terry and Gibbon moved south, entrapping the Sioux between them.

On June 25, Custer arrived in the vicinity of the Sioux encampment and, without waiting for Terry and Gibbon and apparently without realizing the numbers of his enemy (now numbering 7,000 to 10,000 by various estimates, perhaps 1,500 to 2,000 of whom were warriors), rashly sent his men forward to attack in three columns. The left and center columns ran into stiff resistance and were forced on the defensive until two days later, when Gibbon and Terry arrived on the scene. The third column of 210 men, led by Custer himself and moving to the right, soon found itself surrounded by over 1,000 Indians under Crazy Horse. A fight lasting perhaps two hours ensued. When Terry and Gibbon's men arrived on the scene on June 27, they found that Custer's men had been wiped out to the last man. About 50 percent of the 7th Cavalry Regiment had been killed that one day in the Battle of the Little Bighorn.

☆   An American Portrait

George Armstrong Custer—Born in Harrison County, Ohio, in 1839, Custer entered the United States Military Academy in 1857 and was graduated four years later. He stood last in his class of 34 cadets, his negligence and mischievousness being more dominant than his intelligence in his West Point years.

His dubious honor of being the class "goat" notwithstanding, Custer served well during the Civil War and gained fame as a dashing cavalry officer, often being hailed as the "Boy General." First assigned to the defense of Washington, in February 1862 he joined the 5th Cavalry and served as a captain of volunteers and an aide to General McClellan during the Peninsula campaign. In June 1863 he was raised in rank to brigadier general as the head of a Michigan cavalry brigade and thereafter took part in the Gettysburg and subsequent Virginia battles.

His fame as a cavalry officer was enhanced in 1864 when, as a captain in the regular Army, he participated in General Philip Sheridan's campaigns, being brevetted a lieutenant colonel after Winchester and a major general of volunteers in October. In the closing days of the war, Custer was in the van of the pursuit of Robert E. Lee west from Petersburg. He received the Confederate flag of truce on April 9 and was made a major general of volunteers three days after the surrender document was signed at Appomattox on April 12, 1865.

FIGURE 6–2   George A. Custer. (*National Archives, Washington, D.C.*)

Reverting to his regular rank of captain, Custer joined the 5th Cavalry on Indian constabulary duty in the Southwest. In July 1866 he was made lieutenant colonel in the newly organized 7th Cavalry and served in active leadership of the unit until his death, with the exception of one year, when he was suspended from command for being absent from duty.

In November 1868 he was credited with the victory over Black Kettle's Cheyennes in the Battle of the Washita and went on to various duties on the northern Indian frontier. In 1876 he earned the wrath of President Grant for testifying before a congressional committee against Secretary of War William W. Belknap regarding fraud in the Indian service and was deprived of command by the president. But there was such an outcry against this harsh action that Grant relented. Custer was restored to his post just in time to lead the 7th Cavalry to its death on the Little Bighorn River on June 25, 1876. The character and actions of Custer during the Indian wars and in the advance on the Sioux in June 1876 have been the subject of widespread interest and heated controversy down to the present day.

The news of "Custer's Last Stand" stunned the nation in the midst of its centennial celebration, and a clamor for vengeance resulted. Accordingly, the Army poured thousands of men into the Montana Territory, and the Sioux, who had dispersed after the battle to resume their way of life, were subdued in a campaign that ran throughout the winter of 1876–1877. By spring 1877, almost all the Sioux warriors had surrendered and their tribesmen had been herded onto reservations.

Other campaigns were carried out against the non-Plains Indians during these years: the Modoc War of 1872–1873 on the California-Oregon border; the Nez Perce War of 1877 in the Northwest, in which the Army pursued over 800 Indians almost 1,700 miles in three months; and the Bannock, Sheepeater, and Ute Wars in Idaho and Colorado in 1878–1879. The last great Indian campaign was carried out against a band of renegade Apaches and their great war leader Geronimo—Cochise and other Apache leaders having accepted peace in 1872—and ended in 1886. It was directed by General Crook, who, abandoning clumsy wagon trains, used mules instead for greater mobility, enlisted friendly Apaches to his side, and pursued Geronimo and his Apaches wherever they went through mountains and deserts—and even on one occasion across the border into Mexico—until finally running them down.

The last major "incident" of the Indian wars occurred in 1890 in South Dakota at Wounded Knee Creek, when a group of Sioux, caught up in the new Ghost Dance religion that promised a resurgence of Indian glory and immunity to the white man's bullets, left their reservation. They were met by some soldiers at Wounded Knee and told to turn over their rifles and return to their reservation. A scuffle ensued that turned into a frenzied shooting spree by both sides, the soldiers using their four rapid-fire Hotchkiss cannon. When it was over, some 150 Indians, including many women and children, lay dead; 62 soldiers were dead or wounded. The Sioux subsequently returned to their reservation in early January 1891, the tragedy of Wounded Knee perhaps a fitting finale to a campaign between determined foes, the end being predetermined by the soldiers' numerical and technological superiority.

LABOR VIOLENCE AND THE NATIONAL GUARD MOVEMENT

Trial by combat against the Indians and disagreeable occupation duty in the South were not the only onerous challenges facing the Army in the decades following the Civil War, for the nation was not only changing by expanding rapidly into the West, but it was also undergoing a profound internal transmutation as industrialization and urbanization proceeded by leaps and bounds. This meant a diminution of the nation's agricultural predominance that had held sway since colonial times, but, of greater importance, it led to tremendous alterations in the modes of production in manufactured goods. These changes led to diminished personal and vocational security for the country's urban industrial workers as productive units became larger and larger and market forces more and more impersonal. Furthermore, the great influx of European immigrants into the United States (25 million between 1865 and 1914) meant that somehow they had to be assimilated economically and culturally into the nation's life. Finally, all of these changes led to labor violence between the forces of management and organized labor, drawing the nation's military into these domestic confrontations.

After the Civil War, many American laborers began to organize to protect their rights and to go out on strike if necessary to ensure decent incomes and safe working conditions. Most labor–management disputes were nonviolent, but not all. In 1877, the members of the railroad brotherhoods (unions) walked off the job over wage reductions and other issues. Violence soon followed, especially in Pittsburgh. With some two-thirds of America's railroads shut down by the spreading strike, and with the states' governors powerless to do anything either because they had no state militias in existence or because their militias sided with the strikers, the state executives called for federal assistance. President Rutherford B. Hayes ordered 2,000 soldiers and marines into various troubled areas to restore law and order. This set a post–Civil War precedent, and for the next 20 years the military was called upon time and again to undertake the unwelcome duty of using force against American citizens.

Most notable in this regard was the Pullman strike of 1894, in which President Grover Cleveland sent 2,000 soldiers under Major General Nelson A. Miles into Chicago to restore peace and to "assure the unimpeded passage of the U.S. mails" (mail cars were among those that workers refused to handle if a Pullman sleeper car was in the train's makeup). This intervention was carried out despite the protests of Illinois Governor John Peter Altgeld, but it was conducted with great restraint, bringing praise to the Army even though diehard labor unionists saw the move as unconstitutional and unnecessary.

☆ An American Portrait

Nelson A. Miles—Miles, like Alfred H. Terry a non–West Pointer who made it to the top of his military profession in the half-century after the Civil War, was born near Westminster, Massachusetts, in 1839. When the war came in 1861, Miles, a crockery clerk, recruited a company of volunteers for the 22nd Massachusetts Regiment and received his first military commission as a captain of infantry.

Too young and inexperienced to lead his troops during the Peninsula campaign, Miles was assigned to the staff of General O. O. Howard. But he was commended for gallantry at Fair Oaks and was raised to the rank of lieutenant colonel of his regiment. At Antietam the young officer assumed command of his regiment when its colonel was wounded, and within two weeks of the battle Miles had been appointed to regular command of that unit.

Wounded at Fredericksburg in December 1862 and again at Chancellorsville in May 1863 (being presented with the Congressional Medal of Honor in 1892 for his gallant leadership at Chancellorsville), Miles went on to fight at the Wilderness, Spotsylvania Court House, and Petersburg.

At war's end, Miles was made a major general and commander of II Army Corps, this at 26 years of age. He was appointed a colonel in the regulars in July 1866 and was assigned to the infantry. Beginning in 1869 and for 15 years thereafter he served in the West in the campaigns against the Cheyenne, Kiowa, Comanche, Sioux, Nez Perce, and Bannock Indian tribes. In 1880 he was made brigadier general and commander of the Department of the Columbia; in 1886 he succeeded General George Crook in the operations against Geronimo; and in 1888 he was named to head the sprawling Division of the Pacific, in this capacity directing the 1890–1891 winter campaign against the Sioux, which ended with the bloody encounter at Wounded Knee.

In 1894, as commander of the Division of the Missouri in Chicago, Miles and his soldiers were reluctantly drawn into domestic constabulary duty as the Army was called in to restore order and keep the trains moving during the Pullman strike of that year. In the next year, 1895, he became commanding general of the Army, a position in which, during the Spanish-American War, he clashed repeatedly with Secretary of War Russell A. Alger. This problem, combined with his obvious political ambitions, precluded his personally leading the troops at Santiago in 1898 as he wished. He did, however, lead the expedition to Puerto Rico to end Spanish rule there. His actions and attitudes during the war helped convince reformers that serious problems existed in the Army's command structure and led to the creation of a general staff.

Raised in rank to lieutenant general in 1901, the following year, Miles visited the Philippines during the insurrection there and wrote a report critical of American officers and enlisted men in their treatment of the Filipinos. He retired in 1903 but remained active in military and patriotic affairs until his death in May 1925, in his 86th year. Few military leaders, West Point and non–West Point alike, had seen as much action in as many theaters and in as many types of warfare as had Nelson A. Miles in his 42 years of Army service.

But the intermittent labor violence had greater effects on America's military than merely requiring the soldiers to act, all too often, as strikebreakers. The violence of 1877 and thereafter led to the various states either creating or reactivating state volunteer military forces, or militia, now known as the National Guard. By 1879 a National Guard Association had already been formed, and between 1881 and 1892 every state in the Union created its own National Guard units. During the years between 1888 and 1898, 15 states also established naval militias with a total enrollment of over 4,000 men, half the size of the regular Navy.

While the Guard's primary duty was clearly to squelch labor violence (between 1877 and 1903, Guard units were called out over 300 times to police strikes), the National Guard Association and the naval militias, in lobbying for money from Congress, regularly stressed their role as reserve forces for the Army and Navy. They were organizations of citizen-soldiers or -sailors, they said, who would expeditiously answer the nation's call to duty in times of domestic or foreign threat, as they had in the past, a factual but questionable reference to the record of America's militia units in previous wars.

Nevertheless, with strong public support for state-controlled military units in the face of real or potential domestic violence, the Guard and naval militias became major factors in America's armed forces, and the guard became a serious competitor against the regular army for support from Congress. By 1899 there were 100,000 men in National Guard units, as opposed to only 80,670 regulars. This was not an inconsequential fact, since the regulars in both the Army and the Navy during these same years were attempting to reform, upgrade, and professionalize themselves to serve the nation better—this in the face of strong antidemocratic and elitist charges incessantly leveled against America's armed forces.

BIRTH OF THE MODERN ARMY

The post–Civil War Army was ripe for reform on many counts. Many of its persistent internal difficulties resulted from its command structure. Line officers had chronic problems with the staff officers who ran the various Army bureaus. In theory, the bureaus were supposed to serve the officers and men in the field according to their needs. In fact, they often seemed to be serving themselves, with little regard for the real requirements of the 27,000 officers and men stationed at 100-plus posts throughout the country, in coastal defense artillery units, in the South, and along the Mexican border. Commanding generals William T. Sherman (1869–1883) and Philip Sheridan (1884–1888) tried manfully to bring about necessary changes in the Army bureaucracy to make it more modern and professional, but they could make no notable gains.

One piece of evidence of the Army's lack of efficient and realistic planning could be found in its snail-like pace in adopting the new and better weapons systems being accepted elsewhere in the Western world. The muzzle-loading rifle of Civil War vintage was not replaced after the war but only converted to breech-loading. Not until 1872 did the service accept a new rifle, this the .45-caliber single-shot "trapdoor" Springfield (so named because its breech snapped downward like an attic access door). The 1873 Springfield, despite the fact that it fired a black powder cartridge when better rifles firing smokeless cartridges were available, remained the standard infantry shoulder weapon for 20 years. Only in 1893 was the five-shot, .30-caliber Danish Krag-Jorgensen rifle, which fired smokeless cartridges, adopted, and not until 1897 was the "Krag" issued to all the troops.

Likewise, the adoption of Gatling and other machine guns was very slow. Machine guns were not even perceived as having much value for infantry. Rather, having proved vulnerable to quick-firing guns in the Franco-Prussian and Russo-Japanese Wars, they were seen only as offensive adjuncts to artillery and as defensive devices for protecting bridges. Breech-loading artillery pieces were adopted only slowly and even then used black powder.

But dilatory and frustrating as the adoption of modern weaponry may have been, the "armed progressives" in the Army faced even greater problems. These reformers were very much aware of the military advances being made in England and Germany in

FIGURE   6–3 .45-cal. "trapdoor" Springfield rifle.(*Smithsonian Institution, Washington, D.C.*)

particular and the possibility of war against a strong foreign enemy. They fervently believed that the day had passed when a small, poorly trained, and poorly equipped army, officered by seniority-protected line and staff officers deficient in modern military methods and technologies, supplemented by citizen-soldiers, and with no general staff for overall direction, could best serve the nation. What was needed, they argued, were better, more professionally trained officers chosen on the basis of merit and a larger, more professionally trained and better-equipped corps of enlisted men. In a word, the Army badly needed reform from top to bottom to compete with the growing and better-equipped European armies. But bringing these reforms to fruition was a long, hard task.

One of the Army progressives' strongest supporters was William T. Sherman in his years as commanding general. He supported the newly reestablished Artillery School at Fort Monroe, Virginia, and the Engineering School of Application, besides founding the School of Application for Infantry and Cavalry at Fort Leavenworth, Kansas, in 1881. Schools were also founded during these years for the Signal Corps, the Hospital Corps, and the Army Medical Corps. Sherman also backed the professionalism-promoting Military Service Institution in 1878, which began publication of its influential *Journal* and played a leading role in lobbying for the Army's needs. Successors to Sherman backed

FIGURE   6–4 .30-cal. Krag-Jorgensen rifle.(*Smithsonian Institution, Washington, D.C.*)

many other agencies that sought to modernize the Army, such as the Military Information Division in 1889 for policy studies, the Army General Service and Staff College to give further training to rising senior officers, and the top-level Army War College in Washington in 1903.

The year 1903 also saw the long-delayed creation of a general staff to coordinate and supervise all facets of the Army's activities. While the general staff was initially rather small and weak, with undefined responsibilities relative to the bureau chiefs when first created at the urging of Secretary of War Elihu Root, a Wall Street lawyer, the "Root reforms" spelled the beginning of the end for the retention of power by the bureau chiefs and the beginning of a more professional direction and coordination at the highest levels.

☆   An American Portrait

Elihu Root—Born in 1845 in Clinton, New York, Elihu Root never served in the armed forces, but as secretary of war from 1899 to 1904, he instituted the "Root reforms" that laid the organizational groundwork for the modern Army.

Receiving his education at Hamilton College, where his father taught, Root was rejected for military service in the Civil War because of poor health, but went on to law school and by the 1890s had become a prominent lawyer in New York City and a power in the Republican party.

He accepted appointment to the position of secretary of war by President William McKinley primarily to help the nation frame the governments of the territories of Cuba, Puerto Rico, and the Philippines, acquired in the Spanish-American War. He was, however, impressed with the findings of an investigating commission headed by Major General Granville M. Dodge that the Army was badly in need of reform and reorganization, as the lack of planning and operational problems during the recent war clearly revealed.

His reforms were designed to modernize the Army. They were based on his understanding of the writings of Emory Upton and reflected the German model. They also reflected his belief in a need for more businesslike efficiency in the Army. Root's reforms included creating a general staff to plan for war rather than to carry out day-to-day administration, replacing the commanding general with a chief of staff to straighten out the chain of command and weaken the power of the independent bureaus, and creating the Army War College as the service's senior professional school. Despite the fact that Commanding General Nelson A. Miles and other high-ranking staff officers opposed these changes, Root's reform measures, backed by President Roosevelt, were secured in the General Staff Act of 1903. In addition, the Militia Act of 1903, the "Dick Act," created the modern National Guard under federal control with specified standards of training and readiness, the guardsmen available for nine-month call up by the president.

In 1905, Root became secretary of state under the bellicose Roosevelt and strove to improve U.S. relations with Latin America and Japan. After leaving the Department of State in 1909, Root served as senator from New York until 1915 and remained active in diplomatic, political, and philanthropic affairs until his death in 1937.

Root's reforms did not remove all of the inefficiencies and conflicts of authority found in the Army's high command structure, but they constituted positive and necessary steps toward creating a modernized and professional Army leadership and were a notable improvement upon past practices in the service.

One of the intellectual giants of the "armed progressive" movement was Emory Upton. A graduate of West Point in 1861, he had served with distinction in the Civil War. He published *Infantry Tactics* in 1867, adopted by the War Department for the regulars and militia. But Upton's greatest interest lay in the area of military policy. A tour of the world's military systems as a member of a commission to study military reforms resulted in Upton's writing *The Military Policy of the United States,* which was not published until 1904 but was widely circulated in manuscript form in the 1870s.

☆   An American Portrait

Emory Upton—Born near Batavia, New York, in 1839, Emory Upton, the foremost American writer on tactics and military history in the late nineteenth century, attended Oberlin College for one year before transferring to the Military Academy in 1856. Graduated eighth in his class of 45 as a lieutenant of artillery in 1861, Upton, like many young West Point graduates, found his first duty that of drilling volunteers for the defense of Washington in the first weeks of the war. But in the four years of conflict that followed, Upton saw action at Antietam, Fredericksburg, Gettysburg, the Wilderness, Cold Harbor, and finally Petersburg, eventually being promoted to brevet major general.

In the aftermath of the war, Upton secured many assignments, including a five-year term as commandant of cadets at West Point; a two-year trip abroad to study the armies of Asia and Europe; a position as supervisor of instruction at the Artillery School at Fort Monroe, Virginia; and a stint as commandant of the Presidio in San Francisco in 1880. Upton, suffering from terminal cancer, died by his own hand on March 15, 1881.

Upton's ideas on infantry tactics had been adopted at West Point as early as 1867, and he published two more books on military affairs in his lifetime. But undoubtedly his greatest work was "The Military Policy of the United States since 1775," completed in its coverage through the second year of the Civil War and circulated in manuscript form during his lifetime and thereafter. It was published as *The Military Policy of the United States* in 1904, a fitting tribute to a man whose writings on tactics and whose analysis of national military policy made him one of the most influential military theorists during the interwar years.

Upton argued that the real record of the citizen-turned-volunteer-soldier American armies and of the poorly trained and poorly led militia units under dual state–national control revealed both to be politically dominated, weak, ineffective, and wasteful of lives in combat. They simply would not do in the modern world. Rather, Upton urged, drawing on his knowledge of the modern German army, the nation would be best served by a professional army under a general staff leading an "expansible" army of national reserves trained and led by regulars, an idea borrowed from John C. Calhoun. The Guard should be used only to control domestic strife and, if necessary, to repel invasion by a foreign foe, Upton argued.

Upton's ideas did not fare well in the public arena. Whatever the cogency of his arguments and however solidly they were backed by progressives within the officer corps, they ran contrary to the long-standing American fears of a large standing army as a danger to liberty and of an elite officer class as antidemocratic. Reliance upon the citizen-soldier in time of war was a hallowed American ideal, and congressional disposition to spend only as much money on the military as was absolutely necessary was a fact of life.

Upton's reform ideas were rejected by a congressional committee headed by ex-General, now Senator, Ambrose Burnside despite their near-unanimous support by serving generals who testified on their behalf. Upton's reforms also ran into the solid opposition of Senator (and ex-volunteer Major General) John A. Logan, who in 1887—six years after Upton's tragic death by suicide—argued in his book *The Volunteer Soldier of America* that the Army should rely on the citizen-volunteer led by officers trained at the state colleges. West Point and Annapolis, he asserted, should be abandoned because they turned out a "military aristocracy."

Needless to say, Upton's ideas were also uniformly opposed by leaders of the Guard units, who, in 1903, saw themselves recognized by Congress in the Dick Act as America's first-line defenders. In the meantime, having accepted the obvious fact that the guards were not going to be abandoned, the Army regulars began to work with them as trainers and inspectors. The regular Army still preferred reserves and conscription as backups to themselves (especially when, in 1912, the attorney general ruled that the Guard could not be used overseas and when the Mexican intervention of 1916 proved that calling up Guard units was very disruptive of civilian life), but the arguments between defenders of the idea of a regular army of professionals backed by reserves or conscripts versus the National Guard and volunteer devotees continued on into World War II and was still not settled decades later.

The Army's progressives made clear gains in the area of more professional training for officers and men through the service schools. They also gained promotion by examination and service record rather than by strict seniority in 1890. But they made no headway against the existence and expansion of the state-controlled National Guard as the Army's reserve manpower pool in time of national emergency.

BIRTH OF THE MODERN NAVY

The Navy's "dark ages" extended from 1865 to the early 1880s. It was marked by the breakup of the 700-ship Civil War Navy down to a handful of vessels consisting of monitors and sailing vessels. It was dominated by sailing-ship admirals who tended to reject steam-propelled warships, the creation of Benjamin F. Isherwood and his few devoted followers responsible for the Civil War steam-powered vessels. It was not that these sailing admirals were not correct in pointing out that steam-powered vessels had to give a great amount of stowage space to coal, leaving little room for guns, ammunition, quarters, and so on. Likewise, coaling stations were not available where the ships would have to sail. In addition, steam technology was still primitive, and repairs and spare parts were not readily available worldwide. The problem was that the admirals, faced with public indifference and a parsimonious Congress, were unwilling to devote an appreciable amount of the Navy's limited funds to developing ships and ordnance to at least keep them abreast, if not ahead, of the times. With few and inadequate ships, erratic training, subpar crews, poor gunnery, and disenchanted young officers denied rank and influence by seniority-only promotions, the Navy existed on the fringes of national concern until the early 1880s.

But in that decade the American people came alive to the importance of a sizable and modern navy, and the "new navy" was born. Much of the impetus came from the expansion of the nation's markets throughout the world and the need to protect the resulting trade network to ensure America's economic growth and prosperity. Leading the crusade were Secretary of the Navy William H. Hunt (1881–1882) and Admiral John

Rodgers and the Naval Board he headed, which was assigned the task of studying the Navy's needs. Congress turned a deaf ear to much of what Rodgers's board recommended, but it did authorize in 1883 the building of four modern steel vessels, the "ABCDs" (cruisers *Atlanta, Boston,* and *Chicago,* and dispatch boat *Dolphin*). Hunt's successor, William E. Chandler, established the Naval War College at Newport, Rhode Island, in 1885. It soon became the intellectual center of a renaissance in naval strategy, tactics, and policies under the inspired leadership of Rear Admiral Stephen B. Luce. The Naval War College also provided a forum for Captain (later Rear Admiral) Alfred Thayer Mahan, whose ideas and writings popularized naval power not only in the United States but throughout the world.

Mahan lectured at Newport for many years on the subject of naval power, arguing that sea power was the key to the acquisition and maintenance of national greatness because of its function of protecting trade. The importance of gaining command of the sea by decisive battle was the heart of Mahan's message, eagerly accepted by a trade-hungry and power-conscious nation and world. Students at the Naval War College had drunk deeply of Mahan's ideas even before he published his epic *The Influence of Sea Power upon History, 1660–1782* in 1890. His big-navy ideas spread to civilian and military leaders in the United States and abroad and played a leading role in the building of great navies of big-gun ships during the decades spanning the turn of the century.

☆   An American Portrait

Alfred Thayer Mahan—Born at West Point, New York, in 1840, the son of famed instructor Dennis Hart Mahan of the Academy's staff, Mahan spent two years at Columbia College before enrolling at the Naval Academy and being graduated in 1859. During the Civil War he served on blockade duty on the Atlantic and Gulf coasts, and for 20 years after the war was billeted to the varied assignments at sea and ashore required of a rising naval officer.

The turning point in Mahan's military career came in 1885, when, as a captain, he was invited by Rear Admiral Stephen A. Luce to lecture on tactics and naval history at the new Naval War College in Newport, Rhode Island. Here Mahan's lectures drew service-wide fame for their clarity and cogency, and in 1890 they were published as a book entitled *The Influence of Sea Power upon History, 1660–1783*. The book catapulted Mahan and his naval theories to international fame. Mahan's arguments for the necessity of sea power for every great nation, expounded in his *The Influence of Sea Power upon the French Revolution and Empire, 1793–1812,* published in two volumes in 1892, furnished the philosophical basis for the expanding navies of the world in the great power naval race of 1880–1914.

After a second stint as president of the War College, Mahan retired in 1896 but continued writing until his death in 1914 in Washington, DC. During this last period of his life he turned out six more major military and naval books and solidified his position as the foremost philosopher of sea power, a preeminence he still holds today.

Secretaries who followed Hunt and Chandler, such as William C. Whitney (1885–1889), Benjamin F. Tracy (1889–1893), and Hilary A. Herbert (1893–1897), continued the naval expansion program their predecessors had begun. Superior ships of war came off the building ways, among them the 6,000-ton, heavy-armored cruiser *Maine;* the second-class battleship *Texas;* the 10,000-ton battleships *Oregon, Indiana,* and *Massachusetts;* and the 11,400-ton *Iowa,* to be followed by two *Kearsarge*-class 11,500-ton battleships (*Kearsarge* and *Kentucky*) and the *Illinois*-class battleships *Illinois, Alabama,* and *Wisconsin.* By 1898 the American Navy had been reborn, with four first-class battleships plus five building, 14 cruisers, and dozens of smaller ships. All main combat vessels featured swift steam power propulsion and breech-loading rifled guns. The United States Navy was superior to that of most nations and looking to equal the Royal Navy. In 1903 some naval enthusiasts even talked of 45 mighty battleships, one for each state in the Union! By 1916 the Navy had 60,300 men and 77 major combatant vessels with 6-inch or larger main batteries.

The Navy, like the Army, also witnessed a campaign for modernization and professionalism by "armed progressives." The impetus came particularly from younger men blocked by an excess of officers, especially the numerous Naval Academy graduates of 1864 –1868. Advancement in rank was very slow. For example, the top 12 graduates of the class of 1868 served as lieutenants for 21 years on average. Many junior officers simply resigned their commissions in frustration. Others decided to try to change things.

An alleged "naval reform act" of 1882 did nothing fundamental to improve the situation for many younger officers. It mandated only that the size of the incoming classes at Annapolis be reduced. Still only the top 25 percent of the Academy graduates could be offered commissions because with maximum numbers specified for each rank and too many officers, it took two vacancies by death or retirement to produce one promotion, or slot.

In response, the frustrated junior officers decided that two things could and should be done: First, the Navy would have to be enlarged; and second, they would pursue naval careers in fields that were so necessary and functional that the Navy could not get along without them. Accordingly, naval "armed progressives" began a campaign to "sell" the idea of a big navy to businesses involved in naval construction and international trade and to the general public. One of their primary propaganda organizations was the United States Naval Institute, created in 1883 and located on the Academy grounds at Annapolis. In another brilliant propaganda piece, the Theodore Roosevelt–inspired worldwide cruise of the Great White Fleet of 26 vessels from December 1907 to February 1909 became an enthusiastic point of pride for America. In 1909 the supportive Navy League was founded, all of these and other selling efforts being so successful—and their arguments for naval necessity in wartime so well illustrated by the Navy's smashing victories at Manila Bay and Santiago during the Spanish-American War—that by 1914 a navy "second to none" had become a widely accepted goal in American civilian and political circles.

The Navy during these years also both created and took advantage of pride in the country and its navy by deliberately shifting to a recruiting strategy that targeted white nonsailors from the interior of the country as recruits to the service. The campaign proved successful, and naval service thereafter became less an occupation of coastal-based "salts" and more a call to national duty.

These Young Turks also aided themselves and the Navy by developing expertise in such fields as hydroelectronics, ordnance, naval architecture, and scientific management. The Torpedo School had been established at Newport in 1880 and, as has been noted, the Naval War College followed in 1885. To these were added the Office of Naval

Intelligence in 1882 and the naval architecture program at the Massachusetts Institute of Technology in 1893. These created openings in many growing and important fields for young officers. Finally, the "armed progressives" of the new Navy broke the promotion-by-seniority-only bottleneck by the Naval Personnel Act of 1899, wherein "plucking" of unfit captains before advancement to flag rank was put into practice over the determined opposition of the Navy's senior officers.

All of these actions resulted in the creation of a new, modern navy by the second decade of the twentieth century, a navy equipped with many fine ships, the latest in technology, and officers trained and dedicated to America's newly found prowess on the seas.

BIRTH OF THE MODERN MARINE CORPS

In the five decades after the Civil War, the Marine Corps too went through the process of modernization and found its niche as part of America's armed forces, but not without fighting off a number of attempts to disband it.

Due partially to its limited role during the Civil War, an effort was made to abolish the Corps in 1866 and 1867 by the House of Representatives, the attempt being turned back by the strenuous efforts of Commandant Jacob Zeilin with the help of a number of high-ranking naval officers. In the years that followed this brush with extinction, the marines proved their worth as trained infantrymen by their seizure of the Han River forts in the "Hermit Kingdom" of Korea in 1871; by their protection of American nationals in Alexandria, Egypt, in 1882; and by their swift and effective seizure of control in Panama in 1885 during riots by the Panamanians against their Colombian masters. Marines also played a key role in restoring order in Philadelphia during the great railroad strike of 1877.

The Corps' reputation and professionalism were also advanced by the work of Zeilin's two successors as commandant, Charles G. McCawley (1876–1891) and Charles Heywood (1891–1903). During McCawley's tenure, all officers entering the Corps had to be graduates of the Naval Academy. McCawley also reorganized the Marine Corps to improve officer and enlisted men's fighting skills, and, in his best-remembered move, in 1880 appointed John Philip Sousa to lead the Marine Corps Band. In 12 years Sousa turned the band into one of the finest military musical groups in the world and one of the most celebrated bands in America.

Heywood created the School of Application in Washington (later to become the Basic School), instituted mandatory officer promotion examinations, and began a series of advanced officer schools. Yet despite the marines' greater professionalism, no less than four attempts were made between 1894 and 1897 by naval officers to eliminate the Corps, the rationale being that no on-board duties for marines existed in the modern Navy. All four attempts were defeated.

Subsequently the marines more than showed their worth and professionalism, not only in Cuba and the Philippines during and after the Spanish-American War, but also during the Boxer Rebellion in 1900. In addition, the Corps played a crucial role in facing down the Colombian army in 1903 when the Panamanians revolted to ensure that the United States would build a canal across their land. When the Panamanians began to riot in Panama City and attacked the installations of their Colombian overlords, President

Theodore Roosevelt ordered the marines into the city to "prevent landing of any armed forces with hostile intent" (i.e., the Colombian army). Some 475 Colombian soldiers landed but refused to take on the marines. They sailed away. Meanwhile, United States naval squadrons at Colon and Panama City guarded against any further Colombian countermeasures. The Panamanian revolution was quickly over, the new nation of Panama was recognized by the United States, and work began on the Panama Canal, linking at long last the Atlantic and Pacific Oceans. The canal was completed in 1914. President Roosevelt was right when he said, "I took the Canal Zone." Indeed, he had—with the help of America's marines and naval forces.

When riots in Cuba in 1906 threatened that nation's president, marines were sent in to stabilize the situation on Roosevelt's orders, setting a precedent for Marine Corps intervention in the Caribbean that would last for two decades. These constabulary interventions became the Corps' primary function until the 1930s. It is ironic, then, that it was the same President Roosevelt who, aided by senior naval officers, in 1908 made a proposal to remove all marines from all naval ships, thereby destroying their evolving usefulness as amphibious infantry. Roosevelt's bid was turned back by Congress largely because the chairman of the House Naval Affairs Committee, Congressman Thomas Butler of Pennsylvania, was the father of marine hero Major Smedley Butler, decorated for his actions during the Boxer Rebellion.

Freed from this latest threat to its existence, the Corps, with over 9,000 men, continued to carry out its duties as military troubleshooters and wielders of the nation's "big stick" in the Caribbean. In 1910 the marines intervened in Nicaragua; in 1914, at Veracruz (under Colonel John A. Lejeune) in President Woodrow Wilson's dispute with the Mexican government over its right to import arms from abroad; and in 1915 and 1916, on the island of Hispaniola in Haiti and Santo Domingo (the marines leaving Santo Domingo only in 1925 and Haiti in 1934). Thus, by the middle of the second decade of the century, the Marine Corps had reorganized, modernized, and professionalized into an elite 10,600-man special force while fighting off a series of attempts to disband it as useless and superfluous. In the process it had served well in America's major military engagements and had secured a place for itself in America's armed forces table of duties as the nation's amphibious police force in the Caribbean. After distinguished service in World War I, the Corps would finally find its twentieth century military mission as the pioneers and specialists in amphibious operations.

THE SPANISH-AMERICAN WAR

By the late nineteenth century, Spain's once-great empire, stretching from Cape Horn at the tip of South America to the middle of the North American continent, had been reduced to only Cuba and Puerto Rico. Ever since the 1820s, successful revolutions for independence had been carried out as people after people in the old Spanish Empire declared their right to political independence from the Spanish crown. The Cuban people, too, had felt the tug of revolution and freedom, and in the 1860s and 1870s they had tried and failed in their quest for independence. In 1895 they rose up in rebellion once again, this time, they hoped, with the help of an ally to the north, the United States.

Accordingly, the directing Cuban revolutionary council (*junta*) set up its head-quarters in New York City to raise money for the cause; to enlist volunteers; and, above all, to get the United States involved militarily in Cuba's struggle for independence. The key to American intervention, the revolutionaries realized, was effective anti-Spanish propaganda directed at American citizens. In this they were aided by Spanish barbarities in Cuba and by America's "yellow press" popular newspapers tying to outdo one another in circulation by printing the most sensational news possible from home or abroad. The goings-on in nearby Cuba provided excellent grist for their sensationalizing newsmills.

While Congress seemed willing to intervene (even passing a resolution in 1896 that would have given Cuba *de facto* recognition as a country separate from Spain, a claim Spain could not and would not accept), both Presidents Grover Cleveland and William McKinley were very reluctant to go to war with Spain over the independence of Cuba.

But events soon moved beyond McKinley's control. In early February 1898, a letter from the Spanish minister in Washington, Enrique de Lôme, to a friend in Cuba was stolen and subsequently published by William Randolph Hearst's New York *Journal*. Its insulting remarks about President McKinley infuriated the American people and badly strained relations between the United States and Spain. Then, on February 15, 1898, the armored cruiser *Maine* (posted to Havana harbor to evacuate American nationals if necessary and to demonstrate America's interest in events there) was ripped apart by a mysterious explosion and sank. The lives of 260 American sailors were snuffed out in the explosion.

The American press immediately charged that the explosion had been caused by an underwater mine placed against the hull of the ship by the Spanish. Subsequent separate inquiries by Spanish and American investigating teams concluded that there had indeed been an explosion in the powder magazines of the vessel, but neither team could say how the explosion occurred or who had done it. (What caused the explosion has never been positively determined, but recent research indicates that it came either from spontaneous combustion from coal gas—as almost occurred on the battleship *Oregon*—or, more likely, that the Cubans placed the "submarine mine" against the *Maine*'s hull to cause an incident that would force the United States into war with Spain.)

Whatever the cause of the sinking of the *Maine,* Congress began to beat the war drums, and on April 20 it declared Cuba to be free (but added the Teller Amendment stating that the United States had no intention of annexing Cuba) and authorized the president to use the U.S. Army and U.S. Navy to enforce its declaration. A naval blockade of the island was thereupon imposed. Spain reacted with a declaration of war on April 24, 1898, and the United States reciprocated the next day. The Spanish-American War, a "splendid little war," as Secretary of State John Hay later called it, was on. The American people would, indeed, "Remember the *Maine!*"

The Army was unprepared for the war when it came. Scattered over the West and among the East Coast artillery units, the 27,000 men of the Army were inexperienced in tropical warfare and in amphibious operations. The regulars had all they could do just to handle and train the recruits pouring into the service. Before the war was over that summer, the regulars had been expanded to 59,000, and volunteers totaled 216,000 (including 10,000 "immunes," so called because they were allegedly immune to tropical diseases). The volunteers were trained without proper equipment and weaponry in hastily organized camps in the South. Because the law was unclear as to whether or not National

Guardsmen could serve overseas, Guard units were not called up, but if enough members of a Guard unit enlisted as volunteers, the Army kept them together in special volunteer units.

The Navy was much better prepared for conflict. Having been allocated $30 million by Congress during the crisis, the Navy ordered the construction of three battleships and numerous torpedo boats and torpedo boat destroyers and purchased or chartered 50 civilian steamers to be used as transports. It also chartered fast liners to be armed and used as auxiliary cruisers. Additional crewing came from the states' naval militia units.

The Navy's immediate duties were defensive, since it was known that a Spanish fleet, under Rear Admiral Pascual Cervera, had left the Cape Verde Islands on April 29, destination unknown. Accordingly, a "flying squadron" was assembled in Hampton Roads under Commodore Winfield S. Schley to protect the East Coast from attack by the Spanish fleet (an eventuality widely feared at this time), and the North Atlantic Squadron under Rear Admiral William T. Sampson was assembled at Key West to intercept Cervera and bring him to action if possible. The Asiatic Squadron at Hong Kong, under Commodore George Dewey, was ready for action, having been instructed as early as February to stand ready for immediate action by the bellicose Assistant Secretary of the Navy Theodore Roosevelt. A battalion of 647 marines was assembled at the Brooklyn Navy Yard under orders to prepare for action in Cuba. They boarded the USS *Panther* for transportation to Key West and eventually to Cuba.

While the Army was attempting to get itself organized during the first frenzied days of the war and the naval squadrons were assembling in Virginia and Florida, the most glamorous victory of the short conflict took place half a world away in the Philippines, the prized Far Eastern colony of Spain. There Commodore Dewey's Asiatic Squadron steamed into Manila Bay on the night of April 30 and the next morning, in a five-hour barrage of naval gunfire, destroyed the entire Spanish fleet posted there. Two days later, Dewey's marines seized the Cavite Navy Yard and set up a command post there, but Dewey's 1,700 sailors and marines were too few to seize Manila, the capital of the archipelago, so they settled down to await the arrival of army troops, who reached the Philippines two months later.

☆ An American Portrait

George Dewey—Born in Montpelier, Vermont, in 1837, Dewey attended the Naval Academy from 1854 through 1858, being graduated fifth in his class of 15 students. During the Civil War he served as executive officer on the *Mississippi,* played a leading role in the Navy's running by Forts Jackson and Saint Philip to capture New Orleans in April 1862, was with Farragut at Port Hudson on the lower Mississippi, and aided in the attack on Fort Fisher in January 1865.

After the war, Dewey served tours of duty on land and sea and by 1884 had attained the rank of captain. He played an important role in the birth of the "new navy" after 1889 as chief of the Bureau of Equipment (overseeing the design of the new cruisers and battleships being constructed) and as president of the Board of Inspection and Survey after 1895.

Appointed to command the Asiatic Squadron in November 1897, he took command of the fleet at Nagasaki, Japan, as commodore in January 1898, soon thereafter moving the squadron to Hong Kong to be in a better position to attack the Philippines in

FIGURE 6-5   George C. Dewey. (*National Archives, Washington, D.C.*)

the event of war with Spain. Having pushed his men to the limit to prepare for the impending war, Dewey and his squadron were ready for action when informed on April 26, 1898, that the United States and Spain were at war.

Sailing immediately for Manila Bay, on May 1 his squadron destroyed the Spanish fleet anchored there as well as the enemy's land installations. This lopsided victory immediately made the United States one of the major powers in the Far East, showcased the power of the "new navy," induced Congress to raise Dewey to the rank of admiral of the navy, and set off a movement to have him elected president of the United States (a movement that soon fizzled out despite Dewey's enthusiasm for the nomination).

Admiral Dewey went on to serve long and faithfully as president of the General Board of the Navy Department until his death on January 16, 1917. Credited with only one great naval victory, Dewey nevertheless aided in and came to symbolize America's reborn navy and its fighting prowess as the United States moved into the ranks of the major military powers at the turn of the century.

The battleship *Oregon,* stationed at Puget Sound, was ordered to intercept Cervera but took 67 days to make the 15,000-mile trip around South America and through the Straits of Magellan to arrive in the Caribbean. At that time, Admiral Sampson's fleet was on the wrong side of the world and, therefore, unable to block Admiral Manuel Camara's squadron sailing from Spain to attack Commodore Dewey's squadron in Manila Bay. (Camara's squadron was recalled after the U.S. naval victory at Santiago out of fear that an American naval fleet might attack Spain itself.) Both of these incidents illustrated the difficulty of rapid movement between the Atlantic and the Pacific and were used as evidence for the necessity for an interoceanic canal to join the two bodies of water. Naval authorities also pointed out that the inability to unite the Navy's fleets quickly for action was a violation of Mahan's dictum of the necessity of a unified fleet.

Commanding General Nelson A. Miles wanted to train a special force of 80,000 men at Chickamauga Park, Georgia, to invade Cuba in October, after the rainy season was over. But Secretary of War Russell M. Alger, reacting to public clamor demanding immediate action, ordered Miles to have the Army invade Cuba at the earliest possible time. Following orders, the Army began to assemble its men, horses, wagons, ordnance, and so on at the designated—and completely inadequate—port town of Tampa on the Gulf coast of Florida. Here foul-ups of epic proportions began to occur. When Admiral Cervera's fleet was finally located and was no longer a danger to an invasion force, the Army could now move to Cuba. (Cervera had evaded the American naval squadrons completely and had slipped safely into the harbor of Santiago on the southern coast of Cuba but then could not get out, as the Navy had blockaded the harbor entrance.)

Since the Santiago ship channel was narrow and the harbor was mined and guarded by forts, the Navy could not get in to get Cervera. So it asked the War Department to send the Army to destroy the forts and come around behind Santiago at the head of Santiago Bay, thus forcing Cervera out. Alger gave the order, and V Corps, under Major General William R. Shafter, left Tampa on June 14 to carry out the operation. Eight days later the troops made "amphibious" landings at Siboney and Daiquiri, east of Santiago, the men being rowed ashore in boats, their horses hoisted over the sides of the vessels in slings to swim ashore. Fortunately the Spanish did not oppose the landings, which took two days, even though they had 200,000 troops in Cuba. From there the soldiers marched west to San Juan Heights, where Shafter laid out plans for a three-way attack on the Spanish positions there. The attack of July 1 did not go well, but was marked by Colonel Theodore Roosevelt's Rough Riders' charge up Kettle Hill, a sharp engagement at El Caney, and Brigadier General Jacob F. Kent's infantry attack up San Juan Hill, which broke the Spanish defenses. Shafter then wanted to withdraw his forces five miles to save his troops from artillery fire from Santiago and from tropical diseases that were riddling his ranks, but Alger insisted that he hold his advanced position. Shafter resisted.

In the meantime the Navy was blockading Cervera's fleet of four cruisers and two torpedo boat destroyers and had sent the marines to Guantanamo on the eastern tip of the island to seize the port for use as a coaling station. This maneuver was carried out on June 10. But if the Navy could not get in to Santiago Harbor to get Cervera, maybe they could at least ensure that he could not come out. They decided to scuttle the collier *Merrimac* in the harbor channel. This task would be carried out by naval Lieutenant Richard P. Hobson and a skeleton crew. The scuttling took place, but unfortunately the *Merrimac* settled into the mud off the channel, so Hobson's brave attempt came to nothing (although he and his crew were treated as heroes when captured by the Spaniards). The American blockading force of five battleships and five cruisers could only steam in a wide circle outside Santiago Harbor, waiting for Cervera to attempt an escape.

Cervera broke the impasse for both the Army and the Navy at 9:30 on the morning of July 3 when he steamed his outgunned fleet out of Santiago Harbor to turn west and somehow make a break to safety. The American fleet maneuvered into parallel position—with grave difficulty and barely avoiding a number of collisions in the thick black coal smoke disgorged by the ships as full steam was ordered to catch the Spanish—and brought the enemy fleet under intense running gunfire. By 1:30 in the afternoon, Cervera's entire fleet of six ships had been either sunk or beached. Some 600 Spanish sailors had been killed in the four-hour naval battle, and another 1,700 were captured. The American casualty count was only one man killed and one wounded.

Santiago and its 23,000 defenders fell to the Army on July 17 without further fighting, and on July 25 General Miles and 3,000 men landed at Guanica on Puerto Rico, where they were joyfully received by the Puerto Rican populace. By August 13 the entire island had been secured.

In the Far East, meanwhile, VIII Corps consisting of 15,000 regulars and volunteers under Major General Wesley Merritt had begun arriving in the Manila area from the West Coast in late July. The Spanish commander, faced with the loss of the Spanish Asiatic fleet to Dewey on May 1, the subsequent recall of Camara's Spanish fleet, and the overwhelming superiority of American numbers in the Manila area, arranged for an honor-fulfilling but almost comic-opera surrender of Manila on August 14.

Two days before, an armistice had been signed between the United States and Spain. In four months Spain had lost two battle fleets, 23,000-plus troops, Cuba, Puerto Rico, and Manila. In the subsequent Treaty of Paris, the Cubans received their independence and the United States took from Spain the Philippines, the island of Guam in the Marianas (seized by the marines on June 21), and Puerto Rico in the Caribbean. During the Cuban fighting 5,462 Americans had died, only 379 of these being battle casualties; the remainder were victims of disease. With America's great victories at Manila, Santiago Bay, San Juan Heights, and El Caney, and with the incredibly low casualty count, it had, indeed, been a "splendid little war."

But what few Americans realized in the euphoria of victory in 1898 was that the United States had now stepped onto the world stage, especially in the Caribbean basin and the Far East. With this new posture came new and heavy responsibilities that would continually engage the nation and its military in foreign entanglements until finally it found itself in the thicket of European conflict in World War I.

THE PHILIPPINE INSURRECTION AND BOXER REBELLION

When Commodore Dewey and the Asiatic Squadron approached Manila on April 30, they had on board Emilio Aguinaldo, the leader of the Filipino guerrillas then fighting against the Spanish. Aguinaldo and his followers believed that when the United States smashed Spain's military power in the Philippines, it would demand that Spain give up the archipelago and turn it over to the Filipinos themselves. But fearing that a weak independent Philippines would be unable to defend itself and would soon fall victim to the machinations of European powers (especially Germany) just looking for any excuse to seize the potentially rich islands and make them their own to the detriment of the natives there, the United States, in the Treaty of Paris, forced the Spanish government to give up the Philippines. It then kept the archipelago as a dependent state, intending to prepare the islands for eventual independence.

Furious at this decision, Aguinaldo and his insurgents (who had already set up a provisional government) formed into a militia, the *sandatahan,* and in February 1899 fighting broke out between them and the American forces in Manila. The Filipino insurrection lasted for two years and ended only after 20,000 Filipino military and perhaps as many as 200,000 civilians and 4,200 Americans had died. In addition, 2,800 Americans had been wounded out of 125,000 troops posted there.

The Army's campaign against the insurgents ran into many problems, not least the fact that the soldiers were eventually engaged in jungle warfare against a guerrilla enemy. Also complicating their problems was the fact that in the latter months of 1899 the first volunteers were sent home when replaced by 25 regiments of new volunteers recruited especially for the Philippine campaign. Thus General Elwell S. Otis was forced to exchange one army for another in the face of the enemy.

But beginning in November 1899, the Army and Marines launched effective campaigns against the Filipinos' conventional forces, driving Aguinaldo into the mountains of southern Luzon. They also landed troops on the other main islands in the archipelago. General Otis thought the war was over, but the Filipinos changed to guerrilla tactics and fought on, using ambush when possible and blending into the native population when threatened. They also carried out a policy of systematic terror against any Filipino who cooperated with the Americans, even if their fellow countrymen were engaged in extending necessary reforms or humanitarian aid. Atrocities on the part of the Filipinos led to counteratrocities on the part of the American troops.

When General Arthur MacArthur succeeded Otis in May 1900, he took new initiatives to end the frustrating colonial-type war, even if deprived temporarily of part of his command to put down the Boxer Rebellion in China. He moved with dispatch and little mercy against the guerrillas while protecting the nonresisting Filipino civilians from the guerrillas by resettling them and continuing the process of extending humanitarian and educational aid. With regulars replacing the volunteers in 1901, MacArthur also strengthened his hand by using over 11,000 Filipinos to assist the Army in its gradually successful, if merciless, fight against the guerrillas.

☆ An American Portrait

Arthur MacArthur—A native of Springfield, Massachusetts, whose parents moved to Wisconsin four years after his birth in 1845 and whose ancestors had enjoyed distinguished military careers, MacArthur entered the Army in 1862 as a lieutenant in the 24th Wisconsin Infantry. During the war the young officer saw action at Perryville, Stone's River, Chickamauga, Chattanooga, Atlanta, and Franklin and rose steadily in rank to lieutenant colonel. In 1890 he received the Congressional Medal of Honor for gallantry at Missionary Ridge in November 1863.

Reverting to his regular rank of lieutenant at the end of the war, MacArthur soon made captain and for 20 years served on various assignments in the West during the period of the pacification of the Indians and the populating of the area. Called to Washington to serve in the adjutant general's office as a major in 1889, he went on to serve in Texas and the Dakota Territory from 1893 to 1898. With the coming of the war with Spain, he was made adjutant general at the embarkation port of Tampa and of the III Corps at the training site at Chickamauga.

Promoted to brigadier general, MacArthur joined the expeditionary forces sailing for Manila and was appointed provost-marshal-general and civil governor of the city after it fell to the Americans. MacArthur subsequently played a prominent role in putting down the Philippine insurrection from 1899 to 1901, succeeding General Elwell S. Otis as commander of the Division of the Philippines in May 1900.

Raised in rank to major general in 1901 while in the Philippines, MacArthur became a lieutenant general in 1906, three years before his retirement. He died suddenly in September 1912 while addressing a military reunion. He was survived by two sons, Arthur, a naval officer, and Douglas, an Army officer who would become one of the nation's most prominent military leaders of the twentieth century.

With the capture of Aguinaldo in March 1901 and the guerrilla leader's subsequent call to his men to lay down their arms, the war began to wind down. It ended, however, only after soldiers and marines under Army Brigadier General Jacob H. "Hell roarin' Jake" Smith devastated the Moro guerrillas with "kill and burn" tactics on the southeast island of Samar in late 1901 and early 1902. On July 4, 1902, President Roosevelt declared the war at an end. Some soldiers questioned the justice of the recent war against the Filipinos, but the policy of the United States government had been carried out by its armed forces.

In the midst of the fighting against the Filipino insurgents, the United States was also called upon to intervene militarily in China. In 1899, Secretary of State John Hay had signaled America's interest in the Far East when he announced the "Open Door" policy for China guaranteeing equal trading rights for all Western nations and Japan. The Open Door was designed to ensure that China's territorial rights would be respected—that is, that the weakened country would not be dismembered. But a number of Chinese nationalists, resentful of British, French, Portuguese, Russian, German, and Japanese infringements on China's independence and integrity, formed themselves into the Society of Harmonious Fists. These "Boxers," as they were soon called by the Westerners, were determined to drive the foreigners out of their country. With the tacit approval of the Manchu Dowager Empress, they fell upon all foreigners, Christian missionaries, and their converts to Christianity in the countryside and soon placed the foreign legations in the capital city of Peking under siege. Inside the embassy compound were 500 foreigners, 3,000 Chinese Christians, and about 450 troops assigned to the legations. Outside were 140,000 Boxers and imperial troops determined to wipe them out.

The United States quickly sent naval units and marines to the port city of Tientsin. On May 24, 1900, a detachment of 50 marines (plus some soldiers from the Western countries and Japan) commandeered a train and reached Peking, but the Chinese tore up the tracks below the city, so now they too were trapped. When a small relief force of 2,000 men was turned back from retaking Tientsin and the danger of a slaughter in Peking increased, the nations involved decided that something had to be done. Troops were dispatched to China in great numbers, eventually reaching 25,000 men in an "International Relief Force."

From the Philippines came the U.S. 9th Infantry, the 14th Infantry, and some artillery units. Other soldiers were sent directly from the United States. Their numbers reached about 5,000 before the crisis ended. Tientsin was retaken in July 1900, and the international force moved on to the "Forbidden City" 80 miles away, seizing the heart of the capital and lifting the 55-day siege of the Legation Quarter on August 15 after hard fighting. This broke the back of the Boxer Rebellion. American units in China or on their way there were dispatched to the Philippines, although the mopping up continued for some months in the Chinese provinces. In the subsequent Boxer Protocol forced on China, each foreign power was allowed to keep a small armed contingent in the legation area of Peking (an American contingent remained in China until 1938), and China was forced to pay a staggering $333 million in reparations. The United States received only $25 million in reparations and used it all to educate Chinese youths there and in the United States.

Thus America's first role as part of an international military operation on foreign shores ended successfully. But it was a harbinger of things to come. Already America's possession of the Hawaiian Islands (annexed during the Spanish-American War after a long period of reluctance because they were now needed as a vital way station to the Far East), Guam, and the Philippines made the United States a Pacific and Far Eastern power with all the responsibilities that flowed from that new status. The decades of the twentieth century would demonstrate again and again that the steps the nation had taken in 1898 and 1900 without much thought to their consequences would change its relationships not only with the Far East but with the entire world. Within less than half a century America would be forced to stand as the premier defender of the western Pacific against the imperial power of Japan, to be followed by two agonizing conflicts on the Asiatic mainland itself. The Philippine insurrection and the Boxer Rebellion were but the beginning of America's military commitments across the far Pacific.

By 1914, then, the old Army, Navy, and Marine Corps had passed away. Not without considerable difficulty, America's armed forces had expanded, modernized, and professionalized. They had demonstrated their worth in significant clashes of arms. These new, modernized services would soon be called to test their mettle in a great conflict in Europe, a war that would be converted in the minds of the American public into a "war to end all wars."

Suggestions for Further Reading

AMBROSE, STEPHEN E.,   *Crazy Horse and Custer.* Garden City, NY: Doubleday, 1975.

————, *Upton and the Army.* Baton Rouge: Louisiana State University Press, 1964.

ANDRIST, RALPH K.,   *The Long Death: The Last Days of the Plains Indians.* New York: Macmillan, 1964.

BROWN, DEE,   *Bury My Heart at Wounded Knee.* New York: Holt, Rinehart and Winston, 1971.

BRUCE, ROBERT V.,   *1877: Year of Violence.* Indianapolis: Bobbs-Merrill, 1959.

CONNELL, EVAN S.,   *Son of the Morning Star.* New York: North Point, 1984.

COSMAS, GRAHAM A.,   *An Army for Empire: The United States Army in the Spanish-American War.* Columbia: University of Missouri Press, 1971.

FONER, ERIC,   *Reconstruction: America's Unfinished Revolution, 1863–1877.* New York: Harper & Row, Pub., 1988.

FONER, JACK D.,   *Blacks and the Military in American History.* New York: Praeger, 1974.

FRIEDEL, FRANK,   *The Splendid Little War.* Boston: Little, Brown, 1958.

GATES, JOHN M.,   *Schoolbooks and Krags: The United States Army in the Philippines.* Westport, CT: Greenwood Press, 1973.

GRAY, JOHN S.,   *Centennial Campaign: The Sioux War of 1876.* Fort Collins, CO: Old Army, 1976.

HARROD, FREDERICK S., *Manning the New Navy: The Development of a Modern Naval Enlisted Force, 1899–1940.* Westport, CT: Greenwood Press, 1978.

HART, RICHARD, *The Great White Fleet: Its Voyage Around the World, 1907–1909.* Boston: Little, Brown, 1965.

LINN, BRIAN M., *The U.S. Army and Counterinsurgency in the Philippine War, 1899–1902.* Chapel Hill: University of North Carolina Press, 1989.

MAHON, JOHN K., *History of the Militia and the National Guard.* New York: Macmillan, 1983.

MARSHALL, S. L. A., *Crimsoned Prairie: The Wars between the United States and the Plains Indians.* New York: Scribner's, 1972.

MILES, NELSON A., *Serving the Republic.* New York: Harper, 1911.

RICKOVER, HYMAN G., *How the Battleship* Maine *Was Destroyed.* Washington, DC: Naval History Division, 1976.

SEAGER, ROBERT, *Alfred Thayer Mahan.* Annapolis: Naval Institute Press, 1977.

SEFTON, JAMES E., *The United States Army and Reconstruction, 1865–1877,* Baton Rouge: Louisiana State University Press, 1967.

SINGLETARY, OTIS A., *The Negro Militia and Reconstruction.* Austin: University of Texas Press, 1957.

SPECTOR, RONALD, *Admiral of the New Empire: The Life and Career of George Dewey.* Baton Rouge: Louisiana State University Press, 1974.

TAN, CHESTER C., *The Boxer Catastrophe.* New York: Columbia University Press, 1955.

UTLEY, ROBERT M., *Cavalier in Buckskin: George Armstrong Custer and the Western Military Frontier.* Norman: University of Oklahoma Press, 1957.

———, *Frontier Regulars: The United States Army and the Indian, 1866–1891.* New York: Macmillan, 1973.

———, *The Last Days of the Sioux Nation.* New Haven: Yale University Press, 1963.

VESTAL, STANLEY, *Sitting Bull: Champion of the Sioux.* Norman: University of Oklahoma Press, 1957.

WOLFF, LEON, *Little Brown Brother: How the United States Purchased and Pacified the Philippine Islands.* Garden City, NY: Doubleday, 1961.

World War I, 1914–1918

War in the twentieth century has become all-embracing, thanks in large measure to technological breakthroughs in weaponry and to the frightening extension of the concept of the nation at war, in which all citizens are defined as combatants. This new totality of warfare had been foreshadowed in the Civil War in the United States during Sherman's March to the Sea and in the Franco-Prussian War of 1870 and 1871 during the siege of Paris. In each case the distinction between combatant and noncombatant faded almost into nothingness in the face of one army's determination to break the will of the entire enemy nation.

This change in attitude toward civilian casualties, combined with increasingly effective weapons (such as the machine gun; rifled, long-range ordnance armed with various types of lethal warheads; tanks; airplanes; submarines; chemical and biological weapons; and finally shorter-range and intercontinental missiles with nuclear warheads) has led to greater military killing power than ever before. And it is a less discriminating killing power, making little or no distinction between warriors and ordinary citizens, the death toll of noncombatants rising faster than that of combatants. This quantum leap in carnage can be seen in the two great world wars in this century, in which the butcher's bill exceeded humanity's worst fears. World War I produced a total of 8.5 million killed and 37.5 million total casualties, while World War II added perhaps as many as 57 million persons to the roll of the dead alone. Total casualties (dead, wounded, and missing) cannot even be calculated. The specter of Armageddon has been loosed upon the world. Today millions of people live under an ever-present threat of instant annihilation thanks to land-based and sea-based missiles carrying atomic or hydrogen warheads and targeted on their nations' points of vulnerability. These awesome weapons offer no choice to those who would use them but to accept civilian deaths as the price of eradicating military targets.

Yet, ironically, this new scale of lethality has led not to more death and destruction in the last decades of the century, but, rather, to less. The totality of all-out war has forced nations to seek lesser means of persuasion and less destructive forms of war to gain their policy goals. Limited war has become the norm in the decades since the end of World War II, the alternative being mutually destructive and, therefore, self-defeating.

The goal of warfare—the subjugation of the enemy—has not changed in the twentieth century, but the means—virtually unlimited warfare giving way to limited warfare under the threatening shadow of nuclear holocaust—have changed. Therefore, the American people and their civilian and military leaders have had to accept all-out carnage on two occasions in the first half of the century and then the new realities of postwar world relations, including limited wars for limited goals since World War II.

The price has been high, but the American people, reacting according to their cherished beliefs and perceptions (sometimes myopic but grounded in the sustaining belief in the inherent dignity of all persons), have responded to the challenge of two world wars between 1914 and 1945 and then to several lesser military struggles since that time.

Like all powerful nations in the history of the world, America has had to learn in the twentieth century that with power (purposefully developed or born of circumstance) comes responsibility (welcomed or unwelcomed) for the fate of many other nations besides itself. The maintenance of peace is a staggering burden calling for mature wisdom and judgment and for enormous sacrifices in lives and money.

As we have seen, the United States stepped onto the world stage of escalating power confrontations in the Spanish-American War, a war that resulted in America's becoming a Caribbean, Pacific, and Far Eastern power. From these initial hemispheric and transoceanic responsibilities there has been no long-term retreat, even when the United States was also called upon to help defend Europe in World Wars I and II. And because these two successive worldwide conflicts weakened America's longtime European friends, especially France and Great Britain, they forced the United States to take up some of their allies' responsibilities in the Far East, Middle East, and Africa.

In addition, World War II led to the rise of other world powers whose values are clearly at variance with those of the United States, resulting in even greater challenges in attempting to keep the peace in the Western Hemisphere and around the world.

The twentieth century, then, has meant new responsibilities for the United States and its military services, responsibilities not actively sought but nevertheless massive in their dimensions. As befits a free and democratic people, the American response has been generous, though often confused, starting with a questionable and unsuccessful intervention in Mexican affairs beginning in 1914 and leading through two major wars, two "limited" wars, and numerous incidents of hemispheric and worldwide peacekeeping to the present time.

INTERVENTION IN MEXICO, 1914–1917

At the end of the Spanish-American War, American claims to priority status in Latin America, as promulgated in the Monroe Doctrine of 1823, had been reenforced by its acquisition of Puerto Rico. The United States had also gained the right to intervene in Cuba to preserve its independence and to ensure an adequate government there to forestall intervention by any other world power. This right was embodied in the Platt Amendment, included in the new Cuban constitution of 1902 at American insistence. Subsequently, American troops were sent to Cuba in 1906, 1912, and 1917 to preserve order. (In 1934 the United States gave up its right of intervention in Cuba as part of the Good Neighbor Policy promulgated by President Franklin D. Roosevelt.) Similarly, American troops (mainly marines) were dispatched to Haiti, the western one-third of the island of Hispaniola, in 1915; to the Dominican Republic, the eastern two-thirds of Hispaniola, in 1916; and to Nicaragua on the mainland in 1912 and again in 1925 and 1927. But the most dramatic military intervention in Latin America came in Mexico, the scene of smoldering instability from 1910 on.

During that year, the 26-year reign of the despotic president Porfirio Diaz ended in a revolution against him. The rule of his successor, Francisco Madero, was marked by internal unrest and by incidents along the border between the United States and Mexico. This led President William Howard Taft to order a "maneuver division" (initially made up of only 6,700 soldiers but eventually climbing to 13,000 men) to assemble at San Antonio to be available in case of serious trouble. Then, in 1913, Madero was overthrown and subsequently executed by the followers of General Victoriano Huerta. An anti-Huerta force soon gathered under General Venustiano Carranza and Emiliano Zapata. This signaled the beginning of a civil war in that impoverished, unhappy, and misgoverned country.

Unlike Taft before him, who had recognized the Madero government despite his misgivings over how it had come to power (diplomatic recognition being a sign only of internal control by a government, not of external moral approval), the moralistic President Woodrow Wilson refused to recognize the government of General Huerta because it lacked "constitutional legitimacy." This represented a major shift in American policy, quite at variance with the actions of other major countries, which recognized the new regime. But Wilson went even further the next year when he lifted Taft's embargo on sending arms to Mexico, thus allowing the antigovernment forces of Carranza to buy weapons in the United States. He also imposed a naval blockade on Veracruz and Tampico to ensure that Huerta would not be resupplied with arms from abroad.

With this illegal blockade in place, a minor incident in which some American sailors were arrested at the Iturbide Bridge at Tampico while loading supplies (but soon thereafter released) was blown out of all proportion by the actions of the fleet commander, Rear Admiral Henry T. Mayo. Mayo demanded a public apology and a 21-gun salute to the American flag as a sign of respect. Huerta refused. Wilson then made the situation worse by backing Mayo all the way, and Congress authorized the president to use the Army and Navy to force Huerta to meet the American demands.

Soon thereafter, in April 1914, when word was received in the White House that a German merchant steamer was due to arrive at Veracruz with arms for the Huerta government, Wilson ordered the seizure of that Mexican port city. United States Army, Navy, and Marine Corps personnel, to a total of 8,000 men, took part in the bombardment and seizure of Veracruz (five battleships stood offshore), and the two countries stood on the verge of war. Fortunately, the "ABC" powers of Argentina, Brazil, and Chile intervened with offers of mediation. Huerta resigned, Carranza became president, American troops were withdrawn, and the new Carranza government was eventually recognized by the United States.

But not by Francisco "Pancho" Villa, a longtime bandit and one of Carranza's henchmen, who gained control of northern Mexico and set out to goad the United States into intervention so that he could become the "savior" of the Mexican people. Villa instigated a number of incidents along the border that led to the loss of American lives, most notably the execution of 18 American engineers west of Chihuahua in the "Santa Ysabel Massacre" of January 10, 1916. When the Mexican government forces could not bring the bandits to justice in these incidents, and when Villa and over 500 of his men staged an attack on the town of Columbus, New Mexico, a month later, killing eight civilians and eight American soldiers assigned to defend the town, Wilson (with Carranza's reluctant consent) immediately ordered the Army to cross the border "with the sole object of capturing Villa and preventing any further raids by his bands." The War Department added to these objectives three days later "the dispersion of the band or bands that attacked Columbus, N.M."

On March 15, 1916, an advance force of 5,000 officers and men under Brigadier General John J. Pershing, commandant of the Eighth Brigade at Fort Bliss near El Paso, crossed into Mexico in pursuit of Villa and his men. It included the 1st Aero Squadron of eight biplanes under Captain Benjamin D. Foulois and, for the first time, motor trucks in its quartermaster train. Pershing's forces chased Villa across the state of Chihuahua for several months without bringing him to bay, but leading Carranza to protest the presence of the U.S. Army in Mexico. Pershing's men of the "Punitive Expedition" (in time totaling 15,000 men in infantry, cavalry, and artillery units) eventually clashed, not with Villa's men, but with those of President Carranza, especially at Carrizal on June 21. These events almost led to open war, President Wilson on June 16 calling into federal service 132,000 National Guardsmen (almost the total guard contingent from the states) and having them stationed along the border to back up the regulars there and in Mexico.

A six-man joint commission, in the meantime, had begun meeting in July in New London, Connecticut, to work out an American withdrawal. With neither nation intent on war, and with American attention being drawn increasingly to the war in Europe, the Punitive Expedition—the last cavalry-dominated campaign for the Army—was recalled from Mexico by President Wilson on January 30, 1917. Six days later the last American soldier was back across the border, and the incursion had come to an end.

Villa had not been captured (he was assassinated in 1923), but his band had been scattered, and border incidents came to an end. More important, both regular and Guard troops had received much valuable experience in the field and in mobilization and logistics. Weaknesses in both areas had been revealed in this enforced rehearsal for major military actions so they could be corrected before the Army faced infinitely greater problems as it stepped into war in Europe five months later.

BACKGROUND TO THE WAR

The Great War, or World War I (as it came to be called with the outbreak of the second great conflagration in 1939), was brought about by national antagonisms that had been festering and building for decades before the actual outbreak of fighting in 1914. Essentially, the scales of European economic and military power had been thrown out of balance with the creation of Germany out of the numerous German-speaking states by Otto von Bismarck after the Franco-Prussian War of 1870 and 1871.

United at last, Germany was anxious to gain its place among the powers of Europe. Having already taken steps toward economic integration in the decades prior to unification, it quickly became a manufacturing and trading competitor of the first rank. Germany also began to build up its transportation system, especially its merchant marine, and began to look for markets and colonies worldwide in emulation of its older European neighbors.

France looked upon this new Germany with a wary eye, not simply because of its economic progress but also because Germany had been created, so to speak, over the prostrate body of France at Versailles after the Franco-Prussian War. Furthermore, Bismarck had annexed the two key French border areas of Alsace and Lorraine to safeguard Germany's crucial industrial Rhineland. France was determined thereafter to regain both its honor and Alsace-Lorraine whatever the cost.

England was equally uncomfortable over the rise of Germany because of the new nation's manufacturing competitiveness in the world markets and because of its growing maritime prowess, especially on the North Atlantic trade routes. Germany's actions also illustrated that it too wanted a share of colonial claims and riches; this made Britain, with its worldwide empire, uneasy.

Russia was a vast land with weak political leadership, but at the same time it was awakening to a modernized industrial economy in the late nineteenth and early twentieth centuries. It was also plagued with internal problems and the threat of a breakdown of its entire political system (as witnessed by its losses in the Russo-Japanese War of 1904–1905 and the subsequent paralyzing Revolution of 1905). One thing that all thinking Russians could agree on: Austria and, by extension, its new ally Germany could not be trusted, especially as the two German-speaking states wanted to extend their economic and political influence into the neighboring Balkans, the home of various Slavic peoples (plus non-Slavic Rumania) emerging from under Turkish domination and looking to Slavic Russia for aid and guidance.

Faced with these animosities, and additional ones, such as Italy versus Austria and Slavic Serbia versus Germanic and Magyar Austria-Hungary, the major and minor powers of Europe formed alliances or understandings to guarantee their national interests. Germany, Austria-Hungary, and Italy formed the Triple Alliance. England, France, and Russia formed the Triple Entente. All the agreements between these allies were defensive in nature. Still, a wrong move anywhere could quickly convert defensive intentions into offensive actions because of the widespread feeling that each nation had to stand by its friends in time of crisis. Each of these nations felt strongly that its values must not be compromised, and that if war came, its outcome would be swift and relatively painless. This optimism over achieving a swift and decisive victory was based on the fact that each of the nation's armies was being rapidly expanded, and each army had developed a sure-fire plan for military success if war broke out.

Germany had expanded its army from 430,000 men in 1870 to 5.7 million men at full mobilization by 1914; France, from 400,000 to 4.5 million; and Russia and Austria-Hungary, from virtual nothingness to 5.3 million men for Russia and 2.3 million men for Austria-Hungary. These numbers were possible since the Continental powers had adopted a system of a limited army cadre supplemented by a conscript wherein men were conscripted for training and limited service, then served a number of years in the active reserves, followed by more years in the inactive reserves. Continental Europe in 40 years had undergone a phenomenal arms race and was becoming an armed camp. Its armies were far larger, better armed, and better led than ever before. Technology, military professionalism, and unprecedented population growth had created forces of unparalleled destructive potential. And, as mentioned, each nation's military leadership had developed war plans that would guarantee swift victory on the battlefield against its enemies.

Germany, caught between a vengeance-seeking France on its western border and Russia on the eastern side, developed a grand strategy called the Schlieffen Plan, the brainchild of General Alfred von Schlieffen, chief of the German general staff from 1891 until he retired in 1905. Assuming it would take Russia about two months to mobilize against Germany because of its vast distances and primitive transportation system, the plan called for a holding operation in the east while France in the west was swiftly defeated in a grand envelopment across Holland, Belgium, and northern France. As formulated, the Schlieffen Plan called for a vast mobile offensive anchored on the Metz-Thronville forts on the south moving like a sweeping scythe across northern Europe, then sweeping west and south around Paris to complete the encirclement of the entire French army, thus ending the war in the west. The success of the plan hinged on swift movement and timing. It had to be completed in six weeks so that divisions could be moved east (the German government had built the nation's railroads on east-west axes to facilitate such movements) to face the hordes of the Russian army.

Unfortunately for Germany's war plans, General Helmuth von Moltke, Schlieffen's successor, altered the plan significantly by strengthening the left wing (contrary to Schlieffen's dying plea in 1913), thus weakening the critical right wing; by insisting that Dutch territory not be crossed, thus narrowing and pinching the right wing's offensive thrust and forcing the German army to take on the strong Belgian fortress at Liège; and by calling for an offensive into Russian Poland in the east, thus further weakening the time-critical thrust to the west.

France originally assumed that its best chance for victory against Germany lay in a defensive strategy. It would hold its great border fortresses and canalize any German drives between them, destroying the German invaders by skillful counterattacks. But after 1905 the *offense à outrance,* the frontal attack, became ruling doctrine. It was predicated on the French army's mobility on the interior lines and its superior rapid-fire 75-mm field gun. If the German center was attacked in a headlong offensive from Mézières and Espinal and on into Lorraine (with the aid of the British army on the left near the Belgian border and with the Russians moving in on the eastern front), the German offensive through the Low Countries into France could be slowed and stopped by the French offensive thrusts. These war plans became finalized as Plan XVII by General Joseph Joffre, chief of staff of the French army after 1912.

Exactly where and how the German army would be attacked as it swept across the Low Countries and into northern France was never worked out, but the French high command was not concerned. Reflecting the French military's fascination with the offensive, one officer stated, "For the attack only two things are necessary: to know where the enemy is and to decide what to do. What the enemy intends to do is of no consequence." Or as President Armand Fallières said in 1912, "We are determined to march straight against the enemy without hesitation....The offensive alone is suited to the temperament of our soldiers." Such attitudes were typical. The great Napoleon's advice, "In forming the plan of a campaign, it is requisite to foresee everything the enemy may do, and be prepared with the necessary means to counteract it," had long been forgotten.

Russia, too, had plans. If Germany made its initial attacks toward the east, the Russians would abandon the western frontier districts, including Poland, and set up a defensive line near Riga, north of the Pripet Marshes. This was Plan G. If Germany initially attacked to the west, Plan A would be used. This called for a drive through Poland to attack East Prussia to the north and Austrian Galicia to the south.

Austria-Hungary, like Russia, had two contingency plans, each depending upon which moves the enemy made. Plan B would be put into effect in the event of a war with Serbia only. It called for two Austrian armies to invade that Slavic nation to the south while three armies moved north into Galicia as a precaution against a Russian attack there. Plan R, for a war with Serbia plus its Slavic protector Russia (with Germany as Austria's ally), called for two armies attacking Serbia while four armies moved into Russian Poland, there to hold the Russians in check for six weeks until Germany completed its conquest of France and joined Austria-Hungary in defeating Russia.

Britain's plans for its 160,000-man army, small but well trained, called for it to cross the Channel to take up a role as an extension of the French left wing. Assurances to this effect were made to France.

Thus all potential major combatant powers—reflecting the new professionalism of the military but marred by blind spots regarding new weaponry and logistical realities—had detailed plans worked out in case of war. But each plan depended ultimately on timing, movement of troops, logistics, and the enemy's making certain calculable moves. What if the French blew up bridges in the face of the German advance or otherwise obstructed it (as did in fact happen)? What would result if Britain did not reinforce the French left wing on French territory (as happened)? What if Russia joined Serbia against Austria not immediately but later, and Austria-Hungary got caught between war plans (as happened)? What if an initial Russian offensive against East Prussia bogged down or met with defeat (as happened)? No one knew the answers because no one seriously considered the questions. Clausewitz's warnings about the frictions of war had been forgotten.

Into this nightmare world of national antagonisms and intricate military plans came young Gavrilo Princip, a Serbian nationalist, and his six Black Hand cohorts. On June 28, 1914, having crossed the border from Serbia into Austria, they shot to death Franz Ferdinand, the heir apparent to the throne of Austria-Hungary, and his wife in the town of Sarajevo in the Austrian state of Bosnia. Within a month Serbia and Austria, then Russia and Austria, Russia and Germany, Germany and France, Germany and Belgium, and Britain and Germany had mobilized—mobilization being accepted by all nations as a step that meant war—and had declared war. Only Italy stayed out—until bribed in by the Allied powers the next year with promises of Austrian territories—and Turkey and Bulgaria joined the so-called Central Powers of Germany and Austria-Hungary.

The defensive commitments of the Triple Alliance and the Triple Entente, plus the swelling surge of national pride, had at last dragged the European powers into the maw of war. Warriors and citizens in all the countries were convinced that it would be a short, glorious, and decisive conflict. All were wrong. The war lasted four years; brought

65 million men into uniform; eventually involved 30 countries, including the United States, and took 8.5 million lives before peace was reestablished.

TRENCH WARFARE, THE APOGEE OF DEFENSE

While fighting on the 900-mile Eastern Front maintained some movement and flexibility—although remaining indecisive in its outcome for three years despite the great German initial victories over the Russians at the Battle of Tannenberg and the Battle of the Masurian Lakes in East Prussia in August and September 1914 and a summer offensive the next year that drove deep into Russian territory but failed to knock them out of the war—the fighting on the Western Front soon bogged down into trench warfare.

The planned German lightning attack through Belgium and northeastern France was slowed by French resistance and by logistical problems as the German offensive simply overloaded the roads and rails in the area. It was finally stopped by the French and British in August 1914 at the Marne River, only 15 miles from Paris. On September 6 the French staged a desperate counterattack and created gaps in the German line. French and British troops—aided by 6,000 additional troops who drove out to the battlelines from Paris by whatever conveyance was available and took part in the "Miracle of the Marne"—pushed the Germans back beyond the Aisne River, where they halted and dug themselves into defensive trenches. By December 1914 both sides had constructed a series of fortified trenches extending 470 miles beginning at Ostend in Belgium and running south through northeastern France all the way to the Swiss border, an ironic development, since the British scant years before had ceased issuing entrenchment tools to its soldiers as unnecessary and the French had abandoned all instruction in entrenching.

For the next four years this line remained almost stationary as Germans on one side and Frenchmen, Britishers, and Belgians on the other tried fruitlessly—and at a horrible cost in lives—to dislodge the enemy 50 yards to a mile away across "no man's land" from their dug-in positions. Basically, each side was too weak to win and too strong to lose, and no new weaponry or tactic could be devised to break the bloody stalemate. The defensive prowess of the machine gun and artillery was too great for any offensive maneuver or weapon (such as the rolling barrage of artillery or tank) to overcome. Before the fighting ended four years later, millions of men had died in the trenches of the Western Front and many more millions had been wounded as each side tried again and again to break the defensive impasse.

Actually, the trench line snaking across the Western Front was not normally one line but three or more. The front-line trench was 6 to 8 feet deep and 3 to 5 feet wide. It was supported by timbers and equipped with underground dugouts for men and horses, some large enough to bunk over 150 men; these dugouts were largely artillery-proof. There were also dugouts carved into the hills for stores and ammunition, and concrete pillboxes or reinforced bunkers were built as strong points all along the lines. Offensively, from the front-line trenches the soldiers would go "over the top" to attack the enemy across "no man's land," the use of the tactical offense by physical shock being holy writ on both sides. Defensively, the trenches would bristle with machine guns capable of cutting apart attacking infantry with devastating enfilading fire.

In back of the front-line trench 100 yards or so via perpendicular zigzag communication trenches was a support trench, and behind this a reserve trench. If a front-line trench was taken by rifle and bayonet, the defenders would pull back to the next trench to resume their resistance. Out in front of the lead trench were listening posts and, vital to the defensive effectiveness of the trench, fields of barbed wire up to 150 feet in depth (barbed wire was invented in 1874 to enable farmers to keep their livestock penned in) running parallel to the trenches and making a massed attack by infantry virtually impossible.

To overcome the near futility of a successful frontal attack by infantry, the military chieftains on both sides turned to artillery barrages to "soften up" the enemy's lines. For days—or even weeks in some instances—hundreds of thousands of rounds of artillery shells would pound the barbed wire and trenches of the enemy. Then the infantry would climb out of their trenches to attack. This bombardment, of course, ruled out any chance of surprise. But, more important, the defending soldiers would retreat deep into their dugouts until the firing stopped and then emerge with their machine guns, grenades, and rifles to face the attacking infantry making their way across shell-pocked "no man's land" and picking their way through the barbed wire to attack by rifle and bayonet. And since attacking infantry tended to mass toward any opening in the enemy line, plugging this hole left the trailing infantrymen at the mercy of the enfilading and deadly defensive fire.

The French adoption of the rolling artillery barrage creeping ever closer to the enemy's line with the infantry following close behind the falling curtain of shells had little effect on the ability of the defenders to hold their lines, nor did countless attempts to tunnel beneath the enemy's lines or strong points to blow them up. Trench warfare and attacks "over the top" continued, resulting in few appreciable gains—the lines on the Western Front wavering not more than ten miles either way in three years of bloody war—and taking the lives of hundreds of thousands of men. It was war of attrition at its worst.

The futility and human cost of trench warfare and the inability of the high commands to break the deadlock on the Western Front is well illustrated by the major battles of 1914 through 1917. During the first month of the war and the First Battle of the Marne, some 200,000 Frenchmen became casualties while trying to stop the German invasion of their homeland, and in the First Battle of Ypres (a town in Belgium) of October 20 through November 22, 1914, total casualties among the belligerents hit 250,000 men as the Germans attempted to seize the Channel ports of Ostend and Zeebrugge in their "race to the sea."

The next year, 1915, witnessed not only the beginning of the prolonged and disastrous British-French naval and amphibious Gallipoli Campaign at the Dardanelles (the idea of Winston Churchill, First Lord of the Admiralty), in which the Allies suffered about 500,000 casualties and the Turks an equal number, but also the Second Battle of Ypres in April and May, in which the British alone took over 59,000 casualties in thwarting this limited German offensive. Second Ypres is also noteworthy because it was here that the Germans first used poisonous chlorine gas on their enemies. Before the war ended three years later, gas had been accepted as a weapon of war by the Allies too, and more potent phosgene and mustard gas had been added to the belligerents' arsenals. Gas attacks took a million lives during the war, the deadly chemical weapon also causing uncounted instances of misery and ill health to its victims for decades thereafter.

The third year of the war, 1916, saw two of the largest and most deadly battles in military history, Verdun and the Somme. The Battle of Verdun, lasting from February 21 through December 18, consisted of a German attack (codenamed Operation *Gericht*—place of execution) on French positions on the east bank of the Meuse River 40 miles northeast of Paris after a 1,200-gun artillery barrage, followed by a French counterattack. Verdun was marked by the emergence of Henri-Phillipe Pétain as a national hero. The fighting continued into April and beyond even though 81,000 Germans and 89,000 Frenchmen had already died during the first weeks of the battle. It also produced the national slogan *Ils ne passeront pas* (They shall not pass), the final words of General Robert Nivelle's June 23 order of the day. But the cost in human lives in this battle that saw 40 million artillery rounds fired on opposing trenches was appalling. France had 460,000 of its sons killed, wounded, missing, or taken prisoner; German casualties stood at 300,000. Some 420,000 French and German soldiers died in the ten-month Battle of Verdun.

The Battle of the Somme, a futile attempt by the Allies to cut the German line in two, lasted from July 1 through November 19, 1916. Some 1,250,000 Englishmen, Frenchmen, and Germans became casualties. The British suffered 60,000 killed or wounded on the first day alone. Marked by the first use of the tank in the form of 50 British 30-ton Mark I's (6,000 tanks would eventually be built by the Allies during the war) and of the flamethrower, the four-month Battle of the Somme ended with the Allies gaining only 8 miles over a 12-mile front.

The year 1917 witnessed two Russian revolutions, the first against the Romanov czar Nicholas II, and the second against the successor Provisional Government. The second revolution brought to power the Bolsheviks under Nikolai Lenin (original name Vladimir Ilrich Ulyanov) and ensured the weakening or collapse of the Eastern Front to Germany's advantage. Yet trench warfare continued as before on the Western Front, chewing up lives with little or no gain. In late February, the Germans voluntarily withdrew back to the Siegfried Line (the Allied soldiers called it the "Hindenburg Line" in reference to General Paul von Hindenburg, the chief of the German General Staff), shortening their front by 27 miles to make it stronger. But the Allied spring offensives at Arras, the Chemin des Dames, and in Champagne—part of the French commander Robert Nivelle's failed "Nivelle offensive"—led to no break in the stalemated war but, rather, to mutiny in 54 divisions of the French army. Nivelle was replaced by General Pétain, the hero of Verdun, who defused the mutiny by a skillful combination of executions and understanding.

Likewise, the Third Battle of Ypres, or Passchendaele, of July 31 through November 20, 1917—designed by the overconfident British commander Field Marshal Sir Douglas Haig—yielded no appreciable gains for the Allies. The British preceded their slogging advance through the muddy fields of Flanders with an artillery barrage that lasted for two weeks and expended 3 million shells, but their losses still totaled 31,850 men the first day alone. When it was over (the British having 300,000 men killed or wounded, the French 8,500, and the Germans 260,000), the Allied line had been advanced only 9,000 yards.

Then, on November 20, 1917, the British launched a second attack to draw off the Germans from Passchendaele. In this Battle of Cambrai there was no preliminary bombardment to ensure surprise. And nearly four hundred 28-ton, 105-horsepower Mark IV tanks equipped with bundles of brushwood, called "fascines," on their noses to dump into the German antitank ditches ahead of them were used in conjunction with infantry (the idea of Lieutenant Colonel J. F. C. Fuller). The tanks were covered by a curtain of smoke, but the British were unable to follow through on the success of their first day's breakthrough and gained only 10,000 yards for all of their efforts, while taking 4,000 casualties. Furthermore, the ground was retaken by the Germans by December 7. The Battle of Cambrai of 1917 (in which the final British casualty total was 44,000 men; the German total, 50,000) ushered in the era of tank warfare, although only a few, such as Fuller and Winston Churchill, perceived the importance of this new weapon at the time.

The year 1917 ended, then, with the Western Front in approximately the same place it had been established 3 1/2 years before—this despite the loss of hundreds of thousands of lives and the introduction of the tank, rolling artillery barrages, and poison gas. Nor had any carnage-ending changes occurred on the Eastern or Balkan fronts. In the autumn, an Austrian offensive against Italy called the Battle of Caporetto had resulted in the Italian army's being forced to retreat 100 miles, the Italians seeing 305,000 of their men listed as casualties (270,000 having been taken prisoner), but it did not alter the overall situation.

Still, 1917 had foreseen Allied collapse on the Eastern Front with the Bolshevik seizure of power in Russia. It had also witnessed the gradual tightening of the British blockade on Germany, with its attendant shortages and hardships on the home front. It also saw the entry of the United States into the war.

AMERICA GOES TO WAR

As the fighting in Europe stagnated into trench warfare, German hopes for swift victory proved to be chimerical. Accordingly, the Germans, knowing that the British would use their powerful navy to blockade shipping from German colonies and from neutral countries to the Central Powers, that Britain could sustain its industrialized economy only by means of merchant shipping, and that the powerful German High Seas Fleet would be no long-term match for the Royal Navy, early in 1915 turned to a new naval weapon, the U-boat (*Unterseeboot,* or submarine). The U-boat, they hoped, would neutralize Britain's surface fleet power and sink British and Allied merchant vessels off the coasts of Europe.

Although they began the war with only 27 U-boats, the Germans were soon sinking 150,000 tons of Allied shipping each month. Inevitably, neutral ships were misidentified and sunk too. The American public was appalled that the Germans would resort to such an "inhumane" means of warfare, but their disgust was initially balanced by the fact that Britain was blockading neutral European ports and seizing as "contraband" even such nonwar items as food.

But the sinking of a British passenger liner, the *Lusitania,* on May 15, 1915, off the coast of Ireland by a U-boat, with the loss of almost 1,200 lives, including those of 128 Americans, brought heated American protest against the Germans. (The Germans had warned passengers that the liner was liable to sinking and claimed afterward that the British ship was carrying contraband in its holds, a claim now known to be true). The fate of the *Lusitania* moved many Americans, including President Woodrow Wilson, to begin advocating military preparedness to defend American rights. As Wilson would remind the

American people two years later on the eve of a declaration of war, "property can be paid for; the lives of innocent noncombatants...cannot."

The German government backed off from unrestricted submarine warfare in September 1915 by promising not to sink passenger vessels without warning, and the immediate crisis ended. But American trade with Britain and the other allies was beginning to boom (based on extensive American credits that reached $2.5 billion by 1917), and American sympathies still remained basically anti-German and pro-Allied, even though Britain continued to violate American trading rights on the high seas. Nevertheless, the strongest sentiment voiced by the American people was to stay out of the war.

Wilson the moralist preferred diplomacy as a means of ensuring American rights and restoring peace, but he gradually came to realize that the nation had to be militarily prepared in case it was drawn into the conflict raging in Europe. Thus while genuinely proclaiming peace as his goal—and running for reelection as president in 1916 on the slogan "He kept us out of war"—Wilson in his pro-Anglo-Saxon sympathies was actually inching the nation closer to war, this president-directed drift finally culminating in America's entry into the war on the side of the Allies.

A clear sign of America's emerging pro-preparedness stance was the National Defense Act of 1916. This historic act, the most comprehensive piece of military legislation Congress had ever approved, was also partially a response to the disruption in the economy caused by the National Guard's being called up to police the Mexican border because of Pancho Villa's raids. The law of 1916 established the traditional American concept of a citizen army in the form of the National Guard as the nation's basic land force. The Guard, under extended federal control over training and personnel, was to be increased to 475,000 men, and it was liable to be placed in federal service under the president at his will. The act also increased the regular Army to 175,000 men in peacetime and 285,000 in time of war. It established a reserve corps of officers and enlisted men enrolling only individuals, not units, and a volunteer army was authorized in case of war. Thus the Army would consist of regulars, guardsmen, and reserves, plus volunteers during wartime. A Reserve Officers' Training Corps (ROTC) was authorized to operate on the nation's college campuses. In addition, the act gave the president greater control over American industry in time of war. However, reflecting the continuing fear of a professional military establishment, it severely curtailed the development of a general staff by capping the total staff officers allowable at 55 (up from 36) and stipulating that not more than one-half could serve in or near the nation's capital.

Woodrow Wilson may have sincerely believed that his balancing act of insisting on American "neutrality" yet vehemently protesting German "crimes" on the high seas with the use of the U-boat, while at the same time allowing Britain to blockade illegally noncontraband goods flowing to Germany or neutral countries, could be maintained. He may also have seen no contradiction in running for reelection on a peace platform while displaying an anti-German bias and expressing fears that the defeat of Britain and France would swing the balance of power in Europe and on the high seas in favor of "barbaric" Germany. But events were working against Wilson's policy of insisting that all American rights be honored while at the same time trying to stay out of the war.

Early in 1917 the German high command sensed—correctly—that the stalemate on the Western Front could be broken by the impending revolution in Russia (it came within weeks), which would take that troubled nation out of the war and collapse the Eastern Front. (They later expedited the return of the radical Bolshevik leader Lenin from Switzerland for just this purpose.) Believing a breakthrough victory on the Western Front would soon be possible, they decided to unleash their 200 submarines to carry out unrestricted submarine warfare against all shipping, belligerent and neutral, off the coasts of Britain and France. This would cut off these nations from aid, they calculated, and starve them into submission in six months, the ratio of British merchant ships being sunk to U-boats lost then standing at an encouraging 15 to 1. Germany's announcement that henceforth all vessels would be sunk without warning came on January 31, 1917.

This course of action carried the virtual certainty that the United States would join the war, but the Germans assumed that any American aid would be a case of too little, too late. When, therefore, more sinkings occurred (including four American ships), the breaking of diplomatic relations with Germany by the United States brought no curbing of unrestricted submarine warfare, and the British released a month-old intercepted telegram from Arthur Zimmerman (the German foreign secretary) to the German ambassador to Mexico proposing that Mexico join Germany in case of a war with the United States (for which Mexico would receive Texas, New Mexico, and Arizona as compensation). Wilson went before Congress on April 2 and asked for a declaration of war by the United States upon Germany. He stated, "It is a fearful thing to lead this great peaceful people into war....[B]ut the right is more precious than peace," and concluded, "God helping her, she can do no other." Fired with high resolve, although unprepared on land and sea for what lay ahead, four days later, on April 6, 1917, America entered the Great War, "the war to end all wars," the war to "make the world safe for democracy."

Whatever the true issues at stake in World War I—almost all the European belligerents had clearly entered the war to further their own interests and diminish their rivals—the United States steadfastly viewed the conflict as a struggle of good against evil, with "civilization itself seeming to hang in the balance," as Wilson phrased it. As the nation was soon to discover, though, the price of intervention would be high.

SEA POWER HELPS TO TURN THE TIDE

The United States' growth in naval power in the last decades of the nineteenth century was part of a worldwide movement among major and minor powers. The ironclad ship, the precursor of the world's great steel naval fleets, had first made its appearance as ironclad mobile batteries in the Anglo-French forces during the Crimean War of 1854 to 1856. The first clash between ironclad vessels of war took place during the American Civil War in the inconclusive battle between the *Monitor* and the *Virginia* in Hampton Roads in March 1862. The American Civil War also saw the limited use of "Davids," small submersible torpedo boats, by the Confederates. For two decades thereafter, monitors of 2,000 tons with flat decks, single turrets, and two 15-inch Dahlgren smoothbores were the backbone of the minuscule U.S. Navy.

Meanwhile, the European powers continued to experiment with steam-powered ironclads, breech-loading turreted guns, and self-propelled torpedoes. By the 1880s, protected cruisers (no side armor but vital underwater parts protected by thick steel deck plating) and armored cruisers (equipped with side armor) were being used. So were small, faster, and cheaper torpedo gunboats, whose usefulness in warfare was demonstrated in a Latin American war in 1891 and in a Japanese-Chinese naval war in 1894 and 1895. The successes of America's "new navy" in the war against Spain in 1898 provided worldwide confirmation of the effectiveness of the new naval technology of steel ships armed with high-velocity, rapid-fire guns. It seemed to justify naval building programs, as did the massacre of the partially antiquated Russian fleet of 45 vessels by Japan's Admiral Heihachiro Togo's fleet on May 27, 1905, in the Battle of Tsushima during the Russo-Japanese War.

That same year saw the British lay the keel for the *Dreadnought* at Portsmouth. When completed a year later, the 17,900-ton, turbine-powered, 21-knot, elaborately compartmentalized, quad-screwed battleship was armed with ten 12-inch guns firing 850-pound shells, an 11-inch armor belt, and five 18-inch submerged torpedo tubes. As the largest, fastest, and most heavily gunned battleship ever built, it was the wonder of the naval world, making all other battleships obsolete. Its building set off a race by the major nations for superiority in *Dreadnought*-type battleships (soon with 15-inch guns and oil-fueled) and battlecruisers, these to be protected at close range by fast, light cruisers and torpedo-boat destroyers, the assumption being that henceforth great surface fleet engagements would decide control of the seas in the future. Germany immediately began a building program for their *Kriegsmarine* that would give it 58 *Dreadnoughts* in ten years. The United States also played an active role in this international surface naval race as well as in the development of the submarine.

While subsurface vessels probably date back to the sixteenth and seventeenth centuries with the work of the Englishman William Bourne and the Dutch physician Cornelius van Drebbel (the latter's submersible being propelled underwater by oars), the first use of a submersible vessel for military purposes came with the American David Bushnell's round-shaped *Turtle* in 1776, which made three unsuccessful attempts to sink British ships at anchor during the Revolutionary War. Robert Fulton, the genius of American steam-powered river vessels, also invented a submarine, the *Nautilus,* during the time of Napoleon. It was cylindrical in shape with a copper hull and a conning tower and diving planes like those in modern boats. Offered to the French and ready to sail on their behalf in 1800, Fulton's *Nautilus* became a victim first of political squabbling and then, when Fulton offered it to the British in 1804, of Royal Navy disapproval. It never went to war.

During the 1850s an Austrian artillery sergeant named William Bauer built the 52-foot *Seeteufel* (Sea Devil) for the Russians, and during the next decade the French launched their 140-foot *Plongeur* (The Diver) with 23 compressed-air reservoirs for blowing its ballast tanks to return to the surface. During the Civil War, as noted, the Confederates developed their "Davids." These submarines were limited as war vessels by the fact that their only destructive weapons were spar torpedoes (canisters of explosives on the end of a wooden rod), which had to be poked against the side of the enemy's ship to effect an explosion.

Other improvements and designs followed in the late nineteenth century. Swedish-built Nordenfelt submarines of the 1880s were equipped with self-propelled torpedoes; the French-built, 60-foot, cylindrical *Gymnote* was powered by accumulator electric storage batteries; and the French *Narval* at the turn of the century had both a steam engine for running on the surface and an electric motor for submerged running, the steam engine capable of recharging its accumulator electric batteries. The French *Aigrette* (1904) was driven by a diesel engine, which eliminated the danger of explosive fumes within the vessel.

The United States entered the submarine race in 1893. The Irish-American inventor John P. Holland won the first navy contract for such an undersea vessel, but his initial *Plunger* was a dismal failure. His second boat, however, the 55-foot, 9-inch *Holland,* which weighed only 64 tons and was built at his own expense, was a success. It had a surface speed of 7 knots and a cruising range of 1,500 miles. Both the American and British navies put in orders for *Holland*-type boats. The American Simon Lake's boats never matched Holland's in design or acceptance in their early years (one model had three large wheels for running along the ocean bottom, there to release divers to enter enemy harbors, where they would attach explosives to the hulls of the enemy's ships or cut their cables), but six Lake-built boats were purchased by the Navy during World War I.

The Germans were slow in getting into submarine development, although they had built two Nordenfelt boats by 1890. The Krupps steel works then built small boats for Russia after 1902. The German navy accepted the Krupps double-hulled *Karp*-class boat as their U.1 in 1906 and adopted diesel power in their U.19 in 1912. But the high command of the German navy saw the U-boats as threats to the predominance of their surface fleet and could only envision them being used in an auxiliary role in a direct attack on the British fleet, or perhaps using the surface fleet to draw the enemy into a submarine trap.

By the outbreak of World War I in 1914, all the major powers had developed substantive surface and subsurface naval fleets. On the Allied side, Britain, France, and Russia had 32 *Dreadnought*-type battleships, 54 pre-*Dreadnought* battleships, 11 battlecruisers, 420 destroyers and torpedo boats, and 179 submarines. The Central Powers of Germany, Austria-Hungary, and Turkey had 17 Dreadnoughts, 45 pre-Dreadnoughts, 6 cruisers, 178 destroyers and torpedo boats, and 44 submarines. It was obvious that the Central Powers could not directly challenge the Allies by numbers on the surface of the sea. Furthermore, both sides tended not to put their precious Dreadnoughts, their controllers of the seas, in positions where they might be lost to the enemy either by direct action or by mining, as in the shallow waters of the North Sea. Thus the lesser vessels on both sides ended up determining the victory in the crucial war on the seas, and the lesser-strength Central Powers early turned to commerce raiding and the use of submarines as their only viable naval strategy.

By the time the United States entered the war in 1917, the most important strategic naval battle of the conflict—the Battle of Jutland—had already been fought the year before. This battle reenforced the nature of the sea war already underway and determined the U.S. Navy's role within it as antisubmarine warfare became crucial to the Allied cause.

The leaders of both the numerically superior Royal Navy and the technologically superior German High Seas Fleet (created specifically to challenge the British in home waters) realized at the start of the war that control of the North Sea was crucial to the war plans of each. The British had to dominate the North Sea to maintain their blockade of Germany and neutral ports: the Germans had to shut off British commerce with its Dominions and all neutrals. Both awaited the grand sea battle by which each planned to gain naval dominance and thus ensure national victory.

Preliminary skirmishes in the North Sea; in the Falkland Islands far down in the South Atlantic, in which the armored cruisers *Scharnhorst* and *Gneisenau* and three other vessels were sunk; in the Mediterranean; and in the Dogger Bank only led up to the great confrontation of May 31–June 1, 1916, the Battle of Jutland (the Battle of the Skagerrak) off the coast of Denmark. In this one and only great strictly surface engagement in modern times, the German High Seas Fleet was commanded by Vice-Admiral Reinhart Scheer, who had 27 battleships and battlecruisers (14 with 12-inch and 13 with 11-inch guns) and 72 other vessels in his command. Admiral Sir John Jellicoe commanded the 37 Dreadnought battleships and battlecruisers (6 with 15-inch guns, 1 with 14-inch, 15 with 13.5-inch, and 15 with 12-inch guns) and 111 other vessels of the British Grand Fleet. Essentially the Germans attempted to draw the British into a trap. In the ensuing shifting series of engagements the fighting qualities of the battlecruisers proved decisive. They were able to inflict some damage on the Grand Fleet, while suffering some damage themselves, before making a safe return to port.

Regardless of who won the battle in which the British lost 14 ships and 6,000 men and the Germans lost 11 ships and 2,500 men—both sides claimed victory—the importance of the Battle of Jutland lay in the fact that neither side was able to score a decisive victory. Although the High Seas Fleet was still in being and the British were forced to keep their Grand Fleet in home waters and in the North Sea to meet the Germans if they reemerged, British control of the sea lanes was unimpaired, and they continued the tight blockade of the Continent. The Germans, on the other hand, were unwilling to risk the loss of their High Seas Fleet again and, therefore, turned to the use of submarines to starve Britain into submission and break the crushing blockade of their homeland.

With Germany turning to the U-boat as the weapon of choice on the high seas—300 additional U-boats were built by Germany during the war—the Americans, with their horror of submarine warfare and with their rights as a neutral trader at stake, were inexorably drawn into the war, the fateful day of intervention coming in April 1917.

The United States Navy was only partially prepared for war when it came. The Naval Act of 1916 had called for the construction of 156 vessels. These included 10 battleships, 16 cruisers, and 67 submarines, but only 50 destroyers. Wilson had wanted little effort put into antisubmarine warfare (ASW) measures, believing, as many others did, in the inevitability of a big-ship shootout. The authorized vessels were far from being built and on line by April 1917, and adequate crewing was far behind schedule. Only one-third of the Navy's vessels were fit for duty, and only 10 percent of the ships were fully crewed. Furthermore, there were no war plans drawn up (at Wilson's insistence), and no arrangements had been made to cooperate with the British. Secretary of the Navy Josephus Daniels soon suspended the construction of capital ships and put out contracts for 250 destroyers and 400 sub-chasers, a wise move in view of the real nature of the naval war in which the United States would soon be engaged.

Admiral William S. Sims, sent to London to survey the situation even before America's entry into the war, reported that 1.3 million tons of shipping losses had been sustained by the British during the first three months of 1917. And the number of sinkings was rising. The First Sea Lord, Admiral Sir John Jellicoe, warned Sims that if antisubmarine destroyers were not sent to Britain's aid immediately the nation might well face starvation and surrender. Britain's 200 available destroyers—100 more were at Scapa Flow in the Orkneys protecting the Grand Fleet against submarine attack—were simply not sufficient to cover the waters around Great Britain and Ireland plus the vital Mediterranean conduit between England and its colonies.

☆   An American Portrait

William S. Sims—William Sowden Sims was born in Ontario in 1858, the son of American parents. Ten years later his family moved back to the United States, and in 1880 Sims entered the Naval Academy. Following his graduation in 1884, he spent a year in language study in Paris, then six years at sea before being sent back to France for three years as naval attaché.

These experiences made Sims acutely aware of American naval deficiencies. For example, as Sims knew, at Manila Bay, Dewey's squadron had only 141 countable ordnance hits on target out of 6,000 shots expended, and at Santiago the score was 122 hits out of 9,400 shots. When the naval high command turned a deaf ear to his petitions for reform in these and other areas of battle readiness, he took his frustrations directly to President Theodore Roosevelt. Roosevelt was impressed by Sims, made him inspector of target practice and then, after 1907, his naval aide. These positions gave Sims an excellent platform from which to lobby for necessary reforms, especially for continuous-fire gunnery.

Assigned to sea duty as captain of the battleship *Minnesota,* Sims continued to push for reforms and the study of military doctrine, resulting in his attaining the rank of rear admiral and the position of president of the Naval War College in Newport in 1917.

Sent to Europe just before America entered World War I, Sims, now a temporary vice admiral, pushed for American aid to Britain. He was subsequently appointed to direct the American naval war efforts as Commander, United States Naval Forces Operating in European Waters. Raised to the rank of full admiral at the end of the war, Sims returned to Newport to head the War College and push for continued reforms.

Sims retired from the Navy in October 1922 but continued his lifetime dedication to a powerful, modern navy, especially as a devotee of naval air power. He died in September 1936, his beloved Navy much stronger as a result of his four decades of dedication to that service.

Sims cabled home asking that every available destroyer be sent to Britain at once. Despite the initial reluctance of Chief of Naval Operations William S. Benson, the request was honored. Within a month, six American destroyers arrived at Queenstown, Ireland, the first of dozens to follow thereafter. Eventually, 370 ships, including 79 destroyers, were sent to European waters. Convoying of merchant vessels protected by British and American destroyers soon yielded high returns in safe ship passages.

American destroyers, in cooperation with the Royal Navy, conducted ASW patrols out of bases scattered from Scotland to the Mediterranean during the remainder of the war. Their efforts were aided by the development and use of new contact mines equipped with copper tendrils. They also used 300-pound depth charges detonated by increased water pressure as they sank into the sea. Sinkings by German U-boats began to drop dramatically. In April 1917, sinkings had stood at 875,000 tons; by October this figure had been cut almost in half; and by April 1918 the total was down to 278,000 tons. The war against the dreaded and hated U-boats was clearly being won by the American and British destroyers and their companion vessels.

The U.S. surface navy never fired on an enemy surface vessel during World War I, even though a division of battleships joined the Grand Fleet at Scapa Flow and cruisers escorted convoys of men and ships across the North Atlantic. Still, American naval aid was invaluable to the Allied cause. In addition to their ASW duties, American bluejackets laid over 56,000 mines (with 70-foot tendrils that exploded when a sub or ship brushed against them) across the North Sea between June and October 1918. This closed off that vital waterway to the German navy and served as a crushing blow to the German navy's morale. The United States Navy, now grown to over 2,000 ships and over 520,000 officers and men (including 70,000 marines), played a junior, though vital, role in the seaborne phase of the Great Crusade before it ended with the armistice of November 1918.

THE AMERICAN EXPEDITIONARY FORCE

Like the U.S. Navy, the U.S. Army was unprepared for war when it finally came. Since a sizable land force would be needed to fight in Europe and the number of 200,000 regulars and guardsmen was obviously inadequate to the task, Congress in May 1917 passed the Selective Service Act (avoiding the onerous term *conscription* to forestall opposition to the measure), only the second time in its history that the nation had moved to drafting soldiers to fill its ranks. Unlike during the Civil War, conscription legislation this time allowed for no exemptions by purchase or substitution, and no bounties were paid. All men from the ages of 21 to 31 (later expanded to 18 to 45) were required to register, and local draft boards were authorized to exempt from service those men physically or mentally unfit, holding essential jobs, or claiming dependents. Before the war was over, 24 million men had been registered (45 percent of all men) and 2.8 million had been inducted (representing about three-fourths of the "Doughboys" who served alongside the regulars and guardsmen) and put through a six-month training program. Unlike the Civil War, too, this time there were no lateral appointments of prominent citizens to command positions. Some 96,000 officers were trained in special camps and on college campuses—and were quickly dubbed "90-day wonders"—to lead the swelling American land forces.

Some 2 million men (of 4.8 million who served in all branches of service during the war) were eventually sent to Europe to make up 42 divisions in the American Expeditionary Force. These included 200,000 blacks who served in France in segregated units under white officers, three-fourths of them in the rear in labor and supply units. Those black units that did see combat, such as the 92nd Division, did not fare well, being poorly trained and poorly led. Those blacks who married French women during the war were given the choice of being discharged there and staying with their wives or coming home without them when the fighting ended. But the use of black soldiers in combat in World War I was a clear sign of changes that would come during and after World War II, a generation later.

☆   An American Portrait

John J. Pershing—The highest ranking Army officer to serve between George Washington and World War II, "Black Jack" Pershing was born to a poor family in September 1860 in Laclede, Missouri. His childhood education was sporadic, as was his study at State Normal School in Kirksville, Missouri, leading him to apply to West Point to gain a proper education. As he stated to a friend, "I won't stay in the Army. There won't be a war in a hundred years. I'll study law. I want an education now and this is one sure way to get it."

FIGURE 7–1   John J. Pershing. (*National Archives, Washington, D.C.*)

At the Military Academy between 1882 and 1886, Pershing discovered a love for the Army and a flair for leadership, being chosen first captain in his fourth year and being graduated thirtieth in his class of 77 cadets. For five years he served with the cavalry in the West on campaigns against the Indians before being assigned as Professor of military science at the University of Nebraska. Here he not only created an outstanding corps of cadets (who proudly called themselves the "Pershing Rifles"), but he also took a degree in law in 1893. After a year as aide to General Nelson A. Miles in Washington, Pershing was sent back to West Point as an instructor in tactics (here picking up the sobriquet "Black Jack" from the cadets because of his previous command of black troops in the West and his unusually stern demeanor).

With the outbreak of the Spanish-American War, Pershing fought in Cuba at San Juan Hill, Kettle Hill, and Santiago (winning the Silver Star). Then, after being briefly billeted in Washington, he was sent to the Philippines in 1899, where he distinguished himself in campaigns against the Moro tribesmen.

Pershing's star was definitely on the rise. In 1903 he was appointed to the General Staff, in 1904 he was sent to the Army War College, in 1905 he became military attaché to Japan, and in 1906 he was promoted from captain to brigadier general over 862 officers superior in rank, thanks to his achievements and his winning the favorable notice of President Theodore Roosevelt.

After eight more years in the Philippines, in 1914 he was appointed commandant of the Eighth Brigade at the Presidio in San Francisco, he and his brigade being ordered to Fort Bliss, Texas, because of the border incidents with Mexico. The following year he was crushed by the news of the death of his wife and three daughters (his son survived) in a fire at his quarters back at the Presidio. With the outbreak of major trouble with Mexico in 1916, Pershing was ordered to lead the Punitive Expedition into that country and was promoted to major general.

While serving at San Antonio as commandant of the Southern Department, Pershing was called to Washington in May 1917 to assume command of the American Expeditionary Force being sent to Europe. Four months later he was promoted to full general and, in September 1918, in the closing weeks of the war, to general of the armies, the rank once held by Washington. Three years later he was named chief of staff. He retired from the Army in September 1924, gave sound advice to the Army's top officers in the interwar years and during World War II, and died on July 15, 1948, honored as one of America's greatest soldiers.

The first units of the AEF landed in France in June 1917. They were led by crag-jawed, ramrod-straight General John J. Pershing, chosen to command over five other major generals for his no-nonsense approach to military duty. His appointment to lead the AEF was also based on his reputation as a strict but fair disciplinarian, and his leadership of the incursion into Mexico the year before. The number of American Doughboys would increase to 1 million by the summer of 1918 and to 2 million by the time of the November armistice. As they underwent another two months of field training in France before being put into the line (at Pershing's vehement insistence), changes were also taking place at home to make them a more effective fighting force. The dynamic Chief of Staff General Peyton C. March reorganized the entire general staff, including the vital Quartermaster Corps and the Ordnance Department, and added new bureaus for intelligence, war plans, and operations.

☆   An American Portrait

Peyton C. March—Born December 27, 1864, in Easton, Pennsylvania, Peyton Conway March, like Tasker Bliss, was the son of a college professor. His father was a noted philologist at Lafayette College, the school in which March enrolled in 1880 and from which he was graduated with a bachelor's degree in 1884.

That same year March accepted an appointment to West Point, being graduated two years behind his contemporary John J. Pershing and commissioned a lieutenant of artillery in 1888. After eight years of garrison duty, March was sent to the School of Artillery at Fort Monroe, Virginia, in 1896.

With the outbreak of the Spanish-American War in 1898, March was posted to the Philippines, where he was recommended for the Medal of Honor for heroism by General Arthur MacArthur. He went on to serve on MacArthur's staff, helped suppress the Philippine insurrection as a temporary major and lieutenant colonel, and served as provincial governor.

The years 1901 to 1917 saw March occupy various posts as an artillery commander, become an initial appointee to the General Staff in 1903, and serve in the adjutant general's office. With the entry of the United States into World War I, March, then a colonel and commander of the Eighth Field Artillery Regiment, was soon promoted to brigadier general and given command of an artillery brigade in France. He was then advanced to major general and chief of artillery for the AEF.

By the spring of 1918 it was obvious to almost everyone in the Army that the supply and logistical functions were not being performed adequately to support the men overseas despite the efforts of three different chiefs of staff. Accordingly, Secretary of War

Newton D. Baker in March 1918 reorganized the general staff and called March back from Europe to assume the post of acting chief of staff.

Two months later, in May 1918, March was given the temporary rank of general and made chief of staff. Here he worked wonders in logistics by a combination of boundless energy and brusque efficiency. He reduced the powers of the bureau chiefs and created the Air Service, Tank Corps, and Chemical Warfare Service. He galvanized the energy and efforts of the War Department as no predecessor had been able to do. He also made it clear that the chief of staff had primacy over all serving officers and was to be the principal advisor to the Army's civilian chiefs, a view that brought him into direct conflict with Black Jack Pershing during the remaining months of the conflict.

March continued to serve as chief of staff, presiding over the return and demobilization of the men of the AEF, until June 1921, when he retired and Pershing assumed his duties. Thereafter he maintained an active interest in all things military. This included defending the efforts of the War Department during World War I against Pershing's slights in his memoirs by publishing his own volume, *The Nation at War,* in 1932. His interest in the Army continued though World War II and the Korean War. He died on April 13, 1955, in his ninetieth year, in Washington, D.C.

☆   An American Portrait

Tasker H. Bliss—Born on December 31, 1853, in Lewisburg, Pennsylvania, Tasker Bliss was the son of a professor of Greek at the University of Lewisburg (later Bucknell University) and the seventh of 13 children. Partially to relieve the strained family budget, Bliss gained admission to the United States Military Academy at West Point in 1871. He was graduated four years later eighth in his class and was assigned to an artillery unit.

Recalled to West Point in 1876 to teach French and artillery tactics, an assignment that lasted from 1876 to 1880, Bliss was later called to teach military science at the Naval War College in 1885.

His concern for the weaknesses in the Army's organization and his dedication to the idea that the service needed a general staff were the outcome of his seven-year stint in Washington (1888–1895) as an aide to Commanding General John M. Schofield. Although he then spent a number of years as military attaché to Spain, as a field officer in Puerto Rico during the Spanish-American War, and as chief of customs in Cuba as that island was being rehabilitated and modernized, Bliss's interest in army reorganization never flagged.

In 1902 he was called to Washington to advise Secretary of War Elihu Root on staff reforms and was soon promoted to brigadier general and assigned to be the first president of the Army War College. He returned to field duty in the Philippines in 1905, but four years later was recalled to Washington to high staff duty in 1915 and aided Secretary of War Newton D. Baker in building and managing the expanding U.S. Army. On September 22, 1917, he was promoted to general and army chief of staff, in this capacity personally visiting the Western Front and serving as President Wilson's military representative on the Supreme War Council. There he solidly backed General Pershing's demands for more training for his men and maintaining the integrity of the AEF as a single fighting force.

Although he was appointed as a delegate to the Versailles Conference—to his great surprise—Bliss's advice to Wilson was disregarded. He had been relieved as chief of staff and retired as a brevet general in May 1918, spending the decade of the 1920s crusading for arms reduction and for America's joining the World Court. He died on November 9, 1930.

Included in the weapons sent to Europe for the Doughboys' use were the 1903 Springfield rifle (the standard U.S. infantry rifle), the British Enfield rifle modified to fire American ammunition, Vickers-Maxim and water-cooled .30-caliber Browning Model 1917 machine guns, and .30-caliber Browning automatic rifles (BARs), all produced by government and private arsenals. The standard American artillery piece during the war was the French 75-mm gun; American-made 75-mm guns redesigned from French and British models were also used.

Pershing, the American field commander, seeing himself as the American general-in-chief, was loath to operate through the Army's chiefs of staff, including Generals Tasker H. Bliss and Peyton C. March, insisting on answering only to President Wilson and Secretary of War Newton D. Baker. But he did demand, as pointed out, more extensive training for his troops in trench warfare and in offensive operations using the rifle and bayonet before allowing them in battle. Pershing also insisted that his army would fight as a unit, rather than being broken up with its divisions being placed piecemeal in the British and French sectors to shore up those Allied units. Accordingly, the American divisions were placed in the Lorraine sector of the front to the right of the French as both the Allies and Germans prepared for the climactic battles that were sure to come in 1918.

Germany's strategy for 1918 was to take advantage of the collapse of the Eastern Front by shifting troops to the west. Their leaders planned to break through and crush the French and British before the Americans arrived in appreciable numbers and before German morale broke under the strain of the prolonged war and the increasing effectiveness of the Allied blockade. Accordingly, General Erich Ludendorff (nominal deputy to General von Hindenburg but in effective command of the German army) planned a series of hard blows on the Western Front with the 3.5 million men under his command.

FIGURE 7–2   1903 Springfield rifle.(*Smithsonian Institution, Washington, D.C.*)

FIGURE 7–3   .30-cal. Browning 1917 machine gun. (*Smithsonian Institution, Washington, D.C.*)

Tactically, some of the German divisions would be using "Hutier tactics," developed earlier on the Eastern Front by Lieutenant General Oscar von Hutier. These new infantry tactics called for a short but intense artillery barrage before an advance, followed by a rolling barrage behind which small groups of infantrymen, each group with a light machine gun, would cut off enemy strong points. Then the masses of regular infantry would break through with great speed to overwhelm the enemy's infantry lines and artillery.

On March 21, 1918, the Germans launched a major attack north of Saint Quentin on the Somme River against the left sector of the Allied line. Their target was the British army and the long-sought Channel ports. Two great waves of men, proceeding after an intense artillery barrage by 6,000 guns and then following a rolling barrage, jumped off along a 50-mile front. This first attack enjoyed some initial success thanks to the Germans' Hutier tactics and Pétain's unwillingness to send reinforcements to his British allies. But by the end of the month the drive had bogged down because of determined British resistance and a lack of adequate German forces to push their advantage, and Ludendorff was forced to suspend the offensive on April 5.

One month later, a second attack on the British on the Lys River in Flanders had also bogged down (56,000 German and 21,000 Allied soldiers lay dead from these two actions), so on May 27 he launched a diversionary attack on the French at Chemin des Dames ("the Walkway of the Ladies," named for a road built along its crest by Louis XV for his three daughters' walking pleasure) northeast of Paris to draw off British reserves. When his initial thrusts went better than expected, Ludendorff strengthened his drive and was soon at the Marne River, less than 50 miles from Paris, at Château-Thierry.

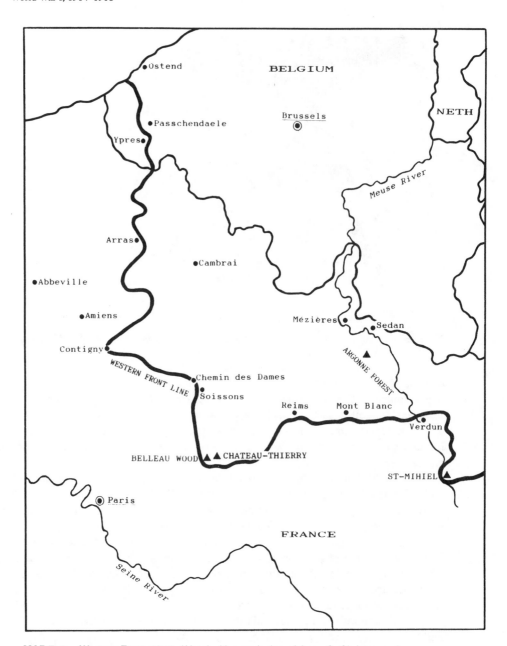

MAP 7–1   Western Front, 1918. (*Used with permission of Anne C, Christensen.*)

It was here in June 1918 that American troops joined their allies to stop the German drive, Pershing finally being forced by the pressure of events to relent and allow his men to be used with Allied forces rather than separately. After the Americans' success in stopping the Germans at Château-Thierry, they went on to capture Belleau Wood (three battalions of marines winning particular praise for their courage in the fight), the American troops showing outstanding élan and fighting skill. But in helping the French block the road to Paris in the Château-Thierry–Belleau Wood operations, the American fighting men paid a high price of almost 10,000 casualties, including over 1,800 men dead. Two subsequent drives by Ludendorff in June and July through the Ameins and Marne salients in the Allied line also failed, thanks in part to ten American divisions being on the line there. These failed offensives left the German forces exhausted and vulnerable to Allied counterattack.

Counteroffensives were exactly what the Allied military high command (consisting of Field Marshal Haig for the British, Marshal Pétain for the French, and General Pershing for the Americans) had been planning to launch as soon as the German drives had spent themselves. The French would now attack and remove the Marne salient in the center sector of the line, the British and French would attack the Amiens salient on the left of the line, and the Americans would attack the Saint-Mihiel salient on the right. This would be followed by a grand offensive all along the front to drive the Germans out of France and out of the war.

The French attack of July 18, 1918, on the Marne salient—in which eight American divisions were included—brought heavy casualties but drove the Germans back 20 miles. The August 8 British-French attack on the Amiens salient, in which the British massed 400 tanks to lead the attack and scored the first armored breakthrough in modern times, collapsed the German positions and forced them back to the Hindenburg Line. Preceded by a four-hour artillery barrage in which more than 1 million rounds were fired, the September 12 attack on the Saint-Mihiel salient by the Americans with 550,000 troops, 260 tanks, and 1,500 airplanes on the Saint-Mihiel salient by the Americans was also an enormous success, with 16,000 prisoners and 443 guns being captured while taking only 7,000 casualties. The American victory in the Saint-Mihiel operation was aided by the fact that the Germans were shortening their lines by abandoning the salient. The long, 470-mile Western Front had now been straightened by the three Allied attacks. It was time for the final blow.

The Allied plan was to hit the Germans so hard that they would be forced back to their border, leaving their supplies behind and thus precluding their being able to fight on. The French would attack in the center, while the British on the left would attack at Cambrai-Saint Quentin. Meanwhile, the Americans were to move through the Meuse River–Argonne Forest section and, in a giant pincer movement with the British, take the key railroad junctions of Aulnoye and Mézières to isolate the German forces on the Hindenburg Line. Jumpoff date for this coordinated operation was set for September 26.

For the Americans to be in position 50 miles away on that day, they had to move 600,000 troops from Saint-Mihiel to their new 24-mile front facing north in only 14 days. That this logistical feat was carried out was due to the brilliant work of Colonel George C. Marshall, chief of operations for the newly designated First Army.

Assembled along the front with the Argonne Forest on the left of the line and the Meuse River on the right, the Americans were able to launch their attack on time with the support of 2,300 guns and 840 Allied planes. Their front was gradually widened to 90 miles as they fought for 47 days against 47 German divisions through four defensive lines to drive through the Argonne Forest and on to the Meuse, in the process giving America its greatest Doughboy hero of the war, Corporal Alvin York of Tennessee, who, in a single engagement, killed 25 Germans and captured 132 more. Some 1.2 million American troops were eventually involved in the offensive. After the heaviest infantry fighting for the longest sustained period of time in American military history, and after the Americans had suffered 120,000 casualties (including 26,667 dead), the front was finally cleared. The American troops crossed the Meuse on November 5 as the French seized Mézières and the British took Aulnoye.

With the Americans and French moving on into Sedan, with German military resistance collapsing all along the front, with the High Seas Fleet in open mutiny and flying the red flag of revolution when ordered to sea for one last suicidal clash, and with civilian demands for peace rising to a crescendo, Kaiser Wilhelm II abdicated (escaping into neutral Holland), and negotiations for an armistice were begun. In the subsequent peace talks the Germans promised to evacuate the Allied territories they still held, give up the key bridgeheads across the Rhine frontier, and surrender their military supplies, including almost all their surface vessels and all of their U-boats. Agreement was reached in a railroad car in the Compiègne Forest on November 8, and all fighting ceased at 11:00 in the morning on the eleventh day of the eleventh month, 1918.

The Great Crusade, the Great War, the "war to end all wars," "the war to make the world safe for democracy"—World War I—was over. Germany and its allies had been defeated, but only at the price of immense physical damage and human loss to all the combatants. The war had resulted in 37.5 million casualties both military and civilian, including 8.5 million dead. Some 261,000 Americans had become casualties, and 50,280 had paid for victory with their lives. (The great influenza epidemic of 1918 had accounted for more soldiers' deaths at home and abroad, some 57,000.) And, without realizing it, America had emerged as the greatest power in the world. How the nation would use this power and what it would mean to its military forces after the boys came home and the cheering stopped were questions still to be answered.

THE EMERGENCE OF AIR POWER

From the beginning of recorded time, man had fought his battles for domination and defense on the two earth surfaces, the land and the sea. World War I changed all that. Henceforth, wars would also be fought in the air, perhaps the final frontier for combat between nations.

Lighter-than-air observation balloons had been used by American forces in both the Civil War and the Spanish-American War, and in 1908 the German army commissioned its first zeppelin (a hydrogen-filled, cylindrical, rigid balloon) for reconnaissance and even bombing missions, but the invention of the heavier-than-air airplane back in 1903 by the Wright brothers soon brought another dimension to war. The airplane had a wider and faster cruising range than balloons for reconnaissance, was less vulnerable to ground-to-air fire, and was eventually fitted with weaponry for offensive purposes.

The United States Army established an Aeronautical Division as part of the Signal Corps in 1907 and purchased its first plane two years later, but it still lagged behind the European nations in this field. In 1914 the Aviation Section of the Signal Corps was formed, but, thanks to a parsimonious Congress, by 1917 it had only two dozen pilots, 1,100 enlisted men, and 224 planes—none of which was designed for combat.

The Air Service, U.S. Army, was established that same year, and by war's end 18 months later, it had acquired 11,000 planes, but their production was too late to give the United States a major role in the air war on the Western Front.

The Air Service in France eventually boasted almost 3,000 planes and 5,000 pilots, but fewer than 700 of the planes were American-made; most were borrowed from the Allies. Nevertheless, the Air Service played a role in the fighting beside the air branches of the Allied powers, initially in an aerial reconnaissance role wherein the aviators were equipped with simplified and improved long-focus light-filtration cameras. Subsequently they began engaging enemy planes in air-to-air combat and in strafing and bombing enemy positions. American aviators recorded almost 800 "kills" of enemy aircraft and 73 balloons while suffering less than 300 losses (most to weather, mechanical failure, and pilot error).

The aviators, organized in pursuit, observation, and bomber squadrons, added a thrilling and romantic aura to the fighting in France (even though the top speed of their planes was only 120 miles an hour and they were normally limited to about 13,000 feet in altitude). The American public thrilled to the exploits of such "aces" as Eddie Rickenbacker, Douglas Campbell, Raoul Lufbery, and Frank Luke, Jr., flying their bi-wing British Sopwith Camels and French Nieuports and Spads. Lufbery was a former member of the famed *Escadrille Americaine,* or Lafayette Escadrille, a group of 38 American volunteer fliers (plus four Frenchmen) who fought for France between April 1916 and February 1918. The great German air hero was Baron Manfred von Richthofen—the Red Baron—with 80 "kills" to his credit before his death in April 1918.

More important for the future, the accomplishments of the aviators produced fanatical devotees of air power. Chief among them were General Hugh Trenchard, commander of the British Royal Air Force; General Giulio Douhet, of Italy; and Brigadier Generals Benjamin D. Foulois and William Mitchell, of the Army Air Service. The latter two American devotees were placed under the firm command and control of Major General Mason T. Patrick as head of the Air Service during the war. Patrick was a much less enthusiastic and more prudent spokesman for air power and its combat use.

Air-power enthusiasts saw the airplane as an offensive weapon, bombing behind enemy lines to crush his ability to carry out warfare (as both sides had done in a limited way with their twin-engine bombers beginning in 1917), the genesis of strategic bombing. Some aviators argued that the airplane would soon make land and sea combat obsolete, and "Billy" Mitchell displayed no hesitancy in arguing that the Air Service should be completely separate from the Army and Navy and under its own unified command.

Mitchell's arguments won few converts in the Army or the Navy, for the Navy by this time had developed its own air force and had 2,000 airplanes and over 1,600 aviators. It had experimented successfully with launching and recovering airplanes from ships and had equipped some of its battleships and cruisers with light seaplanes for reconnaissance duties. It had also located and attacked German U-boats and surface vessels from land bases while protecting convoys during the course of the war.

Whatever the validity of the arguments of Trenchard, Douhet, Foulois, and Mitchell, and whatever the reactions of the land-based and sea-based generals and admirals, control and use of the air was now clearly a part of modern warfare. The interwar decades from 1919 to 1939 would see an extension of the technological possibilities of the use of the airplane, as well as of the submarine and the tank; improved ordnance, antiaircraft guns (first styled "mobile balloon guns"), and field radios; mechanical calculators for cryptography; and other innovations that marked the fighting of World War I.

Improvements in all of these areas would continue even while the world recovered from the bloodletting of World War I, tried vainly to find some means to ensure peace, and finally and reluctantly again took up their weapons to fight World War II in 1939.

Suggestions for Further Reading

BARBEAU, ARTHUR E., and FLORETTE HENRI, *The Unknown Soldier: Black American Troops in World War I.* Philadelphia: Temple University Press, 1974.

BARNETT, CORRELLI, *The Swordbearers: Supreme Command in the First World War.* Bloomington: Indiana University Press, 1963.

BEAVER, DANIEL R., *Newton D. Baker and the American War Effort, 1917–1919.* Lincoln: University of Nebraska Press, 1966.

BRAIM, PAUL F., *The Test of Battle: The American Expeditionary Forces in the Meuse-Argonne Campaign.* Newark: University of Delaware Press, 1987.

CAMPBELL, J. J. M., *Jutland: An Analysis of the Fighting.* Annapolis: Naval Institute Press, 1986.

COFFMAN, EDWARD M., *The Hilt of the Sword: The Career of Peyton C. March.* Madison: University of Wisconsin Press, 1966.

———, *The War to End All Wars: The American Military Experience in World War I.* New York: Oxford University Press, 1968.

FALLS, CYRIL, *The Great War.* New York: Putnam's, 1959.

FREIDEL, FRANK, *Over There: The Story of America's First Great Crusade.* Boston: Little, Brown, 1964.

FUSSELL, PAUL, *The Great War and Modern Memory.* New York: Oxford University Press, 1975.

HART, B. H. LIDDELL, *The Real War, 1914–1918.* Boston: Little, Brown, 1930.

HENRI, FLORETTE, and RICHARD STILLMAN, *Bitter Victory: A History of Black Soldiers in World War I.* New York: Doubleday, 1970.

HORNE, ALISTAIR, *The Price of Glory: Verdun, 1916.* New York: St. Martin's Press, 1963.

HOUGH, RICHARD, *The Great War at Sea, 1914–1918.* New York: Oxford University Press, 1983.

HUDSON, JAMES J., *Hostile Skies: A Combat History of the American Air Service in World War I.* Syracuse: Syracuse University Press, 1968.

KENNEDY, DAVID M., *Over Here: The First World War and American Society.* New York: Oxford University Press, 1980.

MACDONALD, LYN, *Somme.* London: M. Joseph, 1983.

MACKSEY, KENNETH, *Tank versus Tank: The Illustrated Story of Armored Battlefield Conflict in the Twentieth Century.* Topsfield, MA: Salem House, 1988.

MARDER, ARTHUR J., *From the Dreadnought to Scapa Flow,* 5 vols. New York: Oxford University Press, 1961–1970.

MILLER, STEVEN, ed., *Military Strategy and the Origins of the First World War.* Princeton, NJ: Princeton University Press, 1985.

O'CONNOR, RICHARD, *Black Jack Pershing*. Garden City, NY: Doubleday, 1961.

PAXSON, FREDERIC L., *American Democracy and the World War,* 2 vols. Boston: Houghton Mifflin, 1936–1939.

SMYTHE, DONALD, *Pershing: General of the Armies*. Bloomington: Indiana University Press, 1986.

STALLINGS, LAWRENCE, *The Doughboys: The Story of the AEF, 1917–1918*. New York: Harper, 1963.

STONE, NORMAN, *The Eastern Front, 1914–1917*. New York: Scribner's, 1975.

TERRAINE, JOHN, *To Win a War: 1918, the Year of Victory*. Garden City, NY: Doubleday, 1981.

———, *The Western Front, 1914–1918*. Philadelphia: Lippincott, 1965.

VANDIVER, FRANK G., *Black Jack: The Life and Times of John J. Pershing,* 2 vols. College Station: Texas A&M Press, 1977.

WARNER, PHILIP, *Passchendaele*. New York: Atheneum, 1987.

WINTER, J. M., *The Experience of World War I*. New York: Oxford University Press, 1988.

WOLFF, LEON, *In Flanders Field: The 1917 Campaign*. New York: Viking, 1958.

☆8

The Interwar Years, 1919–1939

A collective sense of relief and joy erupted across America on November 11, 1918, as the armistice went into effect, the guns fell silent, and the killing stopped. The Great War was over. It was time to rejoice. It was "over over there." Soon the soldiers would return to giant big-city parades and more modest small-town celebrations.

Most Americans agreed that it was now time to create a peace structure so that never again would young sons, husbands, brothers, and lovers be forced to march off to war, there to die or be maimed in battle. There had to be a better way to quarantine violence between nations. Reason and compromise had to be accepted as the preferred means of pursuing national goals. The price of "going to Armageddon to battle for the Lord" had been too high. An international organization with enforcement powers greater than that of the ineffective World Court at The Hague in the Netherlands had to be devised. President Woodrow Wilson had revealed such a concept back in January, the fitting and climactic last of his Fourteen Points proposed to the warring nations. And the international arms race had to be replaced by international disarmament.

The time was right—indeed, it was overdue, most agreed—to create peace after the bloodiest conflict of modern times, over 8 million corpses bearing mute testimony to the futility of war. But first the matter of the continued fighting in now-Bolshevik Russia, caught up in civil war, the Reds threatening to succeed in establishing a permanent socialist revolutionary regime in that abused land, had to be dealt with.

INTERVENTION IN RUSSIA

Even before the armistice had ended the fighting in western Europe, President Wilson had authorized the sending of American troops into Russia to aid the Allies in supporting the anti-Bolshevik White armies against the Red armies of the Communists, led by Leon Trotsky as war commissar. One Allied expedition had been sent into the Murmansk–Archangel region of northern Russia. Some 5,000 American troops (mostly National Guardsmen from Wisconsin and Michigan, along with 25 sailors and marines from the cruiser *Olympia*) under British command had landed in Russia in September 1918 to face some 20,000 Red Guards (later numbering 35,000). They sustained 550 casualties while guarding supply lines for the Whites and carrying out minor offensive operations, but they were withdrawn in June 1919, their presence having made no appreciable difference in the outcome of the Russian civil conflict on the northern frontier.

A larger force of Allied soldiers, consisting of 8,400 Americans (including 17 female nurses) and constituting the American Expeditionary Force Siberia had landed 3,500 miles to the east at Vladivostock on the Sea of Japan beginning in August 1918. They had been sent there by their governments to attempt to rescue Czech troops trying to fight their way out of Russia to freedom and to aid Admiral Aleksandr V. Kolchak and his White Army forces. At the same time, it was hoped in the West, the Allied force would serve to curb any unilateral Japanese attempts to gain territory in Russia during its second time of troubles. Commanded by Major General William S. Graves (ably assisted by his brilliant young G-2, Lieutenant Colonel Robert L. Eichelberger), the American soldiers, all regulars, along with their Allied counterparts, were too few in number to affect the titanic struggle for empire then underway and, at any rate, were withdrawn in early 1920. However noble the Allies' goals, the interventions in Russia ran contrary to the post-armistice spirit of war-weariness felt by the people of the Allied nations, who only wanted the armies to be demobilized to let the soldiers get on with their lives, whatever the consequences for the Russian people.

More forceful and sustained intervention in Russia between 1918 and 1920 might well have tipped the balance against the Bolsheviks, but peace was in the air in the West. The victorious Allied leaders were more concerned with the postwar settlement in central and western Europe than with the fate of the Russian masses. Above all, high costs and casualties, the price of a spirited and determined Allied intervention, would never have been accepted. Thus Russia was left to its fate as the Allied nations turned their interest and efforts to demobilization and to the peace conference then underway at the Palace of Versailles outside Paris.

DEMOBILIZATION, DIPLOMACY, AND DISARMAMENT

It was necessary for the United States to retain some occupation troops in Europe for a short time. American soldiers moved across the border into Germany within a month of the 1918 armistice and stayed there until January 1923, after the United States signed a separate peace treaty with Germany in 1921. A regiment also served briefly in Austria until 1919. As noted, some troops also served in Russia until 1920. Still, most of the men of the AEF and the expanded U.S. Navy and Marine Corps were brought home and discharged as quickly as possible.

The Doughboys in France were returned to American soil just as rapidly as ships could be found to carry them back across the Atlantic, then mustered out of service by units through demobilization centers scattered throughout the country. Within months, 3 1/4 million men of the 4 million-man Army had been discharged, the Army's pleas for a 600,000-man regular force and a three-month universal military training program having been rejected virtually out of hand by Congress. By the end of 1919, the Army, now an all-volunteer regular force, was down to 225,000 officers and enlisted men. Units of this small force remained in Europe and Russia, were garrisoned on the Mexican border, and were used in putting down strikes and labor violence that broke out in the postwar years, the National Guard units having not yet been reconstituted.

The Navy discharged its men and 12,000 female "yoemanettes" in similar fashion. By 1920 its numbers were down to only 121,845, and the Marine Corps that year stood at 17,165. Whatever the world scene, whatever the nation's obligations in the world, the spirit of peace had triumphed in America, and a strong military, in the minds of most of the citizenry, had become superfluous. This confidence that "war is behind us, peace is at hand" was reflected in Woodrow Wilson's attitudes and actions at Versailles in 1919.

The Allies had accepted the high-flown declarations of principle of Wilson's Fourteen Points in early November 1918 as the basis for postwar negotiations with representatives of the Central Powers. Yet the true vengeful spirit of America's European allies toward Germany and its allies (embodied in various secret treaties entered into during the war to carve up German and Central Power territories when the fighting ended) soon came to the fore as the victors sat down at Versailles in January 1919 to speak of peace and decide the fate of the vanquished.

Seventy delegates from 27 countries (not including any representatives of the Central Powers) were present for the peace conference. Real decision making, however, quickly fell to the "Big Four" (Prime Minister Georges "The Tiger" Clemenceau of France, Prime Minister David Lloyd George of Britain, Prime Minister Vittorio Orlando of Italy, and President Wilson) and then the "Big Three" (when Orlando stormed home, his demands for compensation for Italy being rebuffed; he later returned). Within the Big Four, and then the Big Three, the prevailing sentiment—except for Wilson—was for punishing and crippling Germany.

After the conferees had worked out their treaty—Wilson having scuttled his pious ideas of self-determination for all nations and having accepted the imposition of a Draconian peace on the Germans in exchange for the Allies' agreeing to create a peacekeeping League of Nations—the excluded representatives from Germany were ushered in to the meeting in April and were told that they had to accept the agreement with no possibility of changes being made in the document. They were aghast when they read the proposed terms of peace.

The treaty said that they must accept full guilt for the war. Furthermore, the industrial and mineral-rich Saar Basin and the left bank of the Rhine were to be internationalized, and the right bank was to be demilitarized for 30 miles. Germany would have to pay for all civilian damages caused to all Allied nations during the war (the amount unspecified but an initial $5 billion downpayment due in two years). Further, the output of the Saar and Alsace-Lorraine coal mines would all go to France, and another 25 million tons of coal would be paid to that country annually. Danzig and part of East Prussia would go to re-created Poland to give it an outlet on the Baltic. Further, Germany would lose all its African colonies, could not join the new League of Nations, and was subject to other punishing provisions, including the loss of the Marshall, Marianas, and Caroline islands in the Pacific to Japan.

The German delegation refused to sign the treaty. But with the nation facing starvation (the Allies refused to lift the now-ironclad blockade until the Germans accepted the peace settlement), with the internal danger of Communist takeovers in many German cities becoming very real, and under the threat of invasion, a second delegation was assembled to return to Versailles to sign the treaty. The delegates were still reluctant, but they had to affix their signatures to save the nation from complete disaster.

The German representatives signed on June 28, 1919, in the Hall of Mirrors at Versailles. The treaty was more an outgrowth of Clemenceau's thirst for vengeance and Lloyd George's desire to cripple Germany as a competitor than of Woodrow Wilson's idealism. Wilson got his League of Nations; France got its revenge.

Subsequently, treaties were made with the other Central Powers between 1919 and 1923. Their provisions, along with those of the Treaty of Versailles, changed the map of eastern and central Europe almost completely. Estonia, Latvia, and Lithuania were created on the Baltic out of Russian territory. Poland was re-created from Russian, German, and Austrian territories. Austria and Hungary were emasculated, Czechoslovakia and Yugoslavia being created out of their territories and those of others. It was clearly a case of self-determination for all peoples—but only if convenient and approved by the victorious parties.

Ironically, though, Wilson, who refused to listen not only to General Tasker Bliss but also to his professional, academic, and personal advisors while at Versailles, came home to see his League of Nations and his Treaty of Versailles (the two were inexorably intertwined) rejected by the now-Republican-dominated Senate despite his best efforts to "sell" them to that body. When it appeared certain that he could not get enough affirmative votes in the Senate for its approval, he embarked on a campaign to convince the American people of the righteousness of the treaty and the League. His crusade carried him on an 8,000-mile, 36-stop railroad swing through the nation. But his health broke under the strain and left him an invalid during his last months in office. The United States never ratified the Treaty of Versailles and never joined the League of Nations, the effects of which are still debated to this day.

But if diplomacy as embodied in the Treaty of Versailles must be considered a failure—as were the harsh terms of the treaty itself since they led to the resurgence of Germany in the early 1930s, this time under Adolph Hitler and his Nazi party—American ventures in the area of disarmament were much more successful.

America's love–hate relationship with its military reasserted itself quickly in the aftermath of World War I. As the nation had embraced the rightness of military action in 1917—"God helping her, she can do no other," Wilson had exclaimed—so now it turned to demobilization, disarmament, and isolationism with a vengeance. Undoubtedly some of this extreme reaction sprang from disillusionment when the secret treaties promulgated by the Allies to carve up the Central Powers were released by the Bolsheviks for all the world to see. This information, after all, called into question the whole purpose of the Great Crusade. Likewise, the Draconian provisions of the Treaty of Versailles made it clear that the Allies' purposes were subject to reexamination. When an overwhelming desire to return to "normalcy" (the term was that of Warren Harding, Wilson's successor) also swept the nation, the Americans in the 1920s turned their backs on Europe as "ungrateful" and retreated into isolationism behind their watery moats, the Atlantic and the Pacific.

So, too, with arms. If the nations had not had armies, navies, and weapons of war, the popular argument went, there would have been no war. Therefore, reduce or ban the weapons of war—as well as the number of warriors—and you will reduce or banish war. This typical American reaction, shared by the war-weary European nations, gave birth to three disarmament conferences during the interwar period, beginning with the Washington Naval Conference called by the United States in 1921.

The navies of the world were the logical targets for the disarmers because they had grown to considerable size before and during World War I and were the most visible symbols of overblown militarism. The United States Navy had 16 Dreadnoughts, 13 more building, and 12 new cruisers coming on line. Britain had 33 Dreadnoughts and was preparing to build even more, plus four great battlecruisers. Japan was creating two great naval squadrons of battleships and cruisers, and the French and Italian navies were still formidable and seeking expansion.

Called to Washington in August 1921 to discuss this problem and the expansionist actions of Japan in the Far East were representatives of nine nations. The Harding administration, reacting to a tide of popular opinion in favor of naval reduction, had issued the call. When the delegates met the following month, the American secretary of state, Charles Evans Hughes, seized the initiative in his opening speech by announcing that the United States was willing to scrap 30 battleships (15 existing, 15 building) if the other naval powers were willing to make similar moves. Hughes went on to lay out his ideas on exactly what scrapping should be done by the others. In the absence of any agreed-upon agenda, Hughes's ideas became the basis of negotiations, and three wide-ranging agreements were reached before the conference ended the following February.

The naval disarmament treaty that emerged, known as the Five Power Treaty, set up a ratio of 5 to 5 to 3 to 1.7 to 1.7 in capital ships and carriers. The nations involved were the United States, 525,000 displacement tons in battleships; Great Britain, 525,000 tons; Japan 315,000 tons; France, 175,000 tons; and Italy, 175,000 tons. Aircraft carrier limits were set at 135,000 tons (United States), 135,000 tons (Britain), 81,000 tons (Japan), 45,000 tons (France), and 45,000 tons (Italy), with no carriers over 27,000 tons except 2 carrier conversions from battleships per country (each could be up to 33,000 tons). No capital ships (battleships and cruisers) could be built for 10 years, and none built could be over 35,000 tons and carry guns larger than 16 inches. Cruisers were limited to 10,000 tons and 8-inch ordnance. This 10-year Five Power Treaty effectively ended capital ship construction for a decade, exactly the intention of the proponents of naval disarmament.

The Four Power Treaty (United States, Britain, France, and Japan) formally recognized the signatories' possessions in the Far East, the four nations agreeing to settle all disputes over them by joint conferences. The Nine Power Treaty (the four nations just noted plus the other attendees, Italy, China, Belgium, the Netherlands, and Portugal) pledged to retain the "Open Door" in China, the doctrine first enunciated by American

Secretary of State John Hay in 1899 when the United States became a Far Eastern power with the acquisition of the Philippines after the Spanish-American War. Neither treaty proved to be in the least effective when the Japanese embarked on their path of conquest in Manchuria and China in the 1930s.

But the Five Power Treaty was a reality governing naval ships, and the U.S. Navy was soon cut back to its "treaty strength" and beyond. Congress was only too willing to cooperate for the next decade, the Navy managing, however, to gain one carrier by the conversion of a collier into the inadequate *Langley* and making plans for two new carriers (eventually the *Lexington* and *Saratoga*) built on now-nonallowable cruiser hulls. The Navy did not get the replacement cruisers it begged for until 1929, with the "15-Cruiser Bill." This concession was granted only after the 1927 disarmament conference at Geneva to control cruisers, destroyers, and submarines came to nothing.

But more naval disarmament was in the works. President Calvin Coolidge was converted to building up to treaty strength in cruisers by the failure of the Geneva Conference. But his successor, the peace-loving Quaker Herbert Hoover, saw the Geneva failure not as a call to catch up but as a summons to take more forceful action against naval building. Working with Prime Minister Ramsey MacDonald of Great Britain, the two leaders called the London Naval Conference of 1930. Its deliberations resulted in restrictions on light (6-inch gun) and heavy (8-inch gun) cruisers and on destroyers and submarines. Battleships were further reduced, and the capital ship-building holiday was continued until 1936. But the restrictive London Naval Treaty, for all its high hopes, included an escape clause that allowed any nation to pull out of the agreement when threatened by a nonsignatory power plus an escalator clause whereby if one signatory exceeded its tonnage, all could do likewise. Japan, beginning its expansion into Manchuria in 1931, used the escape clause to scuttle limitations on its navy, the escalator clause thus kicking in to render the naval agreements mute by the mid-1930s.

In the meantime, however, the various naval disarmament agreements had just about gutted the U.S. Navy. By 1933 it had only 101 modern vessels and 90,000 officers and men and stood at only 65 percent of treaty strength. It stood weakest just as the world was about to witness renewed aggression to which it would be called upon to respond.

The Army was worse off than its sister service. Congress did not need international conferences to slash it to the bone. By 1923 it had been cut back to 12,000 officers and 125,000 enlisted men—where it remained until 1936. In 1933, the Army's chief of staff, Douglas MacArthur, observed that the United States stood seventeenth in the world in army strength. But to the proponents of peace and disarmament, such figures for the Army and Navy—the Marine Corps stood at only 16,068 officers and men in 1933— showed that things were going well militarily. Only in selected areas of development did the services fare well during the 1920s and 1930s.

THE NATIONAL DEFENSE ACT OF 1920

Congress in 1920 made its rejection of Elihu Root's expansible-army concept final when it passed the National Defense Act. By this milestone legislation the Army of the United States (AUS) was established. It was divided into the Regular Army, the

National Guard, and the Organized Reserves (Officer and Enlisted). This reflected the idea promulgated in the National Defense Act of 1916 of an army made up of regulars in addition to trained civilians to fit the nation's peacetime and wartime needs. With the professional regulars being at the heart of the AUS as the permanent cadre assigned to train the nonprofessionals, an increase in its authorized strength to 287,000 officers and men was included, although actual numbers would depend upon congressional authorizations.

The act also added three new branches to the Army (Air Service, Chemical Warfare Service, and Finance Department), while the Tank Corps was downgraded and disappeared, henceforth to be part of the infantry. The War Department was given authority over mobilization planning, and the chief of staff and the members of the General Staff were to assume direction of strictly military planning for war, the staff members aiding the chief in supervising the entire Army.

Nine corps areas at home and one each in Panama, Hawaii, and the Philippines were designated field commands, each of the 12 corps to include 6 infantry divisions (1 regular, 2 Guard, and 3 reserve), although the overseas areas did not have their full complement of Guard and reserve divisions. ROTC units were expanded, 31 service schools were authorized, and the Command and General Staff School (Fort Leavenworth), the Army War College (Washington), and the Army Industrial College (Washington, added in 1924) for logistics topped off the Army's educational system. General Pershing complemented these changes when he became chief of staff in 1921 by creating within the General Staff five divisions: G-1 (personnel), G-2 (intelligence), G-3 (training and operations), G-4 (supply), and War Plans (long-range strategic planning). At long last the Army had reached functional reorganization, the record of the AUS with its components and functions meeting and passing the test as it geared up for and fought World War II.

Yet the Army's numbers were always far less than authorized, the regulars standing at about 137,000 for a decade and a half. This meant that most units—corps, divisions, brigades, and regiments—were persistently undermanned, some units existing only on paper. Guardsmen (subject to 48 weekend drills and 15 days of field training each year) totaled approximately 180,000 during these years despite the Guard's authorized strength of 400,000 men. The Guard received about 10 percent of the War Department budget. The organized reserves stood at about 100,000, made up almost totally of officers (subject to schooling and brief active duty stints). Over 300 ROTC units on college campuses trained approximately 85,000 students each year to be junior officers, the smaller Citizens' Military Training Camp (CMTC) program furnishing a much smaller number of reserve commissioned officers annually.

Subsequently during the interwar years, the Army, despite its regulars being used in the onerous duty of evicting the "Bonus Marchers" from the nation's capital dispatch in 1932 and having to delegate 3,000 of its officers and enlisted men to run 1,300 Civilian Conservation Corps (CCC) camps for jobless young men in 1933 and 1934 (part of President Franklin Roosevelt's New Deal program), displayed that it had the organization and flexibility to carry out both military and civilian tasks. It also displayed the ability to expand rapidly and efficiently when called upon to accept greater responsibilities as war clouds gathered in Europe and the Far East in the late 1930s.

AIR POWER CONTROVERSY AND ACCEPTANCE

The devotees of air power came out of World War I determined to sell their gospel of strategic bombing as the single determinant of future conflicts. They would deny the Navy its aircraft carriers, the Army its close air support capabilities and fighter planes as unnecessary. In the United States, Brigadier General "Billy" Mitchell garnered all the publicity he could and finally challenged the Navy to allow him to test his theories by bombing naval ships. The test took place off the Virginia Capes in 1921, Mitchell's bombers flying out from Langley Field 75 miles to the west to launch carefully controlled bombing tests. The Army pilots sank the old 22,500-ton German battleship *Ostfriesland* (only after three days of bombing), and Mitchell argued that the airpower exponents had clearly proved their point. The Navy retorted that the tests really showed how difficult it was to sink a ship by bombs. During the demonstration the weather was clear, the bombers knew the exact location of the target ships, there was no antiaircraft fire, and the ships were at anchor. A moving ship properly compartmentalized with a crew on board to carry out damage control measures and fight back, they argued, would actually be very difficult to sink from the air. Time—and subsequent tests on the battleship *Washington* three years later—would prove them right.

Nevertheless, Mitchell, even though he had deliberately violated some of the conditions agreed upon for the tests, viewed them as absolute vindication of his theories and said so loudly and repeatedly to anyone who would listen. Even when Pershing placed Major General Mason T. Patrick, himself an air power advocate, as head of the Air Service to curb Mitchell's public demands for independence for the Air Service, the fiery Mitchell would not tone down his comments in public. He accused the War Department and the Navy Department of "incompetency, criminal negligence, and almost criminal administration." Brought before a court martial and convicted of insubordination, Mitchell resigned his commission in 1926 and left the Army.

Ironically, in that same year the Army Air Corps was established as an equal combat arm and authorized to build to 17,000 men and 1,800 airplanes. It was considerably enlarged and modernized in the next decade, adding to its inventory in 1934 the all-metal, twin-engine Martin B-10 bomber, in 1936 the Boeing B-17 "Flying Fortress" bomber, in 1937 fast monoplanes with enclosed cockpits and retracting landing gear, and in 1939 the Curtiss P-40 and P-38 "Lightning" fighter planes. With over 40 combat air groups, it was well on its way to becoming a major military component of the armed forces when the nation went into serious war preparedness in 1939.

The Navy, too, had accepted air power as a valuable adjunct to its surface and subsurface fleets during the interwar period, placing its Bureau of Aeronautics under the dynamic Rear Admiral William A. Moffett. During the 1920s the air navy had to "make do" with the old 534-foot *Langley* and the 33,000-ton *Lexington* and *Saratoga,* but it was testing and buying fighter planes, torpedo bombers, and dive bombers and using improved catapults and carrier arresting gear. Over 100 planes were purchased between 1926 and 1930, and Pensacola Naval Air Station, where the Navy's pilots and other air officers were trained, became a coveted assignment for naval officers. These officers ranged from enthusiastic young ensigns enamored of the idea of air combat to aging officers "getting their tickets punched" by winning the gold wings of a Navy aviator.

After 1929, with the Coolidge 15 cruisers being built as well as the 14,500-ton, 765-foot carrier *Ranger* (the first American ship built as a carrier from the keel up), the Navy was clearly in the process of rebuilding. By 1932 it had 342 ships in the fleet (including 15 battleships, 20 cruisers, 22 destroyers, and 82 submarines) with another 16 building. It also included 3 carriers. In 1933, two new 20,000-ton carriers, the 825-foot *Enterprise* and *Yorktown,* were authorized, followed in 1936 by the 14,700-ton *Wasp* and then the 20,000-ton *Hornet.* In 1940, the building of the 20,000-ton, 856-foot *Essex*-class carriers was authorized.

By 1939, then, the Navy was in a full resurgence, with 373 ships in its inventory and 77 building. Naval air was very much a part of this naval renaissance, with five carriers afloat and more on the way. Naval air power had become a vital and accepted part of the fleet. The battleship admirals, members of the "Gun Club" and former young progressives themselves in earlier times, still looked to great gunship duels for control of the seas (despite Admiral Sims's having included carriers in the war games at the Naval War College), but air power was now accepted as a part of modern naval warfare for, at the least, any fleet would be blinded without its aircraft carriers. World War II would prove just how important a part it had become.

ARMOR NEGLECTED

Whatever gains had been made in armored fighting vehicles (AFVs) during World War I, they had made little impact on the Army's high command. By 1920 the Tank Corps of 5,000 vehicles and 20,000 men had all but disappeared, and in that same year the corps was disbanded by the National Defense Act. With the approval of General Pershing, its units were assigned to support the infantry. The 700 Renault and the Mark VIII tanks it had been building with the British during the war were retained, but the Army pursued few innovations in design or tactics.

During the interwar years the Russians and British made notable strides in tank design and tactics. They placed their emphasis on mobility and firepower to restore the offensive in land warfare. The Russians borrowed their BT and later T34, T54, T55, and T62 design ideas (sloped armor, a round turret, and big-wheel suspension) from the American 10-ton 1931 Christie T3 medium tank, the work of the inventive but erratic J. Walter Christie. The Christie T3 was rejected by the U.S. Army, not because of design flaws, but simply because it could afford no more than light tanks armed with machine guns.

The British Royal Tank Corps had some latitude for experimentation through the efforts of its armor genius J. F. C. Fuller, who managed to secure for the Corps an "independent role" in addition to supporting infantry. This was an extension of Fuller's famous Plan 1919, which envisioned tanks breaking through with motorized infantry and mechanized artillery to disrupt and cause damage behind the enemy's lines. Using the 12-ton, turreted Vickers Medium tank capable of speeds of 15 miles per hour as its principal AFV, the British carried out a series of tactical trials of tank warfare methods (using newly developed tank-to-tank radio telephones for communication), the best known and most instructive being the 1930 Salisbury Plain maneuvers.

The Germans, too, made great strides in AFV development and tactics under the inspired leadership of Colonel Heinz Guderian. Using the 10-ton, 35-mile-per-hour PzKw 11D

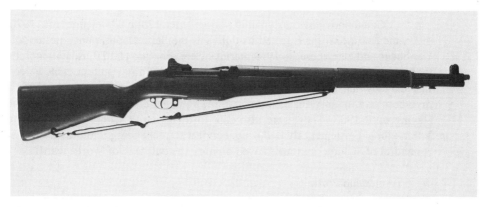

FIGURE 8–1   Garand M1 rifle. (*Smithsonian Institution, Washington, D.C.*)

as their standard light tank and the 18-ton, 25-mile-per-hour PzKw IVC as their medium tank, the Germans, above all, learned the use of concentrated masses of armor to achieve maximum shock effect. Guaderian's tankers also had radio communications systems well integrated into their operating procedures, giving them ground–air coordination lacking in other armies. These tactics and innovations represented the genesis of the Panzer attacks brought into use in World War II.

Yet the Americans still perceived the tank to be only supplemental to infantry. An experimental—and not too successful—mechanized cavalry brigade built around light tanks in the mid-1930s was its only contribution to AFV warfare. On the eve of World War II, the Army's four mechanized regiments were its only commitment to armored warfare. The crash program that produced the inadequate M3 General Grant tank in 1941, with its sponson-mounted 75-mm gun set low on the side of the hull (forcing the tank to full exposure before firing), served as adequate testimony to the Army's neglect of AFV development during the interwar years.

Fortunately, less costly but significant weapons innovations such as the 1935 semi-automatic Garand M1 rifle, 81-mm M1 and 60-mm M2 mortars, 37-mm antitank guns, 105-mm M3 howitzers, and 155-mm "Long Tom" howitzers were made available to the American land armies during the years between the wars. All proved to be superior weapons in combat.

THE MARINE CORPS AND AMPHIBIOUS WARFARE

The men of the Marine Corps during World War I, consolidated into the 4th Marine Brigade in France and proud of their new recruiting slogan "First to Fight," gave more than a fair account of themselves not only at Château-Thierry and Belleau Wood in 1918, but also at Saint-Mihiel and in the Meuse-Argonne offensive. They proved they were more than the "State Department's gendarmes" in the Caribbean and order-keepers on naval vessels and at naval bases; they were also crack infantrymen.

The marines also entered military aviation in the form of the 1st Marine Aviation Air Force, begun in 1917. It reached France the following year and engaged in the final months of the war. Like the Army and Navy, the Marine Corps learned much about technology and tactics during the war and were determined to apply them thereafter.

Commanded by the dynamic Major General John A. Lejeune from 1920 through 1929, the Marine Corps fulfilled its duties as the State Department's police force in the Caribbean and elsewhere. In 1919 marines were sent into Haiti during a revolution there; their numbers were reduced to a handful in 1924, and final pullout came a decade later. In 1926 they made a major incursion into Nicaragua to restore order (and here first used dive-bombing against an enemy force, the initial use of close air support in combat), staying until 1933. They were also sent to Shanghai in China in 1927 to protect the International Settlement there during a civil war, most being withdrawn two years later. A handful of "China marines" stayed on until the outbreak of World War II.

☆ An American Portrait

John A. Lejeune—John Archer Lejeune, commandant of the Marine Corps during its years of modernization, was born in Louisiana in 1867. At age 15 he entered Louisiana State University but left in 1884 when he received an appointment to the United States Naval Academy.

Being graduated sixth in his class of 35 in 1888, Lejeune spent two years as a naval officer before transferring to the Marine Corps. By 1903 he had been advanced to major and given command of the "floating battalion" attached to the Atlantic Fleet, the unit sent by President Theodore Roosevelt to Panama to ensure that province's successful revolution against Columbia. Moving up in rank and responsibility, by 1909 he was a lieutenant colonel and the first Marine Corps officer to be sent to the Army War College.

By the time the United States became involved in World War I, Lejeune had led his marine brigade in the seizure of Veracruz in 1914, had served as assistant to the commandant of the Marine Corps, and had won his star as a brigadier general. He gained a second star as commander of the 4th Marine Brigade in France and was advanced to command of the 2nd Infantry Division, the first time a marine had ever commanded an Army division. He led the division at Saint-Mihiel and in the Meuse-Argonne offensive.

In 1920 Lejeune was named commandant of the Corps, retaining that position for nine years. In this office he laid the foundation for the modern Marine Corps, his most important efforts being directed toward officer education and amphibious warfare doctrine and tactics.

Upon his retirement from the Corps in 1929, he became superintendent of the Virginia Military Institute. He retired from that position in 1937 and died on November 20, 1942, in Baltimore. He was buried in Arlington National Cemetery.

But while carrying out these duties, Lejeune and other Marine Corps staff members were also seriously considering other matters, specifically amphibious landings on hostile shores. After exhaustive studies as to what had gone wrong at Gallipoli, the marines carried out a series of exercises between 1922 and 1925. These revealed that the major problem in amphibious landings was the use of wooden Navy launches to carry the men ashore.

☆ An American Portrait

Smedley D. Butler—Smedley Darlington Butler was born in West Chester, Pennsylvania, in 1881 to a Quaker family. His father served in the House of Representatives for 31 years and was chairman of the House Naval Affairs Committee during the crucial years of the 1920s.

Butler had limited formal education, enlisting in the Marine Corps during the Spanish-American War by claiming to be 18. As a lieutenant he joined the China Relief Expedition created to put down the Boxer Rebellion and was brevetted a captain. During the next 14 years he served in Honduras, Panama, the Philippines, and Nicaragua, earning a reputation as a driving and effective officer.

He won his first Congressional Medal of Honor in 1914 for gallantry at Veracruz and a second a year later in Haiti. Although he received no combat command in France in 1917 and 1918, he was advanced to brigadier general and displayed great efficiency as the commandant of a major military camp at Brest.

After the war he was made commanding general at the evolving Marine base at Quantico, Virginia, leaving between 1924 and 1925 to serve an (unsuccessful) stint as director of public safety in Philadelphia, trying to end vice, prostitution, and gang influence in that city.

Returning to active duty, Butler commanded the Marine Expeditionary Force in China from 1927 until 1929. By 1931 he had been advanced to major general but had incurred the wrath of his Navy and Marine Corps superiors for making indiscreet public accusations, including the unfounded charge that Benito Mussolini had run over a child with his car and refused to stop.

Not surprisingly, Butler was passed over when the post of commandant became vacant in 1931, despite the fact that he was the senior major general on the active list. Thereupon Butler retired to pursue a career in politics. He was unsuccessful in this. During the 1930s he became a leading public figure in the neutrality movement, touring the country to lecture on behalf of isolation and strict neutrality and in 1935 authoring a book entitled *War Is a Racket*.

Surely one of the most colorful and controversial military leaders of the twentieth century, Smedley D. Butler died in June 1940 and was buried in his home town of West Chester, Pennsylvania.

Under Lejeune's successors as commandant in the 1930s, efforts at modernization of the Corps were continued. Amphibious landings received the most attention. The ideas of Earl H. "Pete" Ellis, a staff officer who predicted back in 1913 that the Japanese would seize Pacific islands and that these islands would have to be regained by amphibious assaults, were now acted upon with determination.

A first step was the creation of the Fleet Marine Force as part of the Navy's Pacific fleet to be available with proper equipment for amphibious assaults. Then a manual for landing operations (covering command, ship-to-shore movement, air and naval gunfire, and so on) was prepared and acted upon in exercises to perfect the marines' techniques. The marines also demanded and received better landing boats in the form of "Higgins boats" with retractable flat bow ramps, the forerunners of the famed hinged-bow landing boats of World War II, and LVTs (landing vehicle tracked) for carrying troops right up onto beaches.

By their studies and practice in amphibious warfare during these years the marines found a unique mission and turned it into a specialty that justified their existence in America's military structure. Many Army officers decried the whole thing as foolish; military leaders around the world were in agreement. Amphibious operations, they said, would be unnecessary and suicidal under modern conditions. World War II would prove them wrong. The Army's soldiers would have to learn from the marines the techniques of amphibious warfare as in tandem the two services landed on island after island in the Pacific in their efforts to drive the Japanese back to their homeland between 1942 and 1945.

EXPANSION BY THE AGGRESSORS

The Treaty of Versailles and the other four peace treaties of 1919 through 1923 promised peace but ensured war. Germany had been hemmed in, punished, and impoverished. Austria had been reduced and isolated. Hungary and Bulgaria had been chopped down and humiliated, and Russia was not even considered, other than taking away its western territories to create new and—as time would prove—fragile states. Given time, peace might still have endured. But the United States rejected the League and fled into isolationism, while France and England lacked the will to rebuild and ensure the peace. Germany refused to accept a humbled, second-class existence. Russia's new Bolshevik leaders were determined to build a great nation and expand their ideology worldwide, while Italy, soon racked by troubles, fell under leadership that dreamed of re-creating the glorious Roman Empire. In the Far East, the insurgent and now-industrialized Japanese nation envisioned dominating the vast reaches of the Pacific by whatever means necessary.

In Germany, at the end of the war, the army's general staff was not destroyed; it only changed its name and continued to function, making secret agreements with the Soviets whereby military airplanes, tanks, and shells were made for them in Russia and Germans were trained on Soviet soil. In return, the Germans agreed to train Soviet officers in armor and airborne tactics and to build armament factories for them. From the Treaty of Rapallo in 1922, which reestablished Soviet–German diplomatic relations and brought the two powers closer together, until 1934, Soviet relations with Germany were closer than with any other world power.

Germany's economy, in the meantime, enjoyed some recovery despite the nation's loss of its resources during the war and at Versailles. But the worldwide depression set off by the collapse of Wall Street in 1929 ruined any chance of permanent survival of the German economy and the Weimar Republic. Germany's economic problems opened the door to despair. This, in turn, led to the rise of fanaticism in that troubled republic under the leadership of Adolph Hitler and his Nazis. By 1932 the Nazis were the largest party in Germany's fractured political system, and in the chaos of 1933 Hitler first became chancellor, then dictator, of Germany, announcing the formation of the "Third Reich" with himself as *Fuhrer* (leader).

The leaders of the democracies, even if they had had the will, were powerless to stop these internal developments, and Hitler went on to assume complete power, dispossessing the German Jews and seizing control of the army. Nor did the democratic leaders intervene when Hitler began to violate the provisions of Versailles and move against Germany's neighboring states. In 1935 Hitler announced a return to conscription and universal military training, plus the creation of an air force equal to England's or France's. In March 1936 he sent troops into the demilitarized Rhineland; France and England protested but refused to challenge his action. By the end of that year he had an army of 800,000 men and a navy of 108 vessels built or building. In 1938 he attached Austria to his Third Reich in his *Anschluss* (union) with that country, the move carried out with the help of Austrian Nazi party members.

On September 30, 1938, Hitler won his greatest coup when he, along with Prime Minister Neville Chamberlain of Great Britain, French Premier Edouard Daladier, and Benito Mussolini of Italy signed the Munich Agreement, whereby a part of Czechoslovakia called the Sudetenland, a mountainous area of the country bordering Germany, was awarded to Germany. This transfer of territory took place over the strenuous but futile objections of the Czechs, who realized that it represented their only defensible frontier and contained the bulk of its raw materials and industry. In return, Hitler promised to seek no more territory in Czechoslovakia. Five months later, in March 1939, he seized and annexed the remainder of that country. Despite their pledges to uphold Czechoslovakia's integrity, England and France did nothing. Hitler could now make his next move—into Poland, with the permission of Soviet Russia, which received in return half the Polish territory—a move that finally brought a reaction from France and England, which, too late (after Hitler seized the remainder of Czechoslovakia), had issued guarantees to threatened Poland.

Hitler's ally since the October 1936 signing of the Rome–Berlin Axis was Benito Mussolini, *Il Duce* (the leader) of Italy. Mussolini, like Hitler, had come to political power in the chaotic aftermath of World War I. In 1922 he and his Fascist party henchmen, the Black Shirts, seized the capital city of Rome and control of the Italian government and set out to create the Fascist "corporate state" and to bring glory to Italy through military conquests.

By 1934 Mussolini had amassed sufficient popular backing and military might to provoke an incident with Ethiopia. When Italy's 250,000-man army attacked and seized Ethiopia in six months in 1935 and 1936, that country's emperor, Haile Selassie, appealed for help from the League of Nations. But the Western democracies did nothing effective to stop the Italians. The British Foreign Secretary, Sir Samuel Hoare, and Premier Pierre Laval of France even toyed with a plan to let Mussolini keep two-thirds of Ethiopia without objection, until a public outcry forced them to retreat from their devious and underhanded sell-out of that East African nation. During the fighting, the British left the Suez Canal open to his warships, and United States oil companies furnished the petroleum products for the planes and tanks the Italians used against Ethiopia's primitively armed resistance fighters.

Mussolini then cemented his friendship with both Germany and Japan in 1937 by joining the Anti-Comintern Pact. In the meantime, Germany, Italy, and Russia had interfered in Spain's civil war, the Germans and Italians testing their equipment and tactics by aiding General Francisco Franco's Fascists, and the Soviets sending aid to the Republicans. Then, in March 1939, Mussolini sent his troops into little Albania, across the Adriatic Sea. The democracies finally realized that time was running out on peace. They could probably handle Mussolini, but as for Hitler, they could only hope that his moves toward the east to gain *Lebensraum* (living space) for Germany would provoke war with Stalin and the Soviets. Little did they know the dictator of the Kremlin.

In 1924, Lenin, the leader of the new Soviet state born out of Russia's defeats in World War I, had died, setting off a struggle for control of the absolutist Communist state. The eventual winner of the internal power struggle was the cruel and cunning Josef Stalin, who by 1933 had liquidated millions of civilians to gain absolute control of the Communist party and, therefore, of the entire Union of Soviet Socialist Republics. Stalin continued to liquidate all those who threatened his rule (including much of the Red Army command in his famous party purges of 1935–1938), but he feared the eastward movement of the Germans most of all.

Stalin viewed the West's appeasement of Germany over Czechoslovakia as an ominous sign and knew through his spies in the governments of both London and Paris that the Western democracies' leaders were hoping that he and Hitler would tear each other's country apart. Accordingly, Stalin refused the overtures from England and France to join them against Germany and, instead, signed a nonaggression treaty with Hitler on August 23, 1939, agreeing *sub rosa* that each would seize one-half of Poland and that Russia could have back the independent Baltic states and could not only seize Bessarabia from Rumania but could also control Finland when convenient. Stalin had turned Hitler's path of conquest 180 degrees; it was now directed toward the West. He knew Hitler would eventually come after the Soviet Union to complete his dream of German *Lebensraum,* but for now he had bought time to prepare for that day.

Stalin's diplomatic move gave Hitler the green light to attack Poland. England and France would declare war if he did, he knew, but this time, unlike the years from 1914 through 1918, Germany could fight a one-front war. The Nazi–Soviet Pact of 1939 suited the purposes of both dictators—at least for the time being.

In the meantime, half a world away in the Far East, a fourth aggressor nation, Japan, was on the move. Drawing strength and public support from ancient tales of warrior samurai with their honor code of *Bushido* and from the hard times brought to the Japanese people by the worldwide depression of 1929, the Japanese military chieftains seized power. In September 1931, on the flimsiest of pretexts called the "Mukden Incident," they snatched from China the valuable province of Manchuria (an area rich in oil shale, coal, iron, timber, and arable soil), establishing a puppet emperor, Henry P'u Yi, the last emperor of China's Qing dynasty, and renaming the state Manchukuo. China's friends in the West, who had guaranteed its integrity in the Nine Power Treaty only a decade before, were paralyzed by indifference and economic depression and did nothing except appoint a useless League of Nations commission to investigate Japan's actions. This Lytton Commission recommended in 1933 that Japan be ordered to withdraw from Manchuria. Japan withdrew from the League instead.

During that same year, more of north China was occupied by the Japanese, and in 1937 they invaded China proper, attacking and seizing its major cities of Peiping, Nanking, Shanghai, Hankow, and Canton and forcing its government far inland. In 1936 Japan had joined Germany in the Anti-Comintern Pact, giving both signatories assurance that France and Great Britain would be stretched to the limit if either had to fight to save its homeland in Europe and preserve its Far Eastern colonies at the same time. Japan's throbbing ambition to control the far reaches of the western and southwestern Pacific, plus the Asiatic mainland, now appeared realizable. Only the United States, sitting astride Japan's path of conquest to the south by its bases in the Philippines, stood in the way.

The four aggressor nations, having risen to power in the two decades since World War I, stood posed to strike. And strike they did. On September 1, 1939, Germany attacked Poland from the west, and within two weeks Russian forces had crossed that hapless country's frontier and seized the eastern half of its territory. On September 3, France and Great Britain declared war on Germany. Less than 21 years since the end of World War

I, on November 11, 1918, World War II had begun. Before it ended 6 years later, unprecedented destruction had taken place over vast areas of the globe, and the shape of the entire world had been changed forever.

Suggestions for Further Reading

BUCKLEY, THOMAS H., *The United States and the Washington Naval Conference, 1921–1922*. Knoxville: University of Tennessee Press, 1970.

DAVIS, BURKE, *The Billy Mitchell Affair*. New York: Random House, 1967.

DINGMAN, ROGER, *Power in the Pacific: The Origins of Naval Arms Limitation, 1914–1922*. Chicago: University of Chicago Press, 1976.

GREER, THOMAS H., *The Development of Air Doctrine in the Army Air Arm, 1917–1941*. Washington, DC: U.S. Government Printing Office, 1985.

HAMMOND, PAUL Y., *Organizing for Defense: The American Military Establishment in the Twentieth Century*. Princeton, NJ: Princeton University Press, 1961.

HURLEY, ALFRED F., *Billy Mitchell: Crusader for Air Power*. New York: Franklin Watts, 1964.

ISELEY, JETER A, and PHILIP A. CROWL, *The U.S. Marines and Amphibious Warfare*. Princeton, NJ: Princeton University Press, 1957.

MELHORN, CHARLES M., *Two-Block Fox: The Rise of the Aircraft Carrier, 1911–1929*. Annapolis: Naval Institute Press, 1974.

POGUE, FORREST C., *George C. Marshall: Education of a General, 1880–1939*. New York: Viking, 1963.

ROSKILL, STEPHEN, *Naval Policy Between the Wars*, vol. 2, *The Period of Reluctant Rearmament, 1930–1939*. Annapolis: Naval Institute Press, 1976.

SCHMIDT, HANS, *Maverick Marine: General Smedley D. Butler and the Contradictions of American Military History*. Lexington: University Press of Kentucky, 1987.

SHINER, JOHN F., *Foulois and the U.S. Army Air Corps, 1931–1935*. Washington, DC: Office of Air Force History, 1983.

SPROUT, HAROLD, and MARGARET SPROUT, *Toward a New Order of Sea Power: American Naval Policy and the World Scene, 1918–1922*. Princeton, NJ: Princeton University Press, 1943.

WHEELER, GERALD E., *Prelude to Pearl Harbor: The United States Navy and the Far East, 1921–1931*. Columbia: University of Missouri Press, 1963.

World War II: European Theater, 1939–1945

Hitler's invasion of Poland on September 1, 1939, set off World War II as England and France declared war on Germany two days later. Until December 1941 it was essentially a European conflict pitting Germany and Italy against the countries on their periphery. With the Japanese attack on Pearl Harbor, the conflict became global, the regional war between China and Japan melding into the larger contest.

The major Axis powers as of December 1941 were Germany, Italy, and Japan. The five major Allied powers were Great Britain, France (conquered and under the collaborationist Vichy government, but offering resistance through the Free French movement), China, the Soviet Union (since June 22, 1941), and the United States. At the peak of the conflict, 56 nations were formally at war on one side or the other in a struggle for hegemony over Europe, the Middle East, the Far East, and the great expanses of the Atlantic and Pacific Oceans. It was the largest war, producing the greatest loss of lives and the greatest destruction of property, in the history of the world. When it was over after six years, empires were shaken and trembling, new nations were emerging, the power relationships of the world had been changed forever, and the United States had become one of the two great "superpowers" of the globe, with all the responsibilities that position entailed.

BLITZKRIEG EAST AND WEST

Throughout the summer of 1939, Hitler systematically carried out his thinly disguised plans to invade neighboring Poland. Two German armies were concentrated on the German–Polish border awaiting the signal to attack. At 4:45 A.M. on September 1, 1939,

56 German divisions (including three armored divisions with 3,200 tanks under General Heinz Guderian) began to move across the border into hapless Poland in a giant pincer movement, Army Group North attacking from Pomerania and East Prussia, Army Group South coming in from Silesia and Czechoslovakia. Aiding the *Heer* (army) of the *Wehrmacht* (literally, defense forces) were 1,500 airplanes of the *Luftwaffe* (air force). Within a week the Germans, spearheaded by the Panzer (armored) units moving faster and farther than anyone thought possible (over 11 miles per day) and bypassing Polish defensive units positioned too close to the border to permit maneuverability in the face of the German attacks, had penetrated north and south of Warsaw. By that time, the soldiers of the antiquated Polish army not killed, captured, or scattered were falling back toward the capital. On September 14, German armored units from the north and south met south of Brest-Litovsk, far behind Warsaw. Three days later, Russia (having signed a peace treaty with Japan the day before that assured that it would not be attacked from the rear) invaded from the east "to protect White Russian and Ukranian minorities in Poland."

Guide to Military Formations

Unit and Approximate Numbers	Composition	Commander
Army Group	2 or more armies	General
Army	2 or more corps	General
Corps	2 or more divisions	Lieutenant General
Division, 10,000–19,000	2 or more brigades	Major General
Brigade, 3,000–5,000	2 or more battalions	Brigadier General or Colonel
Regiment, 3,000–5,000	2 or more battalions	Colonel
Battalion, 500–1,200	2 or more companies	Lieutenant Colonel
Company, 150–190	2 or more platoons	Captain
Platoon, 40	2 or more squads	Lieutenant
Squad, 8–12		Staff Sergeant

The Poles in Warsaw were now surrounded and holding out defiantly while appealing in vain for British and French aid. They fought on bravely for ten more days before being forced to surrender. *Blitzkrieg* ("lightning war") had crushed Poland. A new mode of warfare designed to exploit enemy points of vulnerability by superior strength, speed, and maneuverability (tanks combined with mechanized infantry and artillery backed by efficient logistics and covered with overwhelming air power) had entered the battlefield in dramatic fashion. Poland had seen 35 divisions destroyed or scattered, thousands of soldiers and civilians killed, 450,000 men taken prisoner, and the entire nation crushed in only three weeks.

Fortunately for the Allies, Polish cryptologists, who had copied and could decipher the German Enigma coding machine's transmissions, managed to escape to the West, where they shared this knowledge with the French and British. This was the genesis of the British Ultra (for ultrasecret) intelligence network, which, operating from Bletchley Park near London, gave the Allies much valuable information on German military strengths and intentions throughout the war.

In the months thereafter, the Soviets forced Finland to relinquish some disputed territory after a remarkably effective three-month defensive effort by the Finns. The sluggish Russian offensive revealed the ineptitude of its army (which outnumbered its foes five to one) and forced Stalin to reform and modernize his forces. In April of the following year, Denmark was overrun in a single day by German troops. Then Norway fell to the Germans in June 1940, despite heroic defensive efforts by the Norwegians and by British and French troops landed in four locations along the coast to stop the rapid German land movement across the country. Hitler's supply line of iron ore from neutral Sweden through Narvik and down through Norwegian coastal waters was now secure. He had complete control of the Baltic Sea, and his northern flank was secure as he turned on France and its Continental allies.

All this time, the French were positioned behind their Maginot Line extending north from Switzerland along the Rhine, then northwest below Luxembourg to the Belgian border. This grand defensive bastion of concrete and steel forts, casemates, and pillboxes would ensure their right flank, they believed. Their center would be impervious to attack thanks to the thick Ardennes Forest, believed by all to be impenetrable by armor. If the Germans came—and many seriously doubted that this would ever happen during these months, called by many at the time the "Phony War"—then they would come through Belgium, as they had in the last war under the Schlieffen Plan. France's left flank, guarding Germany's expected path into northern France, would be held by French and British troops (a 250,000-man British Expeditionary Force [BEF] was now in France), with Belgian and Dutch troops in defensive positions in front of them. Britain, in the meantime, would blockade the Reich by sea, as it had done during World War I. Little did the semicomplacent Western nations realize that Hitler had every intention of subjugating them in his own good time and by his own plan for invasion.

By May 1940 the Fuhrer had 2,350,000 troops, 2,700 tanks, and 3,200 planes assembled along Germany's western frontier and poised to strike. The Allies had the numerical advantage in men and tanks, but the Luftwaffe outnumbered its French and British air opponents almost two to one in operational aircraft deployed on the Western Front. And Hitler had an invasion plan. Under this plan, drawn up by General Erich von Manstein and designed to fool the Allies completely, Holland, Belgium, Luxembourg, and France would be attacked simultaneously. The main attack would come, not through Belgium, but to the south, through the "impassable" Ardennes region between the Meuse River and the upper end of the Maginot Line. This main armored attack of 44 divisions of Army Group A would cut through the Ardennes and strike past Sedan all the way to the Channel at Abbeville. Meanwhile, German attacks would also be launched by the 30 divisions of Army Group B on Holland and Belgium to the north. If all went well, the Allied armies would be surprised, split, and annihilated.

The plan worked almost to perfection. On May 10, Army Group A, under Colonel General Gerd von Rundstedt, jumped off into the Ardennes. Led by Guderian's Panzers with their 20-ton Mark IV tanks, it reached the Meuse within two days, and by May 20 leading elements had reached Abbeville and the Channel. The Allied armies were cut in two as Guderian swung north toward Calais to catch them between himself and Army Group B.

Army Group B, under Colonel General Fedor von Bock, was also enjoying spectacular success. The Luftwaffe destroyed Dutch and Belgian airfields while paratroop and glider attacks were made at key points in Holland. Some 80 German paratroopers, landing by glider on its roof before its defenders even knew the fighting had begun, seized the vital Belgian fort of Eben Emael north of Liege with ease (having practiced on a mock-up of the fort before the invasion), taking its 1,200 defenders prisoner and opening the Albert Canal for German passage into Belgium. Rotterdam was bombed and deliberately destroyed in what Hitler termed *Schrecklichkeit* ("frightfulness") to send a message of terror to those who would resist his forces. Queen Wilhelmina of the Netherlands fled the country to exile in England; her nation surrendered on May 14. Belgium fell on May 28. Over 300,000 survivors of the British Expeditionary Force and the French army not killed or captured in the German offensives were caught at Dunkirk on the French–Belgian border, with Army Group B sweeping in from Belgium and Army Group A moving up from the south and swiftly capturing Boulogne, Calais, and Gravelines.

In what some have called "the Miracle of Dunkirk," 364,000 British and French troops, ignoring divebomber attacks by fearful Stukas whenever the covering mists and smoke lifted, were taken off the beaches in Operation Dynamo from May 26 to June 4, 1940, by a hastily assembled armada of almost 700 craft and evacuated across the Channel to England. Another 68,000 troops died, were wounded, or were taken prisoner while holding a defensive perimeter for the rescue. Operation Dynamo was the brainchild of 65-year-old Prime Minister Winston Churchill, who had been called to power on May 10, the same day on which the German offensives had begun. Regardless of whether the evacuation should rightly be labeled a miracle, a colossal error by Hitler in stopping the German armored units before Dunkirk (where they could have smashed through the thin Allied defenses), or good luck in that poor flying weather prevented the Luftwaffe from destroying the men on the beaches, the saga of Dunkirk represents one of the most dramatic actions of World War II. Subsequently, General Alan Brooke managed to evacuate 136,000 British and Polish troops from ports in western France. It was from the survivors of Dunkirk and the other remnants of the BEF that a new and more powerful British army emerged, which, with the armies of the Allies, finally crushed Hitler's Third Reich.

On the same day on which Dunkirk fell, June 5, 1940, the Germans launched multiple attacks on the remaining French defensive lines along the Somme and the Aisne. Within five days the Wehrmacht had penetrated as far south as the Seine (through territories they had been unable to take in four years during World War I). Then, on June 10, Mussolini, now convinced that France would fall, launched a 32-division attack across the nation's southeastern border. Paris fell to the Germans on June 14. The German juggernaut rolled on.

The French government of Prime Minister Paul Reynaud resigned from its refuge at Bordeaux, and Marshal Henri-Phillipe Pétain, the hero of Verdun in 1916, took over the government on June 17. He immediately asked for an armistice. One week later it was signed, and three French armies, totaling 400,000 men, surrendered. The capital of the collaborationist Pétain government was established at Vichy, in the southern sector of France left unoccupied by the Germans. On June 24 an armistice was also signed by the Pétain government with Mussolini. In only six weeks, Hitler, with minor and opportunistic help from Mussolini, had smashed Holland, Belgium, and France. Now only Britain stood undefeated among his Western European enemies.

BRITAIN STANDS, THE MEDITERRANEAN TOTTERS

Hitler believed that following the BEF's defeat in France and with its Continental allies defeated, Britain would quickly sue for peace. Plans for the invasion of England, called Operation Sealion, were accordingly not acted upon for weeks on end. When it finally became obvious that Britain, led by the redoubtable Winston Churchill, was not about to capitulate, Hitler set September 15 as the date for the cross-Channel invasion.

But with the Royal Navy still a threat, the Luftwaffe failing to destroy the Royal Air Force as Reichmarschall Hermann Goering, its leader, had promised, and a sizable German army being necessary for the invasion of England, German planning and logistics fell into disarray. The invasion date was pushed back throughout the autumn of 1940. It was finally set for October 1941—after Hitler had defeated Russia, he thought. Operation Sealion was never attempted. It could probably have succeeded in the immediate aftermath of the fall of France, when British ability to resist an invasion was at its nadir. But Hitler did not seize the moment. His hesitancy regarding Sealion was his second great mistake during the war, Dunkirk being his first.

Closely tied to Hitler's failure with Sealion was his loss of the Battle of Britain. Goering promised after the fall of France that the Royal Air Force would quickly be destroyed. With 3,000 bombers and fighters in his Luftwaffe ranged against only 600 to 700 British fighters, only half of which were up-to-date Spitfires and Hurricanes, it should have been. The Luftwaffe enjoyed great initial success during the month of August 1940 in attacking the airfields of Fighter Command in southeast and inland England. Fighter Command was on its last legs until Hitler gave it a chance to recover. On September 7 he switched the focus of the Luftwaffe attacks from the RAF airfields to London in retaliation for an August 24–25 RAF raid on Berlin, ordered by Churchill when Luftwaffe bombers mistakenly bombed London.

London, then, became the prime target and went through the "Blitz" during September 1940. The city and its people suffered considerably, but English will was not broken and Fighter Command was given precious time to recover. Night raids against London and other major cities continued through May 1941. Coventry, a Midlands industrial center northwest of London, for example, saw 70,000 homes destroyed on the night of November 14–15 by 500 Luftwaffe bombers. But Hitler paid the price with over 2,000 planes shot down by Fighter Command, aided by 51 high-level and low-level radar stations along Britain's coasts and very valuable Ultra intelligence that gave the RAF advance warning of the approach and direction of the German planes. And still the country refused to consider surrender. Hitler had made his third great strategic mistake by not destroying the RAF when he had a chance in the first months of the Battle of Britain. Meanwhile, he had turned on Russia.

While Hitler was consolidating his power in Western Europe, attempting to take Britain out of the war by peace diplomacy and air attacks, and preparing to invade the Soviet Union, his Axis partner Mussolini decided on a quick and cheap victory in Greece. Concentrating 162,000 men in Albania in preparation for an attack on neighboring Greece, on October 28, 1940, Mussolini sent his army across the border. Here he met, not glorious victory, but total disaster. Not only was his army stopped, but also by March 1941 the Greeks had counterattacked and seized half of Albania. Hitler, despite having his hands full in preparing for his invasion of the Soviet Union, now had to come to the aid of the Italians.

The German leader had already compelled Bulgaria and Yugoslavia to join the Axis to protect his southern flank as he moved on Russia, but a coup on March 28, 1941, overthrew the Yugoslav government of Prince Paul. Its military leaders renounced the nation's alliance with Germany. Accordingly, Operation Punishment was launched against the Yugoslavs on April 6, 1941, and German army units poured into the country. Only 11 days later it was all over; Yugoslavia surrendered unconditionally in the face of overwhelming German might.

April 6, 1941, was also the date on which Germany invaded Greece. The Greek forces were by then reinforced by 57,000 British troops, but most of the Greek troops were positioned in the west facing Albania. By the end of the month, all of Greece had fallen to the Germans, the British troops being evacuated south to the island of Crete. The Germans then seized Crete by paratrooper drops in May—the only campaign in World War II that employed airborne troops exclusively—but not before the British evacuated 16,000 men (leaving 12,000 to surrender), and not before General Kurt Student's 7th Air Division of 13,000 men, plus 9,000 men of the 5th Alpine Division, had seen 3,600 of their comrades killed and over 2,000 wounded on Crete. Never again would Hitler permit airborne and parachute operations of this magnitude to be launched. Nevertheless, he now held Greece and Crete, thereby threatening the Suez Canal and putting himself in an excellent position to control the eastern Mediterranean and eventually the Near East.

This goal was attainable despite the Italians' loss of Ethiopia, Eritrea, to the north on the Red Sea, and Italian Somaliland, to the south on the Indian Ocean, to the British forces under General Sir Archibald Wavell, commander-in-chief of the Middle East forces, between January and June 1941. (The last Italians in Ethiopia surrendered in November.) The British had also seized Baghdad and Damascus from pro-Nazi forces in May and June.

But these losses were not fatal to the Axis cause because of events that had taken place in the North African deserts. In September 1940, five Italian divisions had moved into Egypt from the area of Cyrenaica in eastern Libya. The British in Egypt had launched a counterattack by their Western Desert Force under Lieutenant-General Richard N. O'Connor in December, and in January 1941 they had taken the port of Tobruk on the Mediterranean coast of Libya, thereby persuading Hitler to send ground forces to aid Mussolini in North Africa. The British had continued to drive the Italians back until they reached El Agheila, almost halfway back across Libya, on February 9. The Western Desert Force, in a remarkable display of desert warfare maneuverability, had advanced 500 miles in two months, in the process destroying nine Italian divisions and taking 130,000 prisoners. But at this point Churchill, against the advice of his Imperial General Staff, had withdrawn most of O'Connor's force to send it to Greece (where it did no good at all, as has been pointed out), leaving the British with only a thin defensive line in Libya. Had these troops not been taken from O'Connor, he possibly could have driven the Italians out of North Africa, thereby denying to the Axis the vital port of Tripoli in Tunisia and severely crippling Hitler's grand strategy.

But within less than a week after O'Connor had arrived at El Agheila, below the "Benghazi Bulge," General Erwin Rommel's Panzer divisions of his Afrika Korps had begun to land in Tripoli. By the third week of March 1941, "the Desert Fox," as he soon came to be called, was ready to move. After seizing El Agheila from the British, Rommel had sent the Italians along the coast road while his 21st Panzer Division units drove across the Benghazi Bulge. The German-Italian forces had regained all of Libya except the port of Tobruk by the end of April. Twice Rommel failed to take Tobruk by assault, but it was obvious that the British were in dire straits in the Western Desert as Rommel moved on into Egypt toward Alexandria. The two battles for strategic Halfaya Pass just east of the Libyan–Egyptian border (the British Operation Brevity of May 15–27, 1941, and Operation Battleaxe of June 15–17) had both gone to Rommel and his Afrika Korps, and it was clear that the southern Mediterranean coast might well fall to the Germans and their Italian allies. If Hitler's invasion of Russia also continued to go well, his dreams of Eurasian and Middle Eastern conquest might well come true.

1941–1942: THE TURNAROUND

Despairing of quickly conquering Great Britain in 1940 and 1941 with the failure of his Luftwaffe air offensive, Hitler looked again to the east, his primary area of concern. Here he had always intended to gain his coveted *Lebensraum* in eastern Europe and southern Russia. By the summer of 1941 he had amassed almost 3 million men on Russia's western border for his second Blitzkrieg attack to the east, Operation Barbarossa.

On the left was Army Group North, with 26 divisions, which was to move through the Baltic states and seize Leningrad. In the middle was Army Group Center, with 51 divisions, including two Panzer armies. It was to strike due east through Smolensk and capture the capital of Moscow. On the right was Army Group South, with 40 divisions, including a Panzer army plus 14 Rumanian divisions and a Hungarian corps, which was to seize the Ukraine, Kiev, Stalingrad, and the oil fields to the south.

Jumping off on June 22, 1941, the 129th anniversary of Napoleon's invasion of Russia and the first anniversary of France's surrender at Compiègne, the three-front offensive went well at first. But by launching a wide-scale invasion against three target areas thousands of miles apart, Hitler had committed his fourth great strategic error, as time would show. By July 14, Army Group North had swept across Lithuania, Latvia, and Estonia and was only 75 miles from Leningrad. By mid-September, Leningrad (the former capital St. Petersburg) was encircled by German troops. The decision was then made to place the city under siege in view of its formidable defenses. The Russians tried desperately to relieve the besieged city of 3 million persons, but failed. Food and supplies had to come into the city across the ice of Lake Ladoga. By Christmas, some 3,500 to 4,000 people were dying every day of starvation and disease. For 900 days the siege of Leningrad went on (over 630,000 persons dying during that time), the Russians also having to beat off an offensive by the Finns that began in July 1941 and was finally halted in December. Leningrad never fell to the Germans, thus holding down troops that would have been invaluable to Hitler's generals farther south on the wide expanses of the Soviet Union.

Army Group Center had also started well, but it was soon slowed in its drive toward Moscow by Russian resistance, mud from heavy autumn rains, and overextended supply lines. By September the Germans had advanced 600 miles, had taken 300,000 prisoners, and had seized Smolensk. By the end of October they were north, south and west of the Soviet capital. By late November they had fought their way into the suburbs in the northern part of the city, but the Russians facing them continued to offer stiff resistance. Then, on December 6, the Soviet army under its brilliant strategist Marshal Georgi K. Zhukov began a counteroffensive, despite previous Russian losses that ran into the millions of men and thousands of tanks and guns.

The Germans were as ill prepared for Zhukov's giant counterblow as they were for the enshrouding Russian winter. Taken completely by surprise, they were driven back both north and south of Moscow. Buoyed up by these successes, and against the advice of his military commanders, Stalin foolishly ordered a general counteroffensive all along the northern and central fronts on January 5, 1942. By dissipating his forces, Stalin allowed the Germans to resist effectively the millions of Russians attacking them, and by the end of March the drive was over, both sides being completely exhausted and bogged down in the mud of the spring thaw. As was the case in the north, German arms in central Russia had slowed to a crawl by mid-1942, and Hitler was clearly in for a long, hard fight if Russia was to be subjugated.

Army Group South also got off to a successful start. By July 11 units under Field Marshal Gerd von Rundstedt were only ten miles from Kiev, deep in the Ukraine. The early medieval Russian capital fell on September 19, and the German armies drove on to seize Kharkov and Rostov. By spring 1942 they were driving toward the Don and Volga Rivers, their eyes on the oil fields of the Caucasus. Beating off two major Russian offensives, the Germans took the Kerch Peninsula in the Crimea, and seized Sevastopol after a 24-day siege on June 30, 1942. The Germans drove on toward the valley of the Don, Stalingrad on the Volga, and the Caucasus as the Red Army tried desperately to stop them.

By August 23, 1942, spearheads of General Friedrich Paulus's Sixth Army had reached the Volga north of Stalingrad, and the Luftwaffe's 4th Air Fleet began to bomb the city. But as the Germans tried to batter their way into Stalingrad, the Russians put up fanatical resistance from the rubble and with heavy and medium artillery situated on the east bank of the Volga. For 67 days the contending armies fought each other night and day in house-to-house and street-to-street combat. During late September and October, Paulus's men launched a second great offensive to seize the city, the climax coming on October 14 to 16, 1942. The Germans were soon exhausted and running low on ammunition and fuel.

On November 23 Paulus asked for permission to withdraw in order to rest his men and resupply them. Hitler angrily refused this request. The Fuhrer's prestige was on the line, and he believed that the Red Army was about to collapse around Stalingrad. He could not have been more wrong. The reality of the situation for Army Group Don (formed after the Russian encirclement) was that four German and Rumanian armies were confined in a narrow salient, their long flanks held only by thin lines of Rumanian and Italian troops. Army Group Don was about to collapse under the pressure of massive Russian counter-offensives. Hitler had been checked at Leningrad and Moscow and was now vulnerable at Stalingrad. He stood on the brink of massive defeat in Russia by November 1942.

So, too, in North Africa, Hitler's forces were about to see the tide of war reversed. After the Brevity and Battleaxe battles of May and June 1941, both sides had been forced to pull back to rest and resupply. But the impetuous Churchill wanted an offensive and a desert victory at any cost. He removed General Wavell for General Sir Claude Auchinleck, Commander-in-Chief, India, to get it. Lieutenant-General Alan Cunningham was placed in command of the newly formed Eighth Army (ex-Western Desert Force). Initially it appeared to be a good move as the British in the fierce Crusader Battles of November and December 1941 swept behind Halfaya Pass, relieved the garrison at besieged Tobruk, and forced Rommel (short on supplies and troops) all the way back to El Aghiela with a loss of 38,000 men (although the ill-prepared Cunningham had to be replaced with Major-General Neil Ritchie before the battles ended).

But Rommel quickly rebuilt his forces—while the British were vulnerable because they were far from their base of resupply in Egypt—and came storming back across Libya in the first six months of 1942. He swept everything before him and advanced into Egypt to the tiny rail town of El Alamein, only 60 miles west of Alexandria. In this 1942 offensive, Rommel lost only 3,360 men to Britain's 50,000. Only the Eighth Army stood between himself and the delta of the Nile, between himself and control of Egypt.

Rommel tried to break through in May, where he inflicted on the British their greatest armored defeat at Knightsbridge and subsequently seized Tobruk, and again in July in the First Battle of El Alamein. He failed, although Churchill subsequently replaced Auchinleck with General Sir Harold Alexander when "the Auck" refused to go on the offensive against Rommel until his men were rested and resupplied. Lieutenant-General Bernard Law Montgomery was given command of Eighth Army, but only because Lieutenant-General W. H. E. "Strafer" Gott, Churchill's first choice, was killed when his plane was shot down by British antiaircraft guns.

The desert war was subsequently decided on August 30 to September 2, 1942, in the Battle of Alam Halfa, Rommel's last attempt to break through the defenses at El Alamein to trap Eighth Army. He failed, largely because Montgomery, through Ultra code decrypts, knew when and where he was going to strike and that he was short on supplies. Rommel pulled back and dug in, never again to go on the offensive.

The Second Battle of El Alamein of October 23 to November 4, 1942, was fierce but anticlimactic and was weighted heavily in favor of the British. Montgomery had almost twice as many men (195,000 to 104,000), over twice as many tanks (1,029 to 489), and almost twice as many artillery pieces (2,300 to 1,200) as Rommel. Furthermore, Rommel's supply lines ran 800 miles back to Benghazi and 1,400 miles back to Tripoli. His Afrika Korps needed 6,000 tons of supplies every day, 20 times the amount needed for Operation Barbarossa. He never got them, thanks in large measure to continued British control of Malta despite persistent air and sea attacks on the island by the Germans, and to Hitler's refusal to sanction an airborne and amphibious German-Italian invasion of the crucial island in July 1942. And Hitler would not let Rommel pull back to refit and regroup. "Defend every inch of ground" was the Fuhrer's order to his African commander. Despite Hitler's orders, the Desert Fox began to retreat back across North Africa on November 4, 1942. Four days later American and British troops landed in Morocco and Algeria on the northwest African coast.

The Germans and Italians in North Africa were now in a closing trap. As in Russia, the tide of the European war was turning. From now on, Hitler and Mussolini would be on the strategic defensive. Victory for the Allies was still 2 1/2 years away, and much bitter fighting remained, but the finger of defeat now pointed at the Axis partners in their brutal friendship.

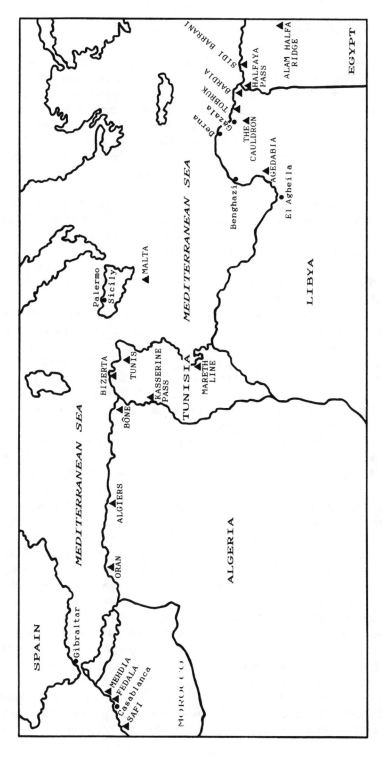

MAP 9-1 North Africa, 1940–1943. *(Used with permission of Anne C. Christensen.)*

ANGLO-AMERICAN STRATEGY FOR COALITION WARFARE

American military planners had been preparing contingency plans for future major conflicts ever since 1919. Until 1938 their plans dealt primarily with aggression by Japan (code named "Orange" in the war-planning scenarios). Plan Orange went through a number of variations in the 1920s and 1930s, but primary emphasis in overall American strategic thinking remained on action in the Pacific. In 1939, however, multi-enemy, multi-ally plans were ordered prepared. These plans were dubbed "Rainbow," from the colors assigned to the various countries that might be friends or foes. As matters worked out, Rainbow 5 (the United States, Great Britain, and France versus Germany, Italy, and Japan) was the plan that fit the situation.

By 1940, with Rainbow 5 as its basis, American strategic planning was focused on three principles: (1) the main American effort would be made in the Atlantic and Europe; (2) a strategic defensive would be maintained in the Pacific, with particular emphasis on guarding the Alaska-Hawaii-Panama Canal strategic triangle, until the European enemies were defeated; and (3) a large-scale ground offensive would be called for in the European Theater, with a projection of American forces onto North African or European soil being necessary.

By early 1941 these assumptions had been reinforced by Admiral Harold Stark's "Plan Dog" memo, accepted by President Roosevelt, which called for secret staff talks with the British looking to a United States–British land offensive. The subsequent staff talks of early 1941 resulted in the ABC-1 Agreement reaffirming the idea of an offensive stance in Europe and a defensive stance in the Pacific, but adding to it the concept of maintaining British and Allied positions in the Mediterranean. By mid-1941, then, months before the United States entered the war, a basic American strategy had been agreed upon, and detailed planning had begun.

The British, too, had been making contingency plans for a war against Germany. Prior to 1939 they reasoned that they would simply erode German strength by blockading and bombing while cutting them off from all means of resupply in the Balkans and the Western Hemisphere. Meanwhile, they would build up their own resources and go on the offensive—somewhere. The German victories of 1939 scuttled these plans. By 1940 the British chiefs of staff had come up with a new set of plans. They would impose a blockade; use strategic bombing to erode German strength, leading to political and military collapse within the Third Reich; and then invade the Continent to receive the German surrender. The German victories of 1940, the lack of an adequate strategic bombing force, the ability of Germany to resupply itself from its conquered territories, and the fact that half of Britain's army strength was overseas rendered this unrealistic plan null and void. Yet included in all of this planning were two vital threads that no one could gainsay: The Mediterranean had to be controlled by the Allies, and Egypt had to be held as a staging area in order for the Empire's forces to make a comeback in that area.

By late 1941 the British had given up all expectation of an economic collapse in Germany from blockade and bombing, although they still hoped for political collapse from within. They now looked to two strategic necessities as the basis of their planning: (1) a second front in the West by an invasion would be essential because the Eastern front could only erode German strength, not defeat Hitler; and (2) the Mediterranean theater was vital to their winning the war. Out of these American and British strategic stances a European strategy for victory was forged in 1941 and 1942, but not without considerable acrimony from the military planners on each side of the coalition.

At the Arcadia Conference held in Washington in December 1941, a meeting of Roosevelt, Churchill, and the British and American chiefs of staff, it was agreed that the Allies would concentrate on Germany first, wear it down, forge a ring of Allied might around it, and then break through the ring at its points of weakness. But while the British talked of possible offensives into Italy, into the Balkans from Turkey, or onto the Continent from the west, they would not commit themselves as to where or when these should take place. The year 1943 was discussed as a likely time. This frustrated their American counterparts, who wanted to get into action as soon as possible and saw themselves being drawn into plans to save the British Empire, not defeat Germany. Out of their frustration came a plan, Bolero-Roundup, which called upon them to concentrate Allied forces in Britain by spring 1943 (Bolero) and invade across the Channel in April of that year with 48 divisions (Roundup). If it looked as though Russia was about to collapse or Germany was crumbling, Sledgehammer, a September 1942 two-division cross-Channel invasion, would go instead. The Americans at Arcadia and for two years thereafter were persistently looking to a solar plexus blow against Germany as their preferred course of action.

But the British were not about to be rushed. They subsequently rejected Sledge-hammer and dawdled on Roundup. The American planners were so frustrated that they asked Roosevelt to suspend the European plans and go all out against Japan instead. Roosevelt refused to adopt this course of action, but he did begin to push the British for a hard commitment in Europe. Public pressure at home demanded that American troops be used in 1942. Revenge for Pearl Harbor and Hitler's successes mandated an American reaction somewhere. Churchill suggested Operation Gymnast, an Allied invasion of North Africa, and Roosevelt agreed. Thus was born Operation Torch (the final name for Gymnast), a decision that hardly pleased the American military planners still looking for a direct attack on the continent. General Dwight D. Eisenhower, chief of army operations and planning on the War Department general staff, remarked glumly that July 31, 1942, the day for the decision for Torch, "could well go down as the blackest day in history." In retrospect it seems obvious that the Mediterranean campaign was the only area of operations available to the Allies in late 1942 where chances of victory were good, but at the time few American military planners would have agreed.

TORCH: THE INVASION OF NORTH AFRICA

Operation Torch called for the seizure of the three largest ports in northwest Africa by simultaneous invasions: Casablanca in Morocco on the "outside" (of the Straits of Gibraltar) and Oran and Algiers on the "inside." The three landing forces were to link up and race east into Tunisia, trapping the Axis forces in North Africa between the British Eighth Army and themselves. D day was set for November 8, 1942.

☆ An American Portrait

George Catlett Marshall, Jr.—Marshall, the organizer of victory during World War II, was born in Uniontown, Pennsylvania, on December 31, 1880. He attended the Virginia Military Institute from 1897 to 1901 and was commissioned a second lieutenant the following year. His first years of service took him to the Philippines during the closing phases of the insurrection there and then to the American Southwest on mapping assignments for the Army.

After a year at the Army Staff College, Marshall spent a number of years in planning and instructing before being sent back to the Philippines in 1913. He first came to the notice of the Army high command as a planner during his years in the archipelago as an aide to Major General Hunter Liggett and with Major General J. Franklin Bell back in the United States. He continued to impress his superiors during World War I when he was assigned as training officer for the 1st Infantry Division, then Chief of Operations for the First Army in France.

Returning to the United States after the war, Marshall served as an aide to General John J. Pershing, Chief of Staff, in Washington from 1919 to 1924 before moving on to become executive officer of the 15th Infantry Regiment in Tientsin, China, for three years. From 1927 to 1932 he was assistant commandant of the Infantry School at Fort Benning, Georgia. Before being named chief of the War Plans Division in 1938, Marshall worked with National Guard units and the Army's CCC project and as commander of the 5th Infantry Brigade. Meanwhile, he won his first star.

After his short stint as chief of the War Plans Division, Marshall was advanced to deputy chief of staff, and on September 1, 1939, he was awarded his second permanent and fourth temporary stars as Army chief of staff. As chief of staff from 1939 through 1945, Marshall directed the buildup and organization of the Army throughout World War II,

FIGURE 9–1 George C. Marshall. (*George C. Marshall Foundation, Lexington, VA.*)

seeing it grow to 8.3 million men. He also undertook a needed reorganization of the War Department and was responsible for Dwight D. Eisenhower's being named to direct the Allied forces in North Africa and then the entire European theater of operations. Marshall hoped for and expected the assignment as commander of the invasion of the Continent in 1944, but President Roosevelt said he needed him in Washington. Marshall thus continued to direct the Army's operations from the nation's capital rather than leading the field armies in battle.

After the war, Marshall chose to retire in his new five-star rank of general of the Army but was called upon by President Truman to serve as his special representative to China to attempt to gain cooperation between Nationalist and Communist forces there. This 1945–1946 mission proved to be a failure, but in January 1947 Marshall accepted appointment as secretary of state, serving until 1949. In these two years he was responsible for the genesis of the European Recovery Program (the Marshall Plan) in 1947, aided in the formulation of the Truman Doctrine of aid to countries threatened by Communism, and played a major role in the negotiations that led to the formation of the North Atlantic Treaty Organization in 1948.

Marshall's retirement from public service in 1949 was very brief. The next year he accepted the post of secretary of defense at the behest of Truman. Here he supervised the rebuilding of American military strength in the first year of the Korean War. In this post he solidly backed Truman in his firing of General Douglas MacArthur for publicly calling for an escalation of the war. Marshall retired as Secretary of Defense in 1951 and two years later was awarded the Nobel Peace Prize for his diplomatic efforts in the postwar years. He died in October 1959 in Washington and was buried in Arlington National Cemetery, one of the most honored military and diplomatic leaders of the twentieth-century United States.

The job of taking Casablanca and Morocco was given to American troops sailing in Western Task Force from Hampton Roads under the command of Major General George S. Patton, Jr. The force consisted of 35,000 men on 39 ships. Center Task Force, with 39,000 men (mostly Americans), sailed in 47 vessels from the Clyde in Scotland. Its commander was Major General Lloyd Fredendall, U.S.A. Its target was Oran. Eastern Task Force of 34 vessels also sailed from Britain. It had 33,000 men (about two-thirds British and one-third American) and was under the American Major General Charles Ryder. Its destination was Algiers. Once the Allied troops had secured Algiers, they would come under the command of Lieutenant-General Kenneth Anderson of Great Britain, and this newly constituted First Army would race east to Tunis. First Army would have two weeks to make the 450-mile dash to seize Tunis before the winter rains and mud arrived and before the Axis could reinforce in large numbers.

But a major concern before the landing was whether or not the French in North Africa would resist the Allied invasion forces since the Vichy government had promised that French troops would defend the North African territories if they were allowed to keep Morocco and Algeria. The British stayed in the background during the secret negotiations between the Americans and the French in North Africa because many French military leaders had not forgotten the Royal Navy's attacks on Oran and nearby Mers-el-Kebir of July 1940 to disable the French fleet. One battleship had been sunk, three other capital ships had been disabled, and over 1,000 French sailors had been killed in the attacks.

Assurances of no resistance could not be gained before the invasion despite attempts to persuade the French military chiefs not to order resistance, but two days after the landings, Admiral Jean François Darlan, commander in chief of all Vichy French forces, in North Africa because of the illness of his son, ordered the French defenders to lay down their arms. Darlan was accordingly appointed to a high civil position (which brought severe criticism in America for the "Darlan deal"), but it did bring 200,000 French military in North Africa over to the Allied side. Darlan was subsequently assassinated as a traitor to Vichy France by a young French royalist on Christmas Eve, 1942, and Hitler ordered the occupation of the remainder of France on November 10 as the French in North Africa ceased their resistance of the Allied landings.

The three landings met stern but brief resistance. Algiers fell first, by 7:00 on the evening of D-Day; Oran was surrendered on November 10; and Casablanca surrendered on November 11, just moments before Patton's major attack on the city was scheduled to begin. But on the other side, Field Marshal Albert Kesselring began sending in troops to Tunisia from Sicily immediately after he received word of the landings. He had to hold Tunisia to save Rommel's army, by this time being driven all the way back across North Africa to the Mareth Line in southern Tunisia. By November 30, some 15,000 Axis soldiers had been ferried in to help hold the country.

By that time First Army was far behind schedule and had outrun its supplies. By November 16, over a week after the landings, it was still 80 miles from Tunis. Logistics, terrain, and the inadequacy of the Americans' General Grant and General Lee tanks against the German Panzer Mark IVs had presented persistent problems and slowed down the whole operation. It was now impossible for First Army to meet its two-week deadline for seizing Tunis. Anderson called a halt on December 2. By late December, Eisenhower, commander of Allied forces in North Africa, realistically brought the campaign to an end as the winter rains and mud came on. The race for Tunisia had been lost. Both sides dug in and began their buildups for the spring.

In February 1943 the Allied front was scattered along a 200-mile front west of Tunis. General Fredendall had no mobile reserves and had placed his headquarters 80 miles behind his front line, which ran along the Eastern Dorsal, a ridge of hills running north and south to the west of Tunis. If the Americans were complacent in their positions, Rommel was not. In cooperation with Colonel General Hans-Jurgen von Armin and his Fifth Panzer Army (rushed in from the Russian front and prepared to launch an attack on the Allied line from Tunisia), Rommel, situated at the 25-mile-long Mareth Line holding off Montgomery's Eighth Army, initiated a bold plan to strike north through the rear of the Allied line all the way to the Algerian coast.

Rommel's troops attacked on February 13, causing great damage and confusion in the Allied lines. The Desert Fox wanted to continue his successful drive but was stopped for two days by Armin's failure to cooperate. When Rommel moved out again, he was challenged, then stopped, at the Battle of Kasserine Pass of February 19–23 by American and British troops. This bloody baptism of fire for the American troops (they took 10,000 casualties and lost 200 tanks) was won not only by their determination and artillery, but also by an uncharacteristic failure of nerve on the part of Rommel, who decided to withdraw when resistance became heated.

Rommel was subsequently removed from command on March 9 for trying to persuade Hitler to abandon North Africa and save his troops. On the other side, Patton replaced the ineffectual Fredendall. The battles for Tunisia went on through March and April, with the Allies attempting to slog through from the west and Montgomery's Eighth Army finally bypassing and breaking through the Mareth Line and fighting its way north. Hitler would not hear of evacuation, even though the Allied naval and air forces were cutting the Axis supply lines to Tunisia and the toll of Italian losses was threatening Mussolini's government in Italy.

☆   An American Portrait

George S. Patton—Undoubtedly the most brilliant, flamboyant, and controversial Allied field commander in World War II, George Smith Patton, Jr., was born in San Gabriel, California, to a wealthy and prominent family whose forebears had played significant roles in American military history. Although his early schooling was irregular, Patton was matriculated into Virginia Military Institute in 1903, leaving a year later to enter West Point. He was not graduated until 1909 because of deficiencies in mathematics, but he nevertheless ranked forty-sixth in his class of 103. Always interested in athletics while at the Academy, in 1912 Patton represented the United States in the Stockholm Olympic Games in the military pentathlon.

Patton served with "Black Jack" Pershing in the expedition into Mexico in 1916, leading a motorized force, then joined him on his staff in France the next year. Displaying a keen interest in the use of the tank in warfare, Patton joined the Army's tank corps and as a lieutenant colonel was given command of the 304th Brigade, which played a prominent role in the Saint-Mihiel offensive. Sensing correctly that the Army had little interest in developing armored weaponry, Patton rejoined the cavalry in 1920 and went on to graduate from the Cavalry School at Fort Riley, Kansas, and the Command and General Staff School in 1924 and 1925. After various other duties, he was appointed to the Army War College in 1931. By 1941 Patton was a major general and commander of the 2nd Armored Division, having rejoined the armored force when the Army showed a renewed interest in this type of land warfare in the late 1930s. By January 1942 he was recognized as one of the Army's top tank men and was commander of the I Armored Corps.

In this capacity he led the American forces at Casablanca as part of Operation Torch in November 1942, and four months later he assumed command of II Corps after the disastrous Battle of Kasserine Pass. By July 1943 he was a lieutenant general and commander of the Seventh Army in Sicily. Here his career almost ended over an incident with two hospitalized American soldiers, but Eisenhower refused to remove him from command because of his value as an aggressive field commander.

Sent to England to "command" the mythical "First U.S. Army Group" as an invasion decoy as part of Operation Fortitude, Patton chafed at his enforced inactivity far from the battlefield. But when returned to field command in August 1944 as head of Third Army in France, he again displayed his fighting élan despite his being under Omar Bradley, his former subordinate in North Africa, as part of Twelfth Army Group. Patton's Third Army swept east, crossed the Rhine in March 1945, and drove into Czechoslovakia and Austria. Patton was soon in trouble again, though, when at the end of the war he urged a continuation of the fighting, this time against the Russians in cooperation with the Germans. He was finally removed from command for suggesting the use of former Nazis in the German government to ward off the danger of communist infiltration. Given command of the Fifteenth Army (a paper force), Patton, although by now a full general, was left with no war to fight and nothing to do. He died on December 21, 1945, as a result of injuries sustained in an auto accident, and was buried in a military cemetery in Luxembourg among his men. He, more than anyone else, shaped the development of American tank warfare during World War II.

Early in May both Allied drives broke through the German-Italian defenses. Both Bizerta and Tunis were taken on May 7, and by May 13 the last Axis units had surrendered. The battle for Tunisia was over. In addition to 40,000 men killed, wounded, or missing (as opposed to the Allies' 66,000), over 250,000 Axis soldiers had been captured. The three-year battle for North Africa had come to an end. Hitler's southern flank had been rendered extremely vulnerable. The seizure of North Africa, combined with Hitler's armies having been halted and subject to massive counterattacks in Russia, closed the ring around Nazi Germany. The only questions now were when and where the next Allied offensives would come in the West.

HUSKY, AVALANCHE, AND SHINGLE: THE CAMPAIGNS IN SICILY AND ITALY

The Allies had already decided where the next blow would be delivered. At their Casablanca Conference of January 1943 four months earlier, Roosevelt and Churchill had fixed upon Sicily. The American chiefs of staff had argued for an invasion of France across the Channel instead, but British logic had again won out. The Anglo-American allies were not strong enough to assault the Continent, but they could attack along the periphery of the Axis empire. Here Sicily was the most obvious choice. For an invasion of the Mediterranean island, Allied supply lines would be secure and an invasion in force would mollify Stalin—who was continually demanding a second front to take the pressure off his armies—and perhaps pressure Italy out of the war.

For Operation Husky the Allies assembled 80,000 men, 7,000 vehicles, 600 tanks, and 900 artillery pieces. Over 3,000 landing craft would be needed to get them ashore in the first 48 hours. They would face nine Italian and two German divisions, a total of 230,000 men. The British Eighth Army under Montgomery would land south of Syracuse on the southeast corner of the island and drive north toward the Straits of Messina. The American Seventh Army under Patton would land on the Gulf of Gela on the southern coast of Sicily and cover Montgomery's left flank. The plans also called for Allied paratrooper and glider landings involving 4,600 men. D-Day was set for July 10, 1943.

The nighttime airborne landings were a tragedy of errors. Some 3,400 American paratroopers under Colonel James M. Gavin were scattered all over southeast Sicily because of inadequately trained air crews, and only 12 British gliders out of 144 landed on target north of Syracuse; the rest fell into the sea or were spread across the Sicilian landscape. Still, the initial landings went well. The Allies beat off Axis counterattacks and managed to drive the Germans and Italians back, while in an incredible blunder off

MAP 9–2   Sicily and Italy, 1943–1945.(*Used with permission of Anne C. Christensen.*)

Gela, shaken American gunners downed 23 of 144 American planes, bringing in 2,000 paratroopers of the 82nd Airborne Division under General Matthew B. Ridgway.

Montgomery began his attack to the north and was soon halted south of Mount Etna. Patton then interpreted his orders to cover Montgomery's flank very liberally. On July 19 he set off across Sicily to seize the port city of Palermo on the northwest corner of the island. Moving fast and encountering light Italian resistance, he seized the city three days later. He then turned his Seventh Army east to drive across the northern shore of the island toward Messina. Here Patton ran into fierce German resistance (and almost lost command for slapping two sick and shell-shocked American soldiers to get them back into combat). Patton's men arrived at Messina on August 17 two hours before the British—to his delight and "Monty's" consternation.

Sicily was in Allied hands, the Allies having suffered 19,000 casualties to a like number of German and Italian casualties. The Germans and Italians had also seen some 90,000 of their men captured, even though 40,000 had escaped across the Straits of Messina into Italy to fight again. Most important, the Americans, after their sometimes mediocre showing in North Africa, had displayed the élan of experienced and battle-tested troops in Sicily and had demonstrated that they could handle mobile and mountain warfare, skills absolutely necessary for their next objective—Italy.

With the deteriorating Italian battlefield situation in Sicily and increasing hardships at home, including 4,000 casualties in Rome when the Allies bombed its rail yards on July 19, the Grand Council of the Fascist Party voted "no confidence" in Benito Mussolini on July 25. Marshal Pietro Badoglio took over and surreptitiously began negotiations with the Allies. A furious Hitler ordered Mussolini rescued and flown to Germany. He also ordered the Wehrmacht to prepare to take over the country. On September 3, 1943, secret surrender terms were signed between the Allies and the new Badolgio government, the surrender to be announced on September 8.

In the meantime, plans for the invasion of Italy, Operation Avalanche, had been worked out. The main contingent of the British Eighth Army was to cross the Straits of Messina and attack Reggio, on the toe of Italy, on September 3. A smaller part of the Eighth Army was to land at Taranto, on the inside of the heel of the boot of Italy, on September 8. The next day the American Fifth Army under General Mark W. Clark was to carry out an amphibious landing at Salerno, south of Naples, at the extreme limit of American fighter plane range from Sicily. The Taranto force was to move up the back side of the Italian peninsula. Montgomery's and Clark's forces were to join up west of the Appennines and fight their way north to and beyond Rome.

☆ An American Portrait

Mark Wayne Clark—Born at Madison Barracks, New York, on May 1, 1896, the son of an army colonel, Mark Clark was reared in army camps. Graduated from West Point in the class of 1917, he was shipped to France. Here he commanded a battalion of infantry and served on the staff of First Army.

After World War I, Clark spent a brief period as a speaker on the Chautauqua circuit before being assigned to the office of the assistant secretary of war. During the interwar period he commanded an infantry regiment, served as an instructor for the Indiana National Guard, and participated in the Army's CCC program. He also was graduated from the Infantry School in 1925, the Command and General Staff School in 1935, and the Army War College in 1937.

By the time America entered World War II, Clark had served as assistant chief of staff at the Army War College and had been advanced in rank to brigadier general. He was soon appointed chief of staff of the Army's ground forces and in October 1942, as a major general and the chief of Allied forces in North Africa, was sent by Eisenhower to negotiate with French officers in North Africa in an attempt to gain their cooperation prior to Operation Torch.

In January 1943, "Wayne" Clark, now the youngest lieutenant general in the Army, was given command of Fifth Army. He commanded the American forces in Italy from the landings at Salerno on September 9, 1943, through 1944, in December of that year succeeding Field Marshal Harold Alexander as commander of Fifteenth Army Group. Considerable controversy still exists over his handling of the Italian campaign. In March 1945, in the closing weeks of the European war, Clark was advanced in rank to general and made U.S. chief of occupation forces in Austria as well as United States high commissioner to Austria, in the latter position winning high praise for his diplomatic skills.

In 1947 Clark was given command of Sixth Army, and two years later was assigned to Fort Monroe, Virginia, as Chief of Army Field Forces. As the Korean War dragged into stalemate, Clark was sent to Tokyo in April 1952 as commander-in-chief of the United Nations Command and of the U.S. Far East Command. In these positions he was forced by the American government to sign the armistice agreement with North Korea even though a victory had not been attained in this limited Far Eastern war.

Clark retired in October 1953 and the next year became president of The Citadel in Charleston, South Carolina, serving in that position until 1965. He died in Charleston on April 17, 1984, and was buried on the grounds of The Citadel.

Clark had 70,000 men, both British and American, in his landing force as he approached Salerno from three North African locations and Palermo on September 9. The Italian surrender was announced by Eisenhower in Algiers and Badoglio in Rome at the same time. The Italian army was of no value to the Allies, however, as it was swiftly and smoothly disarmed by the Germans, the Wehrmacht taking over their erstwhile ally's defensive positions. The landing parties at Salerno, as a result, ran into stubborn German resistance. Within days, Field Marshal Kesselring had four Panzer divisions and the tough Hermann Goering Division contesting their landings. A German counterattack on September 12 and 13 almost drove the Allied invaders back into the Tyrrhenian Sea, naval gunfire offshore finally tipping the balance against the German attackers. The Germans also sank two ships with their new radio-guided gliding bombs, a foretaste of the future, but these had no effect on the outcome of the Salerno invasion. By September 18, when Kesselring pulled his men back to the Gustav Line as Clark was reinforced and the Eighth Army threatened to break through from the south, the Anglo-American forces had already taken 9,000 casualties at Salerno in only nine days of fighting.

Any hope the Allies had of a swift movement up the Italian peninsula was thwarted by the mountainous terrain and the brilliant flexible defensive tactics of Kesselring. Throughout the rest of September and all of October 1943, German defensive maneuvers constantly obstructed the Allied drive north while Kesselring was digging in behind the Gustav Line, a defensive barrier running behind the Garigliano and Rapido Rivers in the west and the Sangro River in the east. The Gustav Line soon became known as the "Winter Line," as the Allies failed to break through the German defenses during one of the worst Italian winters in decades.

By mid-January 1944 the Allies had managed to penetrate the Gustav Line, but they could move no further. In their frustration, the Allied command managed to convince itself that it was militarily necessary to bomb out of existence the great Benedictine monastery of Monte Cassino, located 1,700 feet above the Lisi River and dominating the road to Rome. They believed, incorrectly, that the revered Catholic monastery was being used as an observation post for German artillery holding them up in the center of the Winter Line. Some Allied generals, including Clark, were adamantly opposed to the bombing as unnecessary. Nevertheless, faced with a threat by the Australia–New Zealand force commander that he would withdraw if the monastery was not destroyed, on February 15, 1944, on General Sir Harold Alexander's orders, 600 tons of bombs and artillery turned the famed Christian shrine dating back to the days of Saint Benedict in the sixth century into rubble. Sadly, the bombing did no good because the Germans moved into the rubble and put up an even more effective resistance. Not until mid-May was Monte Cassino taken and the Gustav Line broken.

In the meantime, the Allies had attempted to end-run the Gustav Line by launching an amphibious attack at Anzio, south of Rome. Operation Shingle, with 40,000 American and British troops under Major General John P. Lucas in the initial attack of January 22, 1944, at first met no opposition. But on February 16, Kesselring launched a counterattack with 125,000 men that almost drove the 100,000 Allied troops into the sea. Kesselring's counteroffensive was stopped after five days and 19,000 casualties, but not until three months and 59,000 casualties later (many of disease, exhaustion, and neurosis), on May 23, 1944, were the Allies able to fight their way out of Kesselring's Anzio encirclement.

Then, when the Allied forces breaking out of Anzio joined up on May 25 with their comrades finally penetrating the Gustav Line, Clark did not turn his army east to trap the German forces behind Cassino only 20 miles away, but, instead, and at Churchill's insistence, turned north toward Rome. The propaganda value of taking Rome was deemed more important than capturing or destroying the German armies.

This decision allowed Kesselring to dig in at Valmonte on the Caesar Line, south of Rome, and extricate his Tenth and Fourteenth Armies to fight on. And not until June 4, 1944, did the Allies enter Rome. Then Clark, instead of following the disorganized Fourteenth Army north, set up defensive positions before moving out again against the Germans. For the remainder of the summer the Allies slogged their way up the central portion of the Italian peninsula, being stopped dead in their tracks by rains and by the German defenses during August and September at the Gothic Line north and west of Florence. They finally had to call a halt for the winter near Bologna.

Not until April 1945, with Major General Lucian Truscott now in charge of Fifth Army and General Richard McCreery in charge of Eighth Army, were the Allies able to break through the Gothic Line and advance into the valleys of northern Italy. And not until May 29 did Colonel General Heinrich von Vietinghoff, who had replaced Kesselring, finally surrender to the Allies. This was one day after Mussolini, who had been rescued from his Italian captors back in July 1943 by SS Colonel Otto Skorzeny's commandoes to be installed as Hitler's puppet leader of Italy, was shot to death by Italian partisans. His body and that of his mistress were strung up upside down in a square in Milan for the local Italians to deride and defile.

The war in Italy thus came to an end only in the final days of the war in Europe. It was undoubtedly the most frustrating campaign of World War II, with its high demands for valuable troops, equipment, and landing craft (needed for the Normandy invasion and in the Pacific); and its inception and execution have been marked by controversy ever since. But the Italian campaign drew off thousands of German soldiers from the Russian and Western fronts and made Allied victories there at least marginally easier.

BATTLE OF THE ATLANTIC

Throughout these same years, 1939 through 1944, a naval campaign of epic proportions was taking place on the waters of the Atlantic Ocean, a campaign as crucial to Allied victory as the land battles in North Africa, Russia, Sicily, and Italy.

America, of course, had been rebuilding its naval fleet during the decade prior to its entry into World War II. Thanks to the Vinson-Trammel Act of 1934; the Vinson Act, or "Twenty Percent Naval Expansion Act," of 1938; the Vinson-Walsh Act, or "Two-Ocean Navy Act," of 1940, providing for a 70 percent increase in the size of the Navy; and other legislation, the Navy was almost prepared for trouble when it came.

On the diplomatic front, the United States and 21 Latin American nations signed the Panama Declaration in 1939, soon after the European war began. In it they declared the waters of the Western Hemisphere to be off limits to hostile acts and established an off-shore neutrality zone of 300 miles. Ships and warplanes were to enforce the declaration. Then, as the war heated up, the United States joined other Latin American nations in the Declaration of Havana of June 1940, which stated that an attack on any signatory would be considered an attack on all. A defensive line around the Western Hemisphere had thus been drawn.

But such measures were no help to Britain, struggling to maintain its vital trade in the North Atlantic, Mediterranean, and home waters in the face of an onslaught by German submarines and surface raiders. Accordingly, Roosevelt and Churchill worked out a "destroyer deal" in September 1940 whereby the United States transferred 50 old destroyers to Britain in exchange for 99-year leases on eight British bases, one in Newfoundland and seven in the Caribbean. In addition, Roosevelt as commander-in-chief kept extending the limits of neutrality patrols farther and farther out to sea, their pilots broadcasting the locations of any German submarines spotted on open radio frequencies so that the information would be available to the British.

Roosevelt followed up these steps with a "Four Freedoms" proposal to supply ships and other war materials to nations fighting aggressors. Finally, by the Roosevelt-backed Lend-Lease Act of March 1941, the United States made goods available to the anti-Axis nations on credit. The legislation also included a proviso to construct American air bases in Greenland for North Atlantic patrol duty (by agreement with Denmark) and an extension of the neutrality zone 2,000 miles out to sea, an area well within the announced German war zone.

By late summer 1941 the United States was in an undeclared war on Germany in the North Atlantic, a fact Roosevelt scrupulously hid from the American people. When, therefore, the destroyer USS *Greer* was attacked by U-652 some 200 miles southwest of

Iceland on September 4, 1941, Roosevelt did not reveal that the destroyer had been tracking the German submarine for three hours, but issued an order to "shoot on sight" any hostile craft attacking any American ship or any ship under American escort. Subsequently, on the nights of October 16–17, the USS *Kearney* was attacked by German subs (after she tried to depth-charge them), and on October 31 the USS *Reuben James* underwent the same ordeal and was blown in half and sunk, but Roosevelt never revealed the actions carried out by these naval vessels. He only announced their being attacked.

After the *Reuben James* incident, Congress authorized the arming of American merchant vessels and permitted them to sail into any and all belligerent ports. Neutrality was long dead on the waters of the North Atlantic; the U.S. Navy and merchant marine were clearly acting on the Allies' side. The Navy was thus in a real shooting war with Germany even before Pearl Harbor. Hitler subsequently declared war on the United States after the attack on the American fleet in Hawaii. This step was not demanded by his treaty with Japan but was taken by him to give the German navy every legal right to war on United States naval and merchant vessels to prevent supplies from reaching Great Britain; henceforth, America could no longer claim neutrality while aiding Britain in its war against German submarines and surface vessels.

When World War II had broken out in Europe in 1939, the German navy was not prepared for the great burdens it would be called upon to bear. The year before, Grand Admiral Erich Raeder presented two naval plans to Hitler, one for weapons to be used against commerce (such as submarines and surface raiders), the other, Plan Z, for a great surface fleet for open combat with the Allied navies. Hitler chose Plan Z, with the result that when the war began a year later, Germany was building battleships and cruisers but could not expect to have enough available to control the seas for at least five years. What Germany needed in 1939 and 1940 was submarines to destroy British commerce in the North Atlantic and Mediterranean, but it had less than five dozen boats in commission. Thus, with too few ships of either surface or subsurface types and too few trained men, the German navy nevertheless sailed out to destroy British commerce as its contribution to German victory.

The British turned to convoying early in World War II but still faced major challenges in getting ships through from the Dominions and neutral countries. For example, the German pocket battleship *Graf Spee* sank thousands of tons of shipping in the South Atlantic before three pursuing British cruisers forced her into the neutral port of Montevideo, Uruguay, in the fall of 1939. Compelled to leave the port at the insistence of the Uruguayan government, the captain of the *Graf Spee* scuttled her in December 1939 outside the harbor rather than see her destroyed by the British ships waiting for her on the horizon. Her sister pocket battleship *Deutschland* made it home from southern waters without incident.

After a 1940 hiatus in which Hitler waited in vain for Britain's surrender, in the spring of 1941 Admiral Raeder planned a great surface raiding mission to shut down the North Atlantic to the English. The new 42,000-ton battleship *Bismarck,* the 32,000-ton sister battlecruisers *Scharnhorst* and *Gneisenau,* and the heavy cruiser *Prinz Eugen* were to take part in the operation. The *Scharnhorst* and *Gneisenau* never made it out of port because they needed repairs, but the other two vessels sailed out of Bergen, in occupied Norway, into one of the great naval conflicts of modern times. On May 23, 1941, the ships were spotted moving between Greenland and Iceland by two British cruisers, which proceeded to follow them and broadcast their location. The next day the *Bismarck* met and sank the battlecruiser *Hood,* with her 15-inch guns, and the battleship *Prince of Wales* was badly damaged.

The British Admiralty, shocked and infuriated by the loss of the *Hood,* ordered every available ship after the two German raiders. The *Prinz Eugen* slipped away south, and the *Bismarck* temporarily gave her shadows the slip. But the *Bismarck* was picked up again heading for the French coast, and all available vessels gave chase. On the morning of May 26, 1941, planes from the carrier *Ark Royal* hit the *Bismarck,* their bomb damage jamming her rudders. The crippled giant tried to get away, but the next day the battleships *Rodney* and *King George V* pounded her into helplessness. A cruiser-launched torpedo finally put her down, only 110 of her 2,300-man crew surviving.

Balancing the fortunes of war, the *Scharnhorst, Gneisenau,* and *Prinz Eugen* all managed to slip out of the port of Brest in France in February 1942 and make it safely home through the Channel without even being attacked, one of the most glaring displays of British blundering in the course of the war. But the battlecruiser *Gneisenau* struck a mine and was never repaired, the *Scharnhorst* was later sunk by British vessels in the Battle of the North Cape in the Arctic Ocean off Norway on December 26, 1943, and the new battleship *Tirpitz* was damaged at Kaafiord by midget submarines in the summer of 1943 and was twice bombed at her moorings in Norway in 1944, the second time fatally in November, having never gotten to sea. By 1944, however, German surface raiding was a thing of the past. After the loss of the *Bismarck* in May 1941, Hitler had cooled on surface raiding and had effectively given up on this type of naval warfare in early 1943, dismissing Admiral Erich Raeder as head of the navy. He had turned to the U-boat as his weapon of choice. The unprepared German surface navy had not been able to do the job; whether the now-favored and rapidly building subsurface navy could force the British into submission remained to be seen.

Admiral Karl Doenitz, Germany's U-boat chief, had only 56 boats available when the war began in 1939, far fewer than the minimum 300 he thought necessary, and only 22 were ready for North Atlantic service. With only about 10 boats available at any given time for patrols during the early months of the war, they could do little damage. But by mid-1940 Doenitz had sub bases in Norway and at five locations on the Bay of Biscay on the west coast of France, putting his boats much closer to their targets. And newer and better U-boats were coming on line.

Now Doenitz could send his submarines to sea to hunt the Allied convoys in "wolf packs," coordinated kills, preferably in nighttime surface attacks. They began to enjoy phenomenal success despite the fact that the British had extended their escort patrols farther and farther out to sea. Churchill obtained the 50 American destroyers, but still the sinkings continued, especially in the 600-mile-wide "Black Pit" in the mid-Atlantic beyond the range of long-range patrol planes. The Allies' hopes were dimmed by the fate of convoys that lost up to half their vessels to sub packs in 1940.

Doenitz's sub crews called this the "Happy Time." And well they might, with 217 vessels of over a million tons being sent to the bottom during the summer and autumn of 1940. Doenitz confidently believed that 1941 would close down the merchant trade to Britain across the Atlantic and the Northwestern approaches to the British Isles, but he found that new antisubmarine warfare (ASW) activities and increased land-based coastal air patrols were costing him too many sub losses. He therefore moved his U-boats' areas of operations farther west beyond the range of the patrol planes and continued his naval war of attrition.

☆   An American Portrait

Ernest J. King—Born in Lorain, Ohio, on November 23, 1878, Ernest Joseph King entered the Naval Academy at Annapolis in 1897. He was graduated fourth in his class of 67 in 1901 and two years later was commissioned an ensign and assigned to the Asiatic Fleet. After 14 years of sea duty, teaching at Annapolis, and commanding destroyers, King's naval star began to rise when in 1915 he was appointed to the staff of Vice Admiral Henry T. Mayo, commander of the Battleship Force of the Atlantic Fleet. Here he played an active role in the Navy's duties during World War I. After the war, King reopened the Naval Postgraduate School at Annapolis, then in 1922 underwent training at the submarine school at New London, Connecticut. His administrative talents were recognized when he was appointed commandant of the submarine base at New London the next year.

In 1927, having already garnered experience in battleships, destroyers, and submarines, King was appointed to the Naval Air School at Pensacola, Florida, winning his wings as a naval aviator in only five months, half the normal time for such training. His aviation training was put to immediate use by the Navy when he was appointed as commander of the aircraft squadrons in the Atlantic Fleet the next year. Soon thereafter he was made assistant chief of the Bureau of Aeronautics. Between 1930 and 1932 he commanded the carrier *Lexington,* then moved up to command the Bureau of Aeronautics for three years, between 1933 and 1936. Although by 1939 King was a temporary vice admiral and commander of Aircraft Battle Force, it appeared that his career had reached its zenith when he was appointed to the practically functionless General Board to await retirement.

FIGURE 9–2 Ernest J. King. (*Official U.S. Navy Photo, DOD Still Media Records Center, Washington, D.C.*)

But when World War II began in Europe and President Roosevelt committed the Navy to extensive duties in the Atlantic, King's career was revived. By late 1940 he was commander of the Atlantic Patrol Force, and early 1941 saw him appointed admiral and commander-in-chief of the Atlantic Fleet. When the United States entered the war in December 1941, King was appointed commander-in-chief, United States Fleet (COM-INCH, this acronym seeming more fitting than its predecessor, CINCUS) and set about reorganizing the fleet staff for more combat efficiency. King was soon given the added responsibility of sharing in military war planning at the highest level when President Roosevelt appointed him to the Combined Chiefs of Staff (U.S. Army and Navy chiefs and their British counterparts) after the Arcadia Conference of December 1941. Then, in March 1942, King was also made chief of naval operations, the COMINCH and CNO organizations retaining their separateness but being joined and coordinated by Admiral King.

During the course of the war, King was also called upon to take part in the Allied conferences at Casablanca, Washington, Quebec, Cairo, Teheran, Yalta, and Potsdam. In December 1944 he was advanced to the five-star rank of fleet admiral. In the closing months of the war he performed some final duties by overseeing the abolition of COM-INCH, its duties being transferred to the office of the chief of naval operations (CNO). King left active duty in December 1945, never enjoyed good health thereafter, and died in June 1956 at the U.S. Naval Hospital in Portsmouth, New Hampshire. With his death passed the Navy's organizer of victory in World War II.

By this time, however, on the basis of Roosevelt's policies, the U.S. Atlantic Fleet under Admiral Ernest J. King was carrying out neutrality patrols farther and farther east and was escorting vessels all the way to Iceland. Reykjavik, Iceland, was being used for American air patrols. And the British were using smaller "escort carriers" off Green-land and doing tremendous damage to Doenitz's precious subs. He, accordingly, decided late in 1941 to switch his sub war to the coast of North America, and Operation *Paukenschlag* (drum roll) began.

The U.S. Navy was ill prepared for submarine attacks off the nation's coasts in its early months of action after Pearl Harbor. Its limited number of ships were concentrated in the North Atlantic, and it had built few destroyer escorts for ASW work. As a result, the German U-boats lying offshore from Newfoundland to Florida had easy pickings as unescorted merchant vessels sailing singly made their way up the coast, their silhouettes clearly revealed by the lights of the East Coast cities. The waters off the Carolina Capes, called "the graveyard of the Atlantic" for their shallow, stormy waters, were a favorite haunt. The U.S. Navy, Army, and Coast Guard had only 100 vessels and 200 planes to stop them. In the sub crews' "Second Happy Time" in the first four months of 1942, they sank 87 vessels of over half a million tons. When 23 ships went down off the East Coast in April 1942, tactics were finally changed.

American vessels started using asdic (early sonar) equipment from the British, convoying was instituted, and extended daytime air cover was provided. These methods kept the subs submerged, and the rate of sinkings accordingly declined, so Doenitz sent his subs south to the Gulf of Mexico and the Caribbean. When convoying and air patrols followed even as far south as Brazil, Doenitz recalled his subs from the coast of the Americas to concentrate on the Black Pit, still without air cover, in early 1943.

German shipbuilders were turning out 30 U-boats per month, so Doenitz believed he could now afford appreciable losses and still close down the North Atlantic sea lanes. But the Allies' ASW vessels by this time had radar and radio detection systems. They also operated in antisubmarine groups employing picket lines along the sea lanes. In 1943 air cover from escort carriers (merchant ships converted to small carriers) and from long-range bombers like the B-24, equipped with radar and depth charges, was added.

The turning point in the Battle of the Atlantic came in April 1943. Taking too many losses to the Allies in the North Atlantic, Doenitz switched his U-boats south to central Atlantic waters southwest of the Azores, but there too they met only frustration and death. The U.S. Navy was using "hunter-killer" groups (destroyers, destroyer escorts, and escort carriers) in these waters, and German submarine losses climbed as their number of merchant ship kills dropped precipitously. And Doenitz's sub pens on the Bay of Biscay were now coming under constant attack by the RAF. During 1943 the German navy lost 237 U-boats.

The year 1944 witnessed a continuation of the same effective Allied strategy against the U-boats (hunter-killer groups, larger protected convoys, radar and sonar detection, and almost continuous air cover), and their losses mounted as their sinkings continued to fall. Ultra intelligence was also available to the Allies in seeking out and destroying German U-boats and their supply subs. By 1945 German submarines were no more than an occasional menace as Allied ships carrying men and supplies sailed virtually unchallenged across the North Atlantic, through the Mediterranean, and along the coasts of Western Europe.

During the six years of war, the Germans sank 23.3 million tons of Allied shipping, but the Allies built 42.5 million new tons to replace them during the same period. Some 300,000 safe passages were made by merchant ships across the North Atlantic. The Germans used 1,175 subs during the war. Of these, 785 were lost to Allied naval and air forces (191 to the Americans). Of 41,000 German sailors who served on the U-boats, some 28,000 were killed, and another 5,000 were taken prisoner. The British had 2,177 merchant vessels sunk, and 30,000 mariners died, but in the end it was the technologically and numerically superior Allied ASW crews who won the Battle of the Atlantic. In a very real sense, both Winston Churchill and Karl Doenitz were right. Both had insisted in 1940 and 1941 that the Battle for Europe would be decided on the North Atlantic.

OVERLORD AND ANVIL: THE INVASIONS OF FRANCE

The idea of a cross-Channel invasion of France had been discussed in Allied circles virtually since the fall of Dunkirk in June 1940. The Americans adopted it as a favored strategy upon entering the war, and Stalin had added pressure for such a move by his persistent demands for a second front, this to take the pressure off the Soviet Union. The British, however, were much more cautious in making such a commitment, especially after their disastrous raid on the French port town of Dieppe on August 18 and 19, 1942. In this operation, which included no preliminary air bombardment and only brief naval shelling, over 3,600 of the 6,000 raiders—mostly Canadians—became casualties in only eight hours. The raid clearly illustrated the impossibility of an early cross-Channel invasion. Dieppe also taught the British the danger of going against defended ports and the need for overwhelming force in making amphibious landings against defended shores.

☆   An American Portrait

Dwight David Eisenhower—Although born in Denison, Texas, on October 14, 1890, Eisenhower always considered himself as being from Abilene, Kansas, where his family moved a year later and where he grew up.

After graduating from Abilene High School in 1909, Eisenhower went to work in a local creamery, raising money to put his brother through college, after which his brother was to do the same for him. But Eisenhower received an appointment to West Point two years later and was graduated sixty-first of 164 cadets in the class of 1915, "the class the stars fell on." There followed three years of various assignments, which, to his disappointment, did not include service in France during World War I. Advanced in rank to major, "Ike" was assigned as an aide to Brigadier General Fox Conner, an experienced Army officer. Conner reinvigorated Eisenhower's interest in extensive reading and superior staff work during their three years together from 1922 to 1924.

Eisenhower demonstrated his latent leadership talents when he was graduated first in his class at the Command and General Staff School at Fort Leavenworth in 1926 and again the following year at the Army War College. His outstanding record in these schools won him an assignment in 1930 to the office of the assistant secretary of war, then to the staff of Douglas MacArthur, chief of staff of the Army. In 1936 MacArthur took the rising young staff officer with him to the Philippines as his chief of staff. Here Eisenhower served for three years, he and MacArthur displaying more animosity than heartfelt respect for each other. By 1941 Eisenhower had been promoted to colonel and was chief of staff to Lieutenant General Walter Krueger of the Third Army. After Pearl Harbor he was assigned to the War Plans Division.

The next year Eisenhower was tapped for top field command and sent to England as a lieutenant general and commander of American and Allied forces in England, moving

FIGURE 9–3   Dwight D. Eisenhower. (*National Archives, Washington, D.C.*)

on to become Allied commander-in-chief, North Africa, for the execution of Operation Torch in November 1942. By the end of the next year he had been raised to the rank of general and had been appointed commanding general, Allied Powers, European theater of operations by President Roosevelt. In this position Eisenhower directed Operation Overlord, the breakout from Normandy, and the final defeat of Germany. In the last months of the war he was also awarded the rank of general of the army. He stayed on in Europe after the war as the commander of American occupation forces in Germany.

Known as a high military commander who had managed to gain the cooperation of the always-factious Allied military and political leaders during the war, Eisenhower succeeded George Marshall as chief of staff in November 1945, retaining that post until February 1948. He then left the Army to assume the presidency of Columbia University, returning to uniform in December 1950 when he was appointed supreme commander of the Allied Powers in Europe.

Sought after by both the Democratic and Republican parties as sure presidential timber for the election of 1952, Eisenhower declared himself to be a Republican, won that party's nomination, defeated Illinois governor Adlai E. Stevenson in the election, and was sworn in as the thirty-fourth president of the United States in January 1953. Here he drastically reduced the military budget after 1953 with the end of the Korean War and enunciated the Eisenhower Doctrine of giving financial and military aid to Middle Eastern countries threatened by communism. He left the presidency in 1961 in memorable fashion by warning the country in his farewell address of the threat posed by the "military-industrial complex."

Retiring to his farm at Gettysburg, Pennsylvania, next to the famous Civil War battlefield, Eisenhower died on March 28, 1969, and was buried on the grounds of the Eisenhower Library and Museum in his hometown of Abilene, Kansas.

The debate over the location and timing of the second front had continued until the Trident Conference in Washington in May 1942. Here Roosevelt and Churchill agreed on a cross-Channel attack on France in May 1944. Operation Bolero was already being carried out. It called for turning Britain into a vast staging area for the invasion of the Continent. Over 3 million men, 5 million tons of supplies, 8,000 planes, and 50,000 military vehicles were to be available by May 1944. Planning for the invasion had been carried out by COSSAC (Chief of Staff to Supreme Allied Commander), changed to SHAEF (Supreme Headquarters of Allied Expeditionary Force) when Eisenhower was appointed Commanding General, Allied Powers, European Theater of Operations, on December 31, 1943. Under Eisenhower were Montgomery, who would head the ground forces, and various British generals and admirals heading the SHAEF staff positions.

One of the first decisions made was the choice of Normandy, south of England, as the landing site instead of the Pas-de-Calais area to the northeast. Calais was closer to England but more heavily defended, and Normandy was better suited for resupply and air cover. The British and American bomber chiefs stood in adamant opposition to the whole invasion as a strategic mistake almost right up to the time of its execution; they argued that Germany could be taken out by strategic bombing of its cities, military installations, and industries alone. They had to be dragged into providing air support for Overlord. Ironically, their support during the invasion proved to be critical.

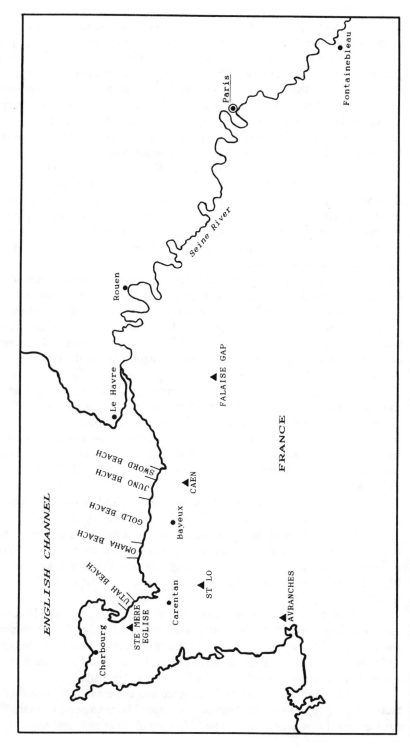

MAP 9–3 Normandy Invasion and Breakout, 1944. (*Used with permission of Anne C. Christensen.*)

243

Planning included not only assembling and training the men in England and gathering all the materials needed for the landing, but also developing special armored vehicles to do demolition work on the German defenses on the beaches. Also part of the plan was the building of two artificial harbors (Mulberry A and Mulberry B) to be floated over and sunk off the landing site to be used for docking and reinforcement until the port of Cherbourg to the northwest was seized. Included, too, was a deception plan called Operation Fortitude. Under Fortitude, a fake "First U.S. Army Group" of no men was "assembled" in Kent in southeast England under the "command" of Lieutenant General Patton (the Allied general most feared and respected by the Germans) to convince them that the landing site would be the Pas-de-Calais across the Channel.

Three weeks before D-day of June 5, 1944 (the date having been pushed back from May), all seemed ready. On June 3 all the assault troops were on board their ships, and the British and American naval forces were in place to support the landings. Bad weather reports indicated that June 5 would not work, but Eisenhower gave the word to go on June 6. Any delay would postpone the whole operation for two critical weeks, and the Allies would then have to start all over.

On June 5 Operation Fortitude was begun, with fake invasion vessels and fake bombers (planes dropping aluminum strips that filled the German radar screens with "planes") moving toward Calais. Fake messages indicating that the Allied invasion was underway were broadcast, and heavy bombing of Calais was carried out. Fortitude fooled the Germans completely. Weeks later, Hitler was still delaying reinforcements for his defenders at Normandy because the "real" invasion site was the Pas-de-Calais. This was Hitler's fifth great strategic mistake.

The German defenses along the Normandy coast were very strong, thanks to the work of Field Marshal Rommel (now head of Army Group B) in building up Hitler's vaunted Atlantic Wall. It stretched along the entire west coast of France, included 15,000 strongpoints, and was manned by 300,000 troops. It included anti-landing-craft and antitank obstacles, artillery emplacements, and machine gun nests. Fortunately for the invading forces, the weather was so bad on the night of June 5 that the Germans did not expect anything to happen.

Operation Neptune, the assault phase of Overlord, consisted of an after-midnight airborne assault by three divisions of British and American paratroopers and glider forces (about 20,000 men) on three key locations. Before sunrise, a massive air bombardment and a 600-ship naval bombardment were directed at the beaches. The 176,000 troops of the first waves debarked from 4,000 landing craft and hit the three beaches of Normandy beginning at 6:30 in the morning. Operation Overlord, the invasion of the Continent, was finally underway.

Farthest to the west on the beaches of Normandy was Utah Beach. Units of the American 82nd Airborne Division dropped behind the beaches during the predawn hours, and then the U.S. Seventh Army Corps under General J. Lawton Collins landed in the early morning hours. Some 23,000 men came ashore on Utah Beach the first day to limited opposition and began to move onto the Cherbourg Peninsula.

In the center of the Allied landing arc was Omaha Beach. Here the Allies ran into their toughest opposition. VI Army Corps under Major General Leonard T. Gerow had been assigned this landing site. It had 100-foot cliffs at each end and only four narrow exits inland. The soldiers not only had to deal with German guns, mines, machine guns, and barbed wire, but they also had to climb into their landing craft 12 miles offshore and endure a prolonged gauntlet of fire even before getting to their assigned beaches. First Army commander Lieutenant General Omar N. Bradley almost called off the whole Omaha Beach operation at 9:00 in the morning, but, as it turned out, SHAEF never received his request. By the end of the first day, the Americans' beachhead was only one mile deep, and 3,000 casualties had already been sustained. Fortunately, a German communications breakdown sent the Wehrmacht's armored reserves to the British beaches to the east, or the Americans on Omaha Beach might have been overrun.

☆　An American Portrait

Omar N. Bradley—Remembered as the "GI's general" of World War II, Omar Nelson Bradley was born in Clark, Missouri, the son of an impoverished school teacher who died in 1908. In 1911 Bradley entered West Point and was graduated four years later, along with Eisenhower, in "the class the stars fell on." He stood forty-fourth in a class of 164. Assigned to the infantry, he served at posts in the West, and during World War I, to his frustration, was never sent to France but was instead given duty guarding copper mines in Montana.

Returning to West Point between 1920 and 1924 as a mathematics instructor and following this up with a year at the Infantry School at Fort Benning, Georgia, Bradley carried out a number of routine assignments well and was sent to the Command and General Staff School in 1928 and 1929. Upon his return to Fort Benning, he caught the attention of George Marshall and was soon tapped to attend the Army War College. By 1939 he was serving directly under Marshall as his chief of staff and was then appointed to command

FIGURE 9–4　Omar N. Bradley. (*Official U.S. Army Photo, DOD Still Media Records Center, Washington, D.C.*)

the 82nd Division with the rank of major general. The next year he was made commander of the Infantry School.

In 1943 Bradley joined Eisenhower in North Africa and was given command of II Corps when Patton was removed to begin planning for the invasion of Sicily. During Operation Overlord, Bradley commanded the First Army and was soon moved up by Eisenhower to take over Twelfth Army Group. Throughout the last year of the war he quarreled bitterly with Montgomery, yet he carried out his European command duties with professionalism and skill while retaining the admiration of the officers and men who served under him.

At the end of the war he accepted the position of head of the Veterans Administration but rejoined the regulars in February 1948 as chief of staff of the Army, receiving the rank of general. In August 1949 he was moved up to chairman of the Joint Chiefs of Staff and was made general of the army the next year. During the Korean War he opposed the expansion of that conflict from his position as head of the Joint Chiefs. He retired from active service in 1953. Bradley was active in various business interests in the years thereafter and died in April 1981 in New York City. He was buried in Arlington National Cemetery, still remembered as one of the most competent and well-liked battlefield commanders of World War II.

To the east on Gold, Juno, and Sword Beaches assigned to the British, things went better, but the fighting was still severe, with the British and Canadian soldiers fighting off German armored attacks. The British did not make it to the city of Caen, their objective, but they were at least holding on during the first crucial hours and days of Overlord. That the Allies were successful in this amphibious landing can be credited not only to the courage of the Allied soldiers but also to the fact that the Allies had complete control of the air. Communications behind the German lines had been severely disrupted by previous air attacks, and Hitler persisted in believing that the Normandy landings were a feint in force, with the real attack to follow in the Calais area.

In the days and weeks that followed, fighting continued to be severe, but the Allies held on and gradually expanded their positions. By the end of June, Cherbourg had been taken, but the British movements to seize Caen as a pivoting point for a swing north and east went slower than expected. The U.S. VII and VIII Corps had a terrible time battling their way south toward Saint-Lô through the *bocage,* a checkerboard of fields and hedgerows that gave ideal cover for the Germans and constantly thwarted armored movement. But a breakout was secured by the end of July, and Allied forces began to roll across France.

VIII Corps and XXX Corps moved west into Brittany to seize the Atlantic ports while the newly organized Third Army, under George Patton, swung around to the east toward LeMans and the Seine. Unfortunately, over 50,000 Germans and most of their armor managed to escape from the Falaise Gap in late August, but the Allies kept driving on, and reinforcements kept pouring in. By the end of July the Allies had taken 122,000 casualties to Germany's 114,000, but the Allies were clearly in France to stay. Some 85 percent of the American casualties were infantrymen in this series of slogging battles. Paris was liberated on August 25, 1944, the Free French leader General Charles DeGaulle given the honor of leading the march into the city.

Not only was the Normandy landing in June a success, but on August 15 the U.S. Seventh Army, under Major General Alexander M. Patch, landed between Cannes and Toulon in southern France in Operation Anvil. The French II Corps followed the Americans onto the beaches, passed through the Seventh Army, and led the advance through Marseilles and up the Rhone River to Lyons and Dijon. On September 12 they joined up with Patton's Third Army moving east. In the meantime, Patch's Seventh Army paralleled them up the Rhone and soon passed Swiss territory to advance in flank with Third Army into Germany.

☆   An American Portrait

Alexander M. Patch—Alexander McCarrell "Sandy" Patch, the only top military commander to serve in combat command in both the European and Pacific theaters during World War II, was born in 1899 at Fort Huachuca, Arizona Territory, the son of an army officer. His father retired on disability the next year, and the family returned to Pennsylvania, where Patch grew up.

In 1908 he entered Lehigh University but left the following year, having won an appointment to the United States Military Academy. Graduated and commissioned a second lieutenant of infantry in 1913, he was sent to France with the outbreak of World War I. Here he directed the AEF Machine Gun School and commanded the 2nd Battalion, 18th Infantry Regiment, in the Meuse-Argonne offensive.

After the war he served at various duty posts and was assigned to the Command and General Staff School in 1924 and to the Army War College in 1931 (where he was a classmate of George Patton). By 1940 he was a colonel and commander of the 47th Infantry Regiment. With the outbreak of World War II, Patch was advanced to major general and commander of the Americal Division in the Pacific, in this capacity directing ground operations in the Guadalcanal-Tulagi campaign as the division replaced the 1st Marine Division on Guadalcanal. Exhausted by these duties, Patch was ordered home by General Marshall and was subsequently tapped to form IV Corps for the European theater of operations.

By March 1944 Patch had been given command of Seventh Army in Sicily, and in August of that year directed the American–Free French landings on the Riviera coast under Operation Anvil. Patch, as a lieutenant general, led Seventh Army until the defeat of Germany and was then ordered to prepare Fourth Army for the invasion of Japan. Shortly after the end of the war, Patch was confined to Brooke Army Hospital in San Antonio, Texas. Here he died of pneumonia on November 21, 1945. He was buried on the grounds of the United States Military Academy, one of America's most respected but least remembered Army commanders of World War II.

Thanks to the success of Overlord and Anvil, by the autumn of 1944 Hitler's armies were under severe pressure in the west while the Russians had long before begun to surge back on the eastern front and threaten the German homeland itself. Equally portentious, the Luftwaffe had lost control of the air, and Allied bomber raids were crushing German cities, factories, and morale in a night-and-day offensive from the skies.

AIR POWER AGAINST GERMANY

The success of air power in the first two years of the European war, most notably Luftwaffe air support in Hitler's drives to the east and west, plus the successes of the RAF in the Battle of Britain, convinced even the most skeptical American leaders that air power had now become critical for success in modern warfare and that the enthusiasts for strategic bombing alone had been dead wrong. Accordingly, General Henry "Hap" Arnold, head of the Army Air Forces (as it was called after June 1941), received support for building up a multi-mission, multi-airplane-type air force from both military and political sources. By the time of Pearl Harbor the Air Forces had over 350,000 men and 2,800 planes and was rapidly expanding. By early 1945 it would have 2.4 million men and 80,000 planes.

☆   An American Portrait

Henry H. "Hap" Arnold—Arnold, the architect of the modern Air Force, was born in Gladwyne, Pennsylvania, in 1886. He joined the corps of cadets at West Point in 1903, on an appointment originally intended for his older brother, and was graduated a second lieutenant of infantry four years later in the middle ranks of his class of 110 cadets. It was at West Point that he picked up the nickname Happy, later shortened to Hap.

After tours of duty in the Philippines and at Governors Island in New York harbor, Arnold entered the Army's neophyte flying contingent in 1911 by enrolling in a two-month flight school operated by the Wright brothers in Dayton, Ohio. For the next six years Arnold carried out both air and infantry duties and in 1917 entered the Air Division of the Signal Corps but saw no action in France.

During the 1920s, Arnold attended the Army Industrial College, testified on behalf of Billy Mitchell at his famous court-martial trial, saw service with the cavalry, and attended the Command and General Staff School at Fort Leavenworth. After 1929, however, he was given air commands and in 1936 was called to Washington as assistant chief of the Air Corps, two years later being made chief, with the rank of major general.

During 1939 and 1940 Arnold played the leading role in allocating aircraft production for the burgeoning Air Corps, in the latter year also accepting the position of deputy chief of staff for the Army. When the Army was reorganized and the Army Air Forces were created as a co-equal combat arm in March 1942, Arnold was named commanding general. He held this position throughout World War II, also taking over command of Twentieth Air Force in the Pacific in April 1944, giving his orders by radio while headquartered in Washington.

While carrying this tremendous load of military duties, Arnold also attended the strategic conferences that shaped World War II. He acted as advisor to President Roosevelt at the Arcadia, Casablanca, First Quebec, and Second Quebec conferences and was with President Harry Truman at the Potsdam Conference. He was forced to miss the Washington and Yalta Conferences because of recurring heart problems. Arnold was advanced in rank to general in March 1943 and to general of the army (joining Marshall, MacArthur, and Eisenhower) in December 1944.

Arnold retired early in 1946, turning over command of the Air Forces to General Carl Spaatz and moving to Sonoma, California. He died there on January 15, 1950, of a fifth heart attack. He was buried in Arlington National Cemetery.

The U.S. Army Air Forces began to build for a European role when Brigadier General Ira Eaker was sent to London to set up a headquarters for Eighth Air Force, as the American contingent was designated. The Eighth Air Force commander was General Carl "Tooey" Spaatz. It took many months of hard work and organization to get the bomber force in a position to help carry the burden of the air war, but by August 1942 Eighth Air Force (now under Eaker as commander) was ready to go.

The American airmen depended heavily on their four-engined B-17 Flying Fortress, an excellent plane for high-altitude flying (despite its limited bomb load) and well configured with 13 .50-caliber machine guns to defend its 10-man crew against enemy fighter planes. They were soon joined by four-engined B-24 Liberators with greater speed and bomb capacity. These two plane types became the backbone of the American high-altitude daylight precision bombing offensive against Germany and the countries under German occupation. Precision bombing targeted specific industrial and military targets, such as airplane factories, electric generating plants, petroleum refineries, and transportation systems to deprive Germany of its warmaking potential; the British preferred area bombing of cities to break the morale of the German people. Eaker and the Eighth, with their Norden bomb sights and their H_2S centimetric radar sets capable of creating a radar map for the plane's crew, began their systematic daylight raids, while the RAF Bomber Command, under Air Chief Marshal Sir Arthur "Bomber" Harris, carried out regular nighttime attacks in their four-engined Lancaster and Halifax bombers.

☆ An American Portrait

Ira C. Eaker—Ira Clarence Eaker was born in Field Creek, in the Hill Country of Texas, in 1896. He was graduated from Southeastern Normal College in Durant, Oklahoma, and entered the Army in 1917. Not satisfied with his life as an infantry officer, he transferred to the Air Corps, winning his pilot rating in 1918. In the 1920s he flew one of the planes in the Pan-American Goodwill Flight of 1926–1927, which brought significant publicity to flying, and two years later he set a world endurance flying record of 151 hours in the air (flying with Carl Spaatz and Elwood Quesada; the former became head of America's European air forces, the latter became head of IX Tactical Air Command during World War II). He also flew the first transcontinental instrument flight in 1936.

In addition to carrying out feats of flying and serving in a number of administrative positions for the Army, Eaker also attended the Air Corps Tactical School at Maxwell Field, Alabama; the Command and General Staff School at Fort Leavenworth; and three universities. He received a degree in journalism from the University of Southern California in 1933. Eaker also penned three books on flying in collaboration with "Hap" Arnold between 1936 and 1942.

Sent to England to observe the RAF after the beginning of World War II, in early 1942 Eaker returned there as head of VIII Bomber Command to organize the first American bomber force in the European theater. In this position he pushed for B-17 Flying Fortress daylight precision bombing raids as the American contribution to the Allied air offensive, and he joined the first U.S. bombing raid on the Continent in August 1942. At the Casablanca Conference of January 1943 he persuaded the Allied coalition leaders to allow the Americans to continue their daylight bombing despite the heavy losses they had been taking.

The next month Eaker was named head of Eighth Air Force. At the end of 1943 he was made commander of the Allied air forces in the Mediterranean, retaining this demanding post until April 1945, when, as a lieutenant general, he was appointed deputy commander of the Army Air Forces.

In 1947 Eaker retired, as he said, "to make room for the younger men," and thereafter pursued a successful business career with the Hughes and Douglas aircraft companies. He also served as a leading spokesman for air power and a strong national defense. In 1979 he received a congressional gold medal as an "aviation pioneer and air power leader," and he was advanced in rank to general by special congressional legislation in 1985. Eaker died at Andrews Air Force Base in August 1987 and was buried in Arlington National Cemetery.

French, Belgian, and Dutch cities and military installations—in addition to cities, installations, and factories in western Germany—came under American air attacks in 1942, but Eaker and his crews wanted more. With additional planes arriving weekly and with their increased proficiency in high-level precision daylight bombing, the men of the Army Air Forces wanted to hit Germany itself and its major cities and facilities in the central and eastern parts of the country. The problem was that neither the British nor the Americans had long-range fighters to escort the bombers deep into Germany. The versatile P-47 Thunderbolt was a fine fighter, but it did not have sufficient range even with drop tanks. German fighters would avoid attacking the American bombers while under escort and then pounce on them with a vengeance just as soon as their fighter escorts turned for home, making the bombers' runs into Germany very costly in men and planes. The British urged the Americans to abandon daylight bombing because of their early losses, but Eaker insisted that daylight raids were much more accurate than nighttime attacks and should be continued. He and the Eighth Air Force got the backing of Roosevelt and Churchill at the Casablanca Conference in January 1943 and the following summer began their campaign in earnest.

☆   An American Portrait

Carl A. "Tooey" Spaatz—Born in Boyerstown, Pennsylvania, in 1891 of Pennsylvania Dutch parentage, Spaatz entered West Point in 1910 and was graduated four years later as an infantry officer. After serving in Hawaii, he took flight instruction and transferred to the Air Service of the Signal Corps, in this capacity joining the 1916 Punitive Expedition into Mexico. As a major in France during World War I he earned the Distinguished Service Cross for downing two German planes—while absent without leave (AWOL) from his assigned training duties.

During the 1920s Spaatz was willing to stand as a vocal defender of Billy Mitchell, and in 1929 he won the Distinguished Flying Cross for his 151-hour endurance flight with Ira Eaker and Elwood Quesada. During the 1930s he served in various staff positions and attended the Command and General Staff School in 1935 and 1936.

Early in 1942 Spaatz was sent to England as the commander of Eighth Air Force, and in August of that year he was named commander of Allied air forces for Operation Torch. He remained in North Africa until the spring of 1944, when he was ordered to

England to command the U.S. Strategic Air Forces in the European theater. In this capacity he became a vocal advocate of systematic analysis of weapons effects and an opponent of "Bomber" Harris's idea of area bombing as opposed to concentrating on specific key targets, such as transportation and synthetic oil facilities. He also opposed diverting Allied bombers to support Operation Overlord, agreeing with Harris that strategic bombing precluded the necessity of an amphibious landing on the Continent. Transferred to the Pacific theater after V-E Day, Spaatz, as head of U.S. Strategic Air Forces in the Far East, supervised the firebombing of Japanese cities and the atomic raids on Hiroshima and Nagasaki.

In February 1946 the blustery Spaatz succeeded "Hap" Arnold as head of the U.S. Army Air Forces, having already been given the job by Arnold of spearheading the drive for air force independence. He was subsequently named the first chief of staff of the new U.S. Air Force. He retired in 1947 but continued to speak out as a proponent of air power until his death in Washington, DC, on July 13, 1974. He was buried on the grounds of the Air Force Academy at Colorado Springs, the service academy he had helped to create.

The raids of Eighth Air Force for the remainder of 1943 proved marginally successful in crippling the German war machine but tragically costly in air crews and planes. June and July saw Allied raids on German cities in the Ruhr Valley, the most famous being the July 27 raid on Hamburg. After American and British bombers had already hit the city in preliminary raids, on that night 739 British bombers dropped 2,917 tons of bombs and started so many fires that a gigantic convection current was created that produced high winds of 150 miles per hour and temperatures of 1,400 degrees Fahrenheit in the city. Half of Hamburg was destroyed (6,200 acres) and perhaps as many

FIGURE 9–5   B-17 Flying Fortress (*USAF Photographic Collection, National Air and Space Museum, Smithsonian Institution, Washington, D.C.*)

FIGURE 9–6   P-51 Mustang. (*USAF Photographic Collection, National Air and Space Museum, Smithsonian Institution, Washington, D.C.*)

as 42,000 people died in this firestorm, which sent flames three miles high. The August 17 raids on Regensberg, with its aircraft factories, and on Schweinfurt, with its ball-bearing factories, both deep in Germany, saw the downing of 53 of the 376 B-17s sent out that day; 47 more were so badly damaged that they never flew again. And when on October 14 another giant raid was staged on Schweinfurt and 60 of 291 Flying Fortresses were lost, all deep raids were suspended until long-range fighter escorts became available.

In the meantime, other Army Air Forces units were also active in the European war. Ninth Air Force was established in 1942 in North Africa. By August 1943 it had grown so large that it was subdivided, units of the Ninth being set to England to supplement the Eighth in its bombing raids on Germany and the occupied countries, its medium bombers becoming especially valuable for low-level short-range attacks on France and the Low Countries. After the fall of France, the Ninth's medium bombers were also used in Allied attacks on the Reich.

The North African units not assigned to the Ninth became the nucleus of the Twelfth Air Force, which by late 1943 began to attack Germany from bases in Italy. In early 1944 it was subdivided, with its heavy bombers and their escorts becoming the Fifteenth Air Force and the mediums, their fighters, and their attack bombers remaining as the Twelfth. The most memorable and tragic mission by the Twelfth was its August 1, 1943, raid on the Ploesti oil refineries in Rumania, the same grim month as the Regensburg and Schweinfurt raids. Flying in from Benghazi in Libya across the German-occupied Balkans and running into overwhelming fighter plane and flak resistance, 54 of the 177 B-24s sent on the mission were shot down (30 percent), 8 had to crash land in Turkey, and half of those that returned had sustained serious damage. Some 446 of the 1,733 crewmen sent on the mission were killed. As in the case of the operations of the Eighth Air Force in England, it was obvious that unescorted long-range missions against the Reich and its territories approached the suicidal. The big P-47 Thunderbolt ("the Jug") did not have the necessary range, and the dual-fuselage P-38 Lightning did not have the maneuverability needed to take on the Luftwaffe's fighters.

The salvation of strategic bombing came in the form of the new, long-range (in excess of 1,000 miles) P-51 Mustang. Powered by the British Rolls-Royce engine, it could reach speeds of 400 miles per hour. Arriving in Europe in December 1943, the Mustangs had turned the whole air war around within months. Bomber loss rates began to fall as the number of downings of Luftwaffe fighters—and, more important, of trained German pilots—soared. And Allied air power in 1944 also gave inestimable—if begrudging—tactical support to Operations Overlord and Fortitude. British and American planes flew over 200,000 sorties to cripple transportation lines behind the German lines in France, kept absolute air control over the landing sites by 14,000 sorties by 8,000 planes on D-Day, and continued their support as the Allied armies broke out of the beachheads and began to drive across France toward Germany. Wherever the land armies fought, Air Forces planes were overhead to control the air above them, to drop airborne troops as needed, and to harass the German defenses with increasing effectiveness.

By early 1945 the American air contingents, along with their British counterparts, were able to range over Germany at will, placing unparalleled bomb tonnage on military and industrial targets and beating down any Luftwaffe attempts to stop them. Eighth Air Force alone could send 1,500 bombers over Germany on any given day. The effectiveness of the Allied air attacks was dramatically demonstrated in February 1945, when an attack by 773 British bombers on Dresden in which 2,600 tons of bombs were dropped created a firestorm in which much of the city was leveled and an estimated 135,000 residents died. When the war ended on April 16, 1945, there was virtually nothing of any importance left to bomb in Germany.

Strategic bombing as a factor in defeating the enemy had never approached the decisiveness that its prewar enthusiasts had claimed, nor did it live up to the exaggerated claims of its enthusiasts thereafter either, but the multi-plane-type, multi-mission Air Forces had played a major role in winning the European war.

ALLIED ADVANCES TO FINAL VICTORY

Having landed successfully in Normandy and having cleared western France of the German enemy, the Allied armies then began advancing into northern France and the Low Countries. Montgomery and Bradley wanted the Allies to move on a narrow front to encircle the Ruhr north of Cologne on the Rhine to make a run on Berlin from the northwest, but Eisenhower preferred to advance into Germany on a broad front, and that was the strategy followed.

As the British Second Army of Montgomery's Twenty-first Army Group seized Brussels and moved on Antwerp by early September 1944, the Americans in the center and to the right of the advancing offensive line, led by armored units using Sherman medium tanks supported by 105-mm self-propelled guns and infantry, continued to press on toward the German border. Despite Patton's Third Army's success in crossing the Meuse at Verdun (crashing through the same areas of America's great World War I victories, this time in days), his movements and those of Lieutenant General Courtney H. Hodges' First Army were delayed by fuel shortages as they waited for Montgomery's Twenty-first Army Group to seize the Channel ports to cut down on the long time and distance all the way back to Cherbourg, from whence their supplies had to be carried. Despite the efforts of Army truckers in what came to be called the Red Ball Express, the Allied drive was bogging down for lack of fuel and other necessities. A closer port had to be secured.

Still looking for a smashing victory on the northern end of the Allied line, Montgomery, with Eisenhower's approval, embarked in mid-September on Operation Market-Garden, an uncharacteristically bold move by the British general to turn the northern end of the Siegfried Line (the "West Wall") by pushing through on a narrow front into Holland. Four key bridges were to be seized by American and British airborne troops as the British 30th Corps pushed north to seize the intervening territories. The 101st and 82nd Airborne Divisions did their work well at Veghel, Grave, and Nijmegen and linked up with the 30th Corps, but the whole operation depended on 30th Corps being able to slash through on an intricate timetable. When 30th Corps was unavoidably slowed down by German resistance, the British 1st Airborne Division was isolated and wiped out by the Germans at Arnhem, taking 7,000 casualties in trying to seize and hold "a bridge too far." The failed operation allowed Field Marshal Gerd von Rundstedt to move 86,000 men into the Schelde Estuary, where they carried on a prolonged defense. Clearing the Channel ports turned out to be a long, hard job. The 60-mile-long Scheldt Estuary was not secured until November 26, and Antwerp was not usable as a port by the Allies for 85 days thereafter. With the whole offensive line being held up, all chances for victory by the end of 1944 had clearly vanished.

But Hitler was not envisioning defeat even at this point. His *Wacht Am Rhein* (Watch on the Rhine) plan was designed to ensure victory even at this late date by superior strategy and execution. It called for a grand offensive across the Seigfried Line through the Ardennes to the sea, recapturing Antwerp, and splitting the Allied armies to destroy them piecemeal before turning to face the Russians advancing in the east. For this bold operation, Hitler's generals scraped together 25 divisions of 250,000 men, 1,900 artillery pieces, and almost 1,000 tanks and other armored pieces and assembled them in complete secrecy behind the Belgian-Luxembourg sector of the Siegfried Line. At 5:30 on the morning of December 16, 1944, the grandiose offensive, the Battle of the Bulge, began.

The Americans in the target sector were exhausted from their November 2 through December 13 battle for the Huertgen Forest, in which they had taken over 30,000 casualties. VIII Army Corps of the First Army was thinly stretched out in its "safe and quiet sector" when, amid low clouds, fog, and heavy snowfall, the German offensive was launched against them.

VIII Corps under Major General Troy H. Middleton was outnumbered 6 to 1 in some sectors and was sent reeling back as four German armies came crashing through, especially the spearheading Panzer Army under Lieutenant-General Hasso von Manteuffel, to capture Antwerp 100 miles to the west.

The key to Allied victory or defeat in the Battle of the Bulge lay in holding the towns of Saint-Vith and Bastogne, vital crossroads for the German advance. Eisenhower hurriedly pumped in all available troops on the periphery of the German salient. If Manteuffel broke through at these towns he could race to Antwerp and split the armies. But the German Panzer leader could not and did not take Saint-Vith in the northern Ardennes because of the stubborn defensive efforts against all odds by the men of the VIII Corps, aided by the 7th Armored Division and the 82nd Airborne sent in to help hold this vital transportation crossroads. They held out for five valuable days and took 6,000 casualties before abandoning the town. Likewise, 30 miles to the southwest at Bastogne, the remnants of the VIII Corps, aided by the 501st Paratroop Infantry Regiment, units of the 10th

Armored Division, and finally the entire 101st Airborne Division, stopped the Germans in their tracks while awaiting rescue—from somewhere. Their rescuers turned out to be the 4th Armored Division, sent by Patton from Third Army to the south. On December 23 the besieged American units were cheered by a break in the weather that allowed supplies to be parachuted in, and three days later armored units of the 37th Tank Battalion under Lieutenant Colonel Creighton Abrams of the 4th Armored Division broke through as Patton had promised. The defenders at Bastogne and Saint-Vith were relieved, while Hitler's Panzer armies ran out of fuel within four miles of the Meuse and found themselves in a deep salient with no relief in sight.

On December 30 the Allies began their counterattacks, First Army from the north and Third Army from the south, and by January 16 the Battle of the Bulge, Hitler's last and greatest gamble, was over. He had lost over 100,000 men (to an Allied casualty total of 81,000), and his last great reserves of German men and equipment were gone. This Ardennes counteroffensive was Hitler's sixth and final great strategic error. He now had little military power left to defend Germany. The end of winter would find the Allies pouring into Germany from the east and west, and there was no way left to stop them.

Spring 1945 found Montgomery's Twenty-first Army Group (mainly British and Canadian in makeup but including Lieutenant General William H. Simpson's Ninth U.S. Army) opposite the Ruhr, Bradley's Twelfth Army Group (including Hodges' First Army and Patton's Third) in the middle, and Lieutenant General Jacob Devers's Sixth Army Group (including Patch's Seventh Army from southern France) across from the Saar.

By the end of March the Rhine had been reached and crossed in many places, and the armies moved across Germany. Keeping promises made by Roosevelt at the Teheran Conference of November and December 1943 and the Yalta Conference of 1945, however, Eisenhower halted the Allied drive toward Berlin at the Elbe to allow the Russians to take the German capital, to the dismay of the British and to the utter disgust of the ever-verbal Patton. By early May, Holland, the Ruhr, Hamburg, the base of the Danish peninsula, Hannover, Linz and Salzburg in Austria, and Munich were all in British or American hands.

In the meantime, the Russians were pouring in from the east. From their defensive stands at Leningrad, Moscow, and Stalingrad, the Russians had moved to the offensive in 1943 and were never stopped for long thereafter as they swept through eastern Europe toward Germany. In January 1943 the Germans at Stalingrad had been forced to surrender, followed by a defeat in the greatest tank battle of the war at Kursk the following July. Kharkov had been recaptured on August 23, 1943, Smolensk had been retaken on September 25, and Kiev had been taken on November 6. Leningrad in the north was relieved in January 1944; Odessa, in the Ukraine, was retaken by the Russians in April; and the Red armies were soon approaching the Polish border. Sevastopol, in the Crimea, fell on May 12. Hitler's unrealistic orders to hold untenable ground and Soviet superiority in men and weaponry were having a telling and disastrous effect on his retreating troops.

In June and July 1944 the Red Army had begun a summer offensive all the way from the Baltic to the Balkans. Poland was entered on July 17, and the Polish home army in Warsaw rose up in rebellion in August and September against the Germans, only to see the Russians halt their offensive movement until the Poles had been wiped out and the city destroyed. The Baltic states fell to the Russians that summer and autumn, and East

Prussia was entered by Russian troops. The autumn of 1944 also saw the Russians move into the Balkan states of Bulgaria, Rumania, and Yugoslavia and into Hungary. Budapest fell in February 1945, and Vienna, on April 14. In the meantime the Russians moved through western Poland and into Germany. East Prussia, Pomerania, and Silesia were soon in the hands of the Red Army. After meeting the Americans on the Elbe at Torgau, east of Leipzig, on April 25, and after a month-long fight, the Russians captured Berlin on May 2. Hitler had committed suicide in his bunker beneath the city on April 30 after naming Admiral Doenitz as his successor. The German troops in Prague, Czechoslovakia, held out for another week. Thousands of them fled west to the American lines and surrendered to escape the Russian army. Following American policy, they were turned over to the Soviets.

On May 4 Montgomery accepted unconditional surrender from representatives of Admiral Doenitz at Luneberg Heath, and the European war formally came to an end on May 8, 1945. In carrying out their part of the last great offensive against Hitler's Third Reich from June 6, 1944, to May 8, 1945, the Western Allies had put 5.4 million troops into Western Europe. The Americans had paid the highest price for victory in the last year of the war, with almost 569,000 casualties, including some 135,000 dead (almost half the total dead in both theaters between 1941 and 1945). The other Western Allies had suffered almost 180,000 casualties, including about 60,000 dead. Unlike its predecessor of 1914 through 1918, this second European war saw the United States bear the heaviest burdens and casualties among the Western Allied forces after 1942. But World War II was not over. The Allies now turned to finish the conflict that had been raging in the Pacific for four long and bloody years.

Suggestions for Further Reading

ABBAZIA, PATRICK,   *Mr. Roosevelt's Navy: The Private War of the U.S. Atlantic Fleet, 1939–1942.* Annapolis: Naval Institute Press, 1975.

AMBROSE, STEPHEN E.,   *The Supreme Commander: The War Years of General Dwight D. Eisenhower.* Garden City, NY: Doubleday, 1970.

ANSEL, WALTER,   *Hitler and the Middle Sea.* Durham, NC: Duke University Press, 1972.

BLAIR, CLAY,   *Ridgway's Paratroopers: The American Airborne in World War II.* New York: Dial Press, 1985.

BLUMENSON, MARTIN,   *Anzio: The Gamble That Failed.* Philadelphia: Lippincott, 1963.

——,   *Patton: The Man Behind the Legend, 1885–1945.* New York: Morrow, 1985.

——,   *Salerno to Cassino.* Washington, DC: U.S. Government Printing Office, 1969.

BRADLEY, OMAR, and CLAY BLAIR,   *A General's Life.* New York: Simon & Schuster, 1983.

CRAVEN, WESLEY F., and JAMES L. CATE, eds.,   *The Army Air Forces in World War II,* 7 vols. Chicago: University of Chicago Press, 1948–1958.

EISENHOWER, DWIGHT D.,   *Crusade in Europe.* Garden City, NY: Doubleday, 1948.

FISHER, ERNEST F., JR.,   *Cassino to the Alps.* Washington, DC: U.S. Government Printing Office, 1977.

GANNON, MICHAEL,   *Operation Drumbeat: The Dramatic True Story of Germany's First U-boat Attacks along the American Coast in World War II.* New York: Harper & Row, Pub., 1990.

GARLINSKI, JOSEF,   *The Enigma War.* New York: Scribner's, 1979.

GELB, NORMAN,   *Dunkirk: The Complete Story of the First Step in the Defeat of Hitler.* New York: Morrow, 1989.

GREENFIELD, KENT ROBERTS,   *American Strategy in World War II.* Baltimore: Johns Hopkins University Press, 1963.

————, ed.,   *Command Decisions.* Washington, DC: U.S. Government Printing Office, 1960.

HAPGOOD, DAVID, and DAVID RICHARDSON,   *Monte Cassino.* New York: Congdon & Weed, 1984.

HASTINGS, MAX,   *Overlord: D-Day and the Battle for Normandy.* New York: Simon & Schuster, 1984.

HICKMAN, HOMER H., JR.,   *Torpedo Junction: U-Boat War off America's East Coast, 1942.* Annapolis: Naval Institute Press, 1989.

HOUGH, RICHARD,   *The Greatest Crusade: Roosevelt, Churchill, and the Naval Wars.* New York: William Morrow, 1986.

HOUGH, RICHARD, and DENIS RICHARDS,   *The Battle of Britain: The Greatest Air Battle of World War II.* New York: W.W. Norton & Co., Inc., 1989.

HUGHES, TERRY, and JOHN COSTELLO,   *The Battle of the Atlantic.* New York: Dial Press/James Wade, 1977.

JACKSON, W. G. F.,   *The Battle for North Africa, 1940–1943.* New York: Mason/Charter, 1975.

LARRABEE, ERIC,   *Commander in Chief: Franklin Delano Roosevelt, His Lieutenants, and Their War.* New York: Harper & Row, Pub., 1987.

LEWIN, RONALD,   *Hitler's Mistakes.* New York: Morrow, 1984.

————,   *Ultra Goes to War.* New York: McGraw-Hill, 1978.

MACDONALD, CHARLES B.,   *A Time for Trumpets: The Untold Story of the Battle of the Bulge.* New York: Morrow, 1985.

————,   *Company Commander.* New York: Ballantine, 1966.

MACDONALD, JOHN,   *Great Battles of World War II.* New York: Macmillan, 1986.

MATLOFF, MAURICE, and EDWIN M. SNELL,   *Strategic Planning for Coalition Warfare,* 2 vols. Washington, DC: Office of the Chief of Military History, 1953–1959.

MILLER, MERLE,   *Ike the Soldier: As They Knew Him.* New York: Putnam's, 1987.

MOSLEY, LEONARD,   *Marshall: Hero for Our Times.* New York: Hearst, 1982.

PARTON, JAMES,   *"Air Force Spoken Here": General Ira Eaker and the Command of the Air.* Bethesda: Adler & Adler, 1986.

POGUE, FORREST C.,   *George C. Marshall: Ordeal and Hope, 1939–1942.* New York: Viking, 1966.

————,   *George C. Marshall: Organizer of Victory, 1943–1945.* New York: Viking, 1973.

RICH, NORMAN,   *Hitler's War Aims: Ideology, the Nazi State, and the Course of Expansion.* New York: W. W. Norton & Co., Pub., Inc., 1973.

SCHAFFER, RONALD,   *Wings of Judgment: American Bombing in World War II.* New York: Oxford University Press, 1985.

SHERRY, MICHAEL S.,   *The Rise of American Air Power: The Creation of Armageddon.* New Haven, CT: Yale University Press, 1977.

SIMPSON, B. MITCHELL, III., *Admiral Harold R. Stark: Architect of Victory, 1939–1945*. Columbia: University of South Carolina Press, 1989.

VAN DER VAT, DAN, *The Atlantic Campaign: World War II's Great Struggle at Sea*. New York: Harper & Row, Pub., 1988.

WEIGLEY, RUSSELL F., *Eisenhower's Lieutenants: The Campaign for France and Germany, 1944–1945*. Bloomington: Indiana University Press, 1981.

WERTH, ALEXANDER, *Russia at War, 1941–1945*. New York: Dutton, 1964.

WHITING, CHARLES, *Kasserine: First Blood*. Briarcliff Manor, N Y: Stein & Day, 1984.

☆10

World War II: Pacific Theater, 1939–1945

There was a certain irony in Japan's attack on the United States naval base at Pearl Harbor on December 7, 1941. Japan had been opened to Western penetration by the "black ships" of Commodore Matthew Perry's naval squadron in 1853. From this enforced first departure from their isolated existence, the Japanese had seldom looked back as they set out to dominate the entire western Pacific region. By 1941 they found that the U.S. Navy, the chosen instrument of their forced entrance upon the world scene, now had to be destroyed if the modernist dream that they had adopted from the West was to be realized.

THE ROAD TO THE PACIFIC WAR

The "restoration" of the Emperor Meiji in 1868, wherein the members of the reactionary feudal aristocracy were shorn of power, signaled the acceptance of a new way of life for Japan, a regeneration keyed on gaining both knowledge and power from the West. Power meant, among other things, acquiring a navy capable of warding off European armed might and ensuring Japanese primacy in the Far East. Accordingly, British warships were purchased, and British naval officers were imported to teach Japan's naval cadets their requisite skills. By the 1890s Japanese shipyards were building naval vessels, the nation's easy victory over the Chinese in 1894 offering confirmation of its expansionist policies.

The world took careful note of the Sino-Japanese War of 1894 and 1895. One result was the Anglo-Japanese alliance of 1902. Then Japan's humiliating defeat of the Russians during the Russo-Japanese War of 1904 and 1905—especially at the Battle of Tsushima under Admiral Heihachiro Togo on May 27, 1905, in which 38 of Russia's ships were sunk, scuttled, captured, or interned—made it abundantly clear that a major naval and imperial power had arisen in the Far East.

Continuing to build and expand thereafter, Japan joined the Allies in World War I and was rewarded with defeated Germany's territories in China plus the Marshall, Caroline, and Mariana Islands in the western and central Pacific, potential springboards to trans-Pacific domination. Then, in 1931, the Japanese army seized Manchuria and six years later invaded China proper via the Yangtse and Yellow River valleys (shooting up an American gunboat, the *Panay,* in the process). This assault occurred only one year after Japan's expansionist military officers had murdered the moderates in the government and seized control of the state.

Armed with its 1936 alliance with the Axis powers and fueled by the Japanese belief that their island nation was destined to rule over the Orient and the western Pacific regions, Japan was determined to continue its expansion both on the Asiatic mainland and in Pacific waters by the outbreak of war in Europe in 1939. By this time its navy had 10 battleships, 10 carriers, 40 submarines, dozens of cruisers and destroyers, and 1,500 naval aircraft, the largest force of its kind in the world. It also had the best torpedoes, highly trained naval officers (graduates of the naval academy at Etajima), and a deep belief in the inevitability of Japanese hegemony over the Far East. Its army had already proved its professionalism in China.

The Japanese government successfully coerced the Vichy government of France into allowing its troops to move into Indochina in 1940. That same year it signed the Tripartite Pact with Germany and Italy, which acknowledged its primary position in the Far East. These actions served clear notice that the Japanese intended to move into the Dutch East Indies, Malaya, the Philippines, and perhaps beyond. With the French and Dutch defeated in Europe and the British overextended in trying to maintain their worldwide empire, its was obvious that only the Americans were in a position to challenge Japanese expansionism.

The U.S. Navy had been building rapidly in the 1930s, and its leaders, as well as the Army's and President Roosevelt, were well aware of these Japanese actions and intentions. Since World War I, American military contingency war plans had concentrated on Color Orange (Japan) in the Pacific, and in April 1940 the Pacific fleet had been transferred from the West Coast to the expanding naval base at Pearl Harbor on the island of Oahu in Hawaii. Here the Navy would be better prepared to meet Japanese aggression if it were to threaten America's trans-Pacific holdings stretching from Hawaii west via Midway, Wake, and Guam to the Philippines (still an American protectorate but promised independence in 1946).

Admiral Stark's Plan Dog memo of November 1940, when accepted by Roosevelt, switched America's primary defensive emphasis under Rainbow Five to the Atlantic war and Hitler. But the United States still had no intention of standing by while the Japanese expanded in the Pacific and threatened American interests as well as those of its friends. In July 1940 President Roosevelt had placed an embargo on strategic chemicals and on aircraft parts and fuel being exported to Japan, and in September 1940 he had added scrap metal to the list. This was a serious blow to the Japanese economy and to its military's plans for expansion because the island nation depended entirely on the importation of these commodities to sustain industrial production and, therefore, its warfare against its Far Eastern neighbors.

One year later, on July 26, 1941, (the day after Japan forced Vichy to grant it the right to occupy Indochina), Roosevelt froze all Japanese assets in the United States and forbade the exportation of oil to Japan (80 percent imported from the United States). Japan was now left with a basic irrefutable choice. Either it could cease its expansionism and withdraw from both China and Indochina as America was demanding in return for lifting its embargoes and unfreezing Japanese assets, or it could gain its necessary raw materials and crude oil elsewhere in order to continue creating its so-called Greater Far East Co-Prosperity Sphere.

The latter was its choice, and this meant that American military power had to be destroyed. American military and naval power in the western Pacific threatened Japan's every move south and southeast to obtain its raw materials and thereby create its Pacific empire. It had to be removed. The American *de facto* demand that Japan cease its expansionism was rejected. This refusal became clear when, on October 18, 1941, the civilian government of Prince Fumimaro Konoye resigned and an army clique led by General Hideki Tojo took over the reins. Despite last-minute attempts to negotiate a compromise settlement—which both sides regarded as futile—it was obvious by early December 1941 that a Japanese-American conflict was about to begin. The American military forces were put on alert; the Japanese prepared to attack. The only question was where and when the war would begin. The "where" was Pearl Harbor; the "when" was Sunday morning, December 7, 1941.

DAY OF INFAMY: PEARL HARBOR

Kichisaburo Nomura was sent to Washington in November 1941 as ambassador to the United States. He was an old friend of the United States and Roosevelt. His honesty and sincerity made him a perfect smoke screen for the Japanese government's fixed intention of going to war. Nomura knew nothing of the impending attack on Pearl Harbor as he negotiated with the United States government. Meanwhile, the Japanese military leaders perfected their plans and put them into operation. While a naval attack force destroyed the American fleet at Pearl Harbor, three armies would quickly seize the Malay Peninsula and Singapore, the Philippines, and the Dutch East Indies. A fourth army would move into Burma from Thailand and close the vital Burma Road from India to China.

The mastermind behind the naval air attack on the Pacific fleet in Hawaii was Admiral Isoroku ("56") Yamamoto. Yamamoto was born in 1884, the sixth son in his 56-year-old father's family. Standing a stocky 5 feet, 3 inches with two fingers missing on his left hand as a result of action at the Battle of Tsushima in 1905, he had been graduated from the naval academy at Etajima, had studied at Harvard, and had served as a naval attaché in Washington. This career naval officer and creator of the Japanese naval air arm was appointed to the position of commander-in-chief of the Combined Fleet in August 1939. He thus became the man fated to lead Japan into war with the United States, despite his open opposition to starting this conflict. Still, he accepted it out of duty to the emperor and his country. However, he had warned Prime Minister Konoye as late as September 1940, "If I am told to fight regardless of the consequences, I shall run wild for the first six months or a year, but I have utterly no confidence for a second or third year."

As a result of his years of study and service in the United States, Yamamoto knew America's industrial and warmaking potential as well as or better than any other of his countrymen. Therein lay his doubts and hesitation. His doubts, indeed, proved to be prophetic.

Yamamoto's idea of a surprise attack on Pearl Harbor to neutralize the American Pacific fleet as the first and crucial stroke of the war received strong support from Commander Minoru Genda. Genda, the most brilliant airman in the Imperial Navy, had thought of a Pearl Harbor attack as early as 1935. Like Yamamoto, he rejected the prevailing idea of a great all-out and decisive naval battle in the western Pacific, arguing that using carrier-based planes in a surprise attack on Hawaii would knock out the U.S. fleet in one bold stroke and give the Japanese the opportunity to expand without American naval interference. The reluctance of the naval general staff to risk six carriers in such an operation was overcome when Yamamoto threatened to resign if the surprise attack idea was rejected.

Accordingly, plans went forward for the Pearl Harbor air assault. Virtually simultaneous invasions of Thailand, Malaya, the Philippines, Wake Island, Guam, and Hong Kong were assigned to the army. Naval pilots practiced their bombing and torpedo attacks on the city of Kagoshima on the island of Kyushu in the south of Japan (a city topographically like Honolulu). Coded reports on the movements of the American fleet at Pearl Harbor were received from the Japanese consul general in Honolulu (including grid reports on the vessels' docking locations and valuable information that the fleet was in port every Saturday and Sunday). The assembled strike fleet in the Kurile Islands in the north went on radio silence so as not to give the Americans any indication of an impending attack by revealing a concentration of Japanese naval vessels.

The carrier strike force was under the command of Vice Admiral Chuichi Nagumo. It included six carriers. Numbered among these were the new 826-foot, 27,000-ton *Shokaku* and *Zuikaku*. On the carriers were 437 planes, 350 for the Pearl Harbor strike, including 140 type 97 "Kate" bombers, 131 type 99 "Val" dive bombers, and 80 Mitsubishi type 0 "Zero" fighters. The carrier strike force was supported by 2 battleships, 3 cruisers, 11 destroyers, 3 submarines, and 8 supply ships for the long journey out to Hawaii and back.

This formidable fleet departed Japanese home waters on November 27, 1941, cruising to the east, far out of the range of American air patrols. On December 1 Nagumo received the message to proceed with the attack, and the 33-ship armada bore due south for Hawaii. By early Sunday, December 7, it had reached its launch point 230 miles north of Oahu.

In port that Sunday morning at Pearl Harbor were 94 naval vessels in a five-square-mile area. These included 7 battleships lined up in "Battleship Row" on the eastern edge of Ford Island, 9 cruisers, and 29 destroyers. Fortunately for the Navy and the nation, missing were the carriers of the Pacific fleet. The *Saratoga* was on the West Coast, the *Lexington* was delivering planes to Midway, and the *Enterprise* was returning from delivering planes to Wake Island.

Despite early warnings (a submarine was spotted and attacked near the entrance to Pearl Harbor and a mobile radar unit on the northern tip of Oahu picked up a large group of planes flying in from the north), when the first Japanese planes began their attacks at 7:55 A.M., the American military personnel on Hawaii were completely unprepared to defend themselves. Likewise, the failure of American military intelligence offices to coordinate their decrypted information and to give proper warning of a probable attack also contributed to the without-warning assault on the military in Hawaii.

The first phase of the Japanese attack lasted from 7:55 to 8:25. It consisted of torpedo and dive bomber attacks on the fleet and strafing attacks on Ford Island Naval Air Station; Ewa Marine Airfield; Kaneohe Naval Patrol Plane Station; and Hickam, Wheeler, Bellows, and Haleiwa Army Air Corps fields. The second phase, carried out between 8:40 and 9:15, consisted of high-level bombing attacks. Phase III between 9:15 and 9:45 consisted of dive-bombing attacks to complete the destruction of the fleet.

When the two-hour raid was over, the Americans had suffered 2,403 persons killed (over 2,000 of them naval personnel) and 1,178 wounded (over 700 naval). Sunk or seriously damaged were 18 warships. These included as lost the battleships *Arizona* and *Oklahoma*, a target ship, and two destroyers; sunk or beached but salvageable were the battleships *West Virginia, California,* and *Nevada,* and a minelayer; damaged were the battleships *Tennessee, Maryland,* and *Pennsylvania,* the cruisers *Helena, Honolulu,* and *Raleigh,* one destroyer, and two minor vessels. The Pacific fleet was a devastated shambles.

Also destroyed were 188 Army and Navy planes, and 159 more were damaged. Still, the carriers were spared destruction by their absence, and, thanks to Admiral Nagumo's sticking to his orders and not ordering a second strike (because he did not know where the *Lexington* and *Enterprise* were and did not want to endanger his fleet), the Pearl Harbor machine shops and repair facilities, plus the 4.5 million barrels of ships' fuel stored in the tank farms in Hawaii, were not destroyed. These overlooked remnants of the otherwise complete Japanese attack remained as the material basis of the Navy's Pacific resurgence thereafter.

Japanese losses were only 29 planes and pilots over the target, although several crashed while landing on their carriers. Also, 1 submarine and 5 midget subs were lost. Yet despite its slight losses in gaining an incredibly deadly first strike, Japan had committed a great blunder. As Gordon Prange has argued in his epic *At Dawn We Slept,*

> By failing to exploit the shock, bewilderment, and confusion on Oahu, by failing to take full advantage of its savage attack against [Admiral Husband E.] Kimmel's ships, by failing to pulverize the Pearl Harbor base, and by failing to seek out and sink America's carriers, Japan committed its first and probably its greatest strategic error of the entire Pacific conflict.

It can also be argued that another strategic blunder was committed in the weeks after Pearl Harbor by the Japanese failure to move immediately to seize the Hawaiian Islands. The army was opposed to the idea because it was too risky, but Admiral Yamamoto, who had originally rejected it as part of the Pearl Harbor plans, in early 1942 reversed himself and advocated taking the islands, thereby to ensure a negotiated peace with the United States and avoid an eventual defeat by a too-powerful America.

As part of his new plan, called "Eastern Operation," Yamamoto called for luring the American fleet out to its destruction, then seizing the American mid-Pacific islands and Hawaii by mid-1943. When the army and the naval board opposed the plan, Yamamoto again threatened to resign. But at least part of his plan was saved when the Doolittle raid by 16 American B-25s flying off the carrier *Hornet* hit Tokyo and three other Japanese cities on April 18, 1942. This convinced the Japanese military chiefs that the American carriers had to be destroyed. It was now agreed in a compromise plan that the fleet would be lured out and destroyed by a combined fleet operation. The Japanese would then take Midway as a stepping stone to Hawaii. Thus was born the Midway operation, which turned the tide for the Americans in the Pacific war on June 4–5, 1942.

BATTLES OF THE CORAL SEA AND MIDWAY

Japanese army units successfully attacked and captured their initial targets of Guam, Wake, and the Philippines. In the Philippines, Americans and their Filipino allies put up a heroic defense of the Bataan Peninsula and the island of Corregidor in Manila Bay from December until April 1942, when they were compelled to surrender. Thereafter they were forced to endure the infamous "Bataan Death March," in which 11,000 men died in six days. Imprisonment for the duration of the war faced the survivors. The Japanese also seized Malaya, Singapore, Hong Kong, and the Dutch East Indies. In the process of carrying out these offensives, the new British battleship *Prince of Wales* and the cruiser *Repulse*, searching without air cover for Japanese transports loaded with troops for the invasion of Malaya, were sunk by enemy aircraft on December 10. Then, in February 1942, the Allied ABDA (American, British, Dutch, Australian) fleet in the Far East was devastated by superior Japanese forces in the Battle of the Java Sea, the American heavy cruiser *Houston* going down at Sunda Strait.

The Japanese army now struck south from their new, giant base at Rabaul on New Britain Island in the Bismarck Island chain to capture Port Moresby in eastern New Guinea and Tulagi in the Solomon Islands. If successful, they would be able to dominate the entire Coral Sea area and threaten Australia itself.

Thus was created the Japanese Operation MO. Dividing his army and supporting naval forces into five groups (two to launch the invasions, two to support the invasions, and one carrier force to enter the Coral Sea and act as a shield against American interference), Admiral Shigeyoshi Inouye launched his attack in early May of 1942. The only Allied forces available to stop him in the southwest Pacific were three small American task forces, one under Rear Admiral Frank Jack Fletcher built around the 20,000-ton carrier *Yorktown* (recently transferred back from the Atlantic), a second smaller force under Rear Admiral Aubrey Fitch built around the *Lexington,* and a third task force under Australian Rear Admiral John G. Crace containing three cruisers and several destroyers. Vice Admiral William F. Halsey's carriers *Enterprise* and *Hornet* were far to the north and out of the picture because of their Doolittle raid on Japan two weeks before, and the carrier *Saratoga* had been torpedoed by a Japanese submarine in January and was out of the war for five months.

After preliminary skirmishes near Tulagi and Port Moresby and between the opposing fleets for three days, the Battle of the Coral Sea—the first naval engagement in history in which the surface ships never exchanged a shot or even saw one another—took place on May 7 and 8, 1942.

The first day of the battle was marked by the sinking of the light carrier *Shoho* from the Tulagi covering force by planes from the *Lexington* and *Yorktown* (the first sinking of an enemy carrier by American naval forces). This was followed an hour later by the sinking by Japanese planes of the American oiler *Neosho* and the destroyer *Sims* south of the American main force. But the Japanese pilots, who had not seen the main American force nearby,

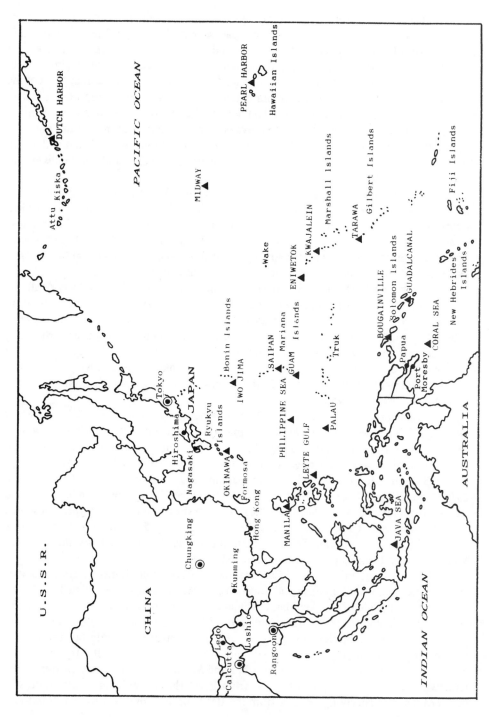

MAP 10-1 World War II—Pacific, 1941–1945. *(Used with permission of Anne C. Christensen.)*

reported that they had sunk a carrier and a cruiser. That evening the American carriers were attacked by Japanese planes, and the Japanese lost 21 of their 27 pilots and aircraft.

The climax of the battle came the next day, May 8, when the *Lexington* was hit and subsequently sank by two explosions occurring some time after the original attack. These blasts came from aviation gas detonations in the interior of the carrier. Most of the crew of 3,000 were saved. Of critical importance, the Japanese pilots reported that they had sunk two carriers. (The *Yorktown* had been hit but continued to function.) Admiral Inouye nevertheless withdrew the entire invasion and landing forces to Rabaul. Late that night Admiral Yamamoto ordered that the Japanese naval units turn around and attack the remaining American fleet, but by this time Admiral Fletcher and his fleet were far beyond their reach.

Thus ended the two-day Battle of the Coral Sea. The Americans had lost 3 ships and 77 planes, and the Japanese had lost a small carrier and 97 planes. It had been a tactical victory for the Japanese but a strategic victory for the Americans because the Japanese invasions had been called off. Port Moresby and Australia were safe—at least for now. And the Japanese believed that two American carriers had been sunk, a vital factor in the Battle of Midway, which took place less than a month later.

Midway Island—actually two small islands making up part of Midway Atoll—is located some 1,150 miles northwest of Hawaii. It was vital to American defense interests as a cable station and as an unsinkable aircraft platform that would serve to defend Hawaii. The fall of Midway—the Philippines, Guam, and Wake already being in Japanese hands—would put the Hawaiian Islands and the whole Pacific defense zone in severe jeopardy. And a Japanese attempt to take the island would both lure out the American Pacific fleet and, if successful, secure a stepping stone to the eventual seizure of Hawaii.

Yamamoto's plans for the Midway operation were complicated. First Carrier Striking Force under Vice Admiral Nagumo (in command at Pearl Harbor) was to approach from the northwest to attack Midway, wipe out its defenses, and destroy the American carriers as they emerged. It was built around four carriers: the 41,300-ton *Akagi,* the 42,500-ton *Kaga* (both having taken part in the attack on Pearl Harbor), and the 20,000-ton *Hiryu* and *Soryu.* These carriers would carry 259 fighters, dive bombers, and torpedo bombers and would have 2 battleships, 3 cruisers, and 11 destroyers as escorts. The Midway Assault Force, or Second Fleet, was to carry 5,000 men in 12 transports escorted by the light carrier *Zuiho,* 2 battleships, and 8 cruisers. It would approach Midway sailing from Saipan in the Mariana Islands.

Far to the north the Second Carrier Striking Force, with 2 light carriers, 3 cruisers, and 6 destroyers, would confuse and draw off American naval forces by striking Dutch Harbor in the middle of the Aleutian chain and then capturing Kiska and Attu at its far western end. First Fleet, led by Yamamoto himself in the giant new 64,000-ton battleship *Yamato* with 8 more battleships, plus cruisers and destroyers, would be stationed to the west to move in and complete the kill on the American fleet. Finally, 16 submarines were to form a barrier between Pearl Harbor and Midway to destroy any carriers (or at least warn Yamamoto) if they emerged from Pearl Harbor, although Yamamoto still believed that any surviving carriers from the Battle of the Coral Sea were still in those distant waters.

☆   An American Portrait

Chester W. Nimitz—Chester William Nimitz, the leader of the American naval war in the Pacific during World War II, was born in Fredericksburg, Texas, on February 24, 1885. Five years later he moved with his mother and stepfather to nearby Kerrville, where he grew up. Applying to West Point only to find that no slots were available, he accepted an appointment to Annapolis in 1901.

Upon being graduated seventh in his class of 114 four years later, Nimitz joined the Asiatic Fleet and saw duty in the Philippines before returning to the United States in 1909 to command submarines. He soon became an authority on diesel engines. This led to further study in Europe and then to duty at the New York Naval Yard. During World War I, Nimitz, now a lieutenant commander, served as an engineering aide to the commander of submarines for the Atlantic fleet. The immediate postwar years saw him placed on the Board of Submarine Design, posted as executive officer of the battleship *South Carolina,* and named superintendent of construction of the Navy's sub base at Pearl Harbor before spending a year at the Naval War College at Newport.

By 1939 Nimitz had commanded the cruiser *Augusta* on Asiatic station and had served as commander of Battleship Division One with his rear admiral's flag on the *Arizona.* He had also advanced from assistant chief to chief of the Bureau of Navigation (in charge of all recruitment, training, promotions, and assignments for the Navy).

It was because of his wide experience on various types of war vessels, his knowledge of the officers in the Navy's key positions as it built to power, and his administrative skills that Nimitz was chosen to assume the post of commander-in-chief of the Pacific Fleet in the aftermath of Pearl Harbor. By March 1942 he also held the position of commander-in-chief of Pacific Ocean Areas, a position that gave him

FIGURE 10–1   Chester W. Nimitz.(*National Archives, Washington, D.C.*)

authority over all military and naval affairs, American and Allied, in the northern, central, and southern Pacific areas. No other military officer in American history has held such wide-ranging authority over such a large war area.

In this position, Nimitz, along with General Douglas MacArthur, the Southwest Pacific Area commander, directed the entire Pacific war until the Japanese surrender in September 1945. Three months later, Nimitz, having been named fleet admiral the year before, assumed the position of chief of naval operations (CNO), replacing Admiral King. After two years as CNO and another two serving the United Nations, Nimitz retired to Berkeley, California, in 1952.

Fleet Admiral Chester Nimitz died at Yerba Buena Island, California, on February 22, 1966, and was buried in Golden Gate National Cemetery not far from his fellow Pacific naval commanders of World War II, Admirals Charles Lockwood, Raymond Spruance, and Kelly Turner.

Admiral Chester Nimitz, commander-in-chief of the Pacific Fleet (CinCPac), was aware of these Japanese moves, thanks to the work of Commander Joseph Rochefort and his cryptography assistants at Pearl Harbor. (Nimitz was not aware, however, of the movement of the First Fleet under Yamamoto far to the west; Yamamoto's presence during Midway did not become known to the Americans until months later.) Rochefort was able to decipher the gathering of the fleets, their targets, the direction of their attacks on Midway, and, finally, the dates of the attacks (June 3 on the Aleutians; June 4 on Midway). This information gave Nimitz an edge on the Japanese, even though they had 10 carriers to his 2 (*Enterprise* and *Hornet,* in addition to *Yorktown* if she could be repaired in time). Furthermore, the enemy had 23 cruisers to Nimitz's 8 and 11 fast battleships to Nimitz's 6 slow battlewagons.

Task Force 16, with *Enterprise* and *Hornet,* returned to Pearl Harbor on May 26 under Admiral Halsey. Halsey being ill, Nimitz gave command of Task Force 16 to Rear Admiral Raymond A. Spruance and sent it off two days later, telling Spruance to place himself on the Japanese striking force's left flank and hit it while its planes were bombing Midway. When Task Force 17 under Admiral Fletcher returned on May 27 with *Yorktown* badly damaged as a result of its beating in the Coral Sea and due for 90 days of repair work, Nimitz gave the naval repair crews just 3 days to get her ready for battle. Three days later she sailed out to join Spruance and Task Force 16 on Nagumo's flank. Altogether the two carrier task forces had 79 fighters, 112 dive bombers, and 39 torpedo bombers. The Japanese submarines arrived too late to observe the carriers' departure, leaving Yamamoto and Nagumo in the dark as to whether or not they were in the Pacific and, if so, how many there were and where. Nimitz further confused them by having a cruiser in the Coral Sea broadcast on carrier air group radio frequencies to convince the Japanese that the carriers were still off the Solomons.

Rear Admiral Robert A. "Fuzzy" Theobald was dispatched with the North Pacific Force of cruisers and destroyers to stop the invasion of the Aleutians (actually Theobald believed the real invasion would come at Dutch Harbor or Alaska, so he stationed his fleet 400 miles south of Kodiak and thus never even made a move against the invasion fleet). Nimitz had the bulk of his power waiting for Nagumo.

☆   An American Portrait

Raymond A. Spruance—Raymond Ames Spruance, born in Baltimore in 1886 but raised by his spinster aunts and grandparents in East Orange, New Jersey, was known throughout his naval career for his quiet intellectualism, absolute integrity, and fighting spirit.

Unable to afford a university education, he accepted an appointment to the United States Naval Academy and was graduated in 1906. He was unhappy at Annapolis and uncertain that he had made the correct career decision, but his tour of duty on the battleship *Minnesota* as part of the worldwide cruise of the Great White Fleet from 1907 to 1909 convinced him he had made the right choice. Although he thereafter pursued advanced study in electrical engineering and served in a number of engineering assignments, Spruance chose to remain a line officer.

During World War I he was advanced to lieutenant commander, but he spent the war years in a shipyard assignment. During the interwar years Spruance spent time both in engineering assignments and in sea commands. He also attended the Naval War College and served two stints on the staff of that institution. The year 1940 found him a rear admiral and assigned to establish the Tenth Naval District headquarters in San Juan, Puerto Rico. By the time World War II broke out, Spruance was back in a sea command as head of Cruiser Division Five at Pearl Harbor, in this capacity serving as surface screen commander to Admiral William F. Halsey in the early wartime Pacific missions, including the Doolittle raid on Tokyo.

Despite his lack of experience with carriers, Spruance was sure-handedly chosen by Admiral Nimitz to replace the ailing William Halsey for the upcoming mid-Pacific confrontation with the Japanese in mid-1942. In the ensuing Battle of Midway, Spruance, as commander of two carrier task forces, proved his mettle as a combat commander.

After a brief period in Nimitz's headquarters, Spruance returned to sea as commander of the Fifth Fleet, in this position playing a leading role in the conquest of the Gilberts, Marshalls, and Marianas, in addition to Iwo Jima and Okinawa. In 1944 he was advanced to the rank of admiral.

After the war, Spruance, the Navy's most effective combat fleet commander, was named president of the Naval War College. He retired in 1948 but returned to serve his country again as ambassador to the Philippines in 1952. He retired a second time in 1955 to Pebble Beach, California, where he died on December 13, 1969, still honored for his integrity and fighting spirit.

Nimitz gave Fletcher and Spruance his Operation Plan 29-42. This directed them to position themselves 200 miles north of Midway on Nagumo's flank and try to catch the Japanese with half their planes off attacking Midway. With luck, they might even catch them while they were recovering their first group of attack planes, forcing them either to let these original attackers ditch in the ocean while they sent up defenders or else recover their attackers before sending up their defenders. Either would eventually be to the Americans' advantage. With the two American task forces on station and the Japanese approaching the 3,000 defenders on Midway, the air and carrier crews of Task Force 16 and Task Force 17 off Midway and Chester Nimitz and his staff back in Hawaii could only sit and wait.

On June 3 the Aleutians were attacked as the radio intercepts indicated they would be, and nine army B-17s from Midway lifted off to attack the invasion force bearing down on them. They scored no hits. But at least Nimitz now knew that the Japanese fleets were coming as scheduled.

The next day, June 4, 1942, saw the climax of the great Battle of Midway. In a confused cacophony of events, Midway Island was severely hit by air attacks; planes from the *Enterprise, Hornet,* and *Yorktown* by dead reckoning and sheer luck found Admiral Nagumo's First Carrier Striking Force; the torpedo bombers made their low-level runs on the Japanese ships and scored no hits but brought the ships' fighter cover down; the dive bombers from the *Yorktown* and *Enterprise* arrived over the Japanese fleet at the same time and began their attacks almost simultaneously, starting giant fires on the *Akagi, Kaga,* and *Soryu* as their planes were being rearmed and bombs and gasoline lines were strewn all over their decks; the *Yorktown* was attacked and badly damaged by planes from the *Hiryu;* the *Hiryu* was attacked and sunk by American carrier planes; and Spruance and Fletcher moved east to get out of the range of any Japanese surface ships.

During the next two days, in the anticlimax of the battle, Japanese surface vessels came east to find the American fleet, then pulled back west. The cruisers *Mikuma* and *Mogami* collided when attacked by an American submarine; then the *Mikuma* was sunk and the *Mogami* badly damaged by American carrier planes. Spruance gave up his chase of the Japanese fleet when he was 400 miles west of Midway, thus thwarting Yamamoto's plan to ambush him; and the *Yorktown* (along with an accompanying destroyer) was sunk by a Japanese sub on her way back to Pearl Harbor.

When the two American task forces returned to Pearl Harbor, they knew they had won a great victory, but they could not know how great a triumph it had been. Midway was secure, all 4 Japanese carriers and 1 cruiser had been sunk, 1 cruiser was badly damaged, 2,500 Japanese had been killed (including a great number of experienced pilots), and 322 aircraft had been lost. The American losses were but 1 carrier and 1 destroyer sunk, 307 men killed, and 147 aircraft lost.

The Japanese had clearly been beaten at Midway in one of the most decisive naval battles in history. What became obvious only with time was that the loss of their four carriers and the high toll of pilot deaths was enough to change the course of the war. From this time forward the Pacific conflict began to turn in the Allies' favor and, as Yamamoto had prophesied, the power of America was about to check, then reverse, the tide of war in the Allies' favor.

THE GUADALCANAL CAMPAIGN

In May 1942 the Japanese seized from the Australians the island of Tulagi and the neighboring islands of Gavutu and Tanambogo off Florida Island in the southern Solomons. The next month they began to build an airfield on Guadalcanal 20 miles to the south across the Sealark Channel. From these points their bombers could strike the islands of New Hebrides, New Caledonia, Fiji, and Samoa. In addition, their surface craft could hit and perhaps sever the vital shipping routes from the West Coast and Hawaii to Australia, now the only location in the South Pacific from which an Allied counteroffensive could

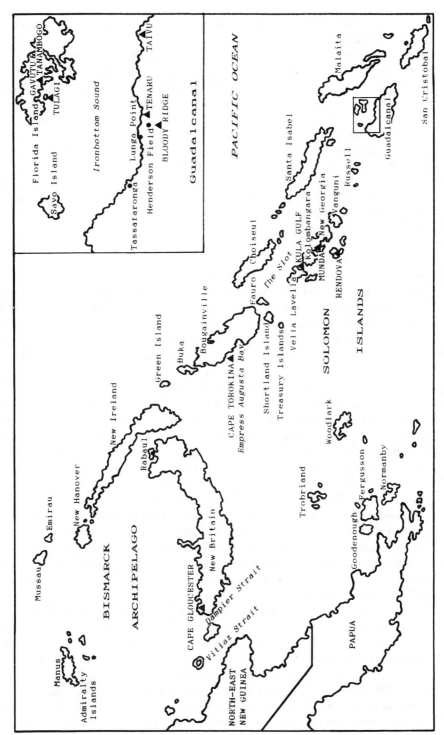

MAP 10–2 Solomon Islands and Bismarck Archipelago, 1941–1944. *(Used with permission of Anne C. Christensen.)*

be launched. The American high command, therefore, decided that these obscure islands had to be retaken.

Guadalcanal (80 miles east to west and 25 miles north to south) and Tulagi to the north (4,000 yards by 1,000 yards) would present a formidable challenge to the 1st Marine Division, ordered to seize them from the enemy. Guadalcanal consisted of hot, wet, and unhealthy jungle infested with crocodiles, lizards, spiders, and scorpions. It was defended by 2,200 Japanese, but 1,700 of these were laborers. Tulagi, across the way, plus the nearby islands, had 1,500 defenders.

Operation Watchtower, the seizure of Guadalcanal and Tulagi, was launched from Wellington, New Zealand, amid terrible chaos. Major General Alexander A. Vandegrift, USMC, finally ordered that large quantities of supplies and ammunition be left behind just to get the invasion force off on time. Most of the 19,000 members of the 1st Marine Division assault force were new recruits assembled from all parts of the Pacific and from the American West Coast.

☆ An American Portrait

Alexander A. Vandegrift—Alexander Archer "Archie" Vandegrift was born in Charlottesville, Virginia, on March 13, 1887, the son of a successful business contractor. From 1905 to 1908 he attended the University of Virginia but then left to join the Marines. By 1909 he had been commissioned a second lieutenant and for the next 14 years served as a member of "the Old Breed" in Nicaragua, Panama, Mexico, and Haiti. In 1923 he became aide to the dynamic General Smedley D. Butler and followed Butler on a number of assignments for 3 years before being dispatched to China.

By 1928 Vandegrift was back in the United States. He spent the next seven years on duty in Washington and at Quantico, at the latter station aiding in the development of amphibious doctrine. From 1935 to 1937 he served with the Marine embassy delegation in China before returning to Washington and the commandant's office. Here he helped manage the Corp's rapid growth for the next four years.

Shortly after the outbreak of World War II, Vandegrift was named commander of the 1st Marine Division and in that capacity directed the long and perilous Guadalcanal campaign. He was relieved from the island, along with the 1st Marines, in December 1942, being awarded the Congressional Medal of Honor for his service there.

In mid-1943 Vandegrift was named commanding general of the 1st Marine Amphibious Corps in the South Pacific area. The following year he was recalled from the war zone to become the eighteenth commandant of the U.S. Marine Corps. In April 1945 he was advanced to general, the first active duty marine to wear four stars. Vandegrift retired in December 1947 and died at Bethesda, Maryland, on May 8, 1973.

On August 7, 1942, the 82 vessels of the American assault fleet sailed around Cape Esperance heading west into the Sealark Channel. They then split, the greater number of marines landing unopposed on Guadalcanal to the south, the smaller number assaulting Tulagi and Gavutu to the north. The Japanese on Tulagi, Gavutu, and nearby Tanambogo put up a fierce resistance for 31 hours, the marines for the first time being subjected to *banzai* (suicide) attacks and to defenders who had to be literally blasted out of their caves because they would not surrender. By the next morning it appeared that all was going well. The Americans had seized the uncompleted Japanese airstrip on Guadalcanal at Lunga Point (renaming it Henderson Field in honor of Major Lofton R. Henderson, a marine air hero at the Battle of Midway) and the northern islands were in the Leathernecks' hands, but a noon air raid by 27 twin-engine Japanese "Betty" bombers that sank an American transport and badly damaged a destroyer was a clear sign that the battle for Guadalcanal had only begun. It would not end until February 1943, six months and 6,300 American casualties later.

The Battle of Guadalcanal consisted of two campaigns fought at the same time. One took place on land as the Japanese placed thousands of troops on the island in repeated attempts to recapture it from the Americans. The second took place on the waters around Guadalcanal as the Imperial Navy ferried in troops, bombarded the marines savagely, and attempted to maintain sea control in the area. Altogether, three major land battles and seven naval battles made up the Guadalcanal campaign.

As the marines on Guadalcanal during the first days on the island strengthened their perimeter and completed the airstrip at Lunga Point amid constant air and naval shelling attacks by the Japanese, the first great naval battle, the Battle of Savo Island, took place on August 9. The day before, Vice Admiral Frank Jack Fletcher, hearing that a Japanese force was moving down through the Solomons chain, pulled out his naval support fleet to protect his three carriers, leaving only a small force of American and Australian cruisers and destroyers under Rear Admiral Victor Crutchley of the Australian Navy to protect the men on the beaches.

Early on the morning of August 9, 1942, a Japanese force of five heavy cruisers, two light cruisers, and one destroyer sailed unseen into Sealark Channel and launched a torpedo and shelling attack on the Allied fleet, inflicting one of the worst defeats on the American Navy in its history. Fortunately, the Japanese broke off the attack without destroying the transports because they did not know the carriers were gone and did not want to get caught by them in the morning light. But four Allied cruisers were sunk or severely damaged and one more cruiser and three destroyers were damaged before the attackers slipped away with only three vessels slightly damaged. Some 1,000 sailors died and another 800 were wounded in the 90-minute, one-sided Battle of Savo Island. And in the aftermath of the battle, Rear Admiral Richmond Kelly Turner, the amphibious fleet commander, pulled his ships out to join Fletcher, leaving 1,400 marines, half their ammunition, and their howitzers and coastal defense guns still onboard the transports as they sailed away. The 18,000 marines on Guadalcanal and Tulagi were now all alone with rations for only one month and ammunition for four days of sustained fighting.

Fortunately, four destroyer-transports slipped in with some supplies on August 15, and on August 20, some 31 Marine aircraft flew in to Henderson Field, the first contingent of the "Cactus Air Force" ("Cactus" being the code name for Guadalcanal). Still, the marines on Guadalcanal, subject to bombing and shelling day after day, and the entire American position in the lower Solomons were in a very precarious position as they faced the first great assault mounted by the Japanese, the Battle of the Tenaru of August 21.

Lieutenant General Haruyoshi Hyakutake had been given 6,000 men and the task of driving the marines off Guadalcanal. His advance force of 915 men under Colonel Kiyono Ichiki had landed at Taivu Point 20 miles east of the marines' position at Lunga

Point on August 18. On August 20, without waiting for the second half of his assigned force, Ichiki led 800 of his men to the west and attacked the marines on their eastern perimeter. Their attack across the Ilu River (not the nearby Tenaru River, but the name stuck) was fierce and unrelenting, but the marines, using machine guns, mortars, artillery, and tanks, held them off and finally flanked them, killing the total Japanese force. Ichiki retreated, burned his regiment's colors, and committed suicide. Suffering fewer than 100 casualties, the marines in the Battle of the Tenaru had won their first victory on Guadalcanal, but greater challenges lay ahead.

Three days later, the Battle of the Eastern Solomons, the second great naval engagement of the campaign, began. As a Japanese amphibious force under Admiral Nagumo, consisting of 3 carriers, 8 battleships, 6 cruisers, and 22 destroyers, came within range of Admiral Fletcher's Task Force 61 (which included the *Saratoga, Enterprise,* and *Wasp*) guarding the American supply routes, a two-day naval aerial fight took place between the fleets on August 24–25, 1942. The American naval units were supplemented by marine fighters from Henderson Field. The Japanese lost a carrier, the *Enterprise* was hit, both carrier forces retired, and the Japanese support ships and transports turned away. The Japanese had lost daytime control of the sea to the Americans, who were now able to pour men and supplies into Guadalcanal. But they still dominated the Solomons by night, moving "down the slot" of the central Solomons to shell the marines night after night and bring in reinforcements on the "Tokyo Express," as the marines called it. They were still determined to wrest Guadalcanal from the Americans.

It was the ability of the Japanese to reinforce their troops on Guadalcanal that led to the second great land engagement of the campaign, the Battle of Bloody Ridge of September 12–14, 1942. On August 31 Major General Kyotake Kawaguchi landed 6,000 men on Guadalcanal—4,000 at Taivu Point east of the marines, and 2,000 at the Matanikau River to their west. His plan called for a three-pronged attack on the marines' perimeter at Lunga Point and Henderson Field. Some 2,000 men would attack from the Matanikau on the west, while 1,000 would attack from the east across the Ilu River. The remaining 3,000, under Kawaguchi himself, would move through the jungle and assault the marines from the south. Tipped off by their own raid on Taivu Point, led by Lieutenant Colonel Merritt A. "Red Mike" Edson, the marines were ready and waiting for the Japanese attacks when they came.

The assaults on the American perimeter were complete failures, thanks to a lack of coordination by the attacking units, who got bogged down making their way through the jungle, and to an incredibly effective defensive effort by the marines in often hand-to-hand fighting along "Edson's Ridge," or "Bloody Ridge," south of Henderson Field, and all along the perimeter. Kawaguchi was forced to withdraw west toward the Matanikau River, his retreating troops undergoing eight days of indescribable misery before reaching the coast.

The Japanese government announced the battle as a great victory. The marines had been "wiped out" on Guadalcanal, they said, and a great victory rally with 30,000 people was staged in Tokyo. But their military leaders knew better and decided that a major effort on Guadalcanal was clearly called for. Some 20,000 troops were ordered to Tenaro, at the northwest tip of Guadalcanal. They were brought in nightly by the "Tokyo Express." At the same time, the Americans were also pouring in reinforcements at a rapid rate (losing the carrier *Wasp* and seeing the battleship *North Carolina* damaged in the process). Vandegrift soon had 23,000 men on the island. These moves by both sides to reinforce themselves for a definitive land battle led to two major naval battles—the Battle of Cape Esperance of October 11–12 and the Battle of the Santa Cruz Islands of October 25–26.

The Battle of Cape Esperance, off the western tip of Guadalcanal, pitted an American cruiser-destroyer force under Rear Admiral Norman Scott against a Japanese force moving "down the slot." It turned into a wild nighttime melee marked by command errors on both sides in which the Americans saw one destroyer sunk and the cruiser *Boise* damaged, but the Japanese reinforcement was temporarily thwarted.

☆ An American Portrait

William F. Halsey—Probably the best known naval officer of World War II, William Frederick Halsey, Jr., was born in Elizabeth, New Jersey, the offspring of a long line of naval officers. After attending the University of Virginia for one year between 1899 and 1900, Halsey accepted an appointment to Annapolis and was graduated in 1904. While there Halsey showed a greater interest in athletics than in academics, ranking in the bottom third of his class.

Like Raymond Spruance, Halsey sailed with the Great White Fleet between 1907 and 1909 (on the battleship *Kansas*). He then went on to destroyer and torpedo duties. When the United States entered World War I, Halsey, now a lieutenant commander, served on destroyers out of Queenstown, Ireland, and won the Navy Cross.

During the interwar period Halsey served in the Office of Naval Intelligence and as a naval attaché in Germany, attended the Naval War College and the Army War College, and spent considerable time at sea on destroyer duty. He also took pilot training at Pensacola, thereafter serving as commander of the carrier *Saratoga* and of the Pensacola Naval Air Station while advancing to the rank of rear admiral.

FIGURE 10–2   William F. Halsey. (*National Archives, Washington, D.C.*)

In 1940 Halsey was made vice admiral and took over command of the carriers in the Pacific fleet. December 7, 1941, found him on the *Enterprise* 150 miles west of Oahu returning from Wake Island. His first fleet actions of the war were carrier task force strikes on the Japanese-held islands in the mid-Pacific. In April 1942 his task force, built around the *Hornet* and *Enterprise*, carried "Jimmy" Doolittle and his Army pilots on their B-25 raid on Tokyo and other Japanese cities. Because of a severe case of dermatitis, Halsey was hospitalized at Pearl Harbor and missed the pivotal Battle of Midway six weeks later.

In October 1942 Halsey was named commander of the South Pacific Force, and for the next two years his carriers and other vessels played a leading role as the American forces moved up the Solomons ladder and into the Bismarck Sea. Halsey's Third Fleet aided MacArthur's landings in the Philippines in August 1944, but he was the subject of criticism for being pulled north during the Battle of Leyte Gulf even though his forces sank four Japanese carriers in the sub battle, the Battle of Cape Engaño. Halsey was also criticized when twice his Third Fleet got caught in typhoons.

Nevertheless, under Halsey's leadership the Third Fleet performed well in the American raids on Formosa, Okinawa, and Japan itself. The Japanese surrender on September 2, 1945, took place on his flagship, the *Missouri,* anchored in Tokyo Bay. Halsey was advanced to fleet admiral the following December.

He retired from the Navy in 1947 to manage the University of Virginia Development Fund and to answer his critics. The colorful and crusty admiral, universally recognized as a superb leader of fighting men, died at Fishers Island, New York, on August 16, 1959.

The Battle of the Santa Cruz Islands took place one week later, after pugnacious Vice Admiral Halsey replaced the cautious Vice Admiral Robert L. Ghormley as commander of the naval forces in the South Pacific. The Japanese were now planning a major land-sea push against Guadalcanal, and Admiral Nagumo's force of 44 ships (including 4 carriers) was the seaborne contingent of this offensive. He was opposed by Rear Admiral Thomas C. Kinkaid, who had only 23 vessels (including the *Hornet* and *Enterprise*). On the morning of October 26 the planes from each of the opposing fleets found their opponent's fleet and attacked. When the two-hour battle was over, the Japanese had suffered 3 ships damaged, but the Americans had lost the *Hornet,* 1 destroyer, and 74 planes, and the *Enterprise* was damaged. The Battle of the Santa Cruz Islands was a clear tactical victory for the Japanese. Whether or not it would turn out to be a strategic victory too depended on the Japanese land force of 20,000 men, including the crack Sendai Division under Lieutenant General Hyakutake himself, now landed at Tassafaronga Point halfway up the coast between Lunga Point and Tenaro and under orders to seize Guadalcanal from the marines once and for all.

The ensuing Sendai Offensive of October 24–26, 1942, was designed to wipe out the marines' perimeter at Lunga Point from four directions at once. It failed, as had the earlier Japanese offensive at the Battle of Bloody Ridge, because of a lack of coordination and a resolute defensive effort by the land and air marines. On October 23 the Japanese force of 2,900 men attacking from the west jumped off 24 hours early and was stopped while taking heavy losses. The next night the 7,000 Sendai attacked from the south and were stopped by 600 marines under Lieutenant Colonel Lewis B. "Chesty" Puller, some reinforcements from the Army's 164th Infantry Regiment, and fierce artillery support. The two other attacks aborted, as did a second Sendai attack the next night. Lieutenant General Kasao Maruyama and what was left of his Sendai Division (about 3,500 men) retreated to Cape Esperance for reinforcement or evacuation. The marines had suffered only 400 casualties in foiling the Sendai Offensive. Yet although both sides were utterly exhausted by this time, neither was willing to back off from Guadalcanal.

During October and November, fresh marines, plus Navy Seabees (men of the construction battalions) and army replacement units began to arrive. By early December all of the men of the 1st Marine Division had been evacuated, and the Army's Major General Alexander M. Patch was on the island with 50,000 men under his command. Even while being replaced, the marines continued with their offensives against the Japanese, and it was clear that General Hyakutake and the surviving Japanese holding out on the western end of the island, now clearly on the defensive, were in desperate need of supplies and reinforcements.

The ensuing three naval battles of Guadalcanal of November 1942 were all marked by furious warfare and many sinkings—adding to the Sealark Channel's name by this time, "Ironbottom Sound." Both fleets suffered many losses (the Japanese lost 2 battleships, 1 heavy cruiser, and 10 transports in the first two battles and scored a tactical success in the third), but the Japanese were not able to reinforce Hyakutake as they planned. On December 12 the Imperial Navy, fearful of more losses, proposed to end the Guadalcanal campaign. By the end of the month the army agreed. The battle for control of the waters around Guadalcanal and thus the battle of the buildup had been won by the Americans, and in January 1943 Patch and his army troops secured all of Guadalcanal as the Japanese evacuated 12,000 to 13,000 survivors (of a total of 36,000 men deployed to the island). Understandably, the departing Japanese soldiers referred to Guadalcanal as "the island of death."

In the long Guadalcanal campaign from August 1942 to February 1943, the Japanese saw 24,000 killed, including 2,300 experienced airmen, the Achilles' heel of the Japanese naval campaign in the Pacific. The marines suffered 4,000 casualties (including 1,200 dead), and the Army took 2,300 casualties. Less than 100 American airmen died. The shipping routes to Australia and New Zealand were now secure, and the Allies were firmly positioned on the outer cordon of the Japanese South Pacific conquests. The Japanese army had suffered its first major defeat in modern times on Guadalcanal. This, combined with the Americans' great naval victory at Midway, meant that the Pacific war had been turned around. As in the European theater, 1942 was the year of decision for the Allied and Axis powers.

CLIMBING THE SOLOMONS LADDER

During 1943 three crucial strategic decisions were made and implemented by the Pacific high command in agreement with President Roosevelt and the Navy and Army chiefs in Washington. These determined the subsequent course of the Pacific war. First, the strategy to be followed in the Pacific would be a two-pronged Allied movement against the Japanese empire. One arm of the movement would advance up from New Guinea and the Solomons toward the Philippines, island-hopping where possible, while a second arm would move west from the Hawaiian Islands, again with the Philippines as the objective. Second, the Army, under General Douglas MacArthur, would carry the load (with assistance from the Navy and Marines) in the Southwest Pacific Theater, while the

Marines (aided by the Army and Navy) would island-hop across the Central Pacific with Admiral Nimitz in supreme command. Third, since these operations—island-hopping evolving as faster and less costly in men than trying to take every Japanese stronghold in the vast Pacific—would call for amphibious operations against defended shores, special-ized landing craft would have to be developed for the operations. Accordingly, the LST (landing ship, tank), LSD (landing ship, dock), LCI (landing craft, infantry), LCT (landing craft, tank) and LVT (landing vehicle, tracked) were procured by the thousands to carry out the amphibious landings across the Pacific.

Following these strategic guidelines, the marines, with the help of the Army and Navy, began to island-hop up the Solomon Islands from their base at Guadalcanal. The Russell Islands, New Georgia Island, with its airfield at Munda, and nearby Rendova were seized between February and August 1943. A key American victory in the area was scored during these months by Lieutenant General George C. Kenney's Fifth Air Force. Learning that a Japanese convoy of seven transports and seven destroyers had left Rabaul on March 1, the feisty general ordered the usual high-level B-17 attacks on the convoy. When two such air assaults sank only two transports, Kenney ordered his twin-engine B-25s and other bombers in to do the job. Their low-level skip-bombing attacks resulted in the sinking of five more transports and four of the destroyers. Approximately 3,000 Japanese troops lost their lives in this Battle of the Bismarck Sea of March 1943.

The Americans also scored a key victory when, having broken the Japanese naval code giving them knowledge of Admiral Yamamoto's movements, they ambushed his plane on April 18, 1943 while he was on an inspection tour of the Solomons. The illustrious Japanese admiral died when American P-38s shot down his plane, which crashed in the jungles of Bougainville. His replacement, Admiral Mineichi Koga, exercised a less sure and less imaginative hand at the helm of the Japanese navy in the Pacific war.

Between October 1943 and April 1944 the men of the 3rd Marine Division and the Army's 37th Division fought for and secured part of the island of Bougainville halfway up the Solomons ladder (the Japanese on the east side of the island remained "withering on the vine" until the end of the war). Seizure of the critical parts of Bougainville, a 125-square-mile mire of jungle, swamps, and mountains, put the large Japanese base at Rabaul in the Bismarck Archipelago within range of American land-based planes. In some of the bloodiest fighting of the Pacific war, marked by furious Japanese counterattacks under General Hyakutake (in command on Guadalcanal the year before during the Sendai Offensive), the island was finally secured, the Americans taking 1,000 casualties while inflicting 7,000 on the Japanese. With the island in American hands, land-based planes flying from Torokina on Bougainville, joined by Navy and Army Air Force planes flying in from the west, soon began daily poundings of Rabaul.

Then, between December 1943 and January 1944, marines of the 1st and 7th Divisions landed on and secured New Gloucester, on the western end of New Britain Island (Rabaul was at the other end), from its 10,000 defenders. This action effectively neutralized Rabaul and gave naval control of nearby Dampier Strait between New Britain and New Guinea to the Allied forces. With tremendous sacrifice and loss of life, the Solomons chain had been brought under American control. In the meantime, MacArthur's forces, having regained control of New Guinea, continued their drive toward the Philippines.

VICTORIES IN NEW GUINEA

While the vicious fighting was raging in the Solomons in late 1942 and early 1943, the Australians were under severe pressure in New Guinea to the west. In July 1942, Japanese troops landed at Gona on the northern coast of Papua (New Guinea). They then began a march across the Owen Stanley Mountain Range to seize Port Moresby, only 300 miles north of Australia across the Torres Strait, which had been their objective in May, when they had been turned back in the Battle of the Coral Sea.

MAP 10–3 Map of New Guinea.(*Used with permission of Anne C. Christensen.*)

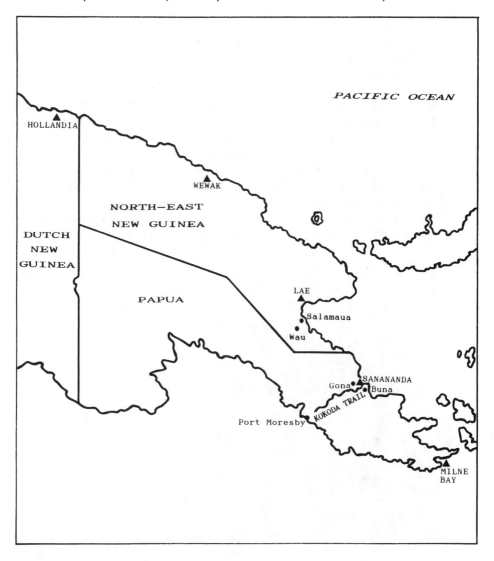

They made their way over the perilous Kodoka Trail with the Australians gamely attempting to stop them. Kenney's Fifth Air Force brought the Japanese infantry under almost incessant attack in aiding the Allies. Meanwhile, a Japanese amphibious attack on Milne Bay, on the far eastern tip of Papua, was turned back by 9,000 Allied troops. The Kodoka Track force of Japanese was finally stopped by mid-September, only 30 miles from Port Moresby. Exhausted and starving, the Japanese soldiers began to retreat back across the track to the northern edge of the island. A second Japanese drive on Port Moresby from Lae and Salamaua in Northeast New Guinea up the coast from Gona was also stopped by the Australians during these months, with valuable logistical help from the Fifth Air Force.

☆   An American Portrait

Douglas MacArthur—Possibly the most famous and most enigmatic military commander of the twentieth century, MacArthur was born at Fort Dodge, Arkansas, on January 26, 1880, the third son of Arthur MacArthur, who would advance to become the Army's highest-ranking officer between 1905 and 1909, and Mary "Pinky" MacArthur of Norfolk, Virginia. Entering West Point in 1899, MacArthur graduated with highest honors four years later as a second lieutenant of engineers, his doting mother having lived in the nearby Craney's Hotel to keep her eye on his progress at the Academy.

During the next ten years MacArthur served in the Philippines, Panama, and stateside; was an aide to his father and to Theodore Roosevelt; and graduated from the Army Engineering School of Application. Marked as a rising talent, he was appointed a member of the War Department General Staff. Sent to France upon America's entry into World War I, MacArthur, now a colonel, served as chief of staff of the 42nd Division (the

FIGURE 10–3   Douglas MacArthur. (*National Archives, Washington, D.C.*)

"Rainbow Division") and participated in the Saint-Mihiel and Meuse-Argonne offensives, winning nine decorations for heroism and being advanced to brigadier general. After the war he was named to lead the Rainbow Division before serving as superintendent of West Point until 1922, introducing a series of badly needed reforms at the Academy.

During the remaining years of the 1920s, MacArthur's military career continued to skyrocket, marked by many important command assignments, service on the "Billy" Mitchell court-martial hearing, advancement to major general, and a one-year stint as head of the American Olympic Committee in 1928. In 1930 MacArthur was advanced to chief of staff of the Army, a post he held for five years.

In 1935 MacArthur accepted the position of military advisor to the Commonwealth of the Philippines, the next year being named field marshal. He retired from the U.S. Army in 1937 but was recalled to active duty in July 1941 as commander of the United States armed forces in the Far East, being advanced in rank to general by December of that year.

Leading the defense of the Philippines against the Japanese from December until he was ordered to Australia in March 1942 by President Roosevelt to serve as commander of the Southwest Pacific Theater, MacArthur spent the next 2 1/2 years driving the Japanese out of New Guinea. In December 1944 he had been made general of the Army; two months before, his Sixth Army had invaded the Philippines. In April 1945 he was named commander of all U.S. Army forces in the Pacific, and it was he who received the Japanese surrender aboard the *Missouri* in September 1945.

From 1945 until 1951 MacArthur commanded the occupation forces in Japan and introduced many long-term reforms in that defeated nation. As head of the U.S. Far East Command, and later as commander-in-chief of the United Nations Command, MacArthur directed the allied forces during the Korean War, executing his greatest military success with the landings at Inchon on September 15, 1950. Seven months later he was relieved of his commands by President Harry Truman for insubordination. He returned to the United States a controversial hero and made an unsuccessful attempt to gain the Republican party's nomination for president in 1952.

MacArthur spent his remaining years serving as chairman of the board of Remington Rand in New York City and writing his book *Reminiscences,* published in 1964. He died on April 5, 1964, and, after a state funeral in the nation's capital, was interred in Norfolk, Virginia, his mother's home town.

Springing to the offensive, troops of the Australian 7th Division and the American 32nd Division were flown in to the Buna-Gona area on the north shore of Papua, where the Japanese had retreated from their Kodoka Track expedition. Under the leadership of Lieutenant General Robert L. Eichelberger, they had driven the Japanese out of Papua by January 1943. Working in tandem with Halsey's offensive up the Solomons ladder, MacArthur next struck at Lae and the Huon Peninsula, 140 miles northwest of Buna-Gona in Northeast New Guinea. On June 30, 1943, the 41st Infantry Division and Australian troops moved on Lae. Throughout July and August they continued to advance, finally securing the village of Lae in September after a one-minute drop of 1,700 paratroopers of the 503rd Airborne Regiment west of the city by Fifth Air Force planes. The Allied troops needed the remainder of the year to secure the Huon Peninsula because 9,000 Japanese soldiers fled into the mountains and had to be dug out.

☆   An American Portrait

Robert L. Eichelberger—Robert Lawrence Eichelberger was one of the most successful Army field commanders of World War II but is all but forgotten today. Born in Urbana, Ohio, in 1886, the son of a prominent lawyer, Eichelberger attended nearby Ohio State University for two years before accepting an appointment to the United States Military Academy in 1905. He was graduated sixty-eighth in his class of 103 four years later.

Assigned to the 10th Infantry, he served in Texas as part of the Maneuver Division in 1911 and was then posted to Panama. The year 1915 found him on the Mexican border as part of the 22nd Infantry Regiment. After general staff duty, Eichelberger, as a major, accompanied General William Graves to Siberia in 1918 and served in that frustrating expedition until 1920. During the 1920s and 1930s he served in China and the Philippines, graduated from both the Command and General Staff School and the Army War College, served on the War Department general staff under Douglas MacArthur and General Milan Craig, and moved to command of the 30th Infantry Regiment at the Presidio in San Francisco.

In 1940, Eichelberger, now a brigadier general, served as a reforming superintendent of West Point. With the outbreak of war, he moved back to field command, first of the 77th Division, then of I Corps. Ordered to Australia in 1942, he began a field-command career under General MacArthur that lasted until his retirement six years later. From August 1942 to January 1943 he carried out a notable campaign in the capture of Buna in New Guinea and in April 1944 was in command at the seizure of Hollandia. During the bloody Philippine campaign he headed the Eighth Army, which carried out 52 amphibious landings before the archipelago was seized from the Japanese. Eichelberger also headed the Eighth Army until 1948 during its occupation duties in Japan.

This fighting general retired in 1948 and received his fourth star in 1950, the same year in which his acclaimed *Our Jungle Road to Tokyo* was published. He died in 1961 in Asheville, North Carolina.

On December 15, 1943, soldiers of the 112th Cavalry Regiment crossed the Vitiaz and Dampier Straits and landed on the western tip of New Britain. With Cape Gloucester falling five weeks later to the Americans and the key Solomon islands also in American hands, the decision was made to bypass now-neutralized Rabaul, tactics now having been switched from "island hopping" to "leapfrogging," bypassing major Japanese installations to strike at weaker and more vulnerable installations behind them, thus ensuring their neutralization without the launching of amphibious assaults against them. Both Rabaul and the Japanese island fortress at Truk, to the north in the Caroline Islands, were thus bypassed. MacArthur turned west to continue his drive toward the Philippines.

With Hollandia, halfway up the northern coast of New Guinea, as their target, American troops moved along the coast while Australian troops moved through the mainland of New Guinea. In a surprise move in February 1944, MacArthur's men seized the Admiralty Islands to the north across the Bismarck Sea, giving the Fifth Air Force bases from which to attack the Japanese stronghold at Madang in Northeast New Guinea. After preliminary bombing, Madang was finally seized on April 24, 1944, after fierce Japanese resistance. The Japanese pulled back up the coast to defend MacArthur's next logical targets, Hansa Bay and Wewak.

But MacArthur leapfrogged over these and struck instead at Hollandia, far up the coast in Dutch New Guinea. After the Fifth Air Force neutralized Japanese air power there, Hollandia was invaded on April 22, 1944, and taken with little difficulty. MacArthur then moved on to seize the Vogelkop Peninsula to the west, while some of his elements, and the Australians, began a major effort to clear out the 55,000-man Eighteenth Japanese Army, trapped between Hollandia and the Australians. This task required the remainder of the summer of 1944.

New Guinea, the Vogelkop Peninsula, and the neighboring islands were at last under effective control after two years of fanatical and effective Japanese resistance. After it became clear that the island of Mindanao in the lower Philippines could safely be bypassed in favor of hitting the island of Leyte farther north, on October 22, 1944, with four divisions behind him and the Fifth Air Force and Halsey's Third Fleet covering him, MacArthur waded onto Philippine soil, fulfilling his promise to the Filipino people of March 1942, "I shall return." Of greater importance than MacArthur's dramatics, American forces now dominated the central and southern Pacific and were within striking distance of the heart of the Japanese empire.

THE CENTRAL PACIFIC DRIVE

As the American and Allied forces in the Southwest Pacific were fighting their way up the Solomons chain and across New Guinea in 1943 and 1944, the American drive across the Central Pacific, directed by Admiral Nimitz, was also being carried out. The target islands in this area were different topographically and botanically from those in the South Pacific. Farther south, the Japanese-held islands were covered with dense jungle and swampy undergrowth; here the target islands were atolls formed from volcanic eruptions. They were marked by coral reefs in their approaching waters, and their soil consisted of volcanic rock. Yet the differences in physical environment signified no difference in the Japanese defenders' determination to fight to the death in the best *samurai* tradition.

The first target in the Central Pacific drive was the Gilbert Islands, 2,500 miles southwest of Hawaii. With these islands in American hands, Nimitz's left flank would be covered for his drive west to the Marshalls, Carolines, and Marianas. Assembled for Operation Galvanic were 35,000 men and a fleet of 200 vessels. Makin Atoll, in the northern Gilberts (the site of marine Lieutenant Colonel Evans F. Carlson's abortive raid of August 1942) was the assigned target of the 27th Infantry Division. The Marines were assigned the task of taking Tarawa Atoll, some 100 miles to the south, and specifically Betio Island within it. The battle for Makin lasted from November 21 through 25, 1943, much too long for the amphibious commander, marine Major General Holland M. "Howlin' Mad" Smith, who thought the Army's drive was too deliberate, especially with a 20-to-1 advantage in numbers over the Japanese defenders. Typically, Smith said so.

On Tarawa the marines ran into furious Japanese resistance from bunkered artillery pieces and machine gun pillboxes, complicated by incredible foul-ups in getting ashore. The Navy lifted its ship-to-shore bombardment 18 minutes early, the naval air strikes were late, the Marine's Higgins boats grounded on the reefs and could not scale the 4-foot seawall, and the beach was a confused mess of men and equipment.

Tarawa-Betio was finally secured by November 23, after the Americans had taken over 3,200 casualties (to the Japanese 4,700). It had been a very expensive lesson for the American military in amphibious warfare against defended islands. For future operations, more and better LVTs ("amtracs," amphibious tractors capable of climbing over coral reefs) would be needed, and UDTs (underwater demolition teams) would have to clear the waters of the landing sites before the troops were sent in. And rockets and high-angle armor-piercing shells would have to be developed to knock out blockhouses and pillboxes because massed naval shelling and bombing could not do the job. Corrective measures were taken immediately.

The second target in the Central Pacific drive was the Marshall Islands, assaulted and secured on February 1–19, 1944. This operation went much more smoothly and resulted in far fewer casualties than the Gilberts operation, thanks to more and better LVTs, better naval and air bombardment, and better land and sea communications through the use of command ships. On February 1–3 the marines attacked Roi and Namur islands while Army troops assaulted Kwajalein and Majuro. Meanwhile, fast carrier task forces hit the giant Japanese naval base at Truk to the southwest, destroying 41 ships and 200 planes, while the Army and Marines also hit Eniwetok Atoll. As in the Gilberts, Japanese resistance was fanatical, but by the time all the Marshalls had been secured in March, the Americans had incurred less than 1,000 casualties.

The next island group targeted was the Marianas, situated only 1,500 miles east of the Philippines and only 1,300 miles southeast of Japan. Control of the wooded and mountainous main islands in the group, Saipan, Tinian, and Guam, would enable the Americans to cut the Japanese waterborne supply routes to the south and place the home islands within the range of the Army Air Force's new long-range B-29 "Super-fortress" bombers.

Saipan, 15 by 5 miles in size and dominated by Mount Tapotchau in the center, was defended by 25,000 Japanese. All were determined to die in the face of an American attack. When, therefore, 20,000 marines from two divisions and soldiers from the 27th Division stormed ashore on June 15, 1944, they met incredible Japanese resistance. After eight days of hard fighting, "Howlin' Mad" Smith of the Marines demanded and got the dismissal of the Army's Major General Ralph Smith because the 27th was again, he insisted, "too slow," and their lethargy was affecting the landings on Tinian and Guam. Nevertheless, by July 6, with Mount Tapotchau finally taken and the Americans sweeping the island, Vice Admiral Chuichi Nagumo, the naval commander (and the commander of the carriers at Pearl Harbor and Midway) committed suicide. His army counterpart, Lieutenant General Yoshitugu Saito, did likewise, but only after the general exhorted his troops to follow him to death and glory.

They did. On July 7 at least 2,500 Japanese soldiers carried out massed *banzai* attacks on the American lines, the soldiers and marines using every weapon available, including 105 millimeter howitzers fired at point blank range, to beat off the frenzied attackers. The island was declared secure on July 9, the Japanese having suffered 29,000 dead, including hundreds of civilians and soldiers who jumped off Marpi Point on the north end of the island onto the rocks below rather than surrender to the Americans. Only 17 Japanese soldiers remained alive on the island. The American casualty toll was 16,000, including 3,400 dead.

Tinian, 3 1/2 miles to the south, fell to the 2nd and 4th Marine Divisions by the end of July. Guam, 100 miles farther south, was assaulted at Asan Point below Agana by the 3rd Marine Division and at Agat farther down the east coast by the 1st Marine Brigade and the 77th Infantry Division on July 21. It was finally secured on August 10, after the Americans again encountered furious *banzai* attacks. The Marianas were now in American hands, with Saipan being prepared as a major B-29 base for the air assault on Japan. While this furious land fighting was going on in the Marianas, to the east of the islands one of the greatest naval battles of the war was also taking place.

THE BATTLE OF THE PHILIPPINE SEA

The decisive Battle of the Philippine Sea was fought on June 19–20, 1944, but it actually began two months before, when Admiral Soemu Toyoda, successor to Admiral Koga as commander of the Combined Fleet, adopted Operation A-GO, a grand plan to smash the encroaching American naval forces by a decisive fleet action in the spirit of the Battle of Tsushima of 1905. As conceived, if the United States fleet attacked the Marianas, it would first be struck by land-based planes and then lured out by the First Mobile Fleet to its defeat in "ceaseless air attacks" using shuttle-bombing tactics whereby Japanese planes from this fleet would attack the Americans, then fly on east to the Marianas for refueling and rearming, hitting the American fleet again on their return flight west to the Mobile Fleet.

The Mobile Fleet under Vice Admiral Jisaburo Ozawa had three carrier divisions. The divisions included 9 flattops with 430 aircraft plus 5 battleships and 13 cruisers. The 55 ships of the Mobile Fleet ships were assembled at Tawi Tawi in the Lulu Archipelago. This Japanese naval force seemed formidable, but a closer look revealed three significant weaknesses. First, while Ozawa's carrier-based planes had a longer range than their American counterparts, giving them an edge in searching for and attacking the American fleet, their air crews had limited training and experience. Second, because of the American submarine campaign being carried out in the western Pacific under the direction of Vice Admiral Charles A. Lockwood, Jr., 21 Japanese tankers had been sunk since January. As a result, the Japanese warships were burning unrefined and volatile Borneo crude oil. Third, 17 of the 25 submarines sent out to scout for the American fleet in May had been sunk by destroyers or aircraft and, therefore, were not available for use against the Americans in the upcoming battle.

On June 6, 1944, an American amphibious force of 127,000 troops with 535 combat and auxiliary vessels left Majuro in the Marshall Islands for the invasion of the Marianas. This was two days after the fall of Rome and the same day as the landings in Normandy. That America could mount this much military power on two sides of the globe simultaneously was vivid confirmation of the now-dead Admiral Yamamoto's warnings as to America's warmaking potential.

The Fifth Fleet covering the Marianas invasion was under the command of Admiral Raymond Spruance. It was made up of three task forces: a southern attack force (Task Force 53), under Rear Admiral Richard L. Conolly; a northern attack force (Task Force 52), under Vice Admiral Richmond Kelly Turner; and Task Force 58, under Vice Admiral Marc A. "Pete" Mitscher, whose job it was to attack enemy ships and protect the invasion forces. Mitscher had 15 carriers and 900 planes in his contingent alone, a far cry from the 3 carriers and 230 planes available at Midway two years before. In addition, he had 7 battleships, 21 cruisers, and 69 destroyers.

As the Japanese in the Mobile Fleet sailed out to meet and defeat this mighty U.S. naval armada, its plan began to unravel when one-third of the 500 land-based planes in the Marianas were destroyed on June 11 by American planes and more were destroyed over the next four days. Sufficient land-based planes to pound the American fleet were now not available.

In the meantime, warned by their subs that the Mobile Fleet was on its way, Spruance and Mitscher were waiting off the Marianas, Spruance refusing to be drawn off to the west because he wanted to cover the Marianas beachheads. On came the Japanese fleet, Ozawa hoping to stand off from the American Fifth Fleet and shuttle bomb it with his 400-plus longer-range planes.

But when the battle began on June 19, there were only 30 land-based planes left in the Marianas, and these were soon destroyed by American aircraft. Furthermore, their airstrips were badly potholed, making them unusable for Ozawa's pilots flying in to rearm and refuel. And when the Americans detected the Japanese attack planes moving in from the west, over 450 fighters were launched to stop them. The result was the eight-hour "Marianas Turkey Shoot" in which the Japanese lost over 400 planes to naval airplanes and surface fleet gunfire. To make matters worse for Ozawa, that same day American submarines slipped in among his Mobile Fleet and sank two carriers, the *Taiho* and the *Shokaku*.

The next day, June 20, when Mitscher's scout planes discovered in late afternoon that the Japanese fleet was slipping away to the northwest, the admiral launched 216 fighters, dive bombers, and torpedo bombers to go after them, even though they were beyond the planes' range out and back and even though they would be returning after dark with pilots who were untrained in night landings. Mitscher then turned northwest to shorten the return distance for the planes after their attacks and hoped for the best. The American planes sank the carrier *Hiyo* and damaged the carriers *Chiyoda* and *Zuikaku*, in addition to a battleship and a cruiser, before turning for home. Many planes ran out of gas and dropped into the sea, but most of them made it back, with Mitscher ordering full illumination of the fleet (despite the danger from lurking enemy subs) and allowing the fuel-starved pilots to land on any available flight deck. Some 49 American aviators died that day, but the Mobile Fleet was badly battered. When American scouts found it the next day, it was 360 miles away and running for home.

Spruance and Mitscher had both crippled the Mobile Fleet and protected the landings in the Marianas in one of the most spectacular events of the Pacific war. Japanese naval power was now critically wounded, and a further disastrous loss of its planes and pilots had taken place. The Japanese navy was in dire straits. Airfields in the Marianas were being prepared for bombing attacks on Japan itself. MacArthur was cleaning up north and west of New Guinea. It was now time for landings in the Philippines.

Nimitz and the Navy—especially Admiral King, the chief of naval operations—wanted to bypass the Philippines and move directly on Formosa to the north, but at a conference held at Pearl Harbor in late July 1944, the ever-elegant MacArthur convinced President Roosevelt that the Philippines had to be retaken, and the die was cast. Plans were drawn up for the invasion of the archipelago.

THE INVASION OF THE PHILIPPINES AND THE BATTLE OF LEYTE GULF

As plans were drawn up for the invasion of the Philippines, Admiral Nimitz showed particular concern over continued Japanese control of the Palau Islands in the western Carolines, 500 miles east of the Philippines. As he saw it, they threatened the left flank of his Central Pacific drive toward the Philippines and MacArthur's right flank as he moved up from the south. Halsey and other commanders wanted to bypass the islands, but Nimitz insisted they be taken, a decision that turned out to be one of the most costly of the Pacific war.

Peleliu, the main island in the group, was defended by 6,500 Japanese in enlarged and defended caves under orders to make no suicide attacks. Rather, they were to contain the Americans on the beaches and then fall back yard by yard, taking every life possible. When the 1st Marine Division hit the beaches on September 15, 1944, they soon found that the three-day preliminary air and naval bombardment had done virtually no damage to the Japanese defenses. The caves and other defense installations along Umurbrogol Ridge, running the length of the 6-by-2-mile island would have to be cleaned out one by one. Before the fighting ended in late November with Palau and nearby Agnaur Island being secured, only 700 of the 6,500 Japanese defenders were still alive on Palau, and over 10,000 Marine and Army casualties had been sustained (1,950 killed and 8,515 wounded), 6,000 from the 1st Marine Division. It had taken 1,600 rounds of light and heavy ordnance to kill each Japanese defender on Palau. It was a gory and unnecessary lesson in island warfare.

In the meantime, after underwater demolition teams and mine sweepers had done their jobs, and after three days of naval and air bombardment, on October 22, 1944, General MacArthur and the U.S. Army returned to the Philippines in landings off Tacloban and Dulag on the southeast coast of the island of Leyte. Sergio Osmena, the president of the Philippines, accompanied MacArthur. Over 132,000 troops of the Sixth Army and 200,000 tons of supplies were landed that first day. Everyone expected an all-out defensive effort by the Japanese in the Philippines; no one expected the great naval battle that would soon be fought and that would spell victory in the Philippines and the virtual annihilation of the Japanese navy.

The Japanese high command had prepared Operation SHO-GO ("Victory Operation") for the defense of the Philippines, Formosa, the Ryukyu Islands stringing down from the home islands, and the home islands themselves. It called for three great fleet actions to drive the American invaders from the Philippines and fatally cripple the U.S. Navy. One fleet, the First Striking Force, which included the giant battleships *Yamato* and *Musashi* plus 3 other battleships, 12 cruisers, and 15 destroyers, was assembled at Lingga Roads near Brunei in Borneo under Vice Admiral Takeo Kurita. It was to sail through the Palawan Passage and cross the Sibuyan Sea in the center of the Philippines, penetrate San Bernardino Strait on the east, and sail around the island of Samar to attack the American invaders in Leyte Gulf from the north.

Part of Kurita's fleet (7 ships, including 2 battleships) under Vice Admiral Shoji Nishimura was to detach south of Palawan and join up with Vice Admiral Kiyohide Shima's Second Striking Force (7 ships, including 3 cruisers) moving down from the Ryukyus. Together they would move through the Sula Strait north of Mindanao and

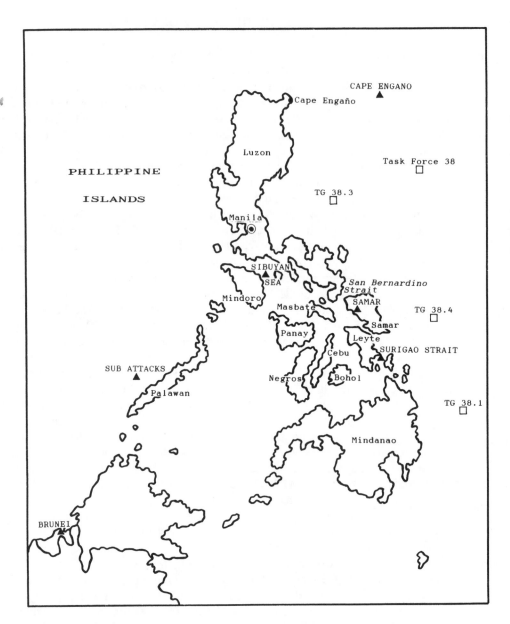

MAP 10–4 Battle of Leyte Gulf, 1944. (*Used with permission of Anne C. Christensen.*)

penetrate Surigao Strait to attack the Americans in Leyte Gulf from the south as Kurita and the First Striking Force moved in from the north.

The Mobile Fleet, still under Vice Admiral Jisaburo Ozawa, with 4 carriers, 2 battleships, 4 cruisers, and 8 destroyers, was the bait to draw Halsey's Third Fleet away from Leyte Gulf. Sailing down from the home islands, it would surely be destroyed, but the success of this complicated plan depended on Ozawa's being able to pull Third Fleet off to the north, away from Leyte Gulf. This part of the plan worked. The others did not.

On the first day of the Battle of Leyte Gulf, October 23, 1944, Kurita's First Striking Force was attacked by American submarines off Palawan on the western edge of the Philippines. Two carriers were sunk and one damaged, but Kurita transferred his flag to the giant *Yamato* and kept on moving toward the Sibuyan Sea. The next day, October 24, his fleet was attacked in the Sibuyan Sea, and, with a third carrier damaged and sinking and the battleship *Musashi* sunk, Kurita turned back toward the west. In the meantime, Nishimura, with Shima 60 miles behind, was discovered and attacked in the Sula Sea. Halsey, believing it was Seventh Fleet commander Vice Admiral Thomas C. Kinkaid's responsibility to cover the Leyte beachhead and that it was his responsibility to go on the offensive if a Japanese fleet approached, took off with Third Fleet in pursuit of Ozawa when the Japanese Mobile Fleet was discovered off to the north. Thanks to the command responsibility split between MacArthur and Nimitz, each admiral thought the other was covering San Bernardino Strait at the eastern end of the Sibuyan Sea. What neither knew was that at sunset Kurita had reversed course and was again heading east for San Bernardino Strait. The only Japanese naval attack expected was that of Nishimura and Shima coming through Surigao Strait to the south.

When Nishimura entered the strait early on the morning of October 25, he had to run a gauntlet of 39 PT boats and five destroyers before meeting up with Admiral Jesse Oldendorf's six old battleships (veterans of the attack on Pearl Harbor) plus cruisers. He suffered heavy damage as Olendorf's ships positioned across the mouth of the strait and "crossed the T" on Nishimura's fleet. They were at a right angle to the Japanese fleet across the top of the T and thus were able to bring all their guns to bear against it, while Nishimura's ships advancing toward them up the T could only bring a portion of their guns to bear on the Americans. Being "crossed" is sometimes avoidable by maneuvering (Scheer did it twice against Jellicoe at Jutland), but Nishimura was unable to effect such maneuvering in the narrow Surigao Straits. As Shima moved up from 40 miles behind, he saw the damage to Nishimura's ships. (Only one destroyer remained, Nishimura having gone down with his flagship, the battleship *Yamashiro*.) Shima's last word from Kurita's force was that they were withdrawing from the Sibuyan Sea, so Shima too decided to turn around.

Leyte Gulf was safe from the south, but then word came that Kurita had broken through San Bernardino Strait and was heading south around the island of Samar toward Leyte Gulf. Only a small carrier task force of 6 escort carriers, 3 destroyers, and 3 destroyer escorts under Rear Admiral Clifton Sprague from Seventh Fleet was standing between him and the destruction of the American forces in Leyte Gulf. Only then did Admiral Kinkaid find out that Halsey by this time was far to the north, attacking Ozawa's Mobile Fleet. Fortunately for the Americans, as Kurita's fleet of 4 battleships, 6 heavy cruisers, and 11 destroyers met the small American force off Samar and attacked, Kurita thought he was taking on Halsey's Third Fleet and, fearing for his safety and losing contact with his own ships in the furious surface and air melee that followed, ordered his ships back through San Bernardino Strait. Halsey's advance ships, returning as quickly as possible from the north, arrived too late, although Third Fleet had sunk 4 Japanese carriers and 5 other ships of Ozawa's decoy fleet.

The Battle of Leyte Gulf, the largest, most complex and far-flung naval battle in history, was over, and the American forces on Leyte were safe. The Japanese had lost 3 battleships, 4 carriers, 10 cruisers, 11 destroyers, 500 aircraft, and 10,000 men, to the Americans' loss of only 5 smaller vessels. The Japanese fleet was still in being, but never again would it be able to enter a major engagement. Yet October 25, the last day of the Battle of Leyte Gulf, contained an ominous warning of future carnage and terror, for on that morning planes from Japan's Special Attack Corps—the *Kamikaze* ("Divine Wind")—launched their first attacks on the American fleet from Clark Field on Luzon, sinking 1 carrier and damaging 4 others. With the coming of the *Kamikaze,* naval warfare entered a new and frightening phase.

THE BATTLES OF IWO JIMA AND OKINAWA

The Sixth Army under General George Krueger and the Eighth Army under General Robert Eichelberger spent the remainder of 1944 and the first months of 1945 regaining the Philippines in assault after assault on the many islands of the archipelago. The main island of Luzon, with the islands' capital of Manila, was not declared secure until March 1945. The Luzon operation stands as the largest single American campaign in the Pacific war, the Americans counting almost 8,000 killed and 33,000 wounded, and the Japanese suffering 192,000 killed. Meanwhile, the marines were given the task of invading Iwo Jima in the Bonin Islands southwest of Japan.

Because the volcanic island of only eight square miles was situated halfway between the Marianas and Japan, it had to be secured as a base for fighters covering the B-29s on their raids on the home islands. The Japanese had spent eight months preparing for the expected American invasion and had done their work well. They had prepared hundreds of concrete blockhouses and over 1,000 fortified caves, and their 21,000 army and navy troops were prepared to fight to the death. The marines of the V Amphibious Force under "Howlin' Mad" Smith had 70,000 men with whom to try to wrest the tiny island from them.

After preliminary bombing and shelling for 75 days, which did only minimal damage, 30,000 marines hit the small beachhead on February 19, 1945. Some 20,000 more would follow. Before the fighting was over on March 26—crowned by the seizure of Mount Suribachi on February 26 by marines from the 28th Marine Regiment— 6,800 Marines and Navy corpsmen lay dead and 20,000 had been wounded. Almost all of the 21,000 Japanese defenders died in place as ordered. For the Marine Corps, Iwo Jima represented the highest ratio of casualties taken to casualties given in its history. In all, 22 marines received the Congressional Medal of Honor in the action on Iwo Jima, 12 posthumously. As Fleet Admiral Nimitz said, "uncommon valor was a common virtue" on Iwo.

For the invasion of Okinawa, the largest island in the Ryukyus chain and only 350 miles south of Japan, Lieutenant General Simon Bolivar Buckner, Jr., had 182,000 men in his Tenth Army command. Vice Admiral Kelly Turner, the amphibious commander, had 1,200 vessels. Before the Okinawa campaign was over, 550,000 men and 1,500 vessels would be involved.

After a six-day preliminary bombardment by Army bombers and Navy planes and surface vessels (the British Pacific Fleet, built around four carriers, having joined the Americans by this time), the initial landings of Operation Iceberg came on April 1, 1945, Easter Sunday and April Fool's Day. The landing forces met little opposition on the beachheads because the Japanese had decided to make their stand inland. But *Kamikaze* planes began their daily attacks on the fleet. The attacks rose to a crescendo first on April 6 and 7, when 335 suicide planes made their assaults on the fleet, and then again on April 12, when 185 *Kamikazes* attacked. By the end of the Okinawa action on June 22, some 1,465 *Kamikaze* pilots had flown to their deaths against the Allied ships, and 120 ships had been hit, 29 had been sunk, and over 3,000 sailors had been killed in their attacks.

As on Iwo Jima, the fighting on land was furious. The Japanese made stout but limited resistance across the center and on the northern part of the island, but moving to the south was different. The Japanese had set up east–west defensive lines, and these, combined with the rugged terrain, made any advance incredibly difficult and costly in lives. It was not until May 18 that Sugar Loaf Hill, the western anchor of the Shuri Line, the Japanese main defensive line, was taken, but at the cost of over 2,600 Americans killed or wounded. And it was not until May 22 that the Japanese began to abandon the Shuri Line and establish a new defensive line seven miles to the south. Despite the fact that they were suffering 1,000 deaths per day under intense artillery and naval fire, in addition to fire from ground troops using tanks, rockets, flame throwers, and dynamite, the Japanese held on until June 22. On that day, General Roy Geiger (who had taken over at General Buckner's death four days before to become the first marine to command an army in World War II) declared the island secure.

In another form of suicide attack, the 64,000-ton battleship *Yamato,* the largest warship ever built, was sent out with 1 cruiser and 6 destroyers with almost all the remaining ships' oil in their bunkers (not enough to return to Japan) to attack the Fifth Fleet and then beach itself on Okinawa and fight until eliminated. Spotted by American submarines while halfway there, the *Yamato* and 4 of her 7 escorting vessels were sunk by 300 American carrier planes on April 7. It was the last Japanese naval action of the war.

The Battle of Okinawa, the bloodiest single campaign of the Pacific war, saw the Japanese suffer as many as 135,000 dead. Civilian deaths numbered about the same, out of a population of 450,000 on the island. The Americans suffered 12,520 dead and 36,630 wounded. The butcher's bill had been ghastly, but the Americans had now secured a base for the invasion of Japan, and the Japanese empire, its army and navy mortally wounded, stood on the verge of total defeat. It was time to apply the *coup de grace.*

The Allies had every expectation that Operation Olympic, the invasion of Japan, would be a very costly affair. The Japanese soldiers had proved time and again that they were willing to die for the emperor in the best *samurai* tradition, and their fanaticism seemed to be increasing. Plans for Olympic were made with Iwo Jima, Okinawa, and the dreaded, death-dealing *Kamikaze* raids fresh in everyone's mind. Would not their defense of their homeland be even more fanatical? Even at this late date in the war, the Japanese home defense plan, Ketsu-Go (decisive battle), called for inflicting such high casualties on the Americans that they would give up and go home.

Operation Olympic called for a November 1, 1945, invasion of Kyushu, the southernmost main island of Japan, by 193,000 men of the Sixth Army, including seven Army and seven Marine divisions. Over 450,000 men would follow, backed up by over

3,000 vessels of the Fifth Fleet, 2,000 carrier-based planes, and 6,000 land-based planes. Eighth Army and First Army would follow in Operation Coronet, with a 14-division invasion of the main island of Honshu in the Yokohama-Tokyo area on March 1, 1946. Allied casualties were estimated to run as high as 1.5 million, and Japanese military and civilian casualties as high as 10 million. Many months of continued bloodshed lay ahead as troops were transferred from Europe to the Pacific to help attain the final victory.

THE CHINA-BURMA-INDIA THEATER

As the Americans and their allies were in the process of first stopping the tide of Japanese expansion in the Pacific and then sweeping the aggressors back from 1942 through 1945, a confusing and frustrating war was also taking place on the Asiatic mainland. The confusion stemmed from a lack of clear and compelling policy goals among the Allies in their war against the Japanese in China, Burma, and India. The frustration lay in attempting to win a clear advantage over the enemy, especially in Burma, a mountainous and jungled region completely unsuited to clear strategic and tactical superiority.

In China the Allies found command resting on the shoulders of Generalissimo Chiang Kai-shek, leader of the Kuomintang party. But Chiang was more concerned with keeping his armies intact to resume the civil war against Mao Tse-tung and the Chinese Communists once the war was over than with fighting the Japanese invaders. Thus he seemed content to marshal all the aid he could get from the United States (flown in from India to China over the Himalaya Mountains—"over the Hump"—by American C-46 "Commandoes" after the Japanese seized the Burma Road from Lashio in Burma to the Chinese capital at Chungking in 1942) to position himself for the postwar situation. This made his cooperation with the Allies less than ideal.

This problem was a source of unending frustration for Lieutenant General Joseph W. "Vinegar Joe" Stilwell, sent to China early in 1942 by President Roosevelt because of his long experience there to command American troops in the China-Burma-India (CBI) theater of operations. Chiang and Stilwell clashed repeatedly, with the often undiplomatic Stilwell making little or no attempt to disguise his contempt for the Chinese leader. Nor did relations improve appreciably when Major General Albert C. Wedemeyer replaced Stilwell in October 1944. Yet popular opinion at home was highly supportive of Chiang Kai-shek, especially by members of the "China Lobby," and the American military in the Far East war had no choice but to cooperate with him as best they could. Their job was made even more difficult because the British were very cool toward supporting Chiang, believing he was hardly a trustworthy ally and that a truly unified China under his leadership after the war would spell serious trouble for their Far Eastern imperial interests.

On the Far Eastern battlefields, American volunteers, members of the AVG (American Volunteer Group), or "Flying Tigers," under Colonel Claire L. Chennault, a retired air corps officer, had been fighting the Japanese since 1941. This group of men, numbering only in the dozens, had captured the imagination of the American people. They ran up an incredible success record of 1,200 kills and 700 probables in their obsolete P-40 Tomahawk fighters with shark's eyes and teeth painted on their noses by their superior hit-from-above-and-run air tactics against Japanese warplanes. The Flying Tigers had evoked considerable sympathy in the United States for the Chinese cause.

Yet whatever the successes of the Flying Tigers (who later became part of the Fourteenth Air Force) and whatever the lack of coordination between the Allies, the overwhelming fact was that in 1942 the Japanese swept through Burma and gave the Allies, in Stilwell's words, "a hell of a beating." The remainder of the war consisted of attempt after attempt to push the Japanese out of this British dependency and open a logistical supply route to China.

In late 1942 a British thrust into Arakan along the Indian border produced few results, with the British and imperial forces being driven out of the area by mid-1943. In the meantime, an offensive in February 1943 into the jungles of northern Burma by the eccentric British general Orde Wingate and his 3,000-man 77th Indian Infantry Brigade, or "Chindits," as he called them, also fell short of appreciable results. Burma was still firmly in Japanese hands, and getting aid to Chiang Kai-shek farther east in China was still very difficult.

The Allies were now unable to agree on the next move. The Americans wanted to conquer northern Burma to reopen the Burma Road from Lashio to Chungking. They also wanted to construct a second road into China from Ledo in northeast Burma and to recapture Rangoon and the railroad running north from it to Lashio. The British preferred to move against the East Indies as a springboard to recapturing Singapore rather than try to penetrate the jungles of Burma again. The Americans won out, and both Allies began to move in reinforcements for a new offensive in northern Burma.

In October 1943 Stilwell began an offensive toward the Irrawaddy River in south central Burma. It soon bogged down, and neither the efforts of General Frank Merrill's "Merrill's Marauders" nor those of Wingate's Chindits could bring anything other than limited success in the face of determined Japanese opposition. (Wingate died in an airplane accident in March 1944.) A second offensive at Arakan, under Lieutenant General William J. Slim's Fourteenth British Army, met with defeat in early 1944. In the meantime, the Fifteenth Japanese Army, under Lieutenant General Renya Mutaguchi, invaded India accompanied by a small "Indian National Army" pledged to throw the British out of India and establish a fascist-style unification government in their place. The Japanese-Indian National Army force moved toward Kohima and Imphal. The siege of these two cities lasted 88 days before the British, supplied by air drops, broke the encirclement on May 12, 1944, forcing the Japanese back into Burma and ruining the dreams of Subhas Chandra Bose, leader of the Indian National Army, to gain control of his homeland. Mutaguchi lost 50,000 of his 84,000 men in this failed invasion.

General Slim then launched an invasion in November 1944 with help from additional troops sent in by Admiral Lord Louis Mountbatten (a cousin of King George VI), supreme commander in Southeast Asia since the autumn of 1943. The invasion cleared central and southern Burma and culminated in the seizure of Rangoon in May 1945. In the meantime, Stilwell (then Wedemeyer after Stilwell had quarreled further with Chiang and was removed) launched a second offensive south from Myitkyina in October 1944. This offensive resulted in the capture of Lashio on March 7, 1945.

But the Allied control of the most crucial territories in Burma did not presage the end of the Far East land war because the Japanese had begun a major offensive in central China in mid-1944. By the end of that year they had gained a land link to Southeast

Asia and had reinforced their holdings in China. Thus in early 1945 the CBI war represented a continuing stalemate, with neither side having gained clear dominance. The war in this peripheral theater simply dragged on until the fall of Japan in August 1945.

THE AIR WAR ON JAPAN

The Fifth Air Force was born from a slap-dash grouping of all bomber and fighter squadrons available and flown to Australia in early 1942 to protect that country from invasion. When officially constituted in September 1942, it had only 80 bombers and 75 fighters operational. But by the end of the year the Fifth had established a base at Dobodura on New Guinea, and its B-17 and B-24 bombers were making raids on Rabaul. Throughout 1943 and 1944, as "MacArthur's Air Force," the Fifth, under General George C. Kenney, gave major support to MacArthur's many campaigns in New Guinea. By early 1944 it had 800-plus fighters, 780 bombers, and over 300 transports in its inventory, and by late 1944 it was on Leyte in the Philippines, where it played an active role in the Army's campaigns to rid the islands of the Japanese. Following the successful fortunes of the American drive on Japan, by mid-1945 it had moved on to Okinawa and to Ie Shima in the Bonin Islands and was preparing for Operation Olympic.

☆ An American Portrait

George C. Kenney—George Churchill Kenney, one of the most dynamic and innovative generals of World War II, was born in Nova Scotia in August 1889 but was reared in Brookline, Massachusetts. He attended the Massachusetts Institute of Technology from 1907 until 1910, studying civil engineering, but left before graduating to begin a successful career as an engineer.

In 1917 Kenney signed on as a flight cadet in the Aviation Section of the Signal Corps and was posted to France. There he flew 75 combat missions with the 19th Aero Squadron and won the Distinguished Service Cross and the Silver Star medals.

Between 1919 and 1933, while carrying out various air and engineering duties for the Army, Kenney attended the Army Air Corps Tactical School, the Command and General Staff School, and the Army War College. He was then moved to the staff of the chief of the Army Air Corps for two years before being appointed to various staff and command assignments between 1935 and 1940.

Early in World War II, Kenney was made commander of the Fourth Air Force, and in August 1942 he was assigned to General MacArthur's headquarters in Brisbane as commander of Allied Air Forces and commander of Fifth Air Force. As head of "MacArthur's Air Force" until June 1944, Kenney played a major role in aiding the Americans and Australians in New Guinea and the Southwest Pacific Command, demonstrating his knack for innovation by low-level, heavily gunned bomber runs on enemy targets, skip-bombing of ships, and the use of parachute bombs.

Advanced to general in 1945, Kenney headed the Pacific Air Command during 1945 and 1946, the Strategic Air Command from 1946 to 1948, and the Air University from 1948 until his retirement in 1951. In his retirement years Kenney wrote four books on the Pacific war. He died at Bar Harbor Islands, Florida, in August 1977.

FIGURE 10–4   B-29 Superfortress. (*Official U. S. Air Force Photographic Collection, National Air and Space Museum, Smithsonian Institution, Washington, D.C.*)

The Seventh Air Force, born of what was left of the Army's Hawaiian Air Force after Pearl Harbor, served in tandem with the Navy's carrier air forces in the drive across the Central Pacific. The Tenth and Fourteenth Air Forces served in the China-Burma-India theater by aiding the British and Chinese land forces there. The Thirteenth Air Force served in the Solomons campaign before joining with the Fifth Air Force in the Philippines.

Naval air in the Pacific also expanded at a remarkable rate. By mid-1943 fast carrier task forces made up of as many as 12 heavy and light carriers escorted by perhaps six battleships and dozens of cruisers and destroyers had been formed to carry the sea war to the enemy. These carriers, crammed with hundreds of planes such as the Grumman F6F "Hellcat" and Vought F4U "Corsair" fighters and Grumman TBF "Avenger" torpedo bombers, were the most formidable weapons in the Navy's arsenal and an indispensable ingredient in the amphibious warfare that marked the Pacific conflict. By 1944 the Navy had 30,000 planes available for the war effort.

Early in 1945 the XXI Bomber Command was created (to be made part of the Twelfth Air Force in July). Its mission was the bombing of Japan, now that bases were available for such a mission. Its commander was 39-year-old Major General Curtis LeMay, the outspoken youngest major general in the Air Forces. During the summer of 1945, some 1,000 B-29 Superfortresses flying out of the Marianas, Okinawa, and Iwo Jima were making almost daily area bombing raids on the cities of the Japanese home islands. They were assisted by carrier-based planes from the American and British navies. The most notable and fearsome accomplishments of the Twelfth Air Force were low-level nighttime raids on Japanese cities, dropping napalm incendiary bombs. On March 9, 1945, they staged a 334-plane fire bombing raid on Tokyo that created a firestorm of 1,800 degrees Fahrenheit, destroying 16 square miles of the city and killing 85,000 people. Firebombing raids on Nagoya, Osaka, Yokohama, and other cities followed, resulting in 260,000 deaths, 412,000 injuries, and the destruction of 40 percent of the built-up areas of the 61 Japanese cities bombed.

☆ An American Portrait

Curtis LeMay—Curtis Emerson LeMay, the architect of the Strategic Air Command, was born in Columbus, Ohio, on November 15, 1906. After graduation from high school, he entered Ohio State University to study civil engineering and distinguished himself as an ROTC student. He left college, however, to join the National Guard and became a pilot in October 1929. Assigned to the 27th Pursuit Squadron at Selfridge Field, Michigan, he completed his college degree, took part in the Army's CCC program, and participated in the Army's 1934 air mail operation.

After service in Hawaii, LeMay reported to Langley Field, Virginia, and the 305th Bombardment Group in 1937. He soon displayed keen innovative talents in air navigation techniques and airplanes, interception of ships at sea. By the time of America's entry into World War II, LeMay had attended the Air Corps Tactical School in Alabama and had assumed command of a bomb group. In 1942, now a lieutenant colonel, he led the 305th Bomb Group to England and again displayed his talents as an innovator by insisting on straight-in bombing and preraid target study. As commander of the 3rd Bombardment Division in 1943, LeMay personally led the famous attack on Regensburg in August.

By 1944 LeMay had been raised in rank to major general and had been sent to the China-Burma-India theater to command the XX Bomber Command. In January 1945 he was given command of the XXI Bomber Command on Guam and ordered to carry out B-29 bombing attacks on the Japanese home islands (in reality, area bombing, not strategic bombing, although no one would admit it). Again LeMay opted for innovative methods by stripping his planes of armament to enable them to carry heavier bomb loads and ordering single-plane, low-level attacks. Planes of LeMay's XXI Bomber Command carried out the frightfully effective incendiary attacks on Japanese cities beginning in March 1945 and dropped the atomic bombs on Hiroshima and Nagasaki on August 6 and 9.

FIGURE 10–5 Curtis E. Lemay. (*Naional Archives, Washington, D.C.*)

After the war LeMay served as commander of U.S. Air Forces in Europe, overseeing the critical Berlin airlift of 1948 and 1949, before being recalled by Air Force Chief of Staff Hoyt S. Vandenberg to rebuild SAC. Serving in this capacity for nine years, LeMay (after 1951 the youngest four-star general since Ulysses S. Grant) breathed new life into his command, moving up in 1961 to become chief of staff of the Air Force.

Before he retired in 1965, LeMay had had many notable quarrels with the Kennedy and Johnson administrations, and especially with Secretary of Defense Robert S. McNamara, over policy and strategy in general and the Vietnam War in particular. LeMay's disenchantment with national policy led him to accept the 1968 nomination for vice president of the American Independence party, led by Alabama Governor George Wallace. LeMay died at March Air Force Base Hospital in California in October, 1990.

The air war, along with the war on land and sea, was cut short when, on August 6, 1945, the *Enola Gay,* a XXI Bomber Command B-29, dropped a single atomic bomb weighing 9,000 pounds on Hiroshima, a city of 340,000 people on the southeastern coast of Honshu. The bomb's explosive power was equal to 20,000 tons of TNT. Perhaps as many as 100,000 Japanese died in the explosion. The Japanese government still refused to surrender, even after the Soviet Union declared war on August 8 and invaded Manchuria. The Japanese still had 2 million men under arms, including 7 regular and 7 reserve divisions and 10,500 operational aircraft, including 5,000 to be used in *Kamikaze* attacks. Therefore, on August 9, a second bomb was dropped on Nagasaki, a city of 250,000 on Kyushu's west coast. Some 35,000 people died. Also, the U.S. Air Forces and Navy since March had been carrying out Operation Starvation, in which over 12,000 mines were dropped in Japan's harbors and inner harbors. This brought industrial production to a halt, and severe food shortages were devastating the Japanese population.

The Japanese government did not know whether the United States had more atomic bombs in its arsenal. They were, however, aware that American submarines now made further sea-based war impossible. Some 288 submarines had sunk 1,150 Japanese merchant vessels and 276 warships by this time. (Of the 8.6 millions tons of the Japanese ocean-going maritime fleet, 54.7 percent—63 percent by number of ships—was sunk by submarines during the war.) And they knew that a massive invasion was about to be launched. In this situation, the Japanese government, after the highly unusual intervention of Emperor Hirohito, accepted the Allied surrender terms on August 14, 1945, V-J Day. Formal surrender documents were signed aboard the American battleship *Missouri* on September 2 in Tokyo Bay, not far from the spot where Commodore Perry had anchored 92 years before and opened Japan to the outside world.

World War II was finally over. Since 1939 the Soviet Union had lost well over 17.5 million military and civilian dead; China at least 5 million; Poland 5.3 million, including the 3 million Jews exterminated by Hitler; Germany 4.5 million; Yugoslavia 1.4 million; France, Britain, and Italy 400,000 each; and the United States 292,000. Total worldwide monetary costs, direct and indirect, were perhaps $4 trillion. The physical damage was inestimable.

During the war over 16.2 million Americans (one-sixth of the nation's men) served in the armed forces, 11.2 million in the Army, 4.1 million in the Navy, 669,000 in the Marine Corps, and 284,500 in the women's auxiliary corps. Approximately 10 million men aged 18 to 44 (later lowered to 38) were draftees, chosen from 36 million registered males. Of the females (all volunteers), over 150,000 served in the WACs (Women's Army Corps), over 100,000 in the Navy's WAVES (Women Appointed for Voluntary Service), over 22,000 in the Women Marines, and over 12,000 in the SPARS (from (s)emper (par)atus, the motto of the Coast Guard. It is also important to note that over 700,000 black troops served in the Army, 500,000 of them overseas, mostly in supply and construction units. Segregation was maintained, but two black divisions, individual platoon and rifle companies, and a fighter group saw action against the enemies of the United States and served well.

Of the 292,131 Americans who died in service, 234,874 were from the Army, 36,950 from the Navy, 19,733 from the Marine Corps, and 574 from the Coast Guard. This represented less than 2 percent of the men and women who served in uniform during the war.

During World War II, America's civilian and military work force of 75 million persons (including greater numbers of women than ever before) produced for American and Allied military use on the sea 1,200 combatant vessels, 2,600 cargo ships, 700 tankers, and 82,000 landing craft. For the air war, 96,000 bombers, 88,000 fighters, and 23,000 transport planes were turned out by the nation's factories. For the land war, 86,000 tanks, 2.4 million trucks and jeeps, 120,000 artillery pieces, and 14 million shoulder weapons were produced. Such prodigious feats of productivity were vivid proof of America's claim to be "the arsenal of democracy" and of Yamamoto's fear of the nation's wartime potential.

WORLD WAR II: WEAPONS AND TECHNOLOGY

As in no other conflict before it, technology and scientific discoveries had a major impact on the outcome of World War II. In most major countries involved in the war, science and the military worked hand in hand to match or exceed the level of each military break-through by the enemy. Aiding the scientists and the military were the research capabilities and facilities of the universities and the productive capacity of the nations' industries. The result was the creation not only of weapons by which to attain victory but also of products and processes that would change the world of war and peace forever.

For example, it was in World War II that the potential of the airplane for military use was fully realized. Every major combatant nation saw quantum leaps not only in the number of warplanes of all types rolling off its assembly lines but also in their tactical use. It was the first war in which long-range bombers could carry their lethal destructive power far behind the enemy's lines to destroy his homefront and his war-sustaining industries. In addition, high-speed fighters, dive bombers, and torpedo bombers were developed by the combatant nations for their warfare on both land and sea. And a glimpse into the future of airpower was provided when, in late 1944, the Germans began limited use of their 540-mile-per-hour jet-propelled Messerschmitt 262 (ME 262) in the European air war. Because of its short range and erratic performance, the ME 262 had no impact on the war, but it was a clear harbinger of air war to come.

Great strides in the use of radar were also taken during World War II. Ground radar to detect enemy aircraft had been developed prior to the war, and the British were greatly aided by this device (plus radio direction broadcasting to their airborne interceptors to guide them to incoming bombers) in the Battle of Britain. As the war went on, MEW (microwave early warning) made the system even better. Of equal importance, the development of centimetric radar with the cavity magnetion valve made radar units smaller and suitable for use in airplanes too. Consequently, there soon followed such important radar devices as H2S, which could create a radar map of terrain; ASW Mk III, which could ferret out a submarine running on the surface; OBOE, a radar system for blind bombing of targets through overcast skies; GEE, a three-station, very accurate navigation system; IFF, whereby a plane could be "identified friend or foe"; and MONICA, a radar unit that warned of the approach of an enemy plane. Radar was also used by the U.S. Navy in its antiaircraft activities through such devices as the Mark 37 fire director, placed aboard ships to complement the Mark 14 and M-9 gyroscopic lead-computing fire-control mechanisms. Asdic and sonar, of course, are underwater radio detection systems that produce visual images. These came into widespread use during the war.

In the war at sea, in addition to many new types of vessels developed for amphibious landings, World War II also saw the development and use of torpedoes employing pure oxygen under compression for propulsion that left virtually no wake, searchlights of incredible candlepower for use by airplanes against subs running on the surface at night; depth charges of Torpex (a very explosive mixture of TNT and RDX) for 50 percent more concussion efficiency; escort vessels equipped with "Hedgehog" depth charges that threw out a pattern of tear-shaped lethal charges to surround an enemy sub; sonobuoys equipped with hydrophones activated by submarine noises; and the German Schnorkel, a retractable air intake and exhaust pipe to allow faster diesel propulsion under water and submersion times measured in days.

On land, tanks with guns from 75 millimeters to 128 millimeters in caliber and sloped armor of 80 millimeters to 150 millimeters in thickness came into use, along with improved tracks, engines, horsepower, stabilizers, durability, and radio communication equipment for armored fighting vehicles. And short-range, rocket-propelled missiles with hollow-charge warheads fired from hand-held bazookas were designed to stop these ever more powerful AFVs.

In the air war, incendiary bombs of napalm with an aluminum naphthenate base were developed and used in the war against Japan. Napalm was also used as an unquenchable incendiary weapon in either hand-held or tank-mounted flame throwers in both theaters of war. And it was the scientists working with military and political leaders who produced the atomic bomb. The development of this weapon was begun in 1943. The success of the scientists' diligence became clear in the cataclysmic explosions over Hiroshima and Nagasaki in August 1945.

It was also the air war that saw the Germans produce the V-1 pilotless, jet-propelled flying bomb guided by a gyroscopic automatic pilot that terrorized England in the latter stages of the war. With a 1-ton explosive warhead, an airspeed of 350 to 400 miles per hour, and a 160-mile range, over 8,000 of these low-altitude V-1s were fired against the English populace. With their low speed and low altitude, however, V-1s could be shot down by antiaircraft fire or swift airplanes.

The successor V-2s, however, were impossible to defend against. They were propelled to an altitude of 50 to 60 miles and then dropped toward their targets at a velocity of 2,200 to 2,500 miles per hour. These characteristics explain the frenzy of the British military to capture the German missile sites east of the English Channel in France and Holland in 1944 and 1945 as a matter of basic defensive necessity. While the V-1s and V-2s were never produced or fired in sufficient numbers to make an appreciable difference on the outcome of the war, they were the prototype of the more accurate, more powerful, and longer-ranged missiles that would mark the world military scene for decades to come.

Similarly, the guided missiles developed by the Germans but never put into production also provided a preview of weapons of the future. These included the Wasserfall surface-to-air radio-controlled missile, with a speed of 1,700 miles per hour and a range of over 16 miles, and the Ruhrstahl X-4 air-to-air missile of 520 miles per hour controlled by electric signals, the forebears of today's wire-guided missiles and torpedoes.

When cryptographic breakthroughs are added in—such as the high-speed Bombe computer used by the British Ultra organization to read the German Enigma signals; the even faster Colossus II programmable electronic digital computer introduced in 1944, which gave instant decrypts of German encoded teleprinter messages; and the Americans' Magic deciphering machine, which broke the Japanese Purple code even before the war began—it becomes obvious that World War II was important not only in deciding the fate of a large part of the world's population. It was also significant in that it brought into close cooperation the scientist and the warrior for the purpose of applying technology to war. In science and military technology, as in the political and economic affairs of nations, World War II opened a new era in the history of mankind, an era of frightening possibilities for human and material destruction.

Suggestions for Further Reading

BLAIR, CLAY, JR., *Silent Victory: The U.S. Submarine War Against Japan*. Philadelphia: Lippincott, 1975.

BUELL, THOMAS B., *The Quiet Warrior: A Biography of Admiral Raymond A. Spruance*. Boston: Little, Brown, 1974.

COFFEY, THOMAS M., *Iron Eagle: The Turbulent Life of General Curtis LeMay*. New York: Crown, 1986.

DAVIS, BURKE, *Marine! The Life of Lt. Gen. Lewis B. "Chesty" Puller, USMC*. Boston: Little, Brown, 1962.

DOWER, JOHN W., *War without Mercy: Race and Power in the Pacific War*. New York: Pantheon, 1986.

DULL, PAUL S., *A Battle History of the Imperial Japanese Navy (1941–1945)*. Annapolis: Naval Institute Press, 1958.

GRIFFITH, SAMUEL B., *The Battle for Guadalcanal*. Philadelphia: Lippincott, 1963.

HIROYUKI, AGAWA, *The Reluctant Admiral: Yamamoto and the Imperial Navy*. Tokyo: Kodansha International, 1979.

HOYT, EDWIN P., *The Battle for Leyte Gulf: The Death Knell of the Japanese Fleet*. New York: Weybright & Talley, 1972.

JAMES, D. CLAYTON, *The Years of MacArthur,* vol. 2, *1941–1945*. Boston: Houghton Mifflin, 1975.

LAYTON, EDWIN T., with ROGER PENEAU and JOHN COSTELLO, *"And I Was There" : Pearl Harbor and Midway—Breaking the Secrets*. New York: 1985.

LEARY, WILLIAM M., ed., *We Shall Return! MacArthur's Commanders and the Defeat of Japan*. Lexington: University Press of Kentucky, 1988.

MANCHESTER, WILLIAM, *American Caesar: Douglas MacArthur, 1880–1964*. Boston: Little, Brown, 1978.

MERILLAT, HERBERT C., *Guadalcanal Remembered*. New York: Dodd, Mead, 1982.

MORISON, SAMUEL ELIOT, *The Two-Ocean Navy: A Short History of the United States Navy in the Second World War*. Boston: Little, Brown, 1963.

NALTY, BERNARD C., *Strength for the Fight: A History of Black Americans in the Military*. New York: Free Press, 1989.

POTTER, E. B., *Bull Halsey*. Annapolis: Naval Institute Press, 1985.

———, *Nimitz*. Annapolis: Naval Institute Press, 1985.

PRANGE, GORDON W., with DONALD W. GOLDSTEIN and KATHERINE V. DILLON, *At Dawn We Slept: The Untold Story of Pearl Harbor*. New York: McGraw-Hill, 1981.

———, *Miracle at Midway*. New York: McGraw-Hill, 1982.

REYNOLDS, CLARK G., *The Fast Carriers: The Forging of an Air Navy*. New York: McGraw-Hill, 1968.

ROSS, BILL D., *Iwo Jima: Legacy of Valor*. New York: Vanguard, 1985.

SPECTOR, RONALD H., *Eagle Against the Sun: The American War with Japan*. New York: Free Press, 1985.

STEPHAN, JOHN J., *Hawaii Under the Rising Sun: Japan's Plans for Conquest After Pearl Harbor*. Honolulu: University of Hawaii Press, 1984.

TUCHMAN, BARBARA, *Stilwell and the American Experience in China, 1911–1945*. New York: Macmillan, 1971.

WEDEMEYER, ALBERT C., *Wedemeyer Reports*. New York: Henry Holt, 1958.

WHEELER, RICHARD, *A Special Valor: The U.S. Marines and the Pacific War*. New York: Harper & Row, Pub. 1983.

WILLMOTT, H. P., *The Barrier and the Javelin: Japanese and Allied Pacific Strategies, February to June 1942*. Annapolis: Naval Institute Press, 1983.

———, *Empires in the Balance: Japanese and Allied Pacific Strategies to April 1942*. Annapolis: Naval Institute Press, 1982.

WINSLOW, W. G., *The Fleet the Gods Forgot: The U.S. Asiatic Fleet in World War II*. Annapolis: Naval Institute Press, 1982.

WOODWARD, C. VANN, *The Battle for Leyte Gulf*. New York: Macmillan, 1947.

Y'BLOOD, WILLIAM T., *Red Sun Setting: The Battle of the Philippine Sea*. Annapolis: Naval Institute Press, 1981.

Cold War
and Korea,
1945–1960

The euphoria of victory was irresistible in August 1945. The two great aggressor nations of Germany and Japan had been defeated and lay prostrate at the Allies' feet. The reactionary forces of German fascism and Japanese militarism had fallen to the forces of freedom. In the process of attaining this great victory, a cooperative bond had been forged among the Allies, a bond to be made permanent in the United Nations, created by 46 states on June 26, 1945. This was to be an assembly of free peoples where reason and discussion would hold sway and where international conflicts would be settled without recourse to bloodletting such as the world had just endured.

Such was the dream. Such was not to be the reality. Hidden just beneath the surface of the Allies' wartime veneer of cooperation and mutual support against common enemies were areas of fundamental conflict and mistrust between the Western democracies and the Soviet Union. On the questions of political philosophies, basic human rights, and, indeed, the very future of mankind, the two sides were in fundamental disagreement. Barely submerged during the war yet clearly visible to the discerning eye, these differences soon surfaced as the exhilaration of wartime victories faded and the triumphant nations got down to the equally serious business of living together in peace.

Before a half decade had passed, the last vestiges of wartime cooperation had vanished, an "iron curtain" had been dropped separating eastern and western Europe, a Communist faction had gained control in China, and the United States found itself in a new type of international conflict called the cold war. This contest of wills and resources would test the nation and its military forces in new and demanding ways for the next 4 1/2 decades, force them into unfamiliar confrontational modes, and demand sacrifices of a type for which there were no precedents.

The American people longed for peace after World War II. They found only continued conflict. The United States found itself, without any desire or design on its part, in the position of leader of the Western democracies and peacekeeper of the world. The burdens of this position proved to be heavy and often perplexing and divisive, but America's citizens sensed that they could not put these burdens down. Like the great "hot" war of 1941 through 1945, the "cold" war that followed proved to be a time of testing of purpose, strength, and will for the American nation.

DEMOBILIZATION AND INTERSERVICE RIVALRIES

Reflecting its usual distrust of ambiguity, the American public after the attack on Pearl Harbor went all out to win its war against the Axis powers. When the hostilities were over, however, this same lack of ambiguity, which demanded either war or peace, surfaced again. It took the form of widespread demands to "bring the boys home" and get back to the business of peace.

The military service chiefs were willing to discharge their men and women as fast as possible, but they realized that occupation duties and other worldwide responsibilities demanded that a considerable number of troops be retained in uniform. Just providing transportation back to the United States was bound to cause some delays. Nevertheless, in an effort to be fair, the Army devised a system of discharge that released the overseas veterans who had seen the most combat first. The plan met with widespread approval, but public pressure demanded that all uniformed personnel desiring separation be released on an accelerated schedule. Accordingly, the system was temporarily speeded up, and by the end of 1945 half of the 8 million troops still in the Army had been discharged.

Even this was not enough. In early 1946 the Army was again forced to expedite its discharges when protests and demonstrations by disgruntled soldiers eager to get home broke out overseas. By mid-year another 25 percent had been released. By 1947, only 680,000 ground troops and 300,000 airmen remained in uniform, a far cry from the 4 million men desired by the Army for postwar duties. By 1950 this number stood at only 591,000, and the Army reserves and National Guard numbered only 186,000 and 325,000 respectively, these in underequipped and undertrained units.

The Navy, too, carried out rapid demobilization in the face of public demands for quick discharges, in addition to President Harry Truman's and Congress' determination to slash spending. The Navy's protests that the nation's new worldwide commitments and basic maintenance of equipment demanded larger force levels and more money fell on deaf ears. By 1947, the Navy's budget stood at only $14.5 billion, down from $45 billion the year before. Thereafter it continued to fall. By 1950 active duty naval rolls showed only 375,000 officers and men, down 90 percent from their wartime high. The Marine Corps suffered the same fate. Within one year from the end of hostilities, three divisions had been disbanded, and the number of men and women in the Corps had dropped from 485,000 to 156,000. By 1947 the total number of Marine Corps personnel had been slashed to 92,000, and by 1950 it stood at less than 75,000 officers and enlisted men.

During these postwar years the leaders of the services were forced to spend much of their time arguing before Congress against continued cuts in men and allocations. They also expended considerable energy arguing among themselves and before public bodies over plans for military reorganization. The Army contended that it should be the nation's only land force. It could and should take over the marines' specialty of amphibious landings—if such were ever needed again in view of the nation's supply of atomic bombs. Atomic weapons, they argued, made such landings unnecessary because the threat of atomic destruction would be enough to persuade any aggressor to desist in his actions. At the same time, the Army Air Forces wanted its independence as a separate and equal service branch. It also sought to have control over all military air operations. This would remove Navy and Marine land-based and sea-based air power from those services entirely. The Navy would lose 30 percent of its men and materiel, and it would be left with only the seaborne duties of surface and subsurface combat and convoy escort. The Marines would lose their air wings and be reduced to minor security duties.

The Army brass seemed reluctantly willing to let their air contingents become independent, in part because they feared that the air element might take over if it were not let go. On the other hand, in a land combat situation, where its commanders would have no direct authority over their supporting air cover, they envisioned problems of command and control that would be bound to arise. In reply, the overconfident Air Forces generals argued that with their power to deliver "the bomb," the other services would properly assume a secondary role anyway. Air power alone would quickly and easily win any future war, and the Navy at this time could not deliver atomic weapons. Some even asked if a navy was necessary in America's military future since the Soviet Union had no naval power to speak of.

The Navy retorted that sea control was still vital to the nation's defenses and that naval air power (including nuclear weaponry) was necessary to carry out its vital seaborne missions. Land-based air power, naval officers argued, lacked the flexibility inherent in the Navy's carrier forces to deliver atomic and subatomic force wherever needed across the broad spectrum of choices found in confrontational situations.

As the military services wrangled over their respective roles in the nation's defense network, wheels were also turning in congressional circles in Washington. The lawmakers wanted to ensure better coordination of the nation's military efforts in order to ensure greater efficiency and save money. The result was the National Security Act of 1947. This act did not unify the services, but it did create the U.S. Air Force as a separate and co-equal branch of the armed forces. However, the new Air Force did not absorb the Navy and Marine air units. Nor did the act do away with the Marine Corps, which remained a subbranch of the Navy.

The National Security Act of 1947 also created the National Security Council (NSC), consisting of the secretary of state, the secretary of defense (a new position with cabinet rank), the secretaries of the three services (now at subcabinet rank), and the heads of other agencies as appointed by the president. The NSC was to advise the president and coordinate and integrate all national security policies.

The act also created a second body known as the National Security Establishment (NSE). Headed by the secretary of defense and made up of the civilian secretaries of the Army, Navy, and Air Force, the NSE was intended to direct the three service branches. The secretary of defense, in turn, was to be advised on policy by the Joint Chiefs of Staff (JCS), one from each of the three services. The JCS were also to advise the president on military matters. Thus the three services were to be executive departments with their own secretaries under a supervising and coordinating secretary of defense, the service chiefs recommending policy to the secretary of defense and the president, and the NSC securing cooperation with the nonmilitary executive departments of the government.

One glaring weakness in this setup soon became obvious: The secretary of defense had little power to enforce cooperation and coordination on the services because the service secretaries had large staffs and direct access to the president through both the NSC and informal channels. They were not loath to use these means of access, thus bypassing the secretary of defense if they so chose.

Accordingly, the National Security Amendment of 1949 was passed. This converted the National Military Establishment into the Department of Defense (DOD) as an executive department, with the secretary of defense holding full cabinet rank and the three service secretaries clearly subordinate to him and heading military, not executive, departments. They were now without cabinet rank and had no seats on the NSC. The Joint Chiefs of Staff, with one additional member, a chairman without a vote but *de facto* the president's military advisor, were still retained in an advisory and coordinating role (the commandant of the Marine Corps was added in 1952).

The lines of responsibility were now clear, at least in theory: the president as commander-in-chief was on top; the cabinet-level secretary of defense was below him; the secretaries of the Army, Navy, and Air Force were one step down; and below them were the three individual chiefs of staff. The acts of 1947 and 1949 still left some amorphous relationships at the highest command levels, but the American military services were now clearly placed under a single controlling cabinet-level civilian secretary of defense by these administrative changes.

These reorganization acts, however, did not bury the question of interservice rivalries, as the policy makers had hoped they would. In 1949 James V. Forrestal, former secretary of the Navy and the first secretary of defense, suffered a nervous breakdown and resigned his office. To replace him, President Truman appointed Louis A. Johnson, a blustery West Virginia lawyer-politician with presidential ambitions. Johnson, among other things, was decidedly pro–Air Force, a sentiment not shared by Secretary of the Navy John L. Sullivan. Sullivan believed that relying on the B-36 bomber with atomic payloads as the primary response weapon in America's arsenal was foolhardy. Sullivan accordingly approved the construction of the 65,000-ton supercarrier *United States* in April 1949. She was intended to be a giant multiple-mission vessel capable of launching and recovering nuclear-capable airplanes, giving the Navy a clear strategic function in the years ahead.

Five days after the keel for the *United States* was laid, Johnson, without consulting Sullivan, cancelled the contract for its construction. He also reduced the number of active carriers from 8 to 4 and air groups from 14 to 6. He was determined to merge the Navy's and the Marines' air arms with the Air Force to save money and attain "real unification." By his cancellation of the carrier contract and these other Draconian steps he was deliberately throwing down the gauntlet to the Navy.

In the ensuing hearings before the House Armed Services Committee, chaired by Georgia's Carl Vinson, an old friend and supporter of the Navy, the Navy's top brass, active and retired (including Admirals King, Nimitz, Halsey, and Spruance), launched spirited attacks on Johnson's and the Air Force's contention that atomic bombs and the B-36 were adequate to ensure the nation's security. In this "revolt of the admirals," they also attacked Johnson personally for his financial ties to the builders of the B-36. The new naval secretary, Francis P. Matthews, a Nebraska banker who had no background in naval affairs but who was appointed by Truman when John L. Sullivan resigned in protest over Johnson's cancelling the carrier contract, stood by Johnson and fired Admiral Louis E. Denfield as chief of naval operations for siding with his naval colleagues.

The whole unseemly affair ended when, while the hearings were in session, the Soviets exploded an atomic device. This made it clear that America's monopoly on the atomic bomb was gone. Henceforth use of atomic weapons by the United States would invite atomic retaliation. The Air Force's major trump card of atomic destruction was now rendered far less imposing, thanks to the new realities of international power. Less-than-atomic force was still needed now that the American atomic monopoly had been broken, and subatomic military power could not be furnished by the Air Force alone. The nation would need the Army, Navy, Marines, and Air Force, each with its own special missions and capabilities, it would seem, to serve the nation's defense needs.

In the long run, the "revolt of the admirals" served the nation well. It forced the policy makers in Washington and the service branches to scrutinize carefully the nation's varied defense needs and come to some well-considered conclusions regarding proper responses to a wide variety of military situations. And unity and coordination had been achieved—at least partially and perhaps sufficiently—at the highest levels. Aiding in this process of necessary reappraisal and, indeed, forcing its pace were a series of events in Europe that clearly indicated that confrontation with the followers of Marx and Lenin was destined to be the emerging political and military reality in the postwar world.

EUROPEAN CONFRONTATIONS AND COMMITMENTS

Even while World War II was being fought to its successful conclusion, there were signs that the Soviets were more interested in furthering their own national and ideological goals than in making certain that the Four Freedoms announced by Roosevelt and Churchill off Newfoundland in August 1941 would become the legacy of the peoples of all nations. Soviet attitudes at the wartime summit conferences, especially at Teheran in November and December of 1943 and at Yalta in February of 1945, gave clear indications that hegemony over eastern Europe was one goal that the Soviets were seeking. Winston Churchill was persistently suspicious of Soviet intentions and tried to ensure at least a *quid pro quo* for any gains they might make, but President Roosevelt naively believed that Soviet contacts and cooperation with the West would change their expansionist attitudes.

Stalin was thus able to persuade Roosevelt to acquiesce in loosely worded agreements subject to wide interpretation that allowed the Soviets *de facto* control over eastern Europe. Only in his last weeks of life in early 1945 did Roosevelt realize that his efforts to convert the Soviets and Stalin to Western ideas had been in vain, but by that time it was too late. Western signatures had been affixed to agreements that would allow governments "friendly" to the Soviet Union to rule in eastern Europe, and Soviet troops had already seized much of the territory under dispute. Trouble was not long in coming between the Soviets and their wartime allies.

According to the terms agreed to at the Yalta and Potsdam Conferences of 1945, Germany and its capital, Berlin, located in the Soviet zone of occupation, were to be divided into occupation zones by the four major powers. The British, French, and American zones were soon unified for administrative purposes, and a German government under Allied tutelage was on its way to being established in western Germany. But in eastern Germany the story was different. The Soviets not only obstructed all attempts to unify Germany but also set up a nondemocratic communist government in the eastern sector that was little more than a puppet state backed by Soviet military power.

In Poland the Soviets refused to permit the people to choose an independent government embracing all political parties, as provided for in the Yalta agreements. A Soviet-dominated communist government was organized and recognized instead. The story was the same in all of eastern Europe as country after country, occupied by Soviet troops, was denied free choice and was coerced into becoming a satellite of the Soviet Union. A saddened Winston Churchill, turned out of office by an ungrateful British public, who preferred the Labour party's promises of socialistic egalitarianism at home to Churchill's realism, well encapsulated what was happening in Europe. In a speech at Fulton, Missouri, in 1946, he warned that an "iron curtain" was being drawn across Europe by the Soviets "from Stettin in the Baltic to Trieste in the Adriatic."

The American reaction to the broken Soviet promises and clear signs of expansionism via military force or through the communist parties of western Europe took the form of "containment." Under this foreign policy, communism would no longer be allowed to spread by surreptitiously undermining free governments or by outright aggression. America would not attempt to free any peoples under communist domination, but Marxism would be stopped where it was. Then, the policy implied, time and communism's own internal contradictions and denial of freedom would eventually lead to its downfall. The idea of containment was spelled out by the diplomat George Kennan, head of the State Department's Policy Planning Staff, early in 1947 and soon became accepted American policy.

This emerging policy of containment was put to the test that same year in Greece and the Middle East, where the Soviets had been attempting to bring Greece and Turkey into their orbit by aiding pro-communist factions during civil wars in those countries. To foil their plans, Congress, at the urging of Truman, extended $400 million in aid to Greece and Turkey as part of what soon came to be known as the "Truman Doctrine" (the decision that the United States would aid countries fighting communist incursions). The next year the same principle was applied to Europe in the form of the Marshall Plan (named after its chief sponsor, Secretary of State George C. Marshall), which extended $16 billion in economic aid to European countries desperate to rebuild after the war. This aid was intended to blunt domestic and foreign communist blandishments. The governments of western Europe eagerly accepted this aid. Moscow refused to participate and forced its satellites to do likewise.

The East–West division of Europe took another giant step in early 1948, when the Soviet Union staged a coup and overthrew the government of Czechoslovakia to replace it with a communist-dominated one more to its liking. One month later it began to close off Berlin to the outside world. The latter action eventuated in the 11-month Berlin Airlift.

After preliminary harassing moves to sidetrack Allied steps to constitute a West German government and to force the British, French, and Americans to evacuate the German capital, located deep within eastern Germany, the Soviets on June 24, 1948, stopped all road, rail, and barge traffic into the city.

The American response was initially tentative. Truman did not even convene the National Security Council or consult with the Joint Chiefs of Staff. Ninety B-29s were sent to England as a show of American force and concern, but these were probably not atomic-armed. (Atomic cores were under the control of the Atomic Energy Commission, not the military, at this time.) Whether the planes were atomic-armed or not, the Soviets were not bluffed and did not lift the blockade. General Lucius D. Clay, the military governor in Germany, had initially called for breaking through the blockade with armed trains, but he subsequently backed off from this aggressive position.

Instead, Clay asked General Curtis LeMay, the Air Force commander in Europe, whether his transports could at least ferry coal into the city. LeMay replied in typical fashion that his planes could deliver anything to Berlin. But the Air Force commandant, General Hoyt S. Vandenberg, and the Joint Chiefs (belatedly consulted) worried over an extended airlift and the effect it would have on the Air Force's ability to carry out its other missions around the world.

American and British leaders finally arrived at a decision to supply Berlin with coal and food. Between June 1948 and May 1949, when the Russians lifted the blockade, the Air Force, with minor British aid, transported 2.5 million tons of cargo into Berlin in more than 275,000 flights involving 300 American and British cargo planes. They landed in the German capital, on the average of three-minute intervals, around the clock. The operation was carried out under the direction of Major General William H. Tunner, who had directed the flights "over the Hump" into China during World War II. Over 5,600 tons of supplies entered Berlin every day while the operation was at its peak. The successful Berlin airlift was a great psychological victory for the Western democracies, but it further poisoned relations between those nations and the Soviets. In the meantime, the Western democracies were already moving toward a collective military alliance to fend off Soviet expansionism.

In 1947 representatives of the United States and 21 Latin American republics had signed in Rio de Janiero the Inter-American Treaty of Reciprocal Assistance (the Rio Pact) to resist any aggression in the Western Hemisphere. Then, in 1948, the United States and five western European democracies had entered into a defensive military alliance in the Brussels Treaty. In April 1949 this blossomed into the North Atlantic Treaty Alliance. The terms of this alliance created the North Atlantic Treaty Organization (NATO), wherein the United States and Canada joined ten European democracies (Great Britain, France, the Netherlands, Luxembourg, Belgium, Iceland, Denmark, Norway, Portugal, and Italy) in a pledge of mutual support on land, sea, or air in the event that any signatory nation was attacked. The expected aggressor was the Soviet Union. Six months later Congress provided $1.3 billion in military aid to NATO countries in the National Defense Assistance Act. At the same time, the United States was also providing military equipment and training advisors to Greece, Turkey, and Iran in the Middle East; to Korea, China, and the Philippines in the Far East; and to various Latin American countries.

By 1950, then, the United States and the Soviet Union had become the effective heads of two blocks of nations eyeing one another suspiciously across central Europe, the Middle East, and the Far East. America's policy of containment had hardened into formal alliances designed to stop the spread of communism. These Western moves were matched by similar moves by the Soviet Union within the communist bloc of nations.

This did not mean, however, that the two superpowers met on equal military terms. While the Russians in 1950 had an army of over 2.5 million men trained and equipped to carry out its nation's policies, especially in Europe, the American army was down to only 640,000 men, thanks to the nation's policy of maintaining only a small military establishment. And with the Soviets having demonstrated the year before their ability to produce atomic weapons, ending America's monopoly on the ultimate offensive and defensive weapons, the military leaders in the United States, if not their civilian counterparts, realized that a giant gap existed between their constitutional duty to protect and defend America's interests and their ability to carry out that duty in the many areas of the world now covered by American commitments. This was as obvious in the Far East as it was in Europe.

THE "LOSS" OF CHINA AND THE KOREAN WAR

The United States had long held a special interest in China. This concern extended back into the nineteenth century to efforts of Christian missionaries to "civilize and Christianize" that populous Asiatic country. Secretary of State John Hay's Open Door policy at the turn of the century had been an overt attempt to prevent the dismemberment and exploitation of China. American interest had not flagged in the decades thereafter as the American people witnessed the rise to power of Sun Yat-sen and the Kuomintang party, the competition and civil war between the Chinese Communists led by Mao Tse-tung and the Kuomintang under Chiang Kai-shek in the 1920s and 1930s, and the renewed civil war between the Communists and the Kuomintang "Nationalists" after World War II.

The activities of the pro-Chiang "China Lobby" in the United States added to pressure on the American government to ensure a "democratic," non-Communist government in China, especially in view of the fact that the Soviets had apparently turned Manchuria over to Mao and were supporting his bid to wrest control of China from Chiang and the Kuomintang.

The problem was that neither Mao nor Chiang would accept anything less than the complete defeat of the other. And Chiang would undoubtedly not be able to win the civil war without direct American aid. General George Marshall, upon his retirement from the Army, agreed to go to China in late 1945 at the behest of President Truman to try to work out a solution, but his year-long efforts were in vain. The China situation would admit of no outside solution, although it appeared that the Communists and Mao might well be winning.

The denouement came in late 1949 when the Chinese Communists not only seized control of the country but also forced Chiang Kai-shek and his followers to seek refuge off the China coast on the island of Taiwan (Formosa). This was followed in early 1950 by a mutual assistance treaty between Mao's newly proclaimed People's Republic of China and the Soviet Union.

This "loss" or "fall" of China to communism by the free world—a charge of dereliction based on the dubious assumption that China might somehow have been "saved" from the communists by the actions of the United States—led to severe recriminations at home against those who had "allowed this to happen." Amplifying these recriminations was a general uneasiness over communist gains and aggressions in Europe and elsewhere since World War II and an increasing paranoia over the idea that communists or "fellow travelers" were operating within the highest levels of government in Washington. The combination of these sentiments created among a great number of American people and the lawmakers who represented them a mood of determination to enforce containment by military action if necessary, thereby to halt the flow of communist victories.

At that moment, on June 25, 1950, the North Koreans launched an invasion of South Korea. The cold war turned hot, interservice squabbling was suspended, the weakness of the American military became obvious in the weeks that followed, and the nation—not without subsequent second thoughts—took up arms to defend a friendly nation halfway around the world.

With the collapse of Japanese control in Korea in 1945, a line had been drawn across the peninsula by the Allies at the Thirty-eighth Parallel, with the Soviets disarming the Japanese and establishing control north of that line and the Americans doing the same to the south. This arbitrary delineation soon became permanent as the Soviets established a communist regime called the Democratic People's Republic under a Russian-trained Korean, Kim Il Sung, and the Americans and United Nations recognizing a free government called the Republic of Korea under nationalist Syngman Rhee, elected under United States–United Nations supervised elections. For two years thereafter the North Koreans had carried out minor insurgency operations against South Korea, but American intelligence sources expected no escalation of the conflict. The last American troops were withdrawn from South Korea in June 1949.

Perhaps misreading American willingness to defend South Korea since Secretary of State Dean Acheson in January 1950, in delineating America's defense line in Asia, did not include Korea and Taiwan (although he did say that the United Nations would be supported in resisting any aggressive moves against either of them), the North Koreans made their move, evidently with the backing of their Soviet supporters. The Soviets, too, apparently did not expect a United Nations reaction since they had walked out of the Security Council in January over the seating of Nationalist China instead of Communist China and thus would not be present to veto any United Nations military reaction to the invasion.

As thousands of North Korean soldiers of that nation's 135,000-man army swept across the Thirty-eighth Parallel, aided by Soviet-built T-34 tanks, they brushed aside all opposition. To attempt to stop them, South Korea had only 95,000 ill-trained and lightly equipped men in its army, which was not much more than a police force. The South Korean capital of Seoul, only 35 miles below the border near the western coast of the peninsula, fell to the invaders within three days, and parallel attacks down the center and along the eastern coast of the country were equally successful. The South Korean army was soon falling back in disarray.

In the meantime, President Truman had taken three important steps. First, he had the matter of the invasion taken before the United Nations, where the North Korean incursion was officially condemned and military action was authorized to resist it. Second, he took steps to defend South Korea. On the very day of the invasion he ordered General Douglas MacArthur, the American Far East commander in Tokyo, to supply the Republic of Korea (ROK) forces with any available war materiel and to consider the best means of

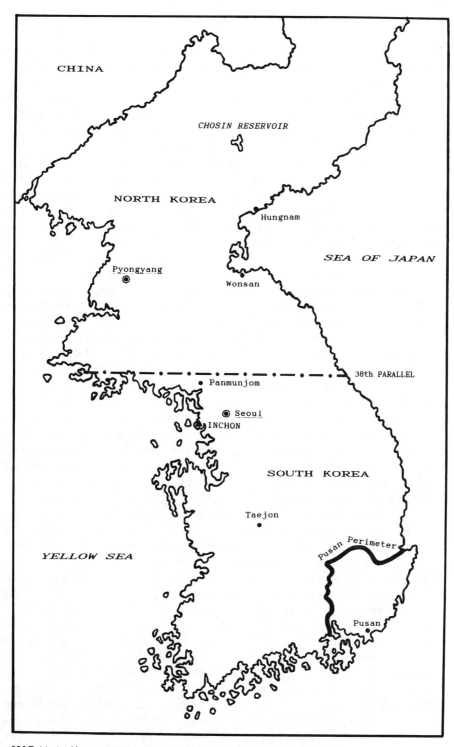

MAP 11-1 Korea, 1950–1953.(*Used with permission of Anne C. Christensen.*)

further aid. The next day he authorized MacArthur to use United States naval and air units below the Thirty-eighth Parallel to aid the ROK forces. And on June 27 he approved the use of American land forces in Korea. By June 30 MacArthur had been authorized to use all forces available to repel the invaders and to save the port of Pusan in the south. Third, Truman had ordered the Seventh Fleet to the waters off Taiwan to prevent either Mao's Communists or Chiang's Nationalists from using the Korean fighting as a pretext to resume their warfare, thus widening the conflict. The United States had now been forced into a shooting war in support of containment, and the United Nations for the first time was using military force to resist aggression. The first phase of the Korean War had begun.

MacArthur's Eighth Army in Japan contained one armored unit (1st Cavalry) and three infantry divisions (7th, 24th, and 25th), but they were woefully understrength and sadly underequipped. His Far East Air Force (FEAF) consisted of short-range jet defensive interceptors designed for air-to-air combat, not for close air support of ground troops. His available naval units were few in number, although the Seventh Fleet was nearby.

With Lieutenant General Walton H. Walker in command of Eighth Army (with ROK elements attached), American troops began arriving in South Korea. But the American and ROK troops could only slow the North Korean People's Army (NKPA) invaders; they could not stop them. Defensive lines of armor, artillery, and infantry were thrown up at key points in the mountainous South Korean terrain, but the NKPA armored and infantry units pushed around and through them, forcing further retreats until it was obvious that the crucial port of Pusan, the last major holding point in the south, was about to be encircled.

By early August, Walker's forces had taken 76,000 casualties (70,000 South Korean, 6,000 American) and were dug in behind the 140-mile "Pusan Perimeter," but, on the positive side, FEAF had gained air superiority over the North Koreans, and Naval Forces, Far East (consisting of U.S. naval units plus ships of other nations), had retained absolute control of the waters around Korea. The United Nations land position in South Korea was still perilous, but MacArthur, now designated United Nations commander over the troops of 21 nations aiding the United States either then or later by furnishing combat units, medical teams, and supplies, was nonplussed over the situation. The enemy had suffered over 58,000 casualties, had no control of the air and sea, had long and tenuous supply lines, and had lost much of his equipment. Walker, in the meantime, was parrying the enemy's uncoordinated thrusts and gaining men and materiel daily. Besides, MacArthur had his staff working on an offensive plan first conceived in the early and darkest days of the war. It was now about to be executed. The second phase of the Korean War was about to begin.

MacArthur's plan, destined to become the greatest strategic victory in his long career, envisioned a grand envelopment to trap the whole NKPA in South Korea. He would launch an amphibious assault at Inchon on the Yellow Sea just 25 miles west of Seoul and recapture the South Korean capital, giving him control of the major rail lines and highways leading through it to the south. This would leave the North Korean invaders with no escape route except through the mountains to the east. X Corps, under Major General Edward M. Almond, was assembled from the 7th Infantry Division, the 1st Marine Division, and 9,000 ROK troops to carry out the Inchon landing and seize Seoul. In the meantime, according to the plan, the reinforced Eighth Army at Pusan was to break out of its perimeter, thus trapping the North Koreans between it and X Corps and destroying them in a giant double envelopment.

MacArthur's plan was both brilliant and dangerous. Inchon could be approached only through mile-wide mud flats, and the tides rose 30 feet in those waters. A low or falling tide would leave his ships stranded in the mud, and resupply could be carried out only on the high tide, every 12 hours. Furthermore, the defenses on the island of Wolmi-Do at the harbor entrance had to be taken out, and the assaulting infantry would have to scale a high seawall to gain access to the city. Most of MacArthur's military colleagues opposed the invasion, some giving it a 500-to-1 chance of success. But the flamboyant general was given the green light by Truman and the Joint Chiefs, and the landings were scheduled for September 15, 1950.

☆   An American Portrait

Lewis B. "Chesty" Puller—Born at West Point, Virginia, on June 26, 1898, of an old and distinguished Virginia family, Lewis Burwell Puller attended the Virginia Military Institute in 1917 and 1918 before joining the Marine Corps. After World War I, during which Puller helped train recruits at Parris Island, South Carolina, he was commissioned a reserve second lieutenant but chose to return to his enlisted rank of corporal in the postwar cutbacks rather than leave the Corps.

After five years' service as an officer of the *Gendarmerie d'Haiti* during the marines' control of that nation, Puller in 1924 was recommissioned as officer in the Corps. After four years of stateside and Hawaiian service, he was sent to Nicaragua in 1928. Here he won the first of his five Navy Crosses, the only marine to ever do so, in his three years of service in that Central American hotspot.

After spending a year at the Army Infantry School at Fort Benning, Puller returned to Nicaragua in 1932–1933 before being sent to China for three years. By the time of Pearl Harbor he was a battalion commander in the 1st Marine Division and moved with his unit to the South Pacific to fight in the Guadalcanal campaign. Always conspicuous for his bravery and his inspirational leadership of his men, Puller had moved up to command the 1st Marine Regiment by the time of the bloody fight for Peleliu in the autumn of 1944. He was returned to the United States to train recruits in November 1944, and by this time he had earned three additional Navy Crosses.

During the Korean War, Puller led the 1st Marines in the amphibious landings at Inchon and subsequently won his fifth Navy Cross during the marines' retreat from the Chosin Reservoir. Subsequently Puller was advanced in rank to brigadier general and was appointed commander of the 3rd Marine Brigade. In 1954, now a major general, he was made commander of the 2nd Marine Division at Camp Lejeune, North Carolina. On November 1, 1955, Puller was promoted to lieutenant general and retired from the Corps. He died in Hampton, Virginia, on October 11, 1971.

The audacious landings at Inchon opening the second phase of the war were a spectacular success. Wolmi-Do was neutralized, and the invading assault forces swept through Inchon and on toward strategic Kimpo Airfield west of Seoul. By September 29, Seoul had been retaken and turned over to President Rhee, while the men of X Corps fanned out to secure the entire area. Meanwhile, Walker's Eighth Army broke out of the Pusan Perimeter and swept north, with 135,000 North Koreans being killed or captured in MacArthur's trap. Some 35,000 North Koreans escaped back across the Thirty-eighth Parallel, but, incredibly, South Korea had been cleared of the enemy in only two weeks' time.

Although Truman had originally intended only that the invaders be removed from South Korea, he was aware that the troops who had managed to escape, when combined with North Korean reserves, could still prove to be a menace to South Korea. He also knew that the reunification of the country was a longstanding United States and United Nations goal. Accordingly, on September 27 he gave permission to MacArthur to allow his troops to move across the Thirty-eighth Parallel but to use only ROK troops as he approached the North Korean borders with China and the Soviet Union. The United Nations subsequently approved this action.

Within a month, American and ROK troops had successfully cleared much of North Korea of NKPA soldiers and were moving in four separate columns (unable to support one another because of the terrain) toward the northern border at the Yalu River. However, resistance was stiffening, and commanders on the scene reported that Chinese soldiers were being discovered among the North Korean defenders. But at a conference on Wake Island on October 15 between Truman and MacArthur, the general discounted such reports, as well as Chinese threats to intervene. MacArthur was wrong. The United Nations forces were racing toward disaster. By late November over 300,000 Chinese "volunteers" from six corps-sized formations had entered North Korea and were overwhelming the American and ROK forces. The third phase of the war had begun.

MacArthur ordered his troops back from the Yalu in the face of the enemy numbers, and subsequently a general retreat was in progress. The United Nations troops suffered grievously due to the dogged enemy pursuit and the enshrouding bitter winter in North Korea, where temperatures dropped to forty degrees below zero and less, but the retreat remained orderly. X Corps was evacuated to Pusan from Wonsan and Hungnam on the Sea of Japan, and the marines broke out of their encirclement at the Chosin Reservoir and fought their way back to Hungnam and evacuation in one of the most heroic and dramatic incidents of the war.

By late December the United Nations forces were back to the vicinity of the Thirty-eighth Parallel, and Lieutenant General Matthew B. Ridgway, flown in to take command (General Walker had been killed when his jeep collided with a ROK truck) had managed to establish a defensive line. But even this could not be held, and on January 4, 1951, the Chinese retook Seoul from the United Nations forces.

☆   An American Portrait

Matthew B. Ridgway—Matthew Bunker Ridgway was born on March 3, 1895, at Fort Monroe, Virginia, the son of a career Army officer. Raised at various army posts, Ridgway entered West Point in 1913 and was graduated four years later. Assigned to Camp Eagle Pass, Texas, he remained at that post through World War I and saw no action on the Western Front.

From 1918 through 1924 Ridgway was back at West Point serving as an instructor in French and Spanish and as athletic director. During the 1920s and 1930s he was assigned to a number of foreign duty stations in China, the Philippines, Nicaragua, Bolivia, and Panama; he also saw stateside duty in Texas, Georgia, and California. These decades also saw Ridgway in attendance at the Command and General Staff School and at the Army

FIGURE 11–1   Matthew B. Ridgway. (*National Archives, Washington, D.C.*)

War College. On the eve of World War II he was serving on the War Plans Division of the General Staff.

Early in the war, Ridgway, now a major general, was given command of the 82nd Infantry Division, then ordered to convert it into an airborne unit, one of the first and destined to be one of the most famous in the Army. After moving the 82nd to North Africa for more training in early 1943 after Operation Torch, Ridgway parachuted in with his men in the airborne assault on Sicily as part of Operation Husky in July of that year. The drop was in many ways a near disaster, but Ridgway and his paratroopers had proved the value of vertical assaults.

Ridgway dropped a second time with the 82nd Airborne Division on June 5, 1944, to hold the area behind Utah Beach as part of Operation Overlord, the Allied landings in Normandy. Subsequently turning over command of the 82nd to General James M. Gavin, Ridgway assumed the post of head of XVIII Corps of the First Allied Airborne Army. Although he played no direct role in the airborne assaults as part of Operation Market-Garden, Ridgway led his airborne troops through the Ardennes campaign and then into Germany in the last months of the war.

After the war, Ridgway served as commander of the Mediterranean theater of operations, chairman of the Military Staff Committee of the United Nations, commander-in-chief of the Caribbean Command, and deputy chief of staff for administration and training.

In December 1950 Ridgway was sent to Korea to replace General Walton H. Walker at one of the most critical points of the Korean War. Displaying his usual command presence, Ridgway ordered a phased pull-back by his United Nations troops to more defensible lines south of the Thirty-eighth Parallel. He then launched a counteroffensive that took him back to and beyond the parallel by the end of February 1951. Here the war became a firefight stalemate, but Ridgway was called away from the battlefield in April 1951 to assume the post of Far East and United Nations commander when President Truman removed General Douglas MacArthur from that position for insubordination.

One year later, in May 1952, Ridgway, now a full general, was named to replace General Dwight D. Eisenhower as supreme commander of the Allied forces in Europe. In October 1953 he was called back to Washington to serve as chief of staff of the Army. In his two years in this position he distinguished himself by fighting against the reduction of conventional forces in favor of reliance on atomic weaponry, by urging a "flexible response" capability for America's armed forces, and by arguing against American military intervention in Vietnam.

Ridgway retired in 1955 and lives today in Pittsburgh, Pennsylvania, one of the last surviving great captains of World War II and Korea.

Ridgway nevertheless managed to reestablish his defensive line and stop the Chinese and North Koreans, now increased in number to 400,000, some 40 miles south of the Thirty-eighth Parallel. Truman and his military advisors now had to decide the next step. Would they accept a basically stalemated military situation and work toward a negotiated settlement, or would they escalate the fighting, perhaps bringing on a major conflict with China or Russia, in order to win the war and reunite Korea? The president and the Joint Chiefs agreed to go with the first option. MacArthur strenuously disagreed. He argued for blockading and launching air attacks on China and for using Chiang Kai-shek's troops in Korea and against the Red Chinese mainland. To his consternation, MacArthur's ideas were rejected by his superiors.

With Ridgway deftly managing some offensive moves toward the Thirty-eighth Parallel, recapturing Seoul, and attempting to establish a solid defensive line, the war entered its fourth phase, the negotiating phase. It would last for two years. Still, the fighting continued, even while Truman began to search for means of attaining a negotiated peace. This displeased the bellicose MacArthur, who began to assume an independent diplomatic and political role in his public and private utterances. Then, in defiance of Truman's orders that all public policy statements be cleared by him before being released, MacArthur wrote in a letter to the Republican leader of the House of Representatives, Joseph Martin of Massachusetts, that he favored the use of Nationalist Chinese troops and that the limited war policy in Korea was wrong. Martin read the letter on the House floor. In response, Truman relieved MacArthur of his command on April 11, 1951, appointing Ridgway in his place as head of the United States and United Nations command.

Since the nation was already becoming disenchanted with the war and its "no-win" philosophy, Truman's "firing" of the general caused a tremendous domestic political uproar. Those who favored a policy of all-out victory in war saw MacArthur as a martyr to Truman's misguided policies; those who already opposed the war as essentially futile and not vital to the nation's interests, or who were inclined to be antimilitary anyway, saw MacArthur as a dangerous demagogue getting his just desserts for insubordination. The general returned home to giant parades and public accolades (fueled by the Republican party, whose leaders were willing to use the issue for partisan gain). All of the nation's confusion over the Korean situation—first styled a "police action," then a "conflict," and only finally a "war"—seemed to crystallize momentarily around the Truman–MacArthur controversy. Yet the excitement eventually died down, and the American people still found that there was a war of sorts going on in Korea, seemingly without resolution.

The soldiers and marines of Eighth Army and their ROK counterparts, now under Lieutenant General James A. VanFleet, had continued to beat off the Chinese and North Korean attacks during the spring of 1951 with vital air support from FEAF in air and land interdiction roles and from Navy and Marine aviators furnishing precision air support to the ground troops. They finally established the Kansas-Wyoming Line north of the Thirty-eighth Parallel after bloody fighting to seize the "Iron Triangle" in central Korea from the communists in a series of battles at "the Punchbowl," "Heartbreak Ridge," and "Bloody Ridge." Here the fighting slowed in late 1951, and steps toward negotiations began.

The peace talks that began at Panmunjon in November 1951 dragged on into 1952, the major issue of contention being the United Nations proposals that prisoners of war would not have to return to their homes upon their release from captivity, an idea vigorously rejected by the communists. Finally, in October 1952, the talks broke down completely while small raids and artillery duels continued sporadically along the Kansas-Wyoming line.

Negotiations were resumed only after Dwight D. Eisenhower promised to "go to Korea" as a part of his bid for the presidency as the candidate of the Republican party. Eisenhower flew to Korea to confer with General Mark Clark, the Far East commander, and decided that further pressure was needed to break the negotiating deadlock in the stalemated war. Accordingly, after his inauguration, Eisenhower sent word through diplomatic channels to China, the Soviet Union, and North Korea that if negotiations were not resumed and an armistice forthcoming he would move decisively, using *every* weapon in the American arsenal in Korea *and elsewhere* to end the stalemate. This threat led to a resumption of the peace talks, and on July 27, 1953, an armistice was signed and the fighting stopped.

In three years 142,000 Americans had been counted as casualties in the war, in which 2 million fighting men had seen action. Over 33,000 had died in action, more than 20,000 had died of other causes, 103,000 had been wounded, and 5,200 were missing. America's allies, mainly South Korea, saw another 61,000 killed. North Korean and Chinese casualty totals stood at between 1.25 and 1.5 million men killed, wounded, imprisoned, or missing. Most of these were Chinese. The armistice line stood approximately at the Thirty-eighth Parallel (slightly south in the west and slightly north in the east), and both North Korea and South Korea were approximately in the same posture as they had been in 1950. The American people continued to ask, as they had been asking for two years, why the war had been fought. What had been gained? The answers were not always clear and convincing, but they were substantive for those who would consider them.

In the first place, the Korean War, decades later often called "the forgotten war," had, in consonance with the nation's evolving policy of containment and its treaty commitments to other nations, successfully resisted an aggressor and defended a friend. Communist expansion by military force had been stopped, and South Korea was free to build its own destiny behind an American protective shield. This was a major achievement and the greatest single justification for the three-year war.

Second, the American people and their military had been introduced to the concept of limited wars for limited ends with major nations using smaller nations as subsidized and equipped proxies under a nuclear umbrella that precluded widening the conflict for all-out and decisive victory. This was difficult for many Americans to accept, raised as they were only on experiences of all-out war for all-inclusive goals, but the limited Korean War was in many ways the prototype for countless conflicts that would occur in the decades to come.

FIGURE 11–2   F-86 Sabrejet. (*Official U. S. Air Force Photo, DOD Still Media Records Center, Washington, D.C.*)

Third, Korea illustrated clearly that reliance on atomic weaponry alone for national defense and the upholding of treaty obligations not only was too dangerous but also hogtied the nation when it was confronted with threats or aggressions that would not admit of atomic war as a solution. A wide range of military responses—whatever the cost—would henceforth be necessary if the United States was going to continue to shoulder the responsibility for defending Western freedoms.

Fourth, while the Korean War was fought with essentially the same weapons and tactics as World War II had been (tanks, artillery, infantry, automatic weapons, and so on), innovations had appeared that illustrated the continuing evolution of military technology. Among these were the use of jet-propelled airplanes such as the F-80 Shooting Star, the F-84 Thunderjet, and the F-86 Sabrejet fighters with more powerful and accurate ordnance such as homing, solid-fuel Sidewinder missiles (although World War II vintage Mustangs and Corsairs performed well in close air support roles). Also new was the use of helicopters such as the Sikorsky HRS-1 for "vertical assault" tactics and rapid evacuation of the wounded, plus the introduction of the heavy M46 and M47 Patton tanks with improved semiautomatic transmissions and better range finders to outduel the Russian T-34s. The use of beam-riding and radar-guided missiles in antiaircraft weapons also came about in Korea.

Fifth, it was during the Korean War that racial segregation came to an end in American military units. An end to segregated units had been mandated in Executive Order 9981 issued by President Truman back in 1948, but little progress had been made. In the maw of combat during the Korean fighting, integration was forced upon the services, and the time-honored military barrier against mixed units came to an end.

The Korean War of 1950–1953 was a valuable lesson in the realities of the world's new political order and in the sense of realism necessary for living in the post–World War II decades. All-out (now nuclear) war was being replaced with limited (non-nuclear) wars in which the aggressor would use nationalistic "wars of liberation" as a preferred and less dangerous means of aggression. Many, if not most, Americans—agreeing with MacArthur that there was "no substitute for victory"—did not realize this in 1953. Policy makers still tended to see the Korean conflict as an aberration, not as the beginning of a trend, but events during the remainder of the decade continued to drive the lessons home.

EXPANDING COMMITMENTS AND TECHNOLOGICAL ADVANCEMENTS

Backed, it would appear, by widespread public support for reliance on atomic power to deter any aggressor (the United States held a giant lead in the development of this type of weapon, and it seemed a good way to hold down defense spending), President Eisenhower and Congress continued to carry out a military policy that placed major emphasis on nuclear retaliation as the ultimate trump card in strategic planning. "Massive retaliation" was the watchword in American foreign policy, as enunciated by Secretary of State John Foster Dulles. Yet the military was expected to be prepared for all exigencies and to win. This left the services with no choice but to fight for more money for weaponry improvements. Technological change, combined with their respective roles as guardians of the peace on land, at sea, and in the air, demanded no less.

Given the major emphasis placed on strategic nuclear weapons, it is hardly surprising that the Air Force's share of the military budget increased appreciably in the 1950s. Missiles and bombers were expensive, as was the cost of maintaining the necessary men, equipment, and bases to sustain the forces of the Strategic Air Command (SAC), the designated deliverer of massive retaliation. The Tactical Air Command (TAC), designed for defensive and tactical air support missions, also made sizable budget demands.

Still, the Army and the Navy, with their missile-armed and nuclear-powered surface and subsurface programs, were also in the "atomic business" strategically and tactically—besides carrying out their substrategic missions—so their budgets, too, continued to grow during the decade. By 1959, federal outlays for the military stood at $44.6 billion, 48 percent of the total budget, and actually marginally higher than during the height of the Korean War in 1953, when it cost $44 billion to support the military. Despite the fact that military spending in 1959 represented 9.5 percent of the gross national product (GNP), a decrease from 13.4 percent of the GNP in 1953, resistance in the White House and in the halls of Congress to this budgetary growth was strong. It was Eisenhower himself who warned of the danger to America of the "military-industrial complex." Yet the American people seemed willing at last to abandon—grudgingly, to be sure—their historic postwar pattern of disarmament. They appeared disposed to sustain such expenses because the communist menace was perceived as greater than ever, and American commitments around the world were necessarily multiplying in the face of this threat.

In Europe, for example, the NATO alliance was built up even during the Korean War. This occurred out of a persistent fear that the Soviets would take advantage of America's involvement in Korea to launch a land attack on western Europe. Accordingly, the number of army divisions in Europe was increased from 1 to 5, fully one-third of the total of 15 divisions in the entire Army. Aid was also extended to the NATO allies through the Mutual Defense Assistance Program to strengthen their forces. At America's behest, West Germany was allowed to rearm and add its divisions to NATO's forces.

In the Mediterranean, the Sixth Fleet was created to guard NATO's southern flank and to provide American naval strength in the eastern Mediterranean, where Soviet incursions in Iraq, Egypt, and other countries appeared to signal their intention to dominate that strategic area. And strong Arab nationalistic-religious feeling against Israel (created in 1948 with strong backing from the United States out of territories taken from the Arabs) made it mandatory that the American military be in a position to respond quickly and effectively in that troubled part of the world.

American interest in Middle Eastern affairs was indicated by the government's role in sitting in on Baghdad Pact committee meetings and in supplying assistance to its signatories (Great Britain, Iran, Iraq, Turkey, and Pakistan) after the formation of that defensive alliance. This interest was again indicated in the formulation by Congress in 1957 of the so-called Eisenhower Doctrine pledging United States aid to any Middle Eastern country threatened by communist expansionism. This doctrine was put into effect the next year when rebellions sponsored by Egypt and its Soviet-leaning leader Gamel Abdel Nasser broke out and the governments of Lebanon and Jordan requested American military aid. Within two weeks almost 6,000 marines and 8,500 soldiers had landed in Lebanon, airborne troops were in Jordan, and more soldiers had moved into Turkey. All the while the Sixth Fleet stood offshore but within striking distance. The crisis passed, and America had proved in the Middle East that force could and would be used to ensure containment.

The American government continued to work with the Middle Eastern Central Treaty Organization (CENTO)—the old Baghdad Pact reformed after Iraq withdrew— and also entered into defense alliances with Turkey, Pakistan, and Iran. Once again, as in western Europe between 1945 and 1950, events were propelling the United States and its military forces into positions of greater responsibility, not through a desire to dominate but in order to preserve certain principles of freedom and self-determination.

In the western Pacific, too, American commitments continued to grow. The United States was already deeply involved in the defense of the Philippines since that archipelago attained its independence in 1946 and agreed to 99-year leases on 23 military installations, including the crucial Subic Bay naval base and Clark Field. And, of course, the nation was committed to the maintenance of South Korean integrity following the armistice in 1953. This commitment took the form of two army divisions stationed there.

In addition, the United States was aiding France monetarily in that nation's attempts to retain control over Vietnam. In 1954 the United States played a leading role at the Geneva Conference setting up two Vietnams, although it was not a signatory to the agreement. Subsequently, the United States joined Australia, New Zealand, France, Great Britain, the Philippines, Thailand, and Pakistan in 1955 in forming the Southeast Asia Treaty Organization (SEATO) mandating aid and consultation in the face of communist aggression in that area of the world. In 1958, acting on a congressional resolution passed three years before, President Eisenhower sent military aid to the Nationalist Chinese on Taiwan when the communists on the mainland began to shell the offshore islands of Quemoy and Matsu, apparently intending to seize them as springboards for the invasion of Taiwan.

Thus, throughout the 1950s, the United States continued to expand its diplomatic and military obligations throughout the world. These necessarily led to major adjustments within the services as they moved to match their capabilities to the duties being thrust upon them, all the while operating within the monetary restrictions imposed by Congress and by the president under his "New Look" military policy. This was no easy task because technology was rapidly changing the way in which wars would henceforth be fought on land, at sea, and in the air. The use of the helicopter for vertical assault tactics was a prime example. Helicopters were used during the Korean War for reconnaissance, casualty evacuation, limited movement of troops, and supervision of units by commanders. And

Sikorsky HRS-1 helicopters used in squadrons proved capable of moving a company of infantry into areas of rough terrain in hours rather than in days, as would be necessary on foot. Helicopter development, especially in the larger helos and attack helos, continued during the 1950s, the marines adopting vertical envelopment tactics as a specialty, as they had adopted amphibious landing tactics during the 1930s.

In land operations, too, work continued on the 52-ton Patton tanks (the heavy Pershing tanks having been withdrawn from service in Korea to the near unanimous approval of the tankers), although the Patton's 90-millimeter gun presented persistent problems. The usefulness of tanks even in the mountainous terrain of Korea proved the continued need for AFVs in the modern modes of war. Accordingly, development continued during the 1950s, culminating in the M60 main battle tank with a 105-millimeter gun, introduced in 1960.

Development also proceeded on armored personnel carriers (APCs) to move infantry swiftly and with comparative invulnerability to and beyond the enemy's lines. This eventually led from the unsatisfactory M75 and M59 models to the "swimmable" M113 Bradley APC introduced in 1960, with its 25-millimeter gun and its TOW (*t*ube-launched, *o*ptically tracked, *w*ire-guided) antitank missile system as a necessary component of mobile land warfare.

FIGURE 11–3   M48 Patton tank. (*Official U.S. Army Photo, DOD Still Media Records Center, Washington, D.C.*)

FIGURE 11–4 M113 Bradley APC. (*Official U.S. Army Photo, DOD Still Media Records Center, Washington, D.C.*)

At sea, the Navy took giant strides in the 1950s, particularly in the nuclear field. It had been working on the idea of a nuclear-powered submarine since the 1940s. Such a vessel would draw its steam power from an atomic reactor that required no oxygen and gave off no exhaust. This would afford it submerged times measured in days or even weeks, making it almost invulnerable to ASW attack. Driving the project was a crusty and demanding naval officer, Hyman G. Rickover.

Success was attained with the launching of the atomic submarine *Nautilus* in 1954 and its successful sea trials the next year. Then, two years later, the *Nautilus* successfully sailed from the Pacific to the Atlantic under the polar ice cap. This feat of sustained underwater navigation was eclipsed two short years later when the *Triton* completely circumnavigated the world underwater, taking 83 days to make the 36,000-mile epic journey.

Nor was the Navy neglecting nuclear power for its surface vessels. In 1957 the keel was laid for the USS *Long Beach,* a nuclear-powered, 17,000-ton cruiser with batteries of guided missiles for ordnance instead of guns. She joined the fleet three years later. In 1958 the keel was laid for CVN *Enterprise,* a 1,123-foot, atomic-powered aircraft carrier with cantilevered decks capable of launching a plane every 30 seconds. Her eight nuclear reactors could power the 90,000-ton giant to a speed of 30 knots and required refueling only every two years. Between 1952 and 1955 the Navy also commissioned four 60,000-ton conventional carriers capable of handling the A-3 Skywarrior strategic bomber. With these carriers joining the fleet, the Navy had the ability to deliver atomic loads by air from nonfixed bases.

The Navy also took a giant step forward in the 1950s by developing the capability of firing guided missiles from submarines while the vessels were submerged. Nuclear submarines with short-range Regulus missiles (which required them to surface for firing) just would not be satisfactory from the point of survivability. Success was attained in 1960

FIGURE 11–5   CVN Enterprise. (*Official U.S. Navy Photo, DOD Still Media Records Center, Washington, D.C.*)

when the *George Washington*, while submerged off the Florida coast, fired a Polaris missile from beneath the sea. Polaris missiles were propelled by a solid-fuel rocket and could deliver both nuclear and thermonuclear warheads. By the end of the 1960s their effective range had been increased from 1,380 to 2,880 miles. The nuclear-powered and nuclear-armed Navy had been born by 1960, and a new and powerful element had thereby been added to the international balance of power.

FIGURE 11–6   B-52 Stratofortress. (*Official U.S. Air Force Photo. , DOD Still Media Records Center, Washington, D.C.*).

In the air, too, there was an ongoing surge of technological improvements in weaponry that set the scene for decades to come. In strategic bombers the six-engine, propeller-driven B-36s (jet engines were added later) and all-jet B-47s in use at the start of the Korean War gave way to the eight-engine, jet-propelled B-52s. More than 700 of these giant intercontinental bombers were delivered to SAC between 1955 and 1962, and many were still in use into the 1990s. The 1950s also saw the advent of the single-seat Douglas A-4 Skyhawk jet attack bomber, first used by the Navy. This rugged plane saw service until 1979. In fighters, the Douglas F-4 Phantom jet was developed in the late 1950s, and the high-altitude, long-range "spy" plane, the Lockheed TR-1, or U-2, became operational in 1957. It had a range of 4,000 miles and could cruise at altitudes of up to 85,000 feet. Even from this height it was able to produce remarkably detailed reconnaissance photos, thanks to developments in aerial photography unimaginable just a decade before.

In the field of missiles, the 1950s witnessed a belated but determined effort by the United States to best any possible opponent. Eisenhower's budgetary restraints—he called for "more bang for the buck"—had only limited effects on American efforts to build better intercontinental ballistic missiles (ICBMs) and intermediate-range ballistic missiles (IRBMs), appropriations for this purpose climbing from $1.4 billion in 1955 to $2 billion in 1958. The early liquid-fueled, 5,000-mile-range Atlas and Titan I ICBMs gave way to the Air Force's Minuteman rocket and the Navy's Polaris. The Minuteman became operational in 1962, and the improved Titan II in 1963. Between 1959 and 1963 some 200 Atlas and Titan I ICBMs were actually deployed, and in that same period 100 Thor and Jupiter IRBMs were also based in Great Britain, Turkey, and Italy.

Tactical nuclear weapons plus air-to-air and surface-to-air tactical missiles (for example, the Nike antiaircraft missile) were developed during the 1950s and brought on line then and into the 1960s. By 1968 some 7,200 tactical nuclear missiles had been deployed in Europe. All things considered, the conclusion becomes inescapable that America's growing worldwide responsibilities in the 15 years following World War II, coupled with the escalating rate of technological change in land, sea, and air weaponry, were pushing America's military to the forefront of the nation's policy and budgetary concerns. Events combined with technology were making the country's armed forces a vital factor in all aspects of its diplomatic policy of containment—this despite any residual heartfelt desire to return to a pre–World War II posture of either war or peace, a choice now long vanished in the postwar era of Cold War confrontation.

MANPOWER AND MANAGEMENT

These changes in responsibilities and technology, in turn, forced the armed services to consider their own organization in order to handle efficiently the burdens they were now compelled to bear. In addition, the tight budget "New Look" policy of the president and congressional reluctance to spend for defense meant that emphasis was necessarily placed on high-cost air and missile weaponry and highly trained men and women to use them. Military pay and retirement benefits were upgraded in 1958 as a matter of necessity in order to retain active duty personnel, but the problem of maintaining a sufficient number of enlisted personnel and adequately training them continued to plague the services. The tight budget policy also mandated that each service strive to gain all it could to carry out its particular missions as it saw them. This resulted in yearly interservice budgetary squabbles over allocations. As a consequence, presidential and congressional steps were taken to enforce coordination and cooperation while at the same time providing for all military contingencies.

For example, two attempts were made during these years to provide less expensive reserve forces to back up the regular forces. Those reservists called up for duty in Korea either as individuals or as units had served well, but their mobilization had caused a number of problems that needed to be remedied. The passage of the Reserve Officer Personnel Act (ROPA) in 1954 had solved the problem of reserve officer rank equity, but other problems remained. Early in the decade, under the 1948 Selective Service Act, a young man between the ages of 19 and 26 faced a total of 81 months of military duty in an active, ready reserve, or standby reserve capacity. Alternatively, he could spend 10 years in the National Guard. But with deferments being generously given and low draft quotas imposed, few men were called to active duty, and "compulsory military service" was that in name only. Furthermore, reserve time mandated neither joining a reserve unit nor participating in regular training.

Congress tried to correct these problems in the reserve system by passing the Reserve Forces Act of 1955, demanding a total of 6 years of active and compulsory reserve duty. A young man could also enlist in the reserves prior to age 18 1/2; in this case he could serve 6 months on active duty and 7 1/2 years in the active reserves. But a combination of budgetary restrictions and inadequate numbers of enlistees joining the reserves resulted in undermanned and underequipped reserve units. The hope was for a reserve and National Guard force of 2,900,000 by 1970, but reserve units totaled only about 700,000 by 1960. Thus the ready and standby reserve system in the military services showed continued distinct weaknesses in numbers and training by the end of the decade. Less than 10 percent of the Army reserves, for example, were engaged in weekend training programs because of low pay and other factors. As military forces they were hardly ready for effective mobilization to flesh out the regulars in time of emergency or crisis.

Congress was more successful in forcing cooperation on the bickering services by increasing the authority of the secretary of defense. By legislation passed in 1958, the military departments were made clearly subordinate to the secretary, who, in turn, was subordinate to the commander-in-chief. Each service retained control over its own men and women, equipment, and logistics, but the secretary of defense could decide functions, priorities, and areas of research and development. At the same time, the Joint Chiefs of Staff were assigned the task of coordinating military matters and establishing unified Army, Navy and Air Force commands in Europe, the Far East, the Pacific, the Caribbean, and Alaska, although overall operational control was in the hands of the secretary of defense operating through the three service secretaries.

Thus, at long last the three branches of service were placed in a regular and enforceable chain of command with direction of each individual service no longer residing in semiautonomous chiefs who could choose to follow or disregard the directions of their respective secretaries. This reform hardly did away with interservice rivalries, as each branch continued to demand its share of the pie in military affairs, budgetary and otherwise; but at least after 1958, increased cooperation and coordination was possible if not always attainable.

The 1950s, then, ended with the American military moving toward limited revitalization as an instrument of containment, with greatest emphasis being placed on nuclear and technological capabilities. Despite resistance, budgets were being expanded and weapons systems of high technological sophistication were being researched, developed, and brought on line. The American people, despite the frustrating war in Korea early in the decade, were also coming to accept their new role in the world and the necessity of the military commitments attendant upon that role. And the Soviets and others who would challenge America and its friends had at least been checked.

Few Americans realized that the nation would soon face a greater challenge to its responsibilities and values in a war in Vietnam—a war that by 1975 would divide the nation and cast a pall over its ideological and military commitments for years to come. Unlike its other cold war tests of courage and will, this time America lost the war, and reverberations of that defeat continued to be felt many years later.

Suggestions for Further Reading

ALBION, ROBERT G., and ROBERT H. CONNERY, *Forrestal and the Navy.* New York: Columbia University Press, 1962.

ALEXANDER, CHARLES C., *Holding the Line: The Eisenhower Era, 1952–1961.* Bloomington: Indiana University Press, 1975.

APPLEMAN, ROY E., *Disaster in Korea: The Chinese Confront MacArthur.* College Station: Texas A&M University Press, 1989.

———, *East of Chosin.* College Station: Texas A&M University Press, 1987.

BLAIR, CLAY, *The Forgotten War: America in Korea, 1950–1953.* New York: Times Books, 1987.

COLLINS, J. LAWTON. *War in Peacetime: The History and Lessons of Korea.* Boston: Houghton Mifflin, 1969.

CROSSLAND, RICHARD B., and JAMES T. CURRIE, *Twice the Citizen: A History of the United States Army Reserve, 1908–1983.* Washington, DC: Office of the Chief, Army Reserve, 1984.

CUMINGS, BRUCE, *The Origins of the Korean War: Liberation and the Emergence of Separate Regimes, 1945–1947.* Princeton, NJ: Princeton University Press, 1981.

DUNCAN, FRANCIS, *Rickover and the Nuclear Navy: The Discipline of Technology.* Annapolis: Naval Institute Press, 1989.

GADDIS, JOHN L., *Strategies of Containment.* New York: Oxford University Press, 1981.

HASTINGS, MAX, *The Korean War.* New York: Simon & Schuster, 1987.

HEINL, ROBERT D., *Victory at High Tide: The Inchon–Seoul Campaign.* Philadelphia: Lippincott, 1968.

HELLER, FRANCIS H., comp., *The Korean War: A 25-Year Perspective.* Lawrence: Regents Press of Kansas, 1977.

HEWLETT, RICHARD G., and FRANCIS DUNCAN, *Nuclear Navy: 1946–1962.* Chicago: University of Chicago Press, 1974.

HOPKINS, WILLIAM B., *One Bugle, No Drums: The Marines at Chosin Reservoir.* Chapel Hill, NC: Algonquin, 1986.

HUSTON, JAMES A., *Guns and Butter, Powder and Rice: U.S. Army Logistics in the Korean War.* Cranbury, NJ: Susquehanna University Press, 1989.

KNOX, DONALD, *The Korean War—Pusan to Chosin: An Oral History.* New York: Harcourt Brace Jovanovich, 1987.

KORB, LAWRENCE J., *The Joint Chiefs of Staff.* Bloomington: Indiana University Press, 1976.

MACGREGOR, MORRIS J., JR., *Integration of the Armed Forces, 1940–1965.* Washington, DC: U.S. Army Center of Military History, 1981.

REES, DAVID, *Korea: The Limited War.* New York: St. Martin's Press, 1964.

RIDGWAY, MATTHEW B., *The Korean War.* Garden City, NY: Doubleday, 1967.

ROSE, JOHN P., *The Evolution of the U.S. Army Nuclear Doctrine, 1945–1980.* Boulder, CO: Westview Press, 1980.

SCHALLER, MICHAEL, *Douglas MacArthur: The Far Eastern General.* New York: Oxford University Press, 1989.

SPANIER, JOHN W., *The Truman–MacArthur Controversy and the Korean War.* Cambridge: Belknap Press of Harvard University Press, 1959.

STOKESBURY, JAMES L., *A Short History of the Korean War.* New York: William Morrow, 1988.

WHELAN, RICHARD, *Drawing the Line: The Korean War, 1950–1953.* Boston: Little, Brown, 1990.

WILSON, JIM, *Retreat, Hell! We're Just Attacking in Another Direction.* New York: William Morrow, 1988.

☆12

Cold War
and Vietnam,
1960–1975

The years 1945 to 1960 had seen the United States shoulder the burdens of worldwide power by becoming the *de facto* leader of the Western democracies and playing an active role in the affairs of Europe, the Middle East, and the Far East. When military force was called for, it was used successfully, especially in Korea. When monetary assistance was needed, it was granted, as called for in the Marshall Plan. When reorganization of America's armed forces was required to carry out the nation's military commitments, it was achieved. When the price tag for strategic and tactical atomic weapons, for technological improvements in subatomic conventional weaponry, and for the men who manned them continued to climb, the money was forthcoming.

Not without much soul-searching over America's new responsibilities in the world and what they meant to the nation in terms of lives lost of its men in uniform, the United States had managed to carry out its perceived destiny as the leader of the free world in the decade and a half after World War II. As its new, young president, John F. Kennedy, said in his inaugural address in January 1961: "Let every nation know, whether it wishes us well or ill, that we shall pay any price, bear any burden, meet any hardship, support any friend, oppose any foe to assure the survival and the success of liberty." Few Americans were heard to take issue with the new president's pledges in 1961.

Fifteen years later this confidence and willingness to bear the burden were gone. Retrenchment, neo-isolationism, antimilitarism, and a pervasive cynicism toward the ideals of democracy and world responsibility had gripped the land. Despite—or because of—the efforts of the nation's leaders to put into practice America's values at home and abroad, the United States had lost a bloody war in Vietnam, had witnessed racial and antiwar violence in its streets, and had seen the government weakened by scandal and a presidential resignation. The divisive war, the domestic hatred and violence, the national disgrace—all were somehow tied together, creating a pervasive sense of a loss of direction. No one could conclusively decipher its origins, and no one could point the way back to shared ideals and an end to the turmoil.

Yet, despite its ideological, political, and spiritual wounds, America's worldwide responsibilities remained. However it faced these responsibilities during the remainder of the century, it was clear by the mid-1970s that America had been changed in a short decade and a half, perhaps permanently, perhaps only temporarily. Its men and women in military uniform shared in its post-1960 agonies and in its ideological confusions. Like the nation itself, the military by the mid-1970s was seeking self-assurance, support, and leadership in the aftermath of America's time of troubles.

KENNEDY AND MCNAMARA

John Kennedy came to the presidency in 1961, defeating Eisenhower's vice president, Richard M. Nixon, by a whisker in the 1960 elections. Partial credit for his narrow victory lay in his charge that the Republicans, under Eisenhower's "New Look" military policy, had allowed a "missile gap" to be opened by the Soviets, a charge later shown to be false. The nation's defenses were in fact adequate, although perhaps overbalanced toward massive retaliation. There had been, it is true, the embarrassment of the Soviets shooting down an American U-2 spy plane deep in their territory the year before. Soviet Premier Nikita Khrushchev had used the incident, clumsy U.S. denials of spying, and the public trial of pilot Francis Gary Powers as an excuse to cancel a summit conference with Eisenhower scheduled in Paris for May 1960. This embarrassing incident, however, was balanced by a proposed agreement between the United States, Great Britain, and the Soviet Union that same year that would ban all nuclear testing in the atmosphere and under water. To a degree, the proposed treaty would deescalate the race in atomic hardware and raised the hope that subsequent agreements might be reached to lessen the risk of atomic war.

Kennedy sounded a new military note when he endorsed and popularized the concept of "flexible response." He was struck by the fact that with the United States and the Soviet Union continuing to stockpile nuclear weapons and having achieved effective delivery systems for them, both nations would find it mandatory to avoid mutual destruction. This being the case, there was an increased likelihood of continued limited confrontations in the Third World, where emerging nations might be induced to accept Soviet aid in their wars of liberation, the Soviets thus advancing their own ideological and national cause on the back of ex-colonial resentments of the West. Given these conditions, the United States should continue to use diplomacy as an instrument of containment and disarmament, but, Kennedy stressed, it had to be prepared at all times to defend itself and its friends against Soviet aggressions, either direct or indirect. Kennedy therefore urged a flexible response capability ranging from full nuclear to limited conventional modes of warfare.

The concept of flexible response in order to lessen reliance on nuclear deterrence was hardly new. The idea had been popularized during the previous decade by many academics, including Dr. Henry Kissinger of Harvard University in his *Nuclear Weapons and Foreign Policy* (1957), and by such high-ranking military leaders as Army Chief of Staff Matthew B. Ridgway and his successor, General Maxwell D. Taylor.

Kennedy's energetic espousal of flexible response led to its public acceptance as basic military policy. Yet missile-delivered massive retaliation remained, of necessity, a vital part of America's defense posture. Surrendering nuclear superiority to the Soviets would open the door to atomic blackmail and render the nation defenseless in the face of a threat of total or near total annihilation. Accordingly, strategic weapons improvements would continue for the next three decades. By 1963 the deployment goals were 1,000 intercontinental ballistic missiles (ICBMs) built around Minuteman and Titan missiles plus 41 submarines capable of firing over 600 missiles on assigned targets. These were part of the nation's Strategic Triad, a combination of land-based intercontinental ballistic missiles (ICBMs), submarine-launched ballistic missiles (SLBMs), and long-range bombers for a balance of retaliatory options. The nation was actually continuing to operate under the threat of mutually assured destruction, even though the acronym *MAD* would not find disfavor until the 1970s.

A second decision made by Kennedy had an even greater impact on the American military for years to come: his appointment of Robert S. McNamara as secretary of defense. A former Air Force lieutenant colonel and one of the new breed of management experts who based their decisions and policies on computer-generated systems analysis and social science game theory, McNamara came to the position of defense secretary after serving as head of Ford Motor Company. He brought with him to the Department of Defense a coterie of academic experts, all sharing a mutual faith in systems analysis and a common critical attitude toward existing Pentagon practices as wasteful and inefficient. To their supporters, they were "defense intellectuals" bringing needed reforms to the American military bureaucracy. To their detractors, they would be known thereafter as McNamara's "whiz kids," who left the American military in an organizational shambles and whose methodologies brought defective civilian decision making into areas of defense policy.

In the area of finance, McNamara introduced the planning-programming budget system (PPBS). Under it, all costs and projections had to be prepared for budgeting by program packages such as strategic deterrence, rather than by existing management categories. Tied to this was the Five-Year Defense Plan, under which all military spending had to be justified according to function or mission, allowing the Office of the Secretary of Defense (OSD) to exercise veto power over both functions and spending because of the secretary's and his staff's preparation of the budget. The objective was to cut costs by buying only necessary items at the best price.

But "systems analysis," whereby weapons systems for the same mission were compared for their total cost effectiveness over their useful life (rather than for their effectiveness in winning wars or deterring aggressors), and "commonality," whereby all service procurements were to be made through a new Defense Supply Agency for mass buying and standardization, resulted in the services' being forced to accept weapons or equipment not suitable for their missions. As a prime example, the Air Force and Navy were both compelled to adopt the TFX fighter plane even though neither could use it because of the compromises built into its design. Forced to work within these rules, America's military leaders quickly became disenchanted with McNamara, his management team, and his budgetary processes.

McNamara's new ground rules, with their inherent bias toward civilianization and centralization of the armed forces, also led to centralization of the services' intelligence functions in the Defense Intelligence Agency. They also resulted in the removal of the technical service branches in the armed forces from their individual chiefs and their placement under new commands and officers answerable to civilian officials of the OSD via the Chiefs of Staff. These included the Army Materiel Command, the Combat Developments Command, the Office of Reserve Components, and the Office of Personnel Operations.

The results of this fundamental shake-up in budgeting and management were far-reaching. Some cost savings were realized, but critics since McNamara's time have been tracing the deleterious effects of his reforms. Many commentators point to the philosophical flaw involved in the processes he introduced. They argue that McNamara's methods tended to consider only those matters that were quantifiable, leaving out all nonquantifiable factors that may have been of equal or greater importance in matters of war and national defense (such as morale, attitudes, courage, leadership, accident, or miscalculation). These commentators point to Clausewitz's authoritative statement that successful warfare consists of breaking the will of the enemy, and they remind their listeners that "breaking the will of the enemy" refers to something that is nonquantifiable. All the factors involved in breaking the enemy's will can never be quantified, the critics argue, but that does not make them invalid. They point out that Ho Chi Minh proved this dramatically in Vietnam when all the "quantifiables" (such as winning every major battle and having far superior firepower) pointed to an American victory, yet America lost because of "nonquantifiables" (its flawed strategy and North Vietnam's will to win).

This basic philosophical flaw notwithstanding, because of the popularity of McNamara's ideas and his personal influence over Kennedy and, later, President Lyndon B. Johnson, his system and conclusions exerted substantial influence over these presidents, the National Security Council, and the Joint Chiefs of Staff. As a result, civilian quantifiers assumed greater control over matters previously left to military leaders. For example, during World War II the president and the secretaries of war and of the Navy surely made basic decisions regarding grand strategy, but they then left the execution of that strategy to the generals and admirals in the field. The same was true in Korea. But in Vietnam, civilian decision making extended as far down as the tactical level, one factor in the loss of that war.

Thus McNamara's revolution not only caused disarray in the armed forces in the wake of his grand reorganization and systemwide adoption of systems analysis, but it was also a factor in the demoralization of the armed forces during and after Vietnam. Yet for good or ill, McNamara's ideas held sway during the Kennedy years and thereafter with other changes and reorganizations following as a consequence. For example, the Army adopted the Reorganization Objective Army Division (ROAD) divisional structure, whereby all divisions (infantry, airborne, armor, and mechanized) contained basically the same organizational structure but with the ability to add brigades of certain types to fit the tactical situation. After ROAD divisions had been established in the Army, they were extended to the reserves and National Guard. Another innovation was the formation of air assault divisions of higher mobility, all equipment being air-transportable. Still another—an innovation strongly supported and encouraged by Kennedy—was the formation of Special Forces units for guerrilla warfare, psychological warfare, and counterinsurgency operations. Special warfare training was also extended to the reserves.

In regard to the reserve and Guard units, McNamara, not convinced of their ability to augment the regulars in an emergency, reorganized their divisions in 1963. When his plan to consolidate reserve and Guard units (reserve units would disappear; reservists would serve only as individuals) was rejected by Congress, McNamara cut the number of active reserve divisions. By a 1967 reorganization plan, the number of paid reservists was reduced to 260,000, while the National Guard was maintained at 400,000. An experiment was also initiated in 1965 creating a Selected Reserve Force of 150,000 reservists and guardsmen with additional training available for quick call-up, but the concept was abandoned in 1969.

Only about 20,000 reservists and guardsmen were called to active duty during the Vietnam War. They served as replenishment and strategic reserve units only. No mass call-up of either reserves or guardsmen was ever instituted, despite the fact that all the reserve and Guard reorganizations had been put into effect to bring the reserves and Guard to greater mobilization and fighting efficiency. The Army's numbers increased to 1.5 million by 1968 because of the war, but its ranks were filled by regulars, enlistees, and draftees, not by its trained and paid reserve and Guard forces, a fact well noted by the American public and part of the reason for the dissatisfaction over the war in Vietnam.

Thus the regulars and reserves in all three services, plus the Guard, were realigned and redesigned during the 1960s, while they were simultaneously being asked to adapt to systems analysis, quantification, and the new budgetary processes. All of this, it must be recalled if one is to appreciate the almost uniform negative reaction of the military to these changes, took place in the midst of an escalating and increasingly unpopular and misunderstood conflict in Vietnam. This war, and other domestic and foreign crises that demanded the use of the armed forces, revealed the strains within the military and between the military and the White House and Congress. Restructuring carried out in peacetime is inevitably accepted in a far different spirit than in wartime. The American military had to bear the twin burdens of Vietnam and McNamara during the 1960s.

KENNEDY AND CONTAINMENT

Three areas in which President Kennedy used the military in upholding containment were Cuba, Germany, and the Far East. The last year of the Eisenhower administration had seen the overthrow of the Cuban dictator Fulgencio Batista by a group of rebels under Fidel Castro. Castro and his supporters had been recognized by the U.S. government as the legitimate government of Cuba almost immediately, but it soon became evident that Castro was intent on spreading his revolution beyond Cuba to other Latin American countries. He also displayed a distinct interest in close cooperation with the Soviet Union, as well as in imposing his own leftist one-party rule on his Caribbean nation.

As thousands of anti-Castro exiles fled Cuba for the United States, American soil became the base for planning to take the island back from Castro and his cohorts. Operating covertly through the Central Intelligence Agency (CIA), plans were soon hatched for an invasion of the island by a Cuban exile group trained in Nicaragua by U.S. agents. The invasion was to be supported by American military forces, the exiles were told. But, unbelievably, American military leaders were not even consulted in planning the invasion.

The CIA-assisted invasion of Cuba (called Operation Zapata) took place in April 1961 and quickly turned into a disaster. The invader-exiles were wiped out or captured near their invasion site, the Bay of Pigs, and no popular uprising by the Cuban people in support of the invading exiles took place. The invasion force had been promised air cover during their landings, and American naval forces with aircraft carriers were positioned just off the Cuban coast. Kennedy, informed of the invasion plans after his inauguration yet harboring doubts about the whole operation, allowed Operation Zapata to proceed—but he then refused to allow the military to aid the invading forces at the moment of their most critical need.

The Bay of Pigs fiasco was exacerbated by Castro's demanding a ransom for his prisoners and the United States' agreeing to pay it, thereby publicly admitting its part in the operation. The disaster had two major results: Kennedy was determined not to be embarrassed again, and Castro was pushed even closer to the Soviets as a means of ensuring that his revolution would not be overthrown by the United States.

The president, shaken by the Cuban debacle, was scheduled to meet with Premier Khrushchev just two months later in Vienna to talk about the status of Berlin. Khrushchev, sensing Kennedy's weakened prestige, demanded that Western troops be withdrawn from the German capital. The American president's reaction was to call 120,000 reserves to active duty and to order the military to prepare for a possible confrontation with the Soviet Union. This included sending additional troops to Europe.

By autumn Khrushchev had backed down on his demands, and containment seemed intact, although during the crisis the Soviets, through their East German clients, had built a high fortified wall across Berlin to keep the East Germans from escaping to the prosperous free section of the city and from there to West Germany. The Berlin Wall soon became a symbol of Soviet and communist enslavement and a permanent feature of politically and ideologically divided Europe. The reserves who had been called up were released by mid-1962.

Kennedy's third test of containment again concerned Cuba. In the summer of 1962 the Cuban refugee community was alive with rumors that the Soviets were moving missiles into Cuba, and American intelligence confirmed reports of Soviet military advisors, personnel, aircraft, and defensive missile emplacements on the island. Kennedy refused to give credence to the rumors and to the persistent warnings from Republican Senator Kenneth Keating of New York that IRBM missile sites were being prepared—until aerial reconnaissance photos revealed the accuracy of these reports. Kennedy became convinced just two weeks before the 1962 off-year elections were to be held—elections in which, it was predicted, his Democratic party was about to suffer serious losses.

Whether the timing of Kennedy's confirmation was fortuitous or politically expedient or both, he went on television on October 22, 1962, to tell the American people of the buildup of the Soviet missile sites and demand that the IRBM sites be removed. He also stated that he would consider any missile fired from Cuba as coming from the Soviet Union and would retaliate accordingly. By the time he went on the air, the Strategic Air Command (SAC) was on 15-minute alert with planes airborne; air defenses in the southeastern sector of the United States were being buttressed; Polaris-armed submarines had silently left their bases for unannounced cruising areas; 30,000 troops were being moved to southeastern ports in the United States; and the Second Fleet was moving toward Cuban waters. Two days later, with the approval of the Organization of American States,

Kennedy ordered a quarantine on the shipment of any offensive weapons into Cuba. Soviet ships carrying missiles into Cuba were ordered not to cross the quarantine line.

Khrushchev backed down. The offending ships turned away, and the Soviet leader agreed to remove any missiles and launching sites from Cuba. In turn, Kennedy agreed to remove certain missiles from Turkey. The crisis passed, the Soviet missiles were removed from Cuba, and the quarantine was lifted on November 20. The danger was undoubtedly never as great as it was portrayed to be by the media because Kennedy and Khrushchev were in constant communication with little chance of miscalculation, and Khrushchev was not about to take the Soviet Union into war over Cuba. Nevertheless, containment, at least for a time, had been upheld. (At a later date, Cuba would be turned into the largest Soviet military outpost outside the USSR.) Of greatest importance for the future, however, the Cuban missile crisis convinced the Soviets that they had to have a major oceangoing naval force to uphold their national interests beyond their home waters. The unprecedented growth to major status of the surface and subsurface Soviet navy can be dated from this incident in October–November 1962, a major dividing line in the East–West confrontation.

Flexible response and threat of massive retaliation appeared to be working to uphold containment in Europe and the Caribbean. In the Far East, however, the picture was much less definitive. In Laos the United States supported a pro-Western government until 1962. It then gave up, and Kennedy agreed to recognize a "neutralist" coalition government that pledged to allow no foreign military forces in Laotian territories. By the end of 1962 American advisors and technicians had left Laos, but it seemed clear that the neutralist government of Prince Souvanna Phouma was unwilling and unable to prevent the continued use of its eastern territories by the North Vietnamese in moving supplies during its war with South Vietnam. Some 7,000 North Vietnamese troops had remained in Laos to assist the Pathet Lao communists there. Ten years later their numbers had grown to 70,000, and the eastern sectors of Laos were neutral in name only.

On the other hand, dispatching U.S. marines and soldiers into Thailand in mid-1962 aided that country's government in maintaining itself against communist invaders from the east and, therefore, its independence. Of much greater importance, however, was the fact that it was in unstable Vietnam, where legitimate nationalist aspirations became entwined with and were used by communist aggressors, that containment began to fail. Here the American government and its military forces became involved in a conflict that escalated from small beginnings into a major commitment that eventually destroyed the American foreign policy consensus that had existed for three decades. Containment began to wither in the killing fields of Vietnam.

INTO THE QUAGMIRE OF VIETNAM

American military involvement in Vietnam lasted exactly 25 years. On May 1, 1950, President Truman authorized the first military assistance to Indochina. On April 30, 1975, the American-supported South Vietnamese government in Saigon fell to Communist North Vietnamese troops, concluding the final chapter in America's attempt to contain Marxist expansion in that Far Eastern country.

At the Potsdam Conference in 1945 it was agreed that with the defeat of the Japanese, the Nationalist Chinese would occupy Vietnam north of the Sixteenth Parallel and British troops would occupy the country south of that line. Vietnam, Laos, and Cambodia were part of the nation of French Indochina, under Japanese control since 1941. When the Japanese left after their defeat in 1945, however, Ho Chi Minh and his Viet Minh party (made up of communists and nationalists) seized control of much of northern and central Vietnam. British troops from India and Free French forces moved in to control the southern portion of the country. The British left soon thereafter, giving the Free French sole control of the south. The French clearly believed that they had a right to reestablish control over all of French Indochina.

Ho Chi Minh, leader of the communists, arguing that he and the Viet Minh represented the true aspirations of the Vietnamese people, who wanted their independence from France, had set up a government in August 1945 called the Democratic Republic of Vietnam (DRV) and claimed sovereignty over all of Vietnam. A March 1946 agreement between Ho and the French that the DRV would be recognized as part of the French Union soon broke down, however, and by the end of the year Ho exercised considerable *de facto* control north of the Sixteenth Parallel while the French ruled in the south.

Early in 1950, Communist China's Mao Tse-tung recognized the government of Ho and began to send supplies to the DRV. The Americans, reacting to the "loss" of China the year before and seeing the Chinese as the great communist menace in the Far East, reacted with alarm to this new threat. President Truman sent a small military assistance and advisory group (MAAG #1) to South Vietnam to aid the French logistically in upholding the government in the south under Emperor Bao Dai. This was followed by considerable monetary aid to the French as they poured men and materiel into Vietnam to try to prevent its conquest by Ho and the Viet Minh.

By 1954 the French were clearly failing in their efforts to bring all of Vietnam back under their flag despite the fact that the United States was paying 75 percent of their war costs. A time of decision for the United States came that same year when the Viet Minh forces under the diminutive, five-foot-tall General Vo Nguyen Giap managed to put a French garrison under siege at Dienbienphu in northwest Vietnam near the Laotian border. France asked for direct American military assistance to save the garrison. The Joint Chiefs were split on the question, and President Eisenhower finally decided against it. The French troops at Dienbienphu fell to the Viet Minh in May 1954.

This was the final blow for the citizens of France in their support of their government's efforts to retain French Indochina. A peace conference was assembled at Geneva to discuss the future of Vietnam. Present at the conference, besides the French and the Democratic Republic of Vietnam under Ho Chi Minh himself, were representatives from the United States, Great Britain, the Soviet Union, the People's Republic of China, Laos, Cambodia, and South Vietnam in the person of Bao Dai. At the conference it was agreed that Vietnam would be temporarily divided at the Seventeenth Parallel with nationwide elections to be held in two years to decide the fate of the country. In the meantime, the Vietnamese people would be allowed to choose where they wanted to live, north or south. The United States, like all the other powers except the principals, did not sign the resulting accord but did agree to support it.

MAP 12-1 Vietnam, 1950–1975. (*Used with permission of Anne C. Christensen.*)

In the aftermath of this Geneva Accord, 800,000 North Vietnamese took the opportunity to move south, but only 100,000 South Vietnamese moved north. And Ho ordered a considerable cadre of his followers to stay in the south to prepare for the overthrow of the Bao Dai regime. Late that year the United States agreed to send a new MAAG to South Vietnam to help prepare the South Vietnamese army to protect the country. The anti-Communist Ngo Dinh Diem, who had been living in exile in the United States, was approved as the new leader of South Vietnam as Bao Dai fled the country. Diem's ascension to chief of state was endorsed by the people of the south in a referendum the next year.

In mid-1956, Diem announced that South Vietnam would not agree to the all-Vietnam elections because Ho had set up a one-party police state in the north and would never allow the people there a free choice of governments. With 15 million people in the north and only 12 million in the south, the results would be a foregone conclusion in Ho's favor. The United States supported Diem in his stand and was cheered when he declared South Vietnam to be a republic.

As the French pulled out in 1956, the weak and untrained South Vietnamese army was badly outnumbered by the rival forces to the north. The Viet Cong (Vietnamese Communist) military consisted of three types of forces: the conventional Viet Minh regulars (who would number over half a million by 1972 despite horrendous losses in battle); the regional forces, or guerrillas, operating in the countryside; and the hamlet, or village, forces, operating as part-time guerrillas out of their homes to wear down the opposition for the North Vietnamese conventional and regional guerrilla units. The regional and hamlet forces also numbered a half million by 1972.

Unfortunately for the American and South Vietnamese military forces in the first phase of the war, they were expecting conventional border attacks from North Vietnam and were unprepared and untrained to counter the guerrillas. This explains Kennedy's haste to organize and train the Special Forces, the "Green Berets," in 1961.

From 1955 through 1958 Ho was willing to cause no undue provocation, allowing his 10,000 operatives in South Vietnam time to prepare for action. When all was ready in 1958, he made his move. Assassinations, sabotage, abductions, and military attacks took place in South Vietnam while Ho's men began carving out base areas there for future operations. The following year he cleverly camouflaged his design to conquer the south by creating the National Liberation Front (NLF), a party alleging that it represented the poor people of all of Vietnam who were engaged in a war of liberation against colonialism and wanted only to be united to live in peace under Ho. Western journalists were inclined to accept the NLF at face value. But Diem was not fooled. He declared that in fact a well-organized state of aggressive war existed in Vietnam and asked for more military aid in view of the desperate situation.

When Kennedy came into office in 1961 he reaffirmed U.S. determination to prevent communist domination of South Vietnam. Reports given him by USAF General Edward C. Lansdale (long experienced in Vietnamese matters through his work with the CIA, as chief of staff under Eisenhower, and then as special assistant to the president) indicated that this could be done with the right kind of aid. Accordingly, the number of military advisors began to climb (reaching 17,000 by late 1963), U.S. Army helicopters began to support the units of the Army of the Republic of Vietnam (ARVN), American military advisors began to accompany ARVN units into the field, and the Green Berets made their appearance in Vietnam.

Believing that American efforts—which now included both fending off the enemy and building up the South Vietnamese state at the same time—called for coordinated planning and policy, the Military Assistance Command, Vietnam (MACV), was created under General Paul D. Harkins in February 1962 to coordinate the work of the State Department, Defense Department, CIA, and the Agency for International Development. Surprisingly, considering that the United States was attempting to fight a war and build South Vietnam simultaneously, by early 1963 American efforts seemed to be paying off. The ARVN forces were more than holding their own. With American assistance in the form of UH-1s (Hueys), they were carrying out effective raids, keeping the Viet Cong guerrillas off balance, and seriously disrupting Ho and Giap's plans for the conquest of the south.

But at this point things started to go awry. A minority of Buddhist priests began to demonstrate against alleged repression by the government of the Catholic Diem, his brother, Ngo Dinh Nhu, and his brother's wife, Madame Nhu; some resorted to self-immolation. These demonstrations and self-immolations brought about two results: Diem and Nhu reacted harshly against the demonstrators, using the army and militia to put them down; and the American media took particular account of the demonstrations and repression, creating a strong anti-Diem atmosphere in the United States.

In August 1963 Kennedy replaced the veteran State Department official and ambassador to South Vietnam, Frederick E. Nolting, with Henry Cabot Lodge, distinguished Republican liberal from Massachusetts. Lodge soon joined the anti-Diem faction in the State Department led by Assistant Secretary of State for Far Eastern Affairs Averell Harriman. Despite a quick trip in October by Secretary of Defense McNamara and the chairman of the Joint Chiefs, Maxwell D. Taylor, and their subsequent positive report that progress was being made militarily, Kennedy was convinced by members of the State Department and Lodge that Diem had to be "removed" because he stood as the barrier to effective nation-building in South Vietnam. Kennedy gave his assent, and the South Vietnamese generals were informed by Lodge through Lucien Conein, a French-born CIA agent, that American aid would be cut unless Diem and Nhu were removed. Soon thereafter the two brothers were captured and assassinated in an army personnel carrier by military officers led by Duong Van Minh, "Big Minh." Kennedy, who afterwards insisted that he had no idea that the South Vietnamese leader would be killed, was himself assassinated in Dallas three weeks later.

Thus, at the same time as Kennedy was removed from the scene by death, to be replaced by Vice President Lyndon B. Johnson of Texas, the act of deposing Diem plunged South Vietnam into governmental chaos instead of aiding the war effort there. Kennedy had done what Ho had never been able to do. He had removed the effective—if corrupt and sometimes cruel—leader of South Vietnam on whom, for good or for ill, victory depended. He had approved Diem's removal at the very time that Ho's forces, both conventional and guerrilla, had been fought to a virtual standstill. It was his successor, Lyndon Johnson, who was fated to reap the whirlwind of Kennedy's tragic decision and lead the American armed forces deeper and deeper into the quagmire until defeat was ensured.

VIETNAM AND JOHNSON

The assassination of Ngo Dinh Diem ushered in a period of continual instability in South Vietnam that lasted for a year and a half. Various generals jockeyed for the position of leader of the nation, causing disarray, confusion, and venality in the ranks of the South Vietnamese army as leadership assignments were made on the basis of personal loyalty and accepted as a means of personal enrichment. The North Vietnamese took full advantage of this political and military chaos, raising their numbers to 100,000 men operating in the south, two-thirds being conventional forces as Giap sent two full divisions of regulars into the fight. The Viet Cong became a second government in the rural areas. South Vietnamese units pursued them during the day, but everyone openly admitted that in the countryside "the night belongs to the Viet Cong." The South Vietnamese–United States program to relocate the villagers in "strategic hamlets" for their own safety simply collapsed in the face of Viet Cong strength. America in 1964 raised its total number of military advisors to 23,000, but this seemed to make little difference.

☆   An American Portrait

Maxwell D. Taylor—Taylor, eulogized at his death by President Ronald Reagan as "a soldier's soldier and a stateman's statesman," was born in the small Missouri town of Keytesville on August 26, 1901, the son of a railroad lawyer. He decided at an early age to pursue a military career. Entering West Point in 1918, Taylor compiled an outstanding record, including service as first captain of cadets, and was graduated fourth in his class in 1922.

FIGURE 12–1   Maxwell D. Taylor. (*Official U.S. Army Photo, DOD Still Media Records Center, Washington, D.C.*)

During the 1920s Taylor served with engineering units in Maryland and Hawaii and was sent to Paris to perfect his skill in French. During the 1930s he attended artillery school at Fort Sill, Oklahoma; attended the Command and General Staff School; taught foreign languages at West Point; was sent to Tokyo to learn Japanese; and was posted to the Army War College. In 1941 and 1942 he served on General George Marshall's staff at the Pentagon and then was assigned as chief of staff of General Matthew Ridgway's 82nd Infantry Division.

When the 82nd was converted into an airborne division, Taylor stayed with it as artillery commander in North Africa and fought in the Sicilian campaign. He also participated in a secret mission behind enemy lines to determine whether or not Marshal Pietro Badoglio's request for the seizure of Rome was feasible; he determined that it was not, and the assault was cancelled. After further service in Italy, he was selected to command the 101st Airborne Division in February 1944.

Taylor parachuted in with his men behind Utah Beach on D-Day, and after the capture of Cherbourg returned with them to England. The following September he parachuted into Holland with the 101st as part of Operation Market-Garden. Taylor had been called back to Washington when his division was surrounded at Bastogne during the Battle of the Bulge, but he returned in January 1945 to lead them to victory over the Germans.

After the war, Taylor was named superintendent of West Point, then U.S. commander in Berlin, assistant chief of staff, and, in 1953, commander of the Eighth Army in Korea. After serving for a time as U.S. Far East commander, in June 1955 he was appointed Army chief of staff by President Eisenhower. Here he clashed repeatedly with the purveyors of Eisenhower's massive retaliation "New Look," finally retiring in 1959 to write *The Uncertain Trumpet,* in which he spelled out the danger of nuclear war and the need for a flexible response doctrine for the military.

Called to Washington to investigate the Bay of Pigs debacle, Taylor so impressed President Kennedy that he was asked to stay on as the president's special military representative. Sent to Vietnam by Kennedy, Taylor recommended that the United States military role should be primarily logistical. In October 1962 Taylor was made chairman of the Joint Chiefs of Staff, serving until 1964 under Kennedy and Lyndon Johnson. Under the latter, Taylor recommended a strategy of counterinsurgency and air strikes on North Vietnam.

In July 1964 Taylor replaced Henry Cabot Lodge as ambassador to South Vietnam, being given overall military responsibility in the country. Resigning one year later, Taylor served as special counsel to the president and as one of the "Wise Men" advising Johnson. In this capacity, he came to oppose General William Westmoreland's demand for escalation of the fighting in 1968. After his retirement he continued to write and speak out on military issues.

Taylor died on April 19, 1987, and was buried in Arlington National Cemetery near the Tomb of the Unknown Soldier, with veterans of the 101st Airborne Division delivering the final salute.

Then, in August 1964, some North Vietnamese patrol boats apparently attacked two U.S. destroyers in international waters within the Gulf of Tonkin. (The full details of this naval engagement are still not clear, and the whole subject is open to widescale discussion and debate. That the patrol boats were there is clear; whether or not they attacked the second U.S. destroyer is the heart of the dispute.) Johnson ordered air strikes on the North Vietnamese patrol boat bases, and 64 sorties were flown from American carriers. He also reported the situation to Congress. The president requested, and received from Congress on August 7, 1964, the authority in the Tonkin Gulf Resolution to take all necessary measures to repel attacks on U.S. forces and to prevent further aggression in Southeast Asia. Virtually without dissent, Johnson was presented with a *carte blanche* in Vietnam by Congress by this action. He was more than willing to use it as the fighting escalated.

Early in 1965 the Viet Cong and North Vietnamese regular army units began a series of savage assaults that threatened to crumble the South Vietnamese army. North Vietnamese units seized control of district capitals as far south as the Central Highlands and the Mekong Delta region in this frustrating war without front lines, in which the enemy was indistinguishable from the civilian nationals. South Vietnamese political leadership was nonexistent. After a Viet Cong rocket attack on Pleiku, Johnson ordered air strikes against military targets in North Vietnam.

Operation Rolling Thunder was begun by the Air Force in February 1965. Its extent was "measured and limited," much to the distress of the military, because Hanoi and the important port of Haiphong, vital to resupply from the Soviet Union, were excluded as targets. McNamara and Secretary of State Dean Rusk insisted on the cities' exclusion out of fear of Soviet or Chinese intervention, not realizing that neither country was willing to risk full-scale war over Vietnam. Nor did the American government realize that the Soviet Union was aiding North Vietnam only to keep the United States involved there and to weaken it militarily, economically, and politically by a protracted war. Further, American policy makers at this time turned a blind eye to signs out of China that Chinese aid to North Vietnam was negotiable.

Rolling Thunder made little appreciable difference, so Johnson ordered two Marine Corps battalions into Danang in the northern sector (the first regular U.S. troops units to be committed), followed by an air squadron in April. This was followed by the dispatching of the 173rd Airborne Brigade to the Bien Hoa air base north of Saigon and the order for the Air Force's B-52s to begin bombing enemy bases in the jungles of South Vietnam. Between July and December 1965, another 180,000 American troops were ordered in to turn the tide.

Despite the fact that at this point American troop ability and morale were excellent and the United States had a clear advantage in firepower, the commitment of more troops was not decisive. The reason lay in the seriously flawed presidentially directed strategy imposed on the military. The generals wanted to gain military superiority over the enemy quickly and decisively and defeat him on all fronts by isolating him from resupply and by using superior firepower to break his will to conquest. But Johnson, loath to admit publicly that the United States was in a real war because it might adversely affect his "Great Society" domestic programs, listened instead to McNamara and Rusk.

These secretaries urged on him a strategy of "graduated escalation," whereby the United States would increase its warmaking efforts in steps. This way Ho Chi Minh would feel the increasing pressure and eventually come to realize that the cost of continuing the fighting was too high in North Vietnamese lives and materiel. He would then give in. According to McNamara's application of systems analysis to the battlefield, a given tonnage of bombs dropped and casualties inflicted on North Vietnam would produce a given reaction on the North Vietnamese leaders. If these steps did not work, the ante would be raised a little higher until the damage done was unacceptable. Ho and North Vietnam would then quit the fight.

This whole strategic theory of attrition by escalation was based on the assumption that Ho would find a certain level of death and destruction intolerable. But the North Vietnamese leader would accept *any* number of casualties (even ratios as high as 10 to 1 or 100 to 1 if necessary), and Ho also knew that war materiel would continue to flow into North Vietnam from the outside.

☆ An American Portrait

William C. Westmoreland—One of the most controversial commanders of the Vietnam era, William Childs Westmoreland was born in Spartanburg County, South Carolina, in 1914, the son of a textile mill manager. After attending public schools in Spartanburg and The Citadel at Charleston for one year, he gained an appointment to the United States Military Academy in 1932. Here he amassed an outstanding record, including receiving the Pershing Award for leadership and being named first captain of cadets his fourth year. He was commissioned upon graduation in 1936.

Prior to World War II, Westmoreland held assignments at Fort Sill, in Hawaii, and at Fort Bragg, and then gained a reputation for leadership in World War II in North Africa, playing a major role in stopping the German breakthrough at Kasserine Pass. He led troops in combat in Sicily, at Utah Beach, and in the final drive into Germany.

In 1946, Westmoreland, after taking parachute training, was named to head the 504th Paratroop Infantry Regiment. He then became chief of staff of the 82nd Airborne Division at Fort Bragg. He also taught at the Command and General Staff College and the

FIGURE 12–2   William C. Westmoreland. (*Official U.S. Army Photo, DOD Still Media Records Center, Washington, D.C.*)

Army War College before commanding the 187th Airborne Regiment in Korea. In the years after Korea, Westmoreland was assigned to the Pentagon, attended graduate school at Harvard University, and was named secretary to the Army General Staff, serving under Maxwell D. Taylor. Now a major general, he took command of the 101st Airborne Division in 1958 and then served as superintendent of West Point between 1960 and 1963 before being named commandant of the XVIII Airborne Corps.

In June 1964 Westmoreland was appointed commander in Vietnam. He urged an expanded American commitment there, including more troops and the bombing of North Vietnam. Although circumscribed by American policy decisions, Westmoreland carried out a deadly war of attrition against the enemy, using superior American firepower and mobility in an effort to achieve victory in the war. His differences with President Johnson and his civilian advisors, now tilting toward deescalation, and his being caught off guard by faulty intelligence reports at the time of the Tet Offensive, resulted in his being recalled in 1968 to become chairman of the Joint Chiefs. He held this position until his retirement in 1972.

Westmoreland returned to South Carolina, where he made an unsuccessful run for the Republican gubernatorial nomination in 1974. Subsequently playing an active role in the debate over the Vietnam War and his place within it, Westmoreland brought a $120 million suit for libel against the CBS television network for a documentary that charged him with suppressing evidence of increasing Communist strength in Vietnam for political purposes. The ensuing trial revealed how the television network distorted testimony in creating its anti-Westmoreland report. The case was settled out of court, with Westmoreland receiving an apology, but no money, from CBS in early 1985. Westmoreland remains in retirement in Charleston, South Carolina.

In the field, General William C. Westmoreland, who had replaced General Harkins the year before, was left with the task of "winning" the war. But his war-of-attrition strategy—some argue this was an erroneous strategy—was circumscribed by a number of crucial factors. First, there could be no rapid buildup of American ground forces to overwhelm the enemy because President Johnson would not call up the reserves and National Guard units. Such a call-up would be an admission that there was a war on, and monies would have to be deflected from his domestic programs. Second, military strategy, and even tactics at times, were being directed from Washington. For example, Johnson himself selected tactical bombing targets for the Air Force. Third, bombing of North Vietnamese cities, especially Hanoi and Haiphong, the pivot points of the North Vietnamese war effort, was not allowed, even though these were the sites of greatest vulnerability for Ho, because of a fear of bringing China and the Soviet Union into the war. Further, periodic suspension of the bombing of other targets was imposed by the White House and McNamara in the hope of bringing Ho to the bargaining table.

Fourth, top American civilian leaders had decided that "neutral" Cambodia could not be touched, even though supplies for the Viet Cong were flowing openly through the port of Sihanoukville and North Vietnamese operatives fully controlled crucial parts of Cambodian border provinces and used them as staging areas for attacks on South Vietnam. Fifth, it was policy that the Americans were to treat the ARVN as an ally and equal partner and, therefore, Westmoreland had no control over the South Vietnamese army strategically or tactically. This was in contrast to the Korean War, in which the ROK military operated under United States–United Nations direction. Sixth, the "war that wasn't a war" was being shown at home on television screens with little or no media censorship, either self-imposed or government-imposed, in place. This meant that the fighting was being interpreted and judged by persons incapable of understanding the total picture. (Lack of media censorship of some kind was also a point in contrast with World War II and Korea.) Seventh, President Johnson, on the other hand, was somehow unwilling or unable to express a justifiable explanation to the American people for the escalating commitment that the nation was being asked to make in Vietnam. As a result, there could be no rallying of American will to a war effort that was rapidly becoming massive and, therefore, increasingly controversial.

Under these virtually impossible circumstances, Westmoreland and the military, though hamstrung by official policy, fought on. Their strategy consisted of holding actions on all fronts while building logistics bases for sustained action. Out from these fortified base camps (and from extended temporary base camps and fire support bases), long- and short-range patrols were sent to flush out the enemy and fix him for vertical assault tactics. Air Force and naval strategic bombing, in the meantime, attempted to cut or at least seriously disrupt the enemy's line of supply, leaving him with inadequate materiel and subject to destruction. Air Force and Marine tactical support was also employed. If the U.S. Army and Marine Corps ground "search and destroy" missions were successful and the enemy was flushed out and defeated, this, in turn, would protect the South Vietnamese civilians so that the complementary rural pacification program would work. Removing "Charlie" from the countryside would also protect the major cities and economic zones so that the South Vietnamese government would be given a chance at stability and governing success. Basically, within this strategy the marines were assigned the northern provinces of South Vietnam, the Army the Central Highlands, and the South Vietnamese the Mekong Delta and Saigon areas in the south.

This attempt at protecting and pacifying South Vietnam called for a major outlay in men and materiel by the United States. Between 1965 and 1967 the U.S. military manpower commitment in Vietnam rose from 25,000 to 500,000 men (mostly regulars, enlistees, and draftees, the Army having two corps and the Marines two divisions and one regiment in the field) and climbed even higher. South Vietnamese military commitments in the same period rose to 340,000 regulars and 300,000 militia, and Korea contributed 48,000 soldiers. Small contingents were sent from Thailand, Australia, New Zealand, and the Philippines.

The logistics buildup reflected the escalation of manpower. By 1967, some 1.3 million persons (American military, South Vietnamese military, allied military, and civilians) were being supplied by the United States, and supplies were flowing into South Vietnamese ports at the rate of 850,000 tons per month. These included 80,000 tons of ordnance and 80 million gallons of petroleum.

The American troops were well equipped in weaponry, with their M16 rifles, 40-millimeter grenade launchers, claymore mines (which shot off hundreds of dartlike projectiles), armored personnel carriers, Patton tanks, and Huey Cobra helicopter gunships. But the enemy, too, was well armed and equipped with the excellent AK47 rifle, mortars, heavy rockets, and Soviet SAMs. The North Vietnamese had no air power, but they made excellent use of what weaponry they had in a war fought essentially on their terms.

FIGURE 12–3 M16 rifle. (*Smithsonian Institution, Washington, D.C.*).

In 1966 Ho Chi Minh publicly proclaimed a strategy of protracted warfare. It was obvious that a quick victory by North Vietnam was now out of the question as American commitments continued to grow. Indeed, in 1966 the war began to turn against Ho despite all the limitations placed on the American fighting men in the field. United States forces moved to locate and defeat Viet Cong forces and base areas. The 4th Infantry Division drove into the Central Highlands near Pleiku, the 1st Cavalry Division and a brigade of the 101st Airborne moved into the coastal provinces, and the 1st Infantry Division cleared the area north of Saigon. In the meantime, pacification of the countryside was making some progress under the Office of Civil Operations and Rural Development Support (CORDS), with land reform, public health, and education initiatives being carried out. And the South Vietnamese army was cleaning out the Viet Cong "shadow" governments in the countryside. Furthermore, overall governmental authority over South Vietnam was regained under General Nguyen Thieu, who won a clear victory in the September 1967 elections.

FIGURE 12–4 AH1 Huey Cobra helicopter gunship. (*Official U.S. Army Photo, DOD Still Media Records Center, Washington, D.C.*)

Yet Westmoreland and the American forces in Vietnam were continually hobbled and even endangered by flawed policy decisions on how the war was to be fought. On the ground the enemy forces continued to build up with impunity in Laos and Cambodia and strike across the border with great force. This was obvious when, equipped with new Soviet-made automatic rifles, mortars, and large anti-aircraft guns, they hit a Special Forces camp at Dak To in the Central Highlands in November 1967 and were repulsed only with the use of massive American firepower, losing 1,600 men. Likewise, they hit the 6,000 marines at Khe Sanh in the northwest corner of the country just below the demilitarized zone (DMZ) with 32,000 to 40,000 men and held them under heavy siege for two months despite being deluged with 75,000 tons of explosives and suffering 10,000 killed. In the air, Operation Rolling Thunder was not working because the North Vietnamese built their military positions around off-limit targets such as schools, hospitals, and dikes. The Air Force was left bombing the jungles, and McNamara could only conclude that further bombing was not "cost effective." Johnson's civilian advisors, including McNamara, were now urging him to deescalate the war.

While the brunt of the fighting in Vietnam was carried by soldiers and marines, the Navy also played an important role. Primary naval support came from Task Force 77, lying 100 miles offshore on "Yankee Station" in the Gulf of Tonkin. From here, Navy planes flew mission after mission against industrial and tactical targets such as roads and bridges in support of the ground troops. The naval aviators, like their Air Force counterparts, were forbidden to bomb Hanoi, Haiphong, and other privileged sanctuaries.

The Navy dispatched the battleship *New Jersey* to Vietnam, her nine 16-inch guns being used against targets on shore. Small naval vessels were also used to interdict junks and other vessels supplying the North Vietnamese by water. And the "brown-water navy," using shallow-draft converted landing craft equipped with machine guns, 20- and 40-millimeter cannons, and 81-millimeter mortars, patrolled the Mekong Delta and the waters around Saigon interdicting enemy supplies. These sailors aided the Army in carrying out raids on enemy posts along the waterways. Some 38,000 naval personnel were on duty in Vietnam by 1968.

Of crucial importance to the final outcome of the war—clearly as important as the encumbrances placed on the military in the field—were domestic conflicts and antiwar pressures being placed on the policy makers back in the United States. The nation since 1962 had seen the black civil rights movement grow and spill over into major violence that eventually involved the use of military force. Some 20,000 regular troops and 10,000 federalized Mississippi National Guardsmen were ordered to Oxford, Mississippi, in September 1962 to put down riots and ensure the registration of a black student at the University of Mississippi. The next year President Kennedy used federalized Alabama guardsmen during racial troubles in that state, and two years later President Johnson ordered Alabama guardsmen and regulars to protect civil rights activists on their march from Selma to Montgomery.

Johnson's and the nation's civil rights problems continued while the war was escalating. In 1964 there was a race riot in Rochester, New York, and a major racial outbreak in the Watts section of Los Angeles in 1965 necessitated the use of over 13,000 California guardsmen to quell the rioting. During 1966 there were racial outbreaks in many major cities, including Chicago, Cleveland, and San Francisco. The rioting in Newark and Detroit in 1967 was especially destructive. Newark's troubles were quelled by guardsmen, but the Detroit situation eventually required 10,000 Michigan guardsmen and 5,000 regulars to restore order. The year 1968 saw further rioting as a reaction to the assassination of black civil rights leader Dr. Martin Luther King, Jr.

Added to Johnson's racial problems at home was the burgeoning antiwar movement. Based on resistance to selective service in particular and the Vietnam conflict in general, the power base of the movement was the nation's college campuses, where concerned students and professors took the lead in demanding an end to the war. The movement was fueled by a lack of candor on the part of the administration as to why the war was being fought and the problems involved in this amorphous type of drawn-out struggle being fought half a world away. The antiwar sentiment was also fed by television coverage of the fighting in Vietnam. Television could show only the horror of the war but not the justification for the killing, which had been going on with increased intensity for more than three years. Nor could television provide any coverage of North Vietnam and its deplorable torture of Americans held prisoner there, which would surely have altered the public's perception of the war.

The first peace marches began in 1965. In October 1967, some 50,000 protestors besieged the Pentagon. These marches were complemented by antiwar activists' attacks on draft boards to destroy records, flights out of the country to avoid military service, and a gradual shift of the media toward opposition to the war, partially out of a distrust and dislike of Lyndon Johnson. With the racial violence of the 1960s, the high rate of inflation caused by Johnson's insistence that the nation could afford "both guns and butter," and the increasingly misunderstood and unpopular war dragging on in Vietnam, matters were approaching a climax.

1968: YEAR OF DECISION

Well aware of the American public's increasing disenchantment with the fighting in Vietnam—indeed, relying on it as America's greatest point of vulnerability—Ho Chi Minh decided in late 1967 to launch a massive offensive in South Vietnam. Such an offensive might seriously undermine or even topple the Thieu government in the south. Furthermore, the offensive could potentially cause a "general uprising" among the people of the south, removing the base of support for American participation in the war. Perhaps if the general offensive met with great success, a series of defeats could then be inflicted on the American forces and push them out of the war altogether. The time seemed right for Ho to test the capabilities of a general offensive, even though that would mean switching his strategy to conventional warfare (as was being carried out at Khe Sanh), but the stakes seemed worthwhile. Giap agreed. Ho already had his best agents in the south prepared to foster antigovernment uprisings. His attacks, he knew, would also raise the antiwar sentiment in the United States to fever pitch. The uprisings and attacks were planned to come during the holiday time of Tet (the Asian lunar New Year), when tradition called for an armistice or at least a reduction in the fighting.

The Tet Offensive began on January 30, 1968, with simultaneous North Vietnamese attacks in the northern and central provinces and in the Saigon and Mekong Delta areas. Over 84,000 Viet Cong and North Vietnamese regulars attacked 36 of the 43 provincial capitals in addition to dozens of other cities and villages. Heavy fighting broke out in Saigon, in Hue (where at least 3,000 civilians were slaughtered in cold blood by the North Vietnamese), and in Dak To, and continued at Khe Sanh. All of the attacks were repulsed. There were no uprisings against the government. The attackers were simply overwhelmed by American firepower and by surprisingly effective resistance by the South Vietnamese troops. Although the estimates vary, probably some 32,000 North Vietnamese were killed and 6,000 captured, compared to only about 4,000 American and South Vietnamese casualties. Ho and Giap had bet everything on one great offensive, and they had been beaten badly, at least on the tactical level. They were forced to retreat. It took months for them to recover, and they faced serious morale problems at home. Yet their tactical bloody defeat turned out to be the overwhelming strategic victory of the long war.

This ironic outcome of the failed Tet Offensive can be explained by three factors: (1) immediately prior to Tet, a series of optimistic briefings from MACV had described the enemy as virtually destroyed; (2) the antiwar sentiment and disenchantment with Lyndon Johnson's policies was so strong in the United States that any perceived loss would be deemed sufficient reason to call off the war effort; and (3) the United States and South Vietnamese *victory* during the Tet Offensive was portrayed as a *defeat* by the American media, finally convincing the American people that a way had to be found to get out of Vietnam. Tet, then, was a great battlefield defeat for the North Vietnamese but a psychological victory of climactic proportions.

Johnson, overwhelmed by Tet, announced on March 31, 1968, a willingness to negotiate an end to all bombing north of the Nineteenth Parallel. (By November he had extended the ban to all of North Vietnam.) He went on television to inform the American people that he would not run for reelection as president that autumn. (One month before, McNamara had left the Johnson administration, and one week before, Westmoreland had been recalled by the president.) The North Vietnamese leaders now knew they would win. American will had been broken.

VIETNAM AND NIXON

It is instructive to note that the two opposing presidential candidates in 1960 (Kennedy and Nixon) had argued how best to carry out America's moral commitments against aggressors. In 1964 the candidates (Johnson and Barry M. Goldwater of Arizona) had argued over how best to win the Vietnam War. And in 1968, Nixon and Hubert H. Humphrey of Minnesota debated how best to get out of the war. Public opinion had switched dramatically. The winner in 1968, Richard M. Nixon of California, asserted during the campaign that he had a plan to take the nation out of the war while preserving national honor. Significantly, he also promised to "bring the nation together," apparently, at least in part, by defusing the antiwar sentiment.

☆ An American Portrait

Creighton Abrams—Creighton William Abrams, Jr., the top American commander in Vietnam from 1968 to 1972, was born in Springfield, Massachusetts, in 1914. After high school he won an appointment to West Point, graduating in the class of 1936 as a lieutenant of cavalry. After four years in Texas with the 1st Cavalry Division, Abrams in 1941 and 1942 served with the 1st Armored Division and the new 4th Armored Division.

Assuming command of the 37th Tank Battalion, he led it from Normandy across Europe, relieving the 101st Airborne Division in December 1944 at Bastogne during the Battle of the Bulge. In doing so, he came to be regarded as one of the best—if not the best—tank commanders in the European theater.

After the war he attended the Command and General Staff College and held various armored commands. During the Korean War he served on the corps level and afterwards attended the Army War College. In the 1960s Abrams commanded the 3rd Armored Division in Europe during the Berlin Wall crisis of 1962 and the federal troops sent by President Eisenhower to ensure the peaceful integration of the University of Mississippi that same year. By 1964 he had commanded V Corps in Europe, had won a fourth star, and had been appointed vice chief of staff of the Army.

In 1967 Abrams assumed one of the most difficult tasks of his career when he was appointed deputy commander of MACV under orders to improve the fighting capabilities of America's South Vietnamese ally. After the Tet Offensive and the departure of General Westmoreland the next year, Abrams became the head of MACV, presiding over American efforts to hold off the North Vietnamese while drawing down U.S. troop strength and turning the war over to the South Vietnamese under President Nixon's policy of Vietnamization. Here he moved away from Westmoreland's "search and destroy" tactics in favor of harassing the enemy at every turn, including carrying out incursions into Cambodia in 1970 and Laos in 1971, while building up the South Vietnamese military forces. Their success in thwarting the North Vietnamese Easter Offensive in 1972 spoke to the wisdom of his efforts.

In 1972 Abrams returned to the United States to assume the duties of chief of staff of the Army during one of its most troubled periods as it attempted to restructure itself after Vietnam, institute the all-volunteer system, and regain the confidence of the American people. He served in this position with distinction until his death two years later. This often unheralded fighting commander, known for his ability to inspire trust in all those with whom he dealt, was interred in Arlington National Cemetery.

While Nixon probably had no fixed plan for ending the war, as he said, he soon developed one. It was called "Vietnamization." Essentially, it meant supplying the South Vietnamese army and militia, now totaling over 1 million men, with the weapons, materiel, and other aid they would need to carry on the war while the Americans gradually withdrew from the contest with honor intact. But it also meant changing the existing strategic and tactical rules of the game. In March 1969, the North Vietnamese bases in Cambodia were bombed by B-52s. In April and May 1970, South Vietnamese soldiers moved into the "Parrot's Beak" in Cambodia, only 30 miles from Saigon, and U.S. and South Vietnamese units also moved into the "Fish Hook" farther north to destroy North Vietnamese supplies there. Some 74,000 South Vietnamese and American troops took part in the operations, with 11,000 North Vietnamese being killed to only 337 American casualties. The privileged-sanctuary policy in regard to Laos and Cambodia was finished, even though the incursions set off renewed antiwar demonstrations at home and commentators decried the violation of the territorial rights of the two "neutral" nations.

By the end of 1970 the number of American troops in Vietnam stood at only 150,000, down from its wartime high in 1968 of 565,000. In 1971 the policies of Vietnamization and renewed pacification of the countryside continued with some success, but the public outcry in America against the war hardly lessened. News of an American combat patrol wiping out the people of the village of Mi Lai back in 1968 and the subsequent cover-up of the incident by the Army had come out the year before. Lieutenant William Calley, the platoon leader, was being portrayed by the media at his trial at Fort Benning as a typical example of this "evil war" laying waste to Vietnam and its people. (Calley was convicted in March 1971 of premeditated murder.) And incidents of drug use, racial violence, and "fragging" of officers—all evidence of low morale—began to be regularly reported at home. Finally, Daniel Ellsberg in 1971 leaked the contents of the top secret "Pentagon Papers" through the *New York Times,* revealing the plans and doubts of America's high civilian and military leaders during the war. The antiwar movement, highlighted by continual antiwar demonstrations and the Kent State "massacre" of 1970 (after prolonged provocation, Ohio National Guardsmen fired into a group of student demonstrators, killing four), could not even be slowed. Protests continued despite Nixon's promise to end the draft in favor of an all-volunteer Army and in spite of his efforts to extricate the United States from the war while hoping to save an ally, South Vietnam.

In April 1972 the North Vietnamese launched their "Easter Offensive," their first major conventional drive since Tet, four years before. Despite throwing 12 divisions (equipped with Soviet-built armor and artillery) across the DMZ into the Central Highlands, the offensive was stopped very effectively by the South Vietnamese with the aid of overwhelming American tactical air power. Equally important and instructive, in retaliation Nixon ordered the strategic bombing of North Vietnam resumed and the mining of Haiphong harbor. Both were carried out, and neither China nor the Soviet Union reacted with anything other than *pro forma* protests.

Then, in October 1972, while Secretary of State Henry Kissinger was carrying out negotiations (he had opened secret talks back in August 1969), North Vietnam renewed its military attacks. Nixon ordered that Operation Linebacker II be carried out. It was a mighty air bombardment of North Vietnam in which 1,800 sorties were flown and 20,000 tons of bombs were dropped in 11 days. Under this pressure, the North Vietnamese came back to the peace table. North Vietnam and South Vietnam signed peace accords, and the United States agreed to withdraw. All other issues were to be left to the Vietnamese themselves. The agreements were weak in regard to the continued independence of South Vietnam, but it was probably the best settlement attainable under the circumstances. The only real guarantee of future security that President Thieu and the South Vietnamese people had was the American promise that it would continue to aid them so that they could defend themselves thereafter.

The next two years were marked by increased North Vietnamese military action in Vietnam and angry recriminations in the United States. Vietnam veterans continued to return home to widespread public indifference if not to outright hostility. Congress passed the War Powers Act stating that it had to approve of all presidential troop deployments within 60 days or the military units had to be returned to their bases. The Army had to adjust to an all-volunteer force, begun in 1970, and the office of president and commander-in-chief was seriously weakened by the Watergate break-in scandal and subsequent congressional hearings, which eventually forced Richard Nixon to resign in 1974 to avoid impeachment. Gerald R. Ford, ex-congressman from Michigan and Nixon's appointed vice president (Spiro Agnew had resigned from the office in disgrace in October 1973 after being indicted for tax evasion), became the thirty-eighth president of the United States.

As North Vietnam increased its military pressure, the South Vietnamese government and armies became demoralized by the shrinking level of American aid, their only hope for holding off the communists. In 1973 U.S. aid amounted to $2.3 billion; Congress lowered it to $1.1 billion in 1974; and in 1975 Congress appropriated only $700 million.

When, therefore, in 1975 the North Vietnamese began a limited offensive northwest of Saigon (at the same time the Khmer Rouge were attacking the Cambodian capital of Phnom Penh) and no American air strikes were mounted to aid the South Vietnamese, the North Vietnamese leaders got the message: The South Vietnamese were on their own. Accordingly, in March they attacked in the Central Highlands and then moved toward Danang. With South Vietnamese resistance crumbling, a general attack was ordered on all fronts, including Saigon.

President Ford begged Congress for $700 million in immediate aid to try to save the country, but it was refused. On April 30, 1975, the last Americans fled Saigon as the North Vietnamese swept into the capital. The Vietnam War was over. America had lost in Vietnam despite the fact that over 2.5 million Americans had served there, over 47,000 had lost their lives in combat (with another 10,000 having died from other causes), and another 150,000 had been wounded. An ally had been abandoned. Perhaps 10,000 South Vietnamese were executed (one estimate places the figure at 65,000) and as many as 50,000 were imprisoned as the North Vietnamese fastened their rule on the south and soon carried out a massive invasion and lengthy occupation of Cambodia. And American national consensus had been shattered.

THE VIETNAM ERA: A CRITIQUE

In the years since the fall of Saigon, the Vietnam War has been studied in the United States with particular passion. The 25-year conflict has been critiqued from every possible angle. Every aspect of strategy, tactics, generalship, and political leadership has been pondered and argued over as the nation has wrestled with its first major military defeat. From this plethora of analyses, six conclusions go a long way toward explaining the nation's failure in Vietnam.

1. The war was fought from start to finish in cold blood, with no clear policy goal established that would satisfy the American people, especially in a protracted war during which they were bound to question whether or not the goal and the costs of attaining that goal were worth the effort. For the American people to support a war, they must be mobilized for the conflict around defined and embracable reasons. These were never spelled out satisfactorily in regard to Vietnam. The closest the nation came to having a purpose for the fighting and dying was Nixon's goal of preserving national honor while helping South Vietnam save itself. But this did not come until 1969, after the war had already been lost. But Johnson, even after three years of intensive fighting, continued to ask the American people to continue to accept a prolonged and bloody conflict in Southeast Asia as a non-war, with "business as usual" at home. By not mobilizing the people, using overwhelming force between 1964 and 1967, or ending the war by 1968 (even with a stalemated limited victory), he thus opened a point of major vulnerability that Ho Chi Minh and the North Vietnamese were able to exploit with great effectiveness. The result of Johnson's non-war decision was that being "for the war" and "against the war" were both considered patriotic acts. No nation can win a major conflict—and Vietnam was a major conflict by 1967—under these circumstances.

2. America's military leaders allowed civilians to dominate military strategy and even tactics to an extent that efficient warmaking became impossible. American civilian leaders have normally and properly determined strategy (Lincoln during the Civil War, McKinley in the Spanish-American War, and Roosevelt during World War II are prime examples), but in no previous war had they dominated tactics as they did in Vietnam. When it became obvious that the Johnson-McNamara parameters imposed on the military and their tactical interference effectively precluded a successful outcome of the conflict and resulted only in additional battlefield deaths and other casualties to no good end, the military chiefs at the highest levels never put their careers on the line by challenging either the strategy or the tactics ordered by their civilian superiors.

3. American civilian and military policy makers never realized that they were fighting a twentieth-century revolutionary war on the part of North Vietnam. Modern revolutionary warfare calls for both guerrilla and conventional warfare used in assigned sequences or places. It also calls for a protracted and ambiguous struggle in which time works for the revolutionary while he deliberately hides his true intentions in order to weaken the willpower of the enemy. The United States and South Vietnam continually placed the balance of their force mobilization on the Viet Cong guerrillas, but the crucial military force was the regulars, who eventually won the victory for North Vietnam. In a word, the United States fought the wrong kind of war against an enemy it did not understand. And perhaps the war could never have been won, since Ho and Giap could always have dropped the war back to a lower level at any time and continued to wear away at American patience by avoiding any clear-cut solution until the United States gave up and went home.

4. By Johnson's promise not to invade North Vietnam and by his bombing limitations, especially regarding Hanoi and Haiphong, he was ensuring American and South Vietnamese defeat. He forced the United States to follow a negative strategy (avoiding defeat) and negative tactics (weakening the Viet Cong and North Vietnamese regulars and guerrillas so they could not do major damage). With a negative strategy and negative tactics the war could not be won. In adopting this strategy and these tactics, Johnson completely underestimated the will of Hanoi and overestimated the response of the Soviet Union and China to America's attacking obviously non-neutral sanctuaries and cutting off North Vietnam's channels of supply. Trapped by these misperceptions, by his distrust of the judgment of the military leaders, by his overconfidence in his civilian advisors, and by his fear of seeing his Great Society programs fail, he doomed the nation to five years of fruitless carnage before he stepped out of the picture with the war already lost.

5. The media, especially television, was allowed to dominate the interpretation of the war, a war that most journalists did not understand either strategically or tactically. President Johnson exacerbated this situation by not explaining regularly, clearly, and forcefully to the American people why and how the war was being fought. The result of this failure was that the media was playing up the war—with all the necessary distortions intendant upon television coverage—while Johnson and his spokesmen were playing it down. Furthermore, American television and the other media coverage carried to the Far East made it very clear to the soldiers, marines, sailors, and airmen there (who were also rotated back to the United States on a regular basis and thus were well aware of domestic sentiment) that a sizable segment of the American public did not support their efforts and sacrifices. The antiwar forces in the United States were undoubtedly a minority, at least until 1968, but television and the print media allowed them an influence both home and abroad far out of proportion to their numbers.

6. Essentially the United States was trying to fight a war against a very determined enemy while at the same time trying to create a nation out of whole cloth, an impossible task under the best of circumstances. Such a goal can be accomplished only if one is willing to carry out both tasks by massive coercion to the point of internal terror, as was done by Ho Chi Minh in North Vietnam, but it could not have been done by the United States in South Vietnam. The nation of South Vietnam could perhaps have been created *after* the North Vietnamese had been beaten decisively—which was possible through 1965—but not while the prolonged, ambiguously portrayed, and privileged-sanctuary conflict with North Vietnam was being carried on.

Other factors also worked against an American–South Vietnamese military victory. Among these was the policy of one-year tours of duty in Vietnam that constantly worked against unit loyalty and effectiveness by removing officers and noncommissioned officers from their men just as they got to know them (even though the rotation policy was advantageous for the domestic-consumption sham that there was not a major war going on). Also, the use of body counts as a way of determining "success" on the battlefields of Vietnam, where there were no conventional front lines or battles by which to measure military victories, was hardly convincing, if not fraudulent. Add to these factors the overcontrol of tactical action, which virtually destroyed squad-, platoon-, and company-level initiative and leadership (thanks to improved communication and to superior officers hovering overhead in helicopters), to say nothing of tactical control all the way back to the White House, where bombing targets were decided by Johnson. All of these factors militated against an effective United States–South Vietnamese war effort. In summary, the United States and South Vietnam had the men and materiel, but the North Vietnamese had the will to win and a strategy to ensure victory.

CONTAINMENT CONTINUED

In the meantime, other events continued to unfold in the overall policy of containment, although it was now seriously weakened by the Vietnam conflict. In 1968 the reserves received their "Bill of Rights," placing the burden on the service secretaries to ensure that the reserves were properly trained and ready for mobilization. The reserves were also given their own assistant secretaries in each of the branches.

In the regular forces, the draft law was extended in 1967, but even the use of a lottery system did not defuse the criticism of selective service, since draftees were sent to Vietnam while reserves and guardsmen stayed home. In addition, those who were drafted tended to come from minority groups and from the lower socioeconomic levels of society, where the escape hatch of college enrollment was less readily available. These problems led to the adoption of the concept of an all-volunteer Army in 1970 (the draft was ended in 1972), which temporarily caused a rush of marginally qualified persons to enlist. Perhaps more important, the all-volunteer concept also meant a long-term increase in the military budget because military pay rates henceforth would have to be comparable to those in the private sector of the economy.

Important changes also occurred in foreign affairs that affected containment. In 1966 Charles de Gaulle, the president of France, believing that the security of his country could not be ensured by NATO and that the nation's expanding nuclear capability would serve it well, ordered all NATO troops out of the country and took all French troops out from under NATO command. Since France was the communications and logistical center of the military alliance, the effectiveness of NATO forces, now forced to be relocated in England, Germany, Belgium, and the Netherlands, suffered thereby. NATO headquarters was moved to Belgium the following year, and the American army headquarters was moved to Germany.

On the military-diplomatic side, in 1969 the Soviets finally agreed to begin talks on arms control. The Strategic Arms Limitation Talks (SALT) began in Finland that year. However, in the absence of clear and verifiable agreements, both countries continued to build and deploy ballistic missiles, with the American combination of Nike, Spartan, and Sprint missiles and their radar systems coming on line for the United States in the 1970s. Whether or not the growing spirit of détente would dominate as the 1970s faded into the 1980s remained to be seen, but military planners were well aware of the fact that the United States had spread—or dissipated—its strength in Europe, the Middle East, and especially Vietnam.

Making the situation even more perilous, the nation found itself confused over its world responsibilities and divided over its domestic priorities, while its leadership reeled from its own incompetence and lack of vision and resolve. All the while, the Soviet Union, the object of containment, continued to expand and modernize its military at an unprecedented rate. Whatever the nation's temper and mood, major challenges faced the now-discredited military as it sought to regain its place in the life of the nation to meet the challenges of the late 1970s, the 1980s, and beyond.

Suggestions for Further Reading

BERMAN, LARRY, *Planning a Tragedy: The Americanization of the War in Vietnam.* New York: W. W. Norton & Co., Inc., 1982.

CABLE, LARRY E., *Conflict of Myths: The Development of American Counterinsurgency Doctrine and the Vietnam War.* New York: New York University Press, 1986.

CHANOFF, DAVID, and DOAN VAN TOAI, *Portrait of the Enemy*. New York: Random House, 1986.

DAVIDSON, PHILLIP B., *Vietnam at War: The History, 1946–1975*. Novato, CA: Presidio, 1988.

FALL, BERNARD B., *Hell in a Very Small Place: The Siege of Dien Bien Phu*. Philadelphia: Lippincott, 1966.

GIAP, VO NGUYEN, *The People's War, People's Army: The Viet Cong Insurrection Manual for Underdeveloped Countries*. New York: Praeger, 1962.

HALBERSTAM, DAVID, *The Best and the Brightest*. Greenwich, CT: Fawcett, 1969.

HALLIN, DANIEL C., *The "Uncensored War."* New York: Oxford University Press, 1986.

HAMMOND, WILLIAM M., *Public Affairs: The Military and the Media, 1962–1968*. Washington, DC: Center of Military History, 1988.

HERRING, GEORGE C., *America's Longest War: The United States and Vietnam, 1950–1975*. New York: John Wiley, 1979.

JOHNSON, LYNDON BAINES, *The Vantage Point, Perspectives of the President, 1963–1969*. New York: Rinehart & Winston, 1971.

KARNOW, STANLEY, *Vietnam, A History: The First Complete Account of Vietnam at War*. New York: Viking, 1983.

KEARNS, DORIS, *Lyndon Johnson and the American Dream*. New York: Harper & Row, Pub., 1976.

KISSINGER, HENRY B., *Nuclear Weapons and Foreign Policy*. New York: Harper & Row, Pub., 1957.

———, *The White House Years*. Boston: Little, Brown, 1982.

KREPINEVICH, ANDREW E., JR., *The Army and Vietnam*. Baltimore: Johns Hopkins University Press, 1986.

LEWY, GUENTHER, *America in Vietnam*. New York: Oxford University Press, 1978.

MATTHEWS, LLOYD J., and DALE BROWN, eds., *Assessing the Vietnam War*. Washington: Pergamon-Brassey's, 1987.

NICHOLS, JOHN B., and BARRETT TILLMAN, *On Yankee Station: The Naval Air War over Vietnam*. Annapolis: Naval Institute Press, 1987.

NIXON, RICHARD, *RN: The Memoirs of Richard Nixon*. New York: Grosset & Dunlap, 1978.

NOLTING, FREDERICK, *From Trust to Tragedy: The Political Memoirs of Frederick Nolting, Kennedy's Ambassador to Diem's Vietnam*. Westport, CT: Praeger, 1988.

O'NEILL, WILLIAM, *Coming Apart: An Informal History of America in the 1960s*. Chicago: Quadrangle, 1971.

PALMER, BRUCE, JR., *The Twenty-Five Year War: America's Military Role in Vietnam*. Lexington: University Press of Kentucky, 1984.

PALMER, DAVE, *Summons of the Trumpet*. Novato, CA: Presidio, 1978.

PARKER, F. CHARLES, IV. *Vietnam: Strategy for a Stalemate*. New York: Paragon House, 1989.

PIKE, DOUGLAS, *PAVN: People's Army of Vietnam*. Novato, CA: Presidio, 1986.

PISOR, ROBERT, *The End of the Line: The Siege of Khe Sanh*. New York: W. W. Norton & Co., Inc., 1982.

SCHANDLER, HERBERT Y., *The Unmaking of a President: Lyndon Johnson and Vietnam.* Princeton, NJ: Princeton University Press, 1977.

SHARP, U. S. GRANT, *Strategy for Defeat: Vietnam in Retrospect.* San Rafael, CA: Presidio, 1978.

SHEEHAN, NEIL, *A Bright Shining Lie: John Paul Vann and America in Vietnam.* New York: Random House, 1988.

SPECTOR, RONALD H., *Advice and Support: The Early Years of the U.S. Army in Vietnam, 1941–1960.* Washington, DC: Center of Military History, 1983.

STANTON, SHELBY L., *The Rise and Fall of an American Army: U.S. Ground Forces in Vietnam, 1965–1973.* Novato, CA: Presidio, 1985.

SUMMERS, HARRY G., JR., *On Strategy: The Vietnam War in Context.* Carlisle: Strategic Studies Institute, 1981, Novato, CA: Presidio, 1982.

TAYLOR, JOHN M., *General Maxwell Taylor: The Sword and the Pen.* New York: Doubleday, 1989.

THOMPSON, SIR ROBERT, *Peace Is Not at Hand.* New York: David McKay, 1974.

WESTMORELAND, WILLIAM C., *A Soldier Reports.* New York: Doubleday, 1976.

☆13

Continued Challenges and Commitments, 1976–

America's time of troubles did not end with the fall of Vietnam. A gnawing sense of malaise, of disenchantment with the nation, its leaders, and its ever-more-costly mission as leader of the free world, pervaded its people's perceptions through the remainder of the 1970s. Groping for a renewed sense of mission and hope, the American voters rejected the continued presidential leadership of Gerald R. Ford and the Republicans in 1976 in favor of a one-term Democratic governor of Georgia, Jimmy Carter, who sparkled with idealism and gave promise of a more moral and responsive presidency and nation.

But for the next four years, despite Carter's valiant attempts to chart a new course for America in the world, a course based on universal human rights, the nation continued to drift. Carter was unable to provide the leadership and sense of direction the times demanded. Accordingly, in 1980 the American people turned to Ronald Reagan, one-time movie actor, former governor of California, and shining light of the conservative wing of the Republican party, to point the way to an America that could be proud of what it was, its mission to posterity unbeclouded by doubts and hesitations.

The aging and popular Reagan appeared to have largely succeeded in his task. By 1989 much of the confusion of the 1960s and 1970s had vanished, and America—at least on the surface—had seemed to have found itself. Reagan retired in honor, passing the baton of political leadership to George Bush of Texas as the United States entered upon the last decade of the twentieth century.

Yet on a deeper level much confusion remained. The question of America's world role had still not been answered satisfactorily. Did it wish to maintain its leadership of the Western democracies in their struggle against the Soviet bloc, a burden that continued to demand tremendous personal and monetary sacrifices? And what of America's long-term allies, to say nothing of former enemies such as Germany and Japan? Should they not take a more active part in their own defense now that they had clearly recovered economically and politically from World War II?

What of the continued troubles in the Middle East, in which Arab was pitted against Israeli and Muslim against Muslim? Was there no solution to that continued turmoil and warfare, a conflict that threatened to draw both America and the Soviet Union into Middle Eastern confrontation? And what of China and Latin America, the former evolving to major status amid domestic chaos, the latter a continued tinderbox of violence with or without Russian and communist aid and encouragement? What of the bloodshed in emerging Africa? What of the new threat of international terrorism?

Never far from the consciousness of the American people was the overarching question: What of the nuclear arsenals of the United States and the Soviet Union—arsenals that promised instant death to millions of people? Would they ever be used? Could agreements somehow be reached to defuse this ever-present threat of annihilation hanging over both nations? How long would the cold war continue, especially after 1985, with the coming to power in the USSR of Mikhail Gorbachev and his new policies of *glasnost* (openness to public debate) and *perestroika* (restructuring)? Were the Soviet Union and its leaders really capable of fundamental change, of rejecting seven decades of Marxist ideology of inevitable world conquest or four centuries of Russian expansionism, thereby to allow the nations of the world to live without the fear of superpower nuclear or conventional confrontation? How would the convulsive changes taking place in the Soviet Union and in its satellites in eastern Europe in the late 1980s affect the balance of power in the Eurasian heartland and worldwide?

Hindered by the lack of a viable public consensus over the answers to these fundamental questions, America's military—constantly, if unfairly, burdened by the public's fear of "another Vietnam"—persisted in attempting to carry out its Constitutional duty of providing for the nation's defense. Thus the military services, whatever their strengths and weaknesses, whether in periods of strong support (under Reagan) or moderate support (under Carter), whether carrying out missions clear or unclear in their intent, continued to shoulder the nation's armed commitments in a world situation filled with challenges and fraught with danger.

SEARCHING FOR AN AMERICAN STRATEGY

The quest for a functional political, economic, diplomatic, and military strategy to ensure the continued growth and safety of any nation has always been a most difficult task. Involved are interests and priorities basic to that nation's survival and well-being. Some are compromisable; some are not. The diplomat and policy maker must carefully weigh all of these historical, intellectual, moral, and economic values before mapping out a course for the future. A workable national strategy must take into consideration various short-term goals and objectives. More important, it must take into account long-term goals and priorities because today's policies will determine tomorrow's well-being.

Even in the best of times policy making is, therefore, a most intricate exercise in judgment. Yet the rapidity of technology growth in communications and weapons systems and the breathtaking sweep of events in the late twentieth century make thoughtful long-range planning incredibly difficult. This is especially true for the policy makers of the United States because of the nation's position in the world. America's leaders must be ever mindful that they hold in their hands the fate not only of their own people but of countless millions of others. With events unfolding around the globe, often at breakneck speed, decisions must often be made in great haste. This, it would seem, makes long-term goals and objectives even more necessary because short-term events can then be measured against them with greater assurance of accuracy as to their consequences. Yet America would seem to have few well-thought-out long-term goals in the late twentieth century.

An absence of a long-term vision and of a sense of urgency appears to dominate American policy making. This is perilous because events in western and eastern Europe, in Latin America, in the Middle East, in China, in the Indian Ocean—indeed, wherever vital American interests are found—often have to be reacted to in a matter of hours or even minutes. Even when circumstances allow for a more leisurely reaction, the absence of long-range goals complicates decision making and invites miscalculation.

Despite this absence of long-term national goals and policies, however, in making military judgments it would appear that at least some *de facto* consensus exists as to what the nation will and will not do. For example, it is clear that the United States will continue to conduct only limited wars for limited ends if at all possible, thus avoiding any chance for misconceptions that might bring on a wider conflict and the possibility of the use of atomic weapons. These limited wars will be entered into only as a last resort, after diplomacy and other forms of settlement have failed. Second, the United States will seek to use negotiations either to avoid war or to limit or terminate military interventions once entered into. Third, the United States will use gradual and incremental military actions to avoid widening the conflict and risking the chance of unlimited war. Fourth, the United States will seek to keep both civilian and military losses to a minimum, the alternative of high casualties being unacceptable to the American public. Finally, the American military forces will be subjected to tight control from both their civilian and their military superiors in order to avoid the dire consequences of miscalculation or the unnecessary use of force.

Granted these limits on the use of military force by the United States in the late twentieth century, and interventionary restrictions based on lessons learned since 1945 and mandated by the availability of strategic and tactical atomic weaponry, the president of the United States, as commander-in-chief and the chief political leader of the country, also has great influence on the American military and its use. For example, during Carter's four years in office from 1977 to 1981, less money and emphasis were placed on the military as a responding agent to international events, yet the concept of a "countervailing strategy" was developed and implemented to deal with Soviet atomic aggression. Essentially, countervailing strategy was designed to give the United States more options in case of less than all-out atomic attack by a shift in targeting of Soviet cities and military installations. Some would be primary and hit immediately in retaliation; some would be secondary and would be destroyed only if Soviet aggression was not halted. With greater control over the use of various types of atomic weapons and with a greater refinement of targets, it was assumed that all-out confrontation would be avoided and Western security attained.

President Reagan retained the countervailing-strategy concept as the heart of his military program but took steps to strengthen the military at the conventional level to implement effective responses at all levels and thus preclude being forced quickly to the atomic level to resist Soviet aggression. As a result, outlays for the military rose from $132.8 billion in his first budget to over $300 billion by 1988 with further escalations planned, 80 percent of these monies being for conventional, non-nuclear warfare. America's "hollow forces" of the late 1970s were no longer so by the end of the 1980s.

Reagan's steps to reinforce Carter's doctrine of a countervailing strategy through a buildup in the nation's conventional forces, aided by new technological breakthroughs in both atomic and conventional weaponry, were successful. By the end of the decade it was obvious that the Soviets were no longer willing to challenge openly the American power that surrounded them in the form of silo-busting MX intercontinental ballistic missiles (ICBMs), missile-bearing Trident submarines, and sea-, land-, and air-based cruise missiles (the last borne by B-52 and B-1 long-range bombers). It was also clear that they were no longer able to expand along their borders and beyond. Further, they were in deep economic trouble at home because of their socialist economic system and their continued expensive arms buildup to match the United States. Faced with the necessity of restructuring both at home and in their satellites, they appeared willing to talk seriously of disarmament.

The cold war was not over, and containment and deterrence remained vital necessities for the United States because the Soviets had developed major nuclear and conventional capabilities since the 1960s and were as strong as ever militarily. They remained a persistent danger to the West, and no one could predict what decisions might emanate from the always secretive Kremlin hierarchy. Still, the Soviet Union was revealing signs of fundamental change, both internally and externally, that might lead to a lessening of tensions between the superpowers and perhaps disarmament and peace by the end of the century.

Yet despite these impressive military and diplomatic gains for the United States in the 1980s, the Reagan presidency contained one great flaw that revealed its blindness toward the long-term consequences of its policies. This fault melded into an old American attitude and led to a movement toward military retrenchment by the end of the decade.

Reagan essentially rebuilt the American military while also accepting vast increases in domestic social spending. At the same time he was leading the fight to cut taxes to spur the sluggish economy. As a result, the federal budget grew from $660 billion in 1981 to over $1 trillion in 1989, while the Department of Defense budget rose from $161 billion to $300 billion during the same period of time. Defense expenditures grew only from 23 percent of federal outlays to 26.1 percent during these years. Department of Defense monies were no higher in constant dollars and rose from only 5.2 percent to 5.7 percent of the nation's gross national product (GNP) during the 1980s.

Although the vast bulk of the increased federal spending went to nondefense items, greater budget outlays were not matched by sufficient revenues. This resulted in unprecedented budget deficits. The federal deficit reached $156 billion in 1988, for a total federal indebtedness of over $2.6 trillion. This meant an expenditure of $214 billion in interest on the debt alone, or 20 percent of all federal outlays. These fiscal problems set off a cry for reducing the debt to curb its deleterious effects on the economy and on the inability of the United States to compete economically in the world market. One legislative consequence of this mounting debt (in 1985 the nation became a debtor nation for the first time since World War I) was the passage of the Balanced Budget and Emergency Deficit and Control Act of 1985 (commonly referred to as the Gramm-Rudman-Hollings Act), which mandated cuts in federal spending to cure the obvious fiscal problems the nation was facing.

The question then became not *whether* cuts would be made but *where* the cuts would come, and here the military became the primary target, especially in view of the cold war "thaw" then taking place. In reacting to thus reduce the military, the American public and their leaders were essentially reverting to an old American attitude. From the time of independence there has been in the United States a basic distrust of the military. For the bulk of the nation's history a sizable military has been seen as relatively unnecessary, a threat to liberty and democracy, an obstacle to reform, and always wasteful of national resources. The armed forces have received full and enthusiastic support only in times of war; thereafter, the nation reverts to its parsimonious posture toward its soldiers and sailors—until the next war.

This traditional pattern changed in the aftermath of World War II and the ensuing cold war in the 1950s because international dangers argued for strong and continued support for America's defense arm. For the first prolonged period in American history the military was seen as vital and worthy of sustained patronage. Monies were generously given to support and expand the armed forces. But in the 1980s, after almost four decades of continued and growing armament, in the aftermath of the Vietnam debacle and with the easing of tensions between the superpowers, the American public began to revert to its traditional pattern of thought regarding the military. Public favor began to evaporate even though the real costs of basic national defense in a constantly dangerous world continued to escalate because of the advanced technology now involved in weaponry and the increased cost of all-volunteer soldiers.

Added to this reversion to the traditional antimilitary outlook were peculiarly "advanced" twentieth-century American beliefs that peace is the normal condition of humans and, therefore, that war (the abnormal and regressive solution to problems) is caused by misunderstanding, since all people desire peace. It follows from these assumptions that the problem of war then becomes solvable by openness, honesty, people-to-people contact, and a willingness to compromise. This being the case, persistence in an ideological, moral, and military standoff with the Soviets itself becomes the problem, not the Soviet Union or its intentions. To remedy this problem, all steps should be taken to reach an openness and an accommodating posture with this Eurasian superpower by abandoning confrontation and military might and by emphasizing mutual goals. In this scenario, the American civilian and military leaders who refuse to move to understanding and compromise become the villains whose influence must be nullified in the name of peace.

Widely publicized cost overruns and wasteful spending by the military were added to the public's perception of how much the military was costing in tax dollars. These ideas were combined in the minds of many with the appealing assumption that every dollar not spent for defense is a dollar available to be spent on the poor, the homeless, the aged, the abused, and the disenfranchised. The pressure to cut military spending became irresistible. The military faced budget cuts by the end of the 1980s—whatever the international situation, whatever the real dangers from many quarters of the globe (since American commitments had not been diminishing but actually growing in the Middle East, southern Asia, and Latin America in the decades of the 1970s and 1980s), whatever the intentions of the Soviet leaders in those areas and in Europe, and whatever the consequences for national security.

As it entered the 1990s, America thus found itself with a confusion of purpose, a basic disagreement over ends and means, and a series of economic problems that admitted of no easy solutions. Few doubted that the nation had to retain its position as leader of the Western world and that its domestic and foreign priorities had to be met, but no leader—political, military, religious, or academic—could rally the nation around a vision that would guide it through the obvious economic, diplomatic, and military troubles it faced as the century drew to a close.

SOVIET STRENGTHS AND STRATEGIES

Whatever the repercussions of the revolutionary events that broke out in the Soviet Union and its satellites in the late 1980s, the threat of Soviet power and maleficent intent remained for the United States and the world. There were few indications that the Communist party had lost its will to govern, or that the Russian dream of hegemony over the vast extent of the Eurasian heartland had been altered.

Historically plagued by insecurity, the Soviet Union had not abandoned its dream of extending its influence in the Far East, the Middle East, western Europe, and beyond. In its leaders' view, Soviet security would be ensured only when the nation's border areas were under friendly influence and control or else effectively neutralized. Gaining control of the resources of the Eurasian heartland and its borders, neutralizing American influence in western Europe, and gaining access to the open seas to protect its sea lines of communication would make the nation impervious to direct non-nuclear attack by the United States or any other "aggressive" power. Part of this overall strategy involved bringing the Third World areas under Soviet control, thereby to isolate and weaken the United States, still seen by the Soviets as their major enemy ideologically, economically, and militarily.

Steps, therefore, had been taken over the last decades of the twentieth century to carry out this grand plan for security. These included not only sending aid to Third World countries, such as those in the Middle East, Africa, and Latin America, to bring them under Soviet influence (complete domination or subservience being unnecessary and perhaps provocative), but also building better diplomatic relations with the North Atlantic Treaty Organization (NATO) countries of western Europe to entice them to loosen their political, economic, and military ties with the United States. This meant keeping pressure on western Europe by maintaining the presence of conventional forces (increasingly equipped with tactical nuclear weapons) and developing economic ties with them.

Beginning in the 1970s and accelerating under Mikhail Gorbachev, the Soviets attempted to convince the Western nations that they sought only peace and cooperation, western Europe's ties with the United States through NATO standing as a stumbling block to its short- and long-term security and independence of action. In the Russian strategic view, American power had to be weakened. Separating the Europeans from the Americans would not only force the American military threat away from the borders of the Soviet heartland, but would also eventually remove it from Europe altogether. Increased Soviet naval strength would help to ensure that it could not be effectively projected into European and Eurasian affairs again.

All of this could be attained only by the maintenance of strong conventional forces operating under an umbrella of nuclear parity or superiority vis-à-vis the United States. Indeed, the historical-military pattern of Soviet military strategy toward the West reflected this and had become clear by the 1990s. Since World War II the Soviet Union had moved from denigrating nuclear power in the immediate aftermath of the war to acceptance of nuclear military power in the 1950s, especially in strategic missiles. In the 1960s and 1970s the Soviets had turned to building up both nuclear and conventional arms to preclude having to rely on nuclear weapons and all-out nuclear war to gain their strategic objectives. This combination of nuclear and conventional weapons allowed them to keep U.S. power at bay while pursuing their long-range strategic goals by befriending, extending economic aid, and attempting to subvert and influence needy and emerging nations on their borders and in the Third World, all the while attempting to wean western Europe and the forces of NATO from their pact of unified resistance with the United States. Should this grand scheme ever fail, it is not inconceivable that the Soviet Union would move to warfare to redress what it sees as the balance of world power shifting against it.

If this turning to overt violence against the United States remains a possibility—if not a probability—then it is incumbent upon the United States in the 1990s that it be able to counter this turn of events by adequate military strength at both the nuclear- and conventional-weapon level. Of greatest importance, the United States, as the leader of the Western coalition of nations, must maintain the will to win the ideological battle against the Soviets by diplomacy, technological development, economic strength, and even military confrontation if that becomes necessary.

That the overt Soviet military threat to the West remains in the last decade of the century is clear. Despite Gorbachev's peace offensive, the Soviet Union increased its military spending after 1985, and new Soviet missiles of greater accuracy were deployed during the decade. The Soviets at the same time were putting into place the world's only active ballistic missile defense system. Some 200 main battle tanks were being produced each month by 1989, and three large, modern aircraft carriers were being built for Far Eastern and Mediterranean service. Weapons destroyed in accordance with the Salt I and Salt II treaties of 1972 and 1979 and other treaties such as the Intermediate Nuclear Forces Treaty of 1987, are being replaced by newer missiles, perhaps fewer in number but by far greater in lethality. The Soviet Union, like the United States, continues to modernize its strategic forces by improving the accuracy of its missiles and putting MIRV (multiple independently targetable reentry vehicles) on their new and existing missiles. For example, the Soviet SS-20 missiles destroyed under the Intermediate Nuclear Forces Treaty were being replaced by 1990 with twice as many powerful SS-24 missiles.

Again, although in January 1989 Gorbachev announced that the Soviet Union intended to reduce its defense spending, weapons procurement, and numbers of men in uniform, the Soviet navy also reflected the new Soviet strategy of fewer but more powerful weapons. While the Russians were reducing the number of ships in their inventory, they were also in the process of producing new and better nuclear submarines, such as the Delta IV, Typhoon, Akula, and Oscar-class boats, giving them about 30 modern submarines as first-class antisubmarine warfare platforms. They were also building the *Tbilisi*-class large-deck carrier, *Kirov*- and *Slava*-class cruisers, and two new classes of destroyers. They were also constructing or improving their naval facilities in Cuba, Angola, Ethiopia, Vietnam, and South Yemen. They were boasting of a Mediterranean squadron, a northern fleet, a southern fleet, and a Pacific fleet, all with improved warmaking capabilities and intended to maintain their interests in the Arctic Ocean, the Mediterranean Sea, the Indian Ocean, and the western Pacific. The numbers of ships in the Soviet navy may well have been declining in the early 1990s, but its quality and lethality was improving as part of the Soviet military-diplomatic strategy still being implemented.

While this naval shipbuilding program was continuing, the Soviets were also upgrading a naval base in Syria as a major staging and repair area for their submarines and cruisers in the Mediterranean. They were also continuing to support and supply Colonel Muammar al-Qaddafi, the Marxist dictator of Libya since his successful coup in 1969 and the author of countless terrorist acts in the Middle East and even in Europe itself. And they were signing a new agreement to support the radical Muslim nation of Iran with economic and military aid and to defend it against its enemies—namely, the United States—while continuing to fish in the troubled waters of other areas of the Middle East.

THE SOVIET UNION, NATO, AND THE FAR EAST

The Soviet Union's strategy in western Europe, directed at the destruction of NATO and the weakening of American influence in Europe, will perhaps prove to be the most crucial area of victory or defeat for the Soviets in the late twentieth century. Aiding and at the same time complicating the Soviet strategy for western Europe is the fact that the nations that are part of NATO are ultimately dependent on the United States for nuclear protection and for a critical amount of conventional defense. There is some resentment toward the United States over this fact, yet the western European democracies simply cannot "go it alone" at this time.

They might, however, be convinced that there is no real threat from the Soviets and that they should cooperate with them economically. This would obviously weaken their ties with the United States. But the negative side for the Soviet Union of this western European quest for independence is that both the French and British have begun modernizing their strategic nuclear forces, upgrading their bomber forces, and acquiring ballistic missile submarines. Thus while a more independent and neutral western Europe might be less dependent on and even at odds at times with the United States in regard to policy relative to the Soviet Union, it could also develop into a source of independent and perhaps hostile strategic thinking while armed with the capability of causing great damage to the Soviet Union in case of conflict.

Whatever the strength of this quest by the western European democracies for a more independent world role, the 1990s will undoubtedly continue to see the United States bound to Europe by the NATO alliance. NATO's land defensive schemes evolved from "Fallback" in the 1950s (calling for a delaying zone across central France and a main defensive line near the eastern border of France) to "Trip Wire" in the 1960s (designating the delaying zone as lying in West Germany and eastern France and the main defensive line across central France). In the 1970s the defensive scheme was "Active Defense" (calling for both the main defensive line and the delaying zone to be tucked together along the French–West German border). "Air/Land Battle" (designating the delaying zone as the western half of West Germany and the main defensive line as running along the French–West German border) became the NATO defense scheme in the 1980s.

These NATO war plans, as they have evolved, clearly reveal that defensively the NATO nations intend to give up very little territory. Whatever conventional forces the Soviets and their Warsaw Pact allies might throw at them, the NATO assumption is that despite the disparity of numbers between NATO and Warsaw Pact forces (approximately 58 NATO divisions could be counted on to be on line in the immediate aftermath of a Soviet ground attack, as opposed to 80 Soviet-controlled divisions), NATO forces equipped with both conventional and tactical nuclear weaponry will be able to impede any Soviet land offense and inflict severe damage on Soviet and satellite follow-on units. They will be able to thwart a Soviet attack even without the use of strategic nuclear weapons; these, however, will be available in the most critical of situations. Thus NATO remains a viable entity in western Europe. This is true not only on land but also in the form of its naval units along its southern flank. NATO deployments force the Soviets to the reality that any aggressive moves to subdue the western Europeans will involve grave risks to their own nation.

Yet a European movement toward independent defensive capabilities of conventional forces backed by nuclear weaponry had become clear by the 1990s. It was complemented by a corresponding bent toward neutrality in any superpower contest between the United States and the Soviet Union. These developments, combined with signs of American unilateral disarmament in response to Soviet blandishments and Soviet economic ties with western Europe, threatened to wean western Europe away from its strong backing of NATO. If this happened, it would be a severe blow to America's forward strategy, which stresses stopping aggression far from America's shores. At the least, it can be said that the Soviet strategy for a neutralized Europe detached from the United States continues without significant alteration.

In the Far East, too, Soviet intentions remain clear in the 1990s. Although the Sino–Soviet split has placed the Soviets and the Chinese in mutually aggressive stances toward one another in that area and has forced the Soviets to increase their land presence from 12 divisions in 1960 to 52 divisions by 1985, their presence on the Far Eastern strategic front remains formidable. This is illustrated by their backing of North Korea and its 750,000-man army, threatening South Korea as never before with aggression from the north. They also support the 1.1 million-man armed forces of Vietnam (Vietnam has the third largest standing army in the world) with $5 billion worth of aircraft and other military equipment in addition to 2,500 Soviet military advisors.

More important for American counterstrategy, the Soviet Pacific fleet is growing rapidly and making inroads into America's dominance in the vital western Pacific rim. By 1990 the Soviets had transformed their former Pacific coastal fleet into a high-seas offensive naval force of some 830 vessels, this fleet scheduled to be augmented in the 1990s by two modern *Kiev*-class carriers, some 32 ballistic-armed submarines among the 130 boats assigned to this fleet (almost equal to the U.S. Navy's total world submarine deployment), and modern fighter planes. Supplementing the growth of this fleet, the Soviets have turned the former American naval base at Cam Ranh Bay in Vietnam into a major facility, their largest naval base outside Soviet territory, and have moved nuclear missiles into Southeast Asia, endangering Japan, the Philippines, and South Korea, as well as Chinese cities and military facilities. From Cam Ranh Bay the Soviets could block the Malacca, Sunda, and Lombok Straits, placing a stranglehold on the flow of oil and vital materials needed by America and its Far Eastern allies.

Supplementing these forces in place on indigenous Soviet Far Eastern territories are 80 cruise-missile-armed Backfire bombers capable of threatening large stretches of the Far East and at least 165 SS-20 intermediate-range land-based nuclear missiles. With a total of 500,000 troops in the Far East alone, and with these extensions of military influence into the western Pacific and economic penetration into Kiribati (formerly the Gilbert Islands) and Vanuatu (formerly New Hebrides) in the central Pacific, the Soviets have given clear notice that their interests in the western Pacific and beyond are a continuing dimension of their existing worldwide strategic plans.

U.S. INTERVENTIONS IN THE MIDDLE EAST AND NORTH AFRICA

The years since 1975 have seen the United States intervene militarily in Middle Eastern–North African affairs on four occasions. American interest in the area remains high because the U.S. Sixth Fleet patrolling the Mediterranean Sea and the forces of Greece and Turkey represent the southern flank of NATO and are therefore vital to the containment of the Soviet Union. American interest also reflects both economic concerns in the area, especially in petroleum crude, and the historical American friendship with and guaranteed support for the State of Israel, created in 1948 with strong U.S. backing but faced with hostility ever since by native Arab states and nonstate Arab groups determined to destroy that Jewish nation.

Modern Iran, under the control of Shah Reza Pahlavi since 1953, experienced turmoil in 1978 that eventually led to a revolution that brought to leadership an exiled fundamentalist Shiite Muslim leader, the Ayatollah Ruhollah Khomeini. The shah and many intellectual leaders of Iran had been pronouncedly pro-Western and pro-American, but the Ayatollah and his followers saw Westernization, modernization, and America in particular as the embodiment of corruption of Muslim ideas.

In November 1979 Iranian militants seized the United States embassy in the capital city of Teheran and took hostages, including 62 Americans, vowing to hold them until the deposed shah was returned to Iran to stand trial. International condemnations and American diplomatic efforts to free the hostages led nowhere. Finally, President Carter ordered that an attempt be made by the American military to rescue the hostages. The result was the military debacle of the decade.

The rescue force of April 1980 consisted of units from all the military services. Army Delta Force special operations troops, Rangers, and antiaircraft experts were joined by Marine pilots and crews of eight Navy helicopters flying off the carrier *Nimitz* in the Gulf of Oman and Air Force pilots and crews of three tanker aircraft and three transports to carry out the complicated secret operation. The Delta Force and Ranger troops were to be flown from Egypt to a location known as Desert One, southeast of Teheran. Here they were to meet and refuel the helicopters, which were then to take the Delta Force personnel and Rangers to Desert Two, closer to the city. The Army rescuers the next day would drive into the capital in trucks to rescue the hostages (whose location in Teheran was not certain), thereafter to flee the capital in helicopters flown to various points in the city. They would be helicoptered to an abandoned air base south of Teheran to be picked up by Air Force transports and flown to safety.

Everything that could go wrong with a mission did. The hostages remained in captivity (to be finally released the next year when the United States agreed to unfreeze Iranian assets in the United States), and angry recriminations followed over the botched military operation. The main problem appeared to be a too-complicated operation involving too many service branches attempting to do a job that was probably impossible anyway. And there was inadequate preparation and rehearsal. All of the services demanding their "piece of the pie," to the detriment of the success of the mission, seemed to be the final negative verdict of the post mortems. The services would eventually learn from the mistakes of the Iranian hostage rescue attempt of April 1980 and not repeat them, but in the meantime a tragedy of greater proportions had taken place in Lebanon.

Lebanon, a French mandate from 1921 until 1941, has been the scene of continual fighting between Muslim and Christian groups, aided by outside Arab nations and subject to Israeli invasions, for most of the years since the French evacuated the country in 1946. The U.S. Marines intervened in 1958 during a Syrian-backed revolt against the government. Then, in 1982, with civil war raging in the country since 1975 and frequent Israeli incursions into Lebanese territory to deny bases for Arab terrorist groups warring against them, American, French, and Italian troops were sent in as a peacekeeping force to protect and evacuate foreign nationals as necessary.

Following a terrorist attack on the American embassy in Beirut in which some 50 people were killed, 1,250 marines of the 24th Marine Amphibious Unit (one battalion) were sent into Lebanon—6,000 marines and 8,500 soldiers had been sent into a much less dangerous situation in Lebanon back in 1958—and assigned the duty of securing Beirut International Airport. The marines were placed under rules of engagement that permitted them to fire their weapons only when directly targeted or attacked, and the marine guards were under direct orders to keep their weapons unloaded. (A sign was posted in the marine area: "The Can't Shoot Back Saloon.") Protecting civilian lives and property and minimizing force seemed to be a greater priority for the nation's civilian and military leaders than safeguarding the lives of the marines, who had been placed in a very precarious situation in war-torn Lebanon.

On the morning of October 23, 1983, a terrorist driving a 5,000-pound truck bomb sped past the Marine guards and into the lobby of the Marine headquarters at the Beirut airport, killing 241 Marines in the subsequent explosion. (Almost simultaneously, a second suicide terrorist in a truck killed 40 French paratroopers in their barracks two miles away.) In the aftermath of the tragedy, Congress, having reluctantly agreed to an 18-month Lebanon deployment just two months before, began to back off in its support of the peacekeeping mission; the remaining marines were evacuated from Lebanon with President Reagan promising to bring the perpetrators of the bombing to justice (which was impossible under the circumstances). The civil war between the Christian and Muslim factions and the Israeli incursions continued, and the American military realized that 241 lives had been sacrificed in the name of duty in the tangled Middle East.

The latter years of the 1980s brought clearer and more positive missions to the American military in the Middle East and more satisfactory results for their fighting forces. The Soviets, in the meantime having invaded Afghanistan in 1979 to shore up a crumbling client regime, found themselves in a prolonged war they could not win. They finally agreed to evacuate in 1989, after suffering 15,000 killed at the hands of the rugged and fiercely independent Afghan tribesmen in the hills.

The North African state of Libya became an independent monarchy in 1952, but in 1969 its government fell to a junta led by Colonel Muammar al-Qaddafi. In the years thereafter, backed politically and militarily by the Soviet Union, Qaddafi's government supplied arms to violent revolutionary groups throughout the Middle East and aided them in their terrorist campaigns against all "enemies of the Arab people." Libya also attacked neighboring Egypt and Chad. The American government refused to move against Qaddafi for his incitement of rebellion and his support of terrorists until May 1981, when it closed the Libyan embassy in Washington. Then, in August of that same year, two MiG-23 Libyan jet fighters began to harass two American Sixth Fleet F-14 jets taking part in exercises in the Gulf of Sidra. The provocative acts by the Libyan jets were apparently ordered to back up Qaddafi's claim to the waters as belonging to Libya. Qaddafi's jets were expeditiously shot down by U.S. Navy pilots.

This incident, which was widely applauded in the United States, hardly deterred the Libyan dictator from his mission against the West in general and the United States in particular. His support of terrorism continued, and he backed the December 1985 attacks on the Rome and Paris airports. When the Americans continued their operations in the Gulf of Sidra and Libya fired antiaircraft missiles at American naval planes, the United States responded in March 1986 by sinking two Libyan ships and bombing a missile installation. Quaddafi still refused to back off.

Finally, when the Libyan dictator ordered the bombing of a West Berlin discotheque in April 1986, killing a U.S. serviceman, President Reagan approved sending American warplanes to attack key terrorist-related targets in the cities of Tripoli and Benghazi. America's European allies had previously refused to join in imposing economic sanctions on Libya, and even at this time the French government would not allow U.S. Air Force jets to overfly its country. But Reagan was undeterred. Although Quaddafi escaped with his life, the wave of terrorism emanating from Libya came to a halt. President Reagan and the American military had clearly demonstrated the effective use of surgical military power, and the armed forces received plaudits from the nation for a job well done. However, its mission of the 1980s in the Persian Gulf offered few opportunities for decisive action and, indeed, was marked by two unfortunate tragedies.

Despite the fact that the Middle East contains 56 percent of the world's crude petroleum resources, after the Organization of the Petroleum Exporting Countries (OPEC) oil embargo of 1973 and 1974, which created such havoc in the industrialized parts of the world, those nations most hurt by the embargo began to take steps to reduce their dependence on Middle Eastern oil by conserving, building up strategic reserves, and developing new sources of crude. By 1985 the OPEC nations were producing only 9.5 million barrels per day, down from 30.9 million barrels per day in 1979. American consumption of Middle Eastern petroleum dropped from 7 percent of domestic use in 1977 to only 2 percent by 1982. Furthermore, the passage of this oil out of the Middle Eastern refineries to its world markets was simplified and made safer from interruption by the building of a Saudi pipeline to Yanbu on the Red Sea and an Iraqi pipeline through Turkey.

Nevertheless, the continued flow of Middle Eastern petroleum to the United States, western Europe, and the Far East, combined with the strategic position of the Middle East in the Soviet–American confrontation, were deemed sufficient reason for major American concern. A mark of American solicitude over the Middle Eastern situation was the creation in 1979 on the orders of President Carter of the Rapid Deployment Joint Task Force (RDJTF) for action in the Persian Gulf. It consisted of three Army divisions, one Marine amphibious force, five Air Force fighter wings, and three Navy carrier task forces. RDJTF was reinforced in 1983 with the creation of CENTCOM (a central command for the Middle East and Southeast Asia), which added one additional Army division and five additional Air Force wings to the forces available for use in the Middle East.

As it turned out, however, it was the Navy that was called upon to exert primary American influence in the Persian Gulf and around the vital Strait of Hormuz, joining the Persian Gulf and the Gulf of Oman between Saudi Arabia and Iran. The Navy was assigned the task of ensuring the safe passage of American-flagged tankers through these waters amid the turmoil of the various Middle Eastern nations at war with one another.

Little action of any consequence occurred until May 17, 1987, when an American guided-missile frigate, the USS *Stark,* on duty in the Persian Gulf, was attacked by an Iraqi F-1 Mirage fighter and hit by two Exocet missiles, killing 37 American sailors. At the time of the attack the *Stark* was clearly in international waters, 80 miles northeast of Bahrain and outside the Iraqi and Iranian declared war zones. Subsequent investigation centered not on the attack itself, because it appeared to have been a case of pilot error, but on the fact that the frigate put up no effective defense. The ship had been cautioned by an AEW (airborne early-warning) plane of the fighter's course toward the ship, and its tactical action officer had warned that the plane's radar was locked onto the frigate, but the *Stark*'s chaff launchers had not been armed, its Phalanx missile system was turned off, its .50-caliber machine guns had not been loaded, and its fire-control radar had not been turned on.

The whole *Stark* incident made the Navy look bad, but the job of guarding the tankers as they entered and exited the Persian Gulf had to continue. On April 14, 1988, the frigate *Samuel B. Roberts* was severly damaged by a mine. Four days later, however, the Navy scored an impressive victory over Iranian forces harassing shipping in Operation Praying Mantis, in which A-6 Intruder attack bombers escorted by F-14 Tomcat fighters sank an Iranian frigate after a U.S. retaliatory attack on oil platforms in the Persian Gulf. The Navy's job in the Middle East was made even more difficult a week later when it was also directed to protect all "friendly, innocent, and neutral" vessels in the area. In June, the Navy, with the assistance of a marine landing party, attacked and destroyed two Iranian oil platforms used to direct attacks on civilian shipping in the gulf.

But tragedy struck the essentially successful Navy–Marine mission of protecting the tankers on July 3, 1988, when the Aegis cruiser USS *Vincennes,* during a battle with attacking Iranian speedboats, misidentified a civilian Iranian airliner over the Straits of Hormuz and shot it down, killing all 290 persons on board.

Nevertheless, throughout the American commitments in this cockpit of Middle East violence, the tankers continued to sail in comparative safety through the troubled waters of the Persian Gulf, the Strait of Hormuz, and the Gulf of Oman to the Indian Ocean and their world markets beyond both before and after the violence subsided. A cease fire was arranged between Iran and Iraq after eight years of war on August 20, 1988. This decreased the danger to the civilian ships of all nations in Middle Eastern waters, and American naval strength was drawn down. Although marred by the *Stark* and *Vincennes* tragedies, U.S. commitments in the Middle East had been upheld by effective use of military power.

THE LATIN AMERICAN TINDERBOX

In all of its Third World interventions since 1975 the United States has labored to stay well within its *de facto* military parameters of avoiding conflict with the Soviet Union, avoiding both military and civilian casualties, escalating its use of force only gradually, rendering financial and material aid to friendly Third World governments to strengthen their military and security forces, and seeking negotiated solutions to conflicts. This same pattern has held true in Latin America.

Latin America, of course, has long been an area of special interest and influence for the United States, going back to the Monroe Doctrine of 1823. Part of the reason is economic, part is political, and part is pure hemispheric propinquity. Although the United States has held to more of a hands-off attitude toward its southern neighbors since the advent of the Good Neighbor Policy of President Franklin D. Roosevelt in the 1930s, memories of American economic, political, and military interference in the region remain a part of the collective memory of the increasingly self-assertive Latin American nations. All are faced with internal economic and political problems of enormous dimensions, leading to dangerous frustrations and to an atmosphere of real and potential violence in the entire region. Latin America is surely the tinderbox of the Third World.

The various Latin American states have been moving toward more democratic systems of government since World War II and, at the same time, have felt the need to lift the burden of poverty from the masses of their people by launching agricultural, industrial, and commercial revolutions in their nations. At the same time, using selective memory—as all nations do to one extent or another, including the United States—the leaders and peoples of Latin America have often used the United States and "Yankee imperialism" as a convenient scapegoat for their failure to attain their dreams. This has forced the United States to act with considerable circumspection in the area, especially since the Soviet Union has systematically attempted to play upon this anti-American feeling and to take advantage of Latin America's political and economic problems to further its own world influence.

Five nations have been of particular concern to the United States. The first of these is Cuba. After the abortive Bay of Pigs invasion in 1961 and the Cuban missile crisis of 1962, American policy centered on leaving Fidel Castro in power but trying to circumscribe his influence in the Caribbean Basin and Latin America. Despite economic stringencies imposed on the island nation, largely caused by Castro's policies of collectivization, the communist dictator has managed to remain in power with considerable economic and military aid from the Soviet Union.

Since 1975, Castro's influence in Latin America has not been great, but he has sent troops to participate in the civil war in Angola and into other African states (apparently for the revenue involved), and he has consistently sent aid to communist forces in El Salvador and Nicaragua. Nevertheless, the United States, assuming that Castro has been a symbol of failure rather than success for the people of Latin America, has made no moves to unseat him. In 1977 it agreed to exchange diplomats with Cuba without granting full diplomatic recognition. Sensitive to the condition of the Cuban people and to the political impact of the Cuban refugees within its borders, the United States forged an agreement with Cuba in 1987 to accept 20,000 Cubans into the country each year; in return, Cuba has agreed to take back 2,500 Cuban criminals and mental patients jailed in the United States since they arrived in the 1980 Mariel boat lift of political prisoners.

With the two governments allowing more and more Americans to visit Cuba after its being off limits during four decades of acrimony between the governments of the two countries, it was clear by the close of the 1980s that relations between the United States and Castro's Cuba had become hardly friendly but increasingly polite. What the future might hold for Fidel Castro in his relations with the long-supportive Soviet Union was open to question, since the Cuban dictator was loudly denouncing the whole drift of Soviet domestic and foreign policy inaugurated by Mikhail Gorbachev as a betrayal of Marxist-Leninism.

One of the oldest independent countries in Central America, El Salvador, whose history goes back to 1821, has been subject to continual violence and civil war since a junta overthrew the government of General Carlos Romero in 1979. The civil war that has raged since the coup has left 50,000 Salvadorans dead, and some 10,000 leftist guerrillas, armed by the communist governments of Nicaragua and Cuba, still control about one-fourth of the country, mostly in the east. The 5.5 million citizens of El Salvador find themselves caught between the leftist guerrillas and right-wing military death squads with no end to the fighting in sight, despite the free election of the moderate Jose Napoleon Duarte as president in May 1984 and the peaceful succession of Alfredo Cristiani the next year.

President Reagan solidly backed the government of El Salvador with military aid during his terms in office, but the U.S. military was not called upon to intervene there, nor is it likely to be ordered to do so because of the growing anti-interventionist sentiment in Congress.

The United States' third problem area in Latin America is Nicaragua, also highly unlikely to be the scene of American military intervention. Like El Salvador, this Central American country of 3.6 million people has been the scene of continual violence for over a decade. Major trouble began in 1974, when president General Anastasio Somoza-Debayle declared martial law after some government officials were kidnapped by Marxist Sandinista guerrillas. Somoza remained in control until 1978, when a general strike set off a civil war that forced him into exile the next year and the Sandinista forces took over the government of Nicaragua.

Since the Sandinista government was backed by the Soviet Union and Cuba and supplied aid to the Marxist guerrillas in El Salvador, President Reagan made it a major policy goal to overthrow the government in Managua. This meant cutting off trade with Nicaragua, sending the Central Intelligence Agency (CIA) to mine Nicaraguan harbors, and, most important, supplying money and weapons to the Contras, an army of anti-Sandinista Nicaraguans attempting to overthrow the government, in addition to sending U.S. troops to neighboring Honduras to train the Contra forces.

In 1985 the U.S. House of Representatives rejected Reagan's request for military aid to the Contras, approving only $27 million in humanitarian aid. The following June it reversed itself and voted $100 million in military aid. But the revelation that the president's national security advisor, Robert McFarlane, and his aide, Marine Lieutenant Colonel Oliver North, had funneled money from the secret sale of arms to Iran to the Contras in Nicaragua resulted in a scandal of major proportions and a resulting decision by Congress against further aid to the Contras.

Through the intervention of other Central American governments, cease-fire talks between the Sandinistas and the Contras were held in 1988, and in the elections of 1990 the Sandinista government of Daniel Ortega was voted out of power in Nicaragua. Still, the final outcome of the civil struggles in Nicaragua and elsewhere in Latin America remained in doubt in the 1990s, as the forces of reaction battled the forces of change (frequently leftist and often Marxist in orientation), as the forces of traditional economic and military privilege battled the forces of egalitarianism, and as economic changes that ensured the destruction of the old order but no guarantee of greater justice in the new continued to occur.

American military forces were not called to action in Cuba, El Salvador, or Nicaragua in the 1970s and 1980s because of the course of events in those countries, but on two occasions, in Grenada and in Panama, American military action was swift and successful, even though it became a comic opera in the first instance.

Grenada, a tiny Caribbean island nation only 133 square miles in size, is the smallest nation in the Western Hemisphere. It had been a British dependency until 1974. It was governed by a Marxist faction led by Maurice Bishop after 1979. The American government under both Presidents Carter and Reagan were unhappy with Bishop's close ties to Cuba, his representatives' pro-USSR and anti–U.S. votes in the United Nations, and his left-wing authoritarianism. But nothing happened until 1983, when another coup occurred, opening the possibility of greater communist influence in the island nation. Reagan then ordered the military into Grenada to expel the Cuban advisors there, to "rescue" some American medical students on the island, to seize the airport with its newly extended runway (allegedly being prepared for Soviet use), and, apparently, to show American and personal strength after the recent death of the 241 marines in Beirut. Operation Fury was launched on the morning of October 25, 1983.

The U.S. invasion forces consisted of a marine amphibious unit of 1,250 men and two Army Ranger battalions. (The marines and rangers were inexplicably landed on each end of the island even though the capital, the students, and everything crucial on the island was in the center.) They were backed by A-7 Navy fighter-bombers from the carrier Independence battle group, Air Force C-130 gunships, five M60 tanks and 13 other armored vehicles, and armed helicopters. Despite the fact that their opponents consisted of only 636 Cubans (43 professional soldiers, the rest construction workers) and a few Grenadians with no combat aircraft, no artillery, and no tanks, two battalions of the 82nd Airborne Division were flown in as reinforcements on October 26, and the island was not secured for three days.

From beginning to end the Grenada operation was characterized by poor planning and execution on the part of the four services involved, but, to their credit, the military leaders learned from their mistakes. The next time they were called upon to intervene with arms in Central America, such blunders in planning, command, and execution were not repeated.

The Republic of Panama has been of special concern to the United States ever since it gained its independence from Columbia in 1903 with American aid. The Panama Canal between the Atlantic and Pacific Oceans, built by the United States between 1904 and 1914, quickly became the most important resource of the new country, and American influence was heavy thereafter in Panama. Despite the fact that the United States considered the canal of crucial importance economically and militarily, growing Panamanian opposition to American ownership of the waterway led the United States in 1978 to agree to a new treaty whereby the canal would pass to Panamanian ownership in the year 2000, with annual payments increased considerably in the interim.

Ten years later, in 1988, the president of the Panamanian republic attempted to discharge the head of the Panama Defense Forces, General Manuel Antonio Noriega, but, instead, found himself overthrown by Noriega. Ruling as a strongman in the country with the use of his own "Dignity Battalion" goon squads and the defense forces and engaging heavily in the illicit international drug trade, Noriega resisted all attempts to strip him of his power. When voted out of office in an internationally supervised election in May 1989, Noriega claimed victory and refused to allow the elected officials to take office.

The United States in early 1988 had indicted Noriega on charges of protecting drug traffickers and permitting their profits to be laundered through Panamanian banks. The United States also froze all Panamanian government assets in the country. After Noriega had annulled the election that turned him out, President Bush called upon the Panamanian people and the army to remove him, but all such efforts were to no avail, although American military presence in Panama was beefed up.

But in late December 1989, after Noriega's men had killed an American serviceman in Panama and the general had declared war on the United States—and before Noreiga was given the opportunity to name the new head of the Panama Canal Commission—Bush ordered a full-scale invasion of the country. The stated purposes of the invasion were to remove Noriega from power and install the duly elected choices of the Panamanian people, to bring him to the United States for trial on the drug charges, to protect the Panama Canal, and to protect the American citizens, both civilian and military, living in the canal zone.

Some 12,000 U.S. Army troops were flown in to Panama in Operation Just Cause to join the 12,000 soldiers and 600 U.S. Marines already there. Most of the fighting against Noriega's troops took place in and around Panama City. Some 24 American servicemen were killed, but within days all organized Noriega opposition had ended, the elected president and vice president of the republic had been sworn into office and had promised to rule according to constitutional principles, and Noriega had taken refuge in the Vatican embassy to escape capture by the American forces. This time the military had performed with precision, the Southern Command headquartered in Panama having ensured solid planning and execution throughout the entire operation.

The American military had proved that it could function well, and the Panamanian people rejoiced in their new-found freedom despite the outcries of the Organization of American States over the actions the United States had taken. Noriega had escaped capture temporarily but, apparently more willing to face American justice than the wrath of the Panamanian people, within days voluntarily surrendered himself to American officials and was flown to the United States to stand trial. The performance of the U.S.

military in the vital Republic of Panama had been outstanding, and the people of Panama had been freed from the hands of a military strongman and criminal.

American interventions in Central America diplomatically and militarily, then, in the 1970s and 1980s had met with some successes and some failures. No one could predict how events in these five countries and the other Latin American nations would turn out as the decade of the 1990s unfolded, but the area showed some signs of evolving to political and economic modernism and stability with a minimum of outside interference and violence. Whatever the paths its various countries would take, Latin America would remain an area of primary American concern, with the U.S. government offering aid and rejecting intervention as far as possible. American military forces were no longer automatically being called up to play the role of policemen of the Caribbean, but they were willing and able to carry out national policy when called upon to do so.

THE STATE OF AMERICA'S MILITARY

The Department of Defense is a cabinet-level department headed by the secretary of defense. It is responsible for the nation's military services through three military departments (Army, Navy, and Air Force) and 13 defense agencies. The four armed services (Army, Navy, Marine Corps, and Air Force) are subordinate to the three military departments. The military departments oversee the recruitment, training, and equipping of their men and women, but operational control is assigned to the eight unified (joint service) and two specified (functional, usually single-service) commands. The unified commands now include the European, Pacific, Atlantic, Southern, Central, Space, Special Operations, and Transportation commands. The specified commands are the Strategic Air Command and the Forces Command. The operational chain of command, as established by the Goldwater-Nichols Department of Defense Reorganization Act of 1986, descends from the president through the secretary of defense through the Joint Chiefs of Staff to the unified and specified commands.

Another major organizational change came about through the Goldwater-Nichols Act. The Joint Chiefs of Staff were reorganized to increase the powers and responsibilities of the chairman and to downgrade the role of the individual service chiefs. The act further established "joint service" officers who, at the rank of captain (or navy senior lieutenant) are chosen by the secretary of defense to be assigned to three years of joint school education and then three years in a joint service assignment. Furthermore, of the 1,000 specified joint duty positions in the services, one-half must be filled by officers with a joint duty specialty. For promotion to brigadier general or rear admiral, service in a joint duty assignment is required, and for promotion to lieutenant general, vice admiral or admiral, evaluation as a joint staff member is mandatory.

As of 1989, the Department of Defense oversaw 3.7 million service personnel, 2.1 million on active duty (764,000 army, 581,000 navy, 575,000 air force, and 195,000 marines) and 1.6 million in the National Guard or reserves (64 percent of these in the National Guard or Army Reserve). It also employed 1.1 million civilians. Fourteen percent of the active duty personnel were officers; 85 percent were enlisted. Some 11 percent of all officers were members of minority groups, while 31 percent of all enlisted personnel fell into that category. The Army had the highest minority total, with 39 percent of enlisted; the Air Force had the lowest, with 24 percent of enlisted. Slightly over 10 percent of all officers and enlisted in the services were women.

Reenlistment rates for first-term service personnel were highest in the Air Force (55 percent) and Navy (54 percent) and lowest in the Marine Corps (26 percent). Reenlistment rates for career service personnel were highest in the Army (94 percent) and the Air Force (88 percent), with the Navy and Marine Corps trailing (76 percent each). The overall Department of Defense reenlistment rates stood at 49 percent for first-termers and 86 percent for careerists.

Of the 2.1 million persons on active duty in 1989, 1.9 million were serving ashore, the rest afloat. Almost 1.6 million were serving in the United States or its territories; 21,000 in other nations of the Western Hemisphere; 344,000 in Europe; 146,000 in the Far East and Pacific Regions; and 6,400 in Africa, the Middle East, and South Asia. These active-duty personnel were serving in 18 army divisions, 3 marine divisions, and 3 marine aircraft wings; in 15 navy carrier air wings and on 192 navy surface combatants, 14 carriers, 99 attack submarines, 37 fleet ballistic missile submarines, and 218 other naval ships; in 19 air force strategic bomber wings, 4 interceptor squadrons, and 21 tactical fighter wings, and flying 334 strategic airlift and 21 tactical airlift planes.

The 1.6 million men and women in the Guards and reserves were contributing 10 army divisions, 1 marine division, 1 marine aircraft wing, 2 navy carrier air wings, 12 Air National Guard interceptor squadrons, and 16 Air National Guard and Air Force Reserve tactical fighter wings. They were also manning 344 Air Force Reserve and Air National Guard tactical airlift aircraft.

America's primary strategic weapons in 1989 were 1,000 landbased ICBMs (950 Minuteman and 50 Peacekeepers), 263 strategic bombers (173 B-52s and 90 B-1s), 544 fleet ballistic launchers (352 Poseidon and 192 Tridents), and 252 strategic defense interceptors in 14 squadrons. Its tactical air forces consisted of 2,638 Air Force, 888 Navy, and 447 Marine Corps authorized attack/fighter aircraft organized into 169 active and 60 reserve squadrons.

Its general-purpose land forces consisted of 21 active and 11 reserve Army and Marine divisions plus 8 active and 20 reserve separate Army brigades, 4 active and 4 reserve army special forces groups, and 1 active Army Ranger regiment. The Navy had 568 ships in its deployable battle forces, including 42 strategic forces, 434 battle forces, 65 support forces, and 27 reserve forces vessels, plus 26 reserve forces ships and other auxiliaries. In airlift and sealift capacities were 401 authorized intertheater aircraft (58 percent being C-141 transports), and in intratheater airlift capacities were 513 authorized Air Force C-130s and 92 Navy and Marine Corps tactical support aircraft. The Navy's Sealift Command included 61 active tankers and cargo ships and 151 reserve ships.

PROSPECTS FOR THE 1990s

The cost of all of these personnel, equipment, and weaponry items was included in a gradually shrinking budget, estimated at approximately $300 billion dollars for 1990. Of this figure, the military services would spend about 26 percent on personnel (including

1.4 million military retirees), 30 percent on operations and maintenance, 28 percent on procurement, and 13 percent on research, development, and testing. And it was generally conceded in Congress and specified by the chairman of the Senate Armed Services committee, Sam Nunn of Georgia, that the military would face cuts of approximately $325 billion over the next several years as a result of the Gramm-Rudman-Hollings budget-reduction legislation. Many of the cuts would of necessity have to come in personnel costs, and this action would have a deleterious effect on the 2.1 million active-duty personnel and their 2.9 million dependents. How deeply the budget ax would fall on operations, procurement, and research and development remained problematic and subject to heated debate in the military and in Congress, with such development programs as the B-2 bomber and President Reagan's Strategic Defense Initiative facing the most severe cuts, if not outright cancellation.

Cutting back on research, testing, and procurement of the most advanced weaponry vital to the nation's security (including necessary research in the area of chemical and biological weapons and defenses against their use and effects) was seen by many as inherently unwise, imprudent, and symptomatic of the nation's lack of long-range vision and long-range planning. Nevertheless, arguing in favor of serious cuts in authorized military appropriations in the decade of the 1990s were the impact of the revelations of waste and fraud in defense acquisitions in the 1980s; the easing of tensions with the Soviet Union in the era of *glasnost* and *perestroika* and the revolutionary events taking place in East Germany, Poland, the Baltic states, Romania, other satellite states, and within the USSR; the concern for the federal deficit and its impact on the American economy both domestically and in foreign trade; and the desire of the American electorate to devote more monies to domestic programs perceived as crucial.

Whatever the outcome of domestic events; whatever the fate of the Soviet Union and its satellite system; whatever the future of western Europe and NATO; whatever might transpire in the Far East, the Middle East, and Latin America; whatever adverse political forces the military might have to endure in attempting to maintain its strength; whatever vision of its strengths and responsibilities to itself and the world the United States might discover and adopt, the nation's armed forces remain on guard.

Having evolved from relative simplicity in strategy, tactics, weaponry, and world responsibility in colonial days to the awesome complexity of technologies and missions in the last decades of the twentieth century; having become professional fighting forces, backed when necessary by citizen-soldiers, -sailors, -marines, and -airmen; having suffered over 650,000 killed in battle, 485,000 other deaths, and 1.5 million wounded in nine major wars and conflicts alone to uphold the nation's values; and having faced combat at home, in the hemisphere, and around the world, the men and women of America's armed forces, proud of their heritage, continue to serve well the people and the government that they are pledged to protect and defend.

Suggestions for Further Reading

BINKIN, MARTIN, and WILLIAM W. KAUFMANN, *U.S. Army Guard and Reserve: Rhetoric, Realities, Risks*. Studies in Defense Policy. Washington, DC: Brookings Institution, 1989.

BRZEZINSKI, ZBIGNIEW K., *Game Plan: A Geostrategic Framework for the Conduct of the U.S.–Soviet Contest*. Boston: Atlantic Monthly Press, 1986.

BUNDY, MCGEORGE, *Danger and Survival: Choices about the Bomb in the First Fifty Years*. New York: Random House, 1988.

CHARLTON, MICHAEL, *From Deterrence to Defense: The Inside Story of Strategic Policy*. Cambridge, MA: Harvard University Press, 1987.

GRAY, COLIN, *The Geopolitics of Super Power*. Lexington: University Press of Kentucky, 1988.

HADLEY, ARTHUR T., *The Straw Giant: Triumph and Failure, America's Armed Forces, a Report from the Field*. New York: Random House, 1986.

HAMMEL, ERIC, *The Root: The Marines in Beirut, August 1982–February 1984*. New York: Harcourt Brace Jovanovich, 1985.

HENDRICKSON, DAVID C., *The Future of American Strategy*. New York: Holmes & Meier, 1987.

HILL, RONALD J., and JAN AKE DELLANBRANT, eds. *Gorbachev and Perestroika: Towards a New Socialism?* International Library of Studies in Communism. Brookfield, VT: Edward Elgar, 1989.

HOLM, JEANNE., *Women in the Military: An Unfinished Revolution*. Novato, CA: Presidio Press, 1982.

HOOPER, EDWIN B., *United States Naval Power in a Changing World*. New York: Praeger, 1988.

HOSMER, STEPHEN T., *Constraints on U.S. Strategy in Third World Conflicts*. New York: Crane Russak, 1987.

JENSEN, LLOYD, *Bargaining for National Security: The Postwar Disarmament Negotiations*. Columbia: University of South Carolina Press, 1988.

JONES, HOWARD, ed. *The Foreign and Domestic Dimensions of Modern Warfare: Vietnam, Central America, and Nuclear Strategy*. Tuscaloosa: University of Alabama Press, 1988.

KUPCHAN, CHARLES, *The Persian Gulf and the West: The Dilemmas of Security*. Boston: Allen & Unwin, 1987.

LAIRD, ROBBIN F., *The Soviet Union, the West and the Nuclear Arms Race*. New York: New York University Press, 1986.

LEHMAN, JOHN F., *Command of the Seas*. New York: Scribner's. 1988.

LEVERING, RALPH B., *The Cold War, 1945–1987,* 2nd ed. Arlington Heights, IL: H. Davidson, 1988.

LUTTWAK, EDWARD N., *On the Meaning of Victory: Essays on Strategy*. New York: Simon & Schuster, 1986.

———. *The Pentagon and the Art of War: The Question of Military Reform*. New York: Simon & Schuster, 1984.

MCNAUGHER, THOMAS L., *New Weapons, Old Politics: America's Procurement Muddle*. Washington, DC: Brookings Institution, 1989.

RYAN, PAUL B., *The Iranian Rescue Mission: Why It Failed*. Annapolis: Naval Institute Press, 1985.

SCHLESINGER, JAMES R., *America at Century's End*. New York: Columbia University Press, 1989.

SCHOULTZ, LARS, *National Security and United States Policy toward Latin America*. Princeton, NJ: Princeton University Press, 1987.

Index